A Life of
KENNETH REXROTH

Linda Hamalian

W·W·NORTON & COMPANY

NEW YORK · LONDON

FRONTISPIECE PHOTOGRAPH: Kenneth Rexroth camping at Ashcroft, Colorado, 1945.

FIRST EDITION

The text of this book is composed in Baskerville, with the display set in Garamond. Composition and manufacturing by The Maple-Vail Book Manufacturing Group. Book design by Marjorie J. Flock

6003566869

Library of Congress Cataloging-in-Publication Data

Hamalian, Linda.
    A life of Kenneth Rexroth / Linda Hamalian.
      p. cm.
    Includes bibliographical references and index.
      1. Rexroth, Kenneth, 1905–   —Biography.   2. Poets,
American—20th century—Biography.   I. Title.
PS3535.E923Z69   1991
811'.52—dc20
[B]   90–38002

ISBN 0-393-02944-1

W. W. Norton & Company, Inc., 500 Fifth Avenue, New York, N.Y. 10110
W. W. Norton & Company, Ltd., 10 Coptic Street, London WC1A 1PU

1 2 3 4 5 6 7 8 9 0

A Life of

KENNETH REXROTH

FOR LEO

CONTENTS

Photographs appear on pages 117–124 and 247–254

PREFACE

Here is a poem Kenneth Rexroth wrote to his third wife, Marthe, the mother of his daughters.

A Dialogue of Watching

Let me celebrate you. I
Have never known anyone
More beautiful than you. I
Walking beside you, watching
You move beside me, watching
That still grace of hand and thigh,
Watching your face change with words
You do not say, watching your
Solemn eyes as they turn to me,
Or turn inward, full of knowing,
Slow or quick, watching your full
Lips part and smile or turn grave,
Watching your narrow waist, your
Proud buttocks in their grace, like
A sailing swan, an animal
Free, your own, and never
To be subjugated, but
Abandoned, as I am to you,
Overhearing your perfect
Speech of motion, of love and
Trust and security as
You feed or play with our children.
I have never known any
One more beautiful than you.

S A MAN'S DECLARATION OF LOVE and admiration for his wife, this poem is an evocative piece of writing. The careful observations about her movements and expressions, the precision of the wording, the effective use of figurative language, the restrained lyricism—all these attributes save the poem from sappiness. Even for those readers who are wary of man celebrating his love of woman in terms of how much pleasure she gives him—to put it simply, perceiving her as a love object—the poem remains satisfying to read. Clearly the persona in the poem, if not the author himself, does not belittle his love with his praise and his passion.

Like many of the women whose lives he touched, when I first met Kenneth Rexroth I was charmed by his weathered good looks, his erudition, and his hip lifestyle. I was twenty-one at the time, living in California with Leo Hamalian, who had asked Rexroth to give a reading at the California Institute of the Arts. Rexroth, who was sixty-six years old, and Carol Tinker, who was forty-one and whom he liked to describe at the time as his "live-in secretary," came to our home after the reading for dinner. I had cooked an elaborate meal straight out of Craig Claiborne's *New York Times Menu Cookbook*, and when we were through with our coffee, Rexroth told me how perfectly I had prepared the broccoli (in a white anchovy sauce, as I recall). I could not believe that this great poet was commenting knowingly on my green vegetables. When Kenneth and Carol returned our hospitality by inviting us to their home in Santa Barbara, he entertained us around a Mongolian hotpot and talked philosophy (mostly Buddhist) and politics (of the conspiracy theory kind) into the early morning hours. I was convinced he was a genius, and a very kind man. In time his poetry became the subject of my doctoral dissertation under the direction of Maurice Beebe at Temple University. This led to an offer from W. W. Norton to write his biography.

I once felt that I could have been a character in his autobiography—not as a spurned lover or former wife or disillusioned daughter, but as one of the young women attracted to his unconventionally glamorous personality and politics, who learned a great deal and experienced deep pleasure from reading his poetry. Wouldn't it have been wonderful to have poems by Kenneth written to me? But now in retrospect I am aware that he was not exactly the man I imagined him to be.

Kenneth Rexroth wrote some of the best poetry of the twentieth century, but like so many creative artists, he led a far from exemplary life. I have not been inclined to codify and categorize his behavior, to measure and weigh it, to tie it all up, neat, and to defy other Rexroth enthusiasts to come up with a different interpretation. I understand there are many ways of knowing a subject, and it was my own romantic perception which stirred me to write about him, even though I ended up disappointed by some of the truths that I had to face about his life. When "A Dialogue of Watching" was first published, it appeared as one poem in a series of seven, all dedicated to Marthe. After Marthe and Kenneth divorced, Kenneth removed the dedication to these poems and scrambled the sequence. There is no way that the ordinary reader could know who inspired this poem. This biography should help the reader to appreciate the making of Rexroth's oeuvre and to understand the changes it underwent as his life affected his art.

It is precisely Rexroth's ability to transform the raw material of his daily life into art—with the beauty of the natural world ultimately his inspiration—that makes his presence always so vivid to me. I like to read him, and I like to quote him. He was wise in spite of himself, and I am aware of how much I owe his trusting spirit. Without his approval to clear the path, this biography would have taken far longer than the five years I devoted to writing it.

For their cooperation, encouragement, and trust, I would like to thank James Laughlin, Katharine Leavitt, Bradford Morrow, Mariana Rexroth, Carol Tinker, Shirley and Frank Triest, and Marthe Whitcomb. Their goodwill and support was crucial to my work.

For generously granting interviews, giving me vital information, and allowing me to quote from their correspondence, I would like to thank following people: Lionel Abel, A. Alvarez, Joe Axelrod, Amiri Baraka, Michael Baranchek, Lee Bartlett, Julian Beck, Lyn Belaief, Stephen Berg, Monica Bethe, Ronald Bladen, Robin Blaser, Herbert Blau, Joseph Bruchac, Stanley Burnshaw, Elizabeth and Sanford Burstein, Nika Cavat, Porter Chaffee, Ling Chung, Richard Collins, Cid Corman, Malcolm Cowley, Robert Creeley, Dale Davis, Robert Duncan, Richard and Betty Eberhart, George Evans, William Everson, Beatrice Farwell, Karen Feinberg, Lawrence Ferlinghetti, Carolyn Forché, Laura Foreman, Morgan Gibson, Elsa Gidlow, Barry Gifford, Allen Ginsberg, Dana Gioia, Herbert Gold, Mitchell Goodman, Michael Grieg, Donald Gutierrez, Sam Hamill, Jessica Hagedorn, Esther Handler, John Handy, Robert Hawley, Joseph Henderson, George Hitchcock, Laura Riding Jackson, Angela Jaffray, Masha Zakheim Jewett, Yuzuru Katagiri, Sanehide Kodama, Ken Knabb, David Koven, Mildred and Samuel Kramer, John Leonard, Philip Levine, Janet Lewis, Robert Lewis, Nettie Lipton, Edward Loomis, Judith Malina, Michael McClure, David Meltzer, Tom Meyer, Josephine Miles, Jeffrey Miller, John Montgomery, Richard Moore, Eric Mottram, Melissa Mytinger, Gloria Oden, Thomas Parkinson, Octavio Paz, Ruth Pokrass, Bern Porter, Ralph Raimi, Kathleen Raine, Carl Rakosi, Belle and Ivan Raner, Lee Rather, Tim Reynolds, Charles Richards, Doren Robbins, Edouard Roditi, Selden Rodman, Lynn Rollins, Jerome Rothenberg, Norman Rush, Aram Saroyan, Derek Savage, James and Margot Schevill, Horace Schwartz, Jack Shoemaker, Darina Silone, Gary Snyder, John Solt, Tree Swenson, Barbara Szerlip, Eloyde Tovey, Bill Triest, Janelle Therese Viglini, Diane Wakoski, Eliot Weinberger, Theodore and Renée Weiss, Philip Whalen, Susan Wiere, Jonathan Williams, Joyce Wilson, and Noel Young.

For their hospitality while I was conducting research, I would like to thank Marjorie and Jeffrey Appel, Helen and Ardavan Davaran, Clayton and Caryl Eshleman, Morton Paley, and Aram and Margaret Tolegian. For crossing borders with me, I would like to thank Camille Billops and

James V. Hatch. For understanding the challenge of coordinating a full-time teaching schedule with writing biography, I thank my friends and colleagues at William Paterson College. They supported me in many intangible ways.

I also wish to thank Kathleen Anderson, Deborah Baker, Robert J. Bertholf, John Bidwell, George Butterick, Amy Cherry, Lilace Hatayama, Donald S. Lamm, Kevin Ray, Arthur Waldhorn, and Arthur Zeiger for their professional advice and support; the New Jersey Board of Higher Education for awarding me a Governor's Fellowship in the Humanities; William Paterson College for awarding me released time for research and writing; and the National Endowment for the Humanities for a Travel to Collections grant.

I am deeply grateful to my husband Leo for carefully reading several drafts of the manuscript. Without his love and companionship, I doubt that I would have written this book.

ACKNOWLEDGMENTS

THE AUTHOR is grateful to Bradford Morrow, the Kenneth Rexroth Trust, and the following publishers for permission to reprint from previously copyrighted materials:

New Directions Publishing Corporation for excerpts from the following works:

Assays Copyright © 1961 by Kenneth Rexroth

Autobiographical Novel Copyright © 1964, 1966 by Kenneth Rexroth

Bird in the Bush Copyright © 1959 by Kenneth Rexroth

Classics Revisited Copyright © 1965, 1966, 1967, 1968 by Kenneth Rexroth

Collected Shorter Poems Copyright © 1966, 1963, 1962, 1952, 1949, 1940 by Kenneth Rexroth

Collected Longer Poems Copyright © 1957, 1967, 1968, Copyright 1952, 1953 by Kenneth Rexroth

Morning Star Copyright © 1974, 1976, 1978, 1979 by Kenneth Rexroth

Natural Numbers Copyright 1944, © 1956 by New Directions Publishing Corporation

New Poems Copyright © 1971, 1973, 1974 by Kenneth Rexroth

100 Poems from the Chinese All rights reserved

100 Poems from the Japanese All rights reserved

Orchid Boat Women Copyright © 1972 by Kenneth Rexroth

World Outside the Window Copyright © 1987 by the Kenneth Rexroth Trust, Copyright © 1947, 1955, 1957, 1958, 1959, 1960, 1961, 1963, 1964, 1966, 1967, 1969, 1970, 1973, 1977 by Kenneth Rexroth

"Vignettes," *The Long Reach: New and Uncollected Poems 1948–1984* by Richard Eberhart, Copyright © 1984 (page 163). [Chapter Thirteen, page 147, note 25]

"A Berry Feast," *The Back Country* by Gary Snyder, Copyright © 1957 (page 13). [Chapter Nineteen, page 235, note 50]

The University of Michigan Press
  Poems from the Greek Anthology translated by Kenneth Rexroth,
      Copyright © 1962
      (page 2) [Chapter Fifteen, pages 171–72, note 7]
      (page 79) [Chapter Twenty-Five, pages 308–9, note 6]

THE AUTHOR is grateful to Bradford Morrow, the Kenneth Rexroth
Trust, and the following institutions for permission to reprint from
materials in their holdings:

Department of Special Collections, University Research Library, UCLA
    Lawrence Lipton Collection
    Henry Miller Collection
    Kenneth Rexroth Collection
    Edouard Roditi Collection

Special Collections, University Library, University of Southern California Kenneth Rexroth Collection

The Poetry/Rare Books Collection, University Libraries, the University
of Buffalo
    Letters from Kenneth Rexroth to Jonathan Williams
        November 25, 1951 [Chapter Nineteen, page 229, note 17]
        May 1, 1951 [Chapter Nineteen, page 228, note 14]
        November 21, 1950 [Chapter Nineteen, pages 228–29, notes
            15, 16]
        October 7, 1958 [Chapter Twenty-Three, page 288, note 1]

Harry Ransom Humanities Research Center, The University of Texas
at Austin
    Letter from Kenneth Rexroth to Judith Malina, October 8, 1951
        [Chapter Nineteen, page 229, note 19]
    Letters from Kenneth Rexroth to C. W. Gardiner
        January 25, 1947 [Chapter Thirteen, page 155, note 55]
        January 2, 1951 [Chapter Eighteen, page 215, note 10]
        September 10, 1946 [Chapter Sixteen, page 192, note 24]
        February 28, 1947 [Chapter Sixteen, page 192, notes 25, 26]

Special Collections, Washington University Libraries, St. Louis
    Letters from Kenneth Rexroth to Babette Deutsch
        January 26, 1949 letter [Chapter Seven, page 74, note 35]
        October 28, 1952 [Chapter Eighteen, page 221, note 24]
        September 17, 1952 [Chapter Eighteen, page 224, note 35]

Robert J. Bertholf and The Literary Estate of Robert Duncan
    Letters from Robert Duncan to Robert Creeley, Special Collec-
        tions, Washington University Libraries, St. Louis

May 18, 1956 [Chapter Twenty-One, page 265, note 24]

November 26, 1957 [Chapter Twenty-Two, pages 273–74, notes 1, 2]

May 22, 1965 [Chapter Twenty-One, page 265, note 21]

Undated letter from Robert Duncan to Marthe Rexroth [Chapter Twenty-One, page 265, note 23]

Letters from Robert Duncan to Kenneth Rexroth. Department of Special Collections, University Research Library, UCLA

May 14, 1956 [Chapter Twenty-One, page 265, note 22]

January 11, 1958 [Chapter Twenty-Two, page 274, note 3]

Interview of Robert Duncan by Linda Hamalian, May 18, 1982, part of which appeared in *Conjunctions* 4, 1984, pp. 85–95

[Chapter Twelve, page 133, note 13]

[Chapter Thirteen, pages 149–50, note 32]

[Chapter Fifteen, page 178, note 34]

Sterling Lord Literistic, Inc. for The Literary Estate of Jack Kerouac

Letter from Jack Kerouac to Kenneth Rexroth, December 13, 1956. Copyright © 1956 by Jack Kerouac. Department of Special Collections, University Research Library, UCLA [Chapter Twenty-One, page 266, note 26]

The Literary Estate of Henry Miller

Letter from Henry Miller to Kenneth Rexroth, March 18, 1945. Department of Special Collections, University Research Library, UCLA [Chapter Twelve, page 134, note 17]

The Trustees of the Ezra Pound Literary Property Trust

Letter from Ezra Pound to Kenneth Rexroth, August 20, 1931, Copyright © 1991 [Chapter Seven, page 75, note 38]

Untitled poem from *An "Objectivists" Anthology* [Chapter Seven, page 74]. Department of Special Collections, University Research Library, UCLA

The Estate of Marie Rexroth

Letters from Marie Rexroth to Kenneth Rexroth. Department of Special Collections, University Research Library, UCLA

September 4, 1948 [Chapter Fourteen, pages 167–68, notes 30, 33]

May 29, 1949 [Chapter Sixteen, page 190, note 14]

June ?, 1949, and October ?, 1949 [Chapter Sixteen, page 196, note 38]

June 5, 1949 [Chapter Sixteen, page 197, note 41]

November 16, 1958 [Chapter Twenty-Three, page 289, notes 4, 5]

n.d. [Chapter Nine, pages 96, 98, notes 30, 37]

n.d. [Chapter Twelve, pages 130, 131, 132, 136, 139, 141, notes 1, 2, 7, 8, 24, 32, 38]
n.d. [Chapter Seventeen, page 208, note 10]
"Tuesday" [Chapter Eighteen, pages 213, 214, notes 2, 3]
Letter from Marie Rexroth to James Laughlin. James Laughlin private collection
April 4, 1951 [Chapter Eighteen, page 218, note 14]

The Literary Estate of William Carlos Williams
Letters from William Carlos Williams to Kenneth Rexroth. Department of Special Collections, University Research Library, UCLA
April 19, 1948 [Chapter Fourteen, page 163, note 17]
September 21, 1945 [Chapter Thirteen, page 142, note 3; Chapter Fourteen, page 163, note 18]
August ?, 1931 [Chapter Seven, page 75, note 41]
July 31, 1942 [Chapter Twelve, page 136, note 23].

THE AUTHOR is grateful to the following individuals for permission to consult and/or reprint from materials in their private collections and/or under their jurisdiction:

Antler, "Rexroth as He Appeared to Exist, March 24, 1968, 9:00 P.M." *Last Words,* Ballantine Books' Available Press, 1968. Copyright © 1986 by Antler [Chapter Twenty-Seven, page 329, note 11]

Robert Creeley
Robert Creeley Letters, Special Collections, Washington University Libraries, St. Louis

William Everson
Letter from William Everson to Kenneth Rexroth, November 31, 1948 [Chapter Fourteen, page 159, note 9]. Department of Special Collections, University Research Library, UCLA

Carolyn Forché-Mattison
Letters from Carolyn Forché-Mattison to Kenneth Rexroth. Special Collections, University Library, University of Southern California
June 30, 1976 [Chapter Twenty-Nine, page 361, note 33]
December 2, 1976 [Chapter Twenty-Nine, page 361, note 34]

Allen Ginsberg
Letter from Allen Ginsberg to Kenneth Rexroth, June 15, 1955 [Chapter Twenty, page 241, note 17]. Department of Special Collections, University Research Library, UCLA

Laura Riding Jackson
    Letter from Laura Riding Jackson to Kenneth Rexroth, May 24,
        1936, Department of Special Collections, University Re-
        search Library, UCLA. [Chapter Nine, page 93, note 20]

James Laughlin
    For graciously granting me permission to quote from his private
        collection of letters written by Kenneth Rexroth and James
        Laughlin

Judith Malina
    Letter from Julian Beck to Kenneth Rexroth, May 5, 1952 [Chap-
        ter Nineteen, page 230, note 23]. Department of Special
        Collections, University Research Library, UCLA

Michael McClure
    Interview with Linda Hamalian, August 12, 1984 [Chapter 20, page
        242, note 18]
    Passage from "PLANH," *Poetry Flash,* August 1982. [Chapter Thirty,
        page 370, note 8]

Bradford Morrow
    For graciously providing access to and granting permission to quote
        from Kenneth Rexroth's unpublished manuscripts and
        letters, and for permission to reproduce photographs and
        paintings

Gloria Oden
    Letters from Kenneth Rexroth to Gloria Oden
        May 6, 1960 [Chapter Twenty-Four, page 301, notes 10, 12]
        June 10, 1960 [Chapter Twenty-Four, page 301, note 11]
        June 1, 1960 [Chapter Twenty-Four, page 301, note 13]
        August 9, 1960 [Chapter Twenty-Four, page 304, note 19]
        February 14, 1961 [Chapter Twenty-Four, page 305, note 24]
        February 17, 1961 [Chapter Twenty-Four, page 305, note 25]
    "Ornette to Rexroth" (unpublished poem) [Chapter Twenty-Four,
        page 301, note 9]

Edouard Roditi
    Edouard Roditi letters, Department of Special Collections, Univer-
        sity Research Library, UCLA

Selden Rodman
    Journal entries on February 11, 1956, and February 13, 1956, Yale
        University Library [Chapter Twenty, page 255, notes 34,
        35]

Letters from Kenneth Rexroth to Selden Rodman
    May 22, 1946, and May ?, 1946 University of Wyoming Li-
        brary [Chapter Sixteen, page 200, notes 46, 47]

Derek Savage
    Letter from Derek Savage to Kenneth Rexroth, June 11, 1947
        [Chapter Sixteen, page 188, note 10]. Department of Spe-
        cial Collections, University Research Library, UCLA

Gary Snyder
    Interview with Linda Hamalian July 25, 1982 [Chapter Nineteen,
        page 234, note 47; Chapter Thirty, page 370, note 12]
    Letter from Gary Snyder to Kenneth Rexroth, n.d. [Chapter Nine-
        teen, page 235, notes 49, 51]
    From "A Berry Feast," *The Back Country* (Copyright © 1957 by Gary
        Snyder; used by permission of New Directions Publishing
        Corp.), page 13 [Chapter Nineteen, page 235, note 50]
    August 10, 1956, letter from Gary Snyder to Kenneth Rexroth,
        Department of Special Collections, University Research
        Library, UCLA [Chapter Twenty-One, page 266, note 25]
    August 27, 1987, letter from Gary Snyder to Linda Hamalian
        [Chapter Twenty-Six, page 324, notes 30, 31, 32]
    May 6, 1986, telephone conversation between Gary Snyder and
        Linda Hamalian [Chapter Twenty-Nine, page 360, note
        30]

Carol Tinker
    Passages from *The Pillow Book of Carol Tinker*. Santa Barbara: Cad-
        mus Books, 1980.
        "Gold Wires" (page 25) [Chapter 28, page 345, note 22]
        "Thank You" (page 42) [Chapter 29, page 356, note 21]
    and for graciously providing access to photographs

Marthe Whitcomb
    For generously granting me permission to quote from her private
        collection of letters written by Kenneth Rexroth and Marthe
        Whitcomb, and to reprint photographs

Jonathan Williams
    Letters from Jonathan Williams to Kenneth Rexroth, Department
        of Special Collections, University Research Library, UCLA
        November 14, 1950 [Chapter Nineteen, page 228, note 13]
        April 17, 1951 [Chapter Nineteen, page 229, note 18]

Janet Lewis Winters
    Letter from Janet Lewis to Linda Hamalian, July 6, 1985 [Note 7,
        page 387]

IN ADDITION, I consulted the archives of the following libraries not mentioned previously:

The Bancroft Library, University of California, Berkeley
The Beinecke Rare Book and Manuscript Library, Yale University
Special Collections Division, Butler Library, Columbia University
William Andrews Clark Memorial Library, University of California, Los Angeles
Special Collections, Morris Library, Southern Illinois University at Carbondale
The Newberry Library, Chicago
Ryerson and Burnham Libraries, The Art Institute of Chicago
Special Collections, University of Connecticut, Storrs.

One

THE EARLY YEARS
1905–1918

E N ROUTE TO CHICAGO on a cold winter's day, Delia and
Charles Rexroth quickly disembarked when their train
stopped in South Bend, Indiana. They had bought tickets for two, but they were about to become three. Their
first child, Kenneth Charles Marion, was born on December 22, 1905.
Although relatives in Chicago had been expecting them for the holidays,
the Rexroths decided to stay in South Bend, where they knew that they
could find comfortable quarters at a reasonable rent. Their first home
was a house on Park Avenue near St. Joseph's River and Central Park.[1]

South Bend was not unfamiliar to the couple. They had lived there
earlier on Chapin Street, near their old family friend, Leo Eliel. An affluent entrepreneur in the wholesale pharmaceuticals business, Eliel owned
a drugstore on West Washington Street. While Charles was struggling
through Northwestern's medical school, Eliel persuaded him to change
his course of study. If Charles would undertake an undergraduate degree
in pharmacology and a doctorate in organic chemistry, Eliel would finance his education and a partnership in one of the largest wholesale
drug houses in Chicago, Kinsolving & Granisson.[2] The career of Charles
Rexroth was to be erratic: he did not complete his education but managed
to rise from salesman to vice-president before alcoholism took over his
life. The Rexroth residences reflected the fluctuations of their finances.
During the five-year sojourn in South Bend, each address was less impressive than the one before. The Rexroths were, in the words of George
Bernard Shaw, a family of "downstarts."

Shortly before Kenneth turned five, his family moved to Elkhart,
where Delia's parents, George and Mary Reed, were living. After a brief
sojourn in a rather grand house on Beardsley Avenue, the Rexroths
moved again, to West Marion Street, not far from where Ambrose Bierce's
family had dwelt prior to the Civil War.[3] This house was made for basic
living: only front porch pillars suggest superfluous decoration. Within
two years, the Rexroths moved to South Second Street, a much loftier

structure that inspired Delia and Charles to decorate it according to the sophistication of the day: orientalia, William Morris furniture, Art Nouveau pieces.

At the age of six, Kenneth met his first love, his "six to nine years sweetheart."[4] Helen Carpenter, a year older than Kenneth, lived next door to the Rexroths with her parents, Ethan and Grace, and her great-grandmother. Delia and Grace would take the two children boating on the placid waters of the Elkhart and St. Joseph's Rivers. At other times, Kenneth and Helen spent hours together reading. Kenneth wanted Helen always by his side. Indeed, he has described his friendship with her as "infantile matrimony," fulfilling his need for duality,[5] a heavy-handed term for what sounds like a boyhood infatuation. Yet for them both, the memory of this childhood attachment lasted throughout their adulthood, for Rexroth as part of the pattern of his emotional life. Despite periodic announcements that he preferred a monastic existence, he would endure only brief periods without the companionship of a woman who was attentive to his emotional needs, and preferred to remain friends rather than sever ties completely with former lovers.[6]

Kenneth grew closer to Helen as the bond between his parents loosened. Delia had purchased a pair of Art Nouveau copper vases for the house on Second Street and had insisted on carrying them home herself from the Elkhart station over the objections of the railroad's baggage man (who Rexroth claimed was Ambrose Bierce's brother).[7] The strain of carrying such weight precipitated a lung hemorrhage that left her unconscious for two days. Her doctor was unable to diagnose the cause of the illness (which would kill her within three years). Plans to have a second child were dropped. Charles turned to other women, began drinking heavily, and extended the duration of his business trips. A merger between Kinsolving & Granisson and the Herkimer Wine Company meant that Charles now had to solicit business with barkeepers and proprietors of liquor stores. Like Oscar Wilde, he could resist everything but temptation. When Delia recovered her fragile health, she sought solace from local lovers.

Nevertheless, Delia and Charles decided their marriage was worth saving and that a European tour *en famille* would rejuvenate it. Charles had a ready-made excuse for an excursion abroad: if the business was to thrive, he had to prospect in distant places for new suppliers of herbs, oils and perfumes. In 1912, the family traveled from Stockholm to Constantinople, spending considerable time in the Balkans. Although Kenneth was only seven years old, the trip stamped indelible images on his memory: he would never forget the poverty of London, the beauty of the Swedish and German countryside, the great monuments of Paris, the landscape of Italy which made him think of the Land of Oz, and Emperor Franz Josef marching in the St. Stephen's Day Parade in Budapest. He would write later in "Un Bel di Vedremo" about

Watching the blue flame of the chafing dish
On Sunday nights: driving over middle Europe
Behind a café au lait team,
The evenings misty, smelling of cattle
And the fat Danubian earth.[8]

Having introduced their son to the splendors of old Europe, on their
return to the Midwest the Rexroths reinforced those first impressions
whenever possible with private tutoring and a cultured life. Furthermore,
the European adventure gave Charles the impetus he needed to risk
capital in a new and growing American enterprise. After stopping briefly
in Elkhart to visit Delia's mother and the Carpenters, the Rexroths made
their way to Battle Creek, where Charles invested in C. W. Post's breakfast
food business.[9] In a burst of confidence, he and Delia rented a huge,
purple-brown Victorian mansion on Garrison Avenue. Where did the
money come for such an elaborate home, lit by crystal chandeliers hanging from eighteen-foot ceilings?[10] Charles gambled, sometimes successfully, and his investment in cereal prospered. During their first months
in Battle Creek, the Rexroths lived well. Both Delia and Charles took to
wearing high-fashioned clothes, and photographs of Kenneth taken at
this time show a bright, wide-eyed boy with a Buster Brown haircut, well
groomed and apparently at ease with the props then popular—whether a
wide-brimmed straw hat placed on the back of his head or a toy soldier's
uniform complete with rifle. The family tooled around in a Stanley Steamer
before Charles wrecked it in an accident.[11]

In their Bohemian moods, the Rexroths entertained circus performers and burlesque artists, but with their family background of political
activism, they also sought the company of social reformers. By Rexroth's
account, Charles's father, George, was a descendant from the Schwenk-
feldians, the German Pietist sect that originated in the sixteenth century.
George Rexroth, a plumber, voted the Socialist ticket and called himself
an anarchist. He was apparently a friend of Eugene Debs, founder of the
Social Democratic Party, who used to visit him when he wanted to relax:
"they used to sit on the front porch of my grandfather's house, with their
socked feet on the railing, drinking whiskey."[12] At Sandusky, Kenneth's
maternal great-grandfather ran a trading post which served as a last stop
on the Underground Railway. His great-grandmother, who lived until
she was ninety-five, was a Socialist and a feminist who defied social convention by retaining her own name when she married, and smoking little
cigars or china pipes. She entertained Rexroth with stories about his
family that sometimes contained more fiction that fact, like the one that
he had Tecumseh blood. (Rexroth continued to believe that his paternal
great-grandparents were part Indian, possibly Iroquois.) By the time the
Rexroths arrived in Battle Creek, it had become a natural stopping point
for lecturers from black and women's rights groups. The great civil rights

pioneer Sojourner Truth had lived there for thirty years, until her death in 1883. The Rexroths had the pleasure of extending hospitality to such distinguished activists as Mrs. Josephine St. Pierre Ruffin and Mary Church Terrell. Thus in his early years Kenneth breathed an atmosphere of political dissent.

On the heels of C. W. Post's death in 1914, Charles's investments in the burgeoning breakfast food industry faltered.[13] The next year was a disaster for the Rexroths. Moneyless and unemployed, Charles moved the family from their Garrison Street mansion to a furnished three-room apartment in a building infested with rodents and roaches. Reduced to pawning or selling their possessions, the Rexroths had little more than their clothes to bring with them. Kenneth's lessons in French and dancing came to an end. Although he was registered in McKinley Public School #5 between 1912 and 1914, he attended sporadically, educated chiefly at home by Delia during this difficult period. Under these cramped physical and financial conditions, daily squabbles inevitably erupted and the emotional climate became unbearable. Charles and Delia once more faced the inevitability of separation. Charles responded to the crisis by drinking until an attack of delirium tremens landed him in the Keely-Cure Santorium.

Charles got a grip on himself and resumed his career as a traveling salesman in the wholesale drug and liquor business. Soon after Kenneth turned nine, the Rexroths moved out of their tenement to an apartment on Bartlett Street, near Carolyn Richter, a classmate of Kenneth's at PS 5. Her father was a pharmacist at the Amberg & Murphy Drug Company and it seems likely that he and Charles were business acquaintances. Kenneth's friendship with Carolyn progressed apace. They began to fantasize about living in the Land of Oz, reforming the world, and protecting themselves against the philistines, a perspective Kenneth would cultivate through the years. Already exposed to the whims of fate at this young age, Kenneth suspected that fortune, not hard work or good intentions, determined whether a person led a life of luxury or poverty, middle-class respectability or humiliating indigence. Privilege rather than intelligence seemed to govern destiny. His reluctance to participate in the world of free enterprise, and his yearning for a comrade to share his vision of the ideal world, took embryonic form.

Frequently, Kenneth and Delia accompanied Charles on his business trips around Michigan—his territory had been drastically modified. Occasionally they would visit Mr. Eliel in South Bend, although he was now powerless to boost Charles's career. But there were exciting trips to New York City, when they stayed either at the Brevoort or the Lafayette, both popular with writers, artists, and journalists living in or passing through Greenwich Village. The Lafayette edged out the Brevoort as "the unrivalled meeting place of high bohemia," reaching its peak of popularity somewhat later in the twenties.[14] Charles and Delia seemed to prefer this ambiance to all others, and they would drag their nine-year-old son to these two hotel cafés, and places like Polly's Restaurant on MacDougal Street, owned by Paula Holliday. There the anarchist Hippolyte Havel, who served as cook and waiter, would address the people who ate his food as "bourgeois pigs."[15] Emma Goldman was an habitué of Polly's, as well as of the Brevoort and the Lafayette, and Kenneth once overheard a debate she started over fellow anarchist and lover Alexander Berkman, who in 1892 attempted to assassinate the industrialist Henry Clay Frick during the Homestead Strike against Carnegie Steel in Pittsburgh. From his father, Kenneth learned about Berkman's fourteen years in prison; many years later, he wrote an introduction for a new edition of Berkman's *Prison Memoirs of an Anarchist.*[16]

The jaunts to New York City ended in 1915 when the Rexroths left Battle Creek for Chicago so that Charles could supervise a chain of drugstores for individual owners who had enlisted in the Army. No one could say that "Charlie," as his friends called him, was not enterprising. Unable to afford a place of their own, the Rexroths first stayed in the rather grand Lincoln Park West apartment of John Rexroth, Charlie's uncle, then moved to an old, dilapidated house on Emerald Avenue behind Chicago's stockyards, the home of Minnie Monahan, Delia's older sister, her husband, and four stepchildren. The circumstances were hardly conducive to repairing a shaky marriage. To make matters worse, Charles was philandering, and the young Kenneth was witness to a sordid scene in a seedy hotel room near Charles's wholesale drug supplier, involving his father unconscious from drink, an outraged Delia, and a woman who seems to have been Charles's lover. Soon afterwards Charles and Delia decided to separate, and Delia found an apartment for herself and Kenneth in Austin, on the outskirts of Chicago. Charles disappeared for three months. Kenneth's life stabilized: he attended Austin Grammar School regularly and the free children's classes held every Saturday at the Chicago Art Institute. His relationship with his mother became closer, and together they would hike through the Forest Preserve and visit the Field Museum, famous for its more than 13 million specimens in the fields of anthropology, botany, geology, and zoology. They also attended concerts together, and although they both missed Charles, this time was especially precious for both.

Charles came back to Chicago in time for Christmas 1915, celebrated at the Monahans' new apartment in a better neighborhood on Indiana Avenue, near 43rd Street. Although he still drank, Delia and Kenneth were glad to see him. He sweetened his return by renting an apartment for them near Washington Park, complete with their own furniture out of hock and shipped from Elkhart. But after two weeks of family reunion, Delia suffered a severe hemorrhage while ice-skating with Charles in the park. She was taken to Oak Forest Tuberculosis Sanatorium and convalesced there through the winter. She did not respond to treatment prescribed for victims of tuberculosis and was given a few months to live when she was discharged. (Years later, Rexroth learned that she had had gangrene of the lung, not tuberculosis.) Sensing that the end was near, she took Kenneth with her to the familiar comfort of Elkhart and rented a small apartment for them on Second Street, again near the Carpenters. That spring, while Delia's strength held out, she, Kenneth, Grace, and Helen Carpenter enjoyed the countryside and each other's company, as they had nearly five years earlier, though both women were without husbands. Charles was in Toledo drumming up business, and Ethan Carpenter had died.

Delia's deterioration was agonizing. In 1916, the year of her death, there was no cure for her affliction, an aerobic infection that first lodged in her lungs and spread gradually to her lower body. Had her illness been properly diagnosed, her suffering might have been mitigated. When she became bedridden, Kenneth was at her side constantly. Delia did not make him go off to school. Instead, she read to him from books on history, the natural sciences, and the lives of great artists and writers. She felt a great urgency to instill in her eleven-year-old son a sense of independence, and implanted in him the idea of the moral value of knowledge, or as Rexroth would later express it, that epistemology is moral. She wanted him to be a writer and an artist, but urged him to make sure, above all else, to think things through for himself. He listened well, caught up by the powerful truth of her advice, and perhaps by a boy's love for his dying mother. He was to remain haunted by her early death throughout his life. In "Delia Rexroth," written for the thirty-first anniversary of her death, he celebrates Delia's own sense of independence, the tenderness that existed between them, and his deep gratitude to her for making the world of art and literature come alive:

I took down a book of poems
That you used to like, that you
Used to sing to music I
Never found anywhere again—
Michael Field's book, *Long Ago*.
Indeed it's long ago now—
Your bronze hair and svelte body.
I guess you were a fierce lover,
A wild wife, an animal
Mother. And now life has cost
Me more years, though much less pain,
Than you had to pay for it.
And I have bought back, for and from
Myself, these poems and paintings,
Carved from the protesting bone,
The precious consequences
Of your torn and distraught life.[17]

In this poem to his mother, reminiscent of the elegiac, almost erotic poems D. H. Lawrence wrote about his mother, Rexroth offers his work as public homage to her struggle to control her "distraught life."[18] Rexroth's sensual evocation of Delia's physical presence, however, suggests that his passionate memory of her would hinder his relationships with other women. By the time this poem was published in 1947, he had been divorced from one woman and separated from another. Like Delia, each of these women had prized her independence, and possessed a strong self-image. Both cared deeply about art, literature, and music, and both provided Rexroth with the kind of emotional and material support and patient understanding that mothers often provide their sons. Even in physical appearance— light-complexioned, regular-featured, red-haired—they must have called up comforting memories of his deceased but hardly forgotten parent. But they could hardly compete successfully with the role Delia had assumed in Rexroth's imagination.

Unable to take full charge of Kenneth, Charles brought him to live with his mother, Mary Moore Rexroth, in Toledo, in a white wooden frame house on Lawrence Street with a large porch on a block with a half dozen similar structures. Charles's father had died by this time. Either Charles refused to acknowledge his mother's state of senility or felt compelled to place his only son in this bizarre environment. Had the consequences of her condition been benign, Charles's seeming indifference would not have been so shocking. Before she married, Mary had been a teacher in a country college, spoke several languages, and was among the better educated women in the Rexroth family. But by the time Kenneth came to stay, her house overflowed with stacks of books, newspapers and magazines decades old, encyclopedias, and in the basement food she had canned so long ago that it was disintegrating.

Far worse than the clutter were the regular beatings she gave Kenneth with the cane she always had beside her. She administered them during the day, with no one else present, the blinds drawn. Kenneth, barely turned twelve, was completely terrorized. His aunt Grace, Charles's sister, flew into a rage of denial when he tried to tell her about this abusive behavior. Reluctant to disturb the accord between Charles and his mother, he remained silent. Not until a next-door neighbor saw Kenneth silently enduring one of these beatings (for once, the window had been left open and the shade up) was he released from this ordeal. Charles insisted that his mother had never laid a hand on him, although he confessed that his own father had beaten him so brutally that he had run away from home. With the help of Minnie Monahan, who had been called from Chicago, Charles found a small apartment, the top floor of an old Victorian house, on Detroit Avenue. It was only two blocks from Lawrence Street, but once father and son moved, Kenneth never saw his grandmother again. Although he would later describe her behavior as "irrational and unmoti-

vated,"[19] he himself would raise his hand against those he loved, taught
in part by her example.

During that first year in Toledo at his grandmother's house, Kenneth
often played truant and frequented Ten Mile Creek, gathering specimens
that he could examine under the microscope his father had given him.
He would also spend long hours swimming and birdwatching. Nature
provided him with a sense of stability and peace, a resource he would one
day tap for his art. In "Gic to Har" he writes:

> Suddenly I remember
> Coming home from swimming
> In Ten Mile Creek,
> Over the long moraine in the early summer evening,
> My hair wet, smelling of waterweeds and mud.
> I remember a sycamore in front of a ruined farmhouse,
> And instantly and clearly the revelation
> Of a song of incredible purity and joy,
> My first rose-breasted grosbeak,
> Facing the low sun, his body
> Suffused with light.
> I was motionless and cold in the hot evening
> Until he flew away, and I went on knowing
> In my twelfth year one of the great things
> Of my life had happened.[20]

He built himself a reflector telescope to gaze at the stars, learning the
constellations whose sparkle and design would pervade the imagery of
his poetry. With the help of his father (when he was in town), and over
the objections of his grandmother—some of the rotting preserves had to
be discarded—he set up a chemical laboratory in the basement. He ran
tests on artist's materials, producing, for example, a complete range of
earth colors. On his own, after studying the Cubist art that sometimes
appeared in general-interest magazines, he painted rudimentary pictures
with futurist color schemes.

He also had the good fortune to spend two summers on a farm near
Milan, Michigan, that belonged to three unusual women, two daughters
and their ninety-two-year-old mother, who had been among "the first
suffragettes and . . . were extreme left-wing Socialists, who didn't believe
in voting or the Socialist party."[21] (Charles owned a mortgage on the
house, but would not foreclose.) Guided by them, Kenneth read books by
some of the writers he had actually glimpsed from a distance in New York
City, like Upton Sinclair and Max Eastman. The three women also introduced him to the work of Herbert Read, whose poems and critical writings were just beginning to be published in the states. (Rexroth continued
to follow Read's career as his politics turned from Marxism to anarchism:
eventually, he wrote an introduction to the New Directions 1948 edition
of Read's novel *The Green Child*.) The young Rexroth also was exposed to

the poetry and prose of Edward Carpenter, who was inspired by Walt Whitman to become a partisan of democracy and an apologist for homosexual love. He read pamphlets by Eugene Debs, and he reread a book that would play an important role in his own imaginative life, *The Research Magnificent* by H. G. Wells.

During his second summer on the farm, Kenneth felt himself drawn to Anglo-Catholicism even though his hosts were clearly antipathetic to organized religion. Delia, however, had died a Roman Catholic. That fall (1918), back home with his father on Detroit Avenue, he began to attend High Mass and listen to Tudor music, an interest he would retain throughout his life. And his love of books was unabated. The librarians at the public library on Adams and Michigan encouraged him to read Arnold Bennett and George Bernard Shaw. Delia Rexroth's influence had taken firm and heightened hold.

He could also pursue less intellectual interests. He hooked up with a local gang of boys who stole bicycles and car accessories. They liked to terrorize the caddies (whom they perceived as rich kids) at the country club golf links in Ottawa Park, an oasis of pine, fir, and maple trees, grassy fields, and a lake. Kenneth's gang was a "group of exceptionalists / Who, after dark, and on rainy days, / Stole out and shat in the golf holes."[22] To earn spending money, Kenneth also operated a popcorn machine on Collingwood Avenue, then an affluent section in Toledo. What he did not manage to sell to the people on the street, he sold to the owners of the nearby burlesque house for their audiences.

In the meantime, Charles's prospects grew dimmer. His proxy drugstore chain crumbled, and for the first time in his life he had to take a job in a factory, first at the Libby-Owens Glass Company, then at the Willys-Overland Plant. He managed to land something more suitable as a drug clerk for the Cooley Drug Company, and tried—without much success—to give his son a sense of home life. He and Kenneth devised a simple household regimen by cooking one-pot dinners, a menu Rexroth cultivated throughout the years for accommodating dinner guests. A woman friend of Charlie's would join them occasionally, but she disappeared after nursing Kenneth through a bout of flu and scarlet fever. When Charles asked a doctor to check Kenneth's condition, the doctor took one look at Charles himself and dispatched him immediately to St. Vincent's Hospital. He died within three days on April 25, 1919, of heart and kidney failure. Like Delia shortly before her death, Charles was received into the Roman Catholic Church. Kenneth was not yet fourteen. Fifty-four years later, he described his father's last days in "Proust's Madeleine":

> I see my father
> . . .
> Whistling "Beautiful Dreamer,"
> His breath smelling richly

Of whiskey and cigars. I can
Hear him coming home drunk
From the Elks' Club in Elkhart
Indiana, bumping the
Chairs in the dark. I can see
Him dying of cirrhosis
Of the liver and stomach
Ulcers and pneumonia,
Or, as he said on his deathbed, of
Crooked cards and straight whiskey
Slow horses and fast women.[23]

The following two weeks for the orphaned adolescent can only be described as ghastly. He was taken in by Aunt Grace and her husband Charles Carsten. Although Kenneth enjoyed the company of cousin Marcella, he soon knew he was on alien ground. Uncle Carsten had already searched his belongings and confiscated a pad of watercolors and a notebook with poems he had written. Carsten admonished Kenneth for "wasting his time," and strongly advised him to think about a sound way to earn a living. Kenneth recalled: "I recognized only too well the enemy with whom I would have to deal, off and on, for the rest of my life."[24] Moreover, he was forced to attend Sunday School at a liberal Protestant church, which offended his developing High Anglican sensibility.

During this chaotic interval, Kenneth was introduced to labor strife. On May 2, 1919, proposals were distributed to all trade unions for three nationwide strikes on behalf of radical labor organizer Tom Mooney, who had been in prison for two years. On May 8, workers struck the Toledo Willys-Overland automobile plant. Unemployed ex-soldiers were deputized to keep order. When the former doughboys clashed with the strikers, two men died and six were seriously injured. Mayor Schreiber called for federal troops to suppress the riots. The Army withheld its troops but the ex-soldiers on guard were ordered to shoot to kill at the next outbreak of disorder. The federal court issued an order restraining the pickets from interfering with the non-strikers and sent thirty-four Secret Service men to enforce the court order. Along with the other members of his gang, whose parents were participating in the strike, Rexroth served as a message runner for the picket lines: "I can remember bicycling furiously past the administration building, convinced that I was going to be blown off my bicycle by a hail of machine gun bullets, but what it was all about, I do not know."[25] The Toledo plant reopened in June, and the workers gradually returned to their jobs. Kenneth had gotten his first taste of leftist organizing.

Two

A Precocious Adolescence
1919–1924

D ELIA'S SISTER, Minnie Monahan, arrived from Chicago to rescue Kenneth. She discovered that Uncle Will, Charles Rexroth's brother, and Uncle Carsten had been siphoning off Kenneth's small inheritance. Minnie straightened things out and took Kenneth home with her to Chicago. The Monahans were still on Indiana Avenue, the address listed on Kenneth's school transcript when he transferred from Edmund Burke Grammar School to Englewood High School, but they subsequently moved again to a nine-room apartment on South Michigan Avenue, just a few blocks from Washington Park and less than a mile from Jackson Park and the beaches along Lake Michigan. The Monahans welcomed Kenneth into their working-class, Irish-Catholic family, whose way of life James Farrell so colorfully describes in his *Studs Lonigan* series. But Kenneth could not get close to the boys in his neighborhood. They weren't like his adventurous Toledo gang: "they were too busy hanging around street corners smoking cigarettes and spitting."[1]

Nostalgic for the time when he and his parents had lived with the Monahans, Kenneth immediately revisited his old haunts. The visit may have also been stimulated by Upton Sinclair's *The Jungle* and H. G. Wells's *The Research Magnificent*, books he had read on the farm in Milan. In "The Bad Old Days, " he writes:

> The summer of nineteen eighteen
> I read *The Jungle* and *The
> Research Magnificent*. That fall
> My father died and my aunt
> Took me to Chicago to live.
> The first thing I did was to take
> A streetcar to the stockyards.
> In the winter afternoon,
> Gritty and fetid, I walked
> Through the filthy snow, through the

Squalid streets, looking shyly
Into the people's faces,
Those who were home in the daytime.[2]

Rexroth is imprecise here about when he came to Chicago, and when his father died. But at fourteen, he knew without doubt that he had to regard himself as an independent adult. That summer of 1919 while camping on the steep bluffs above the Fox River, he saw a group of boys and girls passing in a touring car. In "A Singing Voice," a poem that recalls this experience, Rexroth hears a woman singing to these children in a "high clear soprano" that he would remember over the next thirty years as an "angelic memory," a reminder of his mother. The words of the song, "Tuck me to sleep / In my old 'Tucky home," provide an ironic contrast to the solitary path Rexroth's life had taken.[3] Unlike those children in the car, he was on his own. But faithful to his mother's aspirations for him, he spent the next year acclimating himself to his new home, determined all the while to pursue his own course.

In September 1920, Kenneth enrolled at Englewood High School, a massive post-Civil War structure. Englewood was a middle-class community with a commercial center almost as large as the downtown district. The view from the classroom windows was not pretty: great hulks of mills and furnaces and grain elevators that rose along the banks of the Calumet River. Sections of the area, however, were still wild, and many birds drank from the marsh waters where rare species of aquatic plants grew. Kenneth spent hours walking or bicycling in these open spaces.

Far from exemplary, Kenneth's record reflects the pattern of a truant hostile to authority, of a bright adolescent grown used to a life of instability. In his first semester he failed Latin and science, but he distinguished himself in algebra. In his second semester, he failed algebra but received "G" (presumably for "Good") in Latin and science. He especially liked his Latin teacher, Mrs. Manley, a "female Samuel Johnson," who sprinkled her introduction to Ovid with observations on various topics from "birth control to arctic exploration." She was popular with the brightest students. Kenneth's performance in two subjects was relatively consistent with his developing personality: he received the grades of Good, Satisfactory, and Excellent in English; and failed military training, a sign of the resistant spirit that would lead him to become a conscientious objector.[4] He avoided various extracurricular activities like the English and Chess clubs because he thought they encouraged conformity. After a heated confrontation with the principal, who was fed up with his spotty attendance and truculent attitude, Kenneth was expelled. On May 28, 1922, his shortlived association with the public school system came to an end. Not yet seventeen, he looked to Chicago's flourishing literary community for instruction.

Kenneth had returned to Chicago during the height of the Chicago

Renaissance, that long burst of literary activity from approximately 1912 to 1925, sparked by a memorable event in the world of visual arts—the World's Columbian Exposition of 1893. The promoters of this exhibition brought to Chicago's Palace of Fine Arts what they considered the best of classical masterpieces. They wanted to show the world that Chicago was not a provincial town and that "its citizens bowed to none in the appreciation of art."[5] Twenty years later, in 1913, the famous New York "Armory Show" came to Chicago, and while the works of Picasso, Braque, Kandinsky, and other Expressionists and Cubists met with more ridicule than praise, new seeds for modernism were planted. By the early twenties, indigenous American art was receiving more attention. The first International Water Color Show in 1922 was predominantly American.

Midwest writers were drawn to Chicago, where they felt they had a better chance to express their opposition to an American Dream reserved for the exclusive few, and their belief that urban, industrial life was dehumanizingly exploitative. Journalism was perceived as a literary medium, and writers such as Theodore Dreiser, Sherwood Anderson, and Carl Sandburg were all associated with Chicago newspapers at one time or another. *The Dial*, established in 1880 (and the third magazine to take this name, the first founded in 1840 as the organ of the Transcendentalist movement, the second in Cincinnati in 1869) flourished during this period. So did Harriet Monroe's *Poetry* and Margaret Anderson's *Little Review*. (Harriet Monroe recited her own dedicatory ode for the Columbian Exposition.) All three provided outlets for twentieth-century poets—locals like Sandburg and Vachel Lindsay, as well as exotics like Pound, Yeats, Joyce, Moore, Eliot, Stevens. Dreiser's *Sister Carrie*, Anderson's *Winesburg, Ohio*, Edgar Lee Master's *Spoon River Anthology*, Sandburg's *Chicago Poems* appeared during this period.

Literary groups and saloons—made up of writers and patrons—thrived on the new energy. The first to achieve its own identity was The Little Room, a group that met Friday afternoons after the weekly noontime performance of the Chicago Symphony Orchestra. It was composed mostly of professional writers and artists who named it after a short story in the *Atlantic Monthly* about a room that vanished and reappeared, "reflecting the fact that the group originally had no special meeting place but gathered in the studio of any one of a number of artists."[6] Some people criticized this group for its exclusivity and bias in favor of the standards set by Eastern literati, but among its regulars it numbered Harriet Monroe; the short story writer and novelist Hamlin Garland; and Floyd Dell, until 1914 when he left Chicago for New York City, where he became an associate editor of the leftist periodicals *The Masses* and *The Liberator*.[7] Sculptor Lorado Taft, whose *Fountain of Time* has been standing in Washington Park since 1922, attended regularly.

Although Kenneth could only appreciate The Little Room from afar, he managed to gain access to another freewheeling salon: "the incredible house of Jake Loeb, a more important Middle Western cultural institution in 1923 than the University of Chicago, the Art Institute, the Symphony, and the Chicago *Tribune* put together."[8] An insurance broker, Loeb was a member of the famous Loeb family, which used its wealth to cultivate the arts in Chicago.[9] Esther Czerny, the great-granddaughter of Carl Czerny, the Viennese composer of pedagogical works for the piano, first brought Kenneth to the Loeb salon on Thursday nights. Kenneth had met her at Hyde Park's Sinai Temple, which encouraged intellectually curious adolescents, regardless of their religion, to participate in its various cultural activities, including classes in drawing and acting. After Esther Czerny introduced him to the Loebs, Kenneth began visiting them on his own. There were five in the Loeb family: "Jake; his wife Claire; two daughters, Esther and Sara-Jo; and a son, Myndiert."[10] Along with Esther and Sara-Jo, Kenneth must have been among the youngest to frequent the Loeb soirées.[11]

He apparently watched "the cream of Chicago's intellectuals in the brief postwar period of Chicago's second renaissance" (among them Clarence Darrow, Sherwood Anderson, Carl Sandburg , Vachel Lindsay, Eugene Debs, Ben Hecht, Margaret Anderson) pass through this house, overheard their conversations, noted the titles of books they were discussing so that he could read them for himself. Sherwood Anderson gave him a copy of Gertrude Stein's *Tender Buttons*, which had "an explosively liberating effect" on his mind. Although he changed his mind about her later, he thought she was tremendously innovative. He credits her with leading him to the avant-garde painters who inspired the abstract style that had begun to take shape in his imagination in Toledo where he had experimented with colors in his grandmother's basement, and before that, in the children's art classes he attended at the Chicago Art Institute when he was living alone with Delia in Austin.

He also encountered, most likely at arm's length, the elite of the international art and literary world—D. H. Lawrence for one, who in late August 1923 found Chicago to be "more alive and more real than New York."[12] He met Eleanora Duse, Bertrand Russell, Isadora Duncan, Sergey Prokofiev—as well as leaders of the labor and radical movements in the United States, including Bill Haywood, Carlo Tresca, John L. Lewis, and the Wobbly poet Charlie Ashleigh.

Another locale that attracted the precocious Kenneth was Bughouse Square[13] in Washington Square, the oldest park in the city, located in the Near North Side opposite Newberry Library. A small shady area with a raised concrete dias, its platform provided "an outdoor forum of garrulous hobohemia. On summer nights local and visiting intellectual hoboes and hobophiles expound[ed] unorthodoxy, socio-political and sexual."[14] He also attended an open forum, known by regulars as the Bug Club (as distinct from Bughouse Square) in Washington Park, the largest inland park in Chicago, embracing some three hundred acres.

More than any of the official education and cultural institutions my favorite school
was Washington Park Bug Club. This was a spontaneously evolved public forum
which met every night except in the dead of winter in a shallow grassy amphithe-
ater beside a lagoon off in the middle of the park. Years later it was to be moved
to another part of the park and equipped with a concrete floor, benches, a podium. . . . In those days it looked like something in ancient Greece.[15]

The crowds at the Washington Park Open Forum were tamer, meeting
on Sunday afternoons to hear a variety of characters discuss problems of
the day. At both spots, Kenneth earned a few dollars soapboxing himself.[16]

At Bughouse Square, colorful speakers addressed the crowd: "Anar-
chist-Single-Taxers, British-Israelites, self-anointed archbishops of the
American Catholic Church, Druids, Anthroposophists . . . Socialists, communists (still with a small "c"), IWWs, DeLeonites . . . Schopenhauerians,
Nietzscheans."[17] Chicago had been, after all, the center of the labor movement: the notorious Haymarket tragedy and the Pullman strike are among
the more sordid episodes in the history of American labor strife. The
Industrial Workers of the World was organized in Chicago in 1905 by
Eugene Debs, Daniel De Leon, Vincent St. John, and Bill Haywood. Chicago also saw the strike of forty thousand clothing workers in 1910, led
by Sidney Hillman; the general steel strike of 1919, broken by federal
troops; and the "Herrin Massacre," brought on by an attempt to operate
a strip mine with non-union labor, which occurred in 1922 when Kenneth
was seventeen. By day, the benches in Washington Square were filled with
people reading newspapers or simply sitting in the sun; but on warm
summer nights, up to a hundred people would listen to the impassioned
pleas of the soapboxer (and sometimes to a partner playing the heckler),
who would pass the hat after performing.[18]

In fact, Kenneth preferred several other places to the conventional
classroom. One was the Dill Pickle Club (or "The Pickle," as regulars
called it), a row of remodeled barns on Tooker Alley, near Bughouse
Square. Originally a bona fide club of radical Bohemians, it was allegedly
founded by an ex-Wobbly organizer named Jack Jones in 1916 in an old
barn-garage on the near North Side.[19] Rexroth tells a different history
for The Pickle. He says the club was founded—with the cooperation of
people connected to the Charles Kerr Socialist Publishing Company, the
Chicago leaders of the IWW, and a few artists and writers—by Jones's
former wife, Elizabeth Gurley Flynn, the Wobbly orator known as the
"Rebel Girl" who went on to become Secretary of the Communist Party of
the United States. He also says that Jones, who turned the club into a
private enterprise, was an anarchist who had "blown off two or three
fingers on each hand souping nitroglycerine out of blasting powder in a
frying pan on the kitchen stove" during a strike in the northern Michigan
mines.[20] The Pickle had a crooked, tunnel-like entrance supposed to evoke

a "titillating speakeasy atmosphere," and made its money by giving middle-class barhoppers of Chicago the impression that they were slumming.[21] A great attraction were the plays produced on stage there, including those of Ben Hecht, a habitué. *The Master Poisoner*, his collaboration with Maxwell Bodenheim, was first staged at The Pickle. Until it became a tourist trap, the works of Strindberg, Ibsen, and Shaw were aired before appreciative audiences, as were Yeats's dance plays and Pound's translations of Japanese Noh plays. This was Rexroth's introduction to Modernism.

Kenneth haunted The Pickle on Sunday nights, when Jones ran lectures followed by open forums during which speakers were invited to be insulted, and wit more rude than original was poured out in a loud stream.[22] On Saturdays, Chicago jazz musicians like Louis Armstrong and Bix Beiderbecke played through the night. Local newspapermen of the day would hang out at The Pickle with girlfriends they had picked up on North Clark Street. There remained a central core of people who drifted over from Bughouse Square, soapboxers of politically radical persuasions, including Ben Reitman, longtime lover of Emma Goldman, radical without portfolio, physician to countless tramps and prostitutes, the man who had crowned himself King of the Hoboes.[23] Kenneth's favorite people were the anarchist and former IWW freelance soapboxers who had disassociated themselves from any organized radical movement: "however, whenever there was a hot strike or a free-speech fight they would volunteer their services—as agitators but never as organizers."[24] In retrospect, Rexroth realized that some of them, once "very active Wobs," had grown disillusioned with the "splits and the uproar of the Bolshies."[25] Kenneth looked up to these men, people like Ricky Lewis who had worked as a Wobbly printshop foreman, and John Loughman, the "King of the Soapboxers" and captain of the debating team at Hobo College, a makeshift institution that provided courses in philosophy and literature, economics, preventive medicine, and law. Kenneth felt especially drawn to Loughman, who eventually became state senator.[26] Guided by these models, Kenneth developed his own style as a fledgling soapboxer who was bringing poetry to the people—often the work of Vachel Lindsay, Lola Ridge, Hilaire Belloc, Ernest Dowson, and Algernon Swinburne.

Near the Dill Pickle stood the Radical Bookstore, on North Clark Street, founded in 1914 and operated by Lillian Udell, a former lecturer in literature, and Howard Udell, a Unitarian minister who ran Detroit's Associated Charities until he could no longer ignore how inadequately social workers helped the poor.[27] By the early twenties, Lillian was totally blind and her two daughters, Phyllis and Geraldine, took in laundry to pay their bills. The bookshop stimulated and satisfied Kenneth's developing taste for the European avant-garde. He read Guillaume Apollinaire, whose Cubist techniques were revolutionizing French poetry; and Robert Desnos, the leading exponent of automatism, whose short Surrealist poems of sharp visual details also owed something to Cubism. The Dadaist nihilism of Tristan Tzara remained appealing to Rexroth's anarchism; simultaneously he was attracted to Stefan George's brief autumnal inscapes and quasi-mystical prophecies and to the Futurist Vladimir Mayakovski, whose experimentalist verses combined hard-boiled toughness with great sensitivity, and aggressively avoided sentimentality, "fine writing," clichéd images, and facile musicality.[28] Rexroth may have picked up copies of Wyndham Lewis's *Blast* and Ezra Pound's book on Henri Gaudier-Brzeska at the bookstore. Lewis's paintings of the twenties had a "decided influence" on him, with their "sort of intact half-assembled Analytical Cubism."[29] The bookstore also supplied him with the latest political pamphlets, newspapers, and books.

In a backroom behind the store, people like Bill Haywood, Eugene Debs, and the Irish revolutionary Jim Larkin played chess or checkers. On Saturday night open house, Carl Sandburg was usually on hand "with the guitar, which he mastered as better accompaniment than the banjo for folksinging."[30] The teen-aged Udell sisters were particularly fond of Sandburg and liked Kenneth. He was not indifferent to them but nothing much happened: "all it ever came to was a kiss or two on the stage in a Wedekind tragedy of youngsters like ourselves."[31]

Another backroom was transformed into a stage for the Little Theater, which became the first art theater to tour the United States.[32] On this stage about the size of a large dining-room table, forty-four plays (twenty-five of them for the first time in the United States) were produced for an audience of ninety. The directors experimented with lighting and stage design, and the actors with Stanislavsky's theories. Sometimes Rexroth participated in the Little Theater production of Shaw and Wedekind, even though he was not a regular member of the company.[33] And he would take his acting background—and that includes soapbox experiences—on the road, enlisting people into the IWW whose ranks he himself had joined.[34] In addition, he had acquired a lustier kind of theatrical experience in a burlesque house.

Kenneth started sneaking off to the Star and Garter, located "down the line" on the Levee, the section of town that housed more exotic kinds of entertainment, to watch a big, brawny redhead called Lorelei, a burlesque star who performed the Dance of the Seven Veils at men's smokers. She was reputedly the daughter of "Gentleman Jim" Corbett, the world heavyweight champion who was regarded as a competent amateur actor (he had once played the lead in a production of Shaw's *Captain Brassbound's Conversion*). Her husband, Billy McKenzie, eked out a living as a lampshade decorator.[35] There Kenneth befriended Mick McCann, "the Champion Female Prize Fighter of the United States and the Captain of the Boston Bloomers." McCann offered him a job acting as the second in his female wrestling act at the Star and Garter:

I wore a big bright yellow wig and a pink tie and camped as no fairy would dare do. I beat her with a towel, pumped her arms and legs up and down and blew water in her face between rounds, and tied and untied her tin tits in a long comic routine. Later I got a job as a general relief man and filled in mostly for the candy butcher, but also for the comics and straight men.[36]

Kenneth had first met Lorelei, Billy McKenzie, and Mick McCann at the Green Mask, a Bohemian tea room on Grand Avenue and State Street where weekly poetry readings and lectures were conducted. Ben Hecht (his wife, Rose Kalish, was a star in the productions at the Dill Pickle) and Sherwood Anderson would come to these gatherings, and even Clarence Darrow was known to have appeared once. Alberta Hunter, Jimmy Yancey, and Irene Castle would also stop by.[37] It was run by June Wiener, a former carnival performer who wrote poetry and painted, and Beryl Bolton, a former actress in grade-B movies. Among those who contributed their talents were Edgar Lee Masters, and the writers whose names became synonymous with the Harlem Renaissance—Langston Hughes, Countee Cullen, and Claude McKay. The Green Mask was the first place where poetry was read to jazz. To the improvisations of Dave Tough[38] and other jazz musicians who were attracted to the Mask, the young Rexroth read Whitman, Sandburg, and his new favorites, the avant-garde French poets. Other readers included Sam Putnam, who as an expatriate in France edited *New Review*, and Mark Turbyfull, the poet who when he was still in high school captured Margaret Anderson's attention with a poem called "Amber Monochrome."[39] Sandburg himself sometimes showed up with his guitar, and Vachel Lindsay and Max Bodenheim occasionally participated. The room was decorated with Wiener and Bolton's paintings, "blue nudes dancing with silver fauns under crimson trees,"[40] the shelves with the little magazines of the day and books of free verse. The regulars who preferred the Green Mask were more serious than those who frequented The Pickle. Ogling tourists were not welcome. It was the early days of Prohibition, and liquor was not served. People who got drunk were bounced.[41]

While Kenneth was living with the Monahans, he provided a model for Kenny in James Farrell's *Studs Lonigan*, the young man who helps steal bicycles and who works for Vause's Drug Store, much as Kenneth did. At the time, Rexroth and Farrell did not know one another personally, and although Farrell moved events back three or four years, he captured Kenneth's cocky personality.[42] We first meet Kenny Kilarney when he and Studs are chewing tobacco together:

Kenny Kilarney appeared, and Studs smiled to see him. Kenny was thin, taller than Studs, Irish, blue-eyed, dizzy-faced, untidy, darkish, quick, and he had a nervous, original walk. . . . Kenny gave a rambling talk. . . . Studs laughed, because you had to laugh when Kenny pulled his gags. Kenny was a funny guy. He ought to be in vaudeville, even if he was still young.[43]

A bit later, after Kenny steals a bathing suit for a swim with Studs in Lake Michigan and chalks his initials on the streets of the "ritzy" Hyde Park neighborhood they pass on their way, he advises Studs on the art of seduction, "like he was an older guy with much experience."[44]

At the lake, Kenny proves to be an expert diver and swimmer ("he started a stump-the-leader game on the board but he was too good for them, so they all lost interest").[45] Kenny declares that a good lifeguard could swim all the way to Michigan City or Benton Harbor. "Studs said that Kenny was nuts, but then he couldn't talk as fast as Kilarney, so he lost the argument. Kenny just talked anyway and it didn't matter what he talked about or make him less funny."[46] In the second part of the Lonigan trilogy, *The Young Manhood of Studs Lonigan*, Studs joins the wild celebration on Michigan Avenue of Armistice Day. He and his friends spot Kenny Kilarney on top of one of the lions in front of the Art Institute, flinging tomatoes into the crowd.[47] There can be little doubt that close behind this portrait of Kenny sits an early aspect of Rexroth.

Kenneth lived with the Monahan family for about three years. He remained fond of his cousins, and Aunt Minnie and Uncle Paul, but at seventeen he had grown too independent to blend in with a traditional Chicago-Irish family. He wanted the freedom to come and go as he pleased, and a quiet space to write, paint, and study. Paul and Minnie Monahan did not discourage Kenneth from leaving in 1923. With the money he earned as a soda jerk and delivery boy for Vause's drugstore, his gigs in the burlesque houses, and the tiny income he received from his salvaged inheritance, he rented a two-room apartment at 5427 Prairie Avenue, one block west of Calumet Avenue, in the same South Side working-class neighborhood of closely spaced single-family bungalows.[48] The building belonged to a Jewish family of garment trade unionists and Socialists. Kenneth bought an easel, a supply of paints, put his mother's Medici prints on the wall, and moved in an old, abandoned piano.

That same year Al Capone bought a house at 7244 Prairie Avenue, down the street from Kenneth. (He lived there for eight years before he was convicted in 1931 of income-tax evasion.) Chicago had become a wide-open town that supported a huge trade in liquor, gambling, and prostitution, with gangsters also controlling many legitimate enterprises. Millions of dollars were at stake, and rival gangs blasted each other with sawed-off shotguns and submachine guns trying to protect their territories. Chains of speakeasies and honky-tonks opened up, and Kenneth would move along the fringes of these places.

But mostly he was hanging out at the Green Mask, where he would often be stranded late at night. When his favorite burlesque dancer and her husband invited him to room with them in the nearby West Adams apartment, he accepted the offer. The rent would be cheaper, too. His uncle Paul helped him move his belongings over to West Adams Street. But before long, he discovered that boarding with Lorelei and Billy

McKenzie had its perils. Their circle of friends included petty thieves and a few high-powered gangsters as well. Kenneth decided to move out. McKenzie and Lorelei eventually broke up, and McKenzie left the underworld to lead the more respectable life of an intellectual Bohemian. He and Kenneth remained friends during Kenneth's Chicago years.

The Near North Side was Kenneth's haunt. Close to Chicago's Gold Coast, the real distance was enormous. Young and adventurous people who had come to the city seeking their fortunes settled there. This district was known for little theaters, bookstores, Bohemian and radical clubs. Its rooming houses and old buildings had been cheaply converted into studios for artists. Art stores, antique shops, and rare book stalls were tucked away among the old buildings. South of Chicago Avenue were the slums, home for the "laborer, hobo, the rooming-house family, the . . . bohemian, the criminal, and all sort of shipwrecked humanity."[49] North of Chicago Avenue lived young, unmarried men and women who worked in the nearby Loop as accountants, stenographers, and clerks. The entire district was crisscrossed with business streets.

When Kenneth got bored with writers and artists, he would walk down to Clark Street, an "all night" street of bars, chili parlors, pool halls, dance halls. It ran through the second largest community of Greeks in the country, and he would pass the evening in one of the clubs, "drinking moustike, smoking a narghile, and watching the belly dancers."[50] He liked to join the nightly circle of folk dancers, "holding on to a handkerchief and lunging about like a bear."[51]

He got the money for this entertainment by clerking at A. C. McClurg & Company, the bookstore whose owner published *The Dial.* At the turn of the century, journalists, writers, and devotees would congregate there to exchange ideas and opinions at a spot they called "Saints' and Sinners' Corner." The star of the group was the poet and journalist Eugene Field. By 1924, the Saints' and Sinners' Corner had dissolved, but Kenneth was touched by its history and decided to try his hand in the newspaper world. He soon discovered how unromantic it was, and how all the stories were "puffed and padded with sentimentality."[52] But he knew that with a press card, he would gain access to the more elite sections of society, and that he would have a chance to meet writers.

On his first job as reporter with the City News Service, he earned eighteen dollars a week covering the petty courts, the police stations, and the morgue for the Chicago papers. He quit for one no better, covering conventions for the *Journal of Commerce,* whose offices were down the street from the Green Mask. His colleagues were more congenial here, especially Hi Simons, who had served a prison term as a wartime conscientious objector and written a volume of poems. Rexroth finally struck it lucky with the *Herald and Examiner,* as a part-time reporter. This job enabled him to meet the Chicago writers he had hoped to meet, most of whom, after all, were journalists. He would tag along after them for lunch at Schlogel's, a Chicago institution modeled on the English coffeehouses of Samuel Johnson's time that served as a meeting place for Chicago writers, much as the Algonquin Hotel did for New York writers.[53] Regulars at Schlogel's Round Table, as it was called, included Henry Justin Smith, news editor of the *Daily News,* and his colleagues Keith Preston and Lloyd Lewis. Harry Hansen, the precocious war correspondent and childhood friend of Floyd Dell, often sat beside Ben Hecht. Pascal Covici and Billy McGee, whose bookstore on Washington Street was a new version of the Saints' and Sinners' Corner at McClurg's, made sure to talk to Sherwood Anderson, who stopped by whenever he was in town. Rexroth had already seen many of these men at the Dill Pickle.

During the course of his brief newspaper career (later resumed in San Francisco), Rexroth encountered the seamier side of Chicago life, meeting people who lived on the edge and eked out a marginal life stealing, informing, and selling their bodies. Rexroth developed an appetite for this "lowest low life," and claimed to have preferred from that time on "a saloon frequented by prostitutes and thieves to a coffee bar full of bad poets."[54] Rexroth himself was beaten up by the police because he and two friends were mistakenly suspected of stealing a wallet. Dragged to the police station at 6:00 a.m., they were mugged, fingerprinted, then shown the "goldfish": they were released at ten o'clock that night "having had nothing to eat, drink, or smoke, with black eyes, split eyebrows, torn lips, sprained fingers, burned toes."[55] Still a minor, Kenneth's case was brought to the attention of Judge Henry Horner, later to become governor of Illinois. Horner, however, was already familiar with Kenneth Rexroth.

Admitted to the bar in 1899, Horner was elected judge of the Probate Court of Cook County when he had just turned thirty-five. A member of the Chicago Literary Club, he wrote poetry and literary essays, and collected Lincolnia—he eventually acquired 1,900 books about Lincoln alone and about 350 funeral orations. Among those who would browse through his collection were Carl Sandburg, who was then writing *The Prairie Years.* During his five-year tenure as judge, Horner developed an intense affection for children. His biographer writes: "Once a year all children under guardianship were called in for personal interviews with the judge. When the rights of children were involved, Horner took special care."[56] Kenneth had become one of those children after his case was brought to Horner's attention three years earlier, on April 13, 1921.

When Kenneth came back to Chicago in 1919, the Monahans asked a family friend, David Macdonald, to serve as his legal guardian the following year. Kenneth had inherited a little money from his father and from the grandmother who had treated him so atrociously in Toledo. His small estate was settled in Judge Horner's court.[57] Horner took a personal interest in Kenneth, who immediately informed him that he wanted to be a writer and painter. The judge raised no objection to this precocious adolescent living on his own; and he may have seen Kenneth hanging around the Loeb house where he was often a guest. He did suggest that Kenneth continue his education in a more conventional way—by officially attending college or classes at the Art Institute—but Kenneth resisted. When he moved in with Lorelei, Horner became uneasy. One evening Horner came to West Adams Street, "scared the Feelys [sic] out of their wits," and invited Kenneth to dinner. After he had subjected Kenneth to a brisk lecture on the downward path of crime, the two walked over to the Green Mask and enjoyed the entertainment. Before the evening ended, Horner gave him a telephone number to call in the event of trouble. By the time Horner learned of Kenneth's day-long ordeal at the police station, there was nothing he could do but admonish him for being at the wrong place at the wrong time. However, this was not to be Rexroth's final encounter with the police.

One Thursday evening during a poetry reading at the Green Mask, the police from the East Chicago station busted June Wiener and Beryl Bolton on the charge of keeping a disorderly house. The writer whose work was featured that night was accused of lewd and lascivious conduct and making an obscene exhibition. Rexroth was also arrested because he had invested a small portion of his grandmother's inheritance in the Green Mask, and was hence considered part owner. Apparently one of the police detectives was exacting revenge on June Wiener, who had refused to give her dog to the detective's girlfriend, a woman who (by Rexroth's account) worked upstairs in a brothel operated by the Greek syndicate. June, Beryl, the poet, and Kenneth were each sentenced to a year in jail and a thousand-dollar fine. Kenneth feared that if the police discovered he was a minor, they would boot him off to reformatory school. Even worse, Judge Horner was out of town, and Kenneth was sentenced to the Chicago House of Correction, the municipal prison established in 1871 to supplant the old Bridewell, land known by all as the Bandhouse.[58] There he suffered indignities and abuses—attempted rape, filthy living conditions, vile food, lice.

However, his friendship with two very different types made his tenure bearable. He had a cellmate nicknamed Blackie, doing life on a murder charge. Once Blackie took a liking to Kenneth and cranked up his connections to the restaurant underworld, the food improved dramatically. Kenneth's other friend, a prison guard, was an old-time radical named MacGregor who was a perfect chess partner and who brought him books from the public library. Thus through the winter of 1923–24 Kenneth maintained his sanity, certain that once Judge Horner returned, he would be released. On the day he was set free, though, it was not Judge Horner or Minnie Monahan who greeted him at the gate but an attractive young social worker by the name of Leslie Smith.

Three

FIRST LOVES
1922–1924

KENNETH HAD MET Leslie earlier when he was first living
on his own in the small Prairie Street apartment. A
confirmed truant and ward of the probate court, he
had been classified as a problem adolescent. Leslie, who
was working for the Institute of Juvenile Research, was assigned Kenneth's case. On the day she came to investigate, she was not prepared to
meet a precocious, arrogant, handsome seventeen-year-old, nine years
her junior, who already regarded himself as a poet and an abstract painter.
In her first confusion she mistook Kenneth for his father, while he was
struck by her resemblance to the photograph of Katherine Mansfield on
the dust jackets of her books—"thin exophthalmic, overbred, sensitive."[1]
He invited her in, served her tea, and talked about his problems with
school and money, but "suddenly the atmosphere in the room became
insufferably tense."[2] They went out to nearby Washington Park and headed
for the island in the middle of the boating lake—that very same place
where Studs Lonigan takes his sweetheart (it no longer exists). After
arranging a date with Leslie for the following week, he returned to his
studio and blocked out an abstract portrait of her.

Soon after this encounter, Kenneth moved to the Near North Side,
first to live with Lorelei and Billy McKenzie, and then to his own one-
room studio. Leslie, it so happened, also lived in the same neighborhood.
She introduced him to her friends, who looked like "Virginia Woolf, the
Stracheys, and the second generation of the Fabian Society."[3] Kenneth's
literary taste began to change. The graceful lyrics of Verlaine, and Walter
Pater's philosophic romance *Marius the Epicurean,* became more important than Tristan Tzara's Dada and Blaise Cendrars' surrealism. He lost
interest in the carefully documented novels of Balzac, but together
he and Leslie struggled through the first pages of *A la recherche du temps
perdu,* mangling the French as they read aloud (Nowhere is there evidence
that Kenneth studied French systematically, though he did attend a class
in advanced French "in a hit or miss fashion" at Englewood High because

he had a crush on the teacher.)[4] Kenneth himself broke out with poems, some in imitation of the Decadents, others far better.[5] He made progress on a poem started a year earlier, "a long philosophic epic, or really reverie" that would appear thirty-five years later under the title of *The Homestead Called Damascus*.[6] And the "color chord of [Leslie's] personality: gray-blue, sienna, yellow ochre, pale umber, gray lavender, terre-verte, coral silver" inspired him to experiment further with his painting technique. In the early days of their romance, they wandered together in the dusk and met for tea at the Chicago Art Institute. Kenneth, completely infatuated with Leslie, proposed marriage to her. When she turned him down, he proposed again.

The following spring (1923), Leslie, feeling trapped by Kenneth's obsessive attention, devised what she thought was a foolproof plan to end their relationship. She left Chicago to study at Smith College for the summer. She did not think Kenneth would follow her to Northampton; but still hoping that Leslie would marry him, he hitchhiked east, picking up jobs along the way. In Northampton he worked as waiter, cook, and operator of a stapling machine that stuck bristles into toothbrushes. He rented a cheap hotel room near Leslie's dormitory. When he was free, he would visit the Common Cupboard, a Boston tea room popular with Bohemians.

Leslie abandoned her attempt to sever connections with her persistent devotee, and the couple spent their leisure time together "in totalized, utterly self-abandoned intimacy."[7] The setting of the sixth stanza of "The Thin Edge of Your Pride" (1949) is Paradise Pond behind Smith College ("The minute fingers of the imperceptible air / Arrange a shadow tracery of leaf and hair / About your face"). And from this period grew one of the best-known love poems in the Rexroth canon, "When We with Sappho":

> We lie here in the bee filled, ruinous
> Orchard of a decayed New England farm,
> Summer in our hair, and the smell
> Of summer in our twined bodies,
> Summer in our mouths, and summer
> In the luminous, fragmentary words
> Of this dead Greek woman.
> Stop reading. Lean back. Give me your mouth
> Your grace is as beautiful as sleep.
> You move against me like a wave
> That moves in sleep.
> Your body spreads across my brain
> Like a bird filled summer;
> Not like a body, not like a separate thing,
> But like a nimbus that hovers
> Over every other thing in all the world.

> Lean back. You are beautiful,
> As beautiful as the folding
> Of your hands in sleep.[8]

The passionate, lyrical energy of the first section quoted here is maintained throughout the poem. It reflects a brief idyllic time for Kenneth, away from the Chicago hustle.

Instead of returning to Chicago in the fall of 1923, Leslie headed for New York, where she secured a job as a social worker. Over her protests, Kenneth followed her. Although she settled in East Orange, New Jersey, Kenneth preferred to prowl the Village, seeking the kind of stimulation his parents had found in New York when they took him there as a child. He rented a room on West 13th Street, "one of the most Bohemian nests in the history of the American intellect,"[9] and before long launched himself into the artistic and political swim. Among the people he purportedly met was Communist chief Earl Browder, who had been released from prison in 1920 after serving a year for opposing the United States entry into World War I; the proletarian writer Mike Gold; the painter Marsden Hartley (who was writing poetry at the time); Max Eastman, and the group of people generally associated with *The Liberator* and *New Masses*. In this same building Emma Goldman had lived with Alexander Berkman in a two-room apartment that served as an office for *Mother Earth* and as a gathering place for leftist intellectuals. Known as "the home for lost dogs," the apartment attracted rootless or moneyless people like Kenneth. Rebounding from Leslie's rebuffs, he engaged in a brief affair with an Indian singer.

Leslie continued to remain elusive. After work, when she was not attending classes at the New School, she was studying for the Civil Service Examination to advance her career as a social worker. To disentangle herself from Kenneth's pursuit, she tried not altogether successfully to act like an older sister. "You make yourself look old by not getting enough sleep," she lectured him in a letter of October 7, "by irregular living—and too many cigarettes." She goes on:

I don't like your trying to look old. You're much more attractive as a youth, KR. . . . Why do you dress with such sophistication? It makes you conspicuous—and the unobstrusiveness that comes of simplicity both of manner and appearance would suit you so much better. For anyone of your sensitiveness I should think you would realize the effect you produce on me. It is inharmonious—and somehow being false to the reality that is you.[10]

Kenneth did not react cheerfully to these comments, which set the tone for their next meeting in Washington Square Park the following Tuesday. Kenneth wanted more romance, less advice on wholesome living.

Five days later, on October 12, Leslie wrote again, pointing out that his education had "not been specific or scientific enough to carry [him] through a logical development of ideas." She conceded that he had faced harsh realities prematurely, but she emphasized that he could not expect the love of a woman to solve all his problems. "You can understand," she concludes, "what my ideal of beauty is—the perfection of adjustment that I believe can be worked out between individuals and their environment. . . . I do not believe as you do that unity can ever be found in the reciprocation of love between two persons."[11] To Kenneth, these remarks seemed intolerably patronizing. Leslie was deliberately analyzing their relationship as though it were simply part of her caseload. She knew that she ran the risk of alienating him, that he could respond by withdrawing into himself and becoming paranoid. Indeed, these comments may have sent him, like his character Sebastian in *The Homestead Called Damascus,* in search of solace at the only tea room in the Village (on the corner of Thompson and Washington Square South) that did not cater to gawking tourists:

> . . . sitting in Romany
> Marie's one stormy evening, watching
> The green distorted faces pass the
> Street lamp, watching the distorted
> Silhouettes on the drawn shades of the
> Tenement across the street, [he] listens
> To gitanas on the phonograph
> And drinks a glass of fermented milk.[12]

Both of Leslie's letters had been sent to still another address—this time on West 22nd Street—reflecting the transience of Kenneth's New York life.[13]

His romance with Leslie going nowhere, Kenneth returned to Chicago. He rented a small North Side apartment[14] and went back to helping June and Beryl run the Green Mask. He wrote tortured letters to Leslie, telling her that he was drowning in the agony of her rejection and in desperation was taking drugs. Leslie wrote back: "Why? Why? It *isn't* like you—I won't have it like you! Instead of living up to the noblest that is in you, you seek to destroy the best of you, leaving a warped and twisted mass which no one could endurably recognize."[15] Most important here is Leslie's indirect acknowledgment that their relationship had gone far beyond that of social worker and client. She wrote:

Kenneth, don't you see that as you offer it, [love] is something to hurt me always, nothing can help me in any way. And yet you realize yourself that I am a misfit, that I rebel against the environment that crushes me and have just about as much unhappiness in my life as you have. . . . Have you quite forgotten the times I tried to be kind—or are they all so classified in your mind as blundering cruelties that you cannot feel the passionate longing behind them to make you happy.

When Leslie returned to Chicago, Kenneth had disappeared into the bowels of the Chicago House of Correction. After he was released, at the end of the winter, she insisted that he see a psychiatrist. He complied, but therapy did little to cool his ardor. However, she had acquired two other suitors for her hand, one a surgeon, the other an accountant. Instead of telling Kenneth that she had compromised herself by failing to keep the relationship professional, she informed him that an impecunious Bohemian could not possibly provide her with the lifestyle she now envisioned for herself. She had finally figured out how to extricate herself from the clutch of this hot eighteen-year-old.

Though unwilling to abandon Leslie, Kenneth directed his energy elsewhere. He became involved in a Dill Pickle production of Pirandello's *Six Characters in Search of an Author* after reading it in *Broom,* the little magazine published by Alfred Kreymborg and Harold Loeb. If the actors looked "as if they were moving around in pea soup and the whole thing was far more modernistic than the text of Pirandello warranted,"[16] Kenneth was proud of the costumes, masks, and sets that he contributed to the production. Occasionally he filled in for actors who didn't show up. Much later, when he began to write plays, this experience would prove useful.

About this time, he met a young woman named Nancy Shores who had earned her living as an exhibition dancer before she became the model on the original Breck shampoo bottle. She and Kenneth took to each other immediately, and soon they were spending their evenings in the mass dance halls where Chicagoans flocked during the twenties, thirties, and forties. By 1917, the city counted more than four hundred public dancehalls, but most of them were dives, small stuffy back rooms in bars where, according to the Juvenile Protective Association, men and women became "intoxicated" and "danced indecently" such numbers as "Walkin' the Dog," "On the Puppy's Tail," "Shaking the Shimmy," "The Dip," and "The Stationary Wiggle."[17] Young people looking for a more respectable setting went to the Dreamland Ballroom on the West Side; Marigold Gardens, Guyons Paradise Garden, and the Arcadia on the North Side; and the outdoor dance pavilions White City and Midway Gardens, both amusement parks. Kenneth and Nancy patronized many of them, but favored the most famous one, the Trianon, owned and operated by two brothers from Greece, Andrew and William Karzas. It was styled after its French model in Versailles—tapestries lined the walls, chairs were upholstered in brocaded velvet, and Corinthian marble columns surrounded the dance floor. A domed ceiling reflected a constantly changing display of colored lights, an appropriate setting for Rudolf Valentino's first performance of the tango that year. Men were required to wear coats and ties; women could not wear slacks, saddle shoes, or sweaters. Kenneth and Nancy danced sedately to the music of the country's top bands—Dick Jurgens, the Dorseys, Guy Lombardo, and Lawrence Welk.

During this period Kenneth wrote a love poem ostensibly to Nancy while still carrying the torch for Leslie. Dancing until dawn with Nancy helped him forget his unrequited love, but no sooner had he escorted her home than his thoughts would turn to Leslie, who lived in the same building on Astor Place:

> I pass your home in a slow vermilion dawn,
> The blinds are drawn, and the windows open.
> The soft breeze from the lake
> Is like your breath upon my cheek.
> All day long I walk in the intermittent rainfall.
> I pick a vermilion tulip in the deserted park,
> Bright raindrops cling to its petals.
> At five o'clock it is a lonely color in the city.
> I pass your home in a rainy evening,
> I can see you faintly, moving between lighted walls
> Late at night I sit before a white sheet of paper,
> Until a fallen vermilion petal quivers before me.

When this wistful lyric to Leslie first appeared in *The Art of Worldly Wisdom*, its first line was the title. Reprinted in *The Collected Shorter Poems*, it was entitled "Confusion."[18]

Kenneth was not the only one with two irons in the fire. After an evening of the tango in Kenneth's arms, Nancy announced that she was marrying a stockbroker the following day. Like Leslie, she wanted a good provider, and knew that this young, hustling, aspiring poet-painter had other priorities. When Kenneth turned to Leslie for solace, she steered him back to a psychiatrist. For the next two months he enjoyed his weekly sessions, during which he talked mostly about politics. He also resumed his nearly obsessive reading, concentrating on the Middle English poets and philosophers, especially Duns Scotus, whose incomprehensibility appealed to him. The theological philosophies of St. Thomas, St. Augustine, St. Bonaventure, and Abelard now gripped and comforted his mind more than the social theories of Eugene Debs, Herbert Spencer, Thomas Huxley—or his analyst.

On the surface, Kenneth seemed to defy Leslie's fears that he would isolate himself, although she could not have approved of the company he sought. He still liked burlesque and vaudeville people and also pursued some underground connections made during his stint in the Chicago House of Corrections. For a while he drove for Eddie MacMillan, a "bag man" for Bugsy Moran. They made the rounds of South Side businesses still under Moran's so-called protection, many of them hideouts for petty gangsters. One on Western Avenue was a particular favorite of Kenneth's. Whenever he appeared there with a "date," he was treated as a VIP. Kenneth liked MacMillan, an "intellectual gangster" who eventually (with the help of Ben Hecht) got to play "bad guys" in Hollywood movies.[19]

Not yet nineteen, Kenneth was a high school dropout, a rogue, a budding actor, a card-carrying radical, a poet, painter, and an avid reader.

He was still living on the Near North Side, in a garret studio where he shared a bathroom with a neighbor, his friend Billy McKenzie. McKenzie and his new girlfriend Sherry introduced Kenneth to Sherry's best friend, Milly Tokarsky, a University of Chicago senior a year older than Kenneth.[20] Kenneth, who liked to be called "Rex" during this period, fell in love with Milly, but she did not reciprocate. The two, however, became good friends.[21] Milly was drawn to Kenneth's Bohemian lifestyle, and was quite impressed by the decor of his small apartment. The walls and ceiling were covered with blue and white batik, and paintings, all by Kenneth. With a major in mathematics, a minor in philosophy, a strong interest in the arts, and a father who used to take her to Emma Goldman's lectures, Milly was the perfect companion for Kenneth when he wanted to talk about Newton, Aquinas, Cocteau, and T. S. Eliot's *The Waste Land,* which had appeared in *The Dial* the previous year. (Although initially overwhelmed by the poem's dissociative style and its "authentic accent of current idiom," Rexroth believed that it had a negative influence on his own poetry: Eliot's "weary, disillusioned withdrawal . . . had become extremely infectious.")[22] Kenneth would introduce Milly to his anarchist friends at The Pickle, including John Loughman, whom she admired and respected even though one evening he irreverently mounted a soapbox in Bughouse Square in the name of the IWW in order to buy the makings for a Mulligan stew.

After she was graduated in 1924, Milly hitchhiked to New York in search of work. (She was denied a teaching position in a small town in Oklahoma, and in Wheaton, Illinois, because she was Jewish.) In an amorous mood, Rexroth visited her there, but Milly resisted his advances. He asked her to marry him but she did not take the proposal seriously. Although Milly had enjoyed the visits she and Kenneth made to the Chicago Art Institute and their nightlong talks about books and people, she avoided any romantic attachment, and suspected that had she succumbed, Kenneth would have lost interest in her. He dedicated to her his translation of the Fifth Elegy by the sixth-century Etruscan poet Maximianus, entitled "Maximian, Elegy V" (first published in the *Pacific Spectator* in 1948). The theme of this poem might lead one to suspect that they had been intimate. It describes a young man's erotic adventure with a flirtatious Greek girl. Maximianus uses the occasion to lament his own waning sexual powers. Rexroth's version is a peculiar mix of pathos and fear; an eerily still moonlit sky reminds him of a long-ago tear-filled evening he spent with a lover. She is anguished by their own personal problems, and by "the general chaos / Of the world" as well. He foresees a troubled life for them both, and predicts, perhaps with some vengeance, that she will end up "abandoned on / A parachute of ruin."[23]

Rexroth temporarily lost touch with Milly when, having caught the reckless spirit of the twenties, she left from Canada for Paris. Although she was only twenty-one, she felt that her time for adventure was running out. Had he known anything about the circumstances of her voyage, his fears for her safety would have been justified. She had spent almost all her money for the berth and would have to find work immediately. She assumed that at the worst, the American Embassy would pay her return ticket. As it turned out, Milly was on the same boat as Emma Goldman, and by the time they landed in Le Havre, Goldman, who first noticed Milly innocently wandering around the library and lounges reserved for first-class passengers, had arranged a job for her in Paris as a secretary. Milly and Kenneth would remain lifelong friends, albeit increasingly far apart as the pattern of their lives created physical and emotional distance between them. Strangely enough, Milly was not aware that Kenneth was a poet until he sent her a copy of *The Art of Worldly Wisdom,* which contains "A Prolegomenon to a Theodicy," the long poem dedicated to her.

Kenneth was hardly prostrated by Milly's rebuffs—at least not outwardly so. He stayed on in New York, sacking out in one sublet room after another. He ended up in a commune on Dominic Street set up by Frances Midner, who had run the Washington Square Book Shop, and was part of the crowd associated with *Broom.* The protégé of Jane Heap and Margaret Anderson, Midner had helped select the art for the *Little Review,* and accompanied Djuna Barnes to Paris. She also worked at the Penguin and Unicorn bookshops on Eighth Street. Illustrator Bill Gropper, poet R. E. F. Larsson (whom Kenneth knew in Chicago), and Harriet and Kep Thorpe (whose friendship later on in Chicago would precipitate the circumstances that led to Kenneth's first marriage) were also part of the commune. They were all evicted from the building when excavation for the Holland Tunnel project ruined its foundation. Kenneth returned to Chicago. There he formed several new liaisons, including one with the wealthy daughter of an Army officer who had grown up on an Indian reservation, collected pornography, drank Slivovitz, and played Bartók, Satie, and Stravinsky on the piano. Meta spent her last night as an unmarried woman with Kenneth, just as Nancy had. Kenneth apparently satisfied the need of some women for "one last fling." In fact he seemed eager to accommodate several similar requests.[24]

Rexroth had not recovered from his mother's early death nor the subsequent rejection by Leslie, a woman who was in part a mother surrogate figure. When he felt sufficiently in control of himself to look for her again, he discovered that she had been sent to the Chicago Municipal Tuberculosis Sanatorium after an operation for hyperthyroidism. Unlike Delia, Leslie had been properly diagnosed, and she could look forward to a healthy life as soon as she was pronounced cured. A very respectable future awaited her: she was officially engaged now to a physician with whom she would settle in Omaha. Conceding that their friendship belonged to the past, Rexroth later idealized the experiences they shared, creating some of his most exquisite poetry, such as "The Thin Edge of Your Pride":

After a hundred years have slept above us
Autumn will still be painting in the Berkshires;
Gold and purple storms will still
Climb over the Catskills.
They will have to look a long time
For my name in the musty corners of libraries;
Utter forgetfulness will mock
Your uncertain ambitions.
But there will be other lovers,
Walking along the hill crests,
Climbing, to sit entranced
On pinnacles in the sunset,
In the moonrise.
The Catskills,
The Berkshires,
Have good memories.[25]

Although it may be difficult to comprehend the depth and magnitude of Rexroth's attachment to Leslie—from all outward signs she either resisted or denied her feelings for him—he claims that his relationship with her was the "most profound emotional involvement" of his young life.[26]

Rexroth would continue to seek women destined to leave him—if not for his youth (they were often older than he was) and his emotional neediness, then for his poor prospects as a provider. His good looks and Bohemian lifestyle were powerful attractions, but his appeal to women waned as they got closer to the realities of marriage. Such early disappointments did not bode well for Rexroth's future loves.

Four

THE RADICAL BOHEMIAN /
THE TENTATIVE POSTULANT

1924–1926

WITHIN THE NEXT TWO YEARS, Rexroth stepped up his involvement in "theatrical productions" as a medium of leftist propaganda. He took his talent west, as much to get away from Chicago as anything else. Dusting off his soapbox from his Bughouse Square days, he hitched a ride to Seattle, where his newspaper experience in Chicago led to a stint on *The Industrial Worker*. He moved north and landed a job at the ranger station near Marblemount.[1] He felt a deep connection with this part of the country. The people he met there spoke in the tones and patterns that made sense to him and their voices awoke part of his own authentic idiom. And while he carried out his duties as patrolman (keeping the trails open for stock crews, etc.), he discovered the world of the mountains. One weekend while climbing the western slope of Glacier Peak (11,000 feet), he was overwhelmed by the rugged beauty of the landscape: "To the southwest the great mountain rose up covered with walls of ice. There was no one near me for many miles in any direction. I realized then, with complete certainty, this was the place for me. This was the kind of life I liked best. I resolved to live it as much as I could from then on."[2]

He next explored the headwaters of Skagit River along the Canadian border, and arranged an itinerary that would permit him to climb a peak every evening after work. When he lost his job at Marblemount to a forestry student from the University of Washington, he bought a horse from the district ranger, Tommy Thompson, and joined a pack outfit hauling building materials for a lookout on the summit of Mt. McGregor. Rexroth had gone back on Leslie's advice to quit smoking, but the boss of the outfit, Old Dan as he was called, offered him five dollars more a week if he got rid of his cigarettes. He worked with Old Dan's group for the summer, mostly wrangling horses, cooking, and learning to backpack.

By the end of August, Rexroth had earned $200, had quit smoking (for the time being), and had made another $200 designing a label and writing some copy for the Moses Coulee Apple Growers Cooperative, whose director he had met at a camp near Lake Chelan. After other odd jobs as cook and packer, he turned around and hitchhiked back to Chicago. Several unusual women crossed his path, including two sisters who were acrobats—"they went bouncing around the campsite like a couple of rubber bear cubs."[3] He was almost poisoned by carbon monoxide fumes while working in a corn silo in Wisconsin, an experience that soured him on what he called "eastern" farmwork. This western odyssey would inspire Rexroth to pull up stakes and head for California two years later.

Soon after he returned to Chicago, his friend Harold Mann, a former silk stocking salesman from St.Louis, and fellow anarchist, insisted that they head south to the sun, soapboxing and panhandling to pay their way. They got as far as El Paso, where the poverty was so great that there was no food to spare even if a person could pay for it. But they gained the trust of one of the few well-to-do farmers around, so that by the time they got back to Chicago around Thanksgiving of 1924, they had consumed enough sowbelly and moonshine to last them their lives.

Rexroth and Mann rented a huge floor-through attic apartment at the corner of Ontario and Michigan and went back to their familiar haunts— especially the Dill Pickle. They befriended three young dancers from the Chicago Opera Company and entertained them in their spacious quarters. Rexroth became especially fond of Dorothy Bond, a beautiful young woman with long brown hair, an oval face, a perfect figure, and "spectacular legs and feet." Although she made most of her money as a photo model and by dancing at Ike Bloom's and the Marigold Gardens, she was a University of Chicago graduate who had majored in home economics.[4] Like many of Rexroth's lovers, she left him for a businessman, but she won a special place in Kenneth's memory in part because the businessman threw her over. She became the co-dedicatee (with Leslie Smith) of *The Homestead Called Damascus*.[5]

About this time, Rexroth resumed interest in the avant-garde theories of André Breton and Tristan Tzara, and also immersed himself in the work of the French anarchist Pierre-Joseph Prudhon. He was encouraged in this direction by two friends, Sam Putnam, and Lawrence Lipton, who had landed a job as assistant editor for Frank Harris's *Pearson's* magazine in its new Chicago headquarters.[6] The three young men decided to put their latest thoughts about these theories into action. They wrote free-associational, automatic poetry, and gave lectures during which they read antiphonally from Kant and the telephone directory, while shills in the audience set off alarm clocks and shot at them with blank cartridges. Sometimes they performed dance rituals—in which Dorothy starred—in their attic, decorated with collages made out of rubbish, They staged Roger Vitrac's satirical farce *The Painter* at the Dill Pickle. They rented

evening clothes, painted on Halloween faces, brandished open black umbrellas, and paraded up and down the escalators of The Fair, one of
Chicago's department stores. Lawrence Lipton says: "In Chicago I joined
the Escalator Movement under the name of Gertrude Stein and nobody
suspected anything. From a poet named Rexroth I learned about six
different kinds of sex, all of them subversive."[7]

They carried on like this until one evening a beautiful black woman in
the audience embarrassed them into giving a true account of the philosophy they seemed so energetically to espouse. She accused them of exemplifying the bankruptcy of Western civilization. This woman, it turned
out, was a black nationalist and active member of the Communist Party,
who supported herself by dancing and stripteasing in the big Chicago
burlesque houses. She persuaded Rexroth to attend lecture and discussion groups on the South Side, and to assist her when she herself lectured
at Lincoln Park on anthropology, African history, and the Harlem Renaissance. When she finally revealed that she had been asked to sing the
lead contralto in Rossini's *Stabat Mater,* Rexroth was thunderstruck, never
suspecting that she was a serious musician. This woman was the great jazz
singer Alberta Hunter, the star of Café Society, who went underground
in Los Angeles during the McCarthy period.[8] When she resurfaced, she
had made a new career for herself as a nurse, although eventually (in her
seventies) she got back to singing jazz at the Cookery in Greenwich Village. She pops up in *An Autobiographical Novel* as a dancer and in a South
State Street burlesque house in *The Homestead:*

> Haitian drums or African and horns
> From New Orleans. She rolls her buttocks
> Like kelp on the sea surge or taffy
> In a churn. Rhinestones cover her bee-stung
> Pussy and perch on each nipple. Drums
> Roll as she rolls her belly and her eyes.[9]

In the fall of 1924, Rexroth fulfilled an old dream by visiting Taos,
where he and Harold Mann had hoped to go earlier. He went to several
parties at the home of Mabel Dodge Luhan, but he was not impressed by
the generally hostile environment created by the opposing factions of
D. H. Lawrence followers, nor by Lawrence himself, who would leave the
room in a fit of anger whenever obscene language was used. Lawrence
the man was no favorite of his, even if Rexroth did eventually edit a
volume of his most imagistic poems with an introduction that created a
new American audience for him. Rexroth made a point of telling Lipton
that he could not admire a man who refused to have children, no matter
how great his talent.[10] Nevertheless, it was Lawrence's perspective on the
unifying power of romantic love that Rexroth had hoped to achieve with
Leslie, and to express in his own poetry.

But Rexroth did make friends with, among others, Jaime De Angulo, a Johns Hopkins M.D., who had begun pioneer studies in the language of the Achumawi Indians by working with Achumawi ranch hands in Alturas.[11] Rexroth became interested in Indian language and culture, already familiar to him through the works of Frances Densmore. And he was able to indulge his interest in the "non-Aristotelean syntax of Indian and African languages" when he went over to Santa Fe, where another writer's colony was flourishing. Witter Bynner was in Santa Fe, just beginning to translate Chinese poetry. He encouraged Kenneth to concentrate on Tu Fu, the poet of the T'ang Dynasty (c. 700–800) who would become a major influence on Rexroth's work.[12]

During this Western trip, Rexroth stopped off in Girard, a town in southeast Kansas known for its Socialist and immigrant population and as home to E. Haldeman-Julius, publisher of the joint enterprise of Emanuel Julius Wayland and Marcel Haldeman. They ran the *Appeal to Reason,* a four-page Socialist newspaper dotted with epigrams and rambling anecdotes, boasting a circulation of one hundred thousand by 1899. The publisher also ran a successful reprint business, using some of Socialist Charles H. Kerr's list to turn out nickel-a-copy booklets on numerous topics. One of these booklets, *You and Your Job,* was written by Carl Sandburg. The publisher also wanted to make available to the masses the "great books," in the cheapest editions possible. According to an old friend of Rexroth's, the company was eventually charged with income-tax evasion.[13] Rexroth may have seen Haldeman-Julius publications when he was a child visiting his Socialist grandfather George Rexroth in Toledo.

Rexroth had watched other men in Bughouse Square selling similar kinds of books, and he figured if Chicagoans could be duped, why not the "weed monkeys" further west? After leaving Taos and traveling with a group of Navahos for a while, he split off for Durango to try his hand at peddling a Julius Haldeman booklet on diet. Using a gila monster, a candle, and a bright navel orange, he convinced the small crowd gathered around him that all their aches and pains were caused by constipation and that his book contained a prescription for a remedy. He ran out of wares after three or four towns.[14] He spent the rest of the summer in the western section of the Rockies, picking up temporary jobs as cook or wrangler. He preferred the company of the Hopi, Navaho, Apaches, and Crow Indians to that of his cowboy colleagues, whose jokes had become tiresome. From Jackson Hole he worked his way to Chicago, overseeing a trainload of cattle, a boring, backbreaking job that disillusioned him about a life on the prairie.

With the money he had earned, Rexroth rented an apartment next door to his friend Billy McKenzie, on Chicago Avenue, and created "a perfect room for high thinking"—decorated in blue and white, with reproductions of Greek sculpture and a Vermeer, a desk, an easel, and two

Cubist paintings.[15] He resumed his reading, concentrating on Plato, Euclid, Alfred North Whitehead, and Wittgenstein. This time he discussed his reactions with Billy McKenzie and Sam Putnam. Despite his youth and lack of formal training, Rexroth, or "Rex," as his friends still called him, dominated these conversations. He tried to give the impression that he came from an aristocratic background, and that he was sophisticated beyond his years. He created a variation of this persona for less intellectual purposes. Once when he was behind in rent, his landlady accosted him on the stairway and demanded to be paid. Billy McKenzie, whose rent was also in arrears, was with him and so was Billy's prospective wife, Sherry. Billy was polite and ingratiating, and assured the woman that the money would soon be on its way. When the landlady turned to Kenneth, he threw back his shoulders, pointed his nose in the air, and replied: "I do not bargain with the hoi-polloi," and proceeded upstairs.[16]

Such bravado paved the way for a new venture. His traveling companion, Harold Mann, and Billy McKenzie wanted to open a coffee shop / tea room like the Green Mask. They found a place near Rush Street and named it the Penguin Coffee Shop after the suggestion of a young advertising executive who wandered in while they were renovating the room.[17] The new proprietors wanted to serve good food in a genteel setting that would attract cultivated customers looking for a pleasant atmosphere where they could exchange ideas and discuss poetry. But they soon ran out of funds, and Rexroth decided to give New York City another shot.

He found an apartment in the Village on Grove Street and started up a friendship with Frances Midner, whose commune he had joined during his previous trip to New York. The building, constructed in 1830, had once been very fine, and was an excellent example of Federal architecture. After his four years in Cleveland, Hart Crane came here and lived happily with a good writing table and an uninquisitive landlady.[18] When Rexroth arrived, Crane was still there. Rexroth was in the basement, Crane right above.

When Rexroth moved in, probably the first week of January 1925, Crane was listening endlessly to Bert Williams's "The Moon Shines on the Moonshine" on his old phonograph. This ragtime lyric may have provided Crane with the seeds of those famous lines: "whitely, while benzine rinsings of the moon dissolve." Rexroth later wrote that "Hour after hour, day and night, I could hear coming through the ceiling, 'So still de night, in de ole distillery, de moon shine white on de ole machinery.' "[19]

Noisy parties went on overhead and a general state of "drunken hilarity" prevailed. Although Rexroth enjoyed these distractions, he had to escape the confines of his environment from time to time in order to remain sane. On one occasion, he and Frances Midner took the IRT subway to Van Cortland Park in the Bronx. They were able to share the kind of experience that Rexroth with his acute power of observation often romanticized in his poetry—a walk in the countryside or along the coast that persuades the poet to affirm a natural harmony in the universe. This time the visibility of the planet Mercury—"cold and dark like a / Fleck of iron"—during an eclipse of the moon provides the inspiration:

> At last
> The sun was only a thin
> Crescent in our glasses with the
> Bright planets nearby like watchers.
> Then the great cold amoeba
> Of crystal light sprang out
> On the sky. The wind passed like
> A silent crowd.[20]

However, Rexroth required a more formal solution for his spiritual needs.

Despite the activity around him, Rexroth felt alone. Something about his unorthodox lifestyle repelled and sobered him. He started to attend St. Luke's Anglican Church down at the end of his block, and in the middle of February, he was baptized. After all, his debates about Catholicism with Milly Tokarsky and Samuel Putnam in Chicago were not some kind of aberration in the general flow of his seemingly radical development. Rather, they were an expression of a part of him that would assert itself more insistently with time. He was groping for a spiritual center to his life, which neither his friends and acquaintances, his poetry, nor his painting could give. Perhaps the accumulated crises of his scattered youth, the transience, the losses and rejections had finally worn down this outwardly invincible but sensitive and emotionally bruised young man. With his parents' deathbed conversions hovering over this scene, he decided to undertake a religious retreat.

In honor of the occasion, his Grove Street friends threw a loud and raucous party.[21] Rexroth would not see most of these people again, although in the late forties he met up again with Frances Midner, who expressed nostalgia for the twenties, and was full of memories of her travels and bookstore customers, and of "what she said to Ezra and what Ezra said to Djuna."[22] The following morning, he began his trip in a winter storm. By the time he reached Poughkeepsie, across the river from Holy Cross Monastery in West Park, ten inches of snow had fallen and the thermometer had dropped below zero. To Rexroth, the world must have seemed like a cold, indifferent place and the monastery a warm, welcoming refuge.

Founded in 1884 by Father James Otis Sargent Huntington, Holy Cross Monastery in West Park, New York, is the oldest house of the Anglican Order of the Holy Cross, and is the center in the United States for the training of new members entering the Order. The priests of the Order devote half their time to traveling as preachers, and the rest to studying at the monastery. Overlooking the Hudson River and surrounded by woodlands where the naturalist John Burroughs spent the second half of his life, it operates a guesthouse for those people who come to the monastery for contemplation and the opportunity to share in the life of the monks. When Rexroth arrived that cold winter night, the community was already at evening prayers in the Romanesque chapel built by Ralph Adams Cram. He had a supper of bread, milk, and cheese, and was shown to his eight-by-ten-foot cell, furnished with a cot, a chest of drawers, a washbasin, a table and chair, a crucifix, and a small kneeling bench for prayer. He slept until he was awakened for morning prayer and mass.

Although Rexroth was regarded as a guest and not a postulant, he was expected to lead a penitent life while at Holy Cross, scrubbing down bathrooms and kitchens, eating scanty meals, and sleeping in bare quarters. Like everyone else, he remained silent at mealtimes while a lector read a brief life of the saint for that day and a related section from a religious text. He participated in all the offices and served every morning at mass. He was encouraged to paint in the large studio with a skylight above the kitchen, which was equipped with sophisticated artist's materials, and he was provided with his own typewriter and a desk after his first day. He was free to use the monastery's excellent library with its wide collection of theological texts and up-to-date works of secular philosophy. Daily he painted, prayed, wrote, and walked through the snowbound forest: "if I had been exalted riding night herd or climbing in the Cascades, or fishing in a mountain stream, I spent the days at Holy Cross transfigured. It was all one orderly rapture."[23]

Rexroth used Holy Cross Monastery and the surrounding area as the main setting of *The Homestead*. Several scenes occur on a private estate in the Hudson Valley modeled after the monastery.[24] Occasionally Rexroth used the small cabin that belonged to John Burroughs, who had died in 1921, when he wanted to immerse himself in the total isolation of the woods.[25] He was at peace during this period, and would have stayed on, except for one important matter: he lacked the vocation for the monastic life (despite occasional contrary declarations he would make in the future). He had arrived the Sunday before Lent, and left at the end of Easter week. With him he took the memory of two months of spiritual contentment. The liturgical life reflected for Rexroth "the most ancient responses to the turning of the year and the changing seasons, and the rhythms of animal and human life." It gave him, moreover, a "belief in ethical activism," based on the faith that "there is a greater existence beyond sense and reason."[26]

Rexroth left the monastery, shelved *The Homestead*, and as if to shock himself back into the real world, got passage as a mess steward in a "filthy rust bucket" bound for the ports on the English Channel. But on this trip and all others, he was now sure that he could always tap into a habit of life that "insures the accessibility of bliss of vision, of total knowledge of significance."[27] Through his mature years, images calling up that vision were to weave in and out of his poetry.

When the Ellerman Lines ship docked at Dunkirk, Rexroth decided to visit Paris and return before it pulled out for Plymouth. He wanted to sit outside at Montparnasse cafés like the Dôme, the Select, La Closerie des Lilas, where he could glimpse the writers, painters, and musicians whose work he had been so avidly following with his Chicago friends. When he was not lingering at the Dôme or the Rotonde during his brief leave in Paris, Rexroth "walked systematically through every museum"[28] and roamed the streets until the early hours. Neither Rexroth's antics in the Escalator movement nor his workouts in Chicago dancehalls had prepared him for the decadent sophistication of the Left Bank. Moreover, his command of spoken French was minimal. Rexroth met Alexander Berkman, already dying of cancer and vastly changed from the fire-eater Kenneth had seen as a child. Berkman advised Rexroth that his place was in the United States, specifically the Far West. As if those were the very words he was waiting to hear, Rexroth went back to his ship, and by July 1925 was in Montana picking up jobs again as a fry cook and horse wrangler.

In September he headed for Missoula, where he met a man named Billy Orville, who turned out to be more interesting than any of his European heroes. Like Rexroth, he had started out as a cook and wrangler, and "had all the characteristics which fiction and the movies made standard equipment for a Western old-timer and in addition he was amazingly literate and well informed and one of the wisest men I've ever met."[29] An old man, who walked with a limp, Orville was looking for someone with anarchist sympathies to help him bring in his alfalfa crop and round up his cows. Rexroth, who always needed the extra money, provided Orville with proof that he was a member of the IWW (his red card) and the deal was set. These were the Red Scare years, but Rexroth's family background and recent experience on the soapbox circuit kept him bold. With the help of a Danish anarchist and small Chicago publisher, Steen Heindrikson, Rexroth had become well versed in left and anarchist politics. He was eager to reveal his political affiliations.

Rexroth grew fond of Orville. The work was not very demanding, and the two men enjoyed swapping stories, drinking black fig wine, and fishing together. When the job was over, Rexroth hitchhiked south to El Paso, where he met a man driving to Mexico City. Rexroth accepted an invitation to accompany him, but the roads were in such terrible shape that they had to abandon the car and complete their trip by train. He got to Mexico City toward the end of 1925, when Mexico was beginning to reap the benefits of the revolution. Land distribution had been stepped up, an irrigation system initiated, and a program of rural education implemented. The government sponsored cultural programs, and artists like

Diego Rivera, José Clemente Orozco, and David Alfaro Siqueiros were commissioned to portray Mexican history on public buildings. They painted murals that exalted the revolution and the Indian past. And they were not aloof from the public. They would sit in cafés, like the artists in Paris, drinking, dancing, chatting, and generally having a good time.

Rexroth spent most of his time with the café crowd. He was not impressed by Diego Rivera, but liked Siqueiros and the artist and photographer Tina Modotti, who was usually at Siqueiros's table. Modotti introduced Rexroth to Edward Weston, an acquaintance Rexroth would renew in the late twenties while Weston was living in Carmel, California. When a friend of Modotti's asked Rexroth if he wanted to accompany her to Oaxaca at her expense, he hit the road once more, this time in comfort. For two weeks, he saw all the sights of Oaxaca, danced and sang into the early hours of the morning, and saturated himself so much with Mexican life and culture that his interest in Mexico was completely satiated. The visit had little effect on the development of his work, and the two poems that reflect the experience, "Oaxaca 1925" and "Gradualism," do not evoke the compelling sense of place that marks his better poems. Rexroth never returned to Mexico.

When he got back to Chicago, he was determined to give up the vagabond life. He yearned for the companionship and emotional support that he associated with a good marriage. But he knew all too well that he was not considered a good catch: almost twenty-one years old, he could offer no financial security to a prospective mate. For comfort, Rexroth turned again to the Church, this time serving as an acolyte and teacher in the school of the Church of Ascension on North La Salle Street. He did not give up his vision of himself as a writer, and his earliest printed poem appeared in the *Parish Bulletin* in 1925, an epistle to St. John that hardly hinted at the young writer's interest in such avant-gardists as Gertrude Stein, Tristan Tzara, or for that matter the early T. S. Eliot. Its closing lines read: "A myriad deaths were yours to die alone / Humblest of martyrs, thy humility / Kept thee for very love on Calvary."[30]

Harriet and Kenneth ("Kep") Thorpe, Rexroth's Grove Street roommates in New York City who had settled in Chicago, also attended the Church of the Ascension.[31] Kenneth Thorpe had attended Vanderbilt University, where he had studied with the Fugitives. A poet and the "first principled reactionary" Rexroth had ever met, Thorpe provided him with an entry into Old and Middle English verse.[32] To read and study, Rexroth went to the Newberry Library across from Bughouse Square where he copied by hand an entire anthology of Middle English verse. (Later, in California, he would copy an entire volume of poetry by Yvor Winters.) Over the next year, he often visited the Thorpes in their apartment on Walton Place to argue about theology and poetry. They might discuss John Crowe Ransom, whose stance as a Fugitive Rexroth thought reprehensible, or George Tyrrell, the Jesuit priest who played a prominent part in advocating Modernism—the European intellectual movement that reinterpreted traditional Catholic teaching—which appealed more to Rexroth's interests.

On his way to the Thorpes one evening in mid-December 1926, Rexroth met their friend and neighbor Andrée Schafer.[33] "She was dressed in a dull crimsom coat with a gray wolf fur at the collar and hem; she had deep chestnut hair, an oval face, a pale ivory skin with bright red cheeks, horn-rimmed glasses, and brown eyes with a gaze of incredible angelic purity and seriousness."[34] Rexroth fell in love with her image, and announced to Harriet Thorpe that he intended to marry her. His optimism was infectious and Harriet Thorpe invited Andrée to join them for dinner. Andrée's passions had been aroused no less than Kenneth's. Now twenty-one, Kenneth was handsome but serious-looking, trimly built, his face grown a bit gaunt, his thick hair slicked back from a wide forehead. After that evening the two were inseparable.

Andrée was born on October 14, 1902, in Chicago, a little more than three years earlier than Rexroth. Like the other women who had been important to Rexroth, she was older and had a strong sense of personal identity. Her mother, Emma Josephine Montgomery Schafer, was of Scots, Irish, and English descent. Her father, John Frederick Schafer, of French and German background, earned his living as a clothes designer. While she was in grade school, Andrée's family moved to Milwaukee, but then returned to Chicago where Andrée completed high school. After graduation, she enrolled in the Academy of Fine Arts, where she studied commercial art for a year. However, once she was exposed to the moderns, she became more attracted to the world of fine art. Forced to support herself by decorating lampshades and dinette furniture, she learned how to use watercolors and oils by copying the great works accessible to her, probably at the Chicago Art Institute, which had also been Kenneth's teacher. She functioned this way for several years, solving problems of technique on her own, until she felt confident that she had attained a professional level.[35] By the time she met Kenneth, she had reduced her commitment to commercial work in order to paint.

After a brief courtship, they were married in early January 1927 at the Church of the Ascension by Father Stoskopf and Father J. Russell Vaughan. Kenneth was regarded as a special member of the flock, one who because he had seriously considered the priesthood merited a Solemn High Nuptial Mass. Overwhelmed by the spiritual and emotional intensity of the occasion, he passed out. Apparently during those first months in Chicago Kenneth and Andrée lived in so emotionally charged an atmosphere that Kenneth lost track of the daily events in their lives and the people with whom they socialized. They were totally locked into each other in a meeting of minds and hearts. Their political orientation

was untarnished left, and they had developed the kind of social conscience that acted like a magnet for people needing assistance. They played
host, sometimes reluctantly, to those out of work without a place to sleep,
and those in need of emotional comfort. Interestingly, both had been
deeply moved by Wells's *The Research Magnificent,* a novel of thwarted
idealism.

Moreover, both were deeply committed to their lives as artists, and
they would often paint together on one canvas, creating Mondrian-inspired
geometrical patterns in primary colors. They later explored the technique
espoused by the leader of the de Stijl movement, Theo van Doesburg,
who believed that inclined planes in geometric abstract painting increased
the dynamic effect of composition. Using ads from magazines as models,
Andrée and Kenneth also created collages of striking originality. And
they dreamed of traveling to Berlin to study with Moholy-Nagy at the
Bauhaus. But their interest was not confined to avant-garde art. Whenever they visited the Chicago Art Institute, they would be freshly trans-
ported by the paintings of Corot, Pissarro, and Cazin. Although Andrée
did not write, Kenneth showed her drafts of his poetry which they would
revise together. In the evenings they read aloud to each other, and Andrée would fall into an "excited coma of passion" when Kenneth recited
John Donne's love poems to her. Once she even fainted after Kenneth's
melodramatic reading of Webster's *The Duchess of Malfi.* Unfortunately,
Andrée could also lapse into another kind of unconsciousness, one far
more destructive to her health and to their idyll of happiness.

The doctors who examined Andrée believed that she suffered from
psychogenic epilepsy. She had never experienced a *grand mal* while engaged in strenuous physical activities like swimming, horseback riding,
skiing, and mountainclimbing. Her seizures usually occurred under psychological stress, but Andrée believed that they were organic in origin
because her mother and her aunt had both died of brain tumors. She
expected to die soon of the same cause. Morbidly depressed by the prospect, she tried to take her own life shortly before she met Kenneth. Now
she must have felt life turning around, that there would be many springs
to come when she would happily watch "gray mottled buckeye branches /
Explode their emerald stars, / And alders smoulder in a rosy smoke / Of
innumerable buds."[36]

Their first winter together in Chicago was especially cold and difficult.
Their apartment building was occupied by members of a little theater,
and no one paid rent. Rehearsals for the group's plays always looked like
staff meetings of an Antarctic expedition.[37] The Rexroths kept warm by
burning coal in two small fireplaces, but the plumbing began to deteriorate when the building's steam pipes burst after the furnace was stoked
for one of the theater group's performances. They decided to flee to the
warmer climate of California, planning first to hitchhike as far as the

Rockies, camping, climbing, and fishing as they made their way through the Cascades north of Lake Chelan. They bought two Bergen rucksacks, and with the help of Andrée's sticky fingers, equipped themselves with a perfectly sized tarpaulin and a beautiful Swiss cooking kit. They left as spring arrived, resolved by then to make a new home for themselves out west.

Five

A PROMISING FUTURE
1927–1929

B Y 1927, THE LAST EMBERS of the Chicago Renaissance were dying out. Edgar Lee Masters was in New York City. Ben Hecht, whose plays proved unsuccessful on the Chicago stage, was dividing his time between New York and Hollywood. Vachel Lindsay's popularity was waning, and he would soon commit suicide. Tennessee Mitchell, the first wife of Sherwood Anderson, would overdose on sleeping pills, and Anderson would take up residence in a stone house he had built for himself and his third wife in Marion, Ohio. Carl Sandburg, fired by an inept editor of the *Chicago Daily News*, headed north for Michigan. Jane Heap and Margaret Anderson fell under the influence of the guru George Gurdjieff at Fontainebleau. Floyd Dell and his family were living in a New York suburb. Only Harriet Monroe, an original star of the Renaissance, remained to edit *Poetry* at 232 East Erie Street, with Morton Dauwen Zabel as her associate. She would eventually reject one of Rexroth's Cubist poems on the grounds that she could not "stand behind what [he was] trying to do with the art."[1] New York City's Greenwich Village had become the undisputed center for writers and artists as well as the place for unorthodox lifestyles.

However, Rexroth was untempted by the magic of the Gotham. For all his sophistication and savoir-faire, he did not want to settle in a city dominated by European culture and tradition, no matter how well he had learned that literature and art. Chicago would remain a special place for him because it was the prototypical "American" city; and he was always ready to talk about his days at the Green Mask and the Dill Pickle, or soapboxing in Bug House Square and West Madison Street.[2] But Rexroth saw no future for himself in Chicago and persuaded Andrée that the West Coast would provide them with a better opportunity to succeed as artists. He had already discovered that he was most at peace in the mountains of the Northwest. His decision to move west instead of east would have far-reaching consequences: for his poetry, his push for recognition, his politics, and his influence on the American literary conscience.

The trip west was highly satisfying, though not without mishap. After wandering through northern Wisconsin, Minnesota, and the North Dakota Badlands, the couple ran into a Montana storm that confined them to a tourist camp for a week. At that camp they became friendly with a man who was particularly well informed about Marxism and revolutionary political thought, and said repeatedly there was not one honest politician alive in the United States. He turned out to be Burton K. Wheeler, senator of Montana, who apparently had a passion for the great outdoors. When the weather had dried up sufficiently, Kenneth and Andrée went to Great Falls as his guests. They accompanied Wheeler on a goodwill tour to Shelby, the site of a recent oil discovery. Then they took a freight train to the bottom of Glacier National Park to visit Kenneth's old friend Billy Orville. Kenneth helped him with his spring plowing before he and Andrée resumed their journey to the Cascades. At night they would see and hear baby bears, deer, coyotes, cougars, and martens. They made friends with the Basque shepherds who offered Kenneth a job. So for a while they lived the lives of Gypsies—working, eating venison, trout, and bear-cub steaks, singing and dancing at night, sleeping very little.

Finally they trekked up to Lake Chelan and called on Blackie Edwards, a tramp painter Rexroth had met two years earlier while working as a horse wrangler and cook with a company packing freight for the Forest Service. Kenneth and Andrée stayed with him through the summer. This time they both got work decorating the walls of barrooms and stores with scenes of the natural habitat. They achieved a modest degree of fame, apparently, because before they left, the were offered positions at the prestigious Cornish School. With the money they earned, they hitchhiked to Seattle and Portland, but hoofed it the rest of the way south, mostly along the beaches or on the cliffs. Because the forest was too dense, they camped whenever they could on the beach. They learned to swim in the dangerous surf. They drew portraits of one another, and of the birds, sea, and beautiful driftwood found in that area only. The people they encountered en route in Oregon were friendly, hospitable; however, once across the California state line, they encountered an entirely different species of people.

Seen in retrospect, Kenneth and Andrée were the forerunners of the flower children who flocked to Northern California during the fifties and sixties. Although they were a perfectly respectable married couple and practicing Anglicans, they were hardly conventional. Hitchhikers, obviously without steady employment, each carrying a huge backpack loaded with camping supplies as well as writing pads and drawing paper, they were clearly strangers who represented a warning to the natives that their Pacific paradise might not last forever. No one welcomed their patronage, and one time Andrée put an end to a brawl between Kenneth and a roadside restaurant owner by hitting the assailant over the head with a bottle of ketchup.[3] Out of necessity they existed on cold food purchased in grocery stores. Whenever they tried cooking at a campsite, they were chased away by "straight" campers. Not until they reached the public camps further south in the Redwoods did they feel free to appreciate the natural beauty of the area.[4] They fished and swam in the Eel River, and saw a variety of wildlife at night, including a newt-eating giant tiger salamander, ringtail cats, skunks, and deer. After four days of midsummer glory, they hitched rides south to the ferry that would take them to San Francisco, where presumably a $500 check awaited them.

When informed that no money had arrived at the post office, they walked up Mission Street, "our packs on our backs, wondering what to do."[5] By sheer coincidence, they passed a wholesale furniture store filled with desks, chairs, and various tables that Andrée recognized: she had painted them while working for *Vogue* studio in Chicago. As they stood in front of the store the store owner approached them, and when he discovered why this young couple was so fascinated by his furniture, he offered them each a job after they demonstrated their skills in the workroom. The Rexroths were no longer in danger of being picked up for vagrancy. They rented a small flat in the Western Addition, and postponed their plans to visit Los Angeles and then come back up north to settle near Seattle into what they had heard was an intact, autonomous intellectual community with a Wobbly heritage. Although they had very consciously turned their backs on the intensity—and the exclusivity, to them—of East coast literary and leftist circles, they did not want to live in a cultural wasteland. (Rexroth was fond of saying that one indication of the desperate state of the arts in San Francisco was that George Sterling was the city's most honored poet.) Once settled, they sought out the few people whom their friends in Chicago and elsewhere had urged them to meet, mostly those with either literary or radical political associations.

Among the first people the Rexroths visited was the poet Elsa Gidlow (1898–1986), who had arrived in San Francisco two years earlier and was earning her living as editor of the *Pacific Coast Journal of Nursing*. She published the first volume of lesbian poetry in North America, *On a Grey Thread* (1923).[6] Elsa had come to San Francisco with her companion Violet Winifred Leslie Henry-Anderson, called "Tommy" by those closest to her, a woman fifteen years her senior. Violet and Elsa met in New York, where Elsa was working as an editor and Violet as her secretary for Frank Harris's *Pearson's*. When the magazine moved to Chicago in 1925, Violet and Elsa were attracted to San Francisco.

Gidlow and Rexroth differ about the circumstances of their 1927 meeting. According to Rexroth, shortly after he and Andrée were listed in the telephone directory, they received a call from Gidlow inviting them to join her and Violet Anderson for tea at her Joice Street apartment near Chinatown. Rexroth describes the couple:

[Gidlow] was a slender young woman, with dark hair, eyes that could flash with laughter, a compact, graceful body, and an ivory skin. . . . To me she had a genuine rare beauty. I don't think she used cosmetics, and she usually dressed in tailored suits of Levot or faintly colored, grey tweeds, heather stockings, and "sensible" walking shoes.[7]

Despite a lapse of nearly twenty years during Rexroth's four decades in San Francisco, and the test of physical distance created by Gidlow's move to Marin County and Rexroth's to Santa Barbara, this relationship would endure. It matured into a friendship based on respect for one another's poetry, political orientation, and sexual orientation.

Gidlow's account of their first meeting is quite different. According to her, the Rexroths appeared without invitation at her doorstep.[8] Although Kenneth and Andrée arrived in San Francisco toward the end of summer 1927, not in the spring as Elsa recalls, her account sounds plausible.

One day early in Spring, a young man with a backpack, accompanied by an attractive young lady, appeared at my door. It was Kenneth and Andrée Rexroth, who had been back-packing along the coast and who had just arrived in San Francisco. We gave this strange couple tea and made them welcome. I didn't know anything about him beyond what he told me—that we had met in New York City and that he was a poet and Andrée was a painter. He said that they were thinking of settling in the area and apparently wanted me to help them meet people. What stands out most about that evening is that without warning Andrée toppled over in an apparent seizure. Kenneth put something between her teeth so that she wouldn't bite her tongue and assured us that everything was under control.[9]

Gidlow was particularly impressed with Kenneth's "matter-of-fact han-dling" of Andrée's seizure, his care for her was "tender and efficient."[10] She and Violet Anderson later extended a dinner invitation to the Rexroths, who she says gave a "slightly homeless impression, although resourceful and apparently well able to take care of themselves,"[11] and the friendship was established.

Gidlow took part fully in the literary activities of San Francisco. With a handsome volume of poetry to her credit, she was invited to the homes of the wealthy who wanted to make their city a cultural center. As Gidlow tells it, poets and artists of all sorts were welcomed to these gatherings, like those at "The Cats," the magnificent home in Los Gatos of writers C. E. S. Wood and Sara Bard Field.[12] The parties were less class-bound than their counterparts in Europe, and California's climate and geography made them more expansive. Often they were held outdoors, in country places reachable only by wheels. Gidlow found space for the Rexroths in the car belonging to photographer and conservationist Ansel Adams. Art patron and philanthropist Albert Bender might have ridden with them too, since his heart condition prevented him from driving.[13] Department store owners Leon and Dorothy Liebes also threw parties for artists and writers in their "palatial flat at the top of a handsome building near the Fairmont Hotel,"[14] above the alley where Gidlow and Anderson lived. Through Gidlow, the Rexroths gained a modest entrée into this bohemianized high society.[15] However, Elsa and Tommy really preferred the natural world of the woods, mountains, and beaches outside San Francisco. And Elsa was profoundly dedicated to her writing. These interests further solidified her friendship with the Rexroths.

From 1927 to 1929, Andrée and Kenneth were able to shape for themselves a life that revolved around their commitment to writing, painting, and their love of the natural environment. They would also become increasingly involved in leftist organizations. After a brief spell in a dank basement apartment and a few other equally unsavory places, they rented an apartment on Montgomery Street, the famous Montgomery Block. Sometimes known as the Monkey Block, it became a haven for artists and writers who needed space and light but could not always pay much rent.[16] Ambrose Bierce, Sadakichi Hartmann, Frank Norris, Jack London, and Margaret Anderson had been among the better-known occupants. Diego Rivera and Frida Kahlo moved into sculptor Ralph Stackpole's studio in November 1930, two months before Rivera started painting his allegory of the riches of California on the stairway wall and ceiling of the California Stock Exchange (also known as the Pacific Coast Stock Exchange Luncheon Club), a private club not open to the public.[17] Rexroth described Rivera's project as "spreading the beautiful light of economic meliorism about him": his impressions of Rivera had not improved since his visit to Mexico.[18] Despite great protest, the building was torn down in 1959 and replaced by the Transamerica Pyramid—according to Rexroth, "probably the ugliest building in America."

When Kenneth and Andrée moved in at the end of summer 1927, it had been converted to four floors of rooms 15 by 22 feet. Rexroth felt that theirs was perfect: a kitchenette, a closet, a sink with a detachable shower underneath, and a balcony that the previous tenant had built on. The monthly rent was $20. They were living on a tight budget, but discovered that San Francisco offered free food to people in the know. Near Montgomery Street was the Golden State Dairy, which gave away buttermilk to the poor. At the end of the day the wholesale markets distributed unsold produce and fish to anyone who could carry it away. In Chinatown, the Rexroths could have dinner for fifty cents; the price was the same at the cheap Italian restaurants, with a glass of "red ink" included.

They made a few friends in the Monkey Block, among them an aspiring writer named Porter Chaffee. He saw Kenneth and Andrée frequently during this period, although he never addressed Andrée, who struck him as "pale, rather slight and fragile." Conversations with Rexroth were volatile, according to Chaffee: "He could anger quickly, go off like a firecracker."[19] The Rexroths spent most of their leisure alone, writing and painting, sometimes working on the same canvas.[20] Kenneth regarded his marriage as eminently successful: "Andrée and I seem to grow closer as time goes on. We have done each other a world of good, and neither of us has had to lose any of the precious things that has made his [sic] character. At first it seemed a little premature, in the first weeks I mean, but I believe we have chosen with wisdom."[21]

As the summer waned, they took advantage of the ocean beach, which in those days was "looked on by the natives as forbidden land. No one lived near it. . . . There was nothing . . . at all except sand dunes and a few isolated, shingled beach houses scattered around."[22] Sea life flourished: oyster beds abounded in the Bay, and Hunter's Point provided San Francisco Bay with shrimp. San Francisco was blessed in those days by great tracts of greenery, and Rexroth would mourn their disappearance as the freeways and developers multiplied.[23] They also went rock climbing.

But San Francisco, with all its attractions, lacked the kaleidoscopic change of seasons typical of the Midwest. By mid-autumn, Andrée missed the colorful foliage and crisp air of a Midwestern fall. Fortunately, she and Kenneth discovered that autumn was only a hitchhike away to the Donner Summit from where they could follow trails across to the Feather River Basin. In his autobiography, Rexroth recalls the many times they enjoyed hiking in Yosemite and the Sierras that autumn. Once they hitchhiked down from San Francisco and spent their first night "under an immense fig tree someplace due east of Merced, where the land was just getting hilly. A farmer took us there, and we slept under his fig tree and ate wonderful black Mission figs." To celebrate Andrée's birthday, October 14, they baked a bannock birthday cake stuffed with the black figs and nuts. They fished in the Merced River, and against the advice of those who knew better, "hiked up to Tuolomne Meadows and over Mono Pass and down Bloody Canyon, to the valley and back up to Lee Vining and Bridgeport, and then turned around and went back down to Bishop and around the mountains, through the Mojave." As they began to go down Mono Pass, a real snowstorm began to blow. They managed to get home without mishap. Had they tried to climb Mount Lyell, as planned, they would have perished.

On another occasion, while camping around Hume Lake, they met a work gang of convicts who were building the road that ran down from the upper basin to the bottom of Kings River Canyon. When the couple agreed to mail uncensored letters for them, the convicts showed them the trail that engineers surveying the area had built as far up as Cedar Grove, a trail the convicts had hidden with timber and brush so they would have private access to the river when they were allowed to go fishing. Midway up the path was a cabin containing a bunk and a stove, owned by a man named Put Boyden. In front, the river had created a deep pool calm enough for swimming and filled with fish.

We were alone, twenty
Miles from anybody;
A young husband and wife,
Closed in and wrapped about
In the quiet autumn,
In the sound of quiet water,
In the turning and falling leaves,
In the wavering of innumerable
Bats from the caves, dipping
Over the odorous pools
Where the great trout drowsed in the evenings.[24]

Andrée and Kenneth made good use of this haven.

As winter approached, the Rexroths inquired about skiing trails and equipment, but information was difficult to unearth, perhaps because, Rexroth suspected, Californians did not want to destroy their state's warm and sunny image. The Sierra Club was of little help. Finally, they uncovered some skis buried in the rear of a sporting goods store where they met Leo Eleosser. A world-famous surgeon and a skilled skier, he was among the first people to reach the peak of Mt. Shasta on skis.[25] By Rexroth's account, he was a tiny man with a full head of gray hair who liked to wear a windsor tie. He also owned several dachshunds who followed him everywhere, including the door of the operating room of San Francisco General, where he was chief of surgical services. Eleosser suggested that they either go to Cisco on the Donner Summit Road and then head north on the steep dirt roads built by the PG&E, where they would have open country past Castle Rock Peak; or go north to the Feather River Highway, where there was the best skiing in America.

Those first excursions challenged their ingenuity. Since they did not own ski boots, they invented their own by strapping ordinary boots with Telmark bindings. They made their own down sleeping bags and designed a tent of Egyptian cotton waterproofed with alumina gel. The trails were not as steep as they had expected nor the weather as cold nor the snow as deep. But they were untrained skiiers, developing technique as they went along, and the slopes they had to negotiate as they careened down the mountain to Donner Lake tested their strength and courage. They spent a week skiing these trails, camping in the snow most nights, twice coaxing the owners of inns closed for the winter to let them spend the night. The "distant landscapes of the mountains and the near landscapes of trees and rocks and waterfalls" left Andrée entranced. Taking her watercolors and paper with her, she would "find a sheltered spot in the sun, and sit there and paint water colors on top of eighteen feet of snow."[26] They would repeat and refine this trip during the next few years.

In the spring of 1928, they only had to roam the southeast sector of the city to enjoy nature. Laguna de la Merced and the region around it was half wild. They would hike around San Bruno Mountain past the cow pastures that stretched between Twin Peaks. That first year was marked by intense activity: "skiing and climbing and hiking in the woods and fishing and swimming." And "the creative outpouring never stopped."[27]

During the course of their second year in San Francisco, Andrée's seizures increased alarmingly. Remarkably, she never suffered them while she was physically active. She would go out to the beach at the end of the Geary Street carline and swim for two and three miles at a time, with Kenneth "paddling along behind her, terrified." Nor was she affected in the mountains when they were skiing and rock climbing, even when they stayed away for as long as six weeks. The seizures would begin a short time after they got home. One evening she came into the kitchenette and swept off the shelf her favorite Chinese bowls, which Kenneth had just washed and put away. When she recovered, Andrée was no less amazed than Kenneth that she had done such damage. For an explanation of her behavior, she turned to psychiatrists, but they were more interested in tracking the pathways of her "spasms" of neurotic behavior than in understanding the cause of her epilepsy. One physician prescribed luminol, another Congo Red, a medical dye which turned her bright scarlet, "like a boiled lobster," and which she could only endure for a month or so. To control the seizures, she was given phenobarbitol, which made her groggy for short periods. Nevertheless, during the late twenties she led an active, productive life, "eminently normal in her behavior and vastly superior in intelligence."[28]

With Andrée's encouragement, in 1927 Rexroth had started submitting poetry to ephemeral publications. With the exception of "Saint Joan" (*Parish Bulletin of the Church of Ascension*, Chicago, c. 1925), the first extant works by Rexroth—four poems and one letter to the editor (in which he criticizes William Carlos Williams for not writing a clear enough defense against the "neoclassical polemics" of Yvor Winters)—were printed by Charles Henri Ford in the April, June, and Fall 1929 issues of *Blues*. A Surrealist poet, Ford was looking for fresh voices to distinguish his new avant-garde magazine in Columbus, Mississippi, and Rexroth seemed just right, offering not only his poetry and prose but Andrée's art work and his own as well.[29] A lively correspondence sprang up between Rexroth and Ford in early 1929, when Rexroth first asked Ford about publishing his poems. Ford caught some flak for printing "When you asked for it," but stood by his decision to use it.[30] With two of the other *Blues* poems, this poem would resurface twenty years later in *The Art of Worldly Wisdom*. Examples of Rexroth's Cubist poetry, they mark the beginnings of his career as a published poet.

More work appeared in *Pagany*, edited by Richard Johns. Ford knew Johns and urged Rexroth to submit his work to him.[31] Another friend of Ford's, Norman Macleod, included Rexroth's "She Left Him" in the Autumn 1929 issue of *Morada*, an historically important avant-garde review. Shortly after it appeared, Ford declared Rexroth's poem a success but thought the magazine was poorly edited, citing accident rather than Macleod's editorial skills as responsible for whatever good work appeared between the covers.

Rexroth wanted to cultivate his relationship with Ford and suggested that he might contribute more than his literary talent to *Blues*. When he offered to enlist subscribers, Ford proposed that on ten subscriptions or more at three dollars a year, Rexroth should keep one dollar and Ford two.[32] Rexroth also agreed to design the covers and the layout, with Andrée's collaboration. Delighted with the suggestion, Ford gave them the green light. On June 5, 1929, Rexroth sent along a number of drawings and two cover designs, one by Andrée, the other by him. Ford liked the cover Andrée had designed so much that he considered using it as a permanent logo.[33] And when it appeared as #7, William Carlos Williams also expressed his admiration to Ford: "a swell cover."[34] Rexroth harbored no hard feelings about Ford's preference for Andrée's cover design, and for the next several months, the couple contributed to the production of the magazine, interrupted for Andrée by a debilitating attack of epilepsy.

Although they were barely paying the bills, Rexroth seriously considered starting up a magazine of his own with a new San Francisco friend, Milton Merlin. They planned to call it either *Tension* or *Form*. While helping Ford, he had acquired some practical, albeit limited, experience. Enlisting sponsors would be a problem, he confided to Ford, because he was determined not to share editorial policy with them. "Since we wish to avoid any obligation to opinionated patrons we will finance it ourselves and that may prevent us from ever publishing it."[35] Rexroth was adamant about what he did not want his magazine to be, and the kind of writing he would refuse to publish. Even though his own work had appeared in *Pagany*, Rexroth dismissed it as a "blasphemous sheet." The winter issue of *transition* was "the worst yet." Nor did he approve of the small private-press *The Gyroscope*, run by Yvor Winters, whom Rexroth characterized as "not so hot . . . [who] has identified himself with the neo-classical reaction with a vengeance, conversations, clichés from Valéry and *l'action Française*."[36] Although Winters now favored a more rational and "poetic style, Rexroth had developed a high opinion of his early experimental poems. Rexroth saw them as tightly organized poems with great emotional impact, poems created not out of free association, but in the Cubist mode where there was a "constant recombination of elements." It was the kind of poetry Rexroth himself would seek to create in the thirties, experimenting with "obvious analogies" to the paintings that he and Andrée had done collaboratively.

But he had not yet completely formulated the magazine's purpose. Like the generation of poets before him, Rexroth was determined to reconcile his respect for the intellect with his faith in intuition and the irrational way in which perceptions were acquired. Still under the sway of

Stein and Picasso, Rexroth plunged into the works of Alfred North Whitehead, an influential philosopher who criticized "scientific materialism" for mistaking an abstract system of mathematical physics for the concrete reality of nature, and who argued that true culture made one receptive to beauty and humane feeling. Milton Merlin introduced his former professor of aesthetics, D. W. Prall, to Kenneth and Andrée, and the foursome engaged in intense discussions about the possibility of understanding the nature of existence. For a while, Rexroth considered Stein, Picasso, and Whitehead the three great geniuses of the twentieth century.[37]

Stimulated by the vigor of a new project, and as *Blues* began to founder, Ford expressed an interest in working with Rexroth and Merlin, but it was not to happen. Rexroth was getting closer to articulating his belief that poetry is apocalyptic and a social force, a perspective Ford could not share. Rexroth was also sharpening his skills at speaking his mind. His relationship to Ford and to *Blues* became strained when he suggested to Parker Tyler, Ford's associate on the magazine, that the governing policy behind *Form* or *Tension* should be one based on "militant objectivity, communism and heterosexuality."[38] In any event, Rexroth, scrambling with Andrée to keep their happy but precarious existence intact, was probably too busy to manage a little magazine.[39]

The couple were feeling isolated in San Francisco. They yearned for close friends with whom they could share their artistic struggles and triumphs, argue about the books they were reading, or discuss their increasing identification with leftist politics. When Charles Henri Ford asked them if they would like to see Josephine Herbst, the American novelist of proletarian sympathies, and her husband John Herrmann, who were passing through San Francisco, Rexroth quickly offered to put them up: "we have extra though primitive accommodations.[40] Herbst and Herrmann had recently traded in their Model T Ford for a Whippet, rented their Bucks County House, and set off for a trip around the United States. Taking the southern route, they drove through Taos, Los Angeles, and up the coast. After their stop in San Francisco, Herbst's hometown, they would go to Oregon where her sister and father lived. They were the kind of people with whom the Rexroths could talk about literary matters and politics, the issues of bohemianism versus communism, working-class literature, and coveting celebrity writers for the movement. They seem to have gotten along famously.

Rexroth got wind that Yvor Winters and Janet Lewis had moved to Palo Alto, where Winters had accepted an instructorship at Stanford University. While he knew that his perspective on poetry differed from Winters's, he craved the opportunity for discussion. On a very hot spring day in 1929, he and Andrée set out—uninvited—for the shack Winters and Lewis were renting on Oregon Avenue.[41] By the time they arrived, Andrée had developed a severe headache. Janet Lewis, who thought

Andrée "very nice, very attractive," took her round the back of the house to get her out of the sun and to cool her off: "we poured water over her head at the laundry tub to help that. I remember her thick, short brown hair." Winters was too busy to chat that afternoon and did not emerge from his study. Lewis felt rather defensive about not encouraging them to stay: "I didn't know how to cook, and didn't think it was right of Rexroth to confront us."[42]

Nevertheless, Kenneth and Andrée tried another visit, and this time Winters gave them a hearing. The two men got into a rather heated argument about French poetry, Winters contending that Louis Aragon, Paul Eluard, and Pierre Reverdy—the very writers Rexroth admired—all wrote bad verse. He far preferred Paul Valéry, and proceeded to read a long passage from "The Marine Cemetery" in a style that Rexroth once said caused "duchesses to swoon." Winters also read some of his own poetry, which was "very strict metrically." Rexroth reacted obstreperously to Winters's anti-modern crusade and radical shift to traditional forms. He never told Winters that in the library he had copied *The Bare Hills,* poems that Winters had written before 1929, poems which Winters believed were only of interest from a paleontological viewpoint.[43] For his own library, Rexroth typed the poems, forty pages in all, placed them in a spiral binder, and read them with "undiminished admiration." Rexroth wanted Winters's permission to write about these poems. Winters responded that he could not prevent Rexroth from writing about them, but he would not give him a "lick of help."

Few people in San Francisco really understood what engaged the Rexroths, perhaps because so few literary publications flourished locally. One that did, however, was *Argonaut,* whose book editor was Joseph Henry Jackson. Rexroth had seen him sitting around the bar at Schlogel's, Chicago's version of the Algonquin Hotel's Round Table. Using the Chicago connection, Rexroth wrangled a few assignments from him.[44] Jackson offered Rexroth a modest honorarium for his efforts, but not enough to earn him a living. However, Rexroth kept the books he reviewed, early installments of a vast personal library he would build up over a lifetime.

In fact, Rexroth often complained about the difficulty of procuring the books he considered indispensable to his development as a writer. He was used to Chicago bookstores like McClurg's where clerks (like himself) were expected to help clients locate books. In San Francisco, he encountered salespeople who reported that a book was out of print if the store did not stock it. His opinion of San Francisco bookstores—and book distributers in general—would never improve.

Rexroth struck up a casual acquaintance with the owners of Star Dairy Lunch, near the Hall of Justice on Kearney Street—Pat Dooley, an ex-policeman, and Stewart Delarney—and one of their customers, Jack Brown, a graduate of an English military academy. The restaurant made its money by serving coffee to the police and Hall of Justice personnel during their breaks.[45] When Rexroth walked into the restaurant soon after he and Andrée had moved to Montgomery Street, to his surprise the three men were discussing the philosophical significance of the non-Euclidean geometry of Nikolay Ivanovich Lobachevsky (1792–1856). Reminded of his philosophic sessions with Milly Tokarsky, he fell right into the conversation. Once they discovered that they were all sympathetic to Marxist politics, they formed a study group that met in the Rexroths' Montgomery Street studio, and remained friends for the next several years. All would become involved with the Communist Party for short periods.

Other contacts followed out of the leftist political connections that the Rexroths were cultivating. They became hosts to a young Russian writer, Mark Kliorin, who had come to America ostensibly to improve his English at the University of Washington in Seattle and to act as foreign correspondent for his father, who ran a chain of newspapers throughout China. After graduating from high school, Kliorin had lived in Harbin, where the central office of his father's newspaper was located. An outrageous character, he took over Rexroth's desk, where he wrote futuristic stories and plays at a furious pace. He often set his bedsheets on fire because he was a chain smoker. He made no contributions to household expenses, and expected Andrée to run his errands.[46] When Kenneth and Andrée finally ran out of patience—half their dishes were broken, cigarette burns covered the edges of the desk and dining table, and money was growing scarce—they took him over to Milton Merlin's apartment. Merlin responded by closing up his place and fleeing to Santa Monica, his home town. Purportedly, Kliorin returned to Harbin to work on one of the newspapers owned by his father. The Rexroths never heard from him again.

Six

Santa Monica Respite, New York Journey
1929–1931

FEELING COMFORTABLE and expansive in a rented five-room house in Santa Monica Canyon, on South Westmoreland Avenue, Milton Merlin invited the Rexroths to share his quarters. Also living with him were Nellie and her husband Joseph Rabinowitch, a poet whose work was apparently too avant-garde for American readers. The Rexroths thought it over, packed their belongings, and headed south in late 1929. Once they arrived, they fell into an almost idyllic routine on the sparse income that Andrée earned through her commercial art. Kenneth picked up an occasional odd job. He describes their life in *The Dragon and the Unicorn:*

> Andrée and I were poor and
> Happy together. Sometimes we
> Were hungry and stole vegetables
> From the neighbors' gardens.
> Sometimes we went out and gathered
> Cigarette butts by flashlight.
> But we went swimming every day
> All year round.[1]

Kenneth became as strong a swimmer as Andrée (he liked to swim until the very end of his life). The sea was crystal clear, and they started collecting and photographing all the tidepool and beach life they had never seen before. Kenneth would frequently catch blue cod and red snapper for dinner. Sometimes they hooked little octopi and shocked their less adventuresome friends by eating them for dinner.

Andrée never had an epileptic attack while in the water, but after a long, tiring day she would suffer a series of *petit mals* when she got home. The phenobarbitol she was taking to control the seizures now left her moody, irritable, and disorientated. But skipping the treatment triggered seizures. As in San Francisco, physicians and psychiatrists gave her little relief. Despair over her worsening condition grew into a severe depression which Kenneth was powerless to relieve. Her passion for her work, her sense of adventure, and her idealism was in full accord with his, and the thought of becoming a burden on him was intolerable. One day while Kenneth was out marketing, Andrée locked herself in the bathroom and tried to kill herself by detaching the hose from the hot-water heater and sealing the windows and doors. Kenneth got back just in time to save her. In the suicide note beside her, she said that she was still deeply in love with him but feared that a fatal tumor was growing in her brain. Somehow she came through this episode with her spirits improved, and was able to immerse herself once again in her art.

In the front yard there was an "umbrella-like" mimosa tree and a large sycamore tree just beyond it that made them feel as though they were in a bosky wood. They would bring a table outside, where Kenneth sat and wrote in the fresh ocean air. They both painted, sometimes on the same large canvas.[2] They spent hours studying the lines of the human body, or animals and plants of "things like Hans Arp's sculpture with its tremendous surface tension like an overfed amoeba."[3] Then they discovered Edward Weston's startling photography of halved cabbages, seashells, peppers, and sections of women's bodies. Under his influence, their interest in geometrical painting waned and they switched to exploring organic forms. They went to the beach to draw roots and kelp and to observe the stages of the sun's effect on plants and trees. Later on, Rexroth would visit Weston at his home in Carmel in order to gather information for an article about his work. Although Weston, whom Rexroth had met in Mexico, was not much more than fifty years old and still as energetic as ever, he appeared to be much older to Rexroth, who was half his age. The two men got on well, although Weston objected to Rexroth's description of his radically original camera work as "photographic painting."[4]

Before the Rexroths left Los Angeles, a huge yellow dog and a very large white cat adopted them. They named the dog Proclus, after the Greek neoplatonist, and the cat Cyprian, after the early Christian theologian. Proclus would often swim with them while Cyprian lay beside them on the beach. The Rexroths were also fond of horses. Santa Monica Canyon at this time was lush with sycamore trees and canyon vegetation. Behind the Canyon was the Will Rogers estate and the Uplifter's Club, a kind of semi-wild country club with a golf course and polo grounds. Wilderness stretched up across the Santa Monica Mountains. Few people rode their horses in those early days of the Depression and their owners were willing to let Andrée and Kenneth exercise them. So they rode and hiked in the mountains of the Malibu range, going up into the Topanga and Tujunga canyons, which could be reached only by dirt roads. At night, when the moon was bright, they would go "deep into the mountains through the chaparral to the pines up on top." Rexroth would remember this year as "one of the most pleasurable years in [his] adult life."[5]

They met several glamorous people through Merlin after they moved out of his house to their own quarters in Ocean Park. Merlin knew some of the celebrities living nearby, and introduced the Rexroths to them, people like Myrna Loy, "a very intellectual and lovely woman who in life bore no resemblance to her appearance in black and white movies."[6] Other notables Rexroth claimed to have encountered were Billie Burke, Dolores Del Rio (in her swimming pool), James Cagney (on the beach), and Eric von Stroheim, who was "sweet tempered ... and extremely small." They met camera people, artists, and others connected to movie production. During this time in Los Angeles, artists and intellectuals at all levels of affluence rubbed shoulders, people with millions and people "who were penniless in Ocean Park, many of them foreign directors and actors."[7]

Once again Rexroth turned to the philosophy of Alfred North White-head, who about that time was lecturing at Harvard University. Much influenced by his ideas, Rexroth formulated the "foundations for a philosophy of organic process and of immanent, rather than transcendant deity" that immunized him against the Existential despair of the 1940s. Rexroth would demonstrate his remarkable ability to render plausible the possibility of spiritual presence and a sense of unity in the natural world with such poems as "The Motto on the Sundial," "Toward an Organic Philosophy," and "A Lesson in Geography." Written in the middle and late thirties for little magazines like *Midwest* and *Compass,* and some better-known publications such as *Partisan Review, The New Republic,* and *New Directions,* these poems were later collected in the volume entitled *In What Hour* (1940). The epigraph to this book, which comes from Whitehead, proposes that there is always an alternative to the seemingly inevitable.

In several poems of this period, Rexroth expressed dismay with the fixed and disastrous direction that he felt Western philosophy was taking. In "Value in Mountains," he writes:

> There are those to whom value is a weapon,
> Collectors of negatives and ascertables,
> And those to whom value is horror,
> Themselves collected by evaluation;
> Who, recurrently dispossessed in each judgment,
> Seizing or seized by presented fact,
> Explode in a fury of discreet instants.[8]

Rexroth needed an alternative to this fragmented view, a vision of the whole that restored value to individual perception, something he had sought at Holy Cross Monastery. Although his temperament remained stimulated by Whitehead's concepts, he returned now to the philosophy of St. Thomas Aquinas, who possessed "a sheer perfection of thought which has never been equalled," but with the same reservation that had made him wary during his Chicago days of accepting Thomism, the Truth, and the Catholic Faith as synonomous.[9] However, H. O. Taylor's *The Medieval Mind*, which contained an elaborate discussion of the Scottish theologian John Duns Scotus (c. 1265–c. 1308), had recently been reprinted, and Rexroth renewed his interest in this theologian who had first captured his interest as an adolescent. Scotus had dared to depart from the rational unity of Thomistic thought and doctrine, to question the idea of "harmony" of faith and reason, insisting in its stead that for people of unusual intellectual capacity and "human patience" (that would include Rexroth, of course), the will was higher than the intellect, divine truth and revelation superior to human knowledge and philosophic systems. He believed that the will, unlike the intellect, is not determined by what is intelligible. According to Scotus's intricate explanation ("barbarisms of hair-splitting technicalities," in the words of H. O. Taylor), the will is free and active, and "directs itself toward the goal of blessedness." Guided by the will and the grace of God, human beings are strong, noble, free to think, act, and love. When Rexroth first read Scotus (while living in Chicago), he found him "practically incomprehensible"[10] Ten years later, he could make better sense of him, although he still believed that he might have been attracted to Scotus—and Whitehead for that matter—by their "extraordinary, eccentric, peculiar language."[11]

The opening stanza of *The Homestead Called Damascus* tracks the careers of two brothers (Rexroth's divided self) whose struggle to establish a connection with the drift of human history bears the imprint of Scotus. In so doing, they confront conflicting philosophies and disquieting claims on their consciousness. Although the precise meaning of the stanza cannot be fully articulated by paraphrase, clearly it underscores the inability of various philosophical systems to solve metaphysical dilemmas. The narrator sounds rather cynical and cavalier: "History demands satisfaction, / And never lacks, with or without our help / From the subjects of its curious science."[12] However, if we consider the possibility that the narrator may be thinking of Scotus, we perceive his aspersion of intellectual investigations as a first voluntary step toward belief in God, rather than a statement of mere frustration with logic and deductive reasoning.

Yet the suffering of Thomas, one of the brothers, flows largely from his skeptical frame of mind. He is determined that all shreds of doubt be erased before he can accept the reality of God. He is the "involuntary active man—/ [who] Peers into the black wounds, hammers the frame / That squeezes the will."[13] He requires concrete evidence of Christ's martyrdom. His unceasing scrutiny, however, will never yield the answers that he seeks. While Thomas is all intellect, he is confined to the world of the knowable. Until he exerts his will to become a "voluntary" active man rather than an "involuntary" one, he will be frustrated. He is trying vainly to hack his way to faith with his intellect as his tool, rather than leaving himself open to the mystery of the will, as Scotus advised. In the second half of the poem, Thomas seems to accept the likelihood that the working mind will never arrive at God, and is ready to follow a less rational path. The influence of Duns Scotus may be traced throughout *The Homestead*, especially in the various moments of revelation that the brothers experience in sections III and IV of the poem. Rexroth's later poems would bear the mark of Dun Scotus's mysticism.

It is ironic, of course, that a theologian as dependent on ratiocination as Duns Scotus should deprecate its significance. Rexroth demonstrates a similar orientation. Through Sebastian and Thomas, he expresses his veneration of knowledge and the powers of the mind. The brothers have more than a superficial grasp on the history of ideas and lock horns in complex, philosophical debates. However, by the end of *The Homestead*, their encounters with the mystical world are more potent than the most sophisticated logical discourse. Since childhood, Rexroth himself had experienced such moments of vision, "momentary flashes of perfect communion with others" that had no place in a world where scientific materialism reigned. But the severity and discipline inherent in Duns Scotus's path to blessedness would not wholly satisfy a young man like Kenneth Rexroth. His sensual love of nature, encouraged perhaps by his reading of American poets like Conrad Aiken and John Gould Fletcher, and the classical Chinese poet Tu Fu, pulled him in another direction, for a less ascetic but equally non-rational view of the human being's relation to the cosmos. He would eventually turn to the writing of Jakob Boehme, the German mystic (1575–1624), where he identified what he needed: a way of endowing the natural world with spiritual significance and an explanation of the revelatory moments he had experienced since childhood. Through Boehme, Rexroth saw glimmering the possibility of escaping Scotus's dictum that faith must be willed, and that revelation was not merely apparition but rooted in reality.

While Merlin, Kenneth, Andrée, and another friend, Frank Triest, were discussing Whitehead and Scotus, they were also exploring Marx. Ironically, they often got together in the home of Triest's father, one of the owners of the successful Levi-Strauss Company, a man Rexroth liked despite his credentials as a "dirty capitalist."[14] They tried to get their hands on all the Marxist literature available in English. For Rexroth, this material confirmed something he had already sensed, that within Marxism was a "basic theory of human self-alienation which was the product of the reification of all things—the cash nexus—and that this could only be overcome by revolution at the point of production, and the return of work to the creation of objects of apparent social significance to the worker. This, of course, is the philosophy of the I.W.W., so it was nothing new to me."[15] Rexroth became increasingly involved with Marxist politics. But it would take a trip to New York City before he engaged in Communist Party activities.

Toward the end of 1930, leaving Andrée at home, Kenneth hitchhiked across the country, stopping in Chicago, presumably to visit his family. When he arrived in New York, he encountered all the excitement around plans to create a nationwide organization of revolutionary artists and writers. Just after the stock market crash in 1929, the editors and writers associated with the weekly *New Masses*—among them Mike Gold, Joseph Freeman, Joshua Kunitz, William Gropper, and Josephine Herbst— had founded the New York John Reed Club, an organization of radical artists dedicated to the creation of a new revolutionary culture. It was named after the American journalist and poet made famous by his eyewitness account of the Bolshevik Revolution, *Ten Days That Shook the World* (1919). Reed became the leader of the Communist Labor Party when it split in 1919 from the United States Labor Party. Indicted for treason, he fled to the Soviet Union, where he died of typhus the following year. The *New Masses* crowd considered Reed the appropriate namesake for their organization because he had remained a poet throughout his entire political career. Mike Gold, who had known Reed, and who had been the first to define the term "proletarian realism," thought Reed's example would help destroy the prejudice against the intellectual in the revolutionary labor movement.[16] Rexroth was amused that the *New Masses* people believed they had given their organization a popular American name, but that did not prevent him from attending the meetings.[17]

In November 1930, Gold had brought home a ten-point "Program of Action" from the Kharkov Second World Plenum on Revolutionary Literature. It directed the New York delegation to politicize intellectuals, reach out to "Negro masses," devote more time to Marxist literary criticism, get closer to the workers, and establish clubs that reflected the ethnic diversity of the United States. Members were encouraged to publish mass pamphlets and create "agit prop troupes" of entertainers. Moreover, they were to regard Marxist critics like Edmund Wilson and Waldo Frank as "recruitable," even though they were not party members and appeared bourgeois. The New York club hotly debated these orders from afar, as well as the feasibility of carrying out such plans.

Rexroth responded keenly to the raw enthusiasm generated at these meetings. Here was the community of activist writers he had not yet found in San Francisco or Los Angeles. Rexroth believed that membership could grow quickly if the John Reed clubs asserted their autonomy aggressively against the dictates of the Russian Bolsheviks. The larger their ranks, the better their chances of preventing "a new round of wars and revolutions," which Rexroth was sure would create an international economic crisis far worse than that precipitated by World War I.[18]

Before heading back to California, he was asked to help create John Reed Clubs on the West Coast. On the advice of writer and director Em Jo Basshe (who along with John Howard Lawson and Mike Gold was an associate of John Dos Passos in the New Playwrights Theater), he decided to avoid recruiting in the movie industry. Harry Carlisle was devoting his energy to organizing Hollywood, but according to the playwright John Wexley, this branch of the John Reed Club reputedly served as little more than an intellectual social club. Ever since the Sacco and Vanzetti case, political activity had seemed futile to many writers and artists.[19] Rexroth himself had suffered his own private despair over the execution. In "Climbing Milestone Mountain, August 22, 1937," he imagines "how it looked / That last terrible week, how hundreds stood weeping / Impotent in the streets that last midnight."[20]

Nevertheless, Rexroth was eager to plan strategies for creating a coalition of progressive, liberal, and revolutionary writers and artists. He did not want to struggle with disillusioned former activists, or waste his time with "a bunch of lumpen intelligentsia who sat around, smoked cigarettes, hugged a cup of coffee all night, and discussed what is proletarian art."[21] He had already seen some of them bemoaning their bleak future at the New York headquarters of the John Reed Club and in neighborhood luncheonettes—sometimes referred to by insiders as "coffee pots." He refused to give them much sympathy.

A rather peculiar counterpoint marked Rexroth's stay in New York and deepening involvement in Party activities. Although he immersed himself in the activities of the John Reed Club, he also sought to recapture his New York past. He enjoyed "going about and sitting in beer speakeasies," especially in a place called the German American Athletic Club. But the city familiar to him a decade earlier, especially Greenwich Village, was changing. Real estate values in the Village were rising and the middle class was returning to new apartment buildings and rooming houses reconverted to flats (a pattern that would repeat itself nearly fifty years later). Kenneth met Cecile Boulton, whose sister Agnes was the second wife of Eugene O'Neill. She introduced him to William Lescaze, one of the first architects in the United States to work in the International style and who in 1931 had co-designed one of the best skyscrapers of the pre-World War II era, the Philadelphia Savings Fund Society Building.

One evening, when Rexroth was dining with the Lescazes, Boulton, Malcolm Cowley, and Dorothy Norman, who was to become the editor of the avant-garde publication *Twice a Year,* Mrs. Lescaze introduced them to Buckminster Fuller, "a little guy in a derby hat"[22] whom none of them knew, even though for the promise of one free meal a day he had decorated the still popular Romany Marie's, now located on West 8th Street. Mrs. Lescaze had just met him herself. "He drew pictures of dymaxion houses in all elevations, exteriors and interiors, dymaxion cars, and a variety of other dymaxions."[23] Fuller entertained everyone by predicting that clothing of the future would be triple knit and permanently shaped, making ironing unnecessary. Although his prophecies proved to be accurate, nobody at the table believed a word he said. For Rexroth, such imaginative dinner conversation created a pleasant break from the political agendas that had preoccupied him.

Seven

EARLY DEPRESSION DAYS
1931–1933

WHEN REXROTH RETURNED to Santa Monica, other concerns distracted him from his determination to organize John Reed Clubs. He had no money, and with the onset of the Depression, he sensed that he and Andrée could no longer depend on their friends for help. They were, for stretches of time, indigent, imposing themselves on people like Michael and Yetta Foreman, the owners of an antiquarian bookshop on Skid Row who opened their home in North Hollywood to the young couple for weeks at a time. (Kenneth used to come to the store and play poker with Michael, but Michael stopped playing with him when he discovered that Kenneth was cheating.) On the other hand, Andrée achieved a small success with a one-woman show at the Santa Monica Public Library. The exhibition, consisting of more than twenty works in watercolors and oils, was received well by the press and the public. She was encouraged by this reception and wanted to cultivate the contacts that grew out of the show. But she and Kenneth knew that it was time to return to the familiar hills of San Francisco. She left a number of her paintings at Jake Zeitlin's bookstore, to be handed over to Joe Rabinowitch when Zeitlin wanted to make space for other artists.

Zeitlin had arrived in Los Angeles in the mid-twenties and had worked as a gardner before he bought his own bookstore on West 6th Street. His bookstore, which also served as a small art gallery, became a meeting place for Bohemian Los Angeles, and Zeitlin befriended many of the writers and artists who either lived or passed through Southern California.[1] Not all of them had as little business sense as Andrée, who forgot to give Zeitlin a price list for her paintings. After apologizing for any inconvenience, she asked him to use his own judgment about setting the prices for her paintings: "they were intended to be from \$15 to \$30 including your percentage, whatever that might be," she wrote from San Francisco on December 11, 1931.[2]

Apparently, Zeitlin was not put out, and maintained cordial feelings for the Rexroths from that time on. Although he would not see Andrée again, he and Kenneth much later resumed a long-distance friendship (after a nearly twenty-year hiatus). By then a good deal had changed in Rexroth's life, but not his enthusiasm for good talk and good times. After they spent an evening together in May 1948, Rexroth wrote to say how glad he had been to see Zeitlin, and how much he enjoyed "getting drunk and saying foolish things with and to you."[3] At this time, Zeitlin also looked like a useful connection because Rexroth was seriously considering the possibility of opening a bookstore of his own. Rexroth got some advice about the book business too from his sometime host and provider Michael Foreman, who ran another bookstore, the Golden Bough.

Joe Rabinowitch was acting, more or less, as Andrée's patron and agent; he also provided a poste-restante for the Rexroths' mail until they were firmly settled back in San Francisco. He mailed Andrée paints that she might not find in San Francisco, and the packages her father was sending her, which he thought might "be more pills." He also tried to show her work at the Delzell Hatfield Gallery on 7th Street and several other avant-garde galleries.[4] In addition, Rabinowitch sent the Rexroths typewriter paper and money orders of five and eight dollars at a time, probably for the three oil paintings he bought. His wife Nellie, however, was apparently unaware that he had acquired the paintings, and he asked the Rexroths to veil their requests for money so that Nellie would not find out. "She almost got hold of your last."[5] For Christmas 1931, Andrée would give him a watercolor. Rabinowitch also entertained the hope that he, Milton Merlin, and Rexroth would launch an avant-garde literary magazine entitled *RMR* (the first letters of each of their last names).

After camping in the Sequoias in General Grant National Park, the Rexroths returned to San Francisco, where they found a large apartment at 1106 Gough Street. Frank Triest moved in to help them pay the rent and to get started with their political organizing. At first they resumed the routine they had maintained during their early years in San Francisco: Kenneth writing and painting, Andrée painting, both of them picking up odd jobs, although Andrée seemed the luckier (or the more determined) in finding work. When they were broke, she stole the groceries they needed.

They dreamed of applying to the Bauhaus, the famous school of architecture and design founded in Weimar, Germany, in 1919 by Walter Gropius. They were particularly eager to study with Laszlo Moholy-Nagy, the Hungarian painter and photographer who taught theory and craft there. Both Kenneth and Andrée had been influenced by his vision of a non-representational art consisting of pure visual fundamentals—color, texture, light, and equilibrium of forms. And they were attracted to his egalitarian theories of education, which proposed that "everybody is talented," and that the natural visual gifts of students rather than specialized skills should be cultivated. Apparently they established a correspondence with Moholy-Nagy, but they got no closer than that.

They also corresponded with the French Surrealist painter André Masson, who, in his first one-man show in 1924 at the Galerie Simon in Paris, revealed himself an exponent of hallucinatory automatism. In an attempt to tap into his unconscious, he would let his hand run free on a drawing pad or canvas without plan or premeditation. He and Andrée exchanged two small, canvas boards that depicted a plaster cast of a torso and a single rose in a vase. Masson and Andrée would contribute to one another's paintings, and each painting ended up nearly identical. One became part of the Peggy Guggenheim Collection housed in Stockholm's Gallery of Modern Art.[6]

The Rexroths shared their enthusiasm for these avant-garde painters with a Los Angeles Polytechnic High School buddy of Frank Triest's, John Ferren. Born in Pendleton, Oregon, in the same year as Rexroth, Ferren spent his early childhood in San Francisco and Los Angeles. Although he had no formal training in art, in his late teens he took to sculpting portrait heads of his friends. Between 1925 and 1929, he lived on Telegraph Hill and held a lucrative job carving tombstones in a stoneyard, which gave him time to pursue his more creative impulses. At that point, Kenneth and Andrée were among the few people in town who understood Modernism and encouraged him. Rexroth like to think that he served as Ferren's mentor.

I used to set him all kinds of tasks . . . I would suggest, for instance, a Turkish rug—to study and make a painting out of the relationships of a particular area which was not a repeat and where the pattern was disassociated. . . . Draw this line diagonally across a reproduction of a great painting, analyze color chords and the abstract relationships of the forms. It was a constant emphasis on what really puts pictures together.[7]

At the outset, Ferren painted figures in clean, bright colors and flat designs, then shifted to abstractions of formal structures and high color. He earned enough money to travel to Europe and studied in Paris, Florence, and Salamanca.

By the time he got back to San Francisco in 1930, he was ready for a one-man show. He visited the Rexroths in their Gough Street apartment, sure he would find once again an audience receptive to his interests. Unfortunately, when he returned the hospitality by inviting the Rexroths to his studio, Andrée suffered a seizure and barely missed severing his ear when she threw a sculptor's chisel at him. She also beat him in four rounds of "blindfold" chess that evening, and Ferren never invited her back.[8] He and Rexroth, however, would take long walks together behind the Berkeley hills, discussing art theory and philosophy, returning again and again to the concept that the patterns an artist makes are found in nature's organic forms, and that creating a sense of unity inherent in those patterns was more important than representational approximations of reality. Ferren's reputation was made by 1936; prominent collectors bought his work and his pictures hung in permanent collections of important American museums, including the Whitney.

The two men also talked politics, and as the friendship developed, Rexroth discovered that Ferren did not know the United States very well. Ferren intended to return to Europe and marry Laure Ortiz de Zarate, daughter of the Spanish artist. Although Rexroth knew that his own work was slackening, he proposed that before Ferren's departure they should hitchhike across the South, so that Ferren could get a good sense of what "ailed" the United States. Ferren had enough money for them both—but not Andrée—and their trip was a good one. Together, they crossed northern Arizona and New Mexico, and visited Hopi and Navaho reservations. They went to Taos and Santa Fe and saw Frieda Lawrence, Spud Johnson, Mabel Dodge Luhan, Andrew Dusberg (who put them up in Santa Fe), and Mary Austin. They studied Indian art, "always disassociating material from the actual object." In the deep South, they managed to get along with "crackers and hillbillies and Ku Kluxers and everybody else," and Ferren "learned a considerable amount about American Evil."[9]

They continued all the way to the East Coast and on May 3, 1931, visited William Carlos Williams at his home in suburban Rutherford, New Jersey.[10] Williams was pleased to meet Rexroth, aware that the younger poet greatly respected and admired his work, despite his diatribe against Williams a year and half earlier in *Blues*. He was also somewhat surprised at Rexroth's familiarity with Anglo-Catholic theology.[11] Ferren did not share Rexroth's enthusiasm for Williams, and wrote later that he hoped no evidence of William Carlos Williams would contaminate Rexroth's poetry.[12]

As soon as he got back to California (Ferren left for Europe), Kenneth, Andrée, and Frank Triest set to work in earnest establishing the San Francisco branch of the John Reed Club, an organization of "putative writers and unputative Communists," as Rexroth liked to say. In retrospect, Rexroth said that his involvement with the Communist Party, which lasted until the first half of Roosevelt's first term of office (early 1938), took up "an inordinate portion" of his life and Andrée's.[13] He sought to create "a genuine organization of intellectuals who had been radicalized by the world economic crisis." Kenneth, but not Andrée, was determined to keep the club independent of the Bolshevik influence. He was interested in relating to workers who were indoctrinated in Marxism, mature old lefties, fellow travelers of the Wobblies in Seattle and Oakland. Writers had to be bona fide, and journalists should be feature writers with by-lines. Artists had to be productive painters or sculptors. Many of them were living in his backyard, so to speak, on Telegraph Hill, Russian Hill, and the Montgomery Block. The group first met in one another's homes, then in a rented hall.

At an early meeting, Rexroth declared that more than anything else, he wanted to design relief programs for writers and artists, early versions of WPA projects. He was accused of being a "petty bourgeois idealist," too dense to acknowledge that artists and intellectuals were parasites, eaters of surplus value. True and loyal Marxists, according to Rexroth's detractors, had to be bona fide members of the working class. Some members walked out in protest against Rexroth's position. For Rexroth, this episode epitomized the attitude of Bolshevik bureaucrats who wanted artists to be subservient, the very thing, he believed, true artists could not be. Rexroth would talk at length about the function of the artist in November 1936 at the Congress of Western Writers in San Francisco.

Rexroth also joined the local branch of the League for the Struggle of Negro Rights, in 1932. This Communist front organization was enjoying a surge of popularity: out of 200,000 Communists in the United States, 500 were black. Before the Depression set in, most blacks had shunned the Party, allegedly because they were afraid of losing their jobs. However, by 1930, unemployment was rampant, and the Party, with its anti-racist slogans, had become attractive. During the summer of 1931, more than eight hundred destitute black families in Chicago were evicted from their homes. Two black workers, Abe Grey and John O'Neill, were killed on August 31 when they confronted police who were trying to evict a widow and her children. Outrage spread across and beyond the community. On the day of Grey and O'Neill's funeral, ten thousand people marched through the South Side. That protest provided the impetus to establish an organization more radical than the NAACP, whose goal since its founding in 1909 had been to end racism within the constructs of the legal system. Rexroth helped to set up groups in the Fillmore District (where one day he would make his home).

Most black families in San Francisco lived on Webster and Buchanan Streets between Sutter and Eddy, in the Victorian homes that had been converted into rooming houses: "there'd be a couple . . . and two or three kids in one room with a gas plate in the closet, living on direct relief grocery boxes from the Associated Charities. That's all there was."[14] Aiming to increase aid for the unemployed, the League organized huge demonstrations of both blacks and whites, usually in front of the offices of Associated Charities. Their goals seemed to coincide with the directives of the Party. But Rexroth had to devote many hours convincing the "apparatus" that the blacks who were living in San Francisco had never been members of the industrial working class. Blacks were debarred from the "lily-white" longshoremen's and shipscaler's unions, and, as a result, were unschooled in the ways of organized resistance. Furthermore, Kenneth recalled, "there was a nonsensical row every time we mobilized activity with the aid of the various pastors of the churches, some of whom were extremely militant and very well informed and whose congregations were in many cases literally starving."[15] For accepting assistance from religious institutions, the League was accused of petit bourgeois deviance. Rexroth sensed that those directly reporting abroad regarded their San Francisco comrades as too independent.

Elected co-secretary of the branch, Rexroth helped to organize an acting troupe which performed on a flatbed truck parked at the corner of Ellis and Fillmore Streets (the forerunner of the "people's theater" that achieved such popularity during the sixties). The group performed pieces inspired by Agitprop theater of the German Communist Party, the street theater of the German Blue Blouse Troops: "the actors all wore blue jeans and chambray shirts and moved with the semaphor motion of marionettes and spoke in a rhythmic monotone."[16] Occasionally Rexroth would recite the poetry of Louis Aragon, the French Surrealist who broke with André Breton in 1931 to pledge his allegiance to the Communist Party. The poem he liked to recite most was *Red Front* (translated by e.e. cummings before he became virulently anti-Soviet), exhorting the workers of France at length to rise against the army and the police for freedom.

In the spring of 1932, the League staged a play for the anniversary of the Paris Commune, generally considered to be the first organized uprising of the proletariat against capitalism. The play dramatized the history of the Commune, episode by episode, with a hidden speaker reading brief excerpts from Marx or Lenin. Set on a bare stage of red, black, and white sheets of butcher paper designed by Kenneth and Andrée, it ended with a recording of the "Internationale." Apparently producing this play was the "most fun any of us [Rexroth and his colleagues] ever got out of the Communist movement." After two nights, Sam Darcy, "the local *vozhd*," forbade additional performances, but according to Rexroth, the play had recruited more members for the Communist Party than any amount of "futile soapboxing before factory gates."[17] Rexroth knew that these orders "to abandon formalist Trotskyite petty bourgeois bohemianism" were an institutional response to the subversive power of a drama based on the Paris Commune. An audience inspired by the vision of freedom for individuals might not want to take dictation from any source, no matter how leftist.

Shortly after this episode, Frank Triest drove the Rexroths to Chicago for the first National Conference of the John Reed Clubs, convened at Lincoln Park Auditorium on May 29, 1932. Rexroth, one of the thirty-eight delegates elected to the presidium, was prepared for the inevitable controversies. He had already been through several, including the one surrounding the Reed Club proposal to reduce the work week to five days and the work day to six hours. This did not wash with "the apparatus" because people in the Soviet Union worked longer than six hours a day. Accused of being "Trotskyite anarchosyndicalists," Rexroth and his colleagues knuckled under and concentrated on securing insurance for the unemployed instead.

Several delegates, including Rexroth, believed that the New York club—

led by writers Mike Gold and Joseph Freeman, and artist Bill Gropper—
dominated the organization.[18] Often Rexroth sounded contemptuous of
New York writers. To Malcolm Cowley, he wrote that some future Ph.D.
would correctly deduce that "poetry in the US in the first half of the 20th
century was of value in proportion to the distance of the point of production from the corner of 8th and MacDougal Sts, NYC."[19] One manifesto
devised by the New York group addressed a familiar concern: recruiting
"fellow travelers" and well-known intellectuals who were sympathetic to
the cause and whose affiliation would bring greater credibility to the aims
of the John Reed Clubs. Freeman and Gold believed that writers like John
Dos Passos, Edmund Wilson, and Malcolm Cowley had been driven away
for fear that direct association with John Reed Clubs would entangle them
in bureaucracy and authoritarianism. Rexroth declared that it was probably Gold's boorish behavior that had caused Wilson's estrangement.[20]
Opposed to any attempt to soften the John Reed agenda in order to
attract celebrities, he accused his colleagues of ignoring writers from the
working class.

Rexroth did not endear himself to his comrades at this meeting. Frank
Triest remarked facetiously, "He told them off. . . . He let loose. . . .
Andrée was frightened that they would murder him on the spot."[21] As a
relief from this stressful situation, they decided to park Frank's car in
Chicago and to embark on a hitchhiking holiday. They camped in New
York's Finger Lakes district, and inspired by the delightful weather, ex-
tended their trip to the Maine coast beyond Bar Harbor before returning
to Chicago and then San Francisco.

Back at their Gough Street apartment, Rexroth continued to seek
literary recognition and remuneration for his writing. For the past two
years, he had been cultivating an important literary friendship with the
poet Louis Zukofsky.[22] While living in Madison, Wisconsin, Zukofsky had
written Rexroth in November 1930 that Harriet Monroe, founder of
Poetry, had asked him to guest-edit an issue of the little magazine. Having
seen Rexroth's poems in *Blues,* Zukofsky thought something by him would
enrich the issue. Rexroth was still smarting from a rejection he had received from Monroe: "I have a profound distaste for its [*Poetry's*] policies,
usual contents, and editor, a feeling I do not understand how you can
help sharing. I believe its vaunted reputation to be spurious, and I would
be delighted to lead any demonstration designed to discredit it."[23] Rexroth
went on, somewhat pompously, to declare how much he admired and
respected Zukofsky's work. He would like Zukofsky, he assured him, if
they ever had the pleasure of meeting. Fortunately, Rexroth did not finish
or send this letter.

At Zukofsky's suggestion, Rexroth called on George Oppen (whose
poetry would win the Pulitzer in 1968) and his wife Mary Oppen. But
Rexroth did not trouble to conceal his view of Oppen as Zukofsky's shadow,
and the two did not get along well. Andrée was not enthusiastic about

either of the Oppens, but Kenneth explained to Zukofsky that she did "not go in for liking people very intensively."[24] Rexroth was quite happy that someone like Zukofsky had invited him to contribute to *Poetry*, and decided to send a manuscript consisting of one long poem and a few short ones. He would be satisfied, Rexroth wrote, if the poems gave Zukofsky pleasure, even if they were not accepted for publication. He believed that if Monroe had veto power, his poems would not see print. When Geraldine Udell of the Radical Bookshop had shown *The Homestead Called Damascus* to Monroe, she had dismissed it as a "lot of talky talk."[25] In a note accompanying the manuscript, he told Zukofsky to use whatever sections appealed to him. Little did Rexroth realize how closely Zukofsky would follow the editorial prerogative Rexroth had given him. Encouraged by Zukofsky's interest in his work, Rexroth, on his own, submitted another poem to Monroe. On February 20, 1931, Monroe with "utmost respect" for Rexroth's sincerity, returned the poem because she did not feel it met her definition of poetry.[26]

Between 1930 and 1932, the correspondence between Rexroth and Zukofsky was frequent and intense, and provides a blueprint for Rexroth's literary, political, and religious interests during the early thirties. Only a year apart in age but from entirely different backgrounds, the two poets were mutually grateful to one another for the serious attention each gave the other's work and theoretical ruminations. Born on New York's Lower East Side in 1904, Zukofsky first read Shakespeare, Tolstoy, Ibsen, and Strindberg in Yiddish. Though he was the one with the formal education (an M.A. from Columbia University) and academic connections (he was teaching at the University of Wisconsin while soliciting articles for *Poetry*), he was nonetheless impressed by Rexroth's erudition, and before he had established an ongoing correspondence with Rexroth, assumed that he had undergone a first-class traditional education. Flattered by the assumption, Rexroth quickly filled Zukofsky in on his unusual childhood and upbringing, and added that he shared Zukofsky's enthusiasm for the French avant-garde and for Whitehead's systematic attempt to give the universe coherence. Zukofsky included Rexroth's poems in *Poetry*, and in *An "Objectivists" Anthology*, along with contributions by William Carlos Williams, Basil Bunting, George Oppen, Carl Rakosi, Lorine Niedecker, and Charles Reznikoff. Zukofsky attributed Objectivist characteristics to the entire collection, yet critics rarely if ever mention Rexroth when discussing Objectivist poetry, even though Rexroth once claimed that he was "an unwilling leader" of the movement.[27] In any case, this early correspondence between the two poets reveals some interesting history of the Objectivist movement in its infancy.

Perceived by some critics as antithetical to the symbolism of Yeats and Eliot, the Objectivist movement took its cues from William Carlos Williams's dictum that there are "no ideas but in things." Like Imagists, Objectivists encouraged economy of presentation, preferring the specific detail and concrete word to the metaphor, which "carries the mind to a diffuse everywhere and leaves it nowhere."[28] However, objectivism, unlike imagism, does not dissociate the image "from the movement or the cadenced shape of the poem." An Imagist poem can be explicated by analyzing its images. The construction of an Objectivist poem is more organic; there are no parts to isolate and dissect. Once completed, an Objectivist poem takes on a life of its own, a free-floating entity independent of its maker. Zukofsky called these poems "found objects," arrangements of "one object near another—roots that have become sculpture, wood that appears talisman."[29] Rexroth would dismiss the movement as a spinoff of the "small sensation" caused by Pound's publication of Zukofsky's "Poem Beginning The" in *Exile,* although later he did acknowledge that the "found poems" of Rakosi, Oppen, Reznikoff, and Zukofsky constituted a distinctive school that had produced "some pretty good poetry."[30]

Zukofsky published three versions of a long poem by Rexroth. It appeared twice in An *"Objectivists" Anthology,* each time entitled "Prolegomena to a Theodicy": first in the form as Rexroth composed it, and then in a form edited by Zukofsky in the section entitled "Collaborations." The last part had appeared a year earlier as "Last Page of a Manuscript" in Zukofsky's issue of *Poetry.* Why all these versions? On January 16, 1931, Rexroth wrote to Zukofsky explaining this poem, his major work in the Cubist mode. Rexroth himself refrained from using the word "objectivist" when referring to his work, an indication perhaps that he sensed the marginal nature of his Objectivist connection. The ten-page letter spoke less about any particular line or allusion in the poem than it did about Rexroth's philosophy of poetry. In a sense Rexroth was going through a metamorphosis. He had delved deeply into the art of writing poetry, purifying himself of stale traditions, while he absorbed the ideas of Duns Scotus, Alfred North Whitehead, the French Dadaists, Karl Marx, and Gertrude Stein. As he wrote to Zukofsky: "The most diverse influences have arisen to name the ideas on my page, from Proclus to Bradley or Royce, from Stoicism to the 'organic philosophy.' I really had no idea my brain contained such a horde." Rexroth was really laying the ground for a poetry distinct from either cubism or objectivism.

On September 17, 1931, Zukofsky told Rexroth that he was eager to print as much of his work as space allowed. He read "A Prolegomena" very carefully, and suggested that a good many passages, the ones that contain theatrical rhetoric, be omitted. A month later (October 15), Zukofsky suggested the poem be stripped of lines that reflected T. S. Eliot's influence (he thought that Eliot's women were more authentic), James Joyce's impertinence, and Tristan Tzara's irresponsibility. Zukofsky's suggestions for revisions reflected the same spirit as Ezra Pound's editing of *The Waste Land;* but Rexroth believed that Zukofsky's abridged version rendered the poem meaningless. Zukofsky resolved the conflict by offering to publish both the original and the revised, shortened versions with brief explanatory notes. The original version appears in the major section of *An "Objectivists" Anthology;* the shortened poem in the section entitled "Collaborations," followed by brief notes by Zukofsky and Rexroth. His work took up a disproportionately large space in the anthology.

Another poet whom Rexroth would eventually meet was Carl Rakosi, also a crucial presence in *An "Objectivists" Anthology.* Rakosi was puzzled by Zukofsky's decision to include Rexroth's long, rambling poems, full of inappropriate philosophical phrases. When he asked Zukofsky why he had done so, Zukofsky replied: "You don't understand the appeal of the pattern."[31] Nearly two decades later, a revision of Rexroth's preferred version, now entitled "A Prolegomenon to a Theodicy," along with the other poems Zukofsky had published, appeared in *The Art of Worldly Wisdom.* In the preface, Rexroth too alludes to the patterning of the poems and places them in the tradition of abstract art, comparing the elements of each poem to the "elementary shapes of a cubist painting."[32] Aware of the difficulties facing the reader, Rexroth warned that these Cubist poems had to be understood on an intuitive level as well as a rational one (a variation on T. S. Eliot's contention in his 1929 essay on Dante that genuine poetry communicates emotionally before it is understood intellectually). Rexroth was asking his audience to take the poem as self-referential, and not to expect conventional signals like transitions and symbols. He was divorcing the means of representation from what was presented, just as Cubist painters dispense with shading and foreshortening.

Although Rexroth outwardly disapproved of artists who rigidly molded their work to suit a particular ideology, he nevertheless conceived his own writing within a political context. Like Zukofsky and the Objectivists, he wanted to banish sentimentality and flippancy, and to release poetry from the limitations of "great and noble" subjects. However, he was not interested in poetry of the "bare awareness of sensa." He wanted to reintroduce into poetry a seriousness, "a respect for ends . . . a consciousness of all the implications, the final issues, the guiding purpose." A poetry of responsibility would deal with subjects "worthy of writing, as an integral part of that vast complexus of vital significance we call the universe." Was he achieving that aim with lines from "The Place" such as these?

> all night sheep speak intermittently
> close at dawn
> Utter bounty
> after voluntary limit
> cautiously anticipating
> the single cosine
> unambitious ballistics
> minute focus
> asymptotic object
> before the fracture of the unsuspected calyx.[33]

Even when parodying the Surrealists Tristan Tzara and André Breton, as in "Fundamental Disagreement with Two Contemporaries," Rexroth was not writing the kind of poetry he himself would have defined as vitally significant. Too often the pattern of these poems takes on an obsessive, perseverating quality, reminiscent of Gertrude Stein, or an ingrown elaboration, as in this section of "A Prolegomenon to a Theodicy":

> The grammar of cause
> The cause of grammar
> The being of grammar
> The magnificent being of division
> The gradient of change
> The invisible triangle of difference
> Of division
> The parsed challenge
> If the extended injunction remains it will be almost possible
> to observe the dispersion of the closing and unclosing
> follicles.[34]

The bravado with which Rexroth writes the Preface to *The Art of Worldly Wisdom* belies his struggle to invent a style that did not sacrifice a central aspect of both his poetry and prose: his own, idiosyncratic, personal voice.

Rexroth would not pursue this form much longer. Nearly twenty years later, he told the poet and critic Babette Deutsch that his Objectivist poems were a "literary parallel to the early Eisenstein movie technique, and a prosody which owed much to the short abrupt cadences of primitive song [and to] non-European languages."[35] He stopped writing this kind of poetry because he knew it could not reach a wide audience. But more importantly, he understood that if his love poems, or poems addressed to social issues, or poems that reflected his spiritual yearnings and deep sympathy for the natural world were to reach a wider audience, he would have to abandon the clotted Cubist/Objectivist mode.

Rexroth could be rough on Zukofsky's work. For example, he compared Zukofsky's Preface (originally published in *Poetry* in 1931 and reprinted in the anthology) to "obscure Kabbalistic prose."[36] He believed that Zukofsky had been overly influenced by Pound's *Cantos*, and that the anthology was too much a reflection of Pound's friendships and tastes. Rexroth disliked Pound's poem in *An "Objectivists" Anthology* (pp. 44–45), especially such lines as

> Red hot Mary of Magdala
> Had nine jews an a Roman fellow
> Nah she'z gotta chob much swellah
> Mit der yiddisher Charleston Band
> mit der YIDDISHER
> Charleston BAND.

Pronouncing this a piece of "virulent anti-Semitic doggerel," Rexroth suggested to Zukofsky and Oppen that Pound had written it to ridicule the anthology and its contributors. Rexroth described their reaction to Babette Deutsch:

This made a mortal enemy of Oppen, who could not bear to realize that he was being played for a sucker, and [went] about telling people that I [was] an Antisemite. Pound, on the other hand, wrote Oppen that he would have nothing to do with the Objectivists' Press if "dot Chew Bolschevick Rexwrothsky" had anything to do with it.[37]

Rexroth regretted his involvement with "the cuckoo land of malice which Pound has always surrounded himself." Nonetheless, in 1931 he invited Pound to contribute to a project taking shape in his mind.

While preparing his poems for Zukofsky, Rexroth was planning with his friends Merlin and Rabinowitch to make the previously conceived RMR (Rexroth-Merlin-Rabinowitch) press a reality. It would provide a forum for writers and artists, their peers and contemporaries, while earning them money. They had in mind a series of pamphlets and books no longer than 150 pages. Zukofsky helped by coming up with names and addresses of writers who might be interested, many of them contributors to his own anthology: Charles Reznikoff, George Oppen, Basil Bunting, Rene Taupin, Whittaker Chambers (whose pen-name was George Crosby), and Harry Roskolenko.

From Rapallo, Pound wrote that he favored the project and hoped that Rexroth could "swing it."[38] He added that "How to Read" belonged in Rexroth's series, and if his prospective publisher backed down, Rexroth could have it: "Country needs it/etc." Pound also offered essays on the French poets, Henry James, and the Orientalist Ernest Fenollosa, from whose papers he had made his celebrated translations of Li Po in Cathay. "You naturally want to begin with . . . that which there is against the least salesresistence [sic]." Encouraging and supportive, Pound proposed the names of writers who might contribute to the project, among them Wyndham Lewis, for his designs and not "his polemics"; Man Ray, who would later photograph Rexroth bathing at Big Sur; and painter and writer Hilaire Hiler, who became a friend of Rexroth's. On Pound's advice, Rexroth also approached the expatriate writer Robert McAlmon, who replied that he was not interested in pamphlets, but was willing to send along short stories.[39] Pound himself wrote to Ford Madox Ford, asking him to contribute a small critical piece about his poetry to the pamphlet series devoted to the "in'nerlexshul life of murka, and don't mean more than about 5 quid per pamph to the authors."[40]

William Carlos Williams offered Rexroth "three moderately long compositions, two of which have already been privately printed."[41] He was referring to "The Great American Novel" and "Spring and All." The third was "January: A Novelette," partially published in *transition*. Together they would be called "Writing(s)." However, RMR never got beyond the conceptual stage. Rexroth kept the idea bubbling for almost six years, but political, emotional, and financial crises created barriers insurmountable for an impoverished poet.

In his early correspondence with Zukofsky, Rexroth explained how he sought to balance his life as a Communist with his calling as a poet and a Christian. He felt that capitalism and the Protestant religion together had destroyed this communion between all things living and the divine, and had invented a rampant individualism, a competitive morality that could destroy the world. It was impossible to align himself with the less radical Socialists who, he felt, were weak and bound to a capitalist economy. As a Marxist, it was logical and self-evident to him that the means of production should be controlled by "the workers" (actually Rexroth hated this term). But he differed from orthodox Marxists in other ways. He believed that he himself had nothing tangible to gain one way or the other from a world revolution.

I starve under capitalism, and I would starve under a dictatorship of the proletariat for the same reasons. After all I am interested in perpetual revolution in a sense other than Trotsky's—the constant raising into relevance of ignored values. Poetry has for its mission in society the reduction of what the Society of Jesus named "invincible ignorance," and the true poet is as much to be feared by the proletariat as by the bourgeoisie.[42]

If the world's economy became Marxist, Rexroth thought that people like himself would benefit emotionally and psychologically. People would lead happier and richer lives if they were not forced to compete with one another.

His Christian faith had not yet wavered significantly, though it would soon be tested severely. In the early thirties he accepted the Church as a supernatural institution, and believed it could not be destroyed by Bolshevism. He was not troubled by the demise of institutionalized religion as it existed in Czarist Russia; "its age-long record of consistent simony is appalling." But it was important for him to convince Zukofsky that he was not a neo-Catholic either: "My objection to the neo-Catholics and scholastics is that they seem to have forgotten what the Christian religion is all about. I don't give a hoot in hell if a man is an Aristotelean and seriously doubt if God does either."[43]

He was not preaching to Zukofsky. Rather, he was using Zukofsky as a reactive audience while he sought to reconcile his belief in "the incarnate Son of God" with his commitment to a political system that essentially denied not only the value of his vocation, but his spiritual aspirations as well.

Eight

CRUMBLING INSTITUTIONS
1933–1936

B
Y 1933, ANDRÉE AND KENNETH seemed to be the model of a "serious" young couple: politically committed, dedicated to art, and engaged in social movements to arrest the effects of the Depression. But their life had its lighter side. During Prohibition, California vintners were producing wine for sacramental purposes. They also sold on the QT to the Italian community around Market Street, where some bars had flourished without interruption since 1907. Kenneth would go down to the local grocery every week and buy a gallon of drinkable red for a dollar. At least one neighbor took careful note of this and observed to the FBI that Kenneth carried the wine "from the grocery store to the house in a very open manner."[1]

Both Andrée and Kenneth were painting a mural for the children's waiting room of the Allemany Health Center, whose design was inspired by the animals on the walls of the Altamira caves. (The mural, 100 feet by 8, ended up in the basement of the San Francisco Health Department and was eventually lost.) Before the Federal Arts Project was instituted in 1934, Edward Bruce, a Treasury Department lawyer and a painter in his own right, had kicked off a pilot project called the Public Works of Art. He had been asked by the Assistant Secretary of the Treasury, Lawrence Robert, known as the custodian of federal buildings, to create a program that would put unemployed artists to work.[2] The idea had been brought to Robert by the painter George Biddle, a Harvard classmate of the recently elected president, Franklin D. Roosevelt. Biddle had been impressed by Mexico's example of paying its artists as civil servants to decorate Mexico City's public buildings in the twenties. Directed by art critic Forbes Watson, the PWAP aimed to employ twenty-five hundred artists who would be selected by regional committees and paid salaries of $25 to $35 a week. The artists would work in their own studios and would have complete control over the subject matter and execution of their work. The beautification of the Allemany Health Center was one of the early projects.

The Rexroths became increasingly absorbed in the PWAP (and subsequently in the Federal Arts Project and the Federal Writers' Project).
Kenneth and a number of artists requested a quick and positive response
to their proposal that the federal government employ San Francisco artists to decorate the walls of Coit Memorial Tower on Telegraph Hill.
Erected in 1933, the "simple fluted shaft" designed by Henry Howard
had already become a landmark, providing a spectacular view of the Bay
Area. With Rexroth's help, artist Bernard B. Zakheim organized a meeting of San Francisco artists during which he called them to action by
describing the plight of their colleagues: one was threatening to commit
suicide, another was cleaning toilet bowls. As a result, a bigger meeting
was convened at Maynard Dixon's studio. Artist Shirley Staschen, who
would become a lifelong friend of Rexroth's, first met him there: "He was
very impressive. I'd never seen anything like that before. He stood up
there and talked and talked, with his eyes closed. He talked about the
need to organize . . . how artists would be taken advantage of unless they
did."[3]

Sculptor Ralph Stackpole suggested that the group appeal to Edward
Bruce. With Bruce's approval—which they won even though Bruce came
under heavy attack for "boondoggling"—the artists were given the green
light to paint murals of California life on the interior walls of the tower.
For his part, Zakheim created a colorful, busy, ten-foot-square fresco
entitled "Library," which he populated with portraits of familiar San
Francisco figures, among them Ralph Stackpole; Shirley Staschen, his
assistant during that period; and Harold Mack, a member of the super-
visory committee of the PWAP and a millionaire who let the Coit Tower
artists use his building on Kearny Street as a base for $25 a month.[4] In the
top center of the mural, Kenneth is shown climbing the library ladder.[5]

As recording secretary of the Executive Committee of the Artists and
Writers Union, Rexroth wrote to Edward Bruce (March 25, 1934) for
assurance that plans were being made to keep the more than seven hundred
artists in San Francisco employed "more productively than as common
laborers or subsistence farmers under the new Emergency Program." He
requested more information about proposals for new buildings, such as
the U.S. Mint that was to replace the old mint on 5th and Mission Streets
where Bret Harte once worked. He also wanted to know what provisions
were being made for Western artists to decorate buildings in the capital.
If there were no artists' jobs to be had, what kinds of white-collar positions, he wanted to know, would be available. His sense of urgency was
strong. Rexroth and his colleagues proposed additional projects—books
and pamphlets, as well as the guides to the states—which they hoped
would be funded by the Federal Writers' Project, which soon replaced the
PWAP.

By 1935, the project was offering jobs to countless unemployed writers, editors, and research workers. Among its most important undertak-

ings was the "American Guide" series, which provided handbooks for every state and territory except Hawaii. The state guides were to combine travel information with essays on geography, architecture, and history. Rexroth was on the editorial staff for the California guide, specifically Northern California, and for the city guide to San Francisco.[6] Here was a fine opportunity to demonstrate his concern about natural conservation and to find support for fighting unsound water relocation projects, mining, and residential overbuilding. Along with Rexroth, others listed in the Preface (p. 5) to the San Francisco manuscript were poet, playwright, and painter Madeline Gleason, one of the first people in the 1940s to make poetry festivals a San Francisco tradition. Three other poets, Maxwell Bodenheim, Claude McKay, and Weldon Kees, contributed their skills, as did the novelists Richard Wright, Ralph Ellison, Nelson Algren, Frank Yerby, and Saul Bellow. So did Loren Eisley and Conrad Aiken, who had exerted significant influence on Rexroth's early work.

A poem like "Senlin: A Biography" from *The Charnel Rose* (1918), which anticipated Eliot's *The Waste Land*, typifies the techniques that drew Rexroth to Aiken. This long, quasi-philosophical rumination depicts a young man's sensual love of nature. Ignoring transition, the poem cuts back and forth across history as Senlin meditates on the role of human consciousness in a world where traditional value systems have disintegrated. Although there are two heroes in Rexroth's *The Homestead*, their spiritual search takes them on a similar singular quest. And like Thomas in Rexroth's poem, Senlin concludes that the poet must never cease to pursue awareness, even if it means confronting terror. Furthermore, Aiken's politics matched Rexroth's anarchism and antipathy to bourgeois values. During World War I, when Aiken claimed exemption from military service on the grounds that poetry was an essential industry, not to be classed with "billiard-making, setting up candle-pins and speculation in theater tickets," Washington authorities granted him permission to continue writing.[7]

After his poems appeared in *Blues* and in *An "Objectivists" Anthology*, Rexroth's reputation began to grow. His involvement with the Federal Writers' Project brought him further notice. People interested in poetry and the arts started calling on him when they were in San Francisco. Dorothy Van Ghent and her husband Roger appeared one evening as the Rexroths were finishing their dinner. Dorothy would later become a distinguished scholar in the history of the novel and a professor at the City College of New York, but when she met Kenneth and Andrée she was a recent Mills College graduate who had just returned from a scholarship year abroad in France and Italy.[8] A struggling but published poet herself, she wanted to attend graduate school in the Bay Area. Kenneth liked her appearance, and was somewhat taken aback by the contrast between the small round figure, the short auburn hair, the delicacy of her freckled face ("friends who met her later said she looked like a Gabon sculpture"), and Roger's rough and tough demeanor ("Roger looked like a common laborer from the docks of Antwerp").[9]

When the Rexroths invited them to share whatever remained of their dinner, they plunged in ravenously, consuming everything in sight, including half a cake and almost all the wine. Between eating and drinking, Dorothy went on talking about poetry "as though she wanted to discuss all of modern literature at once," until she became incoherent and passed out (an unfortunate habit that she was unable to control down to her last days). Andrée brought her back to consciousness by forcing hot salt water and mustard down her throat, which caused her to vomit, and then cupfuls of coffee, which sobered her up. Kenneth packed her and Roger off in a taxi. Had the Rexroths known that she was pregnant, they might have discouraged her from drinking so much, and certainly would have thought twice about their liquid remedy. But everyone was too caught up in the excitement of sharing ideas and passions to be sensible. After this tumultuous introduction, the Rexroths and Van Ghents saw each other regularly. An unorthodox connection among this foursome would soon be established, to the detriment of both marriages.

Kenneth enrolled Dorothy on the list of the Federal Writers' Project, and maneuvered several research assignments for her as a copy editor and proofreader so that she could stay home and care for her son Julius, born in June 1935. She also attended graduate school at Mills College, where she devoted one third of her master's thesis to Rexroth's poetry.[10] A brilliant and passionate student, she went on for the Ph.D. She carved out time to pose for the several portraits Andrée painted of her, and to help organize small at-home poetry seminars at the Rexroths' apartment. The more she fell in with the Rexroths' lifestyle, the more dissatisfied Dorothy grew with her own. In time, she and Roger split up. Andrée started to resent Dorothy's frequent visits. Sensing an undercurrent of hostility, Kenneth decided to take his favorite course—he left for the mountains. When he returned, he was in for a shock. Andrée had moved out and was living with Roger Van Ghent. By Rexroth's account, she proposed that the four of them and the baby establish a ménage—and that when neither Kenneth nor Dorothy consented, she suggested that the two start a romance. Apparently Rexroth felt the need to report that Andrée was responsible for his love affair with Dorothy, and that until Dorothy appeared on the scene, his marriage to Andrée was on solid ground. The "perfect" union between Kenneth and Andrée was dissolving.

During a trip to the mountains with the Rexroths, Frank Triest had noticed that the animosity between them was escalating.[11] Kenneth had baked some bread over an open stove, using dried cow dung as fuel, an astonishing experience for Frank that "took him back to prehistoric times." Kenneth was getting supper under way, and as he reached for a frying pan, Andrée said something to him, unintelligible to Frank but apparently provocative. Kenneth flung the frying pan at her. Andrée, who was sitting on the ground, threw her legs up to protect herself, and "the frying pan hit her right in the ass." Instead of being intimidated by his outburst of temper, Andrée laughed off the attack: "she had a way of dealing with him—not taking his little bits seriously."

Using their WPA checks, the Rexroths moved into inexpensive, separate furnished rooms, one block apart, so that they could pursue their affairs more comfortably, yet conveniently see one another. Well-read leftists, sophisticated Bohemians, they were thoroughly versed in the pitfalls of institutionalized marriage, and decided that they could love one another without owning one another. There were no words about divorce. Tiring of Roger, Andrée became involved with the artist Edward Hagedorn.[12] The affair between Kenneth and Dorothy was erratic, but their friendship would endure for another twenty years.[13] Kenneth boasted of other affairs, including one with a Lillian Gish look-alike who paid for her graduate education at Berkeley with the money she had saved while living in the palace of a Japanese prince. The bravado with which he recalls these relationships masks the anguish he had to be feeling as his "total glorified comradeship" with Andrée disintegrated after eight years.

Rexroth's love affairs did not limit his WPA activities. On the surface, he did not appear to be languishing over Andrée. Rexroth initiated a project inspired by the literary magazine he had once envisioned with his friends Milton Merlin and Joe Rabinowitch. In October 1936, an editorial board was formed and met at the office of the Federal Writers' Project, 717 Market Street, in order to mock up a model. Rexroth probably designed the geometric pattern on the cover. The wide range of poetry and prose, typewritten, attracted the attention of journalist John D. Barry. Barry was so enthusiastic about the "sample for a project of creative work" that he urged collectors in an October 26, 1936, news story to get their hands on a copy, even though the publication was not for sale.

In the Introduction, the editors outlined their philosophy: there were not enough regional outlets for good writing, and the WPA should help provide them.[14] They felt that the commercialized magazine world made many themes and ideas taboo because publishers feared to offend their readers and to lose their advertisers. Here was the trail-blazing opportunity to offer original writing in a publication that would not disappear after a few issues, and could afford to pay its contributors well without demanding that they write in a certain style on prescribed subjects.

Rexroth contributed both prose and poetry to this magazine; however, he took credit only for his poetry: "*The Crisis*: Selections from a book-length sequence" and "Hiking in the Coast Range."[15] In the contributor's note, he lists as credits poems published in *An "Objectivists" Anthology*, in *The New Republic* ("At Lake Desolation," a description of the horrors of war and poverty), and in *Partisan Review* ("Remember now there were others before this," a clear and strong statement against any government or institution that feeds on repression of free thought).[16] However, next to an essay entitled "The Possibilities of an Intelligent Regionalism in California" appears the name J. Rand Talbot, the very name Rexroth used when he was arrested and sent to the Chicago House of Correction. The biographical note indicates it is the pseudonym of a writer who "has lived in California for the past twelve years and has travelled extensively throughout the West, working as a . . . sheepherder, camp cook, fire patrolman and a liberal assortment of other jobs peculiar to the region." The entry adds that the author has used this pseudonym for pulp publications.

"Hiking on the Coast Range" was written to commemorate the maritime General Strike of July 16, 1934, against police brutality. A dues-paying member of the National Maritime Union, which he helped to organize,[17] Rexroth had participated in this demonstration. The two names which he cites in the dedication (Sperry and Conderakias) identify the strikers who had been killed on "Bloody Thursday" (July 5, 1934), the culmination of the International Longshoremen's strike, called on May 9, the most widespread strike ever to occur in the United States. In retaliation, the police raided the Kearny Street office of the Artists and Writers Union who were painting Coit Tower, correctly suspecting that many members, like Rexroth, had participated in the protest.[18]

In "Hiking on the Coast Range," Rexroth composed lines of vivid imagery and contemplative lyricism, combining an acute, intense observation of the natural environment with a radical social conscience:

> The skirl of the kingfisher was never
> more clear than now, nor the scream of the jay
> as the deer shifts her covert at a footfall,
> nor the wild rose-poppy ever brighter
> in the white spent wheat, nor the pain
> of a wasp stab ever an omen more sure,
> the blood alternately dark and brilliant,
> of the blue and white bandana pattern.[19]

The poem continues in this vein, skirting sentimentality and the Cubist modes that had marked his recent poetry, gently asserting that our moral sense cannot remain intact when we feel and see the shock of violence. Curiously enough, when the poem appeared in *In What Hour* (1940), Rexroth changed the "wild rose-poppy" to a "butterfly tulip," saving the color red to describe bloodshed only.

The piece signed by J. Rand Talbot projects an entirely different message: publishing regional creative writing magazines would tap a large source of potential readers who were "too poor or too illiterate" to waste time and money on glossy national publications filled with stories and poems that had little do with them. Far more bellicose than Rexroth the poet, J. Rand Talbot praised East Coast literati for creating a regional identity for themselves, but let fly some familiar insults: "Even New York, the most characterless part of the country, manages to express itself under the benevolent dictatorship of the Founding Fathers in the pages of the *New Masses*."[20] And he was no kinder to his California neighbors, colleagues "from the Blue Pacific to the Snow Clad Sierras, throwing oranges one moment and snowballs the next, always sleeping, however warm the day, under two blankets at night . . . every barren village of 10 or 1,000,000 population teems with poetasters and Sunday painters."[21] In one instance, Rexroth is the gentle, caring poet who loves and respects nature, social justice, and the power and resonance of simple English. In the next, he is a cynic on the edge of contempt for the very masses whose world he so wants to save, and whose appreciation and respect for his work he sought. Throughout his life, Rexroth would demonstrate this mixed perspective, weaving a complex pattern of compassion and cool disdain into an almost schizophrenic imago.

Rexroth stayed with the Federal Writers' Project through the publication of the *WPA Guide to California*. Notes and uncompleted manuscripts suggest that his hand can be found in the sections about Mt. Shasta, a tour from the state line to Sacramento, Sequoia National Park, the General Highways and Trails, and a history of the Donner Party tragedy of 1846. In the introduction to the *Guide* reissued in 1984, Gwendolyn Wright (author of *Building the Dream: A Social History of Housing in America*) singled out Rexroth's descriptions of the national parks, forests, lakes, and deserts as "some of the most beautifully written passages in the guide."[22] She also praised his "picturesque portraits of farm hamlets, fishing villages, and coastal promontories." Initially, Rexroth was not pleased with the results. In 1940, he wrote to Weldon Kees that "all [the WPA] Guides, ours in particular, are very very bad."[23] Years later, Rexroth had grown proud of the *WPA Guide to California*, and relished showing it off to younger writers who were unaware of his contributions.

Rexroth worked on several other WPA-sponsored projects, including "A Field Handbook of the Sierra Nevada," a naturalist's guide for which he used the Sacramento State Library to supplement his first-hand knowledge and experience. The table of contents is quite extensive, ranging across flora and fauna of every indigenous kind. After finishing this manuscript, he planned to write a guide to the California White Mountain range, another guide to Sequoia and Kings River National Parks, and a book about California wild life. He also thought Dorothy Van Ghent might write a history of California poetry. None of these projects was ever completed or published.[24]

One of the unpublished manuscripts, "Camping in the Western Mountains," 234 pages of typescript, deserved to see print. It provides an extensive, highly detailed discussion of exactly what a camper requires to survive in the Western mountains: the right packs, food (including spices for dessert), equipment, methods for waterproofing a tent and breaking in hiking boots, first-aid essentials. It is also filled with friendly advice about how to choose horses and burros as trail companions. Contrary to the scoffing of some critics, Rexroth was indeed an authority on life in the woods and mountains, at camp or climbing—whether on horseback, renting and leading a mule, breaking camp, cooking breakfast, or observing the world from a higher altitude.

Through these years (roughly 1935 to 1938), he remained active in the offshoots of the John Reed Clubs. While Rexroth had by this time joined several Communist front organizations,[25] he stated that he was never a member of the Communist Party itself because the cultural front urged him not to join so that he could help them resist Party bureaucracy.[26] On other occasions he declared that Party Secretary Earl Browder denied him membership because he was too much of an anarchist. However, in a statement made on September 30, 1940, to the Fellowship of Reconciliation, he declared that he had joined the Party in 1935 and had withdrawn from it three years later because of "disagreements on moral and physical grounds of the means it used to carry out its objectives." A number of people interviewed by the FBI when Rexroth applied for CO status on February 19, 1943, believed Rexroth was a Party member.

In "Camping in the Western Mountains," he slipped his fundamental political convictions into a seemingly innocent discussion of camping technique. They hardly followed the Party line: "The ideal camp is a miniature anarchist community straight out of Kropotkin. Each goes about his appointed task quietly and efficiently, the functions of the group are shared with spontaneous equality, problems are settled by consultation rather than controversy, and whatever leadership exists is based solely on experience and ability."[27] It is little wonder that the WPA did not publish a manuscript that carries an endorsement of anarchism by one of its most effective writers; his comrades must have been relieved as well.

Rexroth attended the three-day Western Writers Conference on November 13, 1936, sponsored by the League of American Writers, the organization that had absorbed the John Reed Clubs throughout the country. Like many of the other 250 West Coast writers at the meeting, Rexroth had come to give a paper and to hear Upton Sinclair, Mike Gold, John Steinbeck, William Saroyan, Budd Schulberg, Irwin Shaw, Nathanael West, and Harry Bridges, leader of the longshoremen's union. They listened to lectures about "The Writers in a Changing World," "Fascist Trends," "Writing and Propaganda," "Makers of Mass Neuroses," and the importance of regionalism. Rexroth sympathized with the efforts to encourage writers to identify with the region where they lived; a strong sense of place, he thought, constituted one of the writer's essential tools. However, he firmly opposed any kind of factionalism. In a speech delivered earlier that spring at a conference of Midwestern writers in Chicago, Meridel LeSueur had said that she favored the establishing of roots, creating more confident artists and more receptive audiences, but not at the risk of promoting what she called "reactionary regionalism."[28] Rexroth's speech for the conference, entitled "The Function of the Poet in Society,"[29] struck a similar note, but expressed it in a broader context. It was high time, he decided, to spell out the minimal conditions that working artists needed.

Rexroth's address was ignited by genuine passion. Through allusions ranging from Abelard to Walter Savage Landor to T. S. Eliot, he made sure, as always, to let his audience know in his introduction that they were listening to an educated, worldly man who was hardly naive (often a tell-tale sign of an autodidact). After describing himself as "a social outcast [who] identified with the forces striving for a better social system, a system in which the humanity and leisure for vital appreciation of the arts would be the common property of all men," Rexroth admitted that he wrote with a divided personality, a privilege also enjoyed by greater writers with established audiences like William Butler Yeats and T. S. Eliot, whose poetry, though "truly revolutionary in its final implications," was socially ineffective. Yeats and Eliot had evolved for themselves systems based on theosophy and Anglo-Catholicism, severely critical of modern civilization but largely inaccessible to the average person. If Rexroth and his comrades aspired to enlarge as well as enlighten their readers, they had to devise a means of creating a common literary sensibility that permitted honest communication. If they were going to keep the United States in the "civilized world," they had to reach out to "all the producing classes of the west," the workers and the farmers the country depended on. Rexroth pleaded eloquently for the recognition of regional literary magazines devoted to good writing, not "agitational" lyrics or Party-line prose literature. In a sense he was redefining democracy in dynamic terms by asserting that a free country nurtures the creative impulse in all its people, not merely its elite.

One of the writers whom Rexroth had hoped would be in attendance was Yvor Winters. He had encouraged Philip Rahv, editor of *Partisan Review*, to believe that Winters "was very close to coming to us"[30] because Winters had told Rexroth that he favored a new social order of the kind that had inspired the spirit of the convention.[31] Rexroth proposed that Winters address the poet's role in contemporary society, the very topic that had been assigned to Rexroth, but Winters declared that the energy expended at conventions like this one was wasted. Rexroth tried to coax Winters into changing his mind with a long letter that addressed itself, point by point, to Winters's objections—for example, his intolerance of the newly converted, or his need to separate and polarize politics—without success.[32] At the end, Rexroth made a revealing confession: "I may for the moment become angry when I see comrades pursuing what I believe to be mistaken tactics, but in the last analysis I feel that I have no

other friends, that there is no other society of friends in the world today."
Winters felt his mission was to keep alive the kind of literature he thought
had merit. Rexroth, on the other hand, did not want his vocation as a
writer to prevent him from forming a community that aspired to change
the world.

Meanwhile he still believed that somehow his marriage to Andrée
could be saved. Despite their separate living quarters and love affairs,
Rexroth felt great pride in Andrée's growing if modest reputation as a
painter. She had exhibited her work in such San Francisco locations as
the Palace of the Legion of Honor, the Annual San Francisco Art Association Show, Paul Elder's Gallery, and the Oakland Art Gallery. Elsa Gidlow arranged a show of watercolors in her new apartment at 1158 Page
Street. Outside the Bay Area, Andrée's work could be seen in the Santa
Monica Public Library and Jake Zeitlin's bookstore in Los Angeles. In
1936, her paintings were also displayed on the walls of Stanley Rose's
bookshop, a Hollywood hangout for higher-paid and less political writers,
popular with Gene Fowler, Horace McCoy, and William Faulkner, who
often drank in the back room.[33] Rose himself was a proponent of and an
activist for leftist ideology. It pleased Andrée that she could display her
work in a space owned by a man whose political sympathies were leftist.
She would not always be kindly disposed toward art dealers. Although
neither she nor Kenneth had been able to exhibit in New York City after
the Delphic closed, she turned down the opportunity to show her paintings at the Downtown Gallery because she believed it catered to "petty
bourgeois Trotskeyites"[34] of the East Coast, and expected Kenneth to take
a similar stand. Rexroth feared her political views were becoming rigid,
but complied with her wishes. He was still in love with her.

Over the following months, Andrée's epileptic attacks became more
frequent. Phenobarbitol was still the only drug available for controlling
them. Along with the seizures, she suffered from a new affliction, a semi-
amnesiac state commonly known as "fugue." This state could last for
weeks, months, or even years, during which time the epileptic might begin
an entirely different life pattern. Once the fugue was over, Andrée might
remember what occurred prior to, but not during the fugue. She would
often wander out of the house and get picked up by people who were
trying to help her, but later also by men who would persuade her to
accompany them. When she was in such a state, she became highly sexed.
These experiences were "extremely nerve-wracking" for Kenneth, who
would have no notion where she was or what she was doing.[35] She usually
came home as soon she recovered. Eventually, the interval between fugues grew shorter: Andrée would have seizures on the street, and Kenneth would fetch her from the emergency room at San Francisco County.

At home—either in her own room or Kenneth's—she became subject
to short bursts of violence, another sign of what Rexroth regarded as her

"mental derangement." It is possible that Andrée was acting out in these fugues her unconscious feelings about Kenneth. Some of her Communist friends blamed Rexroth, not her epilepsy, for her erratic behavior, and believed that on occasions he had lost his temper and had become abusive. Andrée was still subject to severe bouts of depression, and attempted suicide again, this time by trying to hang herself. Desperate for some kind of reconciliation, Kenneth suggested that they go to the Sierras once more, but she refused. By the time Kenneth had returned from the trip, Andrée had moved into the apartment of her married lover,[36] a man who was more active in the Party than Kenneth, but who could not watch over Andrée's illness. Again, as she had suggested with the Van Ghents, Andrée proposed that the four live together, but Kenneth was still not interested in a ménage-à-quatre. And now, since he no longer wanted to be Andrée's keeper, he rented himself a furnished room in an old Victorian house that was further away, on 1427 Post Street.

Faced by the prospect of an irrevocable separation, both Kenneth and Andrée sank into a period of turmoil and despondency. Andrée would land in the hospital several times after her "binges," as Elsa Gidlow called them, and it was Gidlow who ended up at her side comforting and counseling her. Meanwhile Rexroth, perhaps contaminated by Andrée's example, contemplated suicide—how seriously is hard to say. But one day when Elsa visited him unexpectedly, she had to talk him out of putting a rope around his neck.[37]

Rexroth blamed the growing severity of Andrée's illness for her rejection of him, her angry outbursts, her promiscuity, and her preference for men—he would describe them as psychopathic—whose existence was even more precarious than his. Perhaps only in this way could he deal with his bitterness over her desertion of him, almost as though she were mentally unbalanced and too ill to know any better. Moreover, Rexroth had become highly critical of many organizations dominated by the Communist Party, while Andrée remained fiercely loyal. According to Elsa Gidlow, Andrée's unswerving commitment to the Party contributed its share to their final estrangement. Kenneth refused to concede that he personally bore any major responsibility for the deterioration of the marriage.

In Rexroth's eyes, the American Communist Party was creating an intolerable and divisive brand of nationalism that contradicted an inherent principle of the revolutionary movement. Rexroth detected tell-tale signs: on the walls of the meeting rooms were blown-up pictures of Washington and Lincoln overshadowing Lenin and Stalin; meetings closed with the singing of "America the Beautiful" instead of the "Internationale." Party members who expressed disapproval of the growing authoritarianism emanating from Russia were expelled. The policies of the so-called third period of international communism condemned as an enemy anyone who was not following the Party line to the letter. When the

Presidium of the Communist International declared that Hitler's dictatorship would accelerate the historical process by destroying whatever illusions the German people had about Social Democracy, no one was permitted to say that the price for tolerating such a government would be the loss of human decency and civilization. The faithful were to believe that "after Hitler, our turn!" Rexroth refused to be counted among them, although Andrée stuck to her guns, even as they backfired.

Nine

POTRERO HILL
1936–1939

EXROTH CONTINUED TO WORK with local Communist front organizations, and published poems and book reviews in *New Masses, Partisan Review, The New Republic, Coast,* and *Art Front.* One evening in the spring of 1936, while helping to organize a "strong radical faction" within the Nurses Association, he drove home a friendly public health nurse named Marie Kass, who would become his second wife. She was a "stately woman with bright red hair . . . the color of a dark tree-ripened orange,"[1] a characteristic she may have inherited from her Hungarian father Charles, who also passed on to her his commitment to Socialist politics. Born in England, her mother's birthplace, Marie was six months older than Kenneth. They made a handsome pair: Rexroth's rugged image balanced well with Marie's vibrant good looks. She was working for the Public Health Department in 1936 and epitomized the bright, informed, and independent woman. Kenneth was also attracted to her "sense of humor both ironic and frisky."[2] In his later years, he recounted stories about this aspect of her personality and liked to say that their period of happiness together was born on that mild spring evening. When Kenneth tried to kiss her, she demurred. She didn't object to the overture, but she did mind the discomfort of "necking in a small coop."[3] She proposed instead that they go to the nearby cemetery and salute life among the dead.[4]

During the summer, Rexroth invited her to the poetry seminars that he conducted at his large furnished room on Post Street. Marie attended until she had to leave for a job as nurse at a posh summer camp at Huntington Lake near Fresno.[5] They agreed to meet at the end of the season for a three-week backpacking trip in the high country. This was their first prolonged period of time together, and it set a pattern they would repeat often, camping from six to eight weeks in the mountains after a long burst of work. Since Marie's nursing skills were always in demand, she could often stop and start work as she pleased. Kenneth's more flexible schedule was tied only to his political activities and his WPA projects.

Kenneth never forgot those three weeks in the Sierras. He and Marie got a ride from a ranger up the narrow dirt road to Florence Lake and Blaney Meadows hot springs, and then on to the pass below Mt. Humphries. Rexroth's pack was so heavy that he had a hard time swinging it off the ground and onto his shoulders. Once he managed to hoist the pack onto his back, Marie would pull him to his feet. They swam, sunned, fished, and generally explored the beauty around them. On the spur of the moment they decided to climb Mt. Humphries after they saw a fox terrier scrambling around on the peak. If a dog could make it up there, they could too.

Near the summit we came on the High Sierra polemonium—dense clusters of deep blue flowers with the most beautiful odor I know. . . . In the twilight we passed through clouds of perfume. It was quite dark when we got back to the lake and we picked our way off down the plateau in the moonlight, ate our supper of Golden trout, risotto, and dried fruit, made love, and slept till the sun woke us up.[6]

Marie would take Andrée's place as Kenneth's beloved companion. Though strong and independent, she was more compliant, more adoring than Andrée, and politically akin. An earthy, sensual woman, she was thrilled that a talented, handsome artist like Rexroth was wooing her.

As with Andrée, Kenneth led Marie to those places which afforded him a fertile background to mesh his aesthetics and his politics into what he would describe as "ecological" poetry. Rexroth always felt that his existence was most validated when he slept under the stars and made his way through isolated trails. He was sure somehow that he was "related to chipmunks and bears and pine trees and stars and nebulae and rocks and fossils, as part of an infinitely inter-related complex of being."[7] As it had for his poems to Andrée, the high country served as a rich setting for Rexroth's love poems to Marie. The poems to Andrée, especially the two entitled "Andrée Rexroth" (that appear in *The Phoenix and the Tortoise*) are extraordinary for their piercing natural images, palpable nostalgia and tenderness. ("They are all gone now, the days / We thought would not come for us are here.") By contrast, in the poems inspired by his love for Marie, *In What Hour, The Phoenix and the Tortoise,* and *The Signature of All Things,* the natural world takes on a sensual and erotic component as well. As Donald Gutierrez suggests, "the realized love experience is also a realization of one's unity with the living, circumambient universe."[8] As an example of how love and sexuality become "forms of dynamic nature" in Rexroth's work, Gutierrez cites the third section of "Inversely, As the Square of Their Distances Apart"—where Kenneth and Marie make love at the "wood's edge," reaching their climax like falling meteors, "dark through black cold / Toward each other, and then compact / Blazing through air into the earth."[9] Rexroth describes spectacular sex again in the poem

"Floating," set in a canoe on a river thick with lily pads.[10] Marie proved to be a worthy partner with whom Kenneth could celebrate the earthy communion of passion and spirit.

The two lovers rented an apartment together at 692 Wisconsin Street on Potrero Hill, the top floor of a typical New England saltbox house that stood in the middle of ten acres with a spring running through. It had been built during the Gold Rush "from salvaged ships' timbers by a New England ship's carpenter." All four rooms were the same size, eighteen by eighteen, and from them Kenneth and Marie could see most of San Francisco. They painted the walls and woodwork white, and put down linoleum in a pattern of gray, white, and black tiles "which looked as though it had been designed by Mondrian." For $12 a month, it was a "perfect place" for their needs. Potrero Hill itself had been a Spanish land grant settled right after the San Francisco earthquake by a group of Molokani, a Russian Anabaptist sect, similar to the Mennonites and Doukhobors, who had left their own country where they worked as skilled mechanics and farmers. The Molokani were on their way to South America, planning to start a communal colony, but the demand for their labor was so great and the pay so high after the earthquake that they decided to stay. They were still living on Potrero Hill, as were "Sicilians who were ostracized by the Northern Italians in North Beach," when Marie and Kenneth moved there.[11]

Marie seemed unconcerned that he remained married to Andrée and was surprised when some people—including those at the WPA offices—became uncomfortable when she told them she was living with Kenneth Rexroth.[12] Marie fit into Kenneth's social milieu, and her nurse's salary eased Kenneth's life of semi-genteel poverty. The few occasions when he was in town, John Ferren would stop by, and so would Hilaire Hiler (Hiler Hirschbein), who had recently returned from Paris where he had enjoyed—thanks to money sent by his father—the luxurious life of an American expatriate painter. He converted an old barn on Jackson Street below Montgomery into a studio, which he decorated with the murals he painted—very large neo-naturalistic Native Americans—for the Jockey, a club he had owned in Paris where he liked to play jazz piano. Two Potrero Hill neighbors would stop by—Dorothy Van Ghent and William Saroyan. Both Saroyan and Rexroth had a mutual correspondent in Yvor Winters.[13]

There were many pleasant evenings on Potrero Hill; people would sing, dance to records, argue about literature and politics. Usually Marie, a skillful musician, would play the piano and sing madrigals and motets with the poet George ("Parks") Hitchcock, a favorite camping companion of Kenneth's. Friends would gather round to sing Chinese and Japanese songs too. (The Chinese theater was still live in the thirties, and Rexroth and his friends went often.) And they may have tried singing some of the compositions Kenneth composed under the title "Songs for Marie's Lute-book." One, arranged to the tune of "Greensleeves," seems especially written for this period when they would steal away from the current of world events soon to disrupt their lives:

> Do you forget that this apparel
> You shall not always own?
> Time counts the coin you so imperil
> At last calls home his loan.[14]

James Laughlin, the founder of the fledgling avant-garde publishing house New Directions, visited the Potrero Hill house to "refresh his soul" when he got fed up with running his ski lodge in Alta, Utah, about twenty miles southeast of Salt Lake City. Laughlin had first come across Rexroth's poetry while guest-editing *New Democracy*, Gorham Munson's shortlived liberal monthly. Ezra Pound had advised Munson to hire Laughlin, who was on leave from Harvard after his first year, and who had spent October 1933 through August 1934 in Rapallo listening to Pound talk about art and literature. Pound urged Rexroth and many others to send their poems to the magazine; when it folded, Laughlin decided to start a magazine of his own with all the material he had gathered.[15] With help from his family's Pittsburgh steel fortune, the first issue of *New Directions in Prose and Poetry* (1936) launched what would become one of the most important publishing companies of contemporary writing. Laughlin came to San Francisco and looked up Rexroth: ". . . the doorbell rang and a man who looked like he was six foot twelve in height was standing in the doorway with a shy look on his face. I said, 'Gee, you must be Jim Laughlin. Come on in.'"[16] Although Rexroth dates this meeting too early (in 1933) and has Laughlin editing *New Democracy* when he was still a "brilliant young prep school student at one of the most fashionable prep schools in the country" (he is referring to Choate), it marked the beginning of one of Rexroth's closest friendships.

At Rexroth's home, Laughlin was introduced to several other West Coast writers. He remembers well the time he met Saroyan: Rexroth, in one of his grouchy moods and perhaps envious of Saroyan's meteoric rise to fame, had begun to insult Saroyan, and at a signal from Marie, Laughlin and Saroyan went off to a "nice, rough bar on Market Street."[17] Saroyan and Rexroth soon lost touch but were reunited briefly in 1958 when Saroyan was in San Francisco with his children, Aram and Lucy. Saroyan had been asked if he wanted to write the film script for Jack Kerouac's *The Subterraneans*, and before deciding, he thought he should observe the Beat scene in San Francisco first hand. While he and Aram were driving up a steep San Francisco street, Aram recognized Rexroth from a line drawing he had seen on a record cover. Typically, Rexroth was carrying a sack of groceries. Rexroth and Saroyan spent some time reminiscing before Saroyan asked about Kerouac, who claimed that Saroyan had been a great influence on his work. Rexroth was not enthusiastic about Kerouac's work (more about that later), saying that he preferred Ginsberg's. Rexroth then went on to talk about poetry and jazz and the dangers of show business.

Looking back on this occasion, Aram Saroyan remains amused, since clearly his father, not Rexroth, was the one who might understand the perils of show business. Aram said his father's fondness for Rexroth was renewed after that meeting. Rexroth's apartment (250 Scott Street) was the first "beat pad" Aram had ever seen, with abstract paintings on the wall and a phonograph set up so that you could see all the interior tubes. He recalls that this meeting was one of the very few "during which Pop willingly surrendered the center of attention."[18] Later, Saroyan's suggestion to Arthur Freed of MGM that Rexroth be considered as the screenwriter for *The Subterraneans* was ignored.[19]

The friendship between Laughlin and Rexroth deepened as Laughlin showed an increased interest in Rexroth's poetry. For *New Directions in Prose and Poetry*, II (1937), he chose two of Rexroth's more difficult poems. One was "Organon," a poem William Fitzgerald later described in *Poetry* (November 1940, pp. 158–160) as an "exercise in Whiteheadian objectivity." Laura Riding had expressed a similar opinion about some poems Rexroth had sent her in 1936. Writing from Majorca, she praised the poems for their "intricacy and consciousness," but added that these qualities seemed "to remain private to independent word combinations which in turn are indifferent to the existence of any surrounding poem."[20] The other poem Laughlin published was "Easy Lessons in Geophagy," an ominous, surreal work in four parts that warns of a world crisis that will surpass all others, both natural and man-made. (People have been known to practice geophagy, that is, to eat dirt, when they have been subsisting on scanty and unbalanced diets.) The poem is dedicated to Rexroth's former neighbor in New York City, Hart Crane, and to his friend Harry Crosby, whose career as a poet was blossoming before he shot himself and Josephine Rotch Bigelow in a New York studio apartment in 1929.[21]

By the early forties, Rexroth and Laughlin saw one another regularly during the winters when Laughlin would go west to San Francisco after skiing in Alta. Rexroth took over from Pound as Laughlin's teacher.[22] Laughlin credits Pound with starting his "serious encounter with literature," telling him what to read, criticizing his reactions at his "Ezuversity" in Rapallo. Laughlin had rented a room but would take all his meals with Pound, paying for the food in place of tuition. However, as Pound became "increasingly cranky and absorbed in economics," Laughlin needed someone else to teach him, "so Kenneth became my guru." Whenever he came to San Francisco, Laughlin would stay with Kenneth and Marie for weeks at a time, listening to Rexroth discourse. He came to regard Rexroth

as an "omniscient autodidact and a dedicated teacher." When Laughlin
suggested a formal monetary arrangement for his bed and board, Kenneth and Marie refused to hear of it.

Once, before arriving for a visit, he offered to hire a cook for them,
but Kenneth balked:

Do you know that a good cook—that is an edible one—would cost you $60 a week
at the very least in Frisco? Longshoremen will be getting $1.80 an hour soon on
their new contract. Anyway—I have a queasy stomach and can only eat my own
and Yee Jun's cooking [a favorite Chinese restaurant]. And no cook would use
our poor antiquated kitchen.[23]

On a typical day when Laughlin was visiting, Marie would fix breakfast
before leaving for work. If the men were still engaged in their literary
activities by the time she returned at six o'clock, she would prepare dinner, although Kenneth would frequently be knocking around the kitchen
before she got home. Laughlin wrote memos and used the dictaphone to
manage his new publishing venture back east. Often Laughlin took Marie
and Kenneth for dinner at Nam Yuan, another favorite Chinese restaurant near the Sun Yat Sen monument, or to Joe's on Broadway where
Laughlin would usually order maritata soup made with cream cheese, or
to Jack's in the financial district where the great treat was crab Louis.
Sometimes they went to Bohemian hangouts like Myrto's or Casa Begine,
whose customers stayed long past midnight, talking, playing chess, singing together after many glasses of wine. They also frequented Izzy Gom-
ez's place, immortalized by William Saroyan in *The Time of Your Life,* and
favored by hard-boiled newspapermen for its thick steaks, french fries,
and salads.

Rexroth and Laughlin spent a good deal of time together outdoors.
They went rock climbing down the coast, and in the early spring, Laughlin especially enjoyed camping and skiing in the Sierras, "when there was
still a lot of snow. We climbed into the mountains, and Kenneth would
dig a little cave in the snow, lining it with fir branches where we slept. This
was very fine."[24] Occasionally, Laughlin and Rexroth left town in Marie's
"old beat up car," heading fifteen miles north to Marin County and an
abandoned hutch made of milled lumber and galvanized metal that Marie
and Kenneth were rehabilitating primarily as a refuge for Kenneth. Built
by sheepherders as a shelter, the cabin had been used by anyone who
happened upon it. It had no running water, and heat was provided by a
fireplace which took up most of the south wall. Furnished with only a
table and two benches, it became a cherished retreat where he could write
and meditate in solitude, or be with Marie or bosom buddies like Frank
Triest or Laughlin.[25]

In turn, Rexroth would visit Laughlin at the lodge in Alta, a small
hostel with one ski lift. Rexroth and Laughlin loved to ski together, although their techniques differed. Laughlin skied with an enthusiasm and

passion that he developed into an increasing mastery over method and art. Rexroth, on the other hand, was a strong, rugged skier who, though "he had no technique . . . could handle the skis."[26] The National Ski Association certified him as a guide to the high mountains in 1947. Rexroth liked to be alone: "sometimes he would sit all by himself on a tree stump, meditating. He took off his skis and meditated." And he didn't approve of Laughlin's decision to expand the lodge with additional ski lifts, which he regarded as an unnecessary concession to convenience.

Other visitors also enjoyed hospitality at Wisconsin Street. In February 1937, André Malraux came to the United States on the invitation of several universities (Harvard, Princeton, and Berkeley) and left-wing organizations, including the then pro-Communist review *The Nation*, for which Rexroth would become the San Francisco correspondent. Acting as an unofficial minister of propaganda and foreign relations for the Republican government of Spain, Malraux toured eight cities in North America to raise funds for medical aid. The celebrated writer and fighting commander of the International Air Force in Spain, Malraux by now was a living legend.[27] Except in Washington, he was received warmly everywhere. On the West Coast he was met by Haakon Chevalier, a fellow Marxist and a professor of French literature at Berkeley who had translated *Man's Fate* and *Days of Wrath*. Luminaries like Marlene Dietrich, William Saroyan, Clifford Odets, and Miriam Hopkins welcomed him cordially. After addressing a cheering overflow audience at the Mecca Temple Auditorium, Malraux went north to San Francisco. There he was introduced by Chevalier (who would later regret his involvement with "Red" West Coast organizations) at a large luncheon that Rexroth attended. Malraux spoke eloquently on behalf of the Republican cause, but the following Sunday, when Chevalier organized a breakfast at the University of California Faculty Club, Malraux chose to lecture on art rather than on Spain. His audience of two hundred was rewarded with a foretaste of certain ideas that he would develop much later in his books about art, especially *Museum Without Walls*. Malraux and his new lover and companion on the trip, Josette Clotis, who herself had become very popular with American audiences, spent the night as guests of Kenneth and Marie.[28] Rexroth was eager for fresh news about Spain and Malraux provided it willingly. Rexroth had kept himself informed by reading a British anarchist newspaper originally called *Freedom* (later *Spain and the Revolution*), and whatever news bulletins were being put out by the Independent Labor Party, allied with the POUM *(Partido Obrero de Unificación Marxista)*. But first-hand information from the front was always best, and Malraux was bursting with it.

Involved as they were in San Francisco's political and cultural scene, Kenneth and Marie looked forward to weekends relaxing in the Devil's Gulch shack, or taking longer trips to the Sierras. Their car, however, was gradually becoming unreliable, and sometimes they preferred to hitchhike. Kenneth regarded Marie's bright red hair as a real asset because he had heard that truckdrivers believed that red-headed women brought luck. He would make Marie pull off her cap and put out her thumb. Once in a while a truckdriver treated them to a dinner at one of the roadside truck stops.[29] Living outdoors suited Rexroth, and his appearance reflected it. Tested and toughened by the challenging regimen of mountain climbing, his body was lean and muscled, fairly glowing with rugged good health, a worthy partner for the long-legged and radiant Marie, who also relished this environment, even when it was dangerous. Once while Kenneth was fishing, she picked and cooked wild mushrooms to eat with the trout she knew Kenneth would catch. After dinner she became violently ill. She had eaten the few poisonous mushrooms she had gathered; by mere chance Kenneth had not. First, Kenneth forced salt water down her throat so that she would vomit. Then he gave her cup after cup of coffee and kept her walking around the campfire all night until the danger passed.

During the summer of 1937, Rexroth embarked on one especially long stay in Yosemite to work on his field guides and camping manuals for the WPA, and to write poetry. Marie worked glumly at the Mission Health Center for a month, very much minding the heat and the solitude. To her "dearest dearest" she complained about having the "strangest sensations that [she was] in New York or the 4th dimension or something."[30] In another letter she described some of the more "exciting" aspects of her job, like pulling a little boy out of a sewer and listening to a colleague tell how she "ran smack into a woman screaming in the street with a dead baby in her arms." She sent Kenneth articles from *Time* that might amuse him and reported on who needed help getting on the relief rolls of the WPA. She kept him informed about the growing world crisis: "*The New Republic* this week comes right out and says it is dead set against collective security, and the paper says Russia is having a new purge." Moreover, San Francisco was busy with strike activity, the "marvel of the summer" being that Woolworths "won a union house, minimum $20 a week, and are they happy!" Eleuria had kittens (she had to be taken to the vet because the last kitten was stillborn and not fully delivered), and Marie tried her own hand at domesticity by baking pears with ginger, "but they weren't so wonderful."

Marie not only met her own responsibilities but also vigorously promoted Kenneth's career. She maintained a log of Kenneth's poems and essays that she had sent out—to *New Masses,* to Harcourt Brace, to James Laughlin, to Macmillan (where the editors were interested in the Sierras camping book), and handled the bulk of his correspondence. She kept him posted on what was being said about him and other poets affiliated with the WPA. She also had to receive, once in July, once in August, the investigators from the "relief rolls," suspicious about Rexroth's absence of more than three months. And yet she found time to write a paper called "Socialism and Public Health" which she planned to submit for publication. Meanwhile, her friends took her out to dinner or came over to talk. Elsa Gidlow, who became a good friend of Marie's while remaining close to Andrée, said that Kenneth thought he had found the perfect mate. He told Gidlow that artists and poets should not intermarry, as he and Andrée had, that they needed opposite types to complement their traits and "that's why I am with Marie. Marie is practical and I am impractical."[31] Marie never disagreed with the second half of Kenneth's assessment.

Kenneth had filed for divorce on February 18, 1937, on the grounds that Andrée had deserted him on July 24, 1934 (while their relationship with the Van Ghents was going strong).[32] Although Marie thought it odd that Andrée would want to spend time with her, they saw one another frequently during the summer of 1937. In one of her more gossipy letters (she signed them "Mariska"), Marie says that she made dinner for Andrée, that the two were sharing marvelous evenings together, and that Andrée was looking "most beautiful." Flattered that Andrée sought her company, Marie invited her to a "Communist" gathering of doctors, public health nurses, and social workers sponsored by Mary Schwab, who had a reputation for encouraging "screwball activities." Andrée and Marie, who usually avoided such occasions, made "quite a hit, appearing in public together and nobody knew whether to ask about [Rexroth] or not!"

Marie borrowed *The Autobiography of Alice B. Toklas* from Andrée and enjoyed it, partly because Toklas alludes (unflatteringly) to Robert McAlmon, who had passed through San Francisco in the early winter of 1937 and visited the Rexroths. A cordial correspondence between McAlmon and Rexroth had begun when Rexroth was trying to get RMR off the ground in 1930–31, and they were now fellow contributors to *An "Objectivists" Anthology*. McAlmon suspected that Rexroth, who had attained prominence in leftist circles, was a good contact. Rexroth's poems were appearing in such publications as *Partisan Review* and *New Masses*. "The Apple Garths of Avalon," which Rexroth described as a mildly ironic poem dedicated to George Santayana[33] had just appeared in *American Stuff*, a voluminous collection of work by writers associated with the Project. McAlmon was now living in Santa Barbara and anxious to join the Federal Writers' Project. His Contact Editions Press, which among others had published Ernest Hemingway, Kay Boyle, Djuna Barnes, H.D., and Bryher (Winifred Ellerman, his former wife, whose money supported the Press), was defunct; the wild Paris drinking parties long gone. He thought that Rexroth would help him make the necessary arrangements, especially since Rexroth had invited him to the 1936 Western Writers Conference. McAlmon was too cynical and too ill (with tuberculosis) to carry out procedure, confessing that like their friend Hilaire Hiler, he would "as soon be in a revolution as in Santa Barbara."[34] In the spring of 1937 before Rexroth took off for the mountains, he and his

WPA colleagues were working on a series of poetry pamphlets and a regional literary journal. As he done six years earlier, Rexroth solicited material from McAlmon, but the *Western Review* and *Pacific Weekly* only had brief lives. McAlmon's autobiography, *Being Geniuses Together* (1938), would soon become a lively source of information about American expatriates living in Paris during the twenties.[35] McAlmon returned to Europe and was trapped in occupied France after the war broke out. Rexroth retained a fond memory of McAlmon, whom he regarded as a dedicated and humane writer misunderstood by the bourgeois literary establishment.[36]

Marie would call on Kenneth at his camp in Yosemite periodically, packing their temperamental car with food, magazines, and mail. Often she would come home euphoric, carrying back a bunch of pine and fir boughs whose fragrance filled the house and enabled her to savor her time with Kenneth. But she could not make these weekend trips very often. One trip home took nine hours because she had to negotiate a dirt trail for thirty-five miles. Once she had to turn back after a mechanic advised her that her brakes were faulty. Wonderful as the visits were, Marie paid a high price with those long, arduous trips back and forth while Kenneth remained at camp in the mountains, inconvenienced only by the wait for supplies. In a low moment, Marie confessed mournfully that resuming work after these absences was impossible. At some point, she perceived the inequity implicit in their relationship, but before this happened, she could only articulate dissatisfaction with her job. She clearly took satisfaction in serving as patron to her lover's career as a poet and writer.

Meanwhile, Andrée was struggling to maintain a balanced existence. Once, returning late Saturday night from a visit to Kenneth in Yosemite, Marie found a frantic letter from Andrée begging her to come over to the house because "something terrific" had happened. Marie immediately went over early Sunday morning before breakfast to learn the good news, hoping that some anonymous wealthy investor had decided to buy Andrée's paintings. Instead, Andrée was celebrating the absence of seizures for three weeks, owing to a new medication recently promoted by the American Medical Association. Andrée was convinced that she was cured, but Marie suspected that the drug was merely a new kind of sedative which her body might not tolerate. In a letter to Kenneth, Marie described Andrée's behavior:

She is in a strange condition, goes around in a complete daze, as some one [sic] who is madly in love for the first time, she says nothing seems to effect [sic] her (petty things that happen) and she is apt to get quite drowsy in the p.m. and early evening. She is in a quivering excitable state so that she shivers when she talks of it as though she were cold.[37]

That same Sunday afternoon, Marie and Andrée paid Elsa Gidlow a visit. Marie left at five, but Andrée stayed on, "apparently by some private arrangement," with Elsa and her companion Vivian. (There is no evidence to suggest that Andrée was romantically attracted to either Elsa or Vivian.)

On Louis Zukofsky's recommendation, Rexroth had been serving as Western correspondent for the League of American Writers, sending east brief notes on books, workers, and anti-Fascist activities.[38] A few months after Rexroth returned to San Francisco, he also did a stint as instructor at the Workers' School, a League of American Writers' operation, which among its programs offered workshops for aspiring writers. Thus Rexroth landed in the classroom even though as a youth he could never tolerate one for long. He relished the role of teacher, especially since his students were self-motivated and genuinely eager for his advice. Marie decided to enroll in the class, and both took their student / teacher roles seriously.

One short story that Marie submitted for criticism was called "Sebastian Del Lucca." It takes place in "the little three bedrooms in back of the big surgical ward at County Hospital," in Ward F, and concerns an Italian immigrant who has lost one leg to Berger's disease and resists an intern's advice to amputate the other. Rexroth graded it an "A" and advised Marie to look up Anatole France's "Crainquibille." Marie must have been revising the story for some time because Rexroth also wrote: "smooth continuity and definitely more restrained in wording and more objective in visual effect."[39]

By the fall of 1938, as world crises unfolded, Rexroth had withdrawn from the WPA. Shortly after Germany, France, Britain, and Italy decreed that Czechoslovakia should evacuate the Sudeten, in effect ending Czechoslovakia's independence, Rexroth severed his connections with the WPA.[40] Why did he leave his editorial and writer's position when he was in the very thick of researching and writing his various guides? For one thing, Rexroth did not want to work for a state that he believed was rapidly preparing itself for war (so he said to the state director at the time of his resignation). He also feared that he was being drawn into the internal politics of the WPA bureaucracy. And he sensed very strongly the need to divert more energy into his writing and his painting before "the oncoming disaster made it impossible to continue creative work."[41]

As he was leaving the WPA, Rexroth's ambivalence about the Communist Party turned into strong aversion. Perhaps this juncture in his life most clearly marks the birth of his active pacifist-anarchist activities. He felt totally dissociated from the benevolent belligerence of the Roosevelt administration, which placed people on relief rolls on one hand and geared up for war on the other. And the Soviet system offered no alternative. He could not sanction Stalin's tightening grip on the Russian people, nor on the members of the American Communist Party. Murder and other forms

of violence could never be justified. Endorsing the dictates from Moscow
aimed at disciplining errant Party members was out of the question. Joseph Freeman, for example, it had been rumored, was required to re-
move his work from bookstores because he had referred in his writing to
Trotsky as a "man" instead of as a murderer. Walter Lowenfels was told
to quit writing poetry until the Party could determine whether it served a
political purpose. Rexroth knew that he had to set his own goals without
the official approval or guidance of anybody. When he refused to endorse
Party policy, Marie stood stalwartly beside him.

To escape the turmoil, Marie and Kenneth went deeper and higher
into the Sierras, from Yosemite to Sequoia Park. For weeks at a time, they
searched for sites off the beaten path and blazed trails of their own to
preserve their isolation. When they tired of carrying three weeks of supplies on their backs, they would rent a burro. In the southern Sierras,
they usually chose the burro they called "Bebe," who was, they decided,
"as old as the rocks" because she was marked with the brand of the Kings
River Packing Corporation, dating back to "the days of Jack London."[42]
Bebe was big for a burro, gray, with white markings, "like the donkey in
Chesterton's poem who carried Jesus and bore ever after the mark of the
cross."[43] Apparently no better donkey could be found anywhere. She did
not have to be tethered or hobbled at night because she always stayed
close to the fire, and she warned Kenneth and Marie when other campers
were nearby. Sometimes the burro had to be left behind as they probed
the high country above the timberline and off the trails. They also began
experimenting cautiously with a rope on ice and snow, even though they
preferred "the acrobatics of difficult rock climbing."[44] While the world
lurched from crisis to crisis that winter, Kenneth and Marie enjoyed the
first-rate equipment they had put together, including a goose-down
"mummy bag" and a coffin-shaped tent of Egyptian cotton, waterproofed
and sunproofed to Kenneth's precise specifications, that could "be pitched
into anything upright."

They decided to join the rock-climbing unit of the Sierra Club. They
passed up the club's major expeditions to the High Sierras, but participated in the weekend practice trips. The poem "On What Planet" was
inspired by one of these journeys to Hunter's Hill, with its big overhang-
ing cliff that Sierra Club members used for practice. Rexroth transforms
a landscape of dramatic natural beauty—"White egrets stand in the blue
marshes; / Tamalpais, Diablo, St. Helena / Float in the air"—into a porten-
tous scene: two white owls suddenly fly out of a small cave and are temporarily blinded by the sunlight. Nearly brushing into Rexroth's face,
they "disappear into the recesses of the cliff," omens perhaps that, like
the owls, human beings will not be able to tell day from night once the
firearms of war cast their deadly glare over the horizon. However, the
spell is broken when a new and graceful climber, "a young girl with ash
blond hair / and gentle confident eyes" (actually a Berkeley student with

whom he was barely acquainted) marvels at the spectacular beauty of the sunset, turns to Rexroth, and says: "It must be very beautiful, the sunset / On Saturn, with the rings and all the moons." The poem conveys the feeling that Rexroth's faith in the cosmic harmony of nature has been magically restored by the words of this mysterious young observer.[45] Rexroth would depend on that faith to sustain him through the approaching political storm.

Ten

SUBVERTING THE WAR EFFORT
1939–1942

OR REXROTH, withdrawing from the Communist Party did not mean retreating into political silence and inactivity. During the fall of 1939, he wrote an impassioned letter to *The New Republic* exhorting the United States to remain neutral during the war. He declared that all ordinary people would be bankrupted by the cost of this war which, he believed, would ultimately starve out everyone while "the imperialists on both sides [went] on killing the working class".[1] The magazine (Malcolm Cowley was literary editor, Bruce Bliven managing editor) replied that it differed with Rexroth on only one major point: if the West was to remain free, the United States had to supply Great Britain with munitions.

This response touched off an angry reaction which *The New Republic* printed under the title "More Wrath from Rexroth."[2] Here Rexroth warned the liberals and the radicals that "their honeymoon with the New Deal [was] over." Rexroth called the Roosevelt administration "Anglophile" and eager for war. He forecast the end of all principled conduct, and predicted that soft-spined liberals would meet the same fate as Bukharin, the editor of *Izvestia,* who was secretly arrested in 1937, expelled from the Communist Party, and executed.[3] For emphasis he singled out the two who would be the first to "get it": Malcolm Cowley and journalist Heywood Broun, who had supported Norman Thomas for president in 1932.[4]

Rexroth needed other outlets to vent his frustration. When his San Francisco friends were not available or tired of listening to him, he appealed to Weldon Kees as an audience. He had met Kees, whose short stories and poetry had already appeared in various little magazines including *Poetry,* while Kees was visiting San Francisco in the summer of 1939. Born in Beatrice, Nebraska, Kees had worked in Lincoln for the Federal Writers' Project until 1937 when he left for Denver to take a job at the public library. He served as contributing editor to both *Prairie Schooner* and *Rocky Mountain Review.*[5]

Although in his review of *New Directions 1937,* Kees had described

Rexroth as "lost in a fog of private sources,"[6] Kees welcomed a meeting. He thoroughly enjoyed the evening they spent together that July. In a letter to fellow editor Maurice Johnson of *Prairie Schooner,* he gave his impressions of Rexroth:

He is a German who looks like the best type of Irishman; volatile, anarchistic, and very witty. Marvelous mimic. He cannot merely tell you of someone; he has to imitate him, and he does this excellently. I particularly liked his imitations of Lionel Abel, Harry Roskolenko . . . Ford Madox Ford . . . a duck, a snake he once encountered in the woods, a Communist laying down the law with cliches from the *Daily Worker.*[7]

A lively correspondence had sprung up between them after both appeared in the *New Directions Annual* for 1939. Rexroth knew that Kees, an idealist with a sharp mind, shared his anarcho-pacifist perspective and wanted him to assault the position of *The New Republic.* "Make your letters just as nasty as you can and keep it up. Write personally to the editors and just raise Cain."[8]

More importantly, Rexroth wanted Kees to help him establish a network of pacifists affiliated with organizations like the Fellowship of Reconciliation, the Women's International League for Peace and Freedom, the National Council for the Prevention of War, and the Keep America Out of War Committee.[9] Rexroth believed that U.S. participation in the war would result in "something a lot worse than a heavy fog in a blacked out London. We have got to keep hands joined, or we will never get out on the other side." Rexroth was not alone in this view. Among others who signed a call for neutrality published by the League for Cultural Freedom and Socialism in the Fall 1939 issue of *Partisan Review* were Kay Boyle, Delmore Schwartz, Katherine Anne Porter, William Carlos Williams, Gorham Munson, and James Laughlin.[10] And he spent countless hours mailing postcards, writing bulletins, cutting stencils in the hope of gaining support for the pacifist movement.

Sometimes Rexroth's faith in activism wavered. To Wendell Kees, he wrote:

The working class, for weal or woe, still seeks expression in parties and trade unions. The leftwing communist or anarchist who "boycotts" the TUs and the political movements of the working class simply relegates himself to the categories of scab or crackpot or both. With the stalinists justifying the Finnish invasion there are quite enough eccentric characters around for the time being.[11]

Unquestionably, Rexroth's image of the "revolutionary" had grown tarnished: In "New Objectives, New Cadres," he writes:

> He who sits in his socks reading shockers,
> Skinning cigarette butts and rerolling and rerolling
>   them in toilet paper,
> His red eyes never leaving the blotted print and the
>   pulp paper.

> He rose too late to distribute the leaflets.
> In the midst of the mussed bedding have mercy
> Upon him, this is history.[12]

Nevertheless, there is no substitute for action: "the problem is to control history / We already understand it."

Early in the summer of 1940, he gave concrete evidence of what he meant: he urged the American Friends Service Committee in Philadelphia to send him abroad as a CO to do "foreign reconstruction" of war-damaged schools and hospitals. But he was refused by Eleanor Slater, who suggested that instead he stay at home and work with the Fellowship of Reconciliation.[13] In response, Rexroth appealed to the FOR on behalf of the Japanese-American population. Rexroth suspected that because they were so easily identifiable, Japanese Americans would suffer far more than German Americans. Although the people at the Fellowship of Reconciliation were reluctant to consider this terrible prediction—they told Rexroth he was overly pessimistic—they set up with his assistance an organization called the American Committee to Protect the Civil Rights of American Citizens of Oriental Ancestry.

Rexroth soon discovered that it was not easy to get Japanese Americans to join. The vast majority believed that their country, the United States, would never treat them as dangerous aliens. Many of them, by Rexroth's account, expected Japan to declare war on Germany, not the United States. Once again, Rexroth found himself engaged in frustrating discussions that went nowhere. The Japanese preferred to think that the organization had been formed to help the Filipino migrant workers picking lettuce in the San Joaquin Valley.

Ironically, during this period of intense disaffection and under the shadow of impending war, Rexroth's first volume of poetry, *In What Hour*, was published by Macmillan, a major New York company. Many of the poems had appeared in *New Masses, The New Republic*, and *Partisan Review*. Political poems, love poems, and elegies are scattered throughout the text. Rexroth's deep communion with the natural universe, especially the world of the High Sierras, remains paramount, as in this excerpt from "Falling Leaves and Early Snow":

> In the years to come they will say,
> "They fell like leaves
> In the autumn of nineteen thirty-nine."
> November has come to the forest,
> To the meadows where we picked the cyclamen.
> The year fades with the white frost
> On the brown sedge in the hazy meadows,
> Where the deer tracks were black this morning.
> Ice forms in the shadows;
> Disheveled maples hang over the water;
> Deep gold sunlight glistens on the shrunken stream.

Somnolent trout move through pillars of brown and gold.
The yellow maple leaves eddy above them,
The glittering leaves of the cottonwood,
The olive, velvety alder leaves,
The scarlet dogwood leaves,
Most poignant of all.[14]

Exemplifying the kind of poetry that Rexroth would write best over the next thirty years, the poem mourns a terrible and tragic event—the German invasion of Poland—yet it unfolds against a landscape whose beauty never ceased to inspire him: the tone is contemplative, the measured rhythms are graceful, the reverence for nature is expressed in sharp-edged imagery, the circumstances and events of his own life are delicately meshed with larger, graver issues, and the unabashed idealism is reined in short of sentimentality.

The book was received harshly by some critics, who seemed intent on making Rexroth pay for either his rejection of the Party or his noisy disapproval of the Roosevelt administration. Rolphe Humphries, poetry editor of *New Masses* and a loyal Party member, was condescending. Indeed, as Humphries asserts, a few of the poems like "The Apple Garths of Avalon" or "Dative Haruspices" do resemble Rexroth's early Cubist poems: developed through a series of abstruse allusions, they become abstract and perhaps tiresome. However, Humphries went beyond literary criticism in describing Rexroth as "a simpleminded man, with a liking for outdoors . . . and a decent reverence for nature and the stars."[15] He advised Rexroth to stick with his "direct and immediate" powers of observation, and to avoid the pose of an "erudite indoor ponderer," as he does, by Humphries's account, in "Gic to Har."[16] Insulted by Humphries's remarks, Rexroth wrote a two-page letter which *The New Republic* published in its November 11, 1940, issue. Rexroth protested that the poem was totally grounded in specific and precise recollections of his Toledo childhood.

Moreover, he was annoyed by Humphries's failure to mention those poems that focused on concrete political matters, like the Kronstadt rebellion, the plight of Kropotkin, and the San Francisco General Strike. Rexroth took this opportunity to make clear his disillusionment with Stalin's policies, and those Americans like Humphries whom he suspected of tolerating such tyranny. "Mr. Humphries is welcome to his opinion of my vocabulary," Rexroth wrote with succinct eloquence, "but I came into the Popular Front from the Left, and went out by the same door. Mr. Humphries knows this. He has either locked himself in the burning building or left by some other exit."[17] From another angle, William Fitzgerald was no kinder.[18] Patronizingly, he called the book "hag-ridden by ancestors" like Eliot, Pound, Hart Crane, and Auden, and dismissed Rexroth's political perspective as "presumably Marxian" and a sign of his bewilderment

with the injustice of world events. Moreover, he ridiculed Rexroth's "facile free-association": while eating he recalls the starving Spaniards, trans-
port planes make him think of bombed civilians, and so on. If Rexroth
wrote a response to this insensitive review, it is not recorded.

Fitzgerald's observations were not completely unsupportable, but profoundly out of balance. For example, Eliot's influence is apparent in the
opening lines of "The Motto on the Sundial": "It is September and the
wry corn rattles / Dry in the field." Yet the poem, a moving protest against
the advance of fascism, would be described more than twenty years later
by Richard Foster as "chillingly prophetic."[19] In "Requiem for the Spanish
Dead," first published in *The New Republic* (March 24, 1937), an airplane
in the sky does remind Rexroth of the suffering and hardship of the
Spanish Civil War, but the connection is hardly facile, as Fitzgerald asserts. Amid the glory of a Sierra Nevada night under the "great geometrical winter constellations," the war dead are eulogized, and so is the death
of a child killed by a driverless truck. The "rich and full-bodied" voice of
a young woman leads the lamentation:

> Voice after voice adds itself to the singing.
> Orion moves westward across the meridian
> Rigel, Bellatrix, Betelgeuse, marching in order,
> The great nebula glimmering in his loins.[20]

Rexroth grieves over the large-scale as well as the individual tragedy
without losing faith in the sanctity of life, and the significance of its continuity.

Later, both Horace Gregory and Marya Zaturenska would also mis-
read the poems in *In What Hour* as little more than "regional verse that
reflected the charms of the Pacific Coast, and the meditative if somewhat
belated contact of a poet with the political and esthetic 'conversations' of
his day."[21] His work would continue to be misappraised, or flatly ignored,
by the "east coast literary establishment," an all-inclusive term that Rexroth
called up when he needed to describe his enemies, real and imagined.
However, much later (in 1984), Robert Hass would credit the volume as
the "first readable book of poems ever produced by a resident of [San
Francisco]," adding that it seemed to "have invented the culture of the
West Coast."[22]

The turbulence of Rexroth's public life was heightened by a personal
tragedy: the death of Andrée. Although he seemed content with Marie,
Kenneth had never resolved the resentment and anger he felt over Andrée's
desertion. He had not fully relinquished his psychological ties to her; in
some way he still loved her. On the other hand, while Marie continued to
see her, he had cut off all contact, largely because he felt uncomfortable
about associating with anyone who was as closely tied to the Party as she
was. When she died on October 17, 1940, after a massive seizure, Kenneth
became hysterical. Andrée's live-in Communist lover disappeared, and

Elsa Gidlow was called upon to sign her death certificate.[23] Kenneth refused to take responsibility for her funeral, so that too fell upon Elsa and her friend Vivian. Using the small sum of money that Andrée had received from the Artists Union, Elsa arranged her cremation at Mt. Olivet Cemetery on October 23. Marie and Shirley Staschen were among the small group that attended the perfunctory services. Several days later, Rexroth called Elsa, furious that Andrée had not been given a "proper Christian burial," probably the last thing Andrée would have wished for herself.

To express his grief over her death, Rexroth created a private myth that compensated for the failure of a once impassioned relationship. Over the next few years, he wrote three elegies to Andrée, all set in Mt. Tamalpais, one of their favorite haunts, where according to Rexroth, Andrée's ashes were scattered (he does not say by whom). Each bursts with the sharp and poignant observations of Rexroth's best poems:

> Now once more gray mottled buckeye branches
> Explode their emerald stars,
> And alders smoulder in a rosy smoke
> Of innumerable buds.
> I know that spring again is splendid
> As ever, the hidden thrush
> As sweetly tongued, the sun as vital . . .[24]

He observes sadly that like the "bright trout poised in the current," their precious relationship can only flow with the passage of time. In another elegy, he mourns that "all the years that we were young / are gone."[25] In a third, he alludes briefly to Andrée's illness, and to the site of a hidden camp which she refused to visit; and he laments "the terrible trouble" of her lifetime illness.[26] The general impression evoked by these poems is one of great sorrow for a lost and idyllic innocence. Rexroth romanticized the whole of their relationship, ignoring the bitter fact that it had failed.

On the surface, he did not grieve long for Andrée. Convinced that the "Phony War" would soon turn real, Rexroth had been in a panic over the call to register with his local draft board. He could not assume that at almost thirty-five, he was too old to be called up. He did not want to go to prison "as a lonely crank," and decided to cooperate with the law. He wrote to Weldon Kees: "Under such circumstances I feel one has a responsibility to his species—it is silly to spend one's life talking about 'Mutual Aid'—and then make socks in jail or plant trees while one's species tears itself to pieces."[27]

Nevertheless, Rexroth applied for status as a conscientious objector. He took a job as an orderly in the psychiatric ward of San Francisco City and County Hospital. It was easy to get because most people looking for work landed better-paying jobs in the shipyards, building liberty ships for the convoys carrying armament and supplies to England and the Soviet

Union. Marie, whose recent professional responsibilities had been mainly administrative, resumed duties as a ward nurse. Given their pacifist position, both of them felt that work of this nature made the most sense. Earlier, they had thought that it also made sense to legalize their relationship. That summer (July 6, 1940), with Al Podesta, Shirley Staschen's husband, as witness, they quietly got married at Olivet Presbyterian Church. Shirley bought a wedding cake, and they had a small party at Wisconsin Street.

Rexroth was not prepared to sacrifice his pacifist principles by submitting to the routine of his new workplace. When he first arrived at the hospital, he was impressed with Joseph Henderson, the resident physician in charge of the psychiatric ward. During his rounds, Dr. Henderson "spread a sense of peace" among the patients. But Henderson left not long after Rexroth's arrival and was not replaced. (A few years later, in 1943, Rexroth would meet Henderson again in the examination room for psychiatric disorders at the Army Induction Center.) The sole authority was interns and two psychiatrists from Stanford University and the University of California medical schools, neither of whom Rexroth respected.[28] Fortunately for them all, he rarely encountered these people since he was working the swing shift from four until midnight, a relatively quiet time after the social workers, medical and nursing students, and psychologists had all left. Rexroth decided to organize the orderlies, not about matters like hours, wages, and pensions, but around the issue of overhauling the structure of the non-violent ward. While he was on duty, he radically changed the procedures usually observed: "No patient was put in seclusion, unless he was so completely demented that he ran around, threw himself in all directions, and attacked people. And no one was kept in restraint except people with brain damage from strokes or trauma who were unconscious and would roll out of bed and injure themselves."[29]

Rexroth tried to give the impression that he was a physician: instead of wearing a smock over his clothes, as orderlies were supposed to, he wore whites; and he made his voice sound authoritative, dropping it a half-octave or so. Whenever he could, he would release the patients from their restraints and allow them their freedom, returning them to restraint right before his shift ended. On the following shift, they would often be subjected to brutal treatment. Once Rexroth caught an orderly beating an alcoholic patient whom he had just calmed down. Rexroth, resorting to the violence that he abhorred, had to jump the orderly from behind and pull him back "with a half nelson." The orderly was suspended temporarily.

At the hospital Rexroth discovered that he could repeat a cure that he thought worked only on Andrée. If, during her stammering aura right before a seizure, Rexroth could lay hands on her and massage her temple, he was able to prevent a *grand mal*. On the ward one day he saw an elderly man suffering from a murderous migraine headache. Rexroth put his hand on the old man's head, and told him to give up his headache, to give it to him. The headache disappeared, or as Rexroth said, "Pretty soon I had a headache and his was gone."[30] Rexroth had great success with excited patients just on the edge of losing total control by giving them warm baths followed by back massages. In fact, Rexroth was applying Swedish massage strokes, pressing certain spots "like buttons on a double breasted coat," where the autonomic and central nervous system synapse. He was convinced that these points were analogous with those of the Hindu ethereal nervous system, which he had learned from reading Woodroffe's *The Serpent Power* and possibly D. H. Lawrence's *Apocalypse*. Rexroth took pride in his assumption that before most people in this country considered using acupuncture, shiatsu, and other techniques developed in the East, he was already applying a method grounded in both the East and the West.

Rexroth's contempt for institutionalized psychiatric care, especially as administered by Freudian analysts, lasted for the remainder of his life. He believed that mental illness was, like tuberculosis, a disease of the poor, and not "an indoor sport of the Viennese upper class."[31] He reduced the process of transference and countertransference to the act of selling love. He thoroughly disapproved of the theory that patients who were going to take their therapy seriously should pay for it, often dearly: "the idea that you can lie on a couch for five years, spend twenty thousand dollars, suddenly remember the first time you saw your grandfather's penis, rise illuminated, and walk away in complete mental health . . . is pure bullshit."[32] In Rexroth's opinion, the chief mission for anyone devoted to helping the mentally ill was to keep the establishment from messing up the patient.[33]

As for neurotics, Rexroth felt comfortable with Otto Rank's approach, which he described as the "straighten-up-and-fly-right" school of therapy. Unlike the psychotic, whose contact with reality is tenuous at best, the neurotic, according to Rexroth, had to be given direction, and more often than not, a few lessons about the haves and the have-nots. In addition to working on the ward, Rexroth did some moonlighting at home for people who needed short-term therapy. To help one young woman overcome her neuroses, Rexroth took her out on his back porch, pointed to the apartment of an impoverished family, and proceeded to give a detailed run-down on their very real and tangible problems, which left them without the time or energy to suffer from such "trivial" complaints. This crude approach apparently worked.

After the patients were asleep, Rexroth took advantage of the long and quiet hours ahead. He began translating from the *Greek Anthology*, the collection of Greek epigrams, songs, epitaphs, and rhetorical exercises that includes about 3,700 poems, some written as early as 700 B.C., others as late as A.D. 1000. He had first attempted to translate Greek when he was fifteen years old with the help of Mrs. Manley, his favorite teacher at Englewood High School. Under her guidance, he was able to read, by a

"crossword puzzle method," the opening pages of Plato's *Republic* and a
poem by Sappho, which he refers to as the "apple orchard" poem:

> . . . about the cool water
> the wind sounds through sprays
> of apple, and from the quivering leaves
> slumber pours down . . .

At this time, this accomplishment had so excited him that he could hardly
fall asleep for the next several nights.[34] Now on the ward, the interns,
unaware that their orderly was so scholarly, would ask what on earth he
was doing surrounded by books, papers, dictionaries. One of the books
that he lugged to the hospital from his massive library was *The Latin
Portrait: An Anthology of English Verse Translations from the Greek Poets.*[35] The
translations from poets ranging from Homer to Meleager, with corresponding Greek texts, provided valuable guidance to this industrious
interpreter. For a few hours at least he could lose himself in classical
Greece, far from a public psychiatric ward and the inevitable war.

Eleven

PACIFIST BARRICADES
1942–1943

ON THE SUNDAY OF Pearl Harbor, Marie and Kenneth went hiking in the Spring Valley Water Reservation, which had required a special permit from City Hall. A beautiful area, it attracted an incredible variety of birds. They spent the afternoon birdwatching, eating lunch, and making love. As they packed up their gear and started to hike out to Skyline Boulevard, Rexroth sensed that they would never return. He had had a similar premonition in Kings River Canyon, expressed in "Strength Through Joy" (which, ironically, had become the motto of Nazi Youth):

> This is the last trip in the mountains
> This autumn, possibly the last trip ever.
> The storm clouds rise up the mountainside,
> Lightning batters the pinnacles above me,
> The clouds beneath the pass are purple
> And I see rising through them from the valleys
> And cities a cold, murderous flood,
> Spreading over the world, lapping at the last
> Inviolate heights.[1]

When they reached the highway, they were met by a string of newspaper boys hawking extra editions that announced the bombing of Pearl Harbor.

Back at Potrero Hill, they listened all night long to the short-wave news broadcasts from around the world and were convinced, as many others were, that the Japanese would bomb San Francisco installations. The following evening, San Francisco experienced an air-raid scare that contributed to their fears. Military radio trackers reported that Japanese fighter planes were bearing down on the Bay Area, and later, that they had departed without attacking. Aircraft from the Second Interceptor Command took off and searched as far as 600 miles offshore for the alleged aircraft carrier from which the phantom planes were supposed to have been launched.

After a night of wailing sirens, the Rexroths got into their car and panic-stricken, fled south to the presumed safety of Los Gatos. There they stayed with Frank Triest, who was back home visiting his wife after a stint at sea organizing the Merchant Marines. Grace had had the house completely sandbagged. When it was clear that no bombs would fall, they returned home.

A few evenings after the news about the war was broadcast, the Rexroths got word that Washington was going to order all people of Japanese descent living on the West Coast to be evacuated. They immediately started a chain of phone calls to their friends, asking each one to contact five other people who were willing to help sabotage these orders and to lessen the suffering caused by them. They also worked with the Fellowship of Reconciliation and the American Committee to Protect the Civil Rights of American Citizens of Oriental Ancestry on behalf of the beleaguered Japanese Americans.

Anti-Asian sentiments were not new in the United States. Their history makes unpleasant reading. At the turn of the century even the American Federation of Labor frowned openly on Japanese immigration. In response, the IWW took an opposing position, earning the thanks of a Seattle Japanese newspaper. At their 1907 convention, the Wobblies passed a resolution condemning persecution of Asians in the West as contrary to the interest of all workers. And the IWW's Western weekly, *Industrial Worker,* was sprinkled with items lauding the Japanese for being more militant than their white colleagues. The paper also praised the cleanliness of the Japanese workers: "Compare the bunk house gang of 'stiffs' on the average railroad with that of the next Japanese extra gang. The difference can easily be detected a half mile off especially if the wind is in the right direction."[2] Rexroth inherited the Wobbly abhorrence of racial prejudice against Asians, and without hesitation sprang to the support of Asian Americans suspected of sympathizing with Japan's imperial ambitions.

Kenneth and Marie turned their four rooms on Wisconsin Street into a halfway house for Japanese Americans who opposed the evacuation. Cots were everywhere, and all who stayed with the Rexroths were safe. Soon, however, the zone of operations reached Potrero Hill, and their home could no longer provide sanctuary. When the Ikabuchis—two adolescent sisters and their brother—received their orders to leave, Kenneth and Marie went with them to the Ferry Building where they would be assigned to a bus. Convinced that she would be denied the basic amenities, the older girl, Mari, was hauling a huge roll of toilet paper. The social worker who oversaw their removal wanted them to pay their own fares, and if not them then the Rexroths since they had assumed responsibility for the family. Kenneth refused to have anything to do with transporting the family any closer to Santa Anita racetrack, where they would have to wait until construction of the internment camps was completed.

Discouraged and depressed by the possibility that Potrero Hill might be vulnerable to Japanese attack, Kenneth and Marie moved to 124 Moreland Street. Rexroth feared that the Japanese would take Hawaii, and San Francisco would be placed under strict martial law. They had thought about fleeing to Salt Lake, to be near James Laughlin's lodge in Alta. On December 28, 1941, Rexroth wrote Laughlin that they had sublet 692 Wisconsin Street to "an aesthetic young man who 'simply ignores' the war. . . . Frankly, I have scant relish for living under the military, even for the privilege of a ringside seat at the last act of 'Intolerance,' "[3] a reference to D. W. Griffith's acclaimed film that closes with an allegorical plea for the end of war through divine intervention.

According to the writer and journalist Michael Grieg, an aura of genuine fear and terror enveloped the city as Japanese Americans prepared to move east. Frightened residents were sandbagging their houses in fear of air raids. Federal troops were present, and blackout curtains were common.[4] San Francisco, Rexroth declared, was in a "state of psychological siege," possessing "behind its blustering chauvinism and race prejudice . . . a very healthy respect for the Japanese Navy." Many evacuees, afraid to carry with them anything of Japanese origin, offered Rexroth "all sorts of beautiful things—bonzai, dolls, kakemono, emakomono, prints, calligraphy,"[5] but he felt that accepting anything would associate him with "the collective guilt of the American State." He did, however, arrange with the California State Librarian, Mabel Gillis, to store the evacuees' books and paintings for the duration of the war and to provide the camps with a library service through the mail. Librarians in the counties where camps were located would contact librarians within the camps. Working with a master file of all the books, they could always order a special volume through Sacramento. Batches of books, including those written in Japanese, would be circulated from camp to camp. Rexroth did keep one item that had been left behind: a little stool with a woven raffia seat made by a child who had been attending a class for perceptually handicapped children at the Japanese YMCA.

In the spring of 1942, Rexroth met a young woman named Hazel Takeshita at the home of Shirley Staschen, who was living on Lombard Street with Al Podesta, her first husband. Hazel was convalescing there from an emergency appendectomy and trying to avoid the internment camps. She planned to register at an educational institution on the East Coast where the Japanese were not being harassed. When she mentioned to Rexroth that she wanted to learn how to knit and crochet in order to design dresses for a living, he got a flash of inspiration. Why not ask the correspondence schools which advertised in the newspapers ("We'll show you how to paint a portrait in ten easy lessons") to provide Japanese Americans with educational passes from the internment camps? Much to his delight and surprise, Rexroth learned that several schools would forward registration papers for the cost of processing them. And at the

Whitcomb Hotel, headquarters for the evacuation, he discovered that the people in charge, overwhelmed by their onerous responsibility, agreed to accept registration at any of these correspondence schools as a legitimate exit to the outside world.

Working more closely with the Fellowship of Reconciliation, Kenneth and Marie started moving people swiftly out to the Midwest and South on educational passes. Many people in San Francisco were sympathetic to this exodus of Japanese Americans, and some of them chose to assist the relocation program for students that the American Friends Service Committee had started. Government officials at the racetrack thought Rexroth was involved with the bureaucracy set up by the Quakers, who were sending delegations to small Midwestern colleges, first securing assurance that prospective Japanese students would be treated well. That was not the case at all: as Rexroth put it, "we just shoveled them out."[6]

When Hazel had fully recovered from her operation, she left for Chicago where she stayed with friends of Rexroth, Helen and Harold Mann, his old traveling companion. Living on Goethe Street, right off Clark Street, the Manns were also involved with the War Relocation Authority and personally oversaw the placement of Japanese Americans arriving in Chicago at a fairly steady pace. Rexroth believed Harold was by and large the person responsible for transforming the North Clark Street area, just south of Lincoln Park, into what was known as the Japan town of Chicago until Urban Renewal programs tore it down. In Chicago, Hazel did in fact learn how to knit, crochet, and design. After an unsuccessful marriage which took her to South America, she opened up a knit shop in San Francisco some time around 1958.[7]

According to Rexroth, the evacuation of Japanese Americans from the West Coast sealed the lid on his disaffiliation from "the American capitalist state, from the State as such."[8] The sheer cruelty of the entire process imposed upon Japanese Americans would forever torment him. He would remember the terror of widowed and aged Isei women who had neither children nor friends to look after them, and how the San Francisco Pound officers went about pulling dogs, cats, even canaries from the hands of their screaming owners and exterminating them.[9] He would also recall the terrified Japanese nationals (not American citizens) who were being shipped to a prisoner-of-war camp in Montana, certain that they would be shot. In the long poem *The Phoenix and the Tortoise*, Rexroth heightens the tragedy by viewing it through the eyes of children confronted by the war's casualties, people who closely resembled their Japanese-American neighbors:

> A group of terrified children
> Has just discovered the body
> Of a Japanese sailor bumping
> In a snarl of kelp in a tidepool.

> While the crowd collects, I stand, mute
> As he, watching his smashed ribs breathe
> Of the life of the ocean, his white
> Torn bowels braid themselves with the kelp.[10]

In a war that changed pacifists into fighting men, Rexroth could only redouble his efforts to make his conscientious objection a position of integrity.

Hence, during the early years of the war, Rexroth, with Marie's encouragement, intensified his relationship with such religious, pacifist organizations as the Fellowship of Reconciliation and the Friends Service Committee. He had not been asked by the League of American Writers to sign the call for a fourth (and as it turned out final) writers' congress to be held in New York City from June 6 to June 8 in 1941. Yet he seemed unwilling to give up dialogue with his colleagues, almost as though he could not rest comfortable in his anti-Stalinist position unless he convinced others to share it. Rexroth wrote a long letter to Franklin Folsom, executive secretary of the League of American Writers, acknowledging that like a "petty bourgeois," he had lost his ability to judge the merits and faults of the Soviet Union and the Communist Party.[11] He needed, however, to express his revulsion of the Moscow Trials, and his outrage over the Hitler-Stalin Pact, although he was willing to concede Molotov's temporary truth that many lives would be saved as a result of the agreement. He was completely unwilling to endorse a war, choosing between the lesser of two evils, and predicted that in the twentieth century differences would be settled by warfare rather than diplomacy. Until human beings escaped "from the frozen embrace of this dead economic system," doom and destruction were inevitable.

Rexroth would fulminate more virulently to others, including Malcolm Cowley, who took a rather large dose of verbal abuse from Rexroth. He was annoyed with Cowley, whom he called "Mlle. Irene Castle Cowley," for saying that he preferred a French victory just because he liked the French. "I was under the impression," Rexroth wrote, "the French were on the other side" (i.e., capitalists).[12] He called Cowley a "jolly belligerent," and accused the people on *The New Republic* of confusing their original dream of an international Communist world with their commitment to art and literature: "You think cowboys from Montana and mechanics from Jersey are going to die with a song on their lips for Michael Arlen, Jean Cocteau, Freda Kirchwey and/or Tommy Manville. Nuts to you, big boy."[13] Cowley's co-workers, he said, were masochists happy to "shiver in delighted prospect at the rubber truncheoning they are going to get when the Huns have passed the Alleganies [sic] and the Japs have passed the Sierras."

Rexroth refused to believe that his vision of the world lacked any provision for confronting a monstrous aberration like Nazism. Nor did he ever construct anything resembling a systematic social theory. He felt that his point of view—that an social order built on anarcho-pacifism could nurture the free development of the self—was still viable, if seemingly paradoxical. Shortly after writing those rather belligerent letters to Cowley, he apologized and expressed regret that he might have permanently alienated this helpful and encouraging supporter of his poetry. "Maybe I am slowly growing up and learning," he wrote on December 3, 1941, "that it is idle and tedious to quarrel with others about their ideas. After all, ideas are going to play a very scant role in the world we are entering." And he begged Weldon Kees to tolerate his position, even though Kees believed that Rexroth's pacifism was fanatical. Rexroth looked to Kees, as he did to Cowley, for sound judgment about his work: "I badly need advice about my poetry. Since Van Ghent and I broke up I literally have no one to talk to"[14] (August 8, 1940). Marie, for all her virtues, lacked the sharp critical eye of his former lover.

Rexroth immersed himself in anti-war activity. Besides joining the Fellowship of Reconciliation, he attended meetings of the American Friends Service Committee in the evacuated Japanese YWCA, and worked as a local representative of the National Committee for Conscientious Objectors. Every other week, Marie and Kenneth held pacifist meetings in their own home. The group decided to call itself the Randolph Bourne Council, after the literary critic and essayist who wrote *Untimely Papers* (1919) and *The History of a Literary Radical* (1920), and who was a hero for young COs of World War I. Bourne had been a steady contributor to *The New Republic* from its first 1914 issue, but when he continued to express his anti-war sentiments after the United States entered the war, he lost the space the journal used to allot him. In June 1917, he published his attack on liberal support for the war in the magazine *Seven Arts,* whose anti-war articles led to its suppression three months later. The Randolph Bourne Council meetings at the Rexroths' were attended by former Communist Party members, and "the most intelligent non-Bolshevik radicals in the city."[15] All members had lost their "revolutionary hope" after the Moscow Trials, the Republican defeat in Spain, and the Hitler-Stalin Pact. They were now forced to reevaluate their Marxist and anarchist perspectives.

Dissatisfied with naked political ideology, Rexroth read avidly in theology, philosophy, and mysticism. He studied George Fox (1624–1691), the founder of the Society of Friends; John Woolman (1720–1772), the American Quaker who was among the first to protest against slavery in the United States; and William Penn (1644–1718), who with a land grant from James II established Pennsylvania as an asylum for Quakers escaping persecution. Rexroth also studied the scholastic theologian Hugh of Saint-Victor and his student Richard of Saint-Victor, whose works became standard manuals on the practice of mysticism. He read the great speculative mystic Meister Eckehart (c.1260–?1327) and his student Heinrich Seuse (1295–1366), who became the leader of the Friends of God, a

Delia Rexroth. "Her enthusiasms were genuine; her glamour provincial but real. She had a pretty accurate estimate of her own role in the scheme of things. I don't think she was a bluestocking, although she may have dreamed of becoming an adventuress."

Charles Rexroth. "Young, he was handsome, romantic, and sophisticated and must have swept my mother off her feet. At forty he had become an Elk, a good-time Charlie at poker, drinking and wenching parties, and on fishing trips with his brother Elks."

All quotations in photograph captions are from *An Autobiographical Novel.*

Kenneth and Delia, 1908. "The other children went to nursery school or kindergarten; I didn't go. There were many more books in our house and Medici prints and etchings on the walls, and the furniture was in a different taste."

Kenneth, c. 1909. "When I was four [my mother] got me a library card. . . . In the course of time in early childhood I read the whole series of Lang's colored fairy tales and several children's sets of science and history books." Here Kenneth is enacting a character from a history book.

Kenneth as Huckleberry Finn.

"For a small child I lived an elaborate social life. . . . We had parties at every imaginable occasion: big birthday parties for each of us, Fourth of July, Christmas, Easter, Washington's Birthday, Halloween and St. Patrick's Day celebrations." Rexroth *(front row far left)* dubbed this gathering in Elkhart, Indiana, "The Alka Seltzer Party."

In 1916, after Delia's death in Elkhart, Charles and Kenneth moved to Toledo, Ohio. Kenneth joined a gang that terrorized the caddies who worked at the Ottawa Park golf course. His friends called him "Duke"; his teachers "truant."

Aunt Minnie Monahan. After Charles died in 1919, Delia's older sister took Kenneth to live with her "pure Proletarian Irish" family in Chicago. Minnie herself had started out as a buyer for a local Elkhart department store before she married Paul Monahan, a widower who worked at the Chicago stockyards to support his five children.

In Chicago, Kenneth was living in his own "artist's studio." He wrote poetry, painted watercolors, and took on small roles in experimental theater productions. He hung out at the Radical Bookstore, the Dill Pickle Club, and Bughouse Square.

Portrait of Andrée Rexroth by Kenneth
Rexroth. . . .

"Bathers" by Andrée Rexroth and
Kenneth Rexroth. Note "KRAR" in
lower right-hand corner.

Portrait of Marie
Rexroth by Kenneth
Rexroth, 1935.

Marie Rexroth, July 1940,
shortly after she and Kenneth were officially mar-
ried. Marie relished the
outdoors as much as Ken-
neth, and would often
accompany him on trips
to the High Sierras.

Kenneth Rexroth with his camping buddy and publisher James Laughlin in 1945 at the "old prospecter's hut" in Ashcroft, Colorado. Sometimes they drove north to Devil's Gulch in Marin County where they stayed in an abandoned hutch of milled lumber and galvanized metal that had once been used by sheepherders as a shelter. They skied together at Laughlin's refuge in Alta. *Photo below is courtesy of James Laughlin*

group of devout ascetic Rhinelanders. (C. Gröber's English translation, *The Mystic Heinrich Seuse,* had recently appeared in 1941.) Still not sated with esoterica, Rexroth went on to read Walter Hilton (1340–1396), one of the great English mystics of the fourteenth century, and the Spanish visionary poet St. John of the Cross.

Most important of all was Jakob Boehme, the German philosophical mystic whose writings had first become known to Rexroth during his late Chicago adolescence. Since childhood Rexroth had experienced "occasional moments of vision . . . momentary flashes of communion with others" where time and space did not exist.[16] On the day his mother died, for example, he had been sitting on the front porch basking in the afternoon sun, watching the birds, and looking over the books he had just taken out of the library. Five white dots decorated the binding of one them. When his aunt Minnie came out to give him the sad news, he stared for a long time at the configuration on the book's spine, until "a great sense of peace and well being" came over him, as though he "had died and gone to a heaven which was all one calm limitless vision."[17] Seeking an explanation for such uncanny experiences, Rexroth poured through Ouspensky and Madame Blavatsky, but it was Boehme's *De signatura rerum* that made most sense to him. It had been translated into English in 1912 with the title *The Signature of All Things.*

At the age of twenty-five, Boehme, who earned his living as a shoemaker, underwent a religious experience which inspired a theosophy that would have a marked influence on subsequent thought, notably Idealism and Romanticism. Often regarded as a "nature" mystic, Boehme believed that the unity of nature presented a vehicle for immediate contemplation of the Divinity. Boehme held that the visible world is the image of the invisible world, a doctrine familiar to Platonic thought, and that God can be known once human beings recognize that the spiritual and invisible world is the foundation of the material and visible world.[18] This theory implied an intense appreciation of nature and disciplined contemplation. Boehme was to have a significant influence on Rexroth's work, perhaps most obviously in a three-part poem in his fourth volume of poetry, both of which bear the title *The Signature of All Things.* Rexroth would pass on that influence to other poets like Robert Duncan.

Western thought did not monopolize Rexroth's attention. He turned to anthologies on Buddhism by Paul Carus, who had collaborated at the turn of the century with D. T. Suzuki, the Buddhist scholar, thinker, and chief interpreter of Zen Buddhism to Western readers. (Rexroth's personal library contained over one hundred texts directly related to Buddhism.) Rexroth also explored Arthur Waley's *The Way and Its Power* (1935), a translation of *Tao te Ching,* the Chinese Taoist text. He studied the Tantric Text Society publications and practiced Hatha Yoga and Kundalini Yoga with Marie, experimenting with complicated bodily arrangements and sexual positions as a way of "dephenomenalizing" themselves so that they could approach a purer state of consciousness. Marie and Kenneth began to perceive that the final result of their lovemaking was a kind of spiritual illumination and that marriage was the "last Sacrament available to modern man [sic]" even if, according to Rexroth, "the terrible destruction of interpersonal relations by capitalism and its war-making State" did nothing to help such relationships endure.[19]

An episode at San Francisco County, however, put an end to their experiments with Hatha Yoga. The police brought to the psychiatric ward a new patient who had run away from Western Washington State Hospital where he had been confined for murdering two orderlies. He was in restraint for causing a ruckus in the lobby of the Fairmount Hotel. Diagnosed as a manic-depressive, the patient spoke with an Ivy League accent and sported a dent in his forehead where a polo pony had kicked him. When Rexroth let him out of restraint, the man promptly terrorized the other patients by mugging them for cigarettes. Rexroth took him to the seclusion room, gave him three cigarettes, and told him he would be returned to the ward after Rexroth came back from dinner. Rexroth instructed the relief orderly not to let the patient out of seclusion, but the orderly failed to heed his advice. When Rexroth came back to the ward, the patient attacked him: "Suddenly I was hit from behind on the back of the neck, picked up and thrown over four beds by the patient, who then ran and jumped on me. I was in the narrow space between the bed and the wall. As he jumped, half the ward jumped on him. I crawled under the bed and out."[20] The patient was soon returned to Washington, but Rexroth retained a permanent memento of this experience.

While shaking free of his attacker, he had given himself a crick in the back, the first warning of a herniated disk. Other symptoms, seemingly unrelated, followed. Without warning his calf muscles would start twitching until they cramped and forced him to the floor. Then he developed an acid stomach and a small stomach ulcer. Three weeks after the incident, Rexroth's stomach became permanently distended and he lost control of some of his abdominal muscles. He could no longer engage in the bodily contortions of Hatha Yoga, but he could practice Yogic breathing during meditation. With time, the leg cramps disappeared, but recurring stomach problems would plague him all his life.[21]

The back injury along with gas rationing temporarily eliminated the trips to the Sierras, but when they were able to coordinate their time off from San Francisco County and save enough fuel, the Rexroths drove to the cabin in Devil's Gulch, seeking a measure of peace for themselves in the midst of calamity. Rexroth sometimes meditated there in isolation.

I look back with nostalgia and awe at the nights I spent alone sitting in the lotus posture, doing controlled breathing, and emptying my mind of its detritus. Nothing but the firelight and the sound of the two waterfalls that came down and joined directly under the cabin. I had a pet kingsnake who used to like to lie inside my shirt, and although you can't make a pet of an owl unless you feed him live mice, the same owl came every night to sit on a shattered tree in front of the cabin and sing to me.[22]

His vivid memories of those moments were poured into most of the poems in his next two collections, *The Phoenix and the Tortoise* and *The Signature of All Things*.[23]

Kenneth and Marie were also attending the only Anglo-Catholic church in San Francisco, the Advent of Christ the King. Even though the sermons sounded to them like military propaganda, Rexroth gained comfort from the celebration of the rites, and from communal prayer which induced a state of objectified meditation for him. However, one Sunday a blind white woman came to High Mass accompanied by a five-year-old boy who clearly was the offspring of an interracial couple. After watching the ushers ignore her, Rexroth guided her to a pew. Following mass, he introduced her to the rector, who behaved rudely, ignoring her and the child. The blind woman never returned, and after a while Marie and Kenneth stayed away as well.

On October 13, 1942, two months before Rexroth reached his thirty-seventh birthday, he received notice from his local draft board that his status as Conscientious Objector 4-E had been changed to 1-A, Available for Armed Service. Distressed because he had not been invited to meet with the draft board before his status was changed, he was convinced that he could prove to the board, with the help of "witnesses, friends, and clergy" who would testify to the sincerity of his beliefs, that he was a bona fide CO.[24] He initiated the long and arduous process of appeal. Rexroth intended to keep his job as psychiatric orderly, and in a memorandum submitted to the board on December 18, 1942, declared that he would donate half his monthly salary, approximately $50, to the Fellowship of Reconciliation. He further explained his position:

The draft procedure places the CO in the position of "proving" himself a very saintly fellow, a position I feel is absurd. I am certainly as sinful as the next person, and I have no sense of moral superiority to the young man who is sacrificing his life in the jungles of New Guinea or the deserts of Africa in defense of his ideals. I only hope that I will be able to act with as much courage as he shows, in the position in life to which God has called me.[25]

He had to wait nearly a year before the board made its decision.

On February 19, 1943, the FBI undertook an investigation of his claim. Rexroth was ordered to report to the Army Induction Center for a physical and psychiatric examination. By coincidence, the director of the Center was Dr. Joseph Henderson, the resident whom Rexroth had met on the psychiatric ward of San Francisco County a few years before.[26] Rexroth immediately announced to Henderson that he was a pacifist for personal and religious reasons; moreover, his work as a writer in making the world a harmonious place to live was far more important than donning a uniform. He would be absolutely useless in the Army. He reminded

Henderson that he had already articulated his pacifist position to him a few years ago when Henderson was a resident. Henderson included this information in his report on Rexroth.

However, Henderson also believed that Rexroth could be scattered, hysterical, and capable of emotional explosions.[27] He was sure that the Army doctors would judge Rexroth unfit for service on psychiatric grounds. During the examination, he observed that Rexroth was full of doubts, fears, and objections, and "pathologically stubborn." While he did not claim that Rexroth was suffering from a particular mental disorder, Henderson did report that his condition bordered on psychosis—a preposterous diagnosis in light of Rexroth's rational and coherent views on warfare and militarism. On the other hand, Rexroth could easily have been playing madman during the examination so that Henderson would declare him 4-E. Rexroth's appeal appeared to be an open-and-shut case.

People of all stripes, predisposed or not to Rexroth, stated to the FBI that they knew him to be a pacifist. The owner of a drugstore patronized by Rexroth since 1936 reported that he would habitually hang around the store proselitizing for pacifism, frequently citing passages from the Bible like "Thou shalt not kill" and "Whosoever shall smite thee on the right cheek, turn to him the other." Before Pearl Harbor, the men at the store would ridicule Rexroth's views, asking him what he would do if someone struck him across the face or if he discovered a robber ransacking his home. Rexroth's stock reply was that he would do nothing to harm another person physically. Even after the attack on Pearl Harbor, he continued to assert that he would not participate in the war, that he was "afraid of a gun and would not use one if he had to keep from being killed," even if he discovered someone had broken into his house and was attacking his wife. He would appeal to the intruder's sense of reason, without resorting to violence. Added to his anti-war views articulated as early as 1936, when there was "no ulterior motive" in speaking so, such arguments convinced the informants that Rexroth truly was a pacifist.

Many people questioned by the FBI were openly hostile to Rexroth. Another shopkeeper reported that Rexroth used to announce that it was against his pacifist principles to kill. Although this shopkeeper had little reason to doubt his sincerity, he thought Rexroth was a "crackpot and very peculiar" because he had grown "a six or seven-inch beard, wore a red beret with a high turtle-neck sweater during the summer of 1940 and also displayed other eccentricities at various times." Others described his behavior as unconventional, inclined to extreme statements and physical gestures during arguments. They blamed his artistic temperament for what they called his emotional instability, smoking cigarettes one day but not the next, eating meat at some meals, only vegetables at others. One woman related a story she thought would validate this assessment. In the late thirties Rexroth had been earning some money as a speaker on the flora and fauna of the High Sierras and as a guide on hiking trips. On one of these trips, he had gotten separated from the party and was lost for several days without food. When the interviewee mentioned to him later back in San Francisco that his knowledge of animal life would have prevented him from starving to death, Rexroth was "horrified" that this woman could think he was capable of killing an animal in order to eat. (Rexroth was an erratic vegetarian.) The woman believed him to be a "borderline insanity case," but did not doubt that his religious anti-war convictions were authentic.

Rexroth's unconventional lifestyle probably strengthened his case. Kenneth and Marie had lived out of wedlock for several years. Neighbors would report that they played "funeral-type" music and that Rexroth could be heard "chanting like a priest" for hours. Friends would come to visit at midnight and stay until two or three in the morning. Several "witnesses" sided with Rexroth, testifying to the value of his work as counselor for other COs, his spiritual nature, and his very real sense of integrity. Rexroth himself later said that the investigation had worked in his favor, even if his "moral character" had been tarnished.

Before his appeal was heard, Rexroth visited the Selective Service headquarters to request a precis of the FBI's investigation of his case. By mistake, the clerk turned over the entire file, and Rexroth discovered that he had more enemies than he had suspected. He read letters and statements from his friends who were Communists and fellow travelers. The more virulent letters accused Rexroth of communicating with Japanese submarines off the coast by short-wave radio, of keeping a lover who belonged to a Ukranian nationalist organization, of having been in constant touch with Trotsky.[28] A co-worker at the Federal Writers' Project reported that when she and Rexroth went out for morning coffee breaks together he would recite obscene Latin limericks that made her sick to her stomach. (One wonders why she kept on having coffee with him.) Declaring herself a former member of the Communist Party, she "identified" people on the Writers' Project whom she knew to be Communists. Rexroth was among them. Rexroth believed this woman harbored feelings of frustration and resentment, not only toward him but toward the United States whose government she had once been interested in radically changing. Her limericks anecdote reminded him of "the Moscow Trial defendant who confessed to meeting Trotsky in a Copenhagen hotel which had been out of existence for a generation."[29] Rexroth was also willing to consider the possibility that she was an FBI agent.

As his draft appeal dragged on, Rexroth was feeling increasingly disturbed and isolated. His commitment to pacifist principles was firm, yet his everyday behavior was becoming self-destructive. Fuming and frustrated over what he considered to be harassment by his draft board and then the FBI, he sorely tried everyone's patience, especially Marie's. Paradoxically, while refusing to enlist in a global conflict, he was sowing seeds of discord at home.

Twelve

PRIVATE BATTLES
1943–1944

THE ATMOSPHERE AT HOME became tense. Marie and Kenneth started to have extramarital affairs which only exacerbated the situation. Marie sought professional advice from their friends, San Francisco therapists Jane and Joseph Wheelwright. She spilled out the whole story to them—Kenneth's irascibility, his fits of temper, his infidelities as well as her own. She felt drained of all energy, used up, and incapable of cultivating personal friendships or pursuing her own creative interests. The sessions seemed to help Marie, but when she tried to work out a new understanding with Kenneth, he felt threatened and provoked, sometimes to the point of violence. For Marie, life on Potrero Hill became intolerable. Taking their dog Rex with her, she left Kenneth to stew in his own juices and accepted a job as a field nurse with a traveling medical unit based in Napa, about fifty miles northeast of San Francisco. Marie was relieved to be in the country, out of San Francisco, and on her own.

She did not want a permanent separation. Her love for Kenneth had not abated much, as a letter she wrote from Napa indicates with its private terms of endearment ("To the Dearest Kenneth Bear / A communication par avion by the Marie Bear") and open declarations of affection.[1] She was full of compassion for her husband: "Certainly one thing Joe told me that I hadn't believed before was that you loved me completely and always would, and that you were suffering tremendously." Her quest for self-enlightenment and a way out of this painful predicament led her to works by Otto Rank and Karin Stephens, and Karl Menninger whose *The Human Mind* she thought most useful, despite Kenneth's dismissal of him as vulgar. She mentioned to Kenneth that Menninger sounded rather sensible to her: that it was often a good idea to separate a patient from a person whom that patient loves and hates so strongly that the individual's presence inhibits the progress of the patient's therapy. If, in addition to protecting herself against further confrontations, she required another reason to justify her flight, Menninger's words provided it.

Travel to her job allowed Marie to appreciate the richness of Napa County's vineyards, groves, and orchards. She rented a room at 1017 Seminary Avenue in town, but sometimes slept in the dormitories of Pacific Union College, which stood on the nearby crater of an extinct volcano (about five hundred ministers, doctors, nurses, and teachers of the Seventh-Day Adventist persuasion received their training there). When she had a holiday, she would drive into the nearby foothills of the mountains—at 2,000 feet there were pine trees—and loll under the blossoming trees that she described to Kenneth as "literally the closest thing you could find to resemble your orchard in the poem."[2] Marie is referring to "When We with Sappho," the poem that begins with his translation of the Sappho fragment Kenneth had grappled with when he was fifteen years old, and which was originally inspired by his love for Leslie Smith. Despite this rift in their relationship, or any others that would follow, Marie strongly identified with Kenneth's work. Although their marriage was now in jeopardy, she was comforted by a poem that he wrote during this turmoil, celebrating the transcendent quality of physical love,

> Our bodies move to each other
> As bodies move in sleep;
> At once filled and exhausted,
> As the summer moves to autumn,
> As we, with Sappho, move toward death.[3]

The volume in which it appeared, *The Phoenix and the Tortoise* (1944), was dedicated to Marie.[4]

Since Rexroth was working the night shift at San Francisco County, he and Marie arranged to meet on weekends. He would catch a Greyhound bus north on Thursday and arrive in Napa in time to have lunch with her, drive her to work in their temperamental and worn-out Willys, and tool around the countryside until he picked her up at four. Evidently their sexual passion remained intact. "For Heaven's sake," Marie wrote, "bring my rubber diaphragm! It must be lying around in a box in the bedroom."[5] But soon these weekend visits were not working out: Kenneth had neither the comforts of home nor the freedom and isolation of his long camping trips in the mountains—his other home site—in Marie's tiny apartment. And he could not tolerate the disruption of his schedule created by Marie's constant movement from town to town, even if it meant overnight stays in the country and swimming in Morrow Cove.

During Easter week of 1943, Kenneth wanted to attend a Tenebrae service, feeling a decided need for high ritual to calm his fearful thoughts about the war. In "Wednesday of Holy Week, 1940," he described the strength he had already drawn from this ceremony:

> The voices of the Benedictines are massive, impersonal;
> They neither fear this agony nor are ashamed of it.

Think . . . six hours ago in Europe,
Thousands were singing these words,
Putting out candles psalm by psalm . . .
Albi like a fort in the cold dark,
Aachen, the voices fluttering in the ancient vaulting,
The light of the last candle
In Munich on the gnarled carving.[6]

Marie had telephone all over Napa Valley, unsuccessfully seeking a church
with a Tenebrae service. A Dominican father in Vallejo told her that the
ceremony took "too much manpower." For a solution, Marie proposed
that she join him in San Francisco late Friday and enjoy Easter weekend
on Wisconsin Street (they had returned to Potrero Hill) where she would
also have the chance "to fix up the garden and do all the things that should
be done there."[7] Characteristically, Marie accommodated herself to Kenneth's needs. Although she was determined to work in Calistoga, she
simply could not ignore his complaints, even when her own well-being
was at stake.

Marie thought that if Kenneth would give up San Francisco, their lives
would improve noticeably. "We only go backwards in my returning to the
city—I love my job and the pay is quite adequate. . . . If you do get a 4F, I
would like you to only work at psychiatry for between 5–6 months a year
at the *most*, you could easily be independent then the rest of the year and
with a cabin in the hills or near the mountains here."[8] However, the move
never materialized. They enjoyed Christmas 1943 together in San Francisco, but their problems continued to mount. Money became scarcer,
and Kenneth's CO appeal dragged on. Sexual infidelity on both sides only
widened the growing chasm between them. They were losing their intuitive ability to understand one another, and their arguments grew fiercer.

Kenneth had never fully reconciled himself to Marie's departure for
Napa, which to him was an act of betrayal far more injurious than anything his former political comrades ever did. She stubbornly insisted on
behaving like an individual with a right to her own identity, as someone
who could be sure that at least a part of her life was not totally committed
to supporting his career. Kenneth was losing hope of a meaningful reconciliation. "I am simply stupefied," he wrote to James Laughlin, "at the
thought that her years with me have meant so little that she could do such
a thing."[9] Moreover, he suspected, erroneously, that Marie didn't really
understand his poetry and regarded his painting as a hobby.[10] Spurned
by his muse, Rexroth struck the romantic, ego-bound pose of the misunderstood and lonely artist: "only Blake and Cowper ever got the kind of
wives poets should have, and Blake's was illiterate, and Cowper's wasn't
his wife."[11]

In January 1944, Marie fled to Yosemite Lodge in Yosemite National
Park for some skiing. She kept in touch with Kenneth, and suggested that
he apply for a job there measuring snow accumulation. She missed him,

especially in the evenings when she had no one to dance with "in that wonderful abandoned Rexroth style." Marie stayed away for a while, but before long she was back at San Francisco County earning the larger salary that supported them and trying to love Kenneth without allowing herself to be emotionally consumed by his neediness. No doubt it was a tough fight. For consolation, she reread such poems as "Runaway," in which Rexroth expresses a yearning for loving intimacy with her:

> I wish I could build a fire
> In you that would never go out.
> I wish I could be sure that deep in you
> Was a magnet to draw you always home.[12]

She would later tell him that only in his writing could she recognize that her life with him had had any meaning at all.

The weekly meetings with the Randolph Bourne Council and the Fellowship of Reconciliation slumped into monthly gatherings; occasionally the FOR meetings were held on Sundays with everyone contributing a dish for a potluck lunch. Their friendship with the poet Richard Moore, then a Berkeley undergraduate, was formed at this time (Moore would become part of Rexroth's anarchist-pacifist literary group that flourished after the war). Some people in their social circle, however, had enlisted in the armed forces, including Hilary Belloc, Jr., who had joined the Canadian Navy. Rexroth especially missed hearing from or seeing his painter friends. John Ferren was writing for the Office of War Information, first in Washington, then Algiers and Paris. His wife Inez was living in New York with a newborn son whom Ferren had not yet seen. Phyllis and Dick Ayer, friends from Rexroth's WPA days and among the first "bohemes" to live on Potrero Hill, were in Florida where Dick was serving in the Air Corps. Dick had decorated a section of the wall above the murals painted by Hilaire Hiler in the Aquatic Building in San Francisco. Rexroth believed Hiler, known in his circles as "the handsome frog," was trying to get into the Navy.

Rexroth also missed people like Robert Duncan, who had become a close friend in 1942 just after returning to Berkeley. Ever since Duncan, already an anarchist, had read Rexroth's letters published in *The New Republic* and *Partisan Review* in 1939 and 1940, he had been fascinated with this man who was "obviously older and more knowledgeable than I was—who had the same stand I had on the whole Stalinist-Trotskyite thing on the Left."[13] Duncan also knew that Rexroth admired the work of D. H. Lawrence, from poems he had sent to *The Phoenix*, a magazine edited by his friend Jimmy Cooney. The day Duncan and Rexroth met, Kenneth and Marie were thick into their underground activities with Japanese Americans, and Duncan recalls that Kenneth, "like the Patchens," was in a state of paranoia. "He didn't want anyone to know where he was. He imagined that any moment a Stalinist would come up the stairs—not that they *weren't* shooting people. When we finally got home, he made one of those marvelous dinners of his." The two poets became friends despite Duncan's open homosexuality and Rexroth's sporadic homophobia. In 1944 Duncan was in Ashfield, Massachusetts, staying at Morning Star Farm with his friends Blanche and Jimmy Cooney. With their help, Duncan had hoped to start publishing *The Experimental Review* again, with a contribution from Rexroth's as yet unpublished manuscript "The Phoenix and the Tortoise."

During this period Rexroth struck up another important friendship, this one with fellow anarchist Henry Miller, who was back from his French and Greek sojourns (Miller had been to California once before, but in 1942 he came to stay). Miller, he discovered, was "a much more professionalized person" than he had expected him to be, and he liked his new companion Janina Lepska, "a really ideal little girl. Well read, intelligent, obedient, extremely young, very hot looking. Like all slavs, she gives off a sort of muffed and booted aroma of Venus in Furs."[14] The first time Miller and Lepska stayed over at Potrero Hill, Rexroth expected to hear loud noises emanating from their bedroom, but he was disappointed— "they were tired, or maybe they do it with hatpins." For the next twenty-five years the two men would maintain a cordial relationship based on literary and political affinities, although Rexroth declared that "Henry's overweening conceit we found a little difficult."[15] They reviewed one another's work favorably, and in 1945 after he plunged into the Bacon / Shakespeare controversy that questioned the authorship of several Shakespearean works, Miller turned for advice to Rexroth as "the only scholar" he knew.[16]

The two writers would promote one another's work. Rexroth wrote two essays on Miller at a time when he most needed support from established American writers: the Introduction to *Nights of Love and Laughter* (1955), an idiosyncratic and suggestive essay that links Miller to Restif de la Bretonne, the long-neglected eighteenth-century writer who recorded the sexual side of the Paris underground; and "The Reality of Henry Miller" (*Bird in the Bush*, 1959), where in the face of popular opinion he insists that Miller's descriptions of sex are rather ordinary and normal to the American male. Writing in the *San Francisco Chronicle* (February 10, 1957), Miller praised *One Hundred Poems from the Chinese* and *In Defense of the Earth*.

Miller was persuaded to settle in Big Sur by the Greek artist Jean Varda, who later proudly said—so he told Anaïs Nin—that Rexroth had honored him with the title of "boudoir painter."[17] The Rexroths occasionally visited Miller at Varda's Red Barn at Partington Ridge, and then at Miller's own place at Anderson Creek. There they met the English poet George Barker, the Dadaist photographer and painter Man Ray, whom he described to James Laughlin as "the well known hypochondriac," and Juliet Browner, Ray's "child bride" and chief model.[18] They befriended

Ephraim Donner, "one of the best painters on the peninsula."[19] Born and raised in Vilna, the grandson of a famous rabbi, and an authority on Jewish mysticism, Donner read Hebrew, Polish, German, Spanish, Italian, and French with equal facility, and became a great fan of the poet and novelist Blaise Cendrars. He had been earning his living as a furrier until he returned to Europe, where he wandered around on foot for a year. Like Miller, he was a magnet for the odd and the eccentric. Rexroth gravitated toward him because he represented the anarchist artist grounded in but not stifled by tradition.

On one occasion the Rexroths were brought to Big Sur by a lover's quarrel between George Barker and Elizabeth Smart, best known for *By Grand Central Station I Sat Down and Wept,* a novel inspired by her romance with Barker. Rexroth had met Smart one day in San Francisco, after he followed her out of Paul Elder's bookshop to Union Square, where she was sitting on the grass reading "something very highbrow," her feet bare because she had washed her socks in the drinking fountain. Charmed by her appearance—she was a "beautiful blond who looked rather like a Dutch or Danish girl of about seventeen"[20] and her unusual behavior, Rexroth sat down beside her and opened a conversation. He learned that she had spent all her money on books, and had taken a room in a skid row hotel, "where she was certain to be raped." She would not reveal anything more about herself, although Rexroth surmised from her speech and clothing that her background was British intellectual. When her brave front collapsed and she burst into tears, Rexroth urged her to come home with him. After dinner, when Smart noticed several Barker books on the shelves, she admitted her secret. She had quarreled with her lover, run away, and was too afraid to return. That weekend, Marie and Kenneth drove her back to Big Sur, where the atmosphere was made tense by the presence of Mrs. Barker. Varda, who had just returned from Mexico, decided to make a party out of the situation.

It was a little like being entertained by a hyperactive Brancusi. He roasted a leg of lamb on an open fire; he made a big pot of moussaka; he drank tumbler after tumbler of retsina; he danced acrobatic Greek dances and jumped over the table. Barker drank beer mug after beer mug of Shandygaff, heated with a red-hot poker, and passed out. I danced with the ladies, mostly Barker's wife, to whom I took a great fancy, and at last we all staggered off to bed.[21]

Eventually Barker and Smart ran away together, and Mrs. Barker went to live in New York City.

Finally good news arrived: Rexroth's I-A had been reversed, and he was now again officially classified as 4-E.[22] The threat of incarceration had lifted (his friend Frank Triest had been sentenced to two years in a federal penitentiary). With Marie's encouragement, Kenneth stopped working at San Francisco County. Marie took a better-paying job at Franklin Hospital and the atmosphere in the Rexroth household calmed down temporarily.

But a concern that had been lurking in the background over the past few years surfaced. Aware that Marie's fertile years were numbered, the couple had to face the possibility that they might never have a child of their own.

Two years earlier, Rexroth had written to William Carlos Williams that he wanted a family before it was too late. Williams had replied that if he really wanted a child, he should go ahead, but warned that men often romanticized their fatherly role and then insisted that their wives "keep the kids away from us when we're busy."[23] In 1944, Marie and Kenneth, both approaching their forties, were not sure that they were suited for parenthood. On the other hand, Kenneth was not prepared to accept the possibility that the life of a dedicated and impoverished artist might be incompatible with the emotional and financial demands of parenthood. At the moment, Marie could hardly take time off from her job to start a family, much less to raise one. Apparently she never told even her closest friends why or whether she resisted pregnancy. However, she did let the rumor float that her fertility would improve drastically if she were to have ovarian surgery. The forties, after all, were not an easy time for women to reject motherhood. The arguments flared up, followed by new accusations of sexual infidelity. They would battle for weeks on end, until Marie felt that she had become a bitter and neurotic nag, living a nightmare. How, she asked herself, could they seriously consider having children under these circumstances? She decided to leave again, this time for Europe.

First, she went to Salt Lake City where she got a job as a private duty nurse. She asked James Laughlin if she could come to Alta. Fearful that Kenneth would think he was taking sides, Laughlin did not respond enthusiastically. He didn't believe Marie could be the tyrant that Kenneth claimed she was, but he acknowledged that he may have only seen Marie's good side. He tried to discourage her from coming, and told her to "trot back home" before Kenneth fell apart completely. But Marie insisted on visiting. She and Laughlin climbed a peak together, and talked through her troubles over a bottle of Rhine wine:

Jim was very wonderful to me and tried to make me happy in the mountains. It is very pleasant to see him in his own surroundings. It made me admire him tremendously and he is very lovable—he went to a great deal of trouble to give me a very nice holiday. He has an alpine garden in which he works all day and he does his publishing business all night.[24]

Once removed from Kenneth, her bitterness about him dissolved. She worried about his welfare and urged him to get a job, not full time, but one that would pay for his basic needs. She encouraged him to photograph his paintings by offering to cover part of the cost: "I may be able to help them you with them now altho I never seemed to be able to when I lived with you."[25] Marie remained unshaken in the faith that her husband was a greatly talented writer, a man whose genius needed to be nurtured, and whose often bullish temperament had to be tolerated, at a distance if need be.

Kenneth was not buying this sweetness and light. In his eyes, Marie had left precipitously: one day she had stalled their Willys in the middle of the street and simply vanished. After a month of silence, he had to learn from Laughlin that she was floating around Salt Lake City. Blind to his own responsibility for Marie's unhappiness, Rexroth placed the blame for it on Marshall Olbrich, a brilliant philosophy student who had edited the student literary magazine at the University of Wisconsin at Madison before moving to San Francisco in 1941. Olbrich was a San Francisco figure around whom many stories circulated testifying to his eccentric behavior, which endeared him to many people, but not to Rexroth. Olbrich was the young man "indifferent to the war" who had sublet Kenneth and Marie's Potrero Hill apartment during the time they were living on Moreland Street, and had made himself very much at home. Olbrich turned the bathroom into what was supposed to be a controlled marine environment brimming with odds and ends from the beach, living and otherwise.[26] Also, he ordered by catalogue a ringtailed cat which "spent the nights swinging around the picture molding as it beshat Kenneth's pure white walls." Although Olbrich adapted to the Rexroths' home, he apparently did not think well of Kenneth. He believed that Rexroth became an anarchist because the United States was cooperating with the Soviet Union against the Axis powers, but that he couldn't choose to become a socialist because "he had to be against whatever was in vogue."[27] As far as Rexroth was concerned, it was Olbrich who had persuaded Marie to work in the Napa Valley, and who had finally talked her into leaving him altogether.

But Rexroth could not totally ignore reality. He knew that he was not pulling his own weight, and that the prospect of earning a living as a writer, of supporting himself, let alone anyone else, was dim. He was feeling miserable and sorry for himself. "It is just absurd," he wrote to James Laughlin, "that a person as smart and talented and whatnot as I am should be unable to feed himself. I have worked terribly hard, and done good, permanent work—and I have past [sic] the turn of my life and I am a beggar with no more recognition than the slightest poetaster."[28] Suffering from what he called nervous exhaustion, he did manage to hold down a low-pressure, low-paying job at Gelber's bookstore. Although he was convinced he had written "some of the best love poetry of the 20th century," it was an empty accomplishment, he told Laughlin, if Marie would not stand by him.

This was a weary and forlorn period for Rexroth. To his credit, he could count a fine volume of poetry, a clear political conscience, an ever-expanding breadth of knowledge, and an extraordinary expertise in mountain climbing and camping. But his personal life was a shambles. He had failed twice at marriage. It is possible to imagine Rexroth composing "The Advantages of Learning" under these circumstances.

> I am a man with no ambitions
> And few friends, wholly incapable
> Of making a living, growing no
> Younger, fugitive from some just doom.
> Lonely, ill-clothed, what does it matter?
> At midnight I make myself a jug
> Of hot white wine and cardamon seeds.
> In a torn grey robe and old beret,
> I sit in the cold writing poems,
> Drawing nudes on the crooked margins,
> Copulating with sixteen year old
> Nymphomaniacs of my imagination.[29]

These last two lines wittily suggest that at least some of Rexroth's allegedly notorious affairs took place in his head. And the self-pity projected here is in dramatic contrast with the rugged, energetic mountain climber who appears so frequently in his other work.

Kenneth thought that Marie, confused about her identity and values, was no less responsible than he for their messy marriage. He refused to acknowledge that he had placed an economic burden on her, and he believed that "if she hired a highschool girl to take care of the house it would cost her about twice as much as it does to keep me alive and at my desk."[30] He attributed to her and then ridiculed her aspirations for a conventional, middle-class life, though he himself longed for some of those comforts. He accused her of not being grateful to him for making her immortal in his poetry. He would mock her jealousy, based on her suspicion—which he said was unfounded—that he was having an affair with their mutual friend June Oppen, a sister of poet George Oppen, and a friend of Laughlin's.

The night Marie left him (she stayed with Elsa Gidlow for four days before going to Salt Lake City), she had decided to visit June when she got off work that evening, taking the Divisedero bus that stopped in front of the hospital to Pacific Heights. As she made her way down the steep hill where the bus had let her off to June's house, she saw through the full glass front of the house June and Kenneth embracing passionately. She could not walk away, and she didn't interrupt them. She simply stood there and watched for a while. In the first letter she wrote to Kenneth from Salt Lake City, she described her reaction: "I think it was the first time in my life I really believed you liked to make love to other women—the other times seemed unreal." And what equally upset her was her own behavior, standing outside that house like a spy in the house of love.[31]

Kenneth brushed off Marie's report as an example of "pathological jealousy." It was raining that night; he was not the man with June, and

Marie could not have seen very much since she could not have been closer than one hundred yards. But Marie had written that from her vantage point, she could "practically describe the color of June's nail polish." Later on, he would admit to Laughlin that he had tried to romance June. And he boasted to Laughlin about his other lovers, including Mildred Brock and Dorothy Van Ghent who had resurfaced after quitting her job at the University of Montana and returning to San Francisco in order to write. (Brock and Van Ghent lived with one another for a while.) But Kenneth expected Marie to love him as if these affairs were of little consequence. In a poem that he takes from Martial, he speaks of waiting for Marie after he dies, telling her story, "sweetly in Hell," capturing the attention of famous lovers like Helen and Paris, Laura and Petrarch, Dante and Beatrice, Catullus and Lesbia.

> And when at last I welcome you there
> Your name will stand for memory of living
> On the tongues of all whom death has joined.
> You shall know this when you see my grave snowless
> Winter long, and my cold sleepfellows
> Shifting themselves underground to warm
> Dead bones at my still glowing ashes.[32]

The very thought that he might outlive Marie (she was six months older than he) terrified him, almost as if he feared reliving the painful experience of becoming an orphan.

From Rexroth's perspective, this particular flight of Marie's (he called her various escapes "powders" when he wrote to Laughlin) was going to be even more traumatic once he discovered how she planned to get herself abroad. She was linking up with the establishment—the United Nations Relief and Rehabilitation Administration—expecting to be assigned to a post in France. But once she arrived at their Washington, D.C., headquarters, she was informed that she would have to learn Serbo-Croatian because most of her work would be in the Russian-controlled Balkan refugee camps, some near Cairo. Then she was told to expect a stint in the Greek or Italian camps under British authority. Writing to Kenneth from the UNRRA Training Center at the University of Maryland in College Park, she asked him if he thought she should follow through with these plans. Kenneth believed she was selling out, totally, that she was going over to the enemy. He told Laughlin that he would have preferred "a thousand times she had joined the Army." Marie, on the other hand, saw little difference between taking money from the San Francisco Public Health Department and accepting a salary from UNRRA. She thought the money "smelled as badly" either way. Money aside, she knew her skills as a nurse could ease the suffering of many people.

Marie never left the United States, but she delayed her homecoming to Potrero Hill. She feared that she would only be returning to interminable arguments and recriminations, and that the chances of a genuine reconciliation were slim. In the very first letter she wrote Kenneth after her departure, she says bitterly that her previous attempt to reunite them was "a sweet lovely hallucination," referring to a line in the poem "Past and Future / Turn About" which marks the time that Rexroth had completed *The Phoenix and the Tortoise*. The poem is a sad one, filled with Rexroth's melancholy about the waste and meaningless sacrifice of war: "Who remembers / The squad that died stopping the tanks / At the bridgehead? The company / Was bombed out an hour later."[33]

For Marie to taunt Kenneth with his own words confirms two things: one, she certainly understood his poetry, refuting his accusation that she was indifferent to his writing; and two, her anger had reached such proportions that she was willing to mock his most tender sentiments. Again, Rexroth felt betrayed. He wrote Laughlin that he now had cause to believe that "all these years [he] had been harbouring a voluntary counterrevolutionary stoolpigeon." He begged Laughlin not to publish *The Phoenix and the Tortoise* because it was "Marie's book" and he could not "bear the thought of it with her gone."

However, Kenneth bombarded Marie with letters begging her to come home. Her resolve to work out her own problems melted, and she decided that she was responsible for their latest contretemps. She had sinned by trying to mold Kenneth into something he was not. A gift from James Laughlin had helped her to draw this conclusion. He had given her a copy of *Sunday After the War*, in which Henry Miller analyzes the precarious existence of contemporary artists. She saw herself reflected in Miller's portrait of "proletariat zombies," lacking the sensitivity to understand the kind of suffering talented writers had to endure.[34] She would prove what a renegade and rebel she truly was, and how she "hate[d] this country so much for the way it treats its Rexroths and Millers."[35]

Playing the role of the injured party, Kenneth complained both to Marie and Laughlin that his health was poor, so poor that he might have to check in to a hospital: "I am getting some sort of mysterious cramp and chorea which is very painful and if it increases won't let me work."[36] He didn't have enough money to buy himself a much-needed pair of shoes. He almost took a job as a ratcatcher, a prospect which horrified Marie. She apologized for being unable to send him enough money to quit Gelber's bookstore just yet, but she managed to send an extra ten dollars for his shoes. And while he was at work, "Rex Bear" (Marie had left the dog at home this time) had gone on a biting rampage. Marie encouraged him to hold on until she got back home at the end of October. "How I long," she wrote, "to sit at our table again with the music on and the evening sun coming in the window while you bring in the dinner you have prepared for us."[37] In a mood of girlish contrition mixed with motherly concern, she declared she truly belonged beside Kenneth. "I know I have caused you immeasurable pain and suffering and I can only regret it and try to be better in the future."

After picking up her final paycheck from UNRRA on September 20, Marie stopped in New York City to see James Laughlin, who was in a jam over a San Francisco love affair. He was being blackmailed by his lover's husband, who had discovered a pack of love letters. Laughlin was going to have to call the blackmailer's bluff and figure out a way of explaining those love letters to his own wife and family if they became public. Gossip had already spread, Laughlin suspected, thanks to "June [Oppen] and Kenneth's other upper class ghetto friends" who liked to discuss Laughlin's wild times in San Francisco.[38] Marie wanted to help Laughlin figure out a way of convincing his wife Maggie that his lover's husband was mad, or that he had the wrong man. Marie did not think that "two naive babies as Jim and [herself] could put much over on Maggie."[39] Marie believed Maggie had never visited the Rexroths on Potrero Hill because she didn't approve of them and thought they were "immoral as well [and] not high class enough." To complicate matters, Marie suspected that Kenneth may have had an affair with Laughlin's lover. But she felt she owed Laughlin whatever help she could muster, especially since he had given her such respite in the Utah mountains.

A superficial calm hung over the Rexroth household when Marie returned in late October 1944. Money remained a source of irritation. Kenneth and Marie threw a big party to celebrate the publication of *The Phoenix and the Tortoise,* and to sell copies. Five people bought eight books. When Kenneth spent the small profit on Christmas gifts for her, Marie became furious. She was quite capable of patronizing Kenneth, leaving him ten-dollar bills attached to notes telling him how to spend the money. She had agreed to pay their food bills and rent, but not for Kenneth's clothing and laundry. Looking for a scapegoat after one nasty fight, Kenneth dashed off a hysterical letter to Laughlin full of accusations: New Directions was ignoring orders for his books, the Stalinists were spreading rumors that Laughlin was a Trotskyite publisher and Kenneth a Trotskyite agent, his books were not selling because only Stalinists patronized bookstores. Laughlin endured this letter, and similar ones that followed.

Thirteen

HAPPY DAYS
1945–1947

DESPITE its sluggish reception, *The Phoenix and the Tortoise* won the California Literature Silver Award, as had *In What Hour* four years earlier.[1] Rexroth needed to borrow a suit in order to attend the dinner held in his honor. To his delight, he learned that Ted Weiss, editor of the *Quarterly Review of Literature,* had asked Williams to review the book and that Williams had consented. After cautiously calling the title poem both "deficient and marvelous," Williams praised the book enthusiastically.[2] Obviously the volume had pleased him, partially because it demonstrated sympathy for and accord with his conviction that a "major new attack on the art" was needed.[3] To James Laughlin, he wrote that

"Rexroth (King Red) has finally emerged into something very firm and perceptive—hard to say how good he is now (and how bad I found him formerly). It takes everything a man has to be a good artist and then he only succeeds by luck sometimes."[4]

To help Rexroth distribute the book, Henry Lenoir was selling it to his customers at the Iron Pot, a bar on Montgomery Street that attracted an artists' crowd. Lenoir liked to display the work of his patrons prominently—both those who were struggling and those who had succeeded. Two paintings by Rexroth's friend Dick Ayer and several by Jean Varda had decorated the walls of the Iron Pot.[5] Rexroth asked New Directions to send an advance copy of Yvor Winters, whose advice he continued to seek despite his rejection of Rexroth's friendship nearly fifteen years before. Winters disapproved of these poems—a rich mixture of love lyrics, political poems, satire, and translations from Latin and Japanese[6]—because they did not observe traditional metrical form. He thought the tone of the poems was honest enough but that their structure was terribly weak.[7] The erotic, sensual poems like "Still on Water" and "Lute Music" are written in the free form that Winters objected to. An example of what bothered Winters is the following excerpt from "Floating," which de-

scribes Marie and Kenneth making love in a canoe as it slowly drifts down
a stream thick with lily pads:

> Move softly, move hardly at all, part your thighs,
> Take me slowly while our gnawing lips
> Fumble against the humming blood in our throats.
> Move softly, do not move at all, while time slides away,
> As this river slide beyond this lily bed,
> And the thieving moments fuse and disappear
> In our mortal timeless flesh.[8]

The rhythms and imagery fuse with the poem's subject, creating an inextricable, complex union of form and content. Even though the meter is
fluid, the poem is as fine a "mastering" of the art form as any critic could
expect.

Puzzled by Winters's negative reaction to his finest work, Rexroth
nevertheless persisted in pursuit of his approval. He apparently regarded
Winters as a surrogate for the older brother he never had, a mentor whose
approval was worth having and whose advice was worth heeding. He had
dedicated "The Place" to him when it first appeared in An "Objectivists"
Anthology, rather perversely since this was precisely the kind of poetry
Winters disliked. In the fraternal spirit, he also wrote "A Letter to Yvor
Winters" (published in 1940 in In What Hour), a poem expressing Rexroth's
pacifist connection to Winters; both had "swords that shall not strike,"
and faced with a global war, both could only try to create better poems.
Its five rhymed quatrains prove that he could easily meet Winters's strict
standards of metrical verse. Rexroth continued to visit Winters uninvited,
ignoring Winters's plaintive discouragements. His teaching obligations
and family responsibilities—Lewis and Winters had two children—left
him little time to chat with fellow poets.[9]

Soon after The Phoenix and the Tortoise was published, Kenneth and
Marie thought Winters might welcome them. When they arrived unannounced (just as long before Andrée and Kenneth had done), Janet Lewis
explained to the visitors that Winters would not budge. But they did not
believe her. "It would have been all right," Lewis remarked, "if I had said
that he was at Stanford."[10] She tried to console them by sitting with them
on the lawn for some conversation. They stayed "quite a long time" before
they realized the truth. That visit was their last. As they left, Marie said:
"There's a sign over the gate that says 'Beware of the dog.' It ought to say
'Beware of the Poet.' "[11]

About Winters's crusty views on literature, Rexroth remained ambivalent. He articulated this attitude to Ted Weiss, who in the pages of the
first volume of the Quarterly Review of Literature had written a long and
angry article attacking Winters for denigrating the poetry of Pound, Eliot,
and Stevens in The Anatomy of Nonsense. Rexroth told Weiss that Winters
was "as good as they come these years as a poet," that he was "unquestion-

ably the best of the constipated school of poetry." Weiss would be unwise
to take on Winters as a critic: "I would no more dream of referring to
Winters' critical ideas than I would to Orrick Johns' one leg, or Max
Bodenheim's no balls."[12]

In February of 1944, Winters's new volume of verse, enigmatically
entitled *The Giant Weapon*, had arrived on the anniversary of the day that
Kenneth had met Marie. Together they read aloud selections from it
while troop trains moved through the night in the railroad yards beneath
Potrero Hill. These powerful poems, "fresh from fifteen years of growth
and decay," inspired Rexroth to speculate about the contradictions between writing poetry and killing, between "kisses at the dark train, / and
children born of dead fathers."[13] It occurred to him that the seemingly
small voices of Winters and Lewis were "the giant weapons." They continued to write poetry in the midst of world mayhem; they stood for "the
creative will [that] stirs the seed from the mud." This poem first appeared,
along with two sensuous and erotic lyrics to Marie, in Weiss's *Quarterly
Review of Literature* in 1945.[14]

Twenty-five years later Rexroth would cite Winters as a "very considerable poet," but also as the promoter of "some of the most wrongheaded
and eccentric criticism ever written."[15] The poetry of Janet Lewis he never
ceased to admire. In 1946, he wrote to Lewis to praise *The Earthbound*,
poems written between 1924 and 1944. He told her that he always thought
she was a fine poet, and praised "the handsome job of bookmaking" that
distinguished the volume. Rexroth's touchy relationship with "the crotch-
etty Mr. Winters" did not interfere with the appreciation of his wife's
talent.[16]

After the war ended in 1945, Rexroth's creative energy surged into
other genres. He was writing not only lyrical poetry but also a series of
four verse plays, two set in the Greek heroic age, "Phaedra" and "Iphigenia at Aulis," and two set in Hellenized Bactria, "Hermaios" and "Berenike." (They would be published collectively in 1951 under the title
Beyond the Mountains.) He read "Phaedra" by lamplight one evening at
Pond Farm, Mary and Ham Tyler's communal writers' home—a converted chicken house nestled above a grove of redwood trees—in Guerne-
ville near the Russian River, where Robert Duncan was also living.[17] Other
projects in progress included an anthology of British poets, and a selection of poems by D. H. Lawrence for New Directions. Marie's career also
blossomed; by 1946, she was earning a respectable salary as an administrator with the Health Service and teaching graduate classes at San Francisco County.

Now that gasoline rationing was over, they could go camping in the
Sierras during the winter and summer. Since Marie was tied down to a
full-time schedule, Kenneth would head for the mountains by himself, or
with Frank Triest or James Laughlin. Favorite destinations were Sequoia
National Park and the other side of the Sierras to Bishop where there was

good fishing at Lake Sabrina, especially for rainbow and golden trout (fish often mentioned in Rexroth's poems). On one occasion, Rexroth hiked into the foothills and built a snow camp. At other times he went over trails that no one else knew of. When friends joined him, Rexroth was in charge, leading on the trails, doing the cooking, deciding how much drinking was permissible (very little). What particularly impressed Laughlin were the desserts Rexroth could make out of dried fruits, and his ability to meditate endlessly, in the posture of Rodin's *The Thinker*. There were wild times as well. Once the two men suffered a disastrous venture up Kings River Canyon with two San Francisco State College students. "We had a couple of broads along—I don't know where Marie was. . . . The girls got blisters on their feet, began to complain, they didn't like each other. . . . Kenneth had brought enough food, so we stayed three or four days. The girls kept complaining. It started to rain."[18]Either Marie ignored or accepted Kenneth's resumed duplicity. But for the time being, especially now that more writers and artists were stopping by the Rexroth home, she was content with an arrangement which left her free to pursue her own affairs, yet let her play the role of the poet's wife.

By 1946, Rexroth's reputation as a "man of letters" was established on the West Coast. Once again, his home became a mecca for local and visiting artists and writers. For many COs living at the Civilian Public Service Camp at Waldport, Oregon—a large number of whom were artists—this image was enhanced by his pacifist activities during the war. Through the efforts of various churches to ensure humane treatment for COs, several CPS camps had established special schools to which the COs could request assignment according to their particular interests. Waldport became a fine arts center, with workshops for writers, printers, painters, musicians, and actors. Several artists from other camps had transferred to Waldport, including Adrian Wilson, who became one of the foremost book designers in the United States, and Martin Ponch, who brought *The Compass* with him from the East Coast. Fresno-born poet William Everson was there, printing *Untide,* an arts and anarchist/pacifist newsletter that served as an alternative to the official newsletter of the camp, *The Tide.*[19]

Rexroth liked to joke that the worst experience recorded by the Lewis and Clark Expedition was winter camping on the Oregon coast, the site of Camp Waldport: "the Selective Service decided that would be a very good place for the literary and artistic conscientious objectors in hopes that they would mold away."[20] On their furloughs, the men caught the slow bus to San Francisco, where many of them would call on Rexroth for moral support and sympathetic company. A number of these men, after they resumed civilian life, settled in the Bay Area. Again Rexroth welcomed them to his home, glad to see that the pacifist community had not "molded away."

Released from Waldport on July 23, 1946, William Everson, a friend of Ham and Mary Tyler, moved in with them at their new large communal farm, a place called Treesbank, not far from Pond Farm, on the Russian River and near Sebastopol in Sonoma County. He became a frequent dinner guest at the Rexroths', and started attending the various poetry readings Rexroth organized. After reading a volume of his poetry, Rexroth had written to Everson while he was still at Waldport, largely to offer encouragement. Everson was surprised by Rexroth's letter since he had only known about Rexroth through hearsay and rumor. Had he been aware before he was drafted that Rexroth was a pacifist, he would have gotten in touch with him "just to find a kindred spirit."[21] On furlough, Everson visited Potrero Hill, and a new friendship was formed. Rexroth had kept an eye on the Washington hand press Everson bought from Ed Ottsman, who promised to hold it for Everson until he was released.

There was a steady flow of visitors at Wisconsin Street. Sometimes Rexroth would throw a party, like the one in November 1946 for Philip Lamantia's first book, *Erotic Poems,* for which he had written the introduction.[22] Robert Duncan came to supper, as did Muriel Rukeyser who with five volumes of poetry already to her credit had moved to Berkeley to teach at the California Labor School. George Hitchcock still liked to dine with the Rexroths, and afterwards enjoyed singing with Marie while she played the piano. East Coast people were invited if they had the proper credentials.

On James Laughlin's suggestion, Richard and Betty Eberhart were asked to dinner. Rexroth was reluctant to meet them because Eberhart was in uniform and probably a "scissorbill" (one of Rexroth's favorite expressions). When World War II ended, Eberhart, a lieutenant in the Navy, decided to stay on an extra year and was assigned to Alameda Naval Station to take care of the returning airmen from the Pacific. Even though his poetry was not familiar to Rexroth, he decided to invite them, and wrote Laughlin that in addition to the Eberharts, "we will have Muriel, Morris Graves, Philip, and maybe the Wheelwrights. Very artistical."[23]

The Eberharts remember the first meeting well. They thought Kenneth and Marie's four rooms on the second floor of the Potrero Hill house were charming, with black and white linoleum on the floors, bookcases made of apple crates, and Rexroth's Mondrian-like paintings and pastels on the wall.[24] Rexroth had apparently invited a few more people than he had originally intended, and Eberhart stood out "like a sore thumb" in his Navy blues and crew-cut. Everyone else was wearing sneakers and dungarees, or as Betty Eberhart put it, "they were what you'd call hippies . . . they didn't dress the way the Navy did." The other guests were amused that a Navy man and his wife were part of an evening at the Rexroths, but before long Eberhart opened up and "Betty and Dick" were made to feel welcome. The COs who were there presented no problem for them because Betty Eberhart's brother was also a CO and had gone to prison in Ohio. Philip Lamantia remained vivid in their memory, as did Morris Graves, who "was wafting around like the ethereal person that he was."

Rexroth spent much of the time in the kitchen preparing a stew which he served in a huge dishpan. After that Friday night, the Eberharts and Rexroths became intimate for a while. When Eberhart was off duty on weekends, Kenneth and Marie would take him and Betty on trips so that they could enjoy California's natural beauty. (They passed up one trip to Big Sur because Miller would not welcome Eberhart.)

Often they would drive north up the coast, with Kenneth at the wheel talking non-stop about the majestic panorama. He expected their undivided attention, and complete trust in his ability as both expert guide and chauffeur. In *The Long Reach*, Eberhart has a series called "Vignettes" which includes a concise account of a typical trip:

> Once by the Pacific Betty, Marie, Kenneth and I
> Were driving northward high over the ocean, Kenneth
> Was driving. We were talking of love, of pacifism.
> All of a sudden a spectacular bird, a red bird
> Flew by the front of the car quite near.
> Rexroth let go the wheel, excitedly began
> Giving a lecture. I feigned needing to make a stop,
> Came back, and took the wheel away from him.[25]

Had either of the Eberharts asked outright to share the driving, Kenneth would have become angry and insulted. But he didn't mind their maneuvers to extricate him from the driver's seat, much to Marie's relief.

Although Rexroth and Eberhart came from vastly different backgrounds (when he was twenty-six Eberhart had served as tutor to the son of the king of Siam), they shared a similar sense of adventure. On one expedition to Mt. Tamalpais, Rexroth had Eberhart dangling down its sheer face with a heavy rope tied around his middle. He had to get over the cliff and down by himself. He tried not to appear frightened. After he had managed about fifteen feet, Rexroth said that it would be better if he pushed his legs against the cliff, so that his body would be horizontal. Rexroth let him drop another ten feet, then instructed Eberhart to bounce. "Bounce," he ordered over and over, and Eberhart bounced his way down to the safety of the flat earth. For more sedate excursions, they would go to the cabin at Devil's Gulch.

Rexroth was "at home" Friday evenings. Usually an invitation was required, but it was easy to obtain by telephoning in advance. Started as a literary soirée of sorts, this occasion turned into regular gatherings for philosophical discussion, storytelling, as well as gossip and social banter. Overall they provided what Berkeley poet, professor, and scholar Thomas Parkinson describes as "genuinely intellectual discussions,"[26] as well as a sense of community for San Francisco's poets and philosophical anarchists. True, Rexroth's Friday evenings were not the first forum in the Bay area for this kind of discourse. Since 1936, the University of California at Berkeley had provided a space for poets to test the waters at the weekly readings, sponsored by James Caldwell, often attended by as many as a hundred students.[27] In 1939, Lawrence Hart came to the campus, where he directed a poetry workshop through the Extension division, as Witter Bynner had some twenty years earlier. But the war had scattered this energy, and in 1946 it was up to Rexroth and Josephine Miles, who had been teaching at Berkeley since 1940, to get things rolling again.

The two maintained a cordial if distant friendship throughout their lives, and in the mid-forties offered contrasting milieus where aspiring writers could expect a serious audience. Miles was working within a more traditional and decidedly academic context, but she fully appreciated the new currents surfacing at this time. Through her efforts, Jack Spicer, Robin Blaser, and Robert Duncan taught writers' workshops at the university. Nearby, on Telegraph Avenue, Duncan also organized poetry readings at a run-down rooming house called Throckmorton Manor. Rexroth's "salon," however, had a distinctive edge noticeably absent in Berkeley: a personality and charisma that were formidable. He dominated the discussions and steered them in directions where he could assume authority. He espoused the avant-garde and reinterpreted the classical writers. He vigorously and relentlessly reiterated his opposition to the Eastern establishment, thus clearing the way for the counterculture that would break out in the next decade.

During the height of the war, Rexroth had expressed his pessimism about the future of humanity in a poem called "Gas or Novocain":

> In ten years
> The art of communication
> Will be more limited.
> The wheel, the lever, the incline,
> May survive, and perhaps
> The alphabet.[28]

Stalin's purges, the Moscow Trials, the rise of Franco, the massacre of the Kronstadt sailors had destroyed whatever qualified revolutionary hope in communism Rexroth and others had entertained before the war. The world had seen that humankind could knowingly choose evil over good, while imagining that it was choosing good over evil. What other valid explanation existed for the Holocaust, the atom bombing of Nagasaki and Hiroshima, the British and American destruction of Dresden, the firebombing of Tokyo? This "insight," Rexroth believed, should have made people skeptical of depraved politicians obsessed with power and of phrases like "the war to end all wars" and "fighting for peace." Now, perhaps buoyed by the atmosphere of postwar optimism, Rexroth let himself hope that a free, humane world community might emerge from the debris and that all civilized life would not be obliterated before the twenty-first century. The times were ripe for a new system, free of bureaucrats and ideology: a postwar spontaneous burst of energy that would bring people together in constructive community.

A group of philosophical anarchists, calling themselves the Libertarian Circle, was organized. The first meetings were held downtown in a large studio until the group could afford to rent the top floor of a house on Steiner Street. The price of admission was a bottle of red wine, about forty-nine cents.[29] The goals of this group, in Rexroth's words, were to "refound the radical movement after its destruction by the Bolsheviks and to rethink all the basic principals and subject to searching criticism all the ideologists from Marx to Malatesta."[30] At "educational" meetings held every Wednesday, the group would discuss a single topic or author based on a reading list that Rexroth had developed. It included "the Andalusian Agricultural Communes, the Shop Stewards movement in revolutionary Germany, communalist groups in the United States, the Kronstadt revolt, Nestor Makhno and his anarchist society and army in the Russian Civil War, the I.W.W., Mutualist Anarchism in America." There were works by fifty philosophers, political theorists, psychiatrists, poets, and historians. On the list were six books about Kropotkin, the leading theorist of anarchism, and three about the French Socialist and anarchist Pierre-Joseph Proudhon. Some of the better-known writers whose names appeared were Alexander Berkman, Emma Goldman, William Godwin, Bakunin, McTaggart, and Wilhelm Reich. Engels, Lenin, Tolstoy, Lao-tzu, Plato, Aristotle, Bacon, Plutarch, and St. Simon also were included.[31] This group may have sensed a great chasm between themselves and the administration in Washington, D.C., but felt connected to like-minded groups in Britain, Europe, and Asia. The meetings created an ambiance that would later help to foster the San Francisco Renaissance.

Several of the members of the Libertarian Circle were the poets who came to Rexroth's Friday evenings—among them Muriel Rukeyser, William Everson, Robert Duncan, Jack Spicer, and Thomas Parkinson—and they would lead discussions about their own work. But Rexroth, now in his early forties, was the model literary figure—wise, productive, and sophisticated. He was an inspiring, if sometimes intimidating, mentor. He was also ruggedly handsome, with a big and beautiful lion's head well suited to his new literary status. The breadth of his knowledge could be astounding, the result, in part, of reading the entire *Encyclopaedia Britannica*. On one occasion, while walking with Hamilton and Mary Tyler along the banks of the Russian River, near Duncan Mills, where Frank Triest had been living since his release from the federal penitentiary (where he had been sent for refusing to register with his draft board), Rexroth truly impressed Ham Tyler with what Robert Duncan characterized as his "ideatic memory." While they were walking together, he caught sight of a rare insect and identified it. "Well, Ham," reported Robert Duncan, "was an entymologist and was just flabbergasted. It was so rare that you could pick out one of these things. There was much about Kenneth's almost magical and sympathetic coordinations when it came to nature."[32]

Many old-time Italian anarchists of San Francisco were puzzled by this fresh crop of anarcho-pacifists who revered art and literature, men like the poet Robert Stock, and Ronald Bladen, a young sculptor, painter, and saxophone player from Vancouver, B.C. who supported himself by working in the shipyards and had attended the California School of Fine Arts. Bladen became a steady friend, who appreciated Rexroth's "streetwise" brilliance even though sometimes it seemed to have a charlatan's edge to it.[33] No doubt encouraged by the example of Rexroth, this younger generation intertwined their imaginative life with their political consciousness, establishing what William Everson identified as a "distinct West Coast literary situation" where the "poet's role as *vates* was affirmed, his prophetic stance as refresher and invigorator of stultified literary and social forms was asserted. Anarchism and pacifism were adopted as political programs against the military-industrial complex, and a relaxed bohemianism was favored over against the 'correct' posture of the Academy."[34] The poetics of the established New Criticism, especially its emphasis on detachment and impersonalism, was decidedly out of place in this context. The old-timers may also have been confused by some of Rexroth's antics. Sometimes he would appear at these meetings in a long, flowing black cape and warn those present to beware of falling into the trap of American consumerism, that blood was on them with each new car and refrigerator they bought.

A good share of this emerging sensibility was grounded in a profound respect for the natural world. And to a large extent the work of Jakob Boehme, the German mystic who was so important to Rexroth, affirmed this perspective. Rexroth continued to be "moved by the tremendous beauty of his picture of the universe,"[35] and led discussions about him at Potrero Hill and at the Libertarian Circle. He accepted both the political and aesthetic implications of Boehme's writings: Nature was a sacred paradigm of harmony, and in such a universe human beings were themselves responsible for creating good and for knowing God or the spiritual world. Boehme was an appropriate figure to study, Rexroth thought, since the members of the Libertarian Circle—artists and activists alike— were attempting to work out for themselves an applied philosophy that might make the world a more humane place.

For a poetry compatible with this perspective, Rexroth encouraged the Circle to read Tu Fu (712–770), the renowned Chinese poet of the T'ang Dynasty whom Witter Bynner had recommended more than twenty years earlier in New Mexico.[36] The poetry of Tu Fu expressed a reverence for life, a mystical communion with nature, at the same time revealing a compassion for humanity and a need to articulate his own feelings of loneliness or frustration. As Rexroth said in his essay "Tu Fu, *Poems*" Tu Fu's acute powers of observation invigorated his imagery and made it poignant, startling, and "yet seemingly so ordinary."[37] For example, in "Travelling Northward," Tu Fu depicts the devastation of war:

> Screech owls moan in the yellowing
> Mulberry trees. Field mice scurry,
> Preparing their holes for winter.
> Midnight, we cross an old battlefield.
> The moonlight shines cold on white bones.[38]

The dense, compressed language of this poem celebrates the beauty of nature while it mourns the passage of time, laments the injustices of the world, and expresses compassion for the suffering of humankind. These themes, far from seeming distant to Rexroth, infuse such early volumes as *In What Hour* and *The Phoenix and the Tortoise*. Tu Fu also influenced the development of Rexroth's technique. For instance, Rexroth learned to dramatize moods, moving from one to another by breaking them with an image vitally connected to the natural world. In "Toward an Organic Philosophy,"[39] Rexroth, camping in the Sierra Nevada, observes that spring has taken longer than usual to arrive. He is alone, despondent, yet consoled by the nocturnal activity around him.

> I descend to camp,
> To the young, sticky, wrinkled aspen leaves,
> To the first violets and wild cyclamen,
> And cook supper in the blue twilight.
> All night deer pass over the snow on sharp hooves,
> In the darkness their cold muzzles find the new grass
> At the edge of the snow.

Especially relevant to Rexroth's discussions at the Circle was Tu Fu's belief in the sanctity of nature within an implicitly moral and social context. Although Rexroth would never endorse didactic or agitprop literature, he felt that a good writer had a difficult but essentially moral and ethical role to play in modern society: that of enlarging and intensifying the techniques of rendering experience and evaluating the contents of that experience. Rexroth had articulated this view before the Congress of Western Writers in San Francisco in 1936, and his mind had not changed. He had delivered this speech in order to make a case for a regional renascence of literature in the West. He wanted to establish local outlets, where writers could keep their skills sharply honed and their audience enlightened. Writers, he had warned, would often feel at odds with that part of the population whose power and privilege depended on keeping the levels of communication debased, uncritical, and uncreative—the very antithesis of the kind of communication that exists in the poetry of Tu Fu. And Rexroth followed his own advice. His poetry thereafter would demonstrate his allegiance to Boehme and Tu Fu—their influence is most visible in the title poem of *The Signature of All Things*, where a Western philosopher and an Eastern poet meet on common ground. His translations of Tu Fu published in *The Phoenix and the Tortoise* and in the *Briarcliff Quarterly* reveal how immersed he was at the time in the work of the Chinese master.

Rexroth became interested in journals that had either originated or flourished at Waldport, magazines like Kermit Sheets and Kemper Nomland's *The Illiterati* (the first edition was destroyed by a postal inspector when he came across an illustration of a nude female) and Martin Ponch's *Compass.* Widely distributed throughout the United States and England, these publications attracted contributions from pacifists who had not been sent to Waldport: Kenneth Patchen; the novelist Irwin Stark, who taught at The City College of New York; the British poet Alex Comfort, who was also a physician and experimental physicist (and would much later write *The Joy of Sex);* the anarchist poet George Woodcock, who in London had turned his poetry sheet *Now* into an influential literary magazine with a radical orientation; James Broughton, poet and playwright; and Henry Miller.

Rexroth's contributions to these publications appeared in 1948: for example, "Andrée Rexroth: Mt. Tamalpais" and "As the sun comes in the window" in *Compass,* and "A Christmas Note for Geraldine Udell" in *The Illiterati,* which by then had moved to Pasadena. In all three poems, Rexroth relies on acute observation of the natural world to communicate a particular feeling, memory, or philosophical rumination. The influences of Boehme and Tu Fu are again evident. ("Now/It is almost ten years since/ You came here to stay. Once more, / The pussy willows that come / After the New Year in this / Outlandish land are blooming."[40] Of the three, only the epistle for Geraldine Udell, who ran the Radical Bookshop, a favorite haunt of Rexroth's during his Chicago days, is overtly political in its references to Eugene Debs, Alexander Berkman, and Bill Haywood. In "A Christmas Note for Geraldine Udell," Rexroth expresses his state of frustrated idealism. Although unwilling to surrender all hope that people would one day embrace anarcho-pacifist principles, he was losing his postwar optimism. Yet he understood that just as "the veering wind brings the cold, organic smell / Of the flowing ocean," each setback was balanced by a life that is constantly feeding and renewing itself.[41]

Rexroth's work also appeared in another forum for postwar literary energy, *Circle,* edited by George Leite and designed by Bern Porter.[42] Leite, who had attended Berkeley, had worked on two earlier publications, *New Rejections* and (with Weldon Kees) *No Directions.* The titles were intended to poke fun at Laughlin's young publishing company, a jape that amused more than it annoyed Rexroth. *Circle* was anti-war, anti-authoritarian, and committed to new art forms. Its scope was international, looking particularly to Europe and the French Surrealists, but its editorial policy expressed a West Coast bias. The first two issues were produced on a mimeograph machine, but the third was printed and displayed a cover designed by Rexroth. That issue also initiated a series called "Les Lauriers Sont Coupés," articles by Rexroth devoted to writers whom he thought deserved greater recognition. The first was about Robert McAlmon, and future columns were given to poets Mina Loy and James Daly. Altogether ten issues of the magazine were published, with contributions by many noteworthy writers and artists. Anaïs Nin offered a story, Henry Miller wrote about the art of his friend Jean Varda, and Robert Duncan, Philip Lamantia, Josephine Miles, William Everson, Kenneth Patchen, and William Carlos Williams all contributed poems. Reproductions of paintings and drawings by Max Ernst and André Masson were also included.

Another little magazine that stimulated the flowering of a new West Coast literary tradition was *The Ark*. The magazine had a decided pacifist and anti-state position. Co-edited by Philip Lamantia and Sanders Russell (who in Woodstock had collaborated with Robert Duncan on *Experimental Review*), this magazine reflected "the Rexroth nexus of 1945 and 1946."[43] Its editorial preface opens as follows:

In direct opposition to the debasement of human values made flauntingly evident by the war, there is a rising among writers in America, as elsewhere, a social consciousness which recognizes the integrity of the personality as the most substantial and considerable of values.[44]

Its first and only issue (Spring 1947) included Rexroth's "Advent 1947,"[45] and works by William Everson, Robert Duncan, Thomas Parkinson, Richard Moore, Kenneth Patchen, James Laughlin, Richard Eberhart, British anarchist George Woodcock, Paul Goodman, e e cummings, Robert Stock, and William Carlos Williams. It was illustrated by Ronald Bladen. By the time the magazine was published in 1947 (printing had begun on a hand press in 1945), Russell and Lamantia had quarreled, and Lamantia dropped out.

Although these writers and activists shared common political views, harmony did not always prevail among them. Rexroth was not particularly adept at arbitrating their disagreements. Lamantia would complain to Rexroth about an editorial decision Russell had made on his own. According to William Everson, Rexroth would "chew Sanders out, accusing him of sabotaging the Movement and things like that."[46] Russell in turn would complain to Robert Duncan that Lamantia was "untrustworthy" and carried tales back to Rexroth. Indeed, Everson himself had already experienced some rifts with Rexroth. Among the most serious was the one over Robinson Jeffers, whom Everson regarded as his "master." Rexroth's antipathy toward Jeffers had originated in the thirties when his reputation was at its zenith and Rexroth was working through his Objectivist phase. Rexroth, whom Everson regarded as his "mentor," wanted Everson to disavow his allegiance to Jeffers. Jeffers, he said, wrote poetry of "appalling slothfulness," and espoused an inhumane and elitist philosophy (unlike many people on the left, Rexroth never accused Jeffers of fascism). And rivalries swirled between the editors of *Ark*, who presumed that San Francisco was the heart of this new literary movement, and the editors of *Circle*, who preferred it to be Berkeley. In the final issue of *Circle*, the editors called *The Ark* and *Contours* (another little magazine which came out of Berkeley) little more than "segments of *Circle*," suggesting snidely that both lacked the scope and sophistication of that journal.

Despite these baroque forms of infighting, Rexroth's reputation continued to grow: he served as a major guiding light to these younger writers between 1945 and 1948. "We were all brought up on Daddy Rexroth's reading list," Robert Duncan observed.[47] By now, Rexroth had earned the encomium. He had published two volumes of poetry, and new poems regularly appeared in literary magazines. He had impressed, even awed, his colleagues with what they regarded as his encyclopedic knowledge, his dedication to his craft, and his commitment to a new literary movement that was not politically neutral. It was exciting to be around him. Thomas Parkinson, who regularly participated in Rexroth's discussion groups, said:

[He] had the trick of imaginative projection that allowed him to suggest he was a contemporary of Lenin, Whitman, Tu Fu, Thoreau, Catullus, Baudelaire, John Stuart Mill—they were all so real to him. The amount of labor and confusion that he saved younger people was immense; one could be painfully working his way out of Dublin Catholicism, and he would talk of Buber or Lao Tzu.[48]

Stirred by Rexroth's spirit, the younger writers and artists devoted themselves to creating a public life for art in San Francisco. As Parkinson described them, they were "like coral insects living and dying to create a lagoon where poetry and the other arts could live peacefully and productively."[49] Rexroth generously gave them grounding and direction at large Libertarian Circle meetings, and in the more intimate poetry seminars at his home on Potrero Hill.

About this time Rexroth was writing an introduction to a volume of D. H. Lawrence that New Directions was publishing in 1947. His approach to the project mixed pride and humility. He wrote to Laughlin:

I can't get over it. I can't believe it is really me doing it. Just think—Kenneth Rexroth doing a selection of D. H. Lawrence's poems! I guess that is the way the archeologists felt who found new lines of Sappho and Christ in the scattered papyri of Oxyrhynchus. Or Schliemann, when his shovel cut thru the ninth superimposed town at Troy and found the tenth a ruin of ashes—and fell on his knees and wept.[50]

Through his espousal of Lawrence, Rexroth attracted other Lawrence admirers like Duncan and Everson into his orbit of influence. He showed them how Lawrence entered into and identified with the natural world, then wrote about it from the inside out. He helped to validate their fascination with the exuberance and vitality of his sexually charged prose and poetry. When Everson went through his shortlived Lawrence stage, he wrote erotica which Rexroth particularly liked and which he encouraged Everson to cultivate.

In late fall of 1946, the English writer and critic Cyril Connolly, then editor of *Horizon,* came to San Francisco, and Rexroth sponsored a gathering in his honor, or as he described it to another Englishman, the poet and publisher, Charles Wrey Gardiner, "we fed him and got him drunk and gave him a marihuana cigarette and everything."[51] About twenty-five people showed up, among them Philip Lamantia, William Everson, and Hilary Belloc, Jr., whom Everson regarded as a "professional Anglophile."[52]

Rexroth, who considered himself expert on modern British poetry ever since he had contracted to do the New Directions anthology,[53] took Connolly to task ("savaging him," in Everson's words) for not publishing the writers whom Rexroth liked. True, he respected Connolly for making no concessions to the war hysteria of the 1940's in editing *Horizon.*[54] But Connolly's taste was not always reliable. There happened to be on hand a copy of John Lindsay's recently published *Modern Scottish Poetry.* Connolly picked it up and said to Rexroth, "I thought you had just made up that Scottish Renaissance, but I see you got it off that the jacket of this Faber book, all Americans take Faber too seriously."[55] Rexroth's response was that he would never contribute a single line to Connolly's magazine. But he must have been jesting. In June 1947, "Another Spring" appeared in *Horizon.*

At the gathering, Connolly invited volunteers to read something that they would like to see published in *Horizon.* So Everson and Lamantia each read one or two poems which Connolly did not understand. Nonetheless, he responded bravely that if they were sent to him, he would consider them for publication. Without intending to be rude, Everson reminded Connolly that he had already rejected some of Everson's work, including "The Stranger."[56] Without missing a beat, Connolly explained to Everson that he had liked the poem but could not publish it because it was too sexually explicit for his printer. At last here was something he could praise; surely, he believed, it was a work that moved both him and his host. Unfortunately, Rexroth had never liked "The Stranger," and had actively discouraged Everson from publishing it. Everson had begun to sense danger in what he called "unstructured eroticism" and with "The Stranger" he addressed himself to that issue, even if that meant he was taking an anti-Lawrentian position. When Connolly started to recite "The Stranger" aloud, Rexroth stormed out of the room outraged.

Word had spread east that the West Coast anarchists were flourishing through educational meetings, poetry readings, and even dances with all kinds of music: traditional waltzes, polkas, folk, and post-bop. When held at Fugazzi Hall, the Libertarian Circle meetings attracted as many as two hundred people, not only writers, painters, theater people, but also physicians, college professors, engineers, psychiatrists. Lewis Hill, once a student of Yvor Winters's at Stanford, and more recently director of the Committee for Conscientious Objectors in Washington, D.C., came one day, unannounced, to a well-attended Libertarian Circle meeting. He believed that an even larger audience could be reached. Meetings and little magazines were fine but they could not be the only means of communication and exchange. Why not set up a cooperatively run, listener-sponsored FM radio station which would reach the entire Bay area? Apparently this proposal was not approved immediately because Hill had fogged the issue with sociological jargon. Here is Rexroth's account of the meeting:

It was difficult enough for the younger college educated people to follow. For the elderly Jews, Italians and Spanish—who after all had been reading revolutionary theory all their lives—it was totally incomprehensible. Lew himself was astonishing enough. He was a tall thin man with a long dead white face and a soft, propulsive manner of speaking.[57]

But Hill managed to launch the first listener-sponsored radio station, KPFA/FM, in the United States. With the help of Richard Moore, Eleanor McKinney, and funds contributed by John Marshall of the Rockefeller Foundation, the station, known as Pacifica Radio, was able to stay afloat. A few years later, Rexroth would conduct a weekly book review program for KPFA/FM (and in the process amass a huge collection of reviewer's copies). Other regulars would include Alan Watts on philosophy, Pauline Kael on film, Jaime de Angulo on *Indian Tales* (1953), Hubert Crehan on art,[58] Elsa Knight Thompson on public affairs, and Ralph Gleason on jazz.

What would come to be known as the San Francisco Renaissance was launched. There were now viable outlets—not limited to academic institutions—for a sensibility that linked the life of the imagination with a pacifist-anarchist consciousness, and which rejected the detachment and impersonality of the New Criticism. The literature of Japanese, Chinese, and the Native American would equal that of Europeans in stature. The natural beauty of the West Coast would provide writers with inspiration and instill within them a commitment to promote ecological sanity. Soon the concept of poetry as performance would be revived and poetry/jazz would become popular. The creative energy dammed up by the war would burst into an exciting and spectacular literary movement.

Fourteen

OLD PROBLEMS, NEW SOLUTIONS
1947–1948

ADDING TO THE FUROR created by the new movement was an article that appeared in the April 1947 issue of *Harper's,* "The New Cult of Sex and Anarchy," by Mildred Edie Brady, an economist and freelance writer living in Berkeley. Claiming that her observations were made at close range, she denigrated both the art and intellectual activity that had emerged in the Bay Area. She divided these new Bohemians into two camps: the Millers and the Rexroths. Those who gravitated toward Henry Miller, many of them COs during the war, did so because of his pacifist booklet *Murder the Murderers,* which he dared to publish during the war, and because they admired his uncensored books such as *The Colossus of Maroussi, Sunday After the War,* and *Air-Conditioned Nightmare,* from which they "imbibed an engaging potpourri of mysticism, egoism, sexualism, surrealism and anarchism." This group emulated Miller's lifestyle, living in ramshackle cabins along the coast near Monterey. The members of Rexroth's group were more bookish: they liked to discuss English anarchists and Kropotkin, "leavening the politics liberally with psychoanalytic interpretations from [Wilhelm] Reich."[1] She insisted that their poetry was incomprehensible. She conceded, however, that the new members got along with the old-time anarchists, or as she describes them, "the mustachioed papas and bosomed mamas." She mistakenly reported that Rexroth had embraced anarcho-pacifism when he resigned from the Communist Party after the bombing of Pearl Harbor. In the end, she was convinced, those people who camped around either Miller or Rexroth placed their faith in the irrational, and measured their spiritual and psychological health by the number of orgasms they were capable of having.

Mildred Brady's remarks stirred the Bay Area community, although not everyone took them seriously. As William Everson saw it, the movement was sure to succeed now that it had been attacked in a respectable publication like *Harper's*.[2] Rexroth was not amused by the allegations that he had been a Communist and connected with a sex cult, fearing that they might jeopardize Marie's career as a public health administrator. The editors of *Circle* pointed out the inaccuracies of the Brady article, accused her of cultivating a taste for "sexual cults and aberrations," and reported that she had hastily left for England where she could indulge her interests far from the scrutiny of the American press. In October 1947, Rexroth contacted Julian Cornell, James Laughlin's lawyer in New York City, whom Laughlin described as a person with "all the virtues of the Quakers and a great mountain man,"[3] about the possibility of taking Brady and *Harper's* to court to secure a retraction and damages. With James Laughlin present, Cornell met with *Harper's* and suggested a settlement to avoid the notoriety of a trial. *Harper's* agreed to retract the allegations, but would not consent to monetary compensation. Laughlin and Cornell thought Rexroth could get $2,500 if he pursued the matter, but he eventually lost interest in the legal intricacies of the case and gave his undistracted attention to literary matters.[4]

At Rexroth's urging, New Directions had taken on a volume of Everson's poems entitled *The Residual Years*. It was edited by Rexroth, who created a table of contents that favored Everson's more recent work where Jeffers's influence was far less apparent. He also wrote the jacket copy. Everson was displeased with the final product, complaining that the book had been coarsely produced and was much inferior graphically to Rexroth's recent *The Phoenix and the Tortoise*.[5] And he objected to Rexroth's jacket copy, which praised him as a writer of simple, personal, and sensuous poetry, a poetry that, Rexroth said, was bound to be rejected by critics and academics of established literary circles, where "an emasculated and hallucinated imitation of John Donne is still considered chic." In all, Everson felt as though he was being thrown to the lions.

Understandably, Rexroth did not receive these complaints with equanimity, especially since Laughlin had recently lauded him as "one of the best blurb writers in the biz."[6] Rexroth told Everson that he was a shrinking violet. He also reminded Everson that he had been given the opportunity to set the book by hand himself from which New Directions would have made plates, or to design it for another printer. He pointed out that Peter Beilenson, the man who printed the book, was New Directions' most expensive printer. Everson could not see that Rexroth had scrawled across the top of Everson's May 11 letter, "I bit his ear the affected ass," but he felt the fire of Rexroth's anger. Nevertheless, Everson would not yield to pressure. He did not want to be called the hope of American poetry. "I am *not* Honest Abe the Pome-Splitter," he wrote in a May 13, 1948, letter to Rexroth, adding that his work bore no resemblance to Kenneth Patchen's poetry, to which it had been compared. Furthermore, he now wanted to disassociate himself formally from the influence of D. H. Lawrence.

And finally, he did not want anyone to presume that his philosophy of life matched Rexroth's. Across the top of this letter Rexroth wrote: "I hope I have got rid of this mealy mouthed hypocrit[e]."[7]

Rexroth was irritated by Everson's failure to appreciate the book, and told Laughlin that he had been "played for a sucker."[8] But he was more disturbed by what he regarded as the "neurotic destructiveness" of Everson's behavior, an overblown pride which made it impossible for him graciously to accept Rexroth's gestures of friendship and interest, which included an offer to throw a book party for him. (Rexroth himself was capable of misinterpreting acts of generosity, especially from affluent friends like Laughlin. He once told Marie that they should never allow people like Laughlin to think he was needed by them.) Rexroth's anger was not altogether unjustified—the gist of Everson's remarks suggested that he was afraid to have his name associated with the likes of D. H. Lawrence, Kenneth Patchen, or Kenneth Rexroth. And Rexroth had heard rumors that Everson was telling everyone that he was a dangerous "faker who has a lot of charm and who leads people on and then exploits them." Rexroth felt betrayed. Yet six months later, in November 1948, he would go to the trouble of sending Everson a sheaf of reviews of *The Residual Years*. In response, Everson humbly asked Rexroth to forgive him for "the harsh words and conduct and attitude of last Spring."[9] Their friendship would survive this serious break.

Rexroth's reputation prospered at home and abroad. He had become a charismatic figure for artists and poets, achieving a kind of glamour among sensitive young San Franciscans who enjoyed the "Bohemian" atmosphere of his soirées. His charm and sense of authority belied the turmoil of his private life. He projected the image of a man who knew how to live well, if modestly, of a man who scorned bourgeois values yet was an expert on art, music, and literature. He was also becoming known to a small but important coterie in England. A London edition of *The Phoenix and the Tortoise* was published by Falcon Press in 1947, the same year as the *Selected Poems of D. H. Lawrence* with Rexroth's Introduction. For a time, Rexroth's attention shifted to England, especially after he had signed a contract with New Directions for the anthology of modern British poets. He had also established an overseas correspondence with fellow anarchists and writers like George Woodcock, Alex Comfort, and Derek Savage.

Rexroth had begun a correspondence with Woodcock in 1943 when Woodcock was publishing the literary magazine *Now* in London and serving as an editor of the anarchist paper *War Commentary*. *Now* published a few of Rexroth's letters, which Paul Goodman and Dwight Macdonald told Woodcock were "mythomaniacal."[10] In 1946, Woodcock published "Lyell's Hypothesis Again," a poem that reflects Rexroth's hopes and apprehensions for the postwar years. The title of the poem refers to a theory postulated by the Victorian geologist Sir Charles Lyell, that the surface of the earth developed out of the action of physical, chemical, and biological processes through geological time. Rexroth emphasizes the place human beings share in this process, a factor that by affirming the significance of their lives might help them achieve a metaphysical harmony with the world.

Against a mountain backdrop of spectacular beauty, Rexroth's poem blends acute observations of this environment with ruminations about his personal tragedies and the "impersonal vindictiveness/Of the ruined and ruining world." He makes love to Marie, and noticing the tiny red marks that the redwood cones have imprinted on his lover's flesh, compares them to the lignite in the cliff, suggesting that their lovemaking has secured them a place in the world's evolution. He marvels that for the moment

> We have escaped the bitterness
> Of love, and love lost, and love
> Betrayed. And what might have been,
> And what might be, fall equally
> Away with what is, and leave
> Only these ideograms
> Printed on the immortal
> Hydrocarbons of flesh and stone.[11]

Sadly, he and Marie could no longer achieve this equilibrium. Their marriage was now in its last throes.

In the spring of 1947, Rexroth's stomach ulcer acted up, and his paranoia bloomed. After feuding with anarchist associates like Sanders Russell and George Leite, he cut his connection to their magazine, *Circle*. Although his reputation was secure, Rexroth feared Leite would try to dissuade local magazine editors from publishing his poems. He criticized Leite for teaching at the California Labor School, "the local Stalinist institute," even though he had taught there himself in the late thirties. Although they had been squabbling constantly, Kenneth and Marie decided to isolate themselves in the Sierras in the hope that a month alone in the mountains would mend the relationship. Neither was yet willing to acknowledge that it was beyond repair.

While Marie's days were consumed by her job at the Public Health Department, and her free time by typing manuscripts and correspondence for Kenneth, Kenneth went off on country hikes with a Mills College student from Philadelphia named Prudence Ohmstead, who with a number of friends had been attending the Libertarian Circle meetings regularly. She was a philosophy major who wrote poetry, a bright and attractive young woman who, unknown at first to Kenneth, was severely disturbed. She had for some time been so infatuated with one of her college teachers that she had deluded herself into believing that she had actually had an affair with him and that he had rejected her. Perhaps as a way of acting out her fantasy, she looked to Kenneth for solace and then for sex, both of which he was glad to provide. He depicts this relationship in a poem entitled "Yugao," which first appeared in *Approach* in the summer of 1947.[12]

In this poem, Rexroth describes the peculiar limbo he experiences as he envisions camping with two women in the mountains. Each is encircled with a romantic halo. Pru is a "distraught, imagined girl / . . . / [who] / Struggles like an ice-bound swan, / Out of the imagination, / Toward a body beside me." The body is Marie's, but Marie is unaware of Pru's presence as she lies beside Kenneth, her "bright, sleeping head, nested / In its pillow" breathing peacefully, mistakenly secure in her love for her husband. The title of the poem hints at Rexroth's real meaning. In Hindu cosmology, a yuga is an age of humanity, with each successive age corresponding to a decline in the moral and physical state of human beings. Was this Rexroth's way of expressing his fear that he had descended a stage himself, that the ethical fiber of his life was fast deteriorating, that his claim to being a devoted husband was little more than good material for a poem?

As soon as Kenneth and Marie returned from their month in the mountains, during the summer of 1947, they had to search for another dwelling without much thought to whether they would stay together. Their landlord had sold the house they were renting. Hoping to buy it themselves, they had borrowed $750 from Laughlin but could not come up with the rest of the down payment. From Switzerland, Laughlin had been asking them to return the money if they were not going to use it for the Wisconsin Street house. His marriage to Maggie was over, and until the divorce was settled, his family was keeping him on a short leash, especially since they were unsympathetic to his side of the affair. His request for reimbursement did not sit any better than the cuts he was asking Rexroth to make in the modern British poets anthology. He also refused to offer firm commitments for future projects.

During this extremely stormy period, both Rexroth and Laughlin feared that their friendship, like their respective marriages, was on the rocks. Rexroth thought Laughlin was a tightwad: the $50 advance for the British poets anthology barely covered his expenses. Offended, Laughlin dropped plans for publishing a de luxe Italian edition of *The Phoenix and the Tortoise*, to be printed by the great Mardersteig. When Rexroth dragged up old misunderstandings about expenses during his previous visits to San Francisco, Laughlin decided not to dedicate a small booklet of his own poems to Rexroth. Oblivious to the coolness between them, Rexroth asked Laughlin if he could find a job for him at Alta. Laughlin suggested that he try writing for *Town & Country*, precisely the sort of high-toned, conservative publication that Rexroth detested.

In contrast to his relationship with Marie, Rexroth's friendship with Laughlin survived these tremors relatively unchanged, and soon they were again exchanging literary gossip (Muriel Rukeyser was trotting around San Francisco with "Paul Robeson and sundry millionairess sponsors of the activities of the Communist Political Association")[13] and ideas for future projects. When Laughlin offered Rexroth a $300 advance if he would write "seriously" about Blake, Rexroth proposed that they meet either in the mountains or at Alta to discuss the matter. When Rexroth boasted about his present "girl," Laughlin made him promise "to be good to Marie"—which perhaps in part explains why in December 1947, Kenneth and Marie rented an apartment together, this time at 187 Eighth Avenue, down the block from Marie's mother. There was nothing Bohemian about this neighborhood. They had lived on Wisconsin Street for twelve years; they were not to live together in this rather cramped space for very long.

Rexroth was still seeing Pru, even though she had become schizophrenic. He was worried about her and for advice would frequently telephone his psychiatrist friend, Leslie Farber. Meanwhile her family had urged her to undergo shock therapy at Agnew Hospital. Rexroth believed that it succeeded only in excising her poetic sensibility. Pru's case became so serious, her fantasies and delusions so pronounced, that her family wanted her declared legally insane by a court of law. The potential for embarrassment was enormous, and Rexroth left town, probably for his Devil's Gulch shack, because he did not want to be subpoenaed as a witness on Pru's behalf, no matter how he cared about her. Pru's roommate, Marthe Larsen, a tall, attractive woman with long brown hair, a wide forehead, and an upturned nose, also wanted to avoid a court appearance. Complaining that she was ill, she escaped into the Mills College infirmary. An exceptionally talented philosophy major at Mills, she had been supporting herself since leaving home in Cincinnati at sixteen, getting through college on scholarships and part-time jobs.[14] She often accompanied Pru to Kenneth's literary evenings. Both Marthe and Kenneth were devastated by the outcome of the trial; neither thought Pru was crazy.

When Kenneth invited Marthe out, she accepted. Until then, Marthe had been so busy keeping herself afloat that she had no time for romance. Now she had a proposal from a famous poet, a mature man twenty years her senior. She had liked him all along, and had been impressed with his initial show of kindness toward her troubled friend. She had enjoyed the Rexroth soirées, and participated in the general adulation that many of the younger people expressed for the Rexroth partnership. For Christmas 1947, Marthe chipped in with a group of other Friday night regulars, including Janet Richards,[15] Ronnie Bladen, and Tram Coombs (for whose poetry Rexroth would write an introduction) to buy the Rexroths a tape recorder. She wrote the note that accompanied the gift, saying it was sent with love and in appreciation of all the evenings of music and poetry at the Rexroths'.

Later, Rexroth himself would distort these early days of their relationship. Reminiscing about this period, he romanticized it, downplaying the heedless affair with Pru, ignoring the fact that he was still married to Marie, choosing to focus instead on the memory of a very bright and lovely Mills College senior who had fallen in love with him. He preferred over the harsher reality the fantasy that he and Marthe had avoided the trial by leaving town together and staying in a "remote part of California" in the home of friends who put them "in the same bed."[16]

As though fueled by turmoil, Rexroth's career gathered momentum, in part because he was awarded the prestigious John Simon Guggenheim Memorial Foundation Fellowship, which carried a $3,000 stipend. William Carlos Williams, James Laughlin, Richard Eberhart, Dwight Macdonald, and Muriel Rukeyser were among the people he had asked to serve as referents. When he wrote Williams of his good fortune, Williams sent him a letter of congratulations "of the most floribundous order," expressing his delight and surprise since this was the first time he could remember that his recommendation had ever done anyone any good.[17]

Williams had been mildly surprised to learn that Rexroth regarded himself as a disciple. "I'm glad to have a pal," Williams had written three years earlier, in 1945.[18] "One feels like a lonesome dog most of the time, it's intensely reassuring to feel the warmth of another's sympathetic interest in one's work." In 1946, Rexroth first published "A Letter to William Carlos Williams," which pays homage to the modern American poet he most respected:

> Remember years ago, when
> I told you you were the first
> Great Franciscan poet since
> The Middle Ages? I disturbed
> The even tenor of dinner.
> Your wife thought I was crazy.
> It's true, though. And you're "pure", too.[19]

Williams confused the occasion Rexroth refers to in this poem (which occurred in 1931) with an unpleasant visit from another mysterious poet from Los Angeles. In his letter congratulating Rexroth on receiving the Guggenheim, he alluded to Rexroth's alleged offensive behavior. A few weeks later Williams apologized for his faulty memory after James Laughlin had told him he was "nuts" to think Rexroth could be so rude.[20]

Cheered by the good news, Rexroth told Laughlin that the grant would enable him to live in the mountains for two years and to get the medical and dental care he had lacked for so long. But he quickly changed his mind about holing up in the mountains once he realized that he now had the mobility to give readings and lectures across the country; and more dizzying, to travel to Europe. He worked out a tentative itinerary for an October–November tour that would include stops in Chicago,

Ithaca, Buffalo, New York City, Northampton, and Boston. To make certain that he would attract the "right" kind of publicity, Rexroth wrote his own news release, which he sent to Laughlin along with his itinerary. It announced his most recent publication—his verse play *Iphigenia at Aulis* (in *New Directions*, X) and the *D. H. Lawrence: Selected Poems* with his Introduction; as well as forthcoming publications, including the *New British Poets*, which would surely "make literary history," and *A Signature of All Things,* "a new collection of simple, profound and intensely personal lyrics and elegies"—no room for false modesty in a blurb. He also listed as his current projects a long poem, to be entitled *The Dragon and the Unicorn,* and a translation of one hundred Japanese poems with illustrations by the great Morris Graves. He described himself as someone who was usually out of reach in the mountains of California and advised interested people to book him fast. In his note to Laughlin, he added that he would have distributed this news release himself, but "an anarchist bastard broke my mimeograph past repair." Rexroth believed that he was standing on the threshold of national, perhaps international recognition, and that financial success was imminent.

Before he left for his first East Coast readings, Rexroth took a brief excursion to Southern California in June of 1948. Using the initial stipend from his grant, he visited friends like fellow anarchist Ward Moore in Monterey, and Mary Gordon (whose roommate in Chicago had been Dorothy Day),[21] and Joe Rabinowitch in Los Angeles. He gave readings at UCLA and at a garden party in the home of the anarchist and painter Jim Fitzsimmons. Juliette and ManRay were among the thirty-five people who showed up.[22] Juliette would remember Rexroth as a gallant, dashing, and romantic stranger. Rexroth regarded this trip as successful, especially since he had earned some money, but also because he had managed to persuade Marthe, who had just been graduated from Mills College, to stop in Los Angeles en route to Cincinnati. They stayed at the Hotel Barclay together, and then after some trouble over her train ticket, Marthe left for home, where she would be followed by notes from Kenneth telling her that he loved her and asking her to help with his correspondence. Rexroth also saw his friend Edouard Roditi at this time, although the circumstances of their meeting had little to do with their common literary interests and the inclinations that had cemented their friendship from the start—that writing poetry was a religious experience, which at its best should be about human concerns and should make a political statement without sacrificing the aesthetic. They also agreed that poets of the classical past were more interesting than those of the immediate past.

Born in Paris in 1910, Edouard Roditi had met Rexroth before the war while studying for his doctorate in Romance Languages at Berkeley. By then, Rexroth was familiar with the poetry Roditi had published in *transition* (when he was only eighteen), *Poetry, The Criterion,* and *The Spectator*. Roditi had been a partner in Editions du Sagittaire, which published

André Breton's *Surrealist Manifestos* and several books by such avant-garde poets as Robert Desnos, Renée Crevel, and Tristan Tzara. During the war, Roditi worked as a language specialist in the French short-wave broadcasting section of the Office of War Information, a position that would not endear him to Rexroth. By 1945 he was employed almost entirely as a conference interpreter, perhaps most notably at the Nuremberg International Military Tribunal on War Crimes in 1946. However, throughout his tenure with the U.S. Government Service, Roditi continued to write. New Directions published Roditi's *Poems 1928–1948* a year after his first-rate study of Oscar Wilde, which Rexroth regarded as "most judicious," an "extraordinary production," and "one of the best informed and written pieces of criticism I have ever read by a contemporary."[23] Roditi was equally enthusiastic about Rexroth's work. With Alain Bosquet, Roditi founded and edited *Das Lot,* a German language periodical devoted to publishing new German writers and translations of avant-garde foreign writers. In the March 1948 issue, two of Rexroth's pacifist poems from *In What Hour* appeared in translation: "On What Planet" and "Falling Leaves and Early Snow." Pleased to see his poems in German, Rexroth wrote Roditi on June 3, 1948, that these skillful translations made the poems sound even better.

During the spring of 1948, Roditi was living communally in a house on South Benton Way, near Lafayette Park, and frequented a homosexual bar called Maxwell's on 3rd Street. After Rexroth's reading at UCLA that June, Roditi showed up at Maxwell's with a "good looking tough Irish girl" and she and Rexroth proceeded to get drunk.[24] They were looking for a place to spend the night together, and Roditi invited Rexroth to come back with him and his friend, "a pretty Mexican boy," to South Benton Way. Roditi made up a bed for them in one of the empty rooms. After everyone had gone to sleep, there was a terrific uproar in Rexroth's room; "all hell broke loose." Rexroth came staggering out with a bleeding lip and a loose tooth. He had told his companion that she wasn't as good a lay as the French prostitutes and she had responded by socking him in the mouth. Rexroth hailed a cab and retreated while the woman went back inside and fell asleep. The next morning, she fixed breakfast for everyone at the house, and enjoyed the atmosphere so much that she stayed on for three more days, presumably as a cook. Rexroth never asked Roditi what happened to her.

Back in San Francisco, before leaving for the East, Rexroth finished reading the final batch of proofs of the *British Poets* and for diversion drew a pastel that resembled the cover of Herbert Read's *The Green Child,* which New Directions had just published with an Introduction by Rexroth. He wrote Marthe that the pastel looked very "Gravessy," and that in fact Morris Graves had stopped by one night while passing through San Francisco en route to England. Rexroth had asked Graves if he would illustrate his Japanese translations, and Graves expressed interest. However,

Laughlin was less enthusiastic about the project. Writing from Klosters, he told Rexroth that the translations were "very dull . . . very little IN them. I imagine in the [original] the form supplies a lot of the content. Is that so? Suggest you do them with the Cal Press. That would spread you in to that area of readership."[25] Laughlin later changed his mind about Rexroth's translations, and a good decision that was, too. One of the volumes, *One Hundred Poems from the Japanese,* published in 1955 by New Directions, went into thirteen printings.[26]

Early in the summer of 1948, while touring the United States, Stephen Spender—the only member of the "Auden group" whom Rexroth thought wrote good poetry—stopped at the Eighth Avenue apartment. With Kenneth and Marie pretending that their marriage was still viable, they went to a party at the home of Jean Varda, who Kenneth said had become "a snob with an impossibly British Anglo-Russian wife."[27] Spender was "too too much—funny—underneath you feel he is a pretty good guy—but Good God! underneath what?" During those days, Kenneth and Marie also saw a good deal of Philip Lamantia and his wife Mary. Marthe was in Cincinnati, not enjoying the visit home. Hoping to comfort her, Kenneth confided that family gatherings inevitably were disillusioning. To prove his point, he described a fantasy in which he had taken Marthe to visit his relatives in Ohio. Everyone was seated around a big family table feasting on sauerbraten and potato pancakes. Awakening to reality, he realized dinner would have been "spam and canned pineapple [with] marshmellers."

About this time, a spate of correspondence with James Farrell aroused other childhood memories. Rexroth had initiated the exchange over political matters, including what he thought was a pernicious new wave of influence that American Communists were exerting in organizations like the Writers Mobilization for Peace and the presidential campaign of Henry Wallace. Rexroth wanted to publish his suspicions and hoped to get Farrell's signature. But Farrell was skeptical of such documents: in his opinion they diffused energy, and created the illusion that the signatories had accomplished something important by asserting their views publicly.[28] Farrell was not unsympathetic to Rexroth's perspective; he did not care for Henry Wallace any more than Rexroth (who believed that Wallace thought Siberia was like the "American Wild West of Bronco Billy"). But he told Rexroth that he was misdirecting his energy, that the American Communist Party should exist to ensure the continued existence of anti-Stalinist, liberal, and revolutionary voices in the United States. In March 1948 he had attended a Workers Defense League conference in New York City where this very goal had been articulated. He thought Rexroth should become involved in a protest against the investigations of alleged Communists in Hollywood being conducted by the House Committee on Un-American Activities. Rexroth appreciated Farrell's position. He let Farrell know that he would be coming to New York in the fall, and hoped that they would have a chance to meet. Farrell was eager to get together also, but more to talk about old Chicago than anything else.

Returning to the Bay Area, Marthe took a summer job to sustain her until the fall, when she would start teaching as an assistant in Berkeley's Philosophy Department and studying for her doctorate (she had graduated from Mills Phi Beta Kappa). She and Kenneth continued their affair with the understanding that his marriage was over. But they had very different conceptions about what that meant. In July, Kenneth took off for Sequoia National Forest with Marie, whose suspicions had not yet been fully aroused by the presence of this friendly and warm graduate student in their home. In exchange for access to Rexroth's formidable library, Marthe agreed to apartment-sit and to handle the mail, especially from Laughlin in case he sent word that he would be visiting them. If Marthe felt abandoned, she did not show it, and was glad to receive Kenneth's newsy letters about the Willys breaking down and the nice burro that was carrying their packs. Toward the middle of August, Kenneth left Sequoia for the cabin at Devil's Gulch where he planned on getting some real writing done, and Marie for Oregon where her friend Marney George had a house on the beautiful and isolated coast at Bandon. Marthe stayed at Eighth Avenue until Kenneth and Marie returned in September.

As it turned out, Marie did not remain on Eighth Avenue for long. Her relationship with Kenneth deteriorated into endless recriminations, reproaches, rows, relieved by occasional moments of sweetness and lacerating nostalgia for all the fun, endearment, tenderness, and love of twelve years together. Old battles were rehearsed with fresh vigor, especially over the feasibility of starting a family. It was Marie's fault, Kenneth stormed, that they did not have children. "It was you, not me," he later wrote, "that refused to have them and said evil brutal things about it."[29] For her part, Marie tried to convince Kenneth that she was not jealous of his poet's life, but miserable that she was no longer his wife, "in the real sense of wifehood and marriage—that you cannot share [love] with two women—the relationship is always between two people."[30] Once, in the heat of anger, Kenneth struck her across the mouth to silence her. Marie decided to return to Bandon for the rest of September, sure that she could get a temporary job on the 4:00 P.M. to midnight shift at the local hospital.

After Marie left for Bandon, Kenneth's behavior bordered on hysteria. He tried to catch her at the Red Cross building where she usually taught class until ten o'clock. He couldn't believe that she had abandoned him. He assigned to her actions a cruelty of unbelievable proportions, a "murderous, destructive never ceasing hate" aimed at coveting and destroying the artist in him. He believed that she was acting out of "thwarted maternity."[31] At the same time he ascribed to her the meanest aspirations that his imagination could conjure: a "Wooster cottage in a fashionable suburb, children, and the society of middleaged (at least the women) mildly fashionable professional people."[32] There seemed to be no way to resolve their differences. Any attempt Marie made to help herself Kenneth regarded as an act of betrayal.

Both of them agonized over the collapse of their marriage. Rexroth, for his part, acknowledged to Laughlin his responsibility for Marie's misery: it must have been trying for Marie to leave again, especially since he would be departing soon for the East Coast. He would not acknowledge that she might be glad to see him go even though she had told him that a temporary separation might be the only means of salvaging their relationship. For her part, Marie believed that in time the love between them could come back "great and strong and beautiful," but for the present, she wrote, "how could I feel any love or need or desire in you when all that came from you was ugly and hateful and when you deliberately chose someone else to put in my place?"[33]

Rexroth feared that his sense of vocation was vanishing with his means of support. To Laughlin, he wrote: "The worst thing is the ironic nature of my—whatdoyoucallem? world view? The only thing I have ever found in life that could redeem its basic insuperable horror, is Holy Matrimony. . . . That's what I have written about, over and over. And here I am. I certainly don't want anybody else."[34] In the same letter he added that his disillusionment reminded him of other women whose affections he had shared, especially Mildred Brock, now an "utterly lost and harried woman," and Dorothy Van Ghent, "a smooth bright shell within which is just . . . nothing." They had proved "fatal" to his marriage. If Rexroth regarded matrimony as holy and sacred, it was not obvious in the pattern of his daily life and the demands he placed on Marie, whose role was to serve him, support him financially and emotionally, nurture him and his artistic aspirations. He confided to Laughlin that instead of becoming a poet, he should have worked in his father's wholesale house and become rich and urbane, conveniently forgetting that his father had died poor and alcoholic.

Yet this same "lost and desolate" soul who feared that he might go mad with sorrow after Marie's departure immediately posted word to Marthe that Marie would be gone until October 1 and that Marthe should meet him at the cabin in Devil's Gulch (where Marie had said she had spent some of her happiest summer days in 1945). Marthe had already visited Kenneth there in late August, carrying with her the two one-pound packages of water biscuits, the Cheddar cheese and dried fruit that he had specifically requested (she would soon get used to pleasing Kenneth's discriminating palate). She typed his translations, poems, and letters, a chore that had once been Marie's ("Will you type *all* my translations and send them to Hubert Creekmore, English Dept., University of Iowa. And send also all the Latin translations to L. R. Lind, Latin Dept., University of Kansas.")[35]

In Marthe's presence, Kenneth showed almost no signs of suffering, but he kept Marie and Laughlin apprised of his grief. He wrote Marie that since her second departure for Oregon, his lips had swelled, a rash had broken out on his feet and hands, and his finger pads and toe tips pained him incessantly, "especially the R. big toe which hurts as though I had a splinter in it." He could not believe how cruel she had been: "You marry a poet so you can have a social feather in your cap, and then treat him as though he had the nerves of a ditch digger."[36] To Laughlin, he continued to express maudlin self-pity. However, by early October, a quiet interlude occurred in this painful drama: Marthe had embarked on her graduate studies at Berkeley and Marie had resumed her job as nursing administrator with the San Francisco Health Department. He himself was facing the greatest adventure of his forty-five years. No wonder that his spirits recovered as he headed east on tour.

Fifteen

ON THE ROAD
1948–1949

A WAITING Rexroth in Chicago, his first major stop, were three gifts from Marthe: a pen, a scarf, and a sweater, all of which pleased him, although he was embarrassed over the expense that Marthe could ill afford. He managed to locate his oldest friends, the Thorpes, and went to mass at his old Church of the Ascension (where he and Andrée had married), which he considered "very splendid with a procession of the Blessed Sacrament and *gobs* of incense and—unlike the West Coast Anglocatholic Churches—nary a fairy!"[1] To do further justice to his old Chicago days, he visited the North Clark Street clubs to see the stripteasers perform on the runways behind the bars of the saloons. He was glad to see that black people there now appeared to be as prosperous as white people, until on closer scrutiny he noticed that they looked "just as neurotic." He assured Marthe that he had not sought out old sweethearts.

His fresh observations of Chicago would be incorporated into Part I of *The Dragon and the Unicorn*.[2] He sounded nostalgic without being sentimental, going back to one of his familiar themes—how the idealism of the thirties had been strangled by creeping capitalism:

> The old Chinese
> Restaurants now tourist joints.
> Gooey Sam where we once roared
> And taught the waiters to say
> Fellow Worker, is now plush.[3]

And he noted that the production plant of Time-Luce Incorporated had found an appropriate location, the former site of several "historical brothels." But Chicago had lost its excitement for Rexroth. He admitted to Marthe that he was not a good traveler, that he missed his home, books, cabin, "and everything—including Marie—but that he missed her most of all.[4] Since he knew that Marthe liked Marie (while visiting Cincinnati, she had bought Marie a small knit purse to replace one she had broken), and because he had assured her that a divorce was imminent, he felt it was not obtuse or crude of him to be candid.

After Chicago, Rexroth stopped in Elkhart. First he visited his mother's grave. He had recently published in *Pacific* (Spring 1947) another of his poems to his mother—"Delia Rexroth (California rolls into)"—in which he comes to terms with the inextricable bond he feels toward her, one that crosses the border of life and death. It is a curious poem in the sense that Rexroth demonstrates a remarkable sensitivity toward his mother, the sort of empathy he seemed incapable of developing for Marie:

> I guess you were a fierce lover,
> A wild wife, an animal
> Mother. And now life has cost
> Me more years, though much less pain,
> Than you had to pay for it.[5]

Elkhart was an important stop, creating in Rexroth the sense of connection, albeit temporary, that people often feel when they revisit scenes of a happy childhood. Here was an opportunity to get some grounding after the recent tumultuous months. In nearby Bristol, he visited the house that had belonged to his great-great-aunt Voney and then her grave. He got a ride to the old cottage in Eagle Lake where he had spent summers reading the classics and learning the countryside. He hiked, picking wildflowers, and followed a crystal-clear stream filled with small trout, a scene—he wrote Marthe—that was "like the cabin only better."[6] Rexroth fully appreciated the beauty of the fall season, which he had almost forgotten after more than fifteen years away. One evening he had a whole pickerel for supper, another treat he had missed for many years. Finally he called on his childhood sweetheart Helen Carpenter, who was happily married to Milos Lundt, a physician. They talked about old times, and the spell of these pleasant memories was not broken by the reunion.

His next stop was Columbus, where Marthe had tried to arrange a reading for him through his friend Dick Emerson who was teaching at Ohio State University, and who with Frederick Eckman was running Golden Goose Press. When he arrived, Emerson was away. (The next time Rexroth heard from him, he asked Rexroth to help him find Chinese characters in foundry type.) Two members of the Romance Languages Department came to his rescue, the distinguished critic Eliseo Vivas, and Claude Strauss. As editor of *Cronos*, Strauss knew Rexroth; in 1947, he had published his translation of an epigram by the last major Roman historian, Ammianus Marcellinus (c. 330–395) whose massive *Chronicle of Events* gives vivid pictures of the economic and social problems of the later Roman Empire.[7] Rexroth made the original typically his own.

> Dawn after dawn comes on the wine
> Spilt on books and music,
> And on the stained and tumbled pillows.

And then, while we are paying
No attention, a black man comes,
And roasts some of us, and fries
Some of us, and boils some of us,
And throws us all in the dump.[8]

Rexroth wanted Vivas and Strauss to arrange a reading at the university on his return trip, and he hoped that Vivas would advise Marthe about graduate studies outside California—Rexroth was considering the wisdom of starting afresh with her in a new setting. His love for California had diminished drastically. This change of mood was astonishing: so often his philosophical quests, his desire to articulate his love and passion for nature and his affection for his mother, Andrée, or Marie are inextricably associated with the California landscape. Exposed to alternate ecologies, he wrote to Marthe on the train ride from Columbus to Buffalo that "California always seemed ugly to me" and that it was going to be worse now."[9] The swings in Rexroth's mood were pronounced: one day he was yearning for the old familiar comforts of home, the next he wanted to chuck the whole show.

Buffalo was his next destination. He stayed near the town of Pavilion, halfway between Batavia and Geneseo, at the home of Charles Abbott, director of libraries at the University of Buffalo and founder of the Lockwood Library's Poetry Collection.[10] This time he wrote Marthe enthusiastically about northwestern New York State. It was like "Heaven, just what I've dreamed of for years & missed so much. I'll *never* be able to live in California again."[11] The Abbott farm, "an immense deteriorated estate,"[12] reminded him of the house Thomas and Sebastian inhabit in *The Homestead Called Damascus,* which he now felt inspired to revise (he would do so in Giant Forest seven years later). At the Abbott farm, the gardens were overgrown, the orchids ruined; inside, the walls were covered either by bookshelves or paintings of seascapes and family portraits. The cabinets were stocked with beautiful china and silver, and scattered throughout were an unusual supply of broken lamps. All this Rexroth described as the perfect setting of a "wholesome decadent life." Many nearby houses had been built in the Greek Revival style that had become popular in that part of New York just before the turn of the century, and Rexroth had his eye on one that was selling for $3,500—it had "fine Doric columns all around it" and just about nothing else, not even electricity. This was where he and Marthe should live. "I shall never be able to stand that sterile California landscape & those savage people again."[13] He suggested that Marthe apply for a post at some upstate New York State college. His well-attended reading at Buffalo pleased him, although he was perplexed by the lack of hospitality. The event had been scheduled during a class hour, and at its conclusion, faculty and students quickly moved on without introducing themselves.

He also drew a respectable crowd in Ithaca, despite a rainstorm on the night of his reading. He reported that he had attracted a larger group than Stephen Spender had, and that the Cornell faculty, including David Daiches whom Rexroth especially wanted to meet, were hospitable and appreciative of his performance. He stayed overnight at Telluride House, which he described inaccurately to Marthe as "the highbrow residence club and guest house for visiting notables."[14] This warm reception led him to suggest an alternate plan to Marthe, one that he thought would really "amount to something." He wanted her to ask for an interview with the chair of Cornell's Philosophy Department and with the specialist in Oriental History, to whom Kenneth had spoken. She would learn Chinese more quickly there than at Berkeley because, as he had discovered, the method of teaching foreign languages at Cornell was far more sophisticated.

Throughout the tour, Kenneth feared that Marie might act rashly and abandon the apartment, the dog, their belongings, and sell his books. He had received one "chilling" letter from her, in which she accused him of going from one sexual liaison to another as he traveled eastward. If he didn't hear from Marie again by the time he got to New York City (or "Babylon," as he called it), he wanted Marthe to go over to Eighth Avenue and find out what was happening.

The trip down to New York City was idyllic. As the train steamed south along the Hudson, Rexroth was so overwhelmed that the words to describe what he saw eluded him. The rich fall colors of the leaves, he told Marthe, exceeded his most vivid memories of that "passing light in which he had / Always lived."[15] Even though the railbed of the New York Central was shaky, as the train passed through Amsterdam, Schenectady, and Albany, Rexroth drew pictures of the old farmhouses he could see from his window, each of which he said was illuminated by radiance, as if painted by Pieter de Hooch.

Once he reached New York, his mood turned sour. Laughlin was in Norfolk, and there were many other people he couldn't locate because the welcome party he was expecting at the offices of New Directions did not materialize. Tentative readings at CCNY and the YMHA (which as far as he could tell was controlled by Delmore Schwartz) did not pan out. He did a reading at the Gotham Book Mart, but received no other offers, a depressing disaster for which he blamed Laughlin. However, when Laughlin invited him to spend a few days at Meadow House, his country home, Rexroth's spirits brightened and he promptly caught a bus to Kingston where Laughlin picked him up. En route to Norfolk, Rexroth wanted to see Holy Cross Monastery in West Park again. They stopped off and Rexroth prayed once more in the little chapel that had been the scene of "so many happy hours" twenty years earlier.[16] At Meadow House, he went on long solitary walks through the snowy woods or holed up in

Laughlin's magnificent library. At night, his sleep was interrupted by an Eastern screech owl that cried "like an abandoned woman."

Returning to the city, Rexroth took in the Empire State Building and lunched with Paul Goodman, who, he later decided, was "really a square." He visited poet and editor Paul Mattick, whom he admired tremendously for his book, *The Inevitability of Communism* (1935). Mattick had recently moved to New York City from Chicago with his wife Ilse. Rexroth had been corresponding with Mattick since 1941 over matters that largely concerned his magazine *New Essays* (formerly called *Living Marxism*). Like Rexroth, Mattick was involved with an anarcho-pacifist group similar to the Libertarian Circle in San Francisco. They maintained their friendship over the next several years.

Rexroth also saw Dwight Macdonald. For the past two years there had been correspondence between Nancy and Dwight Macdonald and the Rexroths—mostly about their concerted efforts to send food and vitamins abroad, about anarchist organizations, and about subscriptions to *Politics*, which Macdonald edited from an Astor Place office. The single most gratifying experience in New York, however, was meeting Selden Rodman.

Shortly before Rexroth left for the East Coast, Rodman had sent him his revised edition of a *New Anthology of Modern Poetry* (1946), which included four poems by Rexroth: "Now, on this day of the First Hundred Flowers," "Here I Sit Reading the Stoic," "Remember That Breakfast One November," and "Adonis in Summer." Rodman got more of a response from Rexroth than he bargained for.[17] Rexroth liked the book, especially the Haitian section, but felt obliged to argue over the inclusion of such poets as John Crowe Ransom ("a late anal arch deacon"), Archibald MacLeish, Theodore Roethke (although later on Rexroth would resign from the editorial board of *Black Mountain Review* in defense of Roethke), and Elizabeth Bishop, "another enemy of literature." Rexroth was baffled by Rodman's selection of E. B. White ("Has he got, locked up at the bank, an autographed picture of you fucking a sheep?"). He was glad Rodman had made room for Gertrude Stein, whose *Tender Buttons* had ignited his interest in Cubist poetry; for Robert Lowell, although as far as Rexroth was concerned, Lowell "had already pooped out"; and for his friend Richard Eberhart. But he wondered about the absence of many writers whom he deemed worthy: H. D., ardent Communist Lola Ridge, Kenneth Patchen ("Honey, is you a square?"), and his friend Muriel Rukeyser whom Rexroth would describe many years later as "one of the most important writers of the Left of her time."[18] He also thought Rodman should have included more folksongs, "white and negro—and some of Frances Densmore's translations of Indian songs." And there was not enough William Carlos William or Carl Sandburg.

He was puzzled that Rodman had omitted John Gould Fletcher. Rexroth's concern over the omission of Fletcher is understandable in light of the important influence that *Blue Symphony* and *Preludes and Symphonies* exerted on Rexroth's own early poetry.[19] A regular contributor to *Poetry* and *The Little Review*, Fletcher was included in Amy Lowell's *Tendencies in Modern American Poetry* (1917) as one of the leaders of the Imagist movement. Rexroth was reading Fletcher seriously between the mid-twenties to early thirties, around the same time that he was studying T. S. Eliot, Conrad Aiken, and the French Symbolists, and he was intrigued by Fletcher's attempt to apply techniques of modern music and painting to poetry, by his knowledge of Oriental systems of symbolism, and by his mysticism. Marie and Kenneth had met Fletcher and his wife Charlie May in San Francisco in 1945. After Fletcher returned to his home in Little Rock, Arkansas, a correspondence had sprung up between the two poets, who shared an enthusiasm for D. H. Lawrence, an appreciation for Asian aesthetics, and an aversion to Ezra Pound's *Cantos*. Fletcher had read *The Phoenix and the Tortoise* in the *New Directions Annual* for 1944 and praised it as a "more sensible version of Pound's meter in the *Cantos*."[20]

In addition to these judgments about who deserved a niche in Rodman's anthology, Rexroth described some characteristics of his own work. "My influences are Chinese, Latin, Greek, Burns, Blake, Landor, ballads and folksongs, late Jacobean and Caroline (the stuff Lawes put to music), lyrics *as sung*. I actually don't like *any* contemporary poetry that much. I much prefer 'The Playparty of Indiana' or 'Folksongs of Southern Michigan' to 'Four Quartets.' " He expressed great antipathy toward what he called the "reactionary generation"—i.e., T. S. Eliot, Allen Tate, Donald Davidson—although he was not able fully to exorcise Eliot's influence, particularly in his revision of *The Homestead Called Damascus*, which Philip Whelan described as "gooey Anglicism."[21] He especially objected to Eliot's emphasis on the detached, ironic voice, and told Rodman that his own verse was better when he dropped the so-called impersonality of modern verse and got into his "own bowels and into the physical intimacies of [his] relations with others and the world. Most poetry is best when it is about what the poet thinks of some pink beloved pussy and not at all about H[enry] A. Wallace and J. C. God."[22] Rexroth thanked Rodman for sending him the book, even though he discovered he could buy it at the local drugstore, a convenience which seemed to unsettle him, despite his rhetoric about making literature accessible to all.

Although Rodman disagreed with many of Rexroth's opinions, he respected their spirit of critical integrity.[23] Rodman remained one of the few people who made Rexroth feel welcome when he was in New York. They met for dinners, and Rodman introduced him to interesting people, including the writer Eve Merriam, who was impressed with the enormous enthusiasm Rexroth seemed to have for everything. Apparently the emotional crises brewing back home did not inhibit his behavior in New York. He flirted with the women he met, and "liked to pinch the girls a lot."

Despite their reservations about Ezra Pound, Rodman and Rexroth together visited him in Washington, D.C., where he was incarcerated at St. Elizabeth's Hospital. Pound carried on at great length about how Bernard Baruch was responsible for "the whole mess" the world was in. Rexroth was convinced that Pound had become as "nutty as fruitcake."[24] In Washington, Rexroth recorded his poetry for the Library of Congress, and stopped at the National Gallery, primarily to see Raphael's *Madonna,* one of his favorite paintings.

Rodman consistently supported Rexroth. When he later applied (unsuccessfully) for a third fellowship from the Guggenheim Foundation, Rodman wrote a glowing letter of recommendation placing Rexroth among the less than dozen living American poets whose work—including the translations—was most likely to survive. He called him an incurable Romantic and added:

The whole dull, grey, standardizing, conformist, amorphous weight of contemporary American civilization is pitted against the few remaining individualists in the Emerson-Thoreau tradition, of whom Rexroth is a splendid example. If his isolation makes him occasionally outrageous and shrill, that is understandable, and more power to him.[25]

Although Rexroth may have inwardly cringed at Rodman's linking him to the New England Brahmin tradition, he appreciated the praise.

Rexroth was glad to move on to his reading at Harvard, first stopping briefly in Northampton to revisit the scenes of his pastoral past with Leslie Smith. In Cambridge, he stayed with Dick and Betty Eberhart. He walked around the Yard, chatted with students and faculty about the latest changes that had taken place on the Harvard campus. He was impressed when he learned that Radcliffe students could now enroll in as many classes at Harvard as they wanted to, although there remained a basic inequity between the sexes given the fact that there were only two thousand women students, half the number of men students, "the same old story." He had contempt for the overly refined atmosphere permeating the campus, and was quite proud of the reaction his poetry created in the audience. "Honey," he boasted to Marthe with typical hyperbole, "you should a seen me reading to the Harvards. When I got through with all of them hot poems, there wan't a dry fly in the house."[26]

Cid Corman heard Rexroth tell this story several times during the course of an evening he spent at Rexroth's Scott Street apartment in 1961 or 1962. Unknown to Rexroth, Corman had been seated in the front row of the Poetry Room, one of fifty people in the audience, and had another version of the reading:

[It] was not very impressive, but the poetry was attractive—later I realized loosely Chinese in character. And very KR in thought / substance—some of his still best known poems. And rightly so. BUT he was SWEATING and obviously very nervous—said nothing, in effect, that wasn't on the page. There was no lion-bearding, unless it happened after the reading.[27]

Corman thought Rexroth was expecting a hostile reaction from the Harvard audience. To avoid embarrassing him or provoking an angry response, Corman never told Rexroth he had been there.

In 1948, Rexroth did not divulge such insecurities to Marthe. He wanted to be her guide and mentor. He sounded out the prospects for graduate work at Harvard, but he still felt that Cornell would be the best place for her. He knew that she was struggling to stay in school and to pay the rent. To lighten her load, she thought of dropping her time-consuming course in Chinese. Rexroth urged her to reconsider and apply for a Fulbright Grant to China. But Marthe did drop the Chinese, and Rexroth suspected that if they were going to have a life together, it would be in California, not elsewhere. He certainly could not support them by traveling the poetry circuit: he had not earned more than $25 a reading. Sometimes he received no fee at all.

At a Bard College poetry festival in Rhinebeck, New York, Rexroth mingled with the students, partying, singing, dancing, and drinking. He was amused by the sophisticated but sheltered women students who complained to him about the "old-fashioned" Reichian therapy their parents insisted they undergo. With the exception of William Carlos Williams, Ted and Renée Weiss, the Eberharts, and Jean Garrigue, who were also attending the conference, Rexroth did not care for the other participants. Robert Lowell especially irritated him when he expressed contempt for populist writers like William Vaughan Moody, Carl Sandburg, Lola Ridge, and James Oppenheim. These writers were not "the best" the United States had produced, but Rexroth believed that they deserved a secure place in American letters. Lowell, Rexroth suspected, thought that he had bad taste and that he supported these writers because they were Socialist.

Nor was Rexroth impressed with Bard College faculty, including those who orbited around Mary McCarthy. He thought they were snobs and aristocrats who liked to get "drunk as perch orchard swine."[28] Rexroth claims that he is the model for one of McCarthy's less attractive characters in *Groves of Academe*, Vincent Keogh, the "poet of the masses" who will read at Jocelyn College in Pennsylvania only if his bus fare is paid. Sporting a bright red shirt, the "proletarian poet" flirts with the female student who serves the punch and cookies after the reading, and makes the mistake of thinking that Jocelyn students and faculty alike are interested in hearing about his experiences as organizer for the John Reed Clubs, or seeing scars that proved he participated in the San Francisco Dock Strike. He is described as older than everyone thought, picturesque, "an historical remain, a chipped statue in a square."[29]

William Carlos Williams was puzzled by Rexroth's behavior at the Bard College festival. Although they corresponded sporadically, the two poets had not seen one another since their first meeting in 1931. Rexroth seemed better read, more erudite than Williams remembered, but as he told James Laughlin, Williams thought there was "a loose connection somewhere—a fear. He isn't willing to follow his classical hardness but wants to be a romantic in a bad sense, I think. His writing and himself are not the same person. . . . I can't quite make him out, hard and soft, I can't tell where it begins and ends."[30] Williams had correctly sensed that at Bard, Rexroth was fighting battles that had as much to do with his personal life as they did with literary life.

Rexroth came back to New York City only to catch his train to Chicago. But he realized, "in desperation," that he had not seen Kenneth and Miriam Patchen, who were living in Old Lyme, Connecticut. He took the Greyhound to Wilton, and from there Gertrude Huston, a friend of Laughlin's and art director for New Directions, drove him to Old Lyme. His evening with the Patchens was the high point of his trip. He decided that Patchen was the most "authentic" person in the East and the only poetic competition to Williams.[31] Exhilarated by that visit, Rexroth left the East Coast in an upbeat mood. The trip to this alien country had been worthwhile, if only to meet the Patchens.

Rexroth's first tour of the East hardly bolstered his reputation or his finances. And his hostile attitude toward the East Coast literary establishment hardened: Elizabeth Hardwick and Fred Dupee were "the wits and despots of intellectual life . . . people whose repartee would get them crushed like bugs in the Waterloo Iowa Country club any Saturday night."[32] With a Guggenheim to his credit, he thought his entry into New York's literary circles was guaranteed. Clearly, he had not been treated like a cultural hero as he was in San Francisco. On the other hand, he had enriched himself spiritually on several occasions—the personal meetings with Rodman and Patchen, for example—and he seemed unwilling to reveal the true depth of his disappointment.

The return trip was slow and uninspiring. He stopped again in Chicago where he stayed with his cousins, the Monahans, on Cole Street. His aunt Minnie sensed that all was not right between Kenneth and Marie, but kept silent. Still bitter that he had not been invited to read in his hometown, he got in touch with poet and critic Elder Olsen at the University of Chicago. Olsen informed Rexroth that there was nothing in Olsen's contract that required him to act as a booking agent for obscure California poets.[33] Brushing off the insult, Rexroth saw a few old friends, dined at the German restaurants that he liked so much, listened to jazz and watched the stripteasers in the North Clark Street piano bars and joints. Later, Robert Duncan would say that Rexroth roamed San Francisco's North Beach hoping to recapture his Chicago experience.[34]

During the second week in November Rexroth was in Missouri, where he gave a "short and snappy" lecture at the University of Kansas City. As at Buffalo, the hospitality was indifferent, and he had to book a room in a downtown hotel. He decided to amuse himself by wandering around the tenderloin district, but didn't enjoy the jaunt because "all the inhabitants look like Truman."[35] He was glad to get out of this "nasty and brutish" town and move on to Lawrence, Kansas. There he felt more among friends, and the reading was a success even though the terrain seemed so ugly that he thought it would be the perfect site for setting off all the stockpiled atom bombs. The puddle-jumper to Taos did little to change his opinion. It stopped twelve times before it crossed the border to New Mexico, moving along the edge of a blizzard the whole time. Rexroth alleviated the loneliness and misery by dashing off a sarcastic commentary to Marthe on "the life of Art." The prospect of meeting her in Los Angeles at the Hotel Barclay or, if his money did not hold out, in less glamorous digs in Stockton, kept up his morale.

Rexroth had great expectations of the avant-garde community in Taos, and in fact the reading / lecture there was well attended despite the 8-degree weather. Rexroth ended the performance with some of his translations from the Japanese. Despite Laughlin's initial lack of enthusiasm, Rexroth was devoting more time to Asian poets, and he was gratified by the enthusiastic reception they received in Taos. For a pony, he relied on a popular anthology of tankas, *Oqura Hyakunin Isshu (Single Poems of One Hundred Poets)*, edited by Fujiwara no Teika. Rexroth also owned a card game that was based on this book, and when he was alone would "translate" the cards with the help of dictionaries and numerous translations of the *Hyakunin Isshu* that appear in the bibliography for *One Hundred Poems from the Japanese* (New Directions, 1955).[36] As Sanehide Kodama has shown, some of the tankas from this volume are transformed into the end of "Part 3" of the long poem *The Phoenix and the Tortoise* (1940–44), beginning with these lines, the first three of which are based on a poem by Lady Akazome Emon:

> Would it have been better to have slept
> And dreamed, than to have watched night
> Pass and this slow moon sink? My wife sleeps
> And her dreams measure the hours
> As accurately as my
> Meditations in cold solitude.[37]

Poems by Emperor Sanjo, Ono non Komachi (a contemporary of Lady Murasaki and lady-in-waiting to the empress), and Fujiwara no Sadayori (Vice-Councilor in the middle of the eleventh century) are also incorporated.[38] Rexroth would go on to translate hundreds of poems from the Japanese, which were later collected into some of his most popular volumes.

Rexroth met the luminaries living in Taos at the time, especially the artist Andrew Dusberg, who appeared old and feeble. (Rexroth considered Dusberg, Marsden Hartley, and Arthur Dove the best artists of their generation.) He also saw Mabel Dodge Luhan and Spud Johnson.

Johnson had accompanied Lawrence and Witter Bynner on the journey later described in Bynner's *Journey with Genius* in 1951 and fired Rexroth's imagination with stories about the English novelist.

Rexroth's enthusiasm for readings was about exhausted. The rigors of the road had worn him down, and he was lonely. Before long, Taos lost its freshness and exoticism: it was now dominated by better-known artists and writers who had become local royalty and who had created a spirit antithetical to the ambiance that had attracted Lawrence. He complained to Marthe that most of his audience was filled with "squares"; he assumed he had given them a good time, but he wasn't sure if it mattered. He was miffed at having to pay for his hotel room since he had drawn an audience of about one hundred and fifty. Getting to Taos had cost him a few more dollars than he had been paid.

The last reading was in Salt Lake City. On the westbound train, he was kicked out of the club car because he lacked a Pullman ticket. Rather than dwell on this unpleasant experience, he was comforted by the beauty of the passing scene of snow falling over the Rockies and longtailed magpies "dipping through the storm." Whatever fantasies he entertained about living in rural New York vanished ("Mary McCarthy can have New York"). He spent less than a day in the Utah capital. He was eager to reach Los Angeles, where after some careful penny pinching, he and Marthe could spend the Thanksgiving weekend at the luxurious Hotel Barclay.

While Rexroth was on tour, gossip about his affair gained momentum. It unsettled Marthe, but Kenneth told her she had no choice but to "face the music." Neither of them, he believed, should feel defensive about their relationship. Their detractors were "objective paranoids," and it was best to ignore them, as Trotsky should have ignored his: "Trotsky might have died sooner, but he would have had a happier life."[39] Was he suggesting, after all, that his relationship with Marthe would be intense but shortlived? The ardent tone of his letters to her reveal that he was depending on her unqualified love for him, a kind of love that Marie, for the time being, had withdrawn. On the other hand, during his East Coast trip he was also writing to Marie in a mood reasonably free of acrimony and bitterness. In essence, Rexroth was seeking to salvage one relationship while securing another, without sacrificing either.

Via letters and postcards he had made the same proposals to Marie as he had to Marthe—for instance, starting a new life in upstate New York. Was he simply trying to hold on to her security, or was the emotional bond between them still strong? Marie took the proposal seriously and indicated that the idea of moving east appealed strongly to her. "I am sure I can find work in that vicinity and would be very happy to try it—so if your enthusiasm remains—why don't we do it? I am absolutely serious. You stay there and I will ship the stuff and follow. You see, you have completely transferred your excitement to me."[40] But whenever Kenneth did not hear from Marie, he became agitated and fearful. He would retaliate

by telling her how successful a reading had been, not as a point of information but to illustrate that strangers appreciated his worth even if his
wife did not. Marie did not tolerate such outbursts. How could he make
such degrading accusations, she asked, if he truly wanted to save their
marriage?

Throughout the trip, Marie's interest in Kenneth's career—and general well-being—barely wavered. Marie felt that she was perfectly within
her rights to act as the concerned wife. She was still taking care of his
professional correspondence, even though her administrative responsibilities at the Health Department were growing. She was not going out
much, but had started teaching her evening Red Cross class again. She
wrote chatty letters about visits from friends like Shirley and Frank Triest.

New members of the Libertarian Circle, Michael and Sally Grieg,
Audrey Goodfriend and David Koven, also called on her. They had been
connected to the New York anarchists who had in 1942 published *Resistance*, a "Bulletin of Free Inquiry." Recent refugees from New York City,
they looked forward to meeting Kenneth upon his return. They were
helping to revive the Libertarian Circle meetings: attendance had dropped
to such a low level that people like the poet James Harmon and his colleague Richard Brown thought the Steiner Street meeting room might
have to be given up. They blamed the group's disintegration on poor
management; the job of arranging for speakers and sending out notices
was not being handled efficiently. But the newcomers from New York
soon restored order with lectures on such topics as the anarchist's role in
the Russian Revolution. Marie assumed that Kenneth would be relieved
to hear this news, since he had wearied of feeling responsible for the
group's survival. These four people enormously impressed Marie, especially after they had located in five days a Potrero Hill house where they
could live communally, and landed jobs to pay the rent. But Rexroth's
relationship with these new people proved to be problematic. Soon after
returning to San Francisco in late November 1948, he visited the group
at their home, "the soul of comradely feelings," as Michael Grieg described him.[41] However, his true feelings were quite different: he described them as a bunch of New York Stalinists who presumed to rescue
the Libertarian Circle by running it as if it were a Communist cell.

Rexroth's accusations against them—denied by both Michael Grieg
and David Koven—came at a time when the act of juggling women was
unhinging his self-control and fogging his vision. Actually, Grieg and
Koven never dreamed of taking over the organization; indeed, such an
activity ran counter to their anarchist principles. Both men, however,
fifteen years younger than Rexroth, were his intellectual peers. They
were no less capable than he of articulating and acting upon their beliefs.
They were seeking camaraderie rather than guidance from Rexroth, but
Rexroth was more accustomed to seeing himself as a leader, a kind of
benevolent authority.[42] Moreover, for comfort and emotional support

while Kenneth was on tour, Marie had turned to Dave Koven, and Kenneth could not tolerate the liaison, no matter how responsible he had been in provoking Marie to look for love elsewhere.

Kenneth had landed in San Francisco at the end of a polio epidemic that had stretched Marie's workdays to the very limit. Whatever joy she may have anticipated in his return disappeared as soon as she understood that Kenneth was most definitely entranced by Marthe, and that he expected her to accept his variation on the ménage à trois. Her initial disappointment that Kenneth had spent the Thanksgiving weekend in Los Angeles turned to anger when she learned that he and Marthe had trysted there. Furthermore, she realized that with the money remaining from his Guggenheim Fellowship he was determined to go abroad, whether or not Marie accompanied him. Marthe was in the middle of her first year of graduate studies at Berkeley with neither the money nor the freedom for such a jaunt. On the verge of a great European adventure, Rexroth lacked a heart's companion to join him on his romantic journey.

Unexpectedly, Rexroth was forced to make his own arrangements for the tour. He refused to acknowledge that Marie had good reason to leave him on his own. He decided to make Marie the villain who had betrayed him, as a woman bent on revenge by having one affair after another. He was incapable of tolerating the idea that she might form a friendship with another man, and become irate whenever he suspected that she had. By now Rexroth had developed the reputation of being a womanizer, someone who would "fuck a snake if it would hold still for him."[43] But he would lambast Marie if she showed the slightest interest in another man.

Actually, he had never forgiven Marie for going to Washington, D.C., four and a half years earlier and signing up with the "enemy" to work in the European refugee camps. In his more paranoid moments, Rexroth accused her of turning their friends against him by portraying herself as a "poor martyred woman" who had to support her husband.[44] He developed a litany of complaints. From his perspective, she had done nothing to improve their marriage, while he had earned a Guggenheim so that she could quit work if she wanted to. He had even persuaded himself that he had applied for a Guggenheim primarily so that they could have a baby. Of course, this was hardly realistic: the Guggenheim Foundation would support them at most for two years, and Kenneth knew that Marie's doctor had told her there might be dangerous complications if she were to become pregnant. Moreover, Marie's enthusiasm for Kenneth's other passion—hiking in the mountains—had palled. And now she had summoned the nerve to quarrel with Kenneth about Marthe.

Caught up in her own dilemma, Marie maintained a calmness that kept her from descending into despair. She moved out of the Eighth Avenue apartment. Her resiliency of spirit made her very popular—she told Ivan Rainer, a Libertarian Circle regular, that her depressions never lasted much more than an hour or two[45]—but ironically this very quality

gave her an enormous capacity for tolerating Kenneth's monstrous mon-
keyshines. When she learned (from Marthe) that Kenneth feared she
might dispossess him from their apartment once he left for Europe, she
reassured him in writing that she would do no such thing. Hadn't she
kept everything waiting for him until his return from the East Coast?
Although she was feeling too estranged to live with Kenneth in February
1949, she sent him a check to pay for the month's rent, gas, electric, and
telephone bills. And she gave him $50 more for the following month's
rent, even though by then he would be gone. She was not acting on his
behalf entirely. She wanted to move back into the apartment after he left
in order to enjoy her books and paintings. She also wished to bring home
her friend Marny George, who was having major surgery and would need
nursing after she left the hospital.

By March 25, 1949, Rexroth had cleared out of San Francisco. He was
back on the train, heading for New York, once again writing Marthe long
letters about the ride, the passengers, and the views. He was less charmed
by this journey than the one of the previous fall; indeed, he kept mention-
ing that his favorite places were the Sierras or his Devil's Gulch shack, and
that travel was a form of exile. He dismissed New Mexico as a drab place
populated largely by illiterates and bigots, with "3 races to take out their
frustrations—Mexicans, Indians and Negroes."[46] He did not care for the
people who were sharing the train car with him, mostly Texan mothers
with children who constantly cried, a symptom of vitamin deficiency,
Rexroth believed. Nor was he thrilled with the Italian children on board
who were always scratching their heads, trying to get at the lice in their
hair, Rexroth assumed. Letting his imagination run riot, he got queasy at
the prospect of traveling third class on European trains, and promised to
get himself inoculated. For a libertarian who could survive long nights in
the winter mountains, Rexroth seemed to have lost his bearings.

Nevertheless, he knew this was his time for Europe. He was confident
that the Guggenheim would be renewed a second year (it was), and he
had high hopes that Marthe would join him once her semester ended. He
stopped off in Chicago to see Aunt Minnie and his childhood buddy
Harold Mann, and to visit the Church of the Ascension and the North
Clark Street bars. He became penurious, boasting to Marthe that he had
not eaten in the dining car once. Before boarding, he would buy milk,
fruit, and crackers, in order to save money for the pleasures of Europe.
It was a good omen, he thought, that at each end of his coach car hung
reproductions of Utrillo, a street in Montmartre and a scene from Aix-
en-Provence. In New York, he looked forward to seeing a new volume of
his poetry, published by Decker Press. A year earlier, Rexroth had turned
over to the Prairie City, Illinois, published the short poems he had written
in his late adolescence and early twenties, about the same time he had
written the first versions of *The Homestead Called Damascus* and "A Prolo-
gemena to a Theodicy." Several of these poems had appeared in little

magazines in the twenties and thirties. But Rexroth was not to see this volume until he reached Paris.[47]

He spent about a week in New York City searching for inexpensive passage across the Atlantic. He did not want to fly, and after a few days of anxious inquiry, he got a berth for $200 on a freighter, *The American Scout*, bound for Liverpool. He was exhausted by the New York pace of life and its emotional tension. He became alarmed when his heart began skipping beats, and one morning woke to discover a blood clot on his cornea. He went to a doctor, who reassured him that a rest more than anything else would help these unsettling symptoms disappear.

New York City seemed even worse than before, in part because he felt self-conscious around the very people whom he might have cultivated as friends, Michael Grieg and Dave Koven's acquaintances at *Resistance*. In fact, the editors of *Resistance* had published in May 1947 an abridged version of one of Rexroth's "Letters from America"—scurrilous public missives describing the American political scene—that had appeared in the British anarchist publication *Now*. Persuaded that the *Resistance* crowd knew that his marriage to Marie had disintegrated, he wrote Marthe that these people were "all agog about Marie's affair with Grieg,"[48] in his imagination the successor to Koven. Aware of Rexroth's misimpression, Michael Grieg suspected that Rexroth might have been trying to ease his bad conscience about going off to Europe without Marie, who had refused his offer, and about his affair with Marthe.[49] But Rexroth felt welcome at the Brooklyn apartment of Weldon Kees, a friend of Grieg's. One evening, to Kees's delight, Rexroth put on a "bang-up performance."[50] He was glad to see a fellow anti-Stalinist.

Rexroth also enjoyed visiting with Paul and Ilse Mattick, who more than any others in New York made him feel at home, something he attributed to the German ancestry they all shared. And on April 2, 1949, after exchanging letters for nearly two years, Rexroth finally met Denise Levertov and her husband Mitchell Goodman in their Barrow Street apartment. Rexroth had first written Levertov to ask if she would contribute to his anthology *The New British Poets*. She was not yet married, and he had also asked her to send him a photograph of herself. In return he sent one of himself in the Sierras, and urged her to come to San Francisco, where he was sure Marie would find her a job since she had training as a nurse. A correspondence between Levertov and Rexroth developed, largely one that expressed affection and deep appreciation of each other's work, although Rexroth reacted negatively to Levertov's announcement that she had married. When she met Goodman in 1947, he was still a graduate student at Harvard studying with the renowned scholar of American literature F. O. Matthiesson. Rexroth registered his disapproval of Goodman by calling Matthiesson a Stalinist, and he warned Levertov that she would soon become a typical faculty wife, either pushing a baby carriage or a shopping cart, all at the expense of poetic imagination.[51] But the few hours Levertov, Goodman, and Rexroth spent together passed pleasantly enough.

Before shipping out, Kenneth told Marthe repeatedly how much he wished she were with him, and how fortunate he was to be loved by her. He described the kind of life he wanted her to share with him:

What I want is a very simple life in a wooded and pretty wild part of the country where I can spend almost all my time as I do at the cabin. In the last year I have had so little peace aloneness and meditation and almost no writing. It is certainly not the kind of life I like.[52]

Young, idealistic, and completely in love, Marthe reassured him that even if he had no immediate prospects for leading that kind of life, he should not lose hope. "You don't need a new philosophy," she wrote to him while he was still in New York, "simply the situation in which to let the one you have work for you."[53] Without qualification, she sympathized with him over his disintegrated marriage and his inability to support himself as a writer. She encouraged Kenneth to confide in her, to air his fears and disappointments, adding that she loved and respected him most when he talked about his work, his worries, and what love meant to him. "The most I want Kenneth," she continued, "is to be as much to you as you want me to [be]—on your basis, on your decision as to when the energy I have should be spent and how the love I have for you should be used. . . . You know, of course, that no plans precede, no person or ambition counts at all before you." Indeed, Rexroth was fortunate to have such pure devotion, whether he deserved it or not.

Sixteen

AN AMERICAN IN EUROPE
1949

AFTER LOADING CARGO in Brooklyn, *The American Scout* left harbor on the evening of April 8, 1949. Rexroth had anticipated a long and lingering departure, but before he knew it, New York's skyline disappeared, the lighthouses vanished, and he was looking out at a dark blue sea on a bright clear night. He was pleased with the meals, and the accommodations were far more commodious than he had expected. He wrote Marthe daily, his letters serving as a journal of an uneventful sea voyage. Uninterested in his fellow passengers, he did little more than eat and sit on deck wrapped up in blankets, permitting himself to be lulled into a restful stupor.

Thoughts of Marie, however, continued to agitate him. He was convinced that he, not she, was truly the one who had been wronged because she had been dishonest with him. He explained to Marthe that he would have to overcome his pain and sorrow before he could be a suitable mate again.

When I think that not only was my poetry thrown away and my greatest poem only a delusion but that all those summers in the mountains that I thought were so wonderful were just a hoax, it is more than I can bear. . . . I can't comprehend anyone being given as much love as I have her and just throwing it all away and spitting in my face. . . . I am injured and crippled emotionally.[1]

How much of this line was calculated to arouse Marthe's sense of compassion? Was he aware that by articulating such thoughts to her—a young woman with romantic thoughts of her own—he might suck her deeper into this melodrama? He confessed to her that he still had an "irrational yearning" to be accepted by Marie.[2] Could Marthe help him break free?

Rexroth, who perhaps least of all understood how he had gotten himself into such an emotional morass, blamed Marie for all his suffering. A "liberated" woman herself, she should have more easily tolerated his lovers since he never intended to leave her for any of them. During the long hours at sea, he created for himself an evil icon of an imaginary Marie: she was a spiteful, oppressive surrogate mother, a witch who was determined to cripple him emotionally, ruin him artistically, and villify him to their friends. How dare she threaten to withdraw financial support if he did not reform? If she had her way, it would be impossible for him to write when his fellowship money ran out. By the end of the crossing, Rexroth felt justified in urging Marthe to apply for a Fulbright scholarship or a teaching position abroad so that she could think of joining him as soon as possible.

The day before Easter 1949, as the ship neared the Irish coast, Rexroth remembered his Chicago days when he had played the part of Cuchalain in *At the Hawk's Well*, and regretted that he was not stopping off to pay his respects to Yeats and Maud Gonne, and to a country where, as he recorded in *The Dragon and the Unicorn*, "All along the coast the bells [were] / Ringing in the birth of the / Irish Republic."[3] But in the planning stages of the trip, the prospect of a cold Irish spring had not been appealing.

Liverpool, the first port of call, turned out to offer more than he had expected, despite his first impression that it resembled "something in Dante, fried in rancid grease."[4] He visited the great cathedral and was surprised to find it "almost as handsome / As Sacré-Coeur."[5] He meandered through various neighborhoods including Chinatown, and ate lunch with "two Lancashire and two Welsh whores,"[6] one of whom was called Clarice. He followed her home for a night of sex. If he suffered any remorse over such behavior, he rationalized it away: a man like him in a strange environment could not survive without the warmth of human affection. The next morning he packed a rucksack, and after a tearful goodbye from Clarice, strode off vigorously toward Wales. Clarice would not be his only bedmate during his European tour.

Rexroth developed into a traveler who richly appreciates the significance of the sites he has traveled far to see. Although he knew that the church at Chester was neither the biggest nor the best, he was overcome with emotion when he realized that he was admiring a bona fide eleventh-century arch. He cried with happiness and excitement at the sight of the "spectacular N Wales coast and the beautiful Vale of Conway,"[7] at the newborn lambs, ruined castles, "all sorts of wonderful birds and beautiful flowers everywhere." When he grew tired of walking and could not hitch a ride, he would board the local bus, "the only bargain in Britain." The cost of clothing was prohibitive, and with all his walking and hiking he had started to wear through his socks. He instructed Marthe to send him special hose—size twelve, 120 fibers, orthochromatic. To avoid paying tax and duty, she was to wash them and send them in a box marked "used clothing."

Eating mostly in pubs where the people were warm and friendly, Rexroth sensed that he was perceived as a representative of all America, especially when he was asked about American foreign policy.

> Not having been in the habit
> Of using "we" when I mean the
> State Department, it takes time
> To explain that America
> Is several different persons.[8]

But he got along well with the Welsh: "Never / Will I find better people / Or a more beautiful country,"[9] and when he left, he took with him a feeling that the world could be deeply harmonious. Rexroth maintained this peaceful state of mind as he strode "through the entranced landscape" of Shropshire, whose beauty and charm he had mistakenly assumed A. E. Housman had exaggerated. It was "all just as he says." Rexroth walked and hitched his way to Tintern Abbey, Bath, and Wells. One night he stayed at St. Briavel's Hostel, a ruined castle high above the Wye, its slopes covered with blooming apple trees.

Awaiting his arrival in Cornwall was the family of the writer and critic Derek Savage, whose poems Rexroth had included in *The New British Poets*. He had initiated a correspondence in 1945 to clear up a possible misunderstanding with Savage. Rexroth had disagreed over an article that Savage had written about D. H. Lawrence in the *Briarcliff Quarterly* and had addressed a letter to the editor. To Rexroth's chagrin, the editor showed a personal part of the letter, not meant for publication, to Savage, and Rexroth wanted to apologize. Savage had not taken the slightest affront, and the two discovered that although they disagreed about Lawrence, and more fundamentally about their practice of Christianity, they were both anti-establishment dissidents who shared a firm commitment to pacifism. They also had a friend in common, George Woodcock, who was still editing the anarchist literary review *Now*.

Their differences about Lawrence cast an ironic light on the emotional turmoil that had disrupted Rexroth's life with Marie. Savage had taken issue with Lawrence because he feared that any practical realization of Lawrence's theories could be destructive to human dignity. In a June 11, 1947, letter to Rexroth, Savage had asserted that like Wilhelm Reich, the renegade psychoanalyst, Lawrence was carrying Freudianism to its logical (and comical) extreme:

This is where I can't agree with Lawrence and I suppose you—the glorification of sexuality and the dispersion of "libido" (if you like) which it involves. So that when you say you'd like to have children by half a dozen women, I am quite unresponsive. For to me, that means you would like to have half a dozen wives, which I interpret as being equivalent to half a dozen selves, but if you are half a dozen selves, your self is disintegrated.[10]

Unaware of Rexroth's private affairs, Savage nonetheless verbalized Rexroth's dilemma with eerie precision. Rexroth's vision of what his creative energy could achieve stood at terrible odds with the realities of his life. And in his lonelier moments Rexroth had admitted as much. In "The

Advantages of Learning," he presents himself as a man with few friends, going nowhere, a "fugitive from some just doom."[11] He imagines himself writing poems late at night, in a dirty old robe, trying to keep warm by drinking hot white wine. While he thinks of the next line to write, he is drawing "nudes on the crooked margins, / Copulating with sixteen year old / Nymphomaniacs of [his] imagination."

Constance and Derek Savage were living with their four youngsters in a six-room cottage near an old water mill on what had once been a country squire's estate. About a mile from the sea and a half-mile from the road, it lacked any sort of convenience. During the summer it was perfect, but during the winter the Savages had to haul supplies through fields knee-deep in mud. Rexroth had arrived at the end of April, looking "very scout-like, in hiker's gear with a rucksack."[12] His first view of Mevagissey was depressing. As Derek Savage observed, "he had leaned over a wall look at the harbour: the tide was out, so all he saw was fishing boats apparently stranded in a sea of mud, and at the same time he was approached by an unkempt, ginger-haired female village idiot known locally as 'Mevva' who had an illegitimate son, reputedly the issue of incest."[13] Although Rexroth thought the climate of Cornwall was dreadful, similar to Big Sur in the winter, he spent (as he notes in *The Dragon and the Unicorn*) "three pleasant days of hospitality / And passionate talk" about literature and politics with the Savages.

When Rexroth realized how little money the Savages had, he asked Marthe to send them packages of tinned meat, "good" dehydrated vegetables, dried fruit, tinned butter, Crisco, and all the clothes she could gather, including her own. Rexroth's admiration for the Savages grew as they became better acquainted. In Derek Savage, he discovered an artist whose intelligence he admired—no small matter for Rexroth—and whose opinions he respected even when he disagreed with them. And he summed up Constance Savage as "an educated Kate Blake." The analogy was not a casual one. When she married Blake, Catherine Sophia Boucher was illiterate. But he taught her to read and to share his passion for Milton's *Paradise Lost*, and she eventually helped him print and color the books of his poems that he would later engrave himself. This was the kind of woman Rexroth wanted: a sensitive, perceptive, intelligent woman, eager to devote herself entirely to his writing aspirations. In London one month later, on May 23, he sent Marie a postcard of Blake's *Beatrice Addressing Dante*, one of the drawings on view at the Tate Gallery. When Rexroth saw Blake's deathbed drawing of his wife, he nearly collapsed from the twist he felt in his heart. He stumbled, "leaned against the wall in agony," he wrote to Marie. And he added:

I always thought of that deathbed drawing as the very symbol of my life—a perfect illustration for the Phoenix and the Tortoise. Now I sit on the Thames Embankment amongst this alien, vindictive and dishonest people and try to think of some reason for continuing living. What have you done to us? Does even the tiniest spasm of remorse ever move you?

Marie responded to Kenneth's charge with clearcut anger, impatience, and rejection. She was unwilling to enter his fantasy: she was not Kate Blake and he had better not think that he was William Blake amid the alien English. She no longer wanted to receive his vituperous letters about her alleged intimacy with "[Michael] Grieg, Jews and fairies," and promised to return them to him unopened.

One of the most important things that Blake said, I guess, is that "all that lives is holy." I love you and I always will but I do not want to live with you again. I do not think that black eyes [i.e., shiners] and a "menage a trois" are things that I ever want in my life again. They destroy the holiness of what was and is between us.[14]

Marie had reached a point of no return: she could not tolerate or participate in the delusions Kenneth needed to maintain about himself. But she could not renounce him completely. Marie's complaints about him—his tendency to overrespond to criticism, his refusal to face facts, his capacity to enlarge the most insignificant event into a major catastrophe—sounded exactly like Kenneth's against her. They were deadlocked.

In honor of Thomas Hardy, Rexroth had hiked across Salisbury Plain to Stonehenge, where "the larks [were] throwing / Themselves frantic into heaven."[15] After Cornwall and rural Hampshire, London was quite a contrast. At first, he thought it was the most beautiful city he had ever seen. He would take his tea in Hyde Park surrounded by mothers, babies, students, and retired India Army colonels. He was unimpressed, however, with the British Museum, because he only saw Chinese prints, not paintings, and the original paintings he did see were, in his opinion, dirty and improperly displayed. He attended High Mass at All Saints, a famous Anglo-Catholic church. He was amused to discover that the preacher was an American who spoke "with a phony accent and lots of polysyllables."[16] But the pigeons in the belltower were genuine English: when the bells rang at the Elevation, they all cooed together.

Rexroth hoped to meet other poets whom he had chosen for *The New British Poets,* and had brought a good suit along for such occasions when hitchhiking gear would be inappropriate. He made a vivid impression on Kathleen Raine, who, half expecting a raunchy Bohemian, was surprised by the correct and dignified visitor who called on her at her home in Chelsea.[17] Raine sensed within him a "burning presence" that sprang from two sources: a passion for his work and a personal unhappiness. She told him that she admired the strength and discipline of his poetry, and his way of presenting human beings in a spiritual light. She also thought that his poetry was American in the best sense, capable of carrying its culture across the Atlantic.

Although he had known her only through her poems, he felt certain of her dedication to poetry and to peace. His meeting with this extraor-

dinarily handsome and compassionate woman confirmed his expectations, as revealed in the last three stanzas of "Stone and Flower," dedicated
to her and first published in 1949 in *Approach*, 5.

> Out of the permanent
> Wreckage of a world where
> Wars are secret or not
> But never, never, stop.
>
> Your poems give meaning to
> The public tragedy
> To which they lend themselves
> On their own terms, as when
>
> One sharp, six pointed star
> Of snow falls from the black
> Sky to the black water
> And turns it all to ice.[18]

Usually Rexroth did not write in quatrains, but here they emphasize the
stability and security of his appreciation for Raine, and provide a neat
frame for the sparkling image that her craft and commitment represented to him. Of all the poets Rexroth met during his European tour, he
liked her best and considered her to be among the most talented.

No one else in London made such an impression. One evening, Raine
and Rexroth went to supper with a friend of Raine's and another contributor to *The New British Poets*, David Gascoyne. Although Rexroth regarded "Gravel Pit Field" as one of the finest mystical poems he had ever
read, Gascoyne in the flesh looked paranoid to him. Another disappointment was Alex Comfort, whom he described as boring.[19] He finally succeeded in meeting Brenda Chamberlain, a young Welsh poet whose work
he had said in his Introduction to *The New British Poets* "presage[d] the
growth of a new post-romantic style." In person, she struck him as "schiz-
oid."

Rexroth spent a weekend with Charles Wrey Gardiner, who ran Grey
Walls Press and had published several of Rexroth's poems in his little
magazine *Poetry Quarterly*, including a section of *The Signature of All Things*,
"As the sun comes in the window,"[20] and "I have closed my ears, I refuse,"
a poem that sounds as though it was written in the aftermath of an argument with Marie.

> I am not going to have been
> Where you say I was. You fancy
> You can force me to have lived
> The past you want. You are wrong.[21]

"The tops of the higher peaks" also appeared in this magazine, revealing
many of Rexroth's current concerns and the connections between them:
his deep appreciation of nature, his exaltation of human sexuality, his

belief that the aesthetic sensibility can provide a kind of salvation. The poem describes the power that two kinds of blue flowers held over D. H. Lawrence and Bartolomeo Vanzetti.

> Lawrence was lit into death
> By the blue gentians of Kore.
> Vanzetti had in his cell
> A bowl of tall blue flowers.
> From a New England garden.
> I hope that when I need it
> My mind can always call back
> This flower to its hidden senses.[22]

"This flower" is the blue *Polemonium confertum eximium,* which grows only in the high mountains of the Sierra Nevada, one of Rexroth's favorite habitats, and for him, a temple of nature. Like many of the poets whom he included in his British anthology, Rexroth here struck the pose of a twentieth-century Romantic poet, determined to endow human existence with meaning, and certain that the effort to do so would sorely test his faith and physical stamina.

In addition to editing *Poetry Quarterly* (with Comfort's assistance), Charles Wrey Gardiner published a literary yearbook, *New Road,* and had written *The Dark Thorn,* a book based on his journal of one year which, according to Rexroth, successfully captured the world of British contemporary poetry with its "erotic difficulties, buzz bombs and passionate conversation in intellectual pubs."[23] Rexroth had looked forward to meeting this contributor who, he suspected, endured a kind of isolation from his peers similar to his own. Because Gardiner had lent him a sympathetic ear during the early stages of their correspondence, Rexroth wanted this fellow poet to know that he had "no personal axe to grind" and that he was "totally independent of USA literary politics."[24]

He had already aired his views of the current literary scene to Gardiner, doubtless hoping they would influence his decisions about which writers he should publish. He amicably berated Gardiner—as he had Selden Rodman—for ignoring poets like Charles Henri Ford, Carl Rakosi, Louis Zukofsky, and Muriel Rukeyser, whose friendship he still valued despite her associations with "Stalinist" or "Stalinoid" poets: "Rukeyser's politics are a little misty . . . she runs with the Gipsy Rose Lee crowd—but she is one of the USA's foremost poets."[25] And on more than one occasion he insisted that Edouard Roditi should be approached. They both agreed that Denise Levertov was immensely talented—Gardiner had been the first person to publish her in England, Rexroth the first in the United States. (Before meeting her, Rexroth confessed to Gardiner that he was sure he could fall "madly in love with her.")[26] Rexroth also urged Gardiner to publish a selected William Carlos Williams. During this first meeting with Gardiner, Rexroth found his wife Cynthia "spookier than his daughter."[27] But his impressions of the Gardiners would improve as he became more intimate with them.

With a few significant exceptions, London social life was disappointing. However, he did enjoy dinner at the Reform Club with Herbert Read (who happened to be a favorite of Marie's). Read's poetry was also in the anthology, and Rexroth had recently written the Introduction to the New Directions 1948 edition of *The Green Child*. The meal itself did not excite Rexroth as much as the heady conversation over shared political perspectives.[28] Read warned Rexroth that the entire structure of intellectual life was breaking down in London and Paris. Another day Rexroth ran into Frank Triest's former wife Grace, who proposed dinner together. He appreciated her company and her Indian lover's, but not the restaurant fare, which he likened to "migraine or epilepsy or angina pectoris."[29] But his worst experience would occur at a political meeting of anarchists, the Freedom Group, to which he had been invited.

After an exhausting hunt, Rexroth located the address where the meeting was to convene, a basement room large enough to hold the fourteen people who showed up. He was bored by the speaker, who sounded like a "convalescent Trotskyite . . . an inhabitant of Sierra Leone who had stumbled on a file of *L'Esprit*, *The Partisan Review* and Sartre's thing while out hunting hippopotami."[30] As a guest, Rexroth assumed that his participation would be welcome, but he was ignored. During the reception that followed, he tried to introduce himself to "a youngish school teacher or social worker looking woman," but she turned her back to him. He fared no better with a "gent in reddish tweeds with a public school accent." He finally maneuvered a couple into a corner and vented his frustration on them. "You people are not anarchists," he told them, "you are just exceptionally English. You are even more brutally rude than the rest of your countrymen."[31] He later complained about the London anarchists to both Herbert Read and George Woodcock, and they responded sympathetically. From Vancouver, B.C., Woodcock reported how glad he had been as a rogue male to get out of London and for that matter England altogether.[32] Read commiserated with him but said that he hadn't yet reached the level of despair that so depressed Rexroth. To prove his point, he gave Rexroth an anarchist pamphlet he had just written, and suggested that one day they could find a more positive name for their school of thought. Rexroth consoled himself by strolling in Kew Gardens, but the sight of a "poor smoke begrimed and stunted pine" made him homesick for the trees and foliage of the High Sierras.

The energy which Rexroth expended in describing to Marthe his latest run-in with the British reduced his feelings of rancor. He almost reveled in this newfound opportunity to criticize and to judge other people after enduring Marie's harsh criticism. And since Marie was half-English herself, he discovered an added pleasure in his righteous stance. He told Marthe that Londoners were consumed with "jealousy, cowardice, and the desire to strike first and then run, or at least the desire to have put you in your place. This is a city of 15,000,000 Maries." In another letter, he added, "the sooner this city is reduced to a puddle of radioactive mud, the better for all concerned." The city was rotten, filled with bigots who looked down on the Welsh and the Scots as "subjects," who were "much nicer than the English—emotionally honest, courteous, and creative—all things the English are not."[33] In a compassionate mood, he wondered if Marie, given the nature of the English, didn't deserve sympathy and respect for overcoming her birthright.

Even the local artists and literati were uncivilized. He went to a pub with the Ceylonese poet Tambimuttu, who had been living in England since 1937 and had recently (and in Rexroth's opinion ignobly) been eased out of editing the magazine which he had founded, *Poetry London*. His poetry had not appeared in *The New British Poets* because he had not responded in time to Rexroth's invitation.[34] They sat down with two women. One left them to get some cigarettes. She walked by a table where George Barker was sitting with a painter who offered to sell her ten cigarettes if she should persuade her "rich American friend Rexroth" to treat them all to a nightclub. Spitting mad, she came back to the table and relayed the proposition to the men. Rexroth responded by asking them to step outside. Either cowed or amused by Rexroth's volatile reaction, they explained that they had no money for nightclubs because they had such high taxes to pay. Rexroth was certain that neither of them had ever paid a penny in tax, and that they could afford to go to any nightclub they chose where they could buy all the cigarettes they wanted.

Something about this raw experience in the pub revived a vituperative streak in Rexroth that belied his libertarian principles. He warned Marthe to avoid the kind of people that Marie was cultivating: "*Never* fall into the hands of Jews and Fairies. No fairy will associate with a woman and no Jew with a schiksa unless he can destroy her integrity and make a mock[ery] of her womanhood."[35] Before Rexroth left for Europe, he had gotten into a number of "anti-homosexual scenes"—once singling out a young man named Dunne and ordering the "faggot" out of his presence. Poet Robin Blaser regarded such episodes as a "kind of hysteria and dramatization that made the distance [between them] grow."[36] Several passages in *The Dragon and the Unicorn* also reveal that however enlightened Rexroth was on questions of human liberty, he was capable of expressing homophobic, anti-Semitic, and sexist sentiments, often as a medium for ventilating his hostility toward imaginary or real enemies of Christian heterosexual poets like himself. Regardless of how his readers felt about the politics of the Middle East or how much they admired the philosopher Martin Buber, they must have been offended by the tone of Rexroth's description of fund-raising drives for the recently born State of Israel, "the / Last bourgeois nationalism."

But today ex-radical
And liberal Jews call Buber
A crypto-Christian and traitor
To his blood, and go to parties
At the homes of rich and silly
Women, and hop around by
Candle light, making noises
Like Fanny Brice, while a
Grimjawed, double-breasted
Bureaucrat gathers in the take.[37]

Rexroth repeatedly urged Marthe to get her passport so that they could meet in Europe. She was not responding enthusiastically, but once she told him that her father's health had taken a bad turn, he turned off the pressure temporarily. Other things needed to be discussed anyway, especially what he should do upon his return to the United States. Before leaving San Francisco he had applied for a teaching position with Black Mountain College, and he had received formal notice that he had been appointed to teach creative writing and criticism for one year, from September 1949 to August 31, 1950. The college, established in 1933 in the North Carolina mountains, should have been a perfect place for Rexroth. It was not dependent on an endowment or group of trustees whose opinions and attitudes would have to be taken into account. The Board of Fellows, the school's governing body, was completely indifferent to his lack of formal academic credentials. The faculty itself—which among other remarkable artists and writers included Charles Olson, Buckminster Fuller, Merce Cunningham, and Willem de Kooning—owned the college as a non-stock corporation. Both faculty and students sat on the board. And they maintained the campus and a farm that helped keep the school self-sufficient. Here was an educational institution built on principles of communal learning acceptable to Rexroth. But he did not want to be at Black Mountain alone, and asked Marthe to arrange an itinerary for herself that would get them both back into the United States before the Fall semester started.

But nothing about Kenneth's future would be settled for some months, no matter what requests he made of Marthe. Despite the bitterness between them, Marie remained inexplicably sympathetic to Kenneth and his complaints about the English. She reported that Morris Graves, recently back from England, had suffered there as well. Graves was "safe" now, back home in Seattle. She tried to ease Kenneth's bouts of loneliness by assuring him that his friends like Eli and Beryl Jacobson, who had last seen him at a successful reading in San Diego, missed him. On the other hand, Marie was not urging him to come home. She had gotten used to living peacefully by herself, and for the time being did not want to resume their conjugal life. She had disapproved of Kenneth's decision to depart for Europe when he did, but as long as he was there he ought to derive whatever benefit he could. In response, Kenneth wrote a letter to her before leaving London for Paris, intended to clarify the issues that he wanted settled between them.

Specifically, he spelled out a seven-point program that Marie was to follow if they were going to live together again.[38] First, she must be willing to have a child. Second, she should resume psychological counseling, preferably from their friend Joseph Wheelwright. Third, they should sleep together in the same bed through the entire night (for the past year, Marie had been in the habit of sleeping most of the night by herself). Fourth, Marie would accompany him to the mountains regularly, something she had been decreasingly inclined to do. Fifth, she should be more affectionate and work at removing her sexual inhibitions. Sixth, she should stop exploiting him socially; that is, she should stop presenting herself to their friends as a self-sacrificing wife, the martyred spouse who worked so hard to support her husband. And finally, she had to control her jealous reactions to Kenneth's friendships, and stop "smashing" his love relationships with other women. She was too possessive. He demanded that she address herself to each of these points before they discussed any kind of reconciliation. Rexroth's motives for making such demands were complicated. On one hand, he seemed desperate to save his marriage but incapable of acknowledging that he bore any responsibility for its failure. He knew what had gone wrong in the relationship, but insisted that Marie had to make the necessary adjustments. On the other hand, he may have been trying to devise a clever ruse to end the relationship without appearing to be the instigator.

At the very end of May, with his manifesto in Marie's hands, and his various suggestions for crossing the Atlantic in Marthe's ("the ideal situation would be for you to show up at a French port with bicycle—3 speeds if possible")[39], Rexroth and the Gardiners crossed the Channel to Le Touquet, the fashionable seaside resort in Pas-de-Calais. He was not sorry to say goodbye to England. Cynthia and Charles Wrey Gardiner had arranged to drive a "cute little car about the size of an MG" to Rome, where Martha Gellhorn, a friend of Caresse Crosby's and a journalist who became the third wife of Ernest Hemingway, would be waiting for it. Her boyfriend had paid for the car ferry tickets and insurance so that Rexroth and the Gardiners only had to pay for gas. As soon as Rexroth set foot on French soil he sent Marthe a postcard, followed by letters marveling that his stomach problems had temporarily disappeared although he was still counting on her bringing to him a good supply of Tums.

En route to Paris, Rexroth and the Gardiners stopped in Amiens. The town had been flattened by the war, but the cathedral remained intact. He was overwhelmed by the sight of Le Beau Dieu, the statue of Christ on the central portal of the west facade. Rexroth believed it was the greatest piece of sculpture ever conceived by Western man, perfectly positioned so that it looked out "over the ruins and the sunset." They then moved on to visit the cathedral at Beauvais. After locating the only decent hotel in town, they spent the evening eating and drinking at its bar and restaurant. The townspeople assumed that Rexroth like the Gardiners was English, so all three were treated cordially. The French, he learned, felt sorry for the English, who had suffered such severe food shortages during and after the war.

Imagine Frenchmen buying drinks—and even offering to provide me with a poule—the bar-maid Simone, who was quite a dish. . . . Altogether it was quite an orgy and a very fitting welcome to France. Charles dropped ten years in a night. Cynthia, of course had never seen anything like it.[40]

When he got to Paris, however, Rexroth's mood changed from general unqualified bonhomie to self-pity: Marie's response to his program for reconciliation had arrived.[41] After much thought, she had decided to take Rexroth's missive "at face value" and she addressed it point by point. As for having children, Marie confined her remarks to the events that had shaped their lives over the past year or two. Kenneth's love affairs had made her feel unwanted and unloved, precisely the wrong mood for a woman who is thinking of conceiving a child. At the age of forty-three, Marie felt it was "too late physically and too late emotionally" for motherhood. She did not say that she had never wanted a child, but that she no longer desired one at this time. She said that she would not object if Kenneth conceived a child with someone else.

Psychiatric help was another matter. Marie had already "tried several varieties" in the past two years, but not Joe Wheelwright's kind because he had refused to see her as his patient. Their friend Leslie Farber had also declined. But no matter whose advice she sought, she invariably heard the same reaction. None of her therapists could tolerate her reason for seeking their counsel—that she needed help in order to try to live with Kenneth again. They thought the relationship was doomed to failure. Moreover, Marie wanted from them something they insisted that she figure out for herself: confirmation that she was not solely to blame for the disintegration of the marriage.

She agreed that their sexual life had deteriorated. But she had not been able to spend entire nights in the same bed with Kenneth because she had felt "deep antagonism in [his] very flesh." She objected to Kenneth's demand that she decide "by mail" whether or not to sleep with him. And here Marie dished out to Kenneth some of his own philosophy about sexual freedom. "Can't it possibly be," she asked, "that we give each other enough freedom to make such a choice daily?" As for being more affectionate and less inhibited, she was certainly willing to try both. But she asked him in rather demure language if he could help her out. Wasn't he at all responsible for her lack of enthusiasm?

Marie wanted Kenneth to realize that she could not devote every moment of her life to furthering his welfare, that there had to be more reciprocity between them if their relationship was to be redeemed. She loved hiking and swimming no less than he did, and reminded him that during the summer of 1948 she had been happy to be in the Sierras. "I shouldn't have to tell you," she wrote, "[that] mountaineering with you has been the *best* part of my life. Nothing else in experience can come near it." But he had no right to be affronted if her level of energy did not match his, especially when she was holding down a job that fatigued her. And it was wrong of Kenneth to infer that she thought he was lazy when in fact she explained by the hour to her friends and therapists that she thought Kenneth worked much harder than she did. But he had to acknowledge that writing did not take the same physical toll as the routine of a regular job.[42] Competitive or not, she clearly preferred home to hiking.

More importantly, Marie was afraid to talk to him candidly because he so readily misunderstood her, lost his self-control, and subjected her to verbal and physical abuse. Yes, she admitted, she had discussed their differences with friends, not to paint a picture of the self-sacrificing wife and the brutish husband, but because she was desperately lonely. She would consent to rejoin Kenneth only in an atmosphere that allowed them to articulate their feelings to one another, face to face. She simply could not accept the entire burden of rebuilding their relationship. Throughout Kenneth's stay abroad, they corresponded about this list of conditions. Kenneth threatened never to return if she didn't agree unequivocally to all his conditions. On one occasion Marie wrote that if she did not love and respect him, she would have told him long ago to "do something quite vulgar with them (such as sticking them up you know where)"—precisely what her present therapist was advising her to do.

Kenneth was blinded by the double standard of his perspective: it was all right for him to air his problems to Laughlin, Selden Rodman, Marthe, even Pru, but he expected Marie to hold her tongue. He insisted on candor about his affairs, which he expected Marie to tolerate, while she was supposed to remain faithful. In his eyes, Marie would "not agree to the simplest things to try to save all those years of love, devotion, toil and tears."[43] The day before he had left London, he wrote Selden Rodman that Marie had become "dishonest emotionally," probably because she had not had any children. He said "the real reason" he had gone abroad was to give Marie a chance to straighten herself out: "But from what I hear she is just using the chance to sleep around. Maybe *that* is the best cure."[44]

Meanwhile, he was courting Marthe, and telling her how crucial it was for their future that she join him in Europe as soon as possible. When he learned that her father was not seriously ill, his letters grew increasingly strident as no response from her arrived. He deeply missed the steady companionship of a lover, and from the Dome Terrasse wrote Marthe that she absolutely must come over without delay. He had found a hotel for them in Montparnasse—Hôtel de Chevreuse—that cost less than a dollar a night. What was she waiting for?

Yet Rexroth did not linger in Paris. With the Gardiners he headed south to Albi, the birthplace of Henri de Toulouse-Lautrec and a town Rexroth had been longing to visit so that he could see the Gothic Sainte-Cécile Cathedral, constructed in brick without flying buttresses. The austere cliffs of its outer walls gave it a glowering, fortresslike aspect. Rexroth preferred to describe it as a "vast red dirigible rising into heaven," and like Ezra Pound was enormously impressed by it. For Rexroth, it was close to heaven.

The party toured the Roman ruins of Nîmes, Tarascon, Arles, and Aix, where Rexroth was touched by the sight of young lovers strolling beneath the plane trees near the beautiful fountains on the Cours Mirabeau. His favorite oasis was the Café Mistral, where he could peacefully savor a glass of Châteauneuf du Pape as he watched the passing scene. Provence particularly pleased him, with its red tile roofs clustered around churches and castles on every hill, and its long, desolate limestone uplands that reminded him of Wyoming. Every so often they would drive by a young girl knitting beside a herd of sheep. Everything was wonderful, and for the moment, beyond description or speech.

By the time they reached the Riviera, the Gardiners had become bored with French cuisine, and Rexroth wrote Marthe that they were "always hunting tea and chips and British food." Rexroth himself complained about spending 1,000 francs for "a *very* bad bouillabaise" in a restaurant near Cannes. Nice reminded him of Atlantic City. With summer on its way, noisy Americans were milling all about, and the group was eager to get to Italy. They spent their first night in Diano Marina, about halfway between Monaco and Genoa, in a hotel near a bridge at the end of town. After the French Riviera, the peace was profound. They walked on the broad esplanade along the sea and under arches through the narrow streets paved with flat stones like the ones in Pompeii, "fireflies slashing low above the pavement and circulating amongst them beautiful young girls and handsome boys."[45] Genoa was awful, "like the Italian slums of Detroit." They stopped briefly in Florence at the Pensione Balestra on the Lung'Arno, where both D. H. Lawrence and John Ferren had once stayed. The Gardiners were delighted by the tea and marmalade at breakfast. Rexroth drove by himself up to Fiesole, where in honor of Lawrence he visited the Etruscan Museum and walked along the Arno in the moonlight thinking of Marthe. They quickened the pace of their journey to Rome, which they expected to be the highlight of their odyssey. Rexroth planned on staying with Caresse Crosby, who had bought a castle in nearby Roccasinebalda, and who would be there waiting for him.

Rexroth described Caresse Crosby to Marthe as "an old, old lady," although at fifty-seven she was only thirteen years Rexroth's senior. After

Harry Crosby's death, Caresse had continued the work of Black Sun Press in Paris until the mid-thirties and had also created a paperback publishing company, Crosby Continental Editions, which printed works by Ernest Hemingway, William Faulkner, and Dorothy Parker. During World War II she had moved to Washington, D.C., where she opened an art gallery and resumed her publishing activities. With Selden Rodman acting as intermediary, Crosby had published Rexroth's dance play *Iphigenia at Aulis* in her slick mixed-media magazine *Portfolio* (Spring 1946). Crosby never bothered to send Rexroth a note formally accepting the play for publication, nor did she send him author's proofs, author's copies, or the $50 that Rexroth had told Rodman would be acceptable remuneration. Rexroth discovered his play had been published when he walked into a local San Francisco bookstore in May of 1946. Infuriated, both he and Marie dashed off angry letters to Crosby. And he told Selden Rodman that Harry and Caresse could take *Portfolio* "and stick it, separately or mutually."[46]

I am not one of the professional cunnilinguists or flagellents [sic] of the literary bon ton. I do not enjoy being kicked around by millionairesses. . . . If she cannot run a magazine without reducing its contributors to literal buggary—but then— that is what she does it for, and they in turn simply love it. But not this boy.

Rexroth cooled off soon afterward, and wrote a heartfelt letter of apology to Rodman which was not without its share of humor. "As for sticking *Portfolio*," he wrote, "maybe you could find a more homey use for it in the same precincts—though it is on pretty stiff paper."[47] His opinion of Crosby had not changed, however, and in another letter written in August, he described her as one of those rich women who feed on artists. She did pay him the $50, and in the fall of 1948 when Rexroth and Rodman were in Washington together to visit Ezra Pound in St. Eliza-beth's, Rexroth permitted Rodman to introduce him to her. Now that they were both in Europe, Rexroth agreed that it would be to their mutual advantage if they met in Rome and drove back to Paris together.

The traveling trio parted company in Rome. Rexroth found a pen-sione easily enough, but the Eternal City was a letdown. It was "squalid and pompous." The art, he said, looked much better in expensive books of reproductions and the ruins of ancient Rome looked just like ruins, "just rubble and a few columns." The Romans seemed ugly and evil. However, from the roof of his pensione one evening when the moon was full and swallows filled the sky, he was able to appreciate the classical beauty of the city. He yearned mightily for Marthe and even fantasized that she might be waiting for him somewhere in the city. He would have to make do with Caresse Crosby, who, he discovered, as they drove to Florence, was a pleasant traveling companion, "surprisingly unpreten-tious and even-tempered." In Florence, the people were more attractive than in Rome: they were "noble-visaged." After exploring the great museums of the city, they went up to Ravenna and east to Venice. Once they arrived in town, Caresse had her own agenda and Kenneth was left to do as he pleased. Consumed by his loneliness, he spent 2,100 lire ($6.00) for a nocturnal gondola ride.

> I wonder if it is possible
> To be more alone than in a gondola
> In Venice under the full moon
> Of June. All I have for company
> Are the halves of my heart.[48]

He did, however, enjoy the peace and tranquility of the excursion, which took him past a vast monastery, San Giorgio Maggiore, from where he could hear monks singing matins. And charmed by the fashionable men's shops, he splurged $50 on a raw silk suit and a pair of leather sandals, which was not such an indulgence since this was the first sizable sum he had spent during his trip on anything other than food and lodgings.

Rexroth had no reservations about the art in Venice, overwhelmed especially by the Tintorettos. From a café table on the Piazza San Marco, drinking beer and listening to musicians play "wonderful Italian corn," he wrote to his "honeybear" that if she postponed her trip any further she was "just plain crazy." Before leaving Rome, he had received Marie's second response to his seven-point program. In Venice, he was still brooding over her answers, which he described to Marthe as "so noble and so crooked." He was affronted by her refusal to accept Marthe as part of a ménage à trois, but conceded that "her answer was highminded, self-sacrificing and equivocal." He foresaw difficult times ahead even though he was now assured a second year of Guggenheim money. When that ran out, he would be dependent on Marie again. He and Marthe had better seize what time they could, Kenneth thought, and so did Caresse, who had now become Kenneth's confidante. They should spend a relaxed and happy year together in "some place like Manfredonia" on the south Adriatic coast. Remembering her old wild days in the twenties, Caresse told him in effect that they should gather rosebuds while they could. Again Kenneth urged Marthe to apply for all the grants she was eligible to receive, to "work all the angles" for financial assistance. Meanwhile, he would tap Laughlin.

On their way back to Paris, Caresse and Kenneth drove west through Vicenza, Verona, Bergamo, and Milan, turned north to the Alps, and passed beautiful Lake Maggiore. They stopped on the west side of the lake in a hotel in Domodossola, the last town below the Simplon Pass. The next morning they drove through the Simplon Pass into Switzerland, "a horrible country of stuffy people with beautiful mountains—still unspoiled—but everything else, including the lakes, thoroughly bitched up." Kenneth missed the view of the Matterhorn because it was covered in cloud. They made their way through Dijon and Troyes into Paris again.

The following day he was sipping an aperitif in a café on the Boulevard Montparnasse and writing Marthe that Italy was best suited for long-term living. However, traveling through France made him realize that they could easily spend a few cheap months camping in the woods of Provence with bicycles and canoes. His Guggenheim had been renewed, but he was prohibited from accepting the job at Black Mountain. Besides, he did not want to return to the States. He was despondent and lonely and sorry that he had not taken Marthe with him at the very outset of his trip. It would have avoided this tug-of-war, and she could have helped him with his French. While he read it well enough, to his ear, it sounded like "farting into lettuce." He was growing fearful, he confessed, that she would tell him that she couldn't meet him in Europe.

Perhaps for the first time, Marthe got some sense of what it was like to cross Kenneth. At the end of her first year in graduate school, she had been accepted into a course of study in philosophy that would have earned her a master's degree. Now Kenneth was asking her to abandon it. And while she was willing to free herself from the constraints of bourgeois morality, she was not inclined to self-destruct. How would she get back on track once their romantic year together ended? And she suffered anxieties over Kenneth's marital status. These ignoble insecurities of hers, Kenneth responded, were backing him into a corner and causing him untold psychological and emotional pain.

When I got your brutal letter and opened it at the Am Ex, I fainted dead away to the people's great consternation. It is hard for me to write this—I am sick and shaken all over. I always knew that any relationship I had with a woman would sooner or later founder on the rock of "security"—but I was unprepared for this disastrous—almost totally unexpected smashup.[49]

As soon as Marie granted the divorce, he would marry her. She was wrong to worry about legalities. Their real marriage would start once she arrived in Europe. She could finish her degree in Paris or Florence, but if she decided to forget about it, he would not mind. In effect, Rexroth came dangerously close to accusing Marthe of withdrawing her love for him, and wondered if she had fallen in love with someone else. He attacked her legitimate concerns about her career and their mutual welfare, and carefully absolved himself in advance from any responsibility for the precarious future that awaited them.

Kenneth barraged Marthe with letters, begrudgingly conceding her right to continue her studies. He would try to get information about European universities that might accept her as a transfer student. He warned Marthe that if she insisted upon his return to the States and to a secure job, he would eventually resent her for it. "After all—don't forget—Marie and I loved each other—or at least I loved her—and now it is over—and just for this reason."[50] And if he came home now, he would always feel that he had been forced to throw away the only chance he had

for a magical "wanderjahr in Europe." Was she willing to risk their love
and life together for the illusion of middle-class respectability?

Kenneth threatened to throw himself in the Seine if she left him alone
much longer. To hasten his divorce, he promised Marthe, he would surrender everything to Marie—even his library. He was totally in love with
her, not at all with Marie. He loved her with the same depth and intensity
that he had once loved Andrée, a kind of love he realized now that he
never had with Marie. Finally, putting his money where his mouth was,
he sent Marthe $300 to book her passage and cover whatever expenses
went along with closing her apartment and crossing the continent. In
addition, Marthe had received travel money from a second Schmidlapp
Fellowship recently awarded to her.[51] Whatever insecurities Marthe might
have had about her future, she was basically optimistic about her relationship with Kenneth, and trusted him implicitly, even at a distance. Persuaded that Kenneth might indeed carry out his suicide threat if she did
not join him, she cabled that she was coming.

Ecstatic, Kenneth immediately sent her the return portion of his Santa
Fe railroad ticket to cash in. He unleashed a series of letters filled with
instructions about which travel agencies she should patronize and what
things she should bring with her, namely, "everything" in supply for a
year: stockings (they should be black or dark blue only and medium
weight), shoes, camping outfits, all her clothes. He told her to look up
Raffi Bedayan in Berkeley, who would supply her with all the Army
surplus goods necessary for a trip to the Alps, just as he provided for
Sierra Club members. She could bring a sleeping bag along with a heavy
wool blanket, and perhaps pick up a geared bicycle under $50. Then
there were pharmaceuticals and the like: Ward's therapeutic compound
vitamins, Seconal or whatever sleeping pills she could get, contraceptives,
and "lots of soap." If she were coming by plane and could spare the
weight, she should bring her typewriter. Of course, if she was coming by
boat, she could haul unlimited amounts of baggage with her. And perhaps she could buy him a pair of jeans (34" waist and inseam), some pure
nylon sports shirts, and "a couple of brilliantly striped T shirts—real
loud—green and purple or orange and blue or something similar and a
couple of mediterranean—one blue, one red, or both blue." He drew
pictures of the kind of shirts he had in mind. And also he needed more
Tums.

Kenneth could barely contain his impatience. He had managed, he
told her, to find an "occasional escortee" for meals and walks, a woman by
the name of Catherine Casey, who reminded him of Pru because she was
"full of unreal love affairs." But she had left for Italy, and he said he was
all alone again. He had not yet visited any of the great sites and monuments of Paris, "even the Louvre," so that he and Marthe could see them
for the first time together. Marthe booked passage on a Cunard liner
leaving from Canada, even though there was a strike in Casnada and in

sympathy the British dockers refused to unload Canadian boats. Kenneth told her that he thought it would be unwise for him to meet her in Liverpool. An enforced stay there until the strike was settled could be very costly.

In a calmer tone, he advised her to stop in New York City, look up his friend Paul Mattick, make whatever contacts she could for future readings and book contracts, and inquire with a phone call whether Washington, D.C., had any progress to report on his application for a Fulbright grant that would permit them to stay in Europe for an additional year. He also asked her to type out a selection of the best Chinese poems translated into any language she could read, "not more than one hundred pages worth." And since she was eventually going to be in London for the boat train, she should stay long enough to view the Blakes, the Turners, and the Chinese pictures at the British Museum. He also hoped that she would bone up on her conversational French.

Seventeen

TRUTH AND CONSEQUENCES
1949

AFTER A VISIT with her father, who was still ailing but considerably improved, Marthe journeyed to Quebec and boarded the ship for England. She found herself in unusual company because most of the passengers were returning English war brides married to Canadian and American soldiers. Her mood of anticipation and excitement contrasted sharply with the deplorable condition of her traveling companions, who more often than not had infants and young children in tow without husbands to help them.[1] When she got to Liverpool she immediately took a train to London. An inexperienced traveler, Marthe had difficulty getting around, especially since she was weighed down with baggage (the strike had ended), including twenty-four bars of Sweetheart soap. Kenneth had told her to call Alex Comfort about buying his bicycle, but she was too tired to figure out the British public telephone system. Instead, she took the next boat train to Paris. After the French Customs inspector informed her that "*nous avons de savon ici,*" he quickly passed her though passport control.[2] In two hours, she was in Paris at the height of the French tourist season—the end of July 1949. Kenneth had mentioned that they would be staying at the Hôtel Delambre, but she was not sure whether she should go there or to the Hôtel de Chevreuse. She decided to wait for him at the American Express office on rue Scribe where he picked up his mail daily. He had not left a message for her. She didn't know how much Kenneth's appearance had changed. In his latest letters he had told her that from sitting all day at the Dome drinking beer and writing letters to her, he had developed a paunch. When she sighted him crossing the street in her direction, he appeared rather debonair, trim, very much the expatriate in sandals and white shorts. He was both excited and surprised to see her. He hadn't known exactly when she was to arrive, and Marthe sensed that he was troubled about something.

Indeed he was. Despite his litany of complaints about being lonely, Kenneth had struck up more than one liaison in Paris. Marthe had arrived on a day which he had planned to spend with a French painter, Yvonne duBois. Would Marthe join them? When they met, Marthe liked her well enough. She was an attractive woman close to Kenneth's age, not the first sexual partner Kenneth had taken while waiting for Marthe. He recorded some of these encounters in *The Dragon and the Unicorn*.[3] In that poem he describes a delicious dinner he enjoyed with a blond Bretonne servant girl who is his "only friend on this continent"; he captures the excitement of a Paris Bastille Day celebration that he spent with Yvonne. Rexroth was not exactly unaware of his inconsistent image, and in the poem carries on a dialogue (at least his persona does) with Pilate, who serves as a kind of chorus. One of Pilate's functions is to challenge the validity of objective, factual evidence. "Who," he asks, "can escape from the shadow of his own head?" Seizing upon this concept, Rexroth rationalizes a way of using words that suggest permanence and commitment without being bound to the restrictions inherent in them.

> The years pass, the Summers go,
> And our few days fall away
> From us like the falling stars;
> But that glory of rockets,
> Showered on sky and river,
> On our nightbound eyes and lips,
> Will always last. That is what
> "Always" means, and all it means.[4]

If he saw a contradiction between what he was telling Marthe about his lonely months abroad and his several sexual liaisons, if he saw any duplicity in his behavior, he was not admitting it.

Kenneth pointed out his sexual conquests to Marthe on the street: naturally she was devastated by this unexpected development.[5] She would have gone home immediately if she not felt trapped by circumstance. She had little money of her own, and the Schmidlapp grant required her to follow the detailed itinerary—created by Kenneth—that she had submitted with her application. Having come this far, she was obligated to continue with the trip. So, in August, they set off for the South of France on bicycles. Marthe had to sort things out in her head, alone, and often deliberately lagged behind, dropping far enough back so that she could stop for coffee in villages which Kenneth had already ridden through. She would sit in a café, usually for an hour or so before lunch and then again after lunch. She was committed to Kenneth, but terribly distressed at the same time.

Rexroth described the trip to Laughlin: it was great to travel without "weirdoes like the Gardiners or aged fatal women like Caresse."[6] He did not even hint that he was accompanied by Marthe. He had bought a bicycle in Paris and was going to peddle through the Loire Valley and Dordogne, then all the way to Perpignan and up again through Narbonne

and over to Sete, Nîmes, Arles, Avignon, and Aix. He planned to store
his bicycle in Nice and book a bus tour of Italy. Laughlin was not to know
that Marthe was coming to Europe because he was, in Rexroth's words, a
"neurotic troublemaker," who would try to stop him from divorcing Marie
as he had already assured Marthe he was ready to do. In truth, Rexroth
had not initiated divorce action—otherwise, Marthe would have heard
about it.

Still married to Marie, Kenneth told Marthe after she arrived in Paris
that his divorce had become final. She was puzzled by this unexpected
news but believed him. When they reached Aix-en-Provence, "the city of
small splendors," they were married in a civil ceremony.[7] If Rexroth's
bigamy bothered him, it didn't show. As an anarchist, he had little regard
for the "law" and legal procedures, but as a romantic who appreciated
ritual, he wanted to prove to Marthe that his intentions were serious, even
if that meant deceiving her. For Rexroth, the symbolism of the ceremony
counted more than the ceremony itself. In the Provence sections of *The
Dragon and the Unicorn* based on this experience, he seems oblivious to
anything but the idyllic countryside around him, and paints an indelible
picture of the houses and the landscape, transforming the simple fare he
and Marthe could afford into feasts, capturing the joy of the lives of the
people who lived there. Once they reached Nice, "the / Beverly Hills of
the middle / classes of Europe,"[8] Kenneth and Marthe stored their bicycles and bused to Genoa. Rexroth liked Italian tour buses, but refused to
stay in the expensive hotels recommended by the tour agency. They visited most of the towns he had seen on his first trip, going farther south to
the Sorrentine peninsula. He toyed with the idea of spending the winter
in Venice, Florence, or Manfredonia because for the moment he could
not "bear the prospect of that vast, hysterical worn out boudoir that is
Paris." Although he retained his affection for Provence, he was fed up
with the "beastly" French. He no longer enjoyed their cuisine and con-
cluded that they suffered from the faults that they attributed to Americans: "commercialism, neurosis, inability to relax, execrable taste, general
all round stupid vulgarity and acquisitiveness."[9]

In Florence, Kenneth showed Marthe a letter from Marie forwarded
to him from Paris. She was considering the possibility of joining him in
France, and wanted him to find out if she could get a position at the
American Hospital in Paris or as a private nurse for Americans, who
would pay her fee in dollars. She thought she would have to work part
time only, leaving her free time to "go about" with Kenneth. She seemed
to be unaware that Marthe was now with Kenneth. Marthe read the letter
in a state of shock. Kenneth confessed that there had been no divorce,
and feebly denied having asked Marie to meet him in Europe. Now he
was worried Marie would show up at the American Express office, just as
Marthe had.

Although Marie had expressed very real anger in her letters to Kenneth, particularly when she was addressing herself to his seven-point reform, she had never said flat out that she stopped loving him. While preserving their home on Eighth Avenue as he wanted it, she had done nothing to suggest that she wanted the evidence of his presence disman-tled. She was still keeping an inventory of all the books he was sending from Europe, and she was advising him about various catalogues and notices which she thought would interest him. She had, for example, sent him a catalogue of Chinese books from the Paragon Gallery Book Shop, asking him to read it carefully so that he could let her know which books from the list he wanted. Although she was reluctant to leave San Fran-cisco, she was beginning to miss Kenneth. "I love you," she had written recently, "and am just as incapable of living without you as you say you are. We can, I am sure, be together again. Come home when you are ready—everything is here as you left it."[10] Perhaps Kenneth had de-spaired over Marthe's delay, or had written to Marie in a pique when Marthe pressured him about divorce, marriage, and financial security. But he had conveyed to Marie with the same urgency he had to Marthe that he was miserable, lonely, on the verge of cracking up. Both Marthe and Marie had taken him at his word.

   Kenneth and Marthe could do little else but continue their trip through Italy, circling around to Milan on their way back to France. Though miserable and distraught, they could not ignore the glorious culture around them, and their spirits lifted temporarily. Fresh from viewing Giottos in Padua and the Palladian palaces, theater, and basilica in Vicenza, they lunched in Verona with the great printer Giovanni Mardersteig.

> One of those perfect craftsmen
> In whom absolute devotion
> And respect for a medium
> Has produced a state of being
> Which can only be called saintly,
> A personality like a
> Work of art, a true state of grace.[11]

In Milan, they spent an entire afternoon in the Convent of Santa Maria delle Grazie gazing at Da Vinci's *The Last Supper*. Toward the end of the day, a nun brought a group of young schoolgirls into the refectory to see the renowned fresco. They all hovered in the back of the hall, obediently listening to their teacher's lecture. One girl, however, entranced, moved as close to the work as she could. Marthe and Kenneth looked away, embarrassed, feeling as though they had intruded on the "vision of a saint." Captivated by this twelve-year-old's "untempered sensibility," Kenneth told Marthe that he "would give anything in the world" to have such a daughter. In fact, Kenneth and Marthe's first child was "already alive."[12] That, however, would not be confirmed until they returned to the States.

Kenneth and Marthe returned to Paris in the middle of a cold, rainy night, too late to keep the reservation they had made at the Hôtel Delambre. It was 2:00 a.m. before they secured a room elsewhere. On the wall of the hallway was a sign that Kenneth had seen the first time he toured France with the Gardiners: *Le silence de chacun assure le repos du tous.* Struck by these words, Kenneth had repeated them to Marthe before she arrived, more as a joke with sexual innuendos than anything else. In Part IV of *The Dragon and the Unicorn,* Rexroth cites these words immediately after the passage that describes Marthe and himself making furious love to assure themselves (and the neighboring clientele) that they were still alive after their gruesome night of travel back to Paris. In the context of his running political commentary, these words take on a more ominous meaning: the silence of each decent person assures the tranquility of those who profit from a corrupt establishment—anyone in France, according to Rexroth, "with an / Income of over sixty dollars / A month . . . and this / Includes existentialists, / Poets, artists, Communists, / All colors of labor fakers, From anarchist to royalist. / They all piss through the same quill."[13]

Marthe was morose, and Kenneth intolerant. She was weary of watching him count pennies, always hunting for the cheapest restaurants and hotels. They never went to the theater or to concerts, and in Venice Kenneth thought the price of a gondola prohibitive, especially since he had already ridden on one. More importantly, Marthe had been feeling ill for some time, but mistakenly associated her nausea with the strong coffee she was drinking. By the time they got back to Paris in November, however, she suspected the truth and wanted to go home. She had lost all interest in living a hand-to-mouth existence either on the coast of the southern Adriatic or in a room with cooking privileges on the top floor of a Montmartre hotel. When she insisted that she needed a medical examination in the comfort of familiar surroundings, they quarreled and Kenneth slapped her face. This was the first but far from the last time that he would strike her. The romantic journey was over. After a small farewell party organized by Yvonne and another girlfriend, Leontine, the couple took a train to Bordeaux where they boarded a freighter for New York City.

Arriving in December 1949, Kenneth and Marthe visited the Matticks at their apartment on West 21st Street. Mattick knew something of Kenneth's state of affairs from Marie, who had visited New York City while Kenneth was in Europe that past summer. She had not kept her unhappiness a secret, talking to the Matticks mostly about her problems with Kenneth. Certain that Kenneth would visit Mattick on his way home to San Francisco, Marie had written in mid-November asking him to tell Kenneth that she loved him and longed to be with him again. Marie also wrote to Kenneth when he was in New York, sending him a check for his birthday so that he could buy books from Orientalia Bookstore. Shortly before Rexroth returned to the States, Mattick had told him about Marie's visit in a November 17, 1949, letter. "You are in a terrible fix," he noted, "and in for some great mental miseries."

From New York, Kenneth headed back to San Francisco while Marthe went to Medford, Oregon, to spend Christmas with her friend Elaine Walker. When her pregnancy was confirmed, she moved to Seattle where she could live temporarily with her best friend Ellen King, from Mills College days. Marthe told Kenneth the news and took a job with the Seattle Public Library. Kenneth had gotten back in time to celebrate his birthday and Christmas, but there was little joy in his household. The apartment was crowded with the books he had ordered, and he felt like a stranger sitting at his desk trying to get his life in order. Marie threw a small birthday party for him, but although he was glad to see old friends like Jim Harmon and Ronnie Bladen, he did not enjoy it. Kenneth did not trust Marie's intentions, and suspected that the party was an act of revenge and a scheme to recruit allies. He felt like "Gulliver amongst a lot of hating, envious gloating Lilliputs."[14] His Libertarian Circle had disintegrated, and the hall on Steiner Street was closed.

Yet neither the sharpness nor the poignancy of his observations were dulled or marred by this unhappy scene. While he walked through Golden Gate Park that "unseasonably cold" Christmas Eve of 1949, darkness fell earlier than usual:

> The sky
> Sinks close to shadowy
> Trees, and sky and trees mingle
> In receding planes of vagueness.
> The wet pebbles on the path
> Wear little frills of ice like
> Minute, transparent fungus.
> Suddenly the air is full
> Of snowflakes—cold, white, downy
> Feathers that do not seem to
> Come from the sky but crystallize
> Out of the air. The snow is
> Unendurably beautiful.
> Falling in the breathless lake,
> Floating in the yellow rushes.[15]

Although only weeks before in Milan the prospect of fatherhood in the abstract had greatly appealed to him, Kenneth responded to Marthe's news by urging her to have an abortion. The greater portion of his Guggenheim money and Marthe's Schmidlapp fellowship expended, he faced the same grim circumstances as before, except that Marthe's support was unlikely and he was six months away from fatherhood. How, he asked Marthe, were they going to raise this baby? He was too much of a Bohemian, too much of a fringe person to start a family. And he was also deeply troubled by Marthe's withdrawal and alienation from him, which had grown ominously despite her proclamations that she still loved him.

In Europe, Kenneth had hoped that he and Marthe could eke out two or three years of "peace and independence" from the crises that awaited them at home. Writing to Marthe in Seattle, Kenneth speculated that Marthe would have earned her degree from the Sorbonne, and they would have passed idyllic summers in the French and Italian countryside. They could have managed "even a baby without trouble or scandal or much extra expense."[16] He did not believe he had been tight with funds or obsessed with meeting "interesting people," or the cultural elite, as Marthe had implied. He preferred the town-to-earth inhabitants of Cligancourt, Belleville, Villette—not those who hung around Les Deux Magots and La Closerie des Lilas. He blamed his bursts of impatience and displeasure on Marthe's "disapproving and withdrawing silence" and the confrontations over hotel rooms, food, and how fast to ride a bicycle.

He refused to believe that someone as sympathetic as Marthe could have objected to his spontaneous sexual liaisons, or his intimacy with Yvonne who, as far as he was concerned, had rescued him from a loneliness that had brought him to the brink of psychotic depression. Certainly Marthe had heard Kenneth's views on the sanctity of love and sex, which he would articulate in *The Dragon and the Unicorn:*

> Love is the subjective
> Aspect of contemplation.
> Sexual love is one of
> The most perfect forms of
> Contemplation, as far as it
> Is without ignorance, grasping
> And appetite.[17]

These lines are a stricture against the kind of egotism that he thought unworthy of Marthe. It was a form of jealousy that he could not abide—except in himself.

He lapsed into a lachrymose mood: why go on with this life when he seemed capable only of spreading misery, despair, and destruction? "It is *I*," he confessed to Marthe, "who destroyed Van Ghent, and Pru, and Andrée and so many others—just as I have destroyed you."[18] But he had no intention of losing her. Kenneth asked her to write to Black Mountain once more to see if they were still offering him a position. "Better do that right away," he added, still confident that she wanted to carry on as his amanuensis.

The pace of Rexroth's everyday activities became erratic. His ulcer acted up, often arousing him in the middle of the night. He slept late, and instead of going to his desk, he would bicycle to the park. His letters to Marthe mixed accusations and self-recriminations with requests that she make job inquiries for herself and seek advice on proper exercise for pregnant women. One minute he played the authority figure, the next a

spoiled child. He would announce that the twenty-year gap in age between them was too wide to cross. There was talk about Rexroth teaching
at the University of Washington, but his reputation, though impressive,
did not make up for the absence of academic credentials. He still pon-
dered the possibility of opening a bookstore or returning to Europe with
Marthe on a Fulbright, although he had heard that anyone with a history
remotely connected to the Communist Party did not have a chance of
winning one. Nor could he give up the idea that he and Marthe should
have stayed in Europe. When he was in particularly low spirits, he would
talk about Leontine or Lydia, a working-class woman he had met in Venice during his trip with Caresse Crosby, and how he should have gone off
with one of them to a remote village where he would be nurtured back to
writing. He saw nothing vindictive or odd about revealing such thoughts
to Marthe who tried to placate him as best she could without losing sight
of her own predicament.

As it turned out, the spring 1950 position for literature at Black Mountain College had already been filled, but the Board of Fellows invited him
to conduct a week's seminar. They had been eager all along to have
Rexroth on campus, and when the Guggenheim fellowship prohibited
him from working, Black Mountain suggested that he should live at the
college anyway, to take advantage of its atmosphere and goodwill. He was
further coaxed to go there by letters and by a visit from a member of the
Black Mountain faculty and friend of Dorothy Van Ghent, Mary Carolyn
Richards. A writer, translator of Artaud, and artist herself. Richards assured Rexroth that even though the salary appeared low, she and her
husband, the pianist David Tudor, had managed to save enough money
to spend the summer in Europe the previous year.

Ultimately, Rexroth put too many obstacles in the path of leaving San
Francisco. For one thing he expected the college to cover the cost of
moving his belongings, which included a library now of three thousand
books. The most Black Mountain could pay was $150. Room and board
were free, but the monthly stipend was $100, too low for Rexroth's satis-
faction. Also, in spite of his lifelong interest in creating "a community of
love," Rexroth took a dim view of living on a campus surrounded by
faculty and students. He also worried that his students would steal his
books. He was hardly in an appropriate frame of mind to teach at freewheeling Black Mountain College.

Eighteen

NEW LIVES
1950–1952

GRADUALLY Rexroth reentered the literary scene. He was self-conscious about his break-up with Marie, convinced that she had turned many of their friends and acquaintances against him. He went down to the Black Cat Café to catch up on San Francisco Bohemian life. During the thirties, the Black Cat had been the most popular spot for writers, artists, and other people on the fringe. He discovered that its founder, Charley Habercorn, had died, and that the place had developed a reputation as "a hangout for militant homosexuals." There he ran into Hilary Belloc, Jr.— whom he suspected of conducting an affair with Marie—and Lawrence Clark Powell, who had as University Librarian of UCLA placed the first library standing order for all New Directions books. Powell invited him to give a reading at UCLA in February 1950, and paid him a fee of $35 and his expenses at the Hotel Barclay, from where he wrote Marthe, telling her how much he missed her and how disagreeable Marie had become.

In March, Rexroth visited Marthe in Seattle because he needed to see first hand that she was determined to have their child. When he returned to San Francisco, he finally told Marie the exact state of affairs. For months he had postponed a direct confrontation with her. He had looked forward to the occasion as he would to "walking into a furnace,"[1] and had tried to hide from her his correspondence with Marthe by asking her not to mail letters that would arrive on Saturday when Marie would be home. As soon as Marie learned that Marthe was pregnant, she cleared out, renting a furnished room and making arrangements to move her clothes and other personal belongings. She had no intention of laying claim to any of Kenneth's books, nor to their apartment. Whatever pain and anguish Marie was feeling, she did not change her attitude about Kenneth's writing. "I *know* the most important thing is you and your writing, but no writing had been done in the past year, and I can no longer believe that you will ever have peace enough to write if we return to each other."[2] It was this selflessness that Kenneth dreaded. How much easier she could have made their break-up if she had been destructive or vituperative.

Selfless or not, Marie was not above expressing her anger over Kenneth's failure to contribute any of the Guggenheim money to the Eighth Avenue household expenses, about his violent threats to follow her after work to make sure she was not living with another man. He had ridiculed her for refusing to accept his relationship with Marthe, and accused her of turning all their friends against him. By now the pattern was familiar: she continued to profess enduring love for him. She was convinced that she would "always" be married to him. "You have told me that over and and over," she wrote, "and I would know it without being told. I have never been afraid of that."[3] She and Kenneth had tried meeting for bicycle rides together, but that proved too painful. She went to Mount Hood for a brief vacation and wrote Kenneth a bittersweet letter from there, explaining that he was the only person she could talk to about mountains. What was the news? What was he writing? Who was he helping lately to gain CO status?

Her concern notwithstanding, Marie had given up the fight. She urged Kenneth to "send for Marthe," warning him that he would regret forever not spending the last months of her pregnancy with her. Marie had a regressive quality about her, and built into her marriage to Kenneth was the mutual agreement that somehow she was always the one who was wrong.[4] After Mount Hood, Marie went back to Bandon for a while. At this point, she wanted to be inaccessible.

No longer afraid that he would have to leave his apartment, Rexroth's mood improved. His work, which he had been neglecting, now absorbed his attention. As though to get himself in form, he badgered Laughlin about the delay of *The Signature of All Things,* and drew from him a three-part diagram for how the book should be designed. Because Laughlin was now supervising *Perspectives,* a Ford Foundation magazine, he was, in Rexroth's estimation, slipping under the influence of the "Drop the Bomb Now Boys," the squares who thought the working class did not read enough Proust, and the editors of the *Partisan, Kenyon,* and *Seẁanee* reviews.[5] He also berated Laughlin for excluding his name from the dust jacket of *The New British Poets.* Rexroth accused Laughlin of being ashamed to publish him, that he had been embarrassed to be seen with him in New York City on his last visit there. And sure that the book would sell, he thought it was time for a second edition of *The Phoenix and the Tortoise.*

Dumping on Laughlin had a cathartic effect, and Rexroth shifted his attention to writing poetry. The last significant chunk of his work to be published was *The Art of Worldly Wisdom* (1949), and he felt detached from this particular volume because he had written most of the poems collected in it more than twenty-five years ago. He refers to the book in *The Dragon and the Unicorn:*

> Was it all true once? Just like
> It says? I cannot find the past.

> It is only anecdotes
> For company and the parching
> Of a few more hidden nerves
> Each year.[6]

The Signature of All Things would be published within the year. New work was long overdue. He asked Marthe to start typing the collecting of Chinese poems he had translated so that he could refine what he had done so far. He wanted to resume work on *The Dragon and the Unicorn*, the long poem based on his treks across the United States and to Western Europe.

Rexroth also received a psychological boost from a request by the recently formed Living Theater to produce *Beyond the Mountains*, which Julian Beck and Judith Malina had read in the *Quarterly Review of Literature*.[7] The Becks would eventually open their first season with the four plays included in *Beyond the Mountains*. They had at this point only read "Hermaious." "Iphigenia at Aulis" and "Phaedra" both had appeared in 1946, in, respectively, Caresse Crosby's *Portfolio* (edited by Selden Rodman) and *New Directions in Prose and Poetry*. "Berenike" did not see print until it was published with the other three plays in the New Directions edition. After Marthe typed Kenneth's most recent revisions, she mailed off the manuscript.

In April, Rexroth met Dylan Thomas on his first American trip. He thought Thomas's drinking was disgraceful, but he liked the Welshman, who looked like a cross between a cherub and Charles Laughton, and invited him to stay at the Eighth Avenue apartment. Rexroth thought Thomas's reading at Wheeler Auditorium hilarious. Surprised to see the auditorium more than half full, Thomas asked his audience whether they mistakenly thought that "Henry Miller with illustrations" had been scheduled to appear. He leveled his usual potshots at the academic world by presenting a list of imaginary titles for doctoral dissertations, including "The Influence of W. C. Fields on Virginia Woolf."[8] Rexroth's regard for Thomas rose even higher when he learned that Thomas had shunned a party held in his honor at the home of Berkeley professor Mark Shorer, arranged to give the faculty an opportunity to meet him. Instead, Thomas went to Big Sur with Tram Coombs and Ruth Witt-Diamant, the "greatest victory on the Cultural Front since the John Reed Club."[9] Rexroth learned later on that Thomas did not see many significant distinctions between the groups of people that he had met in the Bay Area. To Charles Wrey Gardiner, Rexroth would write: "At first I thought he was only a pest, the son of a bitch gets up at 8:00 to start drinking! But as the incredible lies he has told about me and everybody else he met here come back to me from NYC, I gather that he is not in full possession of his marbles, and vicious to boot."[10]

Soon after Thomas left San Francisco, Marthe came down from Seattle, finally reconciled to living with Kenneth although it meant occupying the same apartment that he had shared with Marie. Kenneth thought that for someone who had seemed willing to play the role of "mistress-lover," Marthe's unswerving determination to have the baby represented a radical change in her perspective.[11] He understood finally that he was going to be a father, even though he had never thought of himself as the kind of person he believed all women yearned for: a husband, a father, a provider. Waxing philosophical, Kenneth admitted that her "youth and loveliness and sex" had seduced him, and that he had been blind to the emotional dynamite with which they were playing. "Now," he wrote, "we are just where everybody gets who starts fucking unwisely and too well."

Marthe had brought $700 with her, which added to the $700 remaining from Kenneth's Guggenheim constituted the sum total of their assets. Of the two, Kenneth was more agitated about their lack of financial security. Six months pregnant, Marthe did her best to lessen his anxieties, assuring him that the best thing he could do was resume writing and the routine of San Francisco life. But Kenneth's stomach was bothering him again, and he was getting heart palpitations, in part because Marie had cut off contact with him. He wrote to her, and Marthe, resolved to alleviate Kenneth's distress, tried herself to leave messages at Marie's office. For now, Marie wanted to left alone. Kenneth decided that he could only calm down by himself in the mountains.

He took off in the old Willys—Marie was going to buy another car— for Sequoia National Park. By June 3 he had reached campground, too early in the season to get a burro. He decided to go into Kings River Canyon for a week and hike small distances that he could cover in a day. Because the water was too high for fishing, he spent most of the time reading, writing, and sunbathing. Although he was still taking Tums as a precaution, his health was gradually improving. He wrote Marthe postcards and a few letters, all of them expressing his love and concern for her. He also proposed that they could bring their baby to the mountain shortly after the birth. He had seen other infants at camp, mostly a year old or so, and even a two-month-old baby on a bottle.

Marthe was bored and lonely, cut off from her closest friends in Seattle. With her physician's approval but over Kenneth's objections—now the concerned prospective father, he feared that a long bus trip would trigger a miscarriage or premature delivery—Marthe decided to visit Shirley and Frank Triest, who were still living in Duncan's Mills. When she returned, the mailbox was filled with notes from Kenneth instructing her to carry out various chores: write a letter of complaint about his leaking air mattress to the Firestone Company; secure recording tape (plastic tape on metal spools only) from Hi Hirsch so that when Kenneth came back he could begin recording all of his poems; write to the Forest Service about available summer home sites; write for a French-English edition of Petronius; send back the collection of minor Latin poets that Lawrence Clark Powell had let him borrow from the UCLA library; look for a good

book of French idioms, "real ones not the stuff in the back of grammars";
write to various French museums and libraries for references to poetry
and folksongs of the Indo-Chinese area. Also she should locate the executor of the estate of the Lithuanian-born poet O. V. de L. Milosz, whose
poems he and Marthe had translated—Marthe had done the literal translating and Kenneth made the poems—on their eighteen-day freighter
trip from Bordeaux to New York in December 1949.

Fourteen of these translations were printed in 1952, delicate elegies
tinged with irony and faithful to the rhythms and intonations of common
French diction.[12] Rexroth was attracted to these controlled but emotionally laden lines, especially on his voyage home with Marthe, the last segment of a journey that had thwarted his search for love's constancy.

> When she comes—will her eyes be grey or green,
> Green or grey on the river?
> The hour will be new in a future so old,
> New, but not very new . . .
> Old hours where everything has been said, everything seen,
>   everything dreamed!
> I pity you if you know it.[13]

After a sojourn in Giant Forest, Kenneth returned to the apartment
at the end of June. On July 26, 1950, at Children's Hospital, Marthe gave
birth to Mary Delia Andrée Rexroth, named in memory of Kenneth's
mother and his first wife. Marie became the godmother. Three and a half
months later, Marthe was working at two part-time jobs, one in the audio-
visual department, the other in records, at San Francisco State College
downtown. She would get up every weekday at four, Mary's last feeding
for the night. In order to have time with her new baby, Marthe would stay
up with her until she fell back to sleep, and then get ready for work. By
eight o'clock she was out the door on her way to work, leaving Kenneth in
charge of the sleeping baby. During the day, Kenneth would market, take
clothes to the laundry, and prepare dinner before Marthe returned in the
early evening. Even had she wanted to, Marthe could not cook. The
kitchen was indisputably Kenneth's domain. Not so the secretary's desk.
Kenneth still expected Marthe to type his poems, write his letters, and file
his correspondence. And he assumed that she would gladly be a gracious
host, as Marie had been, with one difference. He hoped that Marthe
would have the good sense to dress, eat, and behave according to his
prescription, more like a good daughter than a wife and mother.

Although he and Marthe could not afford a refrigerator—he had not
made a penny on *The New British Poets*—Kenneth thought about buying a
house in the country for "artistic considerations." For the past twenty
years and with the devotion of a missionary, he had grounded his psyche
in the locale of Northern California, a prerequisite for giving his poetry
the sense of place that D. H. Lawrence thought so important (a precursor

perhaps to "bio-regionalism," a philosophy of writing later developed by
Gary Snyder). In this respect, he also felt close to William Carlos Williams,
who had decided after all it was best to stay put in Rutherford, New Jersey.
Again and again, Rexroth would say that all he wanted was a very simple
home in the woods near the coast.

Actually, a house did become available in the spring of 1951 with a
mortgage that Kenneth and Marthe thought they could carry, a wooden
cottage with five rooms, a garage, and a large garden all around, about
ten miles south of San Francisco on the coast. The Veterans Housing
Association was selling it for $7500, $1,000 down payment, $55 a month.
He and Marthe had only seen it from the outside, but they were definitely
interested. Kenneth decided to consult Marie about the matter. While
Marthe was at work, Kenneth took Marie to see the house. She told Kenneth that she would give him $250 toward it, provided that the mortgage
would be held in the name of Kenneth and Marie Rexroth, who were still
legally married. In a helpful spirit, she wrote to James Laughlin asking
him if he could put $500 into the kitty. She feared that Laughlin would
think such an action on her part deranged, and that it was risky for her to
maintain any kind of connection to Kenneth, especially since she still
claimed to love him. But she believed that it was important for Kenneth's
"friends" to help him make his relationship with Marthe work, and that
he would not succeed if he, Marthe, and Mary continued to live in the
small apartment that had once been her home. As far as Marie could tell,
he was trying: "he's doing a good job of minding the baby all day, and that
takes more than courage when you are Kenneth Rexroth."[14] Laughlin
thought Marie was both unusually idealistic and masochistic.

Rexroth himself asked Laughlin if he could have $500 as an advance
against future royalties. Although he had just borrowed $10,000 to cover
New Directions debts—stores were not paying their bills and sales were
down—Laughlin thought he could raise $500, and was apologetic about
not being able to find more. Both Laughlin and Marie believed in Rexroth's
genius, and were appalled that his everyday life had to be so difficult. So
all Kenneth and Marthe had to do was raise was $250, and the house
would be theirs, or rather Kenneth and Marie's.

Marthe was enraged when she learned that Kenneth had consulted
Marie about business that involved the two of them exclusively. She wanted
Marie to have "nothing to do" with any house that she was buying. Kenneth could call her a "scissorbill" if he wanted to, but she regarded this
latest action of his as indiscreet, eminently unkind, and a clear indication
that he did not see her as his equal. She felt betrayed, and was reminded
of the time in Florence when Kenneth told her that Marie had written
that she was making arrangements to join him in Europe. She told Kenneth that he was unsure about who he wished to share his life, and was
"acting with each possible candidate as though she were selected."[15] Marthe
wanted the house to be in the name of Marthe and Kenneth Rexroth.

When Kenneth expressed some fear to her about misrepresenting their marital status, Marthe suggested that the deed be in her name only, Marthe Larsen, which would also require that their bank account be in her name only. Marthe had taken on the formidable task of changing Kenneth's perception of her. If they were to have a life together, their relationship had to be equalized. In the midst of their wrangling, the house was bought by someone else.

Undeterred by this domestic fiasco, Rexroth made remarkable progress on *The Dragon and the Unicorn,* publishing Part I, in *New Directions in Prose and Poetry,* XII, in 1950, and Part II in the following issue. He considered Part II to be the major section and wrote Laughlin that it was "all about Italy, economics, American fairies and the Revolution. Don't say you can't print it, it ain't art. It's a hell of a lot more art than Ez's antisemitism."[16] It is also, in part, an exquisite, if sometimes irreverent, piece of travel writing in verse. He describes the prehistoric art in the Lascaux caves as "Sid Grauman's Cro-Magnum Theatre,"[17] the medieval castle at Carcassonne as "a tiresome visite,"[18] the atmosphere over Avignon contaminated by the "Stink of the Papacy and / The present stink of English tourists."[19] But more often than not the poem remarkably captures the beauty of a particular setting.

> We camp on the Loire, the vélos
> Parked under a rose bush, the
> Sleeping bags under acacias,
> And careen down the swift current,
> Impossible to stand, much less
> Swim against it. Two owls chatter
> In the trees as the twilight
> Comes, lavender and orange
> Over the white reaches of
> Water and the whiter sandbars,
> And the first starlight dribbling
> On the rushing river.[20]

Or it paints the great contrasts of the landscape.

> Chenenceaux, the sun low and
> Fishermen poling a boat
> Under the arches, a boy
> Wading up to his arms along-
> Side in the weedy water.
> Bléré, a foire and carrousel,
> All the world drunker than peach
> Orchard boars . . .
>   . . .
>
> All day southward to Poitiers,
> Through a world of rivers and

Castles, white shorn wheatfields and
Ripening grapes and suddenly
Tile roofs and cream-colored houses,
The mark of civilization,
Of Rome and the South.[21]

Rexroth's impressions are alive; the intensity of his observations energizes the scene. Selecting the details with an unerring eye, he makes his readers hunger for the food that he consumes with such gusto and appreciation, whether it is "Grilled pork chops, fried potatoes, / Tomatoes, beans in vinegar" at a "peasant auberge" not far from Paris, or the "pâtés truffés" of Périgueux, "slabs of spongy white cheese, and great / Heaps of fruit" at a commercial hotel in Albi, or "Plover's eggs and tomatillos / In aspic" at the Café Mistral in Aix-en-Provence.

Rexroth wanted to see the poem printed in its entirety, along with some shorter poems and some translations of Tu Fu, but he would have to wait for that. Archibald MacLeish had written to Laughlin about translating Tu Fu with Harvard scholar Achilles Fang. Laughlin was still puzzled with all "this Tu Fu business"; but Rexroth was not discouraged, and kept bombarding him with other proposals: translations from the Chinese, selected prose of Kenneth Patchen, a book of comedies that would be a companion to *Beyond the Mountains*. He also wanted Laughlin to publish translations of the work of the prolific French novelist and dramatist Nicolas Restif (1734–1806), the writer often referred to as the Rousseau of the Gutter or the Voltaire of the Chambermaids. Rexroth preferred to describe him as the father of Henry Miller's "heart on sleeve fiction." He was drawn to Restif because he saw reflected in him some of his own attitudes and behavior: a fascination with working-class and Bohemian life, especially the women, yoked to a desire for social reform. In *The Dragon and the Unicorn,* Rexroth briefly alludes to Restif while describing a stroll to the Isle St. Louis in Paris, "Where Restif carved his memoirs / And time has forgot itself."[22]

Every so often, Laughlin lost patience with Rexroth, discouraged by his endless criticism of other writers whom he published in his *New Directions Annual*. Rexroth was also reading final proof on his four verse plays and accused Laughlin of placing too high a price on stage rights. Laughlin knew he would lose $500 even if the whole first printing of *Beyond the Mountains*, 1,500 copies, sold out. He felt that a 10 percent fee was justified even if a fledgling theater company like the Living Theater would have difficulty paying it. Laughlin was sure that few publishers would have printed Rexroth's plays without a large subsidy, and suggested with some heat that Rexroth "and his kind" seek someone else to fund their work. However, Laughlin and Rexroth's arguments never lasted very long and he visited Rexroth in San Francisco soon after *Beyond the Mountains* was published. But he built into the visit a measure of self-protection by staying at a hotel. He was traveling with Gertrude Huston, artistic director at

New Directions, and was not sure she and Marthe would get along, especially since Gertrude and Marie were friends (Marie had stayed in Gertrude's apartment while she was in New York City). Rexroth was afraid
Gertrude and Marie would cause trouble between him and Laughlin, but
he was wrong. If Laughlin had wanted to sever his relationship with
Kenneth, he did not need the help of a friend.

In addition to his many writing projects, Rexroth inaugurated a weekly
KPFA book review program specializing in "mature non-fiction, highbrow literature, scholarly works, fine arts, orientalia, poetry."[23] Some lis-
teners turned in for the information; others wanted to hear his latest, and
sometimes outrageous, pronouncements on the state of contemporary
intellectual life. His delivery was rather crude, he admitted to Babette
Deutsch, whose *Poetry in Our Time* he would review for the *New York Herald
Tribune Book Review* in 1952. His voice was no different from the one he
had used long ago when he "came into the City News Bureau from a
speakeasy phone across from the East Chicago Avenue Police Station—
or from a soap box pitching red cards on West Madison Street or out by
the totem pole in Seattle. It gets worse as I get older. I play back tapes and
shudder—sounds just like a B gangster pitcher."[24] He was also writing
reviews for publications like *The New Republic, Art News, The New York
Times Book Review,* and *The Nation.* He tackled studies of Thomas Mann
and Japanese art, poetry by his friend Herbert Read, and the prose of
Miguel de Unamuno.

Early winter 1951, he resumed his Friday night literary evenings,
asking Weldon Kees, who had come to live with his wife Ann on the West
Coast in the fall of 1950, to be the "opening gun." There was a good
turnout even though Rexroth had charged fifty cents admission "to keep
out the people who drop cigarette butts in the goldfish bowl." Kees thought
the audience was better than the one he would have attracted in New
York—"more alert, more ready to laugh at the satirical"—and was delighted when Rexroth gave him the evening's profits less the cost of the
wine he served.[25]

Kenneth also took great delight in his baby daughter Mary, and Marthe
was determined to make her "marriage" succeed, trying in all ways possible to please Kenneth. But she had a difficult time feeling comfortable
around Kenneth's friends and acquaintances, sensing that many of them
could not treat her with the same warmth they had extended to Marie.
She missed her friend Ellen, now married to Warren Tallman (who with
Donald Allen would edit the influential *The Poetics of the New American
Poetry* twenty years later). Kenneth discouraged her from keeping the
friendships she had formed before he had met her. However, in June of
1952, when Kenneth returned to Giant Forest in Sequoia National Park,
he could hardly object to Marthe's inviting Ellen and Warren down to
keep her company at Eighth Avenue. While Marthe was at the office, they
looked after Mary. Kenneth expected Marthe and Mary to join him by

the end of the summer. He was positive that two-year-old Mary would find life in the mountains exciting. When he arrived at camp in mid-June, he was welcomed by birds, chipmunks, deer, and a young black bear that had made itself at home by sitting on the table at Kenneth's campsite. As always, he was delighted amid these surroundings. It provided relief from his San Francisco routine and his self-imposed reading agenda of classic volumes on European and Asian history, philosophy, religion, politics, art, and American folklore and poetry. For the most part, he avoided novels, which he considered "a class of literature for women and men under thirty."[26] He had continued his habit of reading the fifteenth edition of the *Encyclopaedia Brittanica*. But for creative inspiration he needed to renew and sustain the elemental but deep knowledge he gleaned from living in the mountains.

At Giant Forest, Rexroth wrote the final revisions of *The Dragon and the Unicorn*. He mailed his additions and revisions to Marthe, asking her to spell out any questions or criticism she had, and to isolate passages that were confusing or inconsistent. Marthe obliged. She did not care for the stanza in which he lashed out against the British intellectuals and anarchists he had met in London, one of whom he describes as a "blonde barrage / Balloon . . . / . . . a frantic / Imitation of Mary / McCarthy, Rita Hayworth / And Simone de Beauvoir Sartre."[27] Rexroth excused his attack on Mary McCarthy as a form of retaliation for her portrayal of him as the proletarian poet in *The Groves of Academe*. He made no effort, however, to defend his shabby treatment of Hayworth and de Beauvoir, but started to doubt that Laughlin with his "horror of libel suits" would publish this section.[28]

He was struggling with the opening of Part V, which describes his last view of New York City as his train heads west toward Toledo where he lived as a boy.

> New York a grey haze with flights of
> Pigeons wheeling above Harlem
> As the boys on the rooftops
> Whirl long poles and call them home.[29]

Somehow Rexroth misses the beat here, and captures neither the image nor the movement of his observations, the diction—"pigeons wheeling," boys who "whirl long poles"—is not authentic: the language is too ethereal for the urban scenes it describes. And yet by the end of the stanza, the verse goes back on track.

> The Hudson sinks deeper and
> Deeper into the blue until
> Nothing is left but the black
> Outline of the Catskills, the lights
> Of the other shore, the soaring
> Bridge over the long water
> Wan in the end of evening.[30]

Perhaps Rexroth was not at his best with East Coast city images. William Everson drew the boundaries of Rexroth's territory more sharply, maintaining that Rexroth needed the "California earth and sky and sea [to] form the vital imagery infusing his verse with its power."[31] Yet James Harmon made a point of writing from Alaska to tell Rexroth how much he enjoyed reading the poem: "It must be the most difficult thing in the world to control and sustain something like that and make it ALL poetry. . . . Thank you for a real experience."[32]

In his mountain retreat, he was also gathering material for a special edition of Laughlin's *Perspectives.* Already he had lined up contributions from Richard Eberhart, Selden Rodman, George Woodcock, Henry Miller, Kenneth Patchen, and Parker Tyler. He was going to ask Robert Duncan, William Everson, and Philip Lamantia for a poem each. He hoped as well to include an essay on recent American jazz by Darius Milhaud (who was teaching at Mills College), and an essay on Morris Graves. The issue never appeared.[33] Preoccupied as he was, he genuinely missed Marthe and Mary. He suggested that they come before July 7, the beginning of Marthe's three-week vacation. Low on energy—she was holding down two part-time jobs and still rising early to feed Mary—Marthe begged off. She felt too worn out for such a strenuous vacation, but agreed to let Mary go.

In the third week of June 1952, she drove Mary to Fresno where Kenneth picked her up and took her into Sequoia National Park for the first of their many camping trips together. (The old Willys was still running largely because Rexroth had bought another one solely as a source for spare parts.) Mary was almost two years old, too young to be frightened by the bears who came by at night to take a peak at the new visitor. When she missed Marthe, she and Kenneth would play "phoning Mama" with the paprika can. Kenneth asked Marthe to send a big box of good crayons so that Mary could keep herself busy when Kenneth was not free to entertain her. He also asked Marthe to mail the *Penguin Guide to the Stars* so that he could point out the constellations. Over the years, Mary's presence would become the source of some of his best poems, including his autobiographical "A Living Pearl," "Halley's Comet," and "The Great Nebula of Andromeda," all three of which appeared in the 1956 volume *In Defense of the Earth.* "Halley's Comet" celebrates a father's love for his daughter, and the great sense of continuity she represents for him. In "The Great Nebula of Andromeda," Rexroth permits his political attitudes to surface, not in the didactic fashion that sometimes mars a long poem like *The Dragon and the Unicorn,* but as pointed observation. Wakened in the middle of the night by horses stumbling around a campsite, Kenneth stares at Mary, whose sleeping face he compares to a "jewel in the moonlight." He picks up his "glass" to observe "the Great Nebula / Of Andromeda swim like / A phosphorescent ameoba / Slowly around the Pole."[34] But he speculates that man-made world events will prevent Mary from seeing the twenty-first century, and expresses his fear that far away from his idyllic scene, "fat-hearted men" are plotting her murder. Rexroth had not abandoned his pacifist politics, and his mind was always engaged in planning to help young men acquire CO status during the Korean War.

In late June 1952, Rexroth got word from Laughlin that he was in Pasadena and would like to visit. A few days later Laughlin walked into the campsite, "grinning and shambling," and bearing good news. He had finally accepted Rexroth's Japanese translations and had set the publishing date for *The Dragon and the Unicorn*. Marthe had worked hard to get the manuscript in order, and Kenneth showed his appreciation of her efforts by asking her to send books of French poetry, to track down a Greek dictionary, to sew cloth tote bags and waterproof ponchos, to handle correspondence with various letters to magazine editors and publishers. He had also just completed a long-overdue article on Fernand Léger for *Art News* which he wanted Marthe to type up and send off.

When Kenneth returned to Eighth Avenue at the end of the summer, he and Marthe started to argue violently. Kenneth did not approve of the Tallmans, even though they had helped Marthe enormously while Kenneth was away, taking care of Mary, fixing leaky faucets, and providing all around good company. The Tallmans felt very close to Marthe and invited her, Kenneth, and Mary to spend Christmas with them in Seattle, but Kenneth refused. He seemed to be jealous of them, particularly Ellen, whom he erroneously suspected of having sexual designs on Marthe. Now that he was back, he demanded that Marthe's friends leave, and that he, Marthe and Mary settle into a routine like the one they shared before he left for Giant Forest. One significant change did occur. Marthe landed a full-time position in the office of the Dean of Instruction, Rex Bell, at San Francisco State, and her salary was raised to $368 a month.

A temporary peace prevailed, but Rexroth was wary about the future. He confided in Babette Deutsch that he envied her because she was secure in her marriage.

I have always had a German sentimental Browningesque picture of marriage as ending like Baucis and Philemon or the Japanese couple who also became trees. And here I am at 46, married the 3rd time and to a girl of 24. . . . And it is painful to realize that my baby daughter whom I love so much and would like to watch going into life will be twenty when I am sixty-five.[35]

For now, the Rexroth family was a happy if unconventional trio. The relationship between Marthe and Kenneth, seriously troubled almost from the start, appeared to be somewhat more stable, and Rexroth obviously adored his firstborn child.

Nineteen

ALIVE IN THE SILENT DECADE
1953–1955

B Y THE MID-FIFTIES the San Francisco Bay Area was turning into an exciting place for artists and writers and their audiences. The foundations for a counterculture had been established, not only by Rexroth's literary evenings but also by the discussions led by writers like Robert Duncan, Jack Spicer, and Robin Blaser, and by the informal writers' conferences that Josephine Miles had arranged on the University of California's Berkeley campus. Poet Madeline Gleason also arranged a series of readings for San Francisco poets. And Yvor Winters, isolated as ever, was still attracting high-powered graduate students to his Stanford classroom (among Winters's students who achieved distinction were Thom Gunn, J. V. Cunningham, and Herbert Blau, who became the co-director of the Actor's Workshop, for fifteen years the most important and controversial theater company in San Francisco). More informally, the literary scene could be observed in coffee houses and clubs like the Black Cat, the Cellar, Café Trieste, Leo Krikorian's "The Place," Gino & Carlo's, and Henri Lenoir's Vesuvio Bar, considered "the most popular bohemian watering place in North Beach," whose patrons included or would soon include Robert Duncan, Dylan Thomas, Philip Lamantia, Lawrence Ferlinghetti, Michael McClure, Allen Ginsberg, Herb Gold, Philip Whalen, and Jack Kerouac.[1]

Little magazines like *Circle* and *Ark,* as well as Peter Martin's *City Lights,* Horace Schwartz's *Goad,* Leslie Woolf Hedley's *Inferno,* and Richard Emerson's *Golden Goose,* had contributed to the Bay Area's growing avant-garde, politically hip reputation. But the momentum created by this activity did not flow without interference. McCarthyism and the Korean War caused some dispersement. Although they both eventually would return to the Bay Area, Duncan and Spicer left town: Duncan for Majorca; Spicer, who refused to sign the loyalty oath required by the recently passed Levering Act of all state teachers and employees, for Minnesota, New York, and Boston. Even though he had accepted the Mark Twain professorship, Robert Penn Warren also refused to sign the loyalty oath and did not come to the Berkeley campus.[2] In general, however, the San Francisco Bay Area was a magnet for new thought and art. Throughout the early fifties KPFA won increasing public support and provided an uncensored outlet for expression. Other important forums would soon open up, as more people moved west, some for a visit, others to stay.

In November 1950, Floss and William Carlos Williams had called on Kenneth and Marthe for a "fine chicken dinner which Rexroth had prepared himself, followed by an evening of good talk."[3] And many first-timers in town looked up Rexroth or asked to be introduced to him by a mutual friend. In his middle age, he had achieved the status of an established poet with anti-establishment credentials. Alongside his numerous articles and weekly radio scripts, he had written three volumes of poetry, in addition to four verse plays. One of the newer faces who started appearing at his Friday night soirées was Lawrence Ferlinghetti, an aspiring writer with a Ph.D. from the Sorbonne. Ferlinghetti wanted to meet Rexroth because both his poetry and his Introduction to the poems of D. H. Lawrence had bowled him over. Ferlinghetti had been in San Francisco since 1951, and his friends the printer and graphic artist David Ruff and the poet Holly Beye brought him over to Rexroth's. Ferlinghetti had already met Marthe while looking for a part-time teaching position at San Francisco State.[4] Ferlinghetti soon became a regular at Rexroth's, but rarely uttered a word, preferring to sit back and listen to his host's train of thought on any number of literary, artistic, or political ideas. He liked Rexroth well enough, although he was a little overwhelmed by his domineering presence. Rexroth seemed prepared to talk about anyone and anything with equal authority. Or, as Ferlinghetti remembered Thomas Parkinson saying, upon first meeting Rexroth, one got the impression that sometime after the Kerensky regime, Rexroth had left the fledgling Soviet Republic to stagger on by itself.

Ferlinghetti had been "a completely straight Sorbonne student" who did not even know that there were conscientious objectors during World War II.[5] During those Friday evenings, Rexroth told him about the anarchist movement, Herbert Read, the Freedom Press, and Kropotkin. Whatever intellectual bullying took place—it was impossible for example to defend Ezra Pound's poetry in Rexroth's presence—the energy and the passion of the moment was what counted. To top off his other talents, Rexroth was a great storyteller, even if the stories were not always true, and he was full of short and irreverent descriptions of people: university professors were "the munching and belching society"; the New Critics belonged to the "Pillowcase Head Press School of Literature." It was at Rexroth's that Ferlinghetti met James Broughton, Philip Lamantia, and Robert Duncan, whom he liked immediately. For a while Ferlinghetti looked to Rexroth (and to Kenneth Patchen and Henry Miller) as mentor.

The friendship between Ferlinghetti and Rexroth balanced out as

Ferlinghetti's identity was transformed from a "young, punk North Beach poet" to a bookstore owner and best-selling author. Rexroth had told Ferlinghetti that a bookstore selling paperbacks exclusively would never succeed; but as the Pocket Bookshop—which Ferlinghetti founded with Peter Martin—prospered and expanded to become City Lights Books in June 1953, Ferlinghetti earned new respect in Rexroth's eyes, and a relationship was established between two artists who were now positioned to support and promote one another's work.[6] Both were writing book reviews for the *San Francisco Chronicle*.[7] Ferlinghetti tactfully pointed out that while the early Cubist experiments in *The Art of Worldly Wisdom* were hardly Rexroth's best, it did contain "bright, hard gems." He considered the verse plays to be Rexroth's best work to date.[8] The review of *The Dragon and the Unicorn*[9] is less qualified. Ferlinghetti praises it as "trenchant poetry, which has the clarity of Chinese symbols. Sometimes it is classically lyric, sometimes it growls." Ferlinghetti did not object to its discursive segments, perhaps because the anarchist-pacifist perspective Rexroth articulates in those passages was close to, if not identical, with his own. A decade later, despite his reservations about Rexroth, Charles Olson told Ted Berrigan that he admired the poem also: "That Rexroth, there's no accounting for him, but that long poem of his, *The Dragon and the Unicorn*, that's really something! He gets the whole thing down there."[10]

Rexroth reviewed Ferlinghetti's first book of poems, *Pictures of the Gone World*, along with *Stairwells and Marriages* by Holly Beye, whom he described as "one of the most significant women poets of the youngest generation."[11] Rexroth had seen earlier versions of the poems that appeared in *Pictures of the Gone World*, and was convinced that they would speak to a wide audience. He compared them favorably to those by the French novelist, critic, and poet Raymond Queneau (whose acidic and witty work Ferlinghetti had never read), and the French poet and screenwriter Jacques Prévert. He described Ferlinghetti's work as "the folk poetry of the displaced urban intellectual," and praised it for its "genuinely popular diction."

In addition, Rexroth had helped Ferlinghetti get writing assignments for *Art Digest*.[12] And for the second title in his new publishing venture, the Pocket Poets Series (*Pictures of the Gone World* was the first), Ferlinghetti published *Thirty Spanish Poems of Love and Exile*, translated by Kenneth Rexroth in 1956. Ten years later, City Lights Books would publish the first paperback edition of Rexroth's *Beyond the Mountains*. These two men were not merely logrolling. They achieved the rather pleasant position of being able to encourage one another as members of a growing literary community in San Francisco that was changing the way people related to art and poetry. The importance of this accomplishment was extraordinary. Together, they were making poetry accessible, infusing it with an ecological and communitarian philosophy without compromising aesthetic standards, even giving it the status of popular entertainment. It was a truly Western phenomenon. The only person on the East Coast they felt connected to was William Carlos Williams, the poet "who creates Sacramental relationships."

During this period, Jonathan Williams got in touch with Rexroth for the first time. While he was a prep student at St. Albans in Washington, D.C., he bought five copies of *In What Hour* for fifty cents each, the first purchase of what was to be his Rexroth collection. He heard much about Rexroth during a visit with Kenneth and Miriam Patchen in Old Lyme, Connecticut, in May 1950. Soon after this visit, the twenty-one-year-old Williams wrote to Rexroth to tell him how much he appreciated his work, which struck him as a "very rare contribution towards humanity and integrity in the midst of literary wheeze and collapse."[13] He also wanted the benefit of Rexroth's advice about avoiding the draft. Much to his family's disapproval, he had withdrawn from Princeton University and had decided that he wanted to devote himself to painting and writing. While they were willing to adjust to their son's artistic persona, Williams thought it would be wise to apply for admission to the Chicago Institute of Design. But he was concerned about finding a good place to settle. He did not like New York City, and from all reports, including the *Harper's* article about the new cult of sex and anarchy, he did not see California as an alternative. Perhaps Rexroth could suggest a good place for him to live?

Rexroth was pleased to get Williams's letters and the two began a correspondence that would span the next twenty-five years. Rexroth assured Williams that the sex and anarchy article in *Harper's* was a sham: the author was the wife of a "leading Stalinist frontman," an economics professor at Berkeley. The libelous article was dictated, Rexroth alleged, by a directive of the State Central Committee of the Communist Party, which sought to destroy "the petty bourgeois anarchism" that had arisen locally since the end of World War II.[14] Rexroth added that he now had very little contact with Henry Miller—Mildred Brady's other target— although the two autodidacts over the years favorably reviewed one another's work. As for the Chicago Institute of Design, Rexroth had little to say except that when he passed through Chicago in 1949, he heard at a party that the photography faculty was rated among the best in the country. But in general Rexroth was contemptuous of art schools. He felt that in most institutions the style of painting dominant was dated, the "academic abstractionism of the Moholy Nagy, Ozenfant, Mondrian type," the kind of painting he had done himself between 1925 and 1940. He was no kinder to the California School of Fine Arts, which he described as "under a Neo-Dribble & Drip School dictatorship."[15] In the end, Rexroth thought Williams should do what was most expedient, and than for the present Chicago might provide a more liberating atmosphere that his home in Highlands, North Carolina. He was not encouraging about Williams's application for CO status, warning him that if he were thrown into the penitentiary, he would have to watch out for the Communists who would try either to convert or murder him.[16] But he advised him to choose jail over the Army. Based on his experience in some "nasty jails," Rexroth said the trick of getting through a prison term was never to think of "any screw or warden as human."[17]

Williams decided that the Chicago Institute of Design was stagnant, a "Kapital of Kleenex Kulture,"[18] and he left in June 1951 to spend the summer at Black Mountain College, not far from Highlands, Williams's hometown. But first he went out to San Francisco, where he published his first Jargon Press item, a broadside of one of his own poems and an engraving by David Ruff. It was dedicated to Rexroth, whom he met for the first time that month. (Actually he had met Marthe first, since Kenneth was in the mountains the day he came by.) When he got to Black Mountain in July, the environment proved conducive to writing once he became adjusted to Charles Olson's standards and criticism. Under the tutelage of Aaron Siskind and Harry Callahan, Williams also studied photography and resumed work on the broadsides, pamphlets, and books that would appear in his Jargon series, a lifelong publishing venture.

In December 1952, Williams went up to New York City to see a preview of the Living Theater's production of *Beyond the Mountain* at the Cherry Lane Theater. (The plays had their formal New York premier on December 30.) It was a difficult evening. Malina and Beck had been extraordinarily considerate of Rexroth's role as author, and they sent him long, detailed questions about costumes, music, and casting. Yet Rexroth was greatly disturbed when he learned that they planned to present all four plays in one evening.

I think the audience will be worn out half way through—as well as the actors . . . I really know quite a bit about theatre and I assure you you will just be throwing [the plays] away. Ask anyone with practical experience—radio—burlesque—musical comedy or vaudeville—or the movies NOT some highbrow—and you will get the same answer.[19]

Over Rexroth's objections, they did perform all four, with a running time of three and a half hours.[20] Nor could they accommodate Rexroth's request that they use musical compositions by his friend Richard Collins (who played with the Dave Brubeck Octet), which had been used for *Phaedra*, the first play in the series, produced in St. Louis in, June 1951, and directed by James Walsh. William Carlos Williams did not like the production, even though in *The New York Times Book Review* he had written a very favorable review of the printed version, praising Rexroth for "rais[ing] the colloquial tone to lines of tragic significance."[21] Several negative reviews followed, which Beck and Malina attributed to critics of Rexroth's anarchist politics. But they conceded that their efforts, to a large extent, had been unsuccessful.

Beck and Malina had been proud to produce *Beyond the Mountains*. In the theater's lobby where ten of Rexroth's pastels were displayed, they arranged to sell copies of the New Directions edition. Their goal was to draw parallels between the fall of Greek civilization and the disintegration of the present world, and to prevent their audience from becoming a detached, alienated population without any sense of spiritual commitment or social responsibility.[22] With Malina as Berenike, Beck directed in the Noh style, a deliberate attempt to hypnotize the audience into believing that the end of the world had arrived when the barbaric horde of Huns appear on stage during the last part of the play. But that device was not enough to sustain the audience's attention for three and a half hours. Rexroth missed the performance because he could not afford the air fare to New York. Beck remained "enamoured of the plays," and insisted on taking blame for the production's failure.[23]

The Living Theater lost $2,600 on *Beyond the Mountains,* and a large share, temporarily, of Rexroth's goodwill. He had difficulty recovering his pastels and Richard Collins's musical score. The company had not paid New Directions its royalty fees, nor had they returned the unsold copies of the plays. On Rexroth's suggestion, New Directions filed a lawsuit, but after a brief flare of hostility, all was set straight. Beck and Malina had endured a difficult summer in 1952 when their license was revoked after their landlord called in the Fire Department to stop their production of *Ubu Roi,* which offended him. Rexroth excused them for being remiss about his things. He heard from them periodically, and finally met them when he was in New York in 1958. The Living Theater remained eager to produce new Rexroth plays; much later in 1972, there was talk of Rexroth and Beck compiling an anthology of anarchist poetry. Whatever their differences in style and operation, Rexroth, Beck, and Malina shared a kindred spirit.

Jonathan Williams lost his CO appeal, and rather than face a prison term for draft evasion, signed up for the Army. He was trained as a neuropsychiatric technician and was sent abroad to work in the General Hospital in Stuttgart. Discharged in the fall of 1954, he resumed his literary activities, using the printing press at Black Mountain to publish such poets as Charles Olson, Robert Creeley, Joel Oppenheimer, and Robert Duncan. He next went out to San Francisco, where he worked as a shipping clerk for a record company from September 1954 to May 1955. He and Rexroth saw one another frequently. They went hiking together in Marin County, and Rexroth, "who knew everything around him," would reel off the names of the trees, constellations, and minerals in the rocks around and underneath their feet with dizzying accuracy.[24] Alluding to the Devil's Gulch shack, Williams wrote: "No one else knew where to build a hut like Chomei's [the Buddhist monk] in the hills of Marin County."[25] Williams and Rexroth discussed poetry, but they also liked to talk about jazz and Rexroth's impressive collection of recordings by the Dave Brubeck Octet, Dizzy Gillespie, Fats Waller, the Paul Whiteman Orchestra, Joe Vanuti,

Lionel Hampton, Bix Beiderbecke, Earl Johnson, and Pinetop Smith.[26] His taste also ran to Renaissance, Baroque, classical, and romantic: Bach, Scarletti, Vivaldi, Mozart, Liszt, Paganini, Brahms, and Mendelssohn.[27]

Williams enjoyed Rexroth's literary gossip and raunchy humor. Nor did he mind the liberties that Rexroth sometimes took with the facts for the sake of a good story, or to enhance his image. The day Charlie Parker died, Rexroth called up Williams to commiserate and pass along the observation that he hadn't seen Bird since 1920, when he was living on Chicago's South Side. Williams did not bother to tell Rexroth that 1920 was the year Parker was born, nor did he see any reason to dispute Rexroth's claim that one of his favorite suits, a neat brown pinstripe, had been a gift from Al Capone.

Rexroth and Parker had actually met in the spring of 1952, but did not see one another again until 1954, when Parker rushed out to San Francisco to replace a mysteriously vanished Stan Getz on the Stan Kenton tour of the West Coast. He renewed his acquaintance with Rexroth, whom he considered an astute observer of the jazz scene. To Rexroth, Parker appeared to be in the twilight of his career—he died the following year. Rexroth regarded Parker and Dylan Thomas as the two beleaguered, tragic giants of their age:

like pillars of Hercules, like two ruined Titans guarding the entrance to one of Dante's circles. . . . Both of them were overcome by the horror of the world in which they found themselves, because at last they could no longer overcome that world with the weapon of a purely lyrical art.[28]

For Rexroth, Parker was a great contemporary (fifteen years his junior) who had "caught the pulse of our times, the pressure, the confusion, and complexity . . . [the] sadness, sweetness, and love."[29]

Two years earlier, when Dylan Thomas died in New York City in November 1953, Rexroth wrote a memorial for him entitled "Thou Shalt Not Kill." And indictment of society at large, the poem became famous. It is not necessarily an example of his finest work, but it stands out as undisguised and rhetorical social protest, its message so important that William Carlos Williams believed copies of the poem should have been posted on college campuses across the country.[30] Morgan Gibson has described it as a "public sacrament of mourning and righteous outrage."[31] Gibson notes that the poem echoes the "Lament for the Makaris," probably by the Scottish Chaucerian William Dunbar (c.1460–c.1530). A reminiscence of dead poets, the poem provided Rexroth with a refrain—*Timor mortis conturbat me*—for his own elegy.[32] The *Timor Mortis* theme frequently appeared in fifteenth-century lyrics. But for some readers, the poem illustrates the incompatibility between art and politics, and the uneven quality of Rexroth's oeuvre. Occasionally, it borders on the ridiculous:

> Henry Luce killed him with a telegram to the Pope.
> *Mademoiselle* strangled him with a padded brassiere.[33]

Sometimes it sounds like a recitation of clichés:

> How many stopped writing at thirty?
> How many went to work for *Time*?
> How many died of prefrontal
> Lobotomies in the Communist Party?
> How many are lost in the back wards
> Of provincial madhouses?
> How many on the advice of
> Their psychoanalysts, decided
> A business career was better after all?[34]

The poem can also be offensive:

> I want to pour gasoline down your chimneys.
> I want to blow up your galleries.
> I want to burn down your editorial offices.
> I want to slit the bellies of your frigid women.
> I want to sink your sailboats and launches.
> I want to strangle your children at their finger paintings.[35]

Yet it does succeed in communicating one poet's profound grief over the death of a fellow poet by its sheer force of energy and clear vision of where to lay the blame: on a society that corrupts creative energy in the name of progress.

> Who killed the bright-headed bird?
> You did, you son of a bitch.
> You drowned him in your cocktail brain.
> He fell down and died in your synthetic heart.
> You killed him,
> Oppenheimer the Million-Killer,
> You killed him,
> Einstein the Gray Eminence.
> You killed him
> Havanahavana, with your Nobel Prize.[36]

Rexroth had enormous sympathy for Thomas because as far as Rexroth could understand, Thomas's single defense against "the ruin of the world" was the creative act.

He was able to find meaning in his art as long as it was the answer to air raids and gas ovens. As the world began to take on the guise of an immense air raid or gas oven, I believe his art became meaningless to him.[37]

His enthusiasm for Thomas had been renewed when he came to San Francisco for a second visit in 1953, but Rexroth was still appalled by the power of Thomas's self-destruction. He was ambivalent about Thomas in other ways, too. Although Thomas's work showed a progression from writing verse that "hits you across the face with a reeking, bloody heart, a heart full of worms and needles and black blood and thorns, a werewolf heart" to a poetry that reflects "the humility and calm of ecstatic vision,"[38] he did not agree with the conventional view that Thomas's technique was original. Nor did he consider him to be influential. For Rexroth, Dylan Thomas was important because he urged writers to use their hearts and dreams as much as their rational thoughts, and to resist a mechanized mentality by turning to myth, personal religion, and the imagination.[39]

Rexroth was truly shaken by Thomas's death. To some extent, he identified with the career of Thomas, who from the outset tried to earn his living as a poet with no visible means of support. In his Introduction to *The New British Poets*, Rexroth wrote that "after Thomas, literature was wide open to others than the sons of gentlemen, if they could find some way to keep alive."[40] Furthermore, he believed that Thomas's idiom had been formed by a force that had similarly gripped Rexroth as a child: an "uncontrolled, boyish omniverous reading" that included Surrealist texts, sex books, Shakespeare, Blake, Lawrence, "an orgy of literary sensationalism."[41] But Thomas had become a star, earning high fees for his readings. Despite Rexroth's eminent position in San Francisco literary circles, he was still struggling to make ends meet, and persisted in believing that the Eastern establishment either ignored him or disapproved of him outright. The powerful sense of outrage in "Thou Shalt Not Kill" descended from Rexroth's feeling that his own destiny was also woven into the poem, that his own voice would eventually be wiped out, too. Like Thomas, he would be forgotten, a victim of a capitalist society that looked upon art and literature as mere commodities.

When Karl Shapiro, the Pulitzer Prize-winning poet, lectured on Thomas in San Francisco in April 1955, he noted the hundreds of eulogies written after his death. He suggested that the California poets—"the blankety blank type of Bohemian poets who regard everyone as dead"— were among the most extreme lamenters. He ridiculed "Thou Shalt Not Kill" as overblown with conviction, and for blaming Thomas's death "on everything from T. S. Eliot to *New Republic* magazine."[42] Two years later, Rexroth retaliated in his "Disengagement: The Art of the Beat Generation" by reporting that Shapiro "once referred to San Francisco as the 'last refuge of the bohemian remnant'—a description he thought of as invidious."[43] Yet other readers were also defensive and wanted to know why Rexroth regarded them as responsible for Thomas's death, or what was wrong with a suit from Brooks Brothers:

> "You killed him! You killed him.
> In your bad damned Brooks Brothers suit,
> You son of a bitch."

This poem was published by three different presses, and at the Cellar, a former Chinese restaurant that had been converted into a popular jazz club, Rexroth often read it to the accompaniment of the Cellar Jazz Quintet: drummer Sonny Wayne, pianist Bill Weisjahns, tenor saxophonist

Bruce Lippincott, bassists Jerry Goode and Bob Lewis, and trumpeter Dickie Mills. With Ferlinghetti sharing the spotlight, Rexroth packed the place for six nights.[44] He performed in other North Beach clubs as well. Including the Hungry I. Among the people who saw Rexroth perform was Herbert Blau:

There was a riff of old protest in Kenneth's performance, as if eroticizing the Wobblies, whom in his populist mode he'd always admired. Gyrating, perspiring, he assailed the banality of the age of Ike with its Silent Generation and gray-flannel emotion that seemed to make everybody old before his time. . . . Kenneth was talking art, he was also talking politics, and to all those who had sold out the imagination, Kenneth was unsparing.[45]

During the mid-fifties, Rexroth continued to establish friendships with talented younger writers. Gary Snyder was among the closest. Snyder had first seen Rexroth's poetry in Selden Rodman's Modern Giant anthology, but did not pay much attention to him until he was a graduate student at Indiana University. One day in the library he pulled down a copy of *The Signature of All Things*. He was attracted to the "West Coast and California flavors and qualities" of the book, but he was also fascinated by the biographical information on the jacket copy that Rexroth was a mountaineer. In his middle and late adolescence, Snyder loved mountaineering, and worked as a lookout on Crater Mountain and on Sourdough Mountain in Baker National Forest when he was twenty-two.[46] In 1952, Snyder shared a San Francisco apartment with poet Philip Whalen, his Reed College roommate, but the following year decided that he needed to be closer to Berkeley where he was taking classes in Chinese and Japanese. In the fall of 1953 Snyder called up Rexroth and asked to be invited to a Friday night evening. Snyder, who had read a sizable portion of Rexroth's work, was impressed by Rexroth's erudition, especially in the areas of anthropology, American-Indian studies, and in the Far East. He also appreciated Rexroth's carefully conceived anarcho-pacifism, a political perspective that Snyder had already worked out for himself. On a different note, Snyder admired Rexroth's easy familiarity with European culture since Snyder had never found the time to study it. For the next three years, the two men saw each other regularly, nearly every weekend.

Given their difference in age—twenty-five years—and in experience, the friendship blossomed as one between adviser and student, although Snyder was far too well informed to assume the role of apprentice for very long. Rexroth gave Snyder "the nerve to draw on Far Eastern material . . . to draw Buddhist references and imagery into [his] work,"[47] even though Snyder regarded Rexroth's attitude toward Buddhism as ambivalent. Rexroth's "dry, somewhat choppy line" influenced Snyder's verse as well, although not nearly as much as that of Ezra Pound. Rexroth also provided Snyder with a model for "mountain poetry," more commonly referred to as "bearshit-on-the-trial" poetry: a wilderness setting, a lone observer-speaker, a reference to a star that orientates the speaker and the reader, a picturesque local—near a creek, at the foot of a snow-capped mountain, with precise observations of the surrounding nature life, the animals, the flowers. The reader is given "a sense of the beauty, relative permanence, and superiority of the wilderness in contrast to the machinations of men."[48]

Early into their friendship, Snyder sent Rexroth a poem that he had written during his stay on the Warm Springs Reservation in the summer of 1950, specifically inspired by a Warm Springs Indian tribal celebration called "A Berry Feast." He had also integrated his logging experiences into the poem, as well as some "Oriental notions [and] contemporary goings-on in the Northwest."[49] "A Berry Feast" may also be responsible for the earthy label sometimes attached to Snyder's (and Rexroth's) poetry.

> In bearshit find it in August,
> Neat pile on the fragrant trail, in late
> August, perhaps by a Larch tree
> Bear has been eating the berries.[50]

It is the opening poem of *The Back Country,* a book Snyder dedicates to Rexroth.

After first reading *The Dragon and the Unicorn,* Snyder told Rexroth that it could be improved, but that it was a major work, pointing the direction which American poetry had to follow: toward "the Orient, the western half of this country, the non-European cultural tradition of America and the Pacific. With what can be salavaged from the remains of Europe."[51] He also appreciated the poem for its visual imagery, "especially around nature." For his part, Rexroth praised Snyder whenever he had the opportunity, describing him as the "best informed, most thoughtful, and most articulate of his colleagues."[52] He lauds Snyder for his sense of ecology and community, his "Buddhist love and respect for all sentient creatures," and the linguistic sophistication of his style. Snyder and Rexroth's friendship remained solid longer than most of Rexroth's relationships with other poets, although the two men were to have a crucial falling out in the seventies.

The literary scene seemed to be coalescing neatly, but the political currents of the day were growing more conservative. Rexroth was advising young men who did not want to fight in the Korean War, some of them students at Berkeley. Word had spread that he had achieved CO status during World War II. How had he managed to do so? According to one rumor, he got his exemption by declaring himself to be of Japanese descent.[53] Some people thought that he had spent time in a federal penitentiary.

He also attended and spoke at various anarchist meetings, one of them at the Mills Terrace Christian Church in Oakland, organized by Roger

Rush, who was chairman of a group called the Social Action Committee. Rush's son, the writer Norman Rush, got in touch with Rexroth a year or two later, first to express his admiration for Rexroth's poetry but also to ask if Rexroth could help him find material written by the British Personalists—Alex Comfort, George Woodcock, and Herbert Read in particular, the poets Rexroth had included in his *The New British Poets*. Rexroth sent him a large batch of anarchist material which Rush returned before leaving for federal prison in Tucson, Arizona, where he served nine months of a two-year term for being a non-religious conscientious objector. He and Rexroth corresponded during Rush's prison term, and then briefly while Rush attended Swarthmore College on parole. Although their friendship eventually unraveled, Rexroth remained for Rush a model for the man living in opposition, the radical who did not sell out, a person who "knew how the world is put together."[54]

However, no matter how many anarchist-pacifist meetings he attended, no matter how he sought to change the exploitive elements in society, Rexroth grew resigned to the realization that the world would never come close to his ideal. The execution of Sacco and Vanzetti, the Moscow Trials, the Spanish Civil War, the internment of Japanese Americans during World War II, the Cold War of the fifties, and the Korean War all indicated the shrinking possibilities for a world community. He had presented this point of view two years earlier in a poem commemoratins the death of his friend Eli Jacobson. A lay analyst living in Los Angeles who had once been active in the Party, he had remained in Rexroth's eyes in incurable agitprop and an efficient organizer of leftist literary groups:[55]

> Together, we believe we
> Would see with our own eyes the new
> World where man was no longer
> Wolf to man, but men and women
> Were all brothers and lovers
> Together. We will not see it.[56]

The course of events did not embitter him entirely. In his imagination, he relived the days of active commitment, and never regretted the side he had chosen. "Life was good for us," he writes in the poem; even setbacks were tolerable because they were met with "courage and a gay heart." But he doubted that he would live to see any real change.

Through the next coming years, he would express a similar perspective in poems like "The Bad Old Days," "Portrait of the Artist as a Young Anarchist," and "Fish Peddlar and Cobbler":

> We thought that soon all things would
> Be changed, not just economic
> And social relationships, but
> Painting, poetry, music, dance,

> Architecture, even the food
> We ate and the clothes we wore
> Would be ennobled. It will take
> Longer than we expected.[57]

As far as Rexroth could see, the political climate remained stagnant. Yet even though the prospects for a "noble" world were ebbing, he stubbornly refused to surrender all hope.

Twenty

THE BEATS ARRIVE
1955–1956

IN 1953, ANOTHER LITTLE MAGAZINE had been born, not on the West Coast but at Black Mountain College. Charles Olson, the rector, wanted a journal that would publicize the innovative institute and provide an outlet for its community of writers. Cid Corman's *Origin* proved to be less receptive to these new writers than Olson had hoped, and he asked Robert Creeley if he would like to edit a magazine open to all new and experimental prose and poetry that had broken free of the constraints of New Criticism. Creeley accepted and in the process of forming an editorial board thought about tapping Rexroth. In December, Creeley asked Rexroth if he would serve on the advisory board of the newly launched *Black Mountain Review*.[1]

Three years earlier, while he was living in New Hampshire, Creeley had invited Rexroth to contribute to a journal that he hoped to found. It never materialized. Soon afterward, as the American editor for Rainer M. Gerhardt's *Fragmente,* he asked if Rexroth would send some poems to Gerhardt, who was editing the magazine in Freiburg, Germany. The two poets also had a mutual friend in Denise Levertov, and shared an active concern about advancing her career as a poet. Creeley had visited Levertov and her husband Mitchell Goodman—a Harvard classmate—in the summer of 1951 where they were living in a house near Aix-en-Provence. Rexroth confided to Creeley that Levertov was "something they only turn out once in 100 years, one of the few people I ever completely loved at first sight. Everybody, at least all men, who know her speak of her as though they once seen Dante's B[eatr]ice plain."[2] From Aix, Creeley wrote Rexroth to tell him that Levertov seemed well and thriving but unhappy at the prospect of returning to expensive New York; and from Majorca, Creeley addressed Rexroth with a different request. A good friend in San Francisco was battling both emotional and financial troubles. Although her husband was physically abusing her, she could not bring herself to leave him and start a new life. Creeley asked Rexroth if he would mind dropping his friend a note, letting her know that he would be willing to see her. Creeley apologized for asking such a favor but trusted Rexroth as the only one he knew who could help.

Rexroth agreed to become advisory editor for the *Black Mountain Review*, then resigned after reading the first issue. It included his translations of Artaud, one of the poems distinguished by the memorable line "I say shit / to everything." (With Marthe's help, Kenneth had been working full speed on translating from the French. Jonathan Williams published a Jargon Society edition of *One Hundred Poems from the French* in 1955).[3] A devastating attack by Martin Seymour-Smith on Theodore Roethke, blasting both the poets who imitated him and the critics who approved of their imitation, also appeared. Rexroth thought the article was so spiteful and truculent that he no longer wanted to be associated with the publication. That attack further convinced Rexroth that most literary criticism published east of the Rockies—the kind favored by "the castrated rabbits of Puddle, a Magazine of Piddle"—was biased. Disappointed by his decision to resign, Creeley nevertheless urged Rexroth to write *Black Mountain Review* a piece that would explain to readers his objections to the Roethke review. Rexroth declined, and the following issue of *Black Mountain Review* (Winter 1954) contained the announcement of his resignation, as well as Larry Eigner's mixed review of *The Dragon and the Unicorn*. However, this episode itself created no lasting rancor between Rexroth and Creeley. "I wish you well," he wrote Creeley. "I think the magazine lively, interesting, and much too inbred—as is everything you, Olson, Jonathan et al. do. But that is really all to the good—we probably need more, not less literary clique-ishness."[4]

In 1955, Rexroth was seeking a publisher for *The Homestead Called Damascus*, the long poem he had written in the twenties and revised over the summer of 1954 while camping in Giant Forest with four-year-old Mary. The poem tracks the careers of two brothers while they take their own measure amid conflicting philosophies and disquieting claims on their consciousness and try to establish a connection with the drift of human history, from biblical times through the Middle Ages and the Renaissance, up to their own time in the New World. Rexroth told Laughlin that the major figures of the poem—the brothers Sebastian and Thomas, and the narrator—were all aspects of Rexroth, "two doppel-gangers to the 'empiric ego.' "[5] And indeed the poem not only reflects Rexroth's philosophical concerns but also furnishes a stage for the writers who had instructed and inspired him—among whom were Duns Scotus, Jackob Boehme, Tu Fu, Apollinaire, T. S. Eliot, Conrad Aiken, and H. G. Wells.

Rexroth had asked his old friend Lawrence Lipton, who like Rexroth had left Chicago for the West Coast, whether the poem was publishable.[6] Lipton responded positively. Although he believed Rexroth's later work was far more controlled and polished, he thought " 'The Homestead' was something highly developed . . . the same baby minus the mustache."[7] He also accurately perceived the *The Phoenix and the Tortoise* and *The Dragon*

and the Unicorn had their roots—in theme, technique, and philosophy—
in *The Homestead,* and thought *The Homestead* invaluable for the light it cast
on these later long poems. The only stumbling block to publication, as far
as Lipton could tell, was the poem's length, thirty-four manuscript pages
of 1,248 lines: "the editors who might be expected to show the most
interest in the style and content happen to be precisely those who have
the least space at their disposal." He was all too aware that had it not been
for James Laughlin's annual *New Directions in Prose and Poetry,* both *The
Phoenix and the Tortoise* and *The Dragon and the Unicorn* would have remained in manuscript. But Lipton, whose book of poems, *Rainbow at
Midnight,* had just been published by the Golden Quill Press and selected
for its list by the Book Club for Poetry, was confident that he could make
use of the extensive contacts he himself had cultivated with magazine
editors. Although he was contemptuous of university quarterlies—"which
have plenty of space but waste a lot of it on criticism that we could very
well do without . . . the PHDeistic variety"—Lipton assured Rexroth that
he would try the better ones and also try *Origin, Black Mountain Review,*
and the *Dalehousie Review.*[8]

Rexroth himself had approached Creeley in the winter of 1955 about
publishing *The Homestead.* Creeley agreed to take a self-sustained section
of the poem, "The Double Hellas," for his Divers Press. But the press
folded up a year later, after his marriage had dissolved and he no longer
had access to his wife's small trust.[9] Lipton and Rexroth, however, perse-
vered. In 1957, Theodore and Renée Weiss devoted an issue of the *Quarterly Review of Literature* (IX,2) to Rexroth by printing the entire poem and
an introductory essay by Lipton, which he wrote with much help from
Rexroth.[10]

More writing assignments and a little extra money fell Rexroth's way.
He was publishing in *The New Republic, New World Writing,* and *Art News,*
writing articles about Morris Graves, Frederick Turner, and the Renoir
exhibition at the San Francisco Museum of Art. For *The Nation,* he reviewed *The Journals of Jean Cocteau, The Letters of Edward Gibbon,* and *Science
and Civilization in China.* He wrote the Introduction to Henry Miller's
Nights of Love and Laughter.[11] Although Miller and Rexroth no longer had
much in common, they both possessed a marvelous and maddening characteristic which Robert Lowell attributed to John Berryman: they were
both self-centered and unselfish. That quality gave their amusements and
controversies a breathless, commanding rush. Each sensed this powerful
and unusual combination of traits in the other.

For *The New York Times Book Review,* he reviewed William Carlos Williams's *Desert Music,* and a collection of poems by Weldon Kees, who was
now a popular figure in San Francisco. Kees appeared in the *Poets' Follies,*
a kind of vaudeville of poetry readings and music performed by many of
the poets and artists associated with leftist / anarchist groups, people like

Michael Grieg and Adrian Wilson. Rexroth compared Kees to a "Canadian Air force ace playing a twenties-style player piano, singing in a jazz bass, and remembering all the lyrics."[12] Rexroth's favorable review of Kees's poems appeared April 17, 1955, approximately three months before Kees left his car at the Golden Gate Bridge and disappeared.[13]

About this time, Rexroth met another young poet from the East Coast: Allen Ginsberg. Philip Lamantia, who had met Ginsberg in New York City in 1948, had asked Rexroth if he would be willing to help Ginsberg locate a publisher for a manuscript of poems. Ginsberg had shown the poems to William Carlos Williams, who liked them well enough to write an introduction.[14] By now it was common knowledge that James Laughlin kept his ear open to Rexroth's literary opinions, and Ginsberg hoped Rexroth might persuade Laughlin to publish his poems in either a *New Directions Annual* or *Perspective*. With Rexroth's consent, Ginsberg had sent him the manuscript in August 1952. He was especially curious about Rexroth's reaction to a poem called "Metaphysics," which he had shown to William Carlos Williams three years earlier. Williams was so taken by the poem that he used it as a headnote to *Paterson* 5, completed in 1958. Rexroth suggested to Ginsberg that he get in touch with Richard Emerson at Golden Goose Press and Horace Schwartz at Goad Press.

Ginsberg had been living in the Bay Area since 1953. While staying at his friend Neal Cassady's home in San Jose, he would come up to San Francisco most Mondays, and on one occasion caught Rexroth at home on Eighth Avenue after first trying to find the bookstore that he thought Rexroth operated. Rexroth and Ginsberg got along well, and after Ginsberg moved to the city in October 1954, he started attending Rexroth's Friday night gatherings.[15] Rexroth sent Ginsberg over to Robert Duncan's where for the first time he met Jack Spicer and another newcomer to the city, Michael McClure. Based on the work Ginsberg had shown him so far, Rexroth chided him for writing poetry "like a Columbia University intellectual." Hoping for some kind of "breakthrough of understanding," Ginsberg showed him "Dream Record," a poem about Joan Burroughs, but Rexroth thought it was too formal.[16]

The following year, Ginsberg began work on *Howl*, which both he and Rexroth claim was not influenced by Rexroth's earlier "Thou Shalt Not Kill," even though the two poems have a very similar political perspective, and share a similar rhetorical, exhortational style. He had shown parts of it to Rexroth, and in June asked him if he was being visually clear enough in his transitions from image to image, if he was presenting a "mystical eclipse of time" between images with sufficient coherency. He had been looking at how other poets handled this problem, particularly Keats's last poem to Fanny Brawne and Hart Crane's "Praise for an Urn." He also remembered that Rexroth grappled with these difficulties "in recall of dead woman memory, early book."[17] Ginsberg could have been referring to any one of Rexroth's poems about his mother or Andrée. He would have to wait until Rexroth returned from the mountains to discuss these questions of technique face to face.

Between classes at San Francisco State, Michael McClure was writing poetry in a roughly Lawrentian vein. McClure had "formed a great sense of affiliation" with Robert Duncan's work at this time, and wanted to concentrate on a "spontaneous self-forming body related line."[18] In high school, he had read Rexroth's poems and developed a great admiration for his work, thought it "wizardly." But he did not wish to write that kind of line himself. Rexroth's elegy for Dylan Thomas has not impressed him favorably; some of the lines were "pretty hard to take." Yet Rexroth's impact on him was powerful. McClure's memory reveals what Rexroth was like in action:

He was most learned talking about the West Coast. He was perfectly awkward talking about poets he didn't like. And he said he didn't like the actors. He would still speak about them. You would get an idea of how they fit against the Berkeley Renaissance. Everson would remind him of the CO camp. He would talk about Waldport. That would turn into a discussion of anarchist study groups in the city and then some thoughts about the history of anarchists would come up. He would talk about the anarchists of Barcelona. Then he would have reflections on Stalinists including our local Stalinists and condemnations and damnations and vilifications and jokes and gossip. Kenneth was one of the great gossips of all times. He'd love to get it from others. And from there it might go anywhere. That might remind him of something or somebody he liked or didn't like and that might very well remind him of another favorite subject which would be an original song or new poem and from there it might go to a discussion of a painter of the Sung Dynasty and from there it would be a little hop, skip and jump to the T'ang Dynasty and some thoughts about someone who was coming to visit. People would ask him questions as it went. It was extraordinary. You didn't know what to believe and you didn't know what not to believe.

This non-stop energy was called upon when painter Wally Hedrick proposed a group poetry reading at the Six Gallery, an auto-repair garage that bordered the Embarcadero, on Fillmore Street below Union. It had been converted into a space for displaying the work of young Bay Area artists, and had already been the site for a poetry reading by Walter Lowenfels[19] (Rexroth had introduced him), and a reading of *Faust Foutu* by Robert Duncan, who had since left for Majorca. About twenty-five-feet deep and twenty-feet wide, with white walls and a dirt floor, the space had a small stage at one end, perfect for the cozy literary events that were becoming so popular in San Francisco.

Rexroth passed on Hedrick's idea to Ginsberg,[20] and suggested that he call on Gary Snyder, who had recently returned from a working summer on a trail crew at Yosemite National Park and had resumed studying Asian languages at Berkeley. Snyder brought in Philip Whelan. Ginsberg rounded up Michael McClure and Philip Lamantia, and the Six Gallery

Reading, one of the most famous events in San Francisco literary history, was organized. Rexroth was appointed master of ceremonies for this watershed event held on the night of October 13, 1955. With the exception of Whelan (and Rexroth), all the participants were in their twenties. This would be their first reading together. In addition to putting up announcements in all the North Beach bars, Ginsberg sent out one hundred postcard invitations that announced:

Six poets at the Six Gallery. Kenneth Rexroth, M.C. Remarkable collection of angels all gathered at once in the same spot. Wine, music, dancing girls, serious poetry, free satori. Small collection for wine and postcards. Charming event.

Although he was not on the program, Jack Kerouac was both a visible and audible presence that evening. He had recently arrived in town with Neal Cassady to see Ginsberg.[21] Ginsberg and Kerouac had known one another since their Columbia days in 1945, when Kerouac would stay overnight in Ginsberg's dormitory room, the two men talking about books and sex. Kerouac would also visit Ginsberg at his apartment so that he could listen to William Burroughs discuss Spengler, the Kinsey Report, mystics, and drugs. (Rexroth had found Burroughs' book *Junkie* interesting.) In San Francisco, Ginsberg was eager to show Kerouac that the cultural and political revolution about which they had rhapsodized was taking shape.

When Kerouac had been in San Francisco that past September, Ginsberg dragged him to a Rexroth Friday evening. During one of his earlier KPFA book review programs, Rexroth had praised Kerouac's "Jazz of the Beat Generation" (excerpts from his manuscripts *On the Road* and *Visions of Cody*), recently published in *New World Writing*. He ranked Kerouac's prose with that of the misanthropic invective of Louis-Ferdinand Céline and compared Kerouac's perspective to that of the absurdist French dramatist Jean Genet. Rexroth had agreed to look at Kerouac's manuscripts and perhaps bring them to the attention of Laughlin. But Kerouac was not prepared for the scene at Rexroth's. He was excited by the discovery that other poets there—like Gary Snyder and Philip Whalen—knew a good deal about Buddhism. Rexroth coolly informed him that "everybody" in San Francisco was a Buddhist. Kerouac pulled on Rexroth's mustache and then kissed him, an act of affection which Rexroth mistook for mockery. Kerouac had not intended to insult Rexroth, even though he later confessed that he did not care for the way Rexroth dominated the evening's discussions; he regarded Rexroth's monologues mainly as "egocentric blabbing."[22] Nevertheless, Kerouac and Ginsberg respected Rexroth for the important role he played in opening up San Francisco.

Ginsberg went to the Six Gallery with Kirby and Lawrence Ferlinghetti, who was driving his old Austin. (Gregory Corso would later come to town from Cambridge, Massachussetts, where his *The Vestal Lady on Brattle and Other Poems* had been published[23] with monetary contributions from nearly fifty Radcliffe and Harvard students.) Wearing a bow tie and a cutaway coat that he had bought from a second-hand clothing store, Rexroth made his way up to the poets' platform and noticed that a small box once packed with grapes had been placed in a spot where a speaker might ordinarily have expected a lectern. "This is a lectern," he reassured the more than one hundred people sitting in the audience in a voice that almost twanged, "for a midget who is going to recite the *Iliad* in haiku form."[24] The event had gotten off to a rollicking start.

Working the audience, Kerouac collected money for jugs of wine. Lamantia read the poems of his late friend John Hoffman, Michael McClure recited his elegy "For the Death of a Hundred Whales," and Philip Whalen, looking like "a Zen Buddhist Bodhisattva,"[25] read among other poems his "Plus ça Change." Between lines and verses, Kerouac and Cassady led cheers in appreciation of the poets. "Much to Rexroth's annoyance," Gerald Nicosia reports, "[Kerouac] began to yell 'Go!', to moan, gurgle, and beat out the rhythms of the poetry on his jug—what Rexroth execrated as 'fourth-dimensional counterpoint.' "[26] But Rexroth seemed moved by the readings. When Allen Ginsberg got up and recited *Howl*, Rexroth was electrified: "it just blew up things completely."[27] Not even Ginsberg was prepared for what happened.

[He was] rather surprised at his own power, drunk on the platform, becoming increasingly sober as he read, driving forward with a strange ecstatic intensity, delivering a spiritual confession to an astounded audience—ending in tears which restored to American poetry the prophetic consciousness it had lost since the conclusion of Hart Crane's *The Bridge,* another celebrated mystical work.[28]

The last poet to read was Gary Snyder, who delighted the audience with "A Berry Feast," the poem he had earlier shown Rexroth, and seemed to be totally at ease as he mixed bits of street humor, Asian philosophy, and political wisdom into his presentation. Kerouac would capture this memorable and colorful evening in his novel *The Dharma Bums,* published three years later.

In the interim, the media announced the arrival of the "Beat Generation," and labeled Kenneth Rexroth its patron and elder statesman. This was a rather peculiar state of affairs for Rexroth, since such status would suggest that he had achieved the security of success. Indeed, for some time now he had nurtured and cultivated relationships with younger, primarily male poets, although he promoted work by younger women writers as well.[29] However, right up to the time of the Six Gallery Reading, Rexroth had achieved neither financial independence nor substantial recognition from the Eastern literary establishment. Privately, he saw himself as a poet struggling for wider recognition, not a prosperous paterfamilias as the term "father of the movement" implied. He enjoyed playing the role of the hip, erudite mentor, and, initially, was thrilled by the sudden success of these younger poets. A few days after the Six Gallery Reading he told Ginsberg that he would be famous "from bridge to bridge,"[30] but he was still waiting for his own ship to come in.

His position at home was not much clearer. Although his life with Marthe was as shaky as ever, their second daughter, Katharine Ann Helen, had been born on August 31, 1954. Determined not to return to work as quickly as she had after Mary's birth, Marthe obtained a six month's leave from San Francisco State. She had claimed the right this time to devote herself to her newborn child, and to be nourished by the unqualified love that exists between mother and daughter. The family scraped by, with presents from Marie Rexroth, who was now Katharine's godmother as well as Mary's, who was still legally married to Kenneth, and living across the street. Although he frequently quarreled with Marie, Kenneth was psychologically dependent on their relationship, and refused to initiate divorce proceedings.

When Marthe had returned to work in January 1955, she found herself at the breaking point. Kenneth was still expecting her to serve as his secretary, filing his correspondence, typing and editing his manuscripts. He remained inordinately jealous of her friends, and yet saw no reason why she resented his attachment to Marie, and to the various people he would invite over, even though they often kept her up long after she should have retired for the night. Moreover, Kenneth would still boast about his sexual conquests to their friends and Friday evening guests, which she found humiliating and which had begun to alienate several Bay Area writers like Jack Spicer and Robin Blaser.

Toward the end of August 1955, a few months before the Six Gallery Reading, a new domestic crisis severely shook the Rexroth household: Marthe decided to leave Kenneth. Assisted by a colleague at San Francisco State, she packed up the children's things and headed up to Seattle where the Tallmans were still living. Without revealing her destination, she left a letter saying she needed a respite from him. Kenneth became frantic. He alarmed all their friends and acquaintances and telephoned Marthe's family in Cincinnati to inquire if they knew where she was. Marthe, feeling lost and frightened, called him. He urged her to come home. Marthe called Marie as well, who was full of sympathy and understanding (if anyone knew what Marthe was experiencing, it was Marie), but who nevertheless thought it best that Marthe return. Marthe took that advice after she ran out of money in Seattle and couldn't find work. Marie decided the time had finally come to initiate divorce proceedings, assuming that such a gesture would make it easier for Marthe and Kenneth to repair their relationship. Marie testified that her husband had consorted with another woman, and the divorce was declared legal on September 13, 1955, "on grounds of cruelty."

Rexroth had barely survived this emotional crisis by the time of the Six Gallery Reading. Beneath his facade as the public figure who could skillfully and happily fulfill his responsibilities as master of ceremonies, his nerves were frayed. As a relaxant, he turned to translating Lu Yu (1125–1209), a Sung Dynasty poet who captures with apparent ease the array of emotions a man feels when he realizes his life will not turn out as he hoped. "I Get Up At Dawn" is a good example:

> When your teeth decay you cannot
> Grow new ones. When your hair falls
> Out you cannot plant it again.
> I get up at dawn and look
> At myself in the mirror.
> My face is wrinkled, my hair
> Is grey. I am filled with pity
> For the years that are gone like
> Spilt water. It can't be helped.
> I take a cup of wine and
> Turn to the bookcase once more.
> Back through the centuries I
> Visit Shun and Yu the Great
> And Kue Lung, that famous rowdy.
> Across three thousand years I
> Can still see them plainly.
> What does it matter? My flesh,
> Like theirs, wears away with time.[31]

Soon after the Six Gallery Reading, Rexroth invited Whelan, Ginsberg, Kerouac, and Snyder for dinner, but the hospitality he extended ended up by alienating him from them. After clowning around in North Beach, the younger poets, drunk and carefree, got to Eighth Avenue long after they were expected. Trying to make light of their rudeness, Kerouac asked for a drink. Rexroth exploded. Marthe excused herself by saying she had to heat up dinner. Nobody calmed down. Kerouac called Rexroth a "boche."[32] And Ginsberg announced that he was a better poet than Rexroth, with youth on his side. Remembering these remarks in an interview, Ginsberg admitted that they were insensitive. He was high and still charged by the success of reading *Howl*, which he knew was far superior to Rexroth's "Thou Shalt Not Kill."[33]

Before Marthe could bring out the food, Rexroth ordered them to leave. They did so while Kerouac drunkenly shouted "Dirty German" repeatedly. As inwardly confident as Rexroth was about his talent and knowledge, these young men were brimming with a kind of energy, hope, and good humor that antagonized him, and, perhaps, even provoked his envy. In addition, their rough manners were more than he could bear. It was late at night, and he did not want his children's sleep disturbed. He was convinced that Kerouac had frightened Mary.

In February 1956, the Rexroths moved out of their cramped Eighth Avenue apartment to 250 Scott Street in the predominantly black Fillmore District which adjoins Haight-Ashbury, soon to be the countercul-

Marthe with six-day-old Mary in her arms, July 1950.

Kenneth with Mary. *Selden Rodman*

250 Scott Street.

Kenneth reading poetry to jazz, 1956. *Harry Redl*

Kenneth in a pensive mood at his Scott Street home, 1956. *Harry Redl*

Kenneth and Marthe with Katharine on her fourth birthday, 1958. *Harry Redl*

The entrance to the house where the Rexroths
lived off route de Tholonet, two kilometers
outside Aix-en-Provence. A slope of Mont
Ste. Victoire was visible from one window.

Katharine and Mary in Venice, May 1959.

Marie remained a lifetime friend. Here she is on a camping trip with Kenneth in 1960.

Kenneth surveying his day's catch, 1962. Marie was there to share the feast.

Kenneth talking to a favorite burro in Yosemite National Park, 1965.

Carol Tinker and Mary with Gary Snyder at Scott Street, October 1965.

Frank Triest, Kenneth's fellow anarchist and oldest friend.

Kenneth in the library of his
Santa Barbara home on East
Pepper Lane.

Kenneth in a jovial mood in
Kyoto, 1974. He and Carol
Tinker were living in Higashi
yama in the eastern mountains.
The Fugi Evening

Kenneth and Carol Tinker, Santa Barbara.

The gravestone of Kenneth Rexroth in Santa Barbara overlooking the ocean.

KENNETH REXROTH
22 December 1905 – 6 June 1982

As the full moon rises
The swan sings In sleep
On the lake of the mind,

ture neighborhood of the sixties. Ronnie Bladen helped them move to this large second-floor apartment, above Jack's Records Cellar. There were seven large rooms—three bedrooms, a double drawing room, a dining room, kitchen, a separate bath and toilet, and washrooms between the bedrooms. They had two Andrews heaters in the fireplace but still no refrigerator. The apartment was lined with Rexroth's massive and expanding library, orange crates and apple boxes serving as bookcases.

One of the first visitors to their new apartment was Selden Rodman and his young daughter Beebe. The night before his reading at the Poetry Center—February 11, 1956—Rodman dined at Ruth Witt-Diamant's home with among others the Rexroths and poet and playwright James Broughton. Rodman had not seen Rexroth since they visited Ezra Pound at St. Elizabeth's in 1948. He was disturbed by the way Rexroth dominated the literary talk at the dinner table, with "defensive insecurity and atomized posing."

The lack of humility and harshness of judgement are dangerous in one whose biting wit is so infectious. There is a warmth in him and an appealing generosity with the limits of the commanding position he occupies, but it tends to discourage the timorous and all but the most tolerant of his peers.[34]

Rexroth seemed determined that evening to denigrate the latest poetry of Stanley Kunitz, whose *Selected Poems* would win the Pulitzer two years later. He described it as suitable for fashion magazines. When Rodman reminded Rexroth that he had not read any of Kunitz's more recent poems, Rexroth "guffawed and said that he didn't have to."

After his reading, Rodman spent the next afternoon and evening with Rexroth. They first stopped at Ronnie Bladen's studio to see his paintings, then dined at Scott Street. Rexroth behaved like a lamb, and kept insisting that they spend a few more days together. At the Poetry Center, Rodman had read Rexroth's "A Letter to William Carlos Williams." The audience of two hundred responded with deafening applause, and Rodman sensed that Rexroth was extremely gratified: "I think [Rexroth] understood perfectly that I hadn't done this merely for its drama, or to make him feel guilty, but out of respect for the poem and for its sentiment and for his long devotion to the arts in San Francisco."[35] During dinner at Scott Street, Rexroth had "stepped entirely out of the mask"; secure in the esteem with which Rodman regarded him, he was a gracious and kind host.

More of Rexroth's poetry also saw print, including the beautiful Bern Porter edition of *A Bestiary for My Daughters Mary and Katharine*, which reproduced twenty-six handwritten poems, each devoted to one letter of the alphabet and one animal, except for "N," which is "for nothing. There is / Much more of it than something."[36] The one for "S" is typical of the humorous, didactic, and satirical quality of these poems:

The seal when in the water
Is a slippery customer
To catch. But when he makes love
He goes on dry land and men
Kill him with clubs.
To have a happy love life
Control your environment.[37]

One Hundred Poems from the Japanese, which became one of Rexroth's best-
known volumes, had been published by New Directions in 1955. Other
successful collections would soon follow. Rexroth's creative impulse was
at a peak.

He became more involved with the activities at the Poetry Center at
San Francisco State, identifying with it so closely that he often gave people
the impression that he, not Ruth Witt-Diamant, was the director. He was
eager to see it succeed, anxious for a reading there to carry the same
prestige as one at the 92nd Street Y in New York City. A strong Poetry
Center symbolized for Rexroth that another arbiter, and a fairer arbiter
of the literary scene, had broken the power of the center three thousand
miles away. He had not given up his ideal of a proud regional literary
identity. The Center had three primary projects in operation. One was
the workshop in poetry, led by two local poets who alternated between
reading and discussing poetry submitted by the workshop participants—
officially registered San Francisco State students and adults without academic affiliation. As many as forty people would attend a given workshop.
The second was a monthly poetry reading by a local poet, most often on
Tuesday evenings; readers received a token payment of ten dollars. The
third project brought poets with national reputations to San Francisco.
Through an arrangement the Center made with the San Francisco Museum of Art, these poets read at the museum with the public paying an
admission fee while members of the Poetry Center attended free of charge.

Rexroth recommended poets for readings, and he also taught poetry
workshops. Among the poets who read at the museum were Dylan Thomas,
Edith Sitwell (both of whom actually came before the program was officially set up), W. H. Auden (who gave the inaugural reading), Theodore
Roethke (just a few weeks after he received the Pulitzer Prize), Karl Shapiro, William Carlos Williams, Charles Olson, Robert Lowell, Langston
Hughes, Marianne Moore, Louise Bogan, Stephen Spender, Allen Tate,
Randall Jarrell, and Allen Ginsberg. Between the years 1954 and 1959,
local poets who appeared were Robert Duncan (who was assistant director
in 1956–57), Jack Spicer, Holly Beye, Kenneth Patchen, Thomas Parkinson, James Broughton, Michael McClure, Lawrence Ferlinghetti, Gary
Snyder, Josephine Miles, James Schevill (who took over operation of the
Poetry Center in 1961 after Ruth Witt-Diamant retired), and Rexroth
himself. He was a pillar in the Bay Area community, yet he required
steady reassurance that his position was secure.

Twenty-One

REXROTH IN MISERY
1956–1957

I N THE SPRING OF 1956 Robert Creeley went to San Francisco
to gather material for the next and, as it turned out, the
last issue of *Black Mountain Review*—No. 7. He also wanted
to visit his former Black Mountain student Ed Dorn. Creeley sensed that the creative energy around the Bay Area was contagious:
"for a writer there was really no place that could have been quite like it,
just at that time."[1] In April, soon after he arrived, he called up Rexroth,
who had recently suggested to Creeley that he and Charles Olson send
tapes of their poems for Rexroth to play on KPFA. Creeley sent along
thirty minutes' worth of published and unpublished poems and a short
story entitled "The Grace." Rexroth invited Creeley over to Scott Street
for supper with Jim Harmon and Michael McClure, who lived four blocks
away. McClure, his wife Joanna, and baby daughter Jane were living there
with Jim Harmon and his wife Beverly, a good friend of Marthe's. Harmon and McClure were editing *Ark II-Moby I*, which like its predecessor
Ark was devoted to philosophical anarchism and new literary expression.
Philip Lamantia and Ronnie Bladen were also part of the Harmon / McClure
commune.

Life with Kenneth was growing grimmer for Marthe. Nothing had
improved since she had fled with Mary and Katharine to Seattle the year
before. Although she was only twenty-seven years old, she was reeling
under a kind of fatigue that made her feel middle-aged. She struggled to
hold her job at San Francisco State while carrying out the responsibilities
of secretary, editor, and co-translator that Kenneth had imposed on her.
She resented the directives he showered on her from his retreat in Giant
Forest: letters had to be written, books picked up, and foodstuffs purchased and shipped to the mountains or sent with whoever was joining
him for a few days. (The list would include such items as seven pounds of
mixed dried fruit, five pounds of "the best cheddar cheese," two large jars
of plain "not chocolate" Ovaltine, "two dozen dried egg yolk, one pound
of iodized salt, four pounds best semolina paste salad cut macaroni.") She

was wary of Kenneth scolding her, often slapping her like a child in front of her own children. She yearned to share the diurnal lives of her two daughters. She was sick of his extramarital affairs, the trysts he would arrange at home while she was at work and the ones he encouraged people to think he was having elsewhere.[2]

At their very first meeting over supper that April, Marthe and Creeley were drawn to one another. Creeley himself was emerging from the dissolution of his marriage, and was hanging out with Jack Kerouac. As Ginsberg put it, "Once they met, the two Catholic, New England, mill-town writers really loved each other."[3] Creeley was drinking heavily, and Kerouac often rescued him from violent bar scenes created by Creeley's funny but vicious temper. He also needed money, and Marthe was able to get him a freelance typist's job though the Dean's office at State College. (One assignment was typing up *Howl* for a mimeographed edition that was to circulate among the various San Francisco poets.) Creeley was an attractive, romantic, and serious young writer, who in spite of his dangerous antics was yearning for stability. Marthe was a lovely, intellectual young mother, acutely sensitive to the struggles of a poet's life, but miserable in her subservient and at times masochistic relationship with Rexroth. They fell in love, and saw no reason to hide their intent. Marthe declared an open break.

Rexroth was incapable of tolerating this affair of the heart. He would stand on the steps of their apartment waiting for Marthe to come home, and greet her by screaming obscene names. He threatened to use violence against them both if he ever saw Creeley again, and said he was going to kill himself. He was convinced that Creeley was a debauched Svengali who was trying to spirit Marthe off to a mud hut in Albuquerque, New Mexico. Rather than believe Marthe had chosen an open liaison with Creeley, he preferred to think that Marthe had become mentally unbalanced, was undergoing a serious psychological crisis, and had grown to doubt her role as an effective wife, mother, and muse.[4] Rexroth strenuously denied to himself the possibility that his relationship with Marthe might have been shattered largely by his own actions. He relished the gossip about Creeley drinking, his skirmishes with the bouncer at the Cellar, and his arrest for calling a San Francisco policeman a Fascist.

Creeley was spending a good deal of time now with Kerouac, McClure, and Allen Ginsberg, whom he had asked to serve as West Coast editor for the last issue of *Black Mountain Review*. He and Marthe were not able to see one another very often, but he did manage to take her on a picnic near Gary Snyder's cabin in Marin County where Kerouac had brought him to escape the dangers of San Francisco life. By then, Snyder had left for Japan to study Zen and Japanese at the First Zen Institute of America and had let Kerouac occupy the premises. The envy Rexroth must have felt for the rising popularity of these younger poets was now exacerbated by Marthe's falling in love with one of them. (Marthe and Creeley were less than a year apart in age.) His eminence as a creative artist was threatened. His machismo was under siege. He became paranoid and would accuse the McClures or Ginsberg of harboring Creeley and Marthe.

One day, Ginsberg innocently called up to talk about a new poem he was working on.[5] Rexroth's response was to tell him never to call again. "You sons of bitches," he screamed into the telephone, "I know what you're doing. I feel as if I walked into a candystore and got beaten up by a bunch of juvenile delinquents." He slammed down the receiver, but Ginsberg called him back because he could not imagine what had happened, and had never heard Rexroth sound that disturbed. Rexroth decided to explain: "I heard that you and your friends—Kerouac and all— are having orgies with Marthe in your cottage in Berkeley—you, Creeley and Kerouac." Ginsberg denied that Marthe had ever visited him and that mollified Rexroth. Rexroth's behavior became a local scandal; he would talk about his degrading fantasies, "of gangs of people fucking his wife." Rexroth's friends knew they had to treat him with kid gloves.

Rexroth wrote Laughlin that, periodically, "someone with a strong (fake) muffled Negro accent" would call to tell him that Marthe and Creeley were together at the Cellar on Green Street.[6] He seemed to be in a constant manic state: he was a lighted fuse ready to go off at the slightest provocation. He would talk compulsively and obsessively. He told Marthe he no longer believed Katharine was his daughter, that she had betrayed him before she met Creeley. He developed insomnia and the barbiturates that he started to depend on skewed his perceptions even more.

Creeley left San Francisco for New Mexico to stay with his friend Judson Crews, a Texas-born sociologist and poet who ran a small press, Este Es, in Ranchos de Taos, not far from where D. H. Lawrence, a favorite writer of Creeley's, had lived some thirty years earlier. He was hoping to find work there and begin a new life with Marthe and, if possible, the children. Marthe sought therapy from Jane Wheelwright in order to decide once and for all whether she could continue her life with Kenneth. She went away for a few days in the company of Marie, while Kenneth and the children stayed with Shirley and Frank and their children in Sebastopol. To release Marthe from the responsibility of supporting them, Kenneth made up his mind get a book business under way, first with a catalogue, then eventually by opening a retail store. Kenneth believed he could fix their relationship. "I have confidence in you and myself," he wrote Marthe, "and in our ability to make it work. And I am excited by the prospect of ensuring for you at last a better relationship with the children and freedom from the economic burden."[7] They should move to a smaller place with a garden, and he would move his massive collection of books, which Marthe found oppressive, to a separate place. And he would follow an intense schedule of therapy sessions with Joseph Wheelwright.

At present Marthe needed to be free of Kenneth. When he returned to Scott Street, she went to stay at the Triests with Mary and Katharine. Creeley came back from New Mexico to help Marthe move and then returned to New Mexico, expecting her to join him soon. Kenneth brought the Willys up to Sebastopol packed with the children's clothes and left the car there for Marthe's use. Marthe, however, was in love with Creeley, and was extremely wary of Kenneth's attempts at reconciliation. While she had been living with the Tallmans that previous May, she had received long complicated letters from Kenneth begging her to forgive him for all the harm he had done to her. He was not feeling guilty, a wasted emotion that was "neurotic and never comes to anything except noise and ulcer."[8] Rather, he was in a state of true penitence "in the Catholic sense—with the characteristics of sorrow for sin, confession, penance and resolution of amendment of life."[9] He emphasized how attached he was to his children, how relieved he was they knew nothing of the "shameful things" he had done to their mother. He played analyst, describing their initial attraction to one another in terms of a father / daughter relationship—she was the daughter that Marie had refused to give him, and he was the father who would give her the kind of love and security she had not received from her own father. He felt he had trapped her into "marrying" him when she had become pregnant. In this vein, he would go on, page after page. He told her she was his life and his joy. Hereafter, not only would he wash the dishes, a chore he heartily despised, but he would "abandon a life-long principle" and dry them as well. These letters were filled with erotic yearning that Marthe did not want to hear any longer. The poetry Rexroth had been composing then was even more emotional:

> However much I have blotted our
> Waking love, its memory is still
> There. And I know the web, the net,
> The blind and crippled bird. For then, for
> One brief instant it was not blind, nor
> Trapped, nor crippled. For one heart beat the
> Heart was free and moved itself. O love,
> I who am lost and damned with words,
> Whose words are a business and an art,
> I have no words. These words, this poem, this
> Is all confusion and ignorance.
> But I know that coached by your sweet heart,
> My heart beat one free beat and sent
> Through all my flesh the blood of truth.[10]

Marthe did not want to receive a new series of imploring letters, or give in to the idealized picture Kenneth had made of their relationship. As long as she stayed in Sebastopol, she felt she was encouraging Kenneth to think she would return. She decided to leave for New Mexico straight from the Triests' home. Creeley had sent her a $600 check, more than enough to pay the air fare for Mary, Katharine, and herself.

Getting to the airport was not easy. Frank and Shirley tried to remain neutral while Marthe got ready for the trip, but Frank, whose loyalty to Kenneth was unqualified, attempted in his own way to discourage Marthe from leaving. He disconnected the batteries on all four of the cars on the Triests' premises.[11] Marthe became frantic when she discovered that none of the cars were running, and he admitted to his underhanded deed. Now persuaded that Marthe was determined to leave, he reconnected the battery cable and drove Marthe, Mary, and Katharine to San Francisco. Marthe bought the tickets for a flight that left at midnight. She did not want Frank to keep her company while she and the children waited, so she called Rex Bell, her boss at State College, and asked if she could spend the evening at his home. Frank was now free to go over to Kenneth's and tell him what had happened. Kenneth was devastated. He felt Marthe had kidnapped his children and was throwing her life away on a man who specialized in breaking up families. For the next month and more, his life was hell.

One of the people most concerned about Kenneth was Marie. She had stood by him in May when Marthe had split for Seattle. She found doctors to treat his ailments (one thought he was suffering from hyperthyroidism), looked after him when he carelessly swallowed too many sleeping pills. There had also been occasions when she stayed in the Scott Street apartment from 7:00 a.m. to 7:00 p.m. so that Mary and Katharine were not alone in the house with him while Marthe was at work. She had not told Marthe about Kenneth's state of mind when she and the children were in Seattle, and never would because Marthe might use such information against Kenneth if she were ever to fight him before a court of law for custody of the children.[12]

Now, although Marie was sympathetic to Marthe's complaints, she felt it imperative to keep parents and children together. She was prepared to donate $500 to get Rexroth started in the bookstore business and was ready to ask Laughlin, Lawrence Clark Powell, and Lawrence Ferlinghetti to contribute. But Laughlin discouraged her from believing Rexroth was capable of running a business, partly because he was a failure with figures, and also because he would probably buy more books for his own use than for the store. A job in a second-hand bookstore that could make use of his vast bibliographic knowledge was Laughlin's proposed strategy to combat Rexroth's desperation. He believed Rexroth would fight any plan that restricted his freedom, no matter how strongly Marthe indicated that she wanted him to be the main provider. With the help of Dick and Betty Eberhart, however, Laughlin set into motion plans for a reading tour.

Although Marthe had left without saying goodbye to Kenneth, she did not intend to cut him off entirely. She called him and wrote, and gave him Judson Crews's telephone number, which Rexroth used daily to speak to the children and to curse out Marthe and Creeley. Marthe tried to sound calm. She told him that they were living in a four hundred-year-old, four-room adobe house, "very beautiful and safe," which they could have for a month.[13] She was earnest about reassuring him that the children were fine, giving him small details about their eating patterns—in transit Mary had been afraid that she would starve—and the new friends they had made. In San Francisco, Rexroth had kept Mary isolated, and she was happy now to play with Carol Crews, who was her age. Two-year-old Katharine was becoming "more expansive each minute," and they all were enjoying the country around them. She wanted Kenneth to know that Creeley cared a great deal for the children, that they responded well to him, and that he would not interfere with their relationship with their father. Mary was counting on celebrating her sixth birthday, July 26, with her father. Marthe also offered to send along part of her July salary check. In general, she was encouraging and optimistic, not about her future with Kenneth, but about how they could each work out a life for themselves free of the pain and anger that had marred their married life.

Rexroth responded by becoming irrational and hysterical, and he raged to anyone in his presence about the primitive conditions under which he imagined his family was living—Marthe and the children walking around barefoot on dirt floors, using shallow trenches near their hut for a toilet. He appeared to be having a nervous breakdown. Desperate and distraught, he showed up often at Michael McClure's communal house on Scott Street. In the middle of the night, he called up Laughlin and told him that Marthe had kidnapped the children, and that he needed Laughlin to come out immediately to help him get his family back.[14] He described Creeley and Marthe as destitute, living in a $15-a-month shack. In a letter on June 23 he wrote: "I *must* have all the money I can raise right away—for Christ's sake hurry—a really awful disaster is impending. Everyone in SF is prostrate after 8 weeks of lies, tricks, evasions—especially Frank, Marie, & the Wheelwrights whose trust she betrayed to kidnap the children. She is a woman possessed."[15]

At the end of June, soon after Marthe arrived in Albuquerque, Kenneth wanted to go down there, if not to persuade her to return, then to take Mary and Katharine back with him. He had considered legal action in a New Mexico court to get custody of the children, but Dan Scanlan, Laughlin's lawyer, advised against the expensive procedure that would inevitably be long-drawn-out since states did not like to yield to one another. If Rexroth wanted his children to live with him, the best thing he could do was take them back himself. Although Kenneth was not legally married to Marthe (he had, after all, committed bigamy when he and Marthe were married in Aix), apparently his legal rights to the children were strong because he could prove paternity, and because Marthe would be judged harshly for having children out of wedlock. Once the children were in California, Marthe could not reclaim them unless she could prove that Kenneth had been violent and cruel to them. Laughlin sent Rexroth money to underwrite the trip. He suggested that he drive Marie's car to

Santa Fe and rent a car there so that the California license plates would not signal his approach. Laughlin also sent along a letter of introduction to Bob McKinney, publisher of the Santa Fe *New Mexican.* A wealthy man in politics, he could help Rexroth if he landed in jail or fell into serious trouble while snatching the girls.

But Rexroth was not capable of "kidnapping" his own children. Nor was his old anarchist self comfortable with the idea of dragging his case through the courts to win custody. During his occasional tranquil periods, Kenneth gave Marthe the impression that he was coping, however grimly, with these new developments. "I am trying to make SF pleasant for all of us—that is—working on myself." He thought he could run a bookshop and gallery ("by appointment only") and was also looking for a literary agent. In addition to his "literary work," he hoped to earn money by conducting a private ten-session poetry workshop for ten people, "no old ladies, no adult education freaks." Visits to the McClures yielded some relief (their compassion and patience were tested to the limits), and he spent an evening with Hazel Takeshita, the woman he and the Triests had befriended during World War II. His therapy with Jane Wheelwright progressed. Sounding selfless, he expressed his regrets about not being the person to show Marthe the Southwest, and he hoped she would let Mary see as many Indians as possible. He warned her that she had landed in one of the worst public health areas in the entire United States, that she should watch out for dysentery and not give the children candy, "even though Bob thinks it's ok." He reminded her to take special care with Katharine, who was more susceptible to illness than Mary. By his solicitousness, he hoped to convince Marthe that he was not about to go off the deep end, and was capable of putting the needs of his family before his own.

Clearly, Rexroth's poetry revealed his devotion to Mary. Frequently they are camping in the mountains where Rexroth can observe her "beautiful sleeping face / like a jewel in the moonlight."[16] In "Mary and the Seasons," a set of six poems, Rexroth depicts the unqualified joy he experiences when he teaches Mary the names of the stars and flowers, and how her presence in the mountains sharpens his powers of observation, and his appreciation of nature's grandeur and power. Yet one of his most successful poems, "A Sword in a Cloud of Light," is set in the Fillmore District where, on Christmas Eve, he and Mary walk hand-in-hand past the bars and strip joints. It is her welfare, her need for spiritual affirmation, that concerns him.

> I am fifty
> And you are five. It would do
> No good to say this and it
> May do no good to write it.
> Believe in Orion. Believe
> In the night, the moon, the crowded

> Earth. Believe in Christmas and
> Birthdays and Easter rabbits.
> Believe in all those fugitive
> Compounds of nature, all doomed
> To waste away and go out.
> Always be true to these things.
> They are all there is. Never
> Give up this savage religion
> For the blood-drenched civilized
> Abstractions of the rascals
> Who live by killing you and me.[17]

"In relationship to my children," he wrote to Marthe, "the circumstances of their upbringing maternalized me. It is an absolute agony to be away from them *at all* let alone all this time."

With bittersweet joy, he received the news that *Poetry* magazine had accepted for its October 1956 issue his "Seven Poems for Marthe, My Wife," among Rexroth's finest love poems. They brim with an immediacy of heartfelt emotion and sexual yearning that never smack of the self-conscious and self-aggrandizing poet bemoaning life's misfortunes.

> Lying here quietly beside you,
> My cheek against your firm, quiet thighs,
> The calm music of Boccherini
> Washing over us in the quiet,
> As the sun leaves the housetops and goes
> Out over the Pacific, quiet—
> So quiet the sun moves beyond us,
> So quiet as the sun always goes,
> So quiet, our bodies, worn with the
> Times and the penances of love, our
> Brains curled, quiet in their shells, dormant,
> Our hearts slow, quiet, reliable
> In their interlocked rhythms, the pulse
> In your thigh caressing my cheek. Quiet.[18]

These lines sound genuine because the emotion is described with a precision and clarity that duplicates the inner rhythms of the poet's heart and mind. In other poems as well, all of Kenneth and Marthe's struggles are played out, but with grace, subtlety, economy. The setting is everyday, but the atmosphere is idealized.

> Speak to me. Talk
> To me. Break the black silence.
> Speak of a tree full of leaves,
> Of a flying bird, the new
> Moon in the sunset, a poem,
> A book, a person—all the
> Casual healing speech

> Of your resonant, quiet voice.
> The word freedom. The word peace.[19]

In these poems, Rexroth was able to accomplish a harmony of thought and action that he seemed incapable of creating in reality. Burdened with all the suffering Kenneth and Marthe endured, alone and together, these poems remain hopeful, optimistic, although elegiac. This sequence of poems first appeared during one of the most traumatic periods of his life. If ever there was an example of art serving the need to immortalize dreams of love, it is here. Nearly a year later, Rexroth told Henry Miller that the love poems to Marthe and the sequence of poems to Mary, both of which appeared in *In Defense of the Earth*, were the volume's best.[20]

But Rexroth could only maintain a calm exterior intermittently. Nearly every day now he would visit the McClures in a state of hysterical paranoia, during which he talked endlessly about the spiderlike web that Creeley had cast over Marthe, describing for them a life he imagined to be full of debauchery and pain. The entire San Francisco Bay literary community knew what had happened, and on a very real level, Rexroth felt entirely humiliated. With increasing alarm, Marthe heard more and more about Kenneth's wrenching despair. She and Creeley could not ignore the letters and telephone calls they were receiving. People like Robert Duncan, Jonathan Williams, and Denise Levertov, who were not in San Francisco but had learned about the crisis, were in the immensely uncomfortable position of loving, respecting, and admiring both Creeley and Rexroth. From Black Mountain, Duncan wrote to Creeley: "I must stand by Kenneth as best I can."[21] He was afraid that by telling Creeley how lucky Kenneth was to find Marthe, he might have encouraged Creeley, "his companion spirit in writing," to pursue Marthe—that he had inadvertently "put the bee in the bonnet of your Evil demon," as he expressed it. To Rexroth, he declared that his allegiance was to the children and "for proved companionship to you Kenneth, personally."[22]

Rexroth's condition deteriorated to the point where his friends actually feared for his life. He told Frank Triest that he had made out a will and appointed him its executor; he did not think he would be alive much longer. Marie called up Marthe, and begged her to come back. She sent money for the airplane tickets. Though still in love, Marthe and Creeley realized this was no way to start a life together. Perhaps they had also taken some heartfelt advice from Duncan, who believed that it was a "cruel thing in the name of love to take [Mary and Katharine] away from Kenneth."[23] and that the love between them could only be "trusted" if Marthe were truly free of Kenneth, separated from him for a year.[24] Moreover, Marthe understood that no matter how rational and logical she was, she would feel responsible if Kenneth killed himself. She had to go back, at least until the crisis was resolved.

By the end of July, Marthe and the children were once more ensconced on Scott Street, and Creeley, who had brought them there, had returned to New Mexico. For a while he lived rent-free in exchange for doing some farm work—mostly watching and feeding horses and cows. He waited. Marthe suffered. Her hostility toward Kenneth was so overwhelming that she could hardly bear his presence. For a while, she kept her bags packed and out on the bedroom floor, ready to be picked up at any moment. In August, Creeley returned to San Francisco because Marthe was desperate. She was ready to leave again (and did so briefly while Creeley was nearby), but Kenneth insisted that Mary and Katharine must remain with him. Creeley returned to New Mexico alone, with the understanding that Marthe would follow once she had worked out an arrangement with Kenneth and the children. By September, Creeley had taken a teaching job in a small school for boys earning $300 a month, enough to support himself, Marthe, and the children when and if Kenneth released them.

Kenneth was sure that Marthe would never "abandon" the children, even temporarily. He believed that her spirit was shattered, that she was in a state of total nervous collapse, and needed his special care and attention to regain her former strength. He also suspected that Marthe had never fully recovered from the severe postpartum depression she had experienced after Katharine's birth. To compound their miseries, money was a great problem again, and Laughlin was called on to help. Marie also pitched in, by writing to people who could steer some money in Rexroth's direction. Malcolm Cowley came through with $500—which did not have to be returned—from the Artists and Writers Loan Fund of the National Institute of Arts and Letters.

Initially, everyone was relieved that Marthe had returned, because that signaled an end to Kenneth's manic behavior. Friends outside San Francisco dropped Rexroth notes wishing him well. From distant Kyoto, Gary Snyder wrote to say how sorry he was about all the trouble, but was glad to hear that things were turning around. He told Rexroth that Kerouac was afraid that he had angered him by spending so much time with Creeley during the two-week period before Snyder left for Japan. Kerouac wanted Snyder to tell Rexroth that he had stayed close to Creeley then because he feared that Creeley would get into more trouble than he already had if no one looked after him.[25]

Back from Mexico and living in New York City, Kerouac himself wrote to Rexroth in December to tell him how glad he was that Marthe was home "where she belonged," and that he had absolutely nothing to do with the Creeley affair. He also had high praise for the sequence of love poems to Marthe: "I have just been reading your sad and extremely beautiful love poems and I am beginning to think that nothing rarer's been written in America since rare sweet Whitman and magic Melville and the others of that time . . . I love your lyric line."[26] Together, Allen Ginsberg, his companion Peter Orlovsky, Gregory Corso, and Kerouac sent Rexroth best wishes for the new year. All of them preferred to forget that during the time Marthe and Creeley were together in San Francisco, Rexroth had accused them of roping Marthe into orgies. Above all, Kerouac had written this note to say that "I love and appreciate you for the sweetness you have shown me." Over the next few years, it became clear to several people that Rexroth was capable of appreciating neither Kerouac's overtures of friendship nor his latest work, and that the "Marthe / Creeley" affair, as their relationship came to be known, markedly changed Rexroth's attitude toward him.

The very night that Ginsberg had read *Howl* at the Six Gallery, Lawrence Ferlinghetti requested permission to publish it, and it became No. 4 in the City Lights Pocket Poets Series (1956), just about the time that Marthe returned from New Mexico. To save money, Ferlinghetti used an English printer, Villiers. The first edition passed through Customs without incident.[27] On March 25, 1957, however, the second printing was confiscated by Customs officials on the grounds that it was obscene. In the meantime, City Lights had printed a new edition, which removed it from the jurisdiction of Customs. In retaliation, the San Francisco Police arrested Ferlinghetti and Shigeyoshi Murao, the manager of City Lights Bookstore, for selling obscene literature. After a trial that lasted nearly all summer, Judge Clayton Horn ruled that the book had redeeming social value, that it was not obscene. Among the distinguished witnesses who testified in behalf of Ginsberg was Rexroth.

If at this time Rexroth had been brewing any hostility toward the absent Ginsberg (he was in Tangiers) for being the younger poet who had stolen the spotlight or for being a friend of Robert Creeley, he did not show it. Rexroth asserted that the poem belonged to the tradition of prophetic literature, that Ginsberg's voice was like those of the biblical prophets who denounced evil and showed the way out. He pointed out how various aspects of the poem corresponded to specific sections in the Bible, in language and in theme. For example, he compared "Footnotes to *Howl*" to the Benedictus, also known as the Song of Zechariah, a hymn of praise and thanksgiving found in Luke 1:68–79.

The reference is to the Benedicite, which says over and over again, "Blessed is the fire, Blessed is the light, Blessed are the trees and Blessed is that and Blessed is that," and [Ginsberg] is saying, "Everything that is human is Holy to me," and that the possibility of salvation in this terrible situation which he reveals is through love and through the love of everything Holy in man.[28]

He had mentioned *Howl* in his best books list for 1956 in *The Nation* and would continue to speak highly of Ginsberg.

San Francisco became a popular literary city with the East Coast press once it learned about the lively controversy generated by the publication of *Howl*. When *Life* magazine ran its story on the "scene" (September 9, 1957), Rexroth was prominently featured in a photograph reading poetry to jazz in the Cellar. He was described as a poet of national reputation and an "elder statesman" among the city's poets. Three months shy of fifty-two, Rexroth did not take the publicity seriously enough to let it annoy him. At his apartment, he arranged a poetry reading for *Life* photographers that would introduce them to the new sensibility of poets like Michael McClure and Philip Lamantia. Rather than let the East Coast media batten on his "domain," he decided to take up the gauntlet himself and explain to the common reader what this new literary "movement" was all about.

First published in *New World Writing,* No. 11, 1957, "Disengagement: the Art of the Beat Generation," became one of Rexroth's best known essays. It contributed to the success of a whole new generation of poets, not exclusively the "Beats." In the essay, Rexroth took an essentially Bohemian and Existential (though he disliked Existentialism) stance: that the creative act is an effective defense against despair and hopelessness, and that twentieth-century artists could not keep their integrity if they also sought acceptance from the establishment. Poetry should function, these younger poets believed, as a form of personal communication based on clear images and simple language. They rejected "official highbrow culture" in favor of work by William Blake, William Carlos Williams, D. H. Lawrence, Walt Whitman, and Ezra Pound. For inspiration, they looked to the literature and religion of the Far East. They were anti-war and disrespectful of capitalism (Rexroth could have been describing himself). He seemed eager to speak for these poets, who with their youth, energy, and friendship had caught the imagination of the media in a way he had not managed to do for himself.

With all its insight and integrity, the essay backfired on Rexroth: it angered and alienated academics, literary critics, and even some of the writers he praised. It set a precedent for several essays Rexroth wrote over the next twenty years, many of them later collected in *The Alternative Society.* Rexroth was explicit about who he thought were the enemies of literature. Prominent on the list were educators: "From the seventh grade teacher who rolls her eyes and chants H.D. to the seven types of ambiguity factories, grinding out little Donnes and Hopkinses with hayseeds in their hair, everybody is out to de-poeticize forever the youth of the land."[29] Then there are the publishers and editors, as "carefully organized as the Communist Party," who publish "poets alike as two bad pennies. . . . Most of them are androids designed by Ransom, Tate, and Co., and animated by Randall Jarrell."[30] The editors of *Hudson Review* and *Kenyon Review* pretended that poets like Louis Zukofsky and Parker Tyler never existed. He attributed the popularity of T. S. Eliot's essays to their snob appeal, and to Eliot's "usually correct" assumption that "his readers had never heard of the authors he discussed—Webster, Crashaw, or Lancelot Andrewes."[31] A sure sign that the new poets were not entrenched in this mentality was their decision to be disaffiliated; they did not want to appear on the cover of *Time*.

Rexroth named the poets he thought were in the thick of this new movement. (This list making was something Rexroth would continue to do for the rest of his life, often in his poets-of-the-decade essays like "Poetry in 1965" or "Poetry in the '70's." Sometimes poets found their names dropped or added, depending on whether or not they had antagonized Rexroth in one way or another.) From the older generation, in which he placed himself, he included Indiana-born Jean Garrigue; Robert Fitzgerald, best known for his translation of the *Odyssey* and the poems of St. John-Perse; Dudley Fitts, and his friend Richard Eberhart, "who looks superficially as if he belonged with the Tates and Blackmurs but who is redeemed by his directness, simplicity and honesty."[32] The younger poets he mentioned were William Everson, Philip Lamantia, Lawrence Ferlinghetti, Allen Ginsberg, Gary Snyder, Philip Whalen, David Meltzer, Michael McClure, Robert Duncan, Denise Levertov, and Jonathan Williams. He singled out Ginsberg as the most influential, "a poet of revolt if there ever was one." For the time being, Rexroth could not be accused of allowing his personal animus to interfere with his critical judgment. He also placed Robert Creeley on the list.

Rexroth did allow his simmering hostility to surface; but he directed it against Jack Kerouac, whose behavior had irritated Rexroth from the very beginning. Although Kerouac had tried to clarify his relationship to Marthe and Creeley, Rexroth was convinced that Kerouac had acted as a panderer and had deliberately facilitated trysts between the two lovers. He transferred his ill will from Creeley to Kerouac—attacking a personal enemy, in his opinion, would have compromised his integrity as a critic beyond repair. In the "Disengagement" essay, Rexroth's comments about Kerouac were still positive, but they lacked the earlier enthusiasm for his work. He also called him "the most famous 'unpublished' author in America," even though Harcourt Brace had published *The Town and the City* in 1950. In another version of this article which appeared in *The Nation* under the title "San Francisco's Mature Bohemians," Rexroth belittled Kerouac's interest in Buddhism, and compared the results of his automatic writing, his free-association style, to "terrifying gibberish that sounds like a tape recording of a gang bang with everybody full of pod, juice and bennies all at once."[33] A third version of this piece, entitled "San Francisco Letter," appeared in the special San Francisco Scene number of *Evergreen Review* that Rexroth had co-edited. This time Rexroth confined his remarks to fewer writers, describing in depth how the concept of disaffiliation applied to each—Everson, Lamantia, Duncan, Ginsberg, and Ferlinghetti. San Francisco was their haven from the "world of poet-professors, Southern Colonels and ex-Left Social Fascists."[34] Both Kerouac and Creeley were excluded from this essay.

270   A LIFE OF KENNETH REXROTH

But Rexroth would bring back Creeley into the circle of poets to whom he liked to refer in essays such as "The Influence of French Poetry on American" (written in 1958 but first published in French in 1959); "Why Is American Poetry Culturally Deprived?" (in which he describes Creeley's poetry as "haunted by anxiety," a psychological problem that is a "luxury product of the affluent society"); "The Cubist Poetry of Pierre Reverdy"; and "The Influence of Classical Japanese Poetry on Modern American Poetry" (where he states that Creeley's best short poems resemble those of the Japanese poets who were talented enough to merge their modern sensibility with classical forms). However scathing the remarks he made privately to his friends about Creeley, by and large Rexroth maintained aloof approval of Creeley's work.

Kerouac's work fell under harsher and harsher criticism, despite another conciliatory letter from Kerouac written from Orlando, Florida, in early 1958. Rexroth had given *On the Road* a bad review in the *San Francisco Chronicle* (September 1, 1957), and Kerouac hoped that he had written it out of pique rather than critical judgment. The letter seemed to be a true gesture of friendship and admiration, filled with chatter about the new book he was writing, *Dharma Bums,* inspired by the Six Gallery Reading. Kerouac did not mention that Rexroth appears under the name of Reinhold Cacaoethes, a name which Rexroth resented because he thought it sounded like "caca" (slang for excrement). Kerouac had intended the name to be symbolic: in Greek, it means "he who wears a laurel wreath."[35] Kerouac asked Rexroth to control his anger, claiming once again that he had had nothing to do with Marthe and Creeley, that he had only wanted to prevent Creeley from being attacked by a group of North Beach hoodlums. All he had wanted was to help Creeley recuperate from his drinking bouts. Kerouac expressed genuine affection for Rexroth. There were, he said, no ulterior motives behind his desire for Rexroth's friendship. "I have nothing to gain from either your rancor or love, world wise, writer wise, but I do have much to gain from your love, personally," he wrote. But Rexroth was adamant in his anger. "Rexroth wasn't listening," said Ginsberg. "It was some sort of narcissistic, hysterical pig-headedness."[36] To the dismay of Kerouac and his friends, who had expected great support from Rexroth, he continued to badmouth Kerouac in negative, damaging reviews.

In *The Village Voice,* the *San Francisco Chronicle,* and *The New Yorker,* Rexroth had only unkind words for Kerouac and his latest novel, *The Subterraneans.*[37] He predicted that Kerouac's popularity would be a fad, that his work was jejune, politically naive and inauthentic. But his worst hatchet job did not appear until 1959, when *The New York Times Book Review* printed Rexroth's review of Kerouac's *Mexico City Blues.* Rexroth gave a brief, nasty summary of Kerouac's career as a writer. He reduced *On the Road* to a story about driving other people's fast cars. He used *The Subterraneans* as a springboard to accuse Kerouac of sharing Ku Klux Klan attitudes about black people. Turning to Kerouac's poetry, Rexroth expressed contempt for Kerouac's religious impulses: "his Buddha is a dime-store incense burner, glowing and glowering sinisteringly in the dark corner of a Beatnik pad and just thrilling the wits out of bad little girls."[38] And he ridiculed the drug-induced perceptions that Kerouac wove into these works.

Rexroth's vituperation and spleen wiped out whatever critical acumen he brought to the review. Ginsberg was especially distressed: "What he did to Kerouac was not in the class of the unforgivable, because anything is forgivable. But he did irrevocable damage both to Kerouac's feelings and sensitivities, and also to the very crucial matter of the United States reception of Kerouac's heart and mind."[39] Rexroth had definitively alienated the Beat poets, although the flow of communication did not stop abruptly or permanently.

On the other hand, the critics would have a field day with Rexroth for having defended, promoted, and supported this new generation of disaffiliated poets. Citing Rexroth as the most articulate and outspoken of the poets on the San Francisco scene in an article entitled "The Innocent Nihilists Adrift in Squaresville," novelist Eugene Burdick described Rexroth like this: "he has a mustache, a sad bulldog face, sloping eye sockets, and an unerring taste for the waspish extreme and offensive statement." Rexroth demonstrated the "rigid petulance of the conforming eccentric."[40] In *The New Republic,* Norman Podhoretz labeled Rexroth "the godfather of the San Francisco Renaissance," and accused him of engaging in "publicistic impulses," maintaining that the poets he was pushing had not written anything at all revolutionary.[41] Rexroth's essays were lively but "intellectually irresponsible." Commenting on the special *Evergreen Review* issue devoted to San Francisco and Rexroth's "Letter from San Francisco," Dan Jacobson registered incredulity before Rexroth's hope that Ginsberg's generation of people would soon be running the world.[42] Linking Kerouac, Ginsberg, and Rexroth, Jacobson believed that all three encouraged their readers "to indulge in the violent and delinquent activities of Mr. Kerouac's heroes." Jacobson thought that neither Kerouac, Ginsberg, nor Rexroth had been "modest, disciplined, and serious enough" to make such demands. But Rexroth would remain the "Daddy-O" of the Beat Generation for years to come.

Rexroth did not mind taking advantage of the fame, or notoriety, that he had earned for himself. He gave frequent poetry readings, often to jazz accompaniment, in clubs like the Cellar, the Black Hawk, and the Tin Angel—engagements which generated extra income, in part from the Evergreen and Fantasy Record recordings made of them. He appeared at poetry and arts festivals like the Pacific Coast Arts Festival, sponsored by Reed College in spring 1957. At a conference like this, Rexroth would perform various activities—giving poetry workshops, participating in panel discussions with titles like "The Artist on His Art," and reading his poetry to jazz. Rexroth had six musicians accompanying him: Dick Knight (tenor saxophone), Philip Whalen's Reed College friend Robert Crowley (trumpet), Lee Rockey (drums), George Cole (piano), Hank Wales (bass), and his dear friend Dick Collins (trumpet). Other writers who attended the festival were Theodore Roethke (who was on the Reed faculty), Carolyn Kizer, Mark Shorer, David Wagoner, and James Wright. Among the painters was the self-educated Mark Tobey, whom Rexroth described as a compassionate painter in touch with the "tradition of the Zen landscapists."[43] And despite his contempt for the East Coast press, he agreed to let *Time* feature him in an article called "The Cool, Cool Bards." In the article, he was identified as "the man who started the poetry and jazz trend," the poet who believed that poetry and jazz would return poets to their audience.[44] According to the *Time* reporter, when Rexroth first read "Thou Shalt Not Kill" to jazz at the Cellar, five hundred fans tried to push their way into the club, which had a seating capacity of forty-three. The article did little to change Rexroth's attitude toward *Time*, whose staff writers, he told Marthe, had no understanding of what poetry and jazz was all about.

All this crazy-cat—bohemian poet—shit is just evil editorial policy. All that was put into the *Time* story in the NYC office—including purportedly direct quotes from me. Not a single one of which, not just I didn't say—but none were in the story when it left SF.[45]

But he did feel that the spotlight might open up new, and lucrative, prospects. Perhaps his life at home would soon improve.

Twenty-Two

ON THE EDGE
1957–1958

EXROTH'S RISING REPUTATION did little to mend matters with Marthe, however. Having forsaken her position at San Francisco State, she took temporary jobs to keep the household afloat. In November 1957, she accepted a position with the California Teachers Association. Throughout this period of attempted adjustment, she was not happy with her dual responsibilities. She was chiefly concerned with Mary and Katharine, who needed a stable and peaceful home. She gradually stopped writing to Robert Creeley, who had hoped all during the fall of 1956 that Marthe would come back to him. In late January 1957 he started a new life with Bobbie Hall who, like Marthe, had two young daughters.

Marthe and Kenneth squabbled constantly, largely because Marthe's chance at a freer and happier life was ruined by her return to San Francisco, and because Kenneth was acting the part of the wronged husband, ready to remind Marthe of her "transgression" and quick to accuse her of still loving Creeley, whose character he continued to run down in private. Rexroth kept insisting that Creeley had taken advantage of Marthe while she was suffering from a prolonged postpartum depression. He would become thoroughly nasty about Creeley's reputation, blaming him for breaking up numerous families. He spread a rumor that Creeley had promised Denise Levertov he would leave his wife and children if Denise came to New Mexico to live with him. Somehow, Marthe and Kenneth maintained the semblance of a home through the winter; but their friends could not ignore his outbursts of hostility, and were frustrated in their efforts to help. Even Robert Duncan, who had been very supportive, lost his compassion as Rexroth's bitterness and discontent seeped into other aspects of his life: "Rexroth is mad—without inspiration, but made ugly by a deranged hatred," Duncan wrote Robert Creeley.[1]

Rexroth had been scheduled to read at the Poetry Center on May 26, 1957. He insisted that the admission charge be waived. Duncan, who was working as assistant to Ruth Witt-Diamant, could not understand why

Rexroth objected to the Poetry Center's attempt to cover the cost of Rexroth's $50 fee and of renting space from the Telegraph Hill Community Center. Rexroth assumed that the community funds ordinarily used to cover such costs were diverted into salaries for Duncan, Ruth Witt-Diamant, Ida Hodes (her other assistant), and toward what he regarded as exorbitant honoraria for poets like W. H. Auden, Charles Olson, and Marianne Moore, none of them from the Bay Area. He was particularly annoyed that he had not been invited to read during the same season as Olson and Moore. When Duncan tried to explain how the Poetry Center allocated funds, Rexroth responded by declaring on KPFA that Marianne Moore was a racist, and that Charles Olson, a great admirer of Pound's *Cantos,* carried a Fascist Party card. He threatened to harm Moore if she ever appeared in his doorway. Angered by such malice, Duncan lost his trust in Rexroth. Rexroth for his part considered his friendship with Duncan finished. (Across the back of an April 9, 1957, letter from Duncan, Rexroth scrawled, "This represents the end of relationship with Duncan.")

When Rexroth's reading fell through, he wrongly accused the Poetry Center of canceling it because he had recently criticized the Archbishop of San Francisco for supporting censorship. Rexroth's behavior seemed a by-product of his misery. During his bouts of insecurity and rage, he became petty, although his envy of the royal welcome enjoyed by other poets was understandable. Duncan did not want to abandon Rexroth, but he had to protect himself against future disasters of the same stripe. Moreover, he now believed that he had made a mistake in urging Marthe to come back from New Mexico, and that "in her decision to stand by Kenneth it was not a 'home' or a reconciliation she was standing by but a hopeless sense of his need—that must go thru terror and misery."[2] At the end of the year he wrote a disengaging letter to Rexroth, wishing him well "for the new year, and for a new distant friendship."[3]

Amid such turmoil, Rexroth managed to wrest periods of calm. When he took Mary and Katharine with him to Giant Forest for the last two weeks in June 1957, he achieved an inner serenity that not only made him feel optimistic about his future with Marthe, but also moved him to write some of his finest poetry. He and the children hiked, fished, read aloud to one another, and devised ingenious ways to prevent the bears from eating their supplies. (During the first night, one got their oatmeal and bread.) Katharine, who was only three years old, was very impressed by the bears and the waterfalls, and walked about "open-mouthed and wide-eyed while Mary [gave] her lectures on the sights,"[4] or as Rexroth describes the scene in "Homer in Basic," Mary, imparting her appreciation for the natural world and the *Iliad,*

teaches Katharine
The profound wisdom of seven

> And Katharine responds with
> The profound nonsense of three.
> Grey haired in granite mountains
> I catch baby fish.[5]

And in August, Kenneth, Mary, and Katharine went as guests of James and Ann Laughlin to Snake River Ranch in Wilson, Wyoming. This was the setting of "Fish Peddler and Cobbler," one of Rexroth's better-known poems, typical of his lifelong concerns. A splendid natural landscape sparks a reminiscence about a lover, in this case Rexroth's first wife Andrée, and a nostalgia for the years when Rexroth still hoped that the world would soon become a more decent place. The poet looks to the natural world as a paradigm of peace and harmony, and a reassurance that his wishes are not futile. And he takes joy in his family.

> On the long sand pass we ride
> Through the fields of lavender primrose
> While lightning explodes around us.
> For lunch Mary catches a two pound
> Grayling in the whispering river.
> No fourteen thousand foot peaks
> Are named Sacco and Vanzetti.
> Not yet.[6]

Kenneth hoped that in his absence, Marthe would relax, free of domestic responsibilities. But Marthe did not need a rest from Mary and Katharine; she simply wanted a long respite from Kenneth's bursts of vituperation.

In the fall of 1957, Rexroth accepted several well-paying engagements in Los Angeles. While he was there, he frequently saw Lawrence Lipton, who was responsible for arranging the series. Their friendship had been resurrected by Lipton's hard promoting of *The Homestead Called Damascus*, which appeared the *Quarterly Review of Literature* while Rexroth was still in Los Angeles. From his base in Venice, Lipton had also done his best to publicize the San Francisco scene: interviewed in February 1957 by an assistant editor of *Newsweek* and a CBS newsman for Radio KLAC, he spoke at length about Rexroth's pivotal role in the literary renaissance. He brought together at his house a group of Los Angeles poets and artists to hear a tape Jim Harmon had made of Rexroth reading at the Cellar. Lipton was eager to start a poetry / jazz scene of his own and hoped to use the Cabaret Concert, a club that seated about one hundred people around tables and had a small theater stage. He wanted to open the club with Rexroth, but it took practically the entire year to work out arrangements, largely because Rexroth wanted to bring his own musicians and insisted that they all be paid as respectable a wage as Kenneth Patchen and his musicians had received—"very hincty [snooty] music, but he's the greatest."[7] He told Lipton that "no stripper on Main Street" would work for

the $35 fee that Lipton proposed for an evening's performance. Rexroth
spelled out just how much time and energy was involved, especially in
rehearsal. He also wanted to make clear that no matter how casual and
spontaneous they might appear, these performances required careful
preparation. Lipton complied, making sure to play recordings to the LA
musicians—with whom Rexroth consented to work as long as his longtime
friend Dick Collins oversaw everything—of the music which Rexroth would
expect them to know, for example, Chinese classical music, Jimmy Blan-
ton's "Sophisticated Lady," and Milhaud's polytonal "Saudades do Bra-
zil," as well as songs like "I Dream of Jeannie" and "St. James Infirmary
Blues."

Rexroth gave a number of performances, some to jazz, others straight,
reading largely from *In Defense of the Earth.* The poems he wrote for Mary,
Katharine, and Marthe were the ones his audiences liked most. Many of
the readings took place in private homes, one in the house of Harry Ely's
aunt (years later, Ely, a librarian and musician, would become Marthe's
third husband); another in the home of his hosts Mae and Sol Babitz,
violin editor of *International Musician,* the official journal of the American
Federation of Musicians. But Rexroth most enjoyed reading in coffee
houses like Venice West. His appearance at the Los Angeles Poetry Center scored so great a success that Rexroth wished he had gambled on
getting a cut of the gate instead of the $50 fee.[8] He was genuinely thrilled
to send the profits—the "gold"—with his letters to Marthe, which usually
included individual notes to Mary and Katharine as well. With each reading, Rexroth's enthusiasm waned. He liked the art form, but not the
nightclub types with whom he had to conduct business.

He also visited Dick and Betsy Collins in nearby Long Beach. Collins
was working with Rexroth on a new book of music for his act—he liked
Scriabin for evoking the mystical. They joked about finding a name for
the musicians who played for him—"The Crusaders," "Dick Collins and
his Jade Spotters."[9] And he got to see his old friend Jake Zeitlin, with
whom he spent a few hours downtown in an espresso house near Zeitlin's
bookstore. Through Sol Babitz, he had the great pleasure of meeting Igor
Stravinsky—"very splendid, a real gutsy man at 75."[10] Over dinner, Rexroth
and Stravinsky discovered that they both regarded Paestum, the ruin
which rises stark above the Salerno Plain, with the only extant examples
of classical Greek wall painting, as more splendid than the Parthenon or
Agrigento.[11] For Rexroth, the Temple of Ceres at Paestum was the epit-
ome of harmony and beauty; as he states in *The Dragon and the Unicorn,* a
perfect example of art:

> This is the order of the spheres,
> The curve of the unwinding fern,
> And the purple shell in the sea;
> These are the spaces of the notes
> Of every kind of music.

                    The world is made of number
                    And moved in order by love.[12]

Rexroth and Collins worked out a composition from Stravinsky's *Apollo Musagetes* and *Persephone* to accompany this section of *The Dragon and the Unicorn*. Rexroth performed this composition at the Jazz Concert Hall in late fall of 1957. Collins was unable to play that evening, but some of the finest musicians in the area backed up Kenneth, including Shorty Rogers, Marty Paich, Bill Holman, and Stu Perkoff.[13] Stravinsky was in the audience.

In San Francisco, Marthe kept up a strong front, filling Kenneth in on San Francisco news, especially the flak raised by the *Time* article that had featured him prominently. For example, the *Time* staffwriter had attached the wrong middle initial to *San Francisco Chronicle* music critic Ralph Gleason, a mistake Gleason found amusing and indicative of East Coast pretention. Aware that Marthe faced the heavy burden of working and running the household alone, Kenneth sought to avoid the impression that he was kicking up a storm in Los Angeles, enjoying one merry evening after another. He told Marthe that he was often tired and that he spent his free hours reading and writing. But that was not exactly the case. During his three weeks in Los Angeles and Venice, he had fired up an affair with Susan Wiere, who was part of the artistic and literary group circulating around Lawrence Lipton. Marthe and Mary and Katharine had celebrated Thanksgiving at home with the Triests, waiting in vain for Kenneth's phone call.

Susan (Cain) Wiere was a former showgirl who had married a member of the Wiere Brothers Circus. While living in Europe during the early fifties, she was stimulated by her surroundings to lead a more intellectual life. When she returned to the United States, she registered for classes at UCLA. She soon met the Lawrence Lipton crowd, which turned out to be a rather exclusive group that was serious about being establishment dropouts. To be part of the clique, Susan learned, she had to do three things: smoke pot, love jazz, and criticize society intelligently. More than able to meet the challenge, Susan stopped attending classes but kept her job at the UCLA library.[14] She moved to Ocean Park, close to Lipton's Venice house on Park Avenue, and got into junk sculpting and poetry. She never claimed to be a bona fide Beat. She liked to keep her house clean and her life in order.[15] She would often assist Lipton by typing for him or running errands. Once Lipton asked her to deliver a manuscript to the Babitz house in Santa Monica Canyon. There she met Kenneth and felt an "immediate connection," even though she was awed by his reputation as a poet, and had heard that he was a "lecherous old man."

As Rexroth wrote Lipton after he returned to San Francisco in December 1957, he had fallen in love with Sue 'pretty obsessively."[16] Much of this "desperate constant obsession" was a reaction to the turmoil at home.

He was enraptured by Susan—who called him "sexy Rex." As a former showgirl and a young and beautiful woman keen on art and literature, she fulfilled his need for an unconventional partner who respected his work and took joy in his presence. Before coming down to Venice, Rexroth had joked with Lipton about hitching up with a "nymphomaniac with a cottage on the beach." His affair with Susan was better than anything he had imagined. He slowly steered her away from the Lipton crowd, which he regarded as undisciplined. Sue herself was beginning to feel somewhat detached from her surroundings: the drug scene had intensified, along with the general philosophy that the crazier you were, the more art you would produce and the better it would be.

Susan helped Rexroth feel confident that he could live a life of "peace, productivity, love and happiness," and he did not want to give her up.[17] He commemorates their early days of love in "This Night Only," set on a moonlit Malibu beach.

> We have   only this
> Our one forever
> So small   so infinite
> So brief   so vast
> Immortal   as our hands that touch
> Deathless   as the firelit wine we drink
> Almighty   as this single kiss
> That has no beginning
> That will never
> Never end.[18]

The poem was written to accompany Erik Satie's *Gymnopédie #*1. Sue thought that Kenneth read better to classical music than to jazz. Rexroth himself thought that the arrangement he and Collins had worked out for the poem sounded "Sinatroid." Sinatra actually attended Rexroth's reading at the Jazz Concert Hall, with the idea of doing some jazz and poetry himself one day. His companion that evening was Shirley MacLaine, who remarked that Rexroth sounded like "John Donne in the fourth dimension."[19]

Rexroth returned to San Francisco in time for his fifty-second birthday and Christmas. He was not sure when he would see Susan Wiere again. By mid-January 1958, he was off to New York, where he accepted the $1,000 Shelley Prize from the Poetry Society of America at an "exceptionally and remarkably awful" awards dinner.[20] He stayed in town for more than a week, making arrangements to return later that year to give a poetry / jazz performance at the Five Spot on the Bowery. He saw little of James Laughlin, although they had a working lunch at the New Directions office. He also spoke with the editors at Doubleday about writing an autobiography. He lined up a list of short assignments too for *The Nation, Art News,* and a piece on jazz and poetry for *Esquire,* whose editor, Arnold Gingrich, Rexroth had last seen in 1926 when Gingrich suggested the name for the Penguin Café in Chicago. In Gingrich's office, Rexroth knocked off the article—an informative essay for the non-professional, that appeared originally in the March 29, 1958, issue of *The Nation,* and in another version for the *Esquire* audience two months later.

In the article, Rexroth briefly traces the history of jazz poetry, following it back to the French poet Charles Cros reciting, "not singing," his poetry to music played by a *bal musette* band, and to Negro revival meetings. In defining it, he emphasizes the importance of integrating voice and music until the lines of poetry function as another instrument, "with its own solos and ensemble passages, and with solo and ensemble work by the band alone." Rexroth adds that a chief merit of the form is its capacity to reach an audience far larger than the one attracted by an ordinary poetry reading: "it returns poetry to music and to public entertainment as it was in the day of Homer or the troubadours." Rexroth also mentions that Langston Hughes had read jazz poetry in Chicago during the twenties, Jack Spicer had experimented in the form with a trio led by bassist Ron Crody, and Kenneth Patchen had been successfully performing jazz poetry with Allyn Ferguson and the Chamber Jazz Sextet.[21]

Rexroth's mood turned upbeat as new moneymaking opportunities arose, and the chances of keeping his San Francisco household together looked rosier. He put his affair with Susan Wiere on the back burner, and still hoped for a full reconciliation with Marthe. For Marthe, however, money was no longer a major issue. She proposed that they separate. Now that there seemed some chance of widespread (i.e., East Coast) recognition and healthy remunerations for his work, Marthe suggested that he stay in New York. "You are there and I am here," she wrote in a letter on January 20, 1958, "and won't you please, please let there be at least a minimum of physical truth to what is so completely true: that we are irreparably apart and separate; that we are killing each other together."

Rexroth ignored this proposal, but made sure to tell Marthe that he was suffering from a severe cold and laryngitis. After he wrapped up his business in New York, he flew to St. Louis where he arranged with Jay Landesman, editor of the avant-garde magazine *Neurotica,* to read at the Crystal Palace that spring. Rexroth then went on to Los Angeles, where he gave a reading and stayed with Susan in Venice. From there, he reiterated by letter to Marthe how much he wanted to save their marriage, but that she was a free agent, and if she only had scorn and contempt for him, he was prepared to go on without her but not without his children. Perhaps his relationship with Susan Wiere had given him the strength to consider a future without Marthe. His obsession with Creeley, however, was still very much intact, and he went so far as to wonder whether Marthe had resumed that relationship. But he insisted that he still wanted to make the marriage work, in a way which would give Marthe "a chance to be free" and to develop her interests.[22] He flew back to San Francisco on February 3. His bleak reunion with Marthe was brightened only by a visit from Denise Levertov and Mitchell Goodman, who were passing through town. Rexroth had recently hailed Levertov as the best poet of the new avant-garde in his review of her *Here and Now* for *Poetry* (November 1957). He had not gotten back in time for Levertov's reading at the Poetry Center, but he cooked an elegant steak dinner in her honor.

Within two months, Rexroth was off again carrying out the plans he had made during the winter. His final destination was New York's Five Spot. The first stop was St. Louis, for poetry and jazz at the Crystal Palace. The reading was a great success, and he got along well with the trio of young musicians that Jay Landesman had hired to work with him. Every night of his performance, the nightclub was jammed, and he was immensely pleased by this reception, even though he was making less money than he would have had he opted for a percentage of the gate. (It cost a dollar to get through the door.) The audience was filled with Bohemians and "all the *riche*."[23] His single real complaint about St. Louis—aside from the cold weather—was the general hostility he encountered among academics. He failed to secure a reading at any of the nearby colleges. However, two radio shows as well as a spot on television were arranged, and the *Post-Dispatch* ran a good-sized story too. He was also excited by all the large mansions in St. Louis—including "a palace next to T. S. Eliot's birthplace" that could be bought for $12,000, $2,000 down, and he actually toyed with the idea of moving there. As cities went, St. Louis was a hospitable place.

Rexroth stayed in St. Louis for three weeks. Originally he was guaranteed a one-week engagement, working an hour and a half five nights for $100; but when he turned out to be such a hit, the group (Lovey Powell) scheduled to follow for the next two weeks agreed to split their set with him. He also initiated another close relationship, this time with a friend of the Landesmans, Esther Handler. Recently separated from her husband, a physician, she was in St. Louis, "moving in the Landesmans' world" of affluent Bohemians.[24] Jay Landesman thought Kenneth and Esther might like to meet, and invited Esther to one of Kenneth's rehearsals at the Crystal Palace. When Landesman picked up Esther to bring her over, Kenneth was waiting in the car. At first, neither was impressed with the other. But they spent the day together with Jay, who was clocking Kenneth's running time, and discovered that they were compatible in taste and temperament. Thus started a romance that would evolve into an enduring relationship as "very good friends." Soon afterward Esther and her husband reached a reconciliation, and eventually Esther completed a doctorate in Oriental Studies at the University of Pennsylvania under the direction of Samuel Kramer, who was married to Milly Tokarsky, Rexroth's old girlfriend. However, when they first met, Kenneth let Esther believe that his rocky relationship with Marthe was nearly hopeless. Over the next several months, Kenneth and Esther frequently wrote intimate letters to one another in which they painstakingly delved into their emotional crises.

Nevertheless, he often longed for Marthe and the children. He missed his life in San Francisco, and was very sad that he would not celebrate Easter with his family, or that he would not be able to go with Mary to All Saints Church. Sometimes he felt so homesick that he "could bawl like a calf." He yearned for the routine of their lives, "their flat . . . walking Katharine to school, bicycling together in the park, Friday night, KPFA tapes, each move the same week after week."[25] Rexroth had a great capacity for focusing on some asects of his life and blotting out others. He was still full of declarations of love and devotion to Marthe.

Actually, until Kenneth left for New York City, he and Marthe kept making honest efforts to bury old feuds and move on to a more harmonious life together, although Kenneth did not refrain from practicing his "character analysis" (as Marthe would call it) on Marthe ("I still think you are haunted by a feeling that I think you have not become in these ten years what I expected you to become"). Marthe sent pictures of herself, and of the children sitting on Marie's lap. Kenneth was glad to get the photographs but puzzled that the children were not sitting on Marthe's lap ("You are my wife, not she. I love you, not her"), and complained that Marthe looked too thin and should hire someone to help her with the house, not only with the children.[26] Marthe sent Kenneth his favorite coffee from Raffeta, and was spending what little free time she had typing Kenneth's essays, which would appear in *Bird in the Bush: Obvious Essays* (New Directions, 1959). They exchanged their ideas on whether or not Kenneth should apply for a teaching job, or for another fellowship, so that they all might live abroad for a year. Marthe was not willing to let Kenneth maintain illusions about his attitude toward the academy. He had been presenting himself, after all, as a non-academic. Would actively seeking a position and getting one, Marthe wanted to know, be "too damning to the philosophy behind the poetry and writing in general"?[27] (In 1954, he had made inquiries to various institutions—Stanford, Deep Springs College, Haverford, Reed, Antioch, Oberlin, Swarthmore, Wellesley, Bard—without receiving one positive response.) There is no evidence that these remarks were not exchanged in good faith, between two people who appeared to be making plans to spend the coming years together.

Rexroth left St. Louis for his engagement at the Walker Art Center in Minneapolis. After rehearsing for only two and a half hours with a new trio, he entertained a crowd that overflowed the concert hall into all the rooms on the ground floor of the museum. By April 12, he was back in New York City, complaining about how expensive everything was and how horrified he was by the prospect of spending the next three weeks there. New York was "pure Hell." He visited his former war-resister coun-

selee Norman Rush and his wife Elsa, and was appalled by their impoverished conditions:

They live in the slums of the East Side just around the corner from the 5 Spot on
$30 a week! 3 generations got their heads broken & went to jail, breaking out of
the Lower East Side. Now their children and grandchildren go back, smear white-
wash over the roaches & bedbugs, pin Roualts on the wall & call it the East Village.
There simply are no such dwellings in SF.[28]

Rexroth was worried about the Pepper Adams Quintet, scheduled to
accompany him at the Five Spot, where he was slated to perform for
twelve nights, between April 17 and April 30. This group was much more
vehement than his Crystal Palace trio, and accustomed to playing, Rexroth
assumed, before people who kept talking during the show. His repertory
included several poems of his own, as well as those of Carl Sandburg, Tu
Fu, Ruthven Todd, Pablo Neruda, Ferlinghetti, and Lawrence Durrell,
and he expected undivided attention. But when he learned that Joe Ter-
mini, the owner of the Five Spot, would guarantee him a minimum of
$600, he was elated. "Isn't it nice," he wrote to Marthe, "to have a Father
Bear who can make some money?"[29]

At least New York was not ignoring his presence this time. He was a
guest on "The Long John Nebble Show," as well as Mike Wallace's highly
popular television program, "Night Beat." Word spread that Rexroth's
performance was worth attending. Over lunch, the editors at *The New
Yorker* asked Rexroth if they could feature him in the "Talk of the Town."
The column was written by Louise Bogan, who had met Rexroth in San
Francisco where she was scheduled to give several readings during the
fall of 1955. (Rexroth was there to greet her as her Oakland Ferry docked
in San Francisco. He had reviewed her work in 1937 and then in 1956.)
She wrote a studied mix of news reporting and commentary that reflected
a general puzzlement about what was to be gained from combining poetry
and jazz. Bogan called Rexroth the leader of San Francisco's "boiling
poetry revival" and a founder of "the poetry-read-to-jazz movement,"
thus adding to the myth. He was portrayed as a boastful self-educated
eccentric with "eyes that slope down like the sides of a sharply peaked
roof."[30] (Rexroth liked to say his eyes appeared that way after he was
roughed up by the Chicago police in the early twenties.)

Over lunch, Bogan accepted Rexroth's invitation to his Five Spot de-
but. To Bogan's amusement, Rexroth confessed that he would be wearing
dark glasses to feel relaxed, but also to see his material if he needed to
("you get swinging, and you don't know what you're talking about"). She
thought it even funnier when the MC for the evening, Ivan Black, acci-
dentally pushed Rexroth's script off the music stand and Rexroth lost his
cool and bawled him out, right there in front of the audience.

Undeterred by Bogan's modulated enthusiasm, people were lining up in front of the door as late as 2:00 a.m. Alice Denham described the Five Spot scene, "the musicians' and writers' ethnic pub," like this:

[There were] various writers blustering at the bar—Truman Capote surrounded by his fans, Allen Ginsberg surrounded by orbiting poets, and several pale editors. All surpassed their images in paunch. Rexroth was reading and Larry Rivers was sitting in with [Charles] Mingus. They sat at a table for two in the dark urban forest beneath a pinpoint lamp. . . . They couldn't hear Rexroth's poetry through the jazz. Everybody clapped wildly and the important people drifted away, leaving the place cozy.[31]

Rexroth was especially happy when poet and San Francisco neighbor Bob Kaufman dropped by. The son of a German-Jewish father and a black Catholic mother, Kaufman now lived in San Francisco after spending nearly twenty years traveling around the world, sometimes in the merchant marine. Closely associated with the Beat poets, he had become a popular figure in the San Francisco literary scene, and a symbol of what Lawrence Ferlinghetti describes as "poetic resistance."[32]

Although annoyed that his poetry was often drowned by the music, Rexroth liked being in the spotlight. If he was aware that some of his friends and acquaintances thought his performance amateurish—by Ronnie Bladen's account, he seemed to do everything by rote—he did not let on. In an interview for *Chelsea* that was never published, he told Jerome Rothenberg and David Antin that when he worked on tour with different groups, he could not always get what he wanted.[33] The New York musicians were too "funky." For his Chinese translations, he wanted them to listen to tapes of Chinese music and build jazz around it, but he admitted that "there's a tendency for it to come out like 42nd Street chop-suey music." Nor did he think that his East Coast audience was very sophisticated: "I like to throw out some patter before we start, to relax them. . . . They'll sit right below the bandstand and never crack a smile. . . . All the music and literary references go right by them." But he insisted that poetry with jazz was the only way to return poetry to its audience.

Rexroth ruined his lucky roll when he panicked over the news that Robert Creeley was in San Francisco, staying with Robert Duncan and Jess. In a fit of paranoia, he telephoned Marthe and demanded to know how she had spent her Easter holiday. Furious at the inquisition, Marthe gave Kenneth a full report in her next letter. She explained in minute detail the process of getting the children to baby-sitters, herself to work, and all the laundry, mail ("your mail"), clothes, umbrellas, boots, and groceries up and down the two long flights of stairs every day. She gave him a step-by-step account of how she learned that Creeley was in town, and how she wasted an hour of her therapy time talking about her fear of telling him that Creeley was in town, and of not telling him because if he found out about it from someone else he would suspect her of hiding from him clandestine meetings with Creeley. She assured him that she and Creeley had no wish to stir up old fires, "the one thing you in your sick turmoil could never be asked to dig."[34] Whatever progress they had made in mending their relationship unraveled. If he was going to continue "these busy little jaunts" across the country, reading poetry to jazz, she wanted a smaller apartment in Berkeley, closer to her friends, and near better schools for Mary and Katharine. "After all," she wrote, "what you are interested in is a place to have your books and pictures and mail taken care of."

Kenneth had learned of Creeley's whereabouts while visiting Denise Levertov and Mitchell Goodman at their West 15th Street apartment. Neither of them had intimated that Creeley had seen Marthe, and they were shocked by the bitter invective Rexroth released against Creeley, whom he still believed capable of exerting evil power over Marthe, making her behave like a "bird hypnotized by a snake." Levertov was so upset by Rexroth's diatribe that she asked him to leave. Correspondence between Levertov and Rexroth fell off for a few years after this episode. Nevertheless, Levertov understood that Rexroth did not allow his personal animosity toward Creeley to get in the way of judging his poetry.[35]

When Rexroth calmed down, he was filled with remorse. He decided to take Bob Kaufman's advice: keep cool, otherwise Creeley would give him a heart attack long distance. He begged Marthe's forgiveness for this latest flare-up and hoped that "the last blockages in our complete giving of ourselves to one another [would be] gone, removed, forgotten."[36] He expressed how betrayed he felt by the Beat writers, how "rotten and dishonest and disloyal" they had been.[37] Now he thought he was ready to trust her completely, and pay no attention to rumor and gossip. Without realizing how unbalanced he sounded, he wrote that if he truly had believed Creeley was with Marthe again, he would have flown back immediately to San Francisco and killed him. But he was feeling purged, and was anxious to get through the few college engagements he had to honor if he wanted to cover his New York expenses. He wanted a warm welcome home.

Rexroth enjoyed these college readings, especially the one John Ciardi invited him to give at Rutgers. The Five Spot crowd had worn him out: "another week of hard bop & abstract expressionist artists juiced in the audience may drive me nuts. . . . What swine they are!"[38] Rexroth found the students extremely knowledgeable about jazz but was not particularly taken by their adulation of the hipster. "The hipster is a louse on jazz," he told Rothenberg and Antin during their recent interview, "a mimic of jazz and Negroes who believes the Negro is born with a sax in his mouth and a hypodermic in his arms. That's despicable. In Jazz circles it's what they call Crow Jimism." He was glad to meet Ciardi, with whom he had been corresponding since late 1955, initially over an engagement at the San Francisco Poetry Center, canceled because Ciardi became ill that winter. Rexroth shared with Ciardi his latest thoughts on the progress of modern poetry. He had reiterated his detachment from the metaphysical tradition and the standards for good poetry set by the Fugitives, but on a less serious note added that he wrote poetry chiefly "to seduce women and overthrow the capitalist system."[39] There was literary gossip, too. By Rexroth's account, William Carlos Williams was going strong with poems like "Asphodel, That Greeny Flower," even with "a body only about ⅗s alive. And no monkey glands like Yeats had grafted onto him."[40] He voiced his overall antipathy to Pound, but in a rare moment conceded that the Noh plays were "his best job" and *Homage to Sextus Propertius* was an excellent poem.

Rexroth and Ciardi mutually respected one another's poetry and translations. Rexroth would praise Ciardi on his book review program and reviewed his *I Marry You* for *The New York Time Book Review*.[41] Ciardi was generous about promoting his West Coast friend in his book *How Does a Poem Mean?* with Rexroth's translation of "A Friend Advises Me to Stop Drinking" by the Sung Dynasty poet Mei Yao Ch'en, a poem Rexroth was particularly proud of for its "real simple, this is jes me folks, sort of tone."[42]

> There's not much pleasure
> In a sour stomach and
> Bad breath. I really know that I
> Ought to stop. If I don't do it,
> I don't know what will happen to me.[43]

And Rexroth began his "Classics Revisited" articles for *Saturday Review* in 1964, primarily through Ciardi's efforts as poetry editor.

Before returning to San Francisco, Rexforth read at Bard and Dartmouth, where he had a chance to stay over with his friends the Eberharts in their spacious home near the campus. He had reached Hanover in a state of exhaustion, but recovered soon enough to fill the Eberharts in on his newly acquired success and fame. Even *Variety* had covered his Five Spot act. Then, in Philadelphia, he paid a visit to his old friend Milly Tokarsky Kramer, who was raising a family and teaching mathematics part time. He also saw Esther Handler and her husband Joseph. Rexroth had already been able to send Marthe $800 from New York City and was developing a plan that would free Marthe from working. With the Shelley Memorial Award in 1958, and a Chapelbrook Award and the Eunice Teitjens Award from *Poetry* magazine the previous year, he thought his reputation could provide them some security. He felt confident that he was on the verge of providing Marthe with the kind of life she deserved.

Rexroth was home by the middle of May, and he and Marthe decided that it was time to formalize their union. After endless confrontations with Kenneth playing the role of a "completely moral and wronged husband," her self-esteem had eroded, and her power of resistance had all but failed. As Kenneth hoped, Marthe had lost her will to break free. They were married in June 1958 in the San Francisco Unitarian Church, and regarded the ceremony as a recognitioin of their connubial status of eight years. Later that June, Kenneth took Mary and Katharine to Lawrence and Kirby Ferlinghetti's cabin in Big Sur while Marthe worked at the California Teachers Association. Again the idea was to allow her rest and relaxation, but again she missed the children, whom she began to fear were growing up and moving away from her. Kenneth kept Marthe informed about how well he was caring for them, that they were healthy, keeping out of the sun, eating properly. The surf was too strong for swimming, but they enjoyed fishing for rainbow trout and watching the wildlife around them. Mary was starting a flower collection, and Kenneth asked Marthe, if she did not have too much baggage, to bring their flowerpress along when she came to visit.

He visited a few people, like the artist and Jewish mystic Ephraim Doner and his family, who were living in nearby Monterey. Doner was a good source of information to tap for an essay he was writing on Martin Buber, entitled "The Hasidism of Martin Buber." He doubted that any journal would publish it because he suspected that he could not "say *anything* about Jews without being accused of antisemitism and magazine editors are terrified of the subject."[44] He wrote the essay to work through his relationship with Buber's philosophical writings, especially *I and Thou*, which Rexroth had read many years ago on the recommendation of Hugh MacDiarmid, whose Scottish dialect poems Rexroth had included in *The New British Poets* anthology. MacDiarmid and Rexroth shared a leftist-anarchist political perspective that left its mark on their poetry, as well as an actual physical resemblance: a broad high forehead, a mass of thick hair (though sometimes Rexroth cropped his short), and large downcast eyes. Essentially Rexroth came to terms with Buber's transcendent "life of dialogue," which ultimately requires of human beings a sense of personal responsibility to others, where "magnaminity, courage, and the love and trust of other men" are extolled virtues, "along with humility, simplicity, and joy."[45] In the essay, Rexroth tries to reconcile his identification with Buber's philosophy and his disapproval of Buber's Zionism. Broadly informed and objective in tone, it remains a personal essay, a piece Rexroth wrote for himself, not on assignment. He was proud of it and sent it home to Marthe with the hope that she would like it, and, incidentally, type it up for him. It appeared the following year in Kenneth's first collection of essays, *Bird in the Bush*.

Kenneth and Marthe began making serious plans for 1959. Marthe was determined to take a year's leave of absence in order to spend time with Mary and Katharine. Kenneth proposed a year abroad—in Aix-en-Provence or Diano Marina, which might inspire Marthe to fall in love with him again. He wanted it to be a "new honeymoon."[46] If they were not going to Europe, Kenneth proposed that they move to the country and start a mail-order book business. Kenneth thought no better life was possible for them than a home on the Monterey Peninsula, where they would never have to leave for work, "with the children always around and chickens and ducks and goats and a horse a piece."[47] Marthe regarded the proposal as unrealistic, but was willing to consider it seriously inasmuch as they had been talking about it ever since they had known one another. She thought if she returned to graduate school for better credentials, her future—and the children's—would be more secure. As different as their prospective solutions might be, the Rexroths were making a genuine effort to salvage their life together.

Twenty-Three

A CHANGE OF SCENE
IS NOT ENOUGH
1958–1960

A N AWARD FROM the Amy Lowell Foundaton set the course for the following year. The $2,000 fellowship, known as the "Amy Lowell Travelling Poetry School," required recipients, "poets of American birth and of good standing or able promise, preference again being given to those of progressive literary tendencies," to spend their fellowship year abroad. Armed with the first installment of $500, Marthe, Mary, Katharine, and Kenneth left San Francisco for Aix-en-Provence in mid-September 1958. It took some research and some help from friends to find L'Atelier Vallons des Gardes, route du Tholonet. Nestled in a little ravine, the house, for which they paid the equivalent of $65 a month, was about two kilometers from Aix. It was actually one large room with a kitchen, a bathroom, and a set of stairs that led to two small bedrooms. It had "peach blossom" walls, "as they call them in the Cézannes," Rexroth told Jonathan Williams,[1] and a mottled tile roof. A slope of Mont Ste. Victoire was visible from the window. Potable water had to be carried in from town. For bathwater, there was a well but it ran dry, sometimes as often as every other day. Sizing up the situation fast, Marthe walked over to the local gas station where she picked up a 1935 Fiat for $100. Every two weeks, she drove Mary and Katharine to the Elizabeth Arden salon in Aix for a shampoo. Kenneth refused to conduct business with the local people; his limited French was useful for textual work, but his spoken French was no better than it had been ten years ago.

The family soon settled into a routine. Marthe would take the children every morning to school. They had arrived too late to attend the public school, so Marthe enrolled them in a nearby private Catholic school where they were required to wear white gloves every Wednesday. Often she would bring along a book and after dropping off the children, go to the

Deux Garçons Café for a coffee. She also took long walks, or went marketing before picking up the children. They would stop at the Deux Garçons for hot cocoa, and then come home. In San Francisco, Kenneth had insisted on cooking, but here in Aix he bowed to Marthe. They hired a woman to clean the house three times a week and paid her $16 a month. They also bought a rabbit with the intention of cooking *lapin au moutarde* one day, but the family made a pet of "Pierre Lapin." About once a month they drove the thirty kilometers to Marseilles, and toured the interesting towns and nearby sites like Arles, Nîmes, Aigues Mortes, and Vaucluse. Most days, however, Kenneth stayed home to write, paint, or record tapes on an old-fashioned wire recorder for his book program of KPFA. Although he was not producing as much poetry as he had expected, he reported to G. d'Andelot Belin, Jr., co-trustee of the Amy Lowell Estate, "a lot seem[ed] to be germinating."[2]

Friends in San Francisco took care of their mail and looked after their apartment. Janet and Charles Richards proved to be particularly helpful. Janet Richards had met Andrée Rexroth in 1938 through their mutual friend Leslie Farber, who at the time was a resident at Stanford University hospital where Andrée had years before enrolled in a program for epileptics. An aspiring writer, she remained friends with Kenneth after he and Andrée had separated. She and Charles had entertained Kenneth and Marie, and later Kenneth and Marthe.[3] Now they kept them regularly informed about San Francisco life and mailed them parcels of books that were sent to Kenneth for review. Marie, firmly established in her role as faithful friend to both Kenneth and Marthe, volunteered to send items that could not be gotten in France, including newspaper clippings and Kenneth's raincoat. She told them that everyone listened to Kenneth's KPFA reports on life in Provence, and that the "main topic of conversation at the Ferlinghettis' Friday night"[4] was the ruckus caused by the first broadcast: the difference in electric voltage in American equipment accelerated the tape and made Rexroth sound like "Harry Truman in a high voice."[5]

The Rexroths ran into a wall of Provençal provincialism. The first Sunday in their new home, they decided to call on their next-door neighbors, whom they noticed had two little girls about the same age as Mary and Katharine. But as soon as they got close to their neighbor's house, the entire family came out and in English began screaming at the Rexroths, telling them they were trespassing and ordering them to disappear immediately. They herded the Rexroths off their property "like sheep," the man of the house treading so close on Kenneth's heels that Kenneth threatened to knock him down if he did not keep his distance.[6] Dismissing these neighbors as strange or eccentric, the Rexroths tried calling on others who lived up the valley in the opposite direction. Again, they were ordered off the property, but this time four little girls—who attended the same school as Mary and Katharine—approached them, and to the Rexroth

girls' delight, agreed to come over for tea. The visit was reasonably pleasant until the guests broke some toys and demanded to see how much
money the children had. When the children held out the few francs that
Marthe and Kenneth had given them to save for Christmas presents, the
four girls burst out laughing. They never visited the Rexroths again, and
poked fun at Mary and Katharine at school, calling them dirty little Americans with only a few sous to show off. Marthe also got her share of
taunting (while the nuns watched silently) when she picked up the children from school. None of their French neighbors became any friendlier
as the weeks and months passed. The only local people who spoke to the
Rexroths were shopkeepers.

Through Walter Lowenfels, the Rexroths got in touch with the Surrealist writer Louis Aragon. Renaud de Jouvenal, another poet, who would
translate Rexroth into French, introduced them by letter to his wife's
friend, Madame Françoise Leclerc, who lived in Provence and had volunteered to help them when they reached Aix.[7] They also struck up an
acquaintance with Edwina and Barney Rubinstein, expatriates from Boston who owned a beautiful two-story farmhouse about five kilometers
from Aix. Independently wealthy, they devoted themselves to painting.
The two couples met one evening at the Deux Garçons. The Rubinsteins
had two sons, Mark, who was Katharine's age, and Daniel, a few years
older than Mary. The families were so compatible that Marthe and the
children moved temporarily into their friends' home when Kenneth went
up to London in February to be interviewed by A. Alvarez for the BBC.

Alvarez liked Rexroth immediately and took him pub-hopping after
the broadcast. Rexroth "talked at length about W. H. Auden's pornographic epic, which he had read with great enjoyment." He quoted to
Alvarez "with great relish" Auden's parody of Housman's "Terence, This
Is Stupid Stuff": "The cow lets fall at even / A golden stream of shit, / And
Terence you lie under / And never mind a bit, / Though once you hated
it."[8] Rexroth received twenty guineas for the program on February 3,
1959, and another five guineas for being interviewed by Cynthia Judah
on "Tonight" the evening before.

A heavy snowstorm hit their area of Provence, and Marthe and Edwina had to walk three miles to pick up the children from school and bribe
a taxi driver to get them home. The snow was over Katharine's head.
Weary of the cold himself, Rexroth had brought back a custom-tailored,
heavy green woolen suit from London, which Marthe referred to as his
"shooting." It had about twenty pockets intended for fishing and hunting
paraphernalia, and made him so uncomfortably hot that he would wear
it outdoors in wintertime only. (With a green Alpine hat on his head,
Rexroth sometimes sported that suit when he traveled to New York City.)

The Rexroths could not become part of the local life in Aix, and at
first this indifference to his presence shook Rexroth's self-image. He took
pride in his ability to adapt to all cultures, and had by this time romanti-

cized his visit to Europe ten years earlier where, he said, he met everybody "from Roger Blin to Greco to Montero. People simply spoke to one another across the tables at the Deux Magots or the Dome."⁹ He believed the French had drastically changed since the war, and that Provence was now no more than a suburb of Paris. He decided that the French behaved uncivilly not only to foreigners, but to one another as well. "By popular demand," they had turned themselves into a Fascist country, and their "government functioned on the basis of satisfying the petty malice of every class against every other." He chose to ignore the fact that the United States had alienated the French people with the continued presence of American troops in France after World War II, treating France like a conquered nation rather than an ally. Nor had the execution of Ethel and Julius Rosenberg, the escalation of the Cold War, and the violent struggle for civil rights by Black Americans enhanced the image of the United States abroad. Whether or not he liked it, Rexroth was in French eyes a bona fide American.

Nevertheless, from this six months' experience, Rexroth gleaned a modest collection of beautiful poems entitled "Aix en Provence," primarily organized around the theme of the changing seasons, moving from fall when the Rexroths first arrived, through Christmas, winter, and spring. With a painter's eye, Rexroth describes the gold, orange, green, and purple colors of autumn, the "pure bright limestone gray" of Cézanne's Mont Ste. Victoire in December, and the almond buds "ready to burst" under the half moon of an early spring evening. He also incorporated into one stanza the cool reception the French gave them:

> At Mass
> As the Bishop passed our row
> He gave his ring to our girls
> To kiss. But the professors
> And the Gaullist intellectuals
> Still snub us on the street.¹⁰

And he did not hide the antagonism that he himself had cultivated over the months:

> Lewd sycophancy and
> Brutalized indifference
> Rule the highbrow terrasses
> And the once militant slums.
> Clowns and torturers and cheap
> Literary adventurers
> Parade like obscene dolls. This
> Is no country I ever knew.¹¹

Unlike the longer polemical excursions of *The Dragon and the Unicorn*, the poem inspired by his earlier trip to France, Rexroth's commentary and complaints here are sparse and muted, a recognition—learned perhaps

from translating classical Chinese and Japanese poetry—that he could
convey his feelings more effectively by reducing the rhetoric. In later
poems associated with this period—"High Provence," "Camargue,"
"Leaving L'Atelier Aix en Provence"[12]—Rexroth confines himself to
creating brilliant imagery that evokes romanticized, idealized moods and
memories of life in Provence. "Camargue" is one example:

> Green moon blaze
> Over violet dancers
> Shadow heads catch fire
> Forget forget
> Forget awake aware droppings the well
> Where the nightingale sings
> In the blooming pomegranate
> You beside me
> Like a colt swimming slowly in kelp
> In the nude sea
> Where ten thousand birds
> Move like a waved scarf
> On the long surge of sleep.[13]

In March 1959, the Rexroths left for Italy, and on the recommendation of Tom and Ariel Parkinson, stayed for six weeks in Vicenza at a
convent at the top of Monte Berico, where a lay order of sisters ran a farm
and pensione. "This is a real Paradise," he wrote Laughlin, "and everyone
is happy after the hideous nightmare of Fascist France under the Troisième
Empire."[14] Rexroth enjoyed the paradoxical quality of the place: it was
both pious and sensuous. Enveloped "in the essential odor of Mediterranean civilization," he could take a bath in a room from where he could see
"cherry trees full of nightingales" and hear from "downstairs in the chapel"
the sisters saying compline just before retiring.[15] During the day he could
look out on the rich farmland and orchards, the walled hillside dotted
with nuns milking cows.

The Rexroths did not put the children in school for this short period
of time. But Kenneth felt secure about the decision: he used to say that
"children were safest in a convent or a whorehouse."[16] He worked steadily
on his autobiography, a project in which the editors at Doubleday had
already expressed interest during his last visit to New York. With a tape
recorder, he reminisced about his childhood and adolescence to Mary,
his captive audience. He sent these tapes to KPFA because he was not
getting enough books for review—packing and mailing them had proved
cumbersome and far too expensive. When she wasn't exploring the city,
Marthe took over most of the correspondence, which included a very
pleasant exchange with Louis Zukofsky, who sent her a package of clothes,
including a corduroy jacket that his son Paul had outgrown.

Rexroth also wrote articles and painted. He received some unexpected criticism from readers of The Nation. Over the past two years he

had reviewed books about such various writers and topics as Henry James, H. G. Wells, jazz poetry, the letters of Vincent Van Gogh, Lawrence Durrell, the San Francisco literary scene, the letters of William Blake, Charles Baudelaire, Arthur Rimbaud, Simone Weil, Wallace Stevens, and Japanese poetry. Many readers thought them stimulating enough, but some complained that Rexroth devoted too much discussion to his own ideas instead of evaluating the book under review. Other readers had grown weary of Rexroth's vociferous disapproval of the New Criticism and its advocates, specifically his attacks on Allen Tate, John Crowe Ransom, and Robert Penn Warren. And, as Robert Hatch, the books editor, reminded him, Rexroth had a tendency to repeat himself, especially with references to the *Vaticide Review* (for *Partisan Review*) and college professors who lacked virility. "You pay the price of saying things in memorable ways," Hatch wrote; "people remember them."[17] Under notice that the editor's pencil would be exercised, Rexroth continued to write for the magazine. He was not as quick as before to resign out of principle from a position that brought a small but steady income.

The Rexroths left Vicenza in early May for Venice. There were no signs that they were reaching a meaningful reconciliation. In Provence, each had entertained a private jealousy about the Rubinsteins: Kenneth suspected Barney and Marthe of having an affair; and Marthe thought Edwina's fascination with Kenneth's work was excessive. Their arguments had remained intense, and Rexroth reported to Laughlin that "the domestic situation is quite hopeless."[18] Their month and a half in Vicenza proved far more pleasant than the stay in Provence, but the peace between them was fragile. Rexroth allowed the clash between his joy in the surroundings and his trepidation about the future to color the poems he wrote at Monte Berico. In a reverie about the nineteenth-century lyric poet Giacomo Leopardi who had so effectively drawn upon the beauty of the Italian landscape, Rexroth reveals that, unlike Leopardi, he cannot give himself over to such magnificence:

> It would carry me off, too,
> If I knew where I wanted
> To go, or if I just wanted
> To go nowhere at all.[19]

This indecisive tone strikes an uncharacteristic note, and suggests that Rexroth was too preoccupied with his emotional life to explore these new sources of inspiration confidently. In "Ascension Night," a poem that expresses quiet satisfaction with life at Monte Berico, Rexroth hints at the approach of an impending disturbance:

> Downstairs in the chapel,
> The sisters are saying compline.
> Next door in the bedroom,
> My girls are all asleep.

> The last penny rocket
> Rises from the street fair.
> Moonlight over the Alps
> In a stormy sky.[20]

As long as the family was suspended in the time warp of another life, they could stay together. But the forecast was unstable.

Venice was the last prolonged stop in Italy, where by chance Rexroth heard on the radio "La Vie en Rose," the song broadcast constantly during his 1948–49 European trip. In "Rose Colored Glasses," the poet casts an ironic eye on the song's universal appeal: the pickpockets and prostitutes who have had the misfortune to fall into the hands of the police sing it, children playing hopscotch underneath a clothesline heavy with clothes too grimy to wash clean sing it, a mother and a son on a vegetable barge sing it. Rexroth got a kick out of noting the healthy role that romance played in the imagination of people—including himself—whose everyday routine or future prospects warranted a bleaker view of life. Before too long, Rexroth sensed that he and Marthe would have to drop the illusion that everything would be all right.

The family headed north to England, where Rexroth thought it was "nicer to be / Fed intravenously."[21] They were made to feel very welcome by Constance and Derek Savage, who had exchanged their primitive cottage in Mevagissey for Lawn House, an old Georgian thirteen-room manor. Both taught part time from October to June, and were not paid between school terms. For income, they turned their home each summer into a guesthouse. The people who booked rooms during the season came from all walks of life. Many were artists, art students, writers, actors; but there were also doctors, dentists, architects, and people from as far away as Australia and Fiji.[22] The Rexroths rented two rooms for June, July, and the first two weeks in August. The families got along well. The Savages now had four children: Chris was about Mary's age, and there were two younger boys, Ted and Perry, who were closer to Katharine. Romer, their sixteen-year-old daughter, helped her parents run their summer operation. Rexroth was not properly impressed with Romer's efficiency around the house until the day she cooked him a steak he had brought home from the local butcher exactly to his specifications.

Savage introduced Rexroth to the writers and artists living nearby: Colin Wilson, the precocious author of the popular philosphical study *The Outsider,* and Stuart Holroyd, whom Rexroth interviewed for KPFA. He taped Savage reading a selection of his own poems as well. Rexroth himself gave a poetry jazz performance in the village hall where Savage and his friends ran a local film society. A foursome of Rexroth and Mary, Savage and Chris, embarked on a tour of Lincoln, Nottingham, and Birmingham in Savage's automobile. Since Rexroth's driver's license was invalid in England, Savage was at the wheel. Their pace was not leisurely. Rexroth insisted on seeing everything of architectural, historical, literary, or geographical interest, but had no wish to meet new people. In Ross-on-Wye in Herefordshire, old friends of Savage invited the group to spend the night. Savage and Chris would have been pleased to do so, but Rexroth indicated that he wanted to leave by pacing back and forth outside the house and threatening to continue the trip without Savage and his car if necessary. They made their way to Stratford-on-Avon, Ludlow, and Ely, spending no more than a day or two in each town. Savage seemed more amused than offended by Rexroth's boorish behavior, attributing it to his American upbringing. In the eyes of the English, as in the eyes of the French of Provence, he was distinctly a New World type. If Savage had any doubts about Rexroth's Americanness, they were forever dissolved during a Sunday morning communion service in an ancient parish church in Ludlow. Just as the priest stood with the chalice raised in invitation, Rexroth got up with his camera and clicked off a picture.

The marital disharmony between Kenneth and Marthe did not escape the Savages' notice. Although Kenneth remained for them a likable, admirable, and courageous man and poet, they were shocked by his generally abrasive treatment of Marthe. They regarded Marthe as kind, generous, honest, sweet—all the qualities they wanted in a friend. Savage also noticed that Rexroth devoted all his fatherly attention to Mary, leaving none for Katharine. He paid little attention to any other children in the household. This was particularly obvious when Marthe went alone to London for a short vacation. On one memorable occasion, after Mary and Ted got into a serious tangle, Rexroth refused to accept the possibility that Mary was partly to blame—she was caught trying to strangle Ted. Nevertheless, the families were sorry to say goodbye to one another, and the Savage children missed Mary and Katharine so much at first that they refused to allow their names to be mentioned. A small flurry of correspondence followed; for their generous hospitality, Rexroth sent the Savages a big package of books, and until 1960 continued to send signed copies of his own books.[23] Soon afterwards they lost touch with another. Both Rexroth and Savage realized that they did not share as many attitudes as they once had. And Savage disapproved of Rexroth's preference for heretical and Christian mystics like Jakob Boehme, George Fox (the founder of the Quakers), and William Blake, whose works reinforced what Savage considered to be Rexroth's overdeveloped ego.

The Rexroths were back in San Francisco by September 1959, in time for Marthe to resume her duties at the California Teachers Association and for Mary to start school. Rexroth's absence had not diminished his presence. While he was away, people could still hear his voice over KPFA and read his articles and book reviews in *The Nation*, *The Saturday Review*, *The New York Times Book Review* (including a review of Muriel Rukeyser's *Body of Waking*), *Art News*, and *New World Writing*. Even *Mademoiselle* had published his poem "Aix-en-Provence" in March. Rexroth continued to ride a new wave of popularity after his return. He cultivated his usual forums, but now the "square" publications solicited him. David Cecil and Allen Tate selected "Lyell's Hypothesis Again" for their *Modern Verse in English*.[24] "Raccoon," which contains the salient advice that "Some of life's sweetest pleasures / Can be enjoyed only if / You don't mind a little dirt,"[25] appeared in William Cole's *The Fireside Book of Humorous Poetry*.[26] For *Poetry for Pleasure*,[27] the editors of Hallmark Cards selected two translations from the Chinese and "For Mary" from *In Defense of the Earth*.

But perhaps most curious of all, Rexroth accepted an offer from the *San Francisco Examiner*, owned by the conservative Hearst corporation, to write a column on anything that caught his fancy. Beginning January 31, 1960, Rexroth's column appeared every Sunday, and after May 1961, every Wednesday and Sunday. He wrote the column in an informal, off-the-cuff style on widely varied topics: the immorality of capital punishment, the virtues of drinking wine with dinner, spending Thanksgiving in the Sierras, understanding the latest avant-garde theater in town. The column was regarded as a good source of publicity. As a result, Rexroth was given free tickets to the opera, invited regularly to all art gallery openings and other cultural events, and dined at many of San Francisco's finer restaurants without ever seeing a bill afterwards.

Nor did the call for Rexroth to participate in conferences and to give readings across the country abate. Less than three months after his return from Europe, Rexroth flew down to the University of Texas at Austin in November to deliver a paper entitled "The Poet as Translator" at a three-day symposium on translation. Other speakers—there were ten altogether—included three distinguished scholars: Roger Shattuck, William Arrowsmith, and, from the BBC, Donald Carne-Ross. Published two years later, in Rexroth's second collection of essays, *Assays*, and in Shattuck and Arrowsmith's *The Craft and Context of Translation*,[28] "The Poet as Translator" is a lengthy, erudite, highly readable exposition of Rexroth's perspective on what it means to actually translate a poem, a landmark in the Rexroth canon. He makes several points: that translation is a far more complex process than transliteration; that some of the best translations have been done by people not the least bit fluent in the language they are working in. Temporarily burying the hatchet, he cites Pound's masterful. "The River-Merchant's Wife: A Letter" as a perfect example of a poet's "very high degree of imaginative identification" with the original poem. Rexroth believed that when he worked on his translations from the Chinese, the French, the Spanish, or the Latin, he was honing his own skills as a poet by projecting himself into the mind and the heart of another poet.

The symposium went well. It was a congenial gathering, with dinner the night after Rexroth's talk at Roger Shattuck's home, and a party given by classicist and translator William Arrowsmith, to whom Rexroth confessed that the conference was far more intellectual than he expected, and that he had stayed up the entire night before writing a paper solid enough to pass muster.[29] Through the years, Rexroth's critics contended that he liked to let his readers believe he was an expert in all the languages he translated. If they had read this essay carefully, they would have realized that Rexroth made no such claim.

The trip to Texas also gave Marthe and Kenneth some much-needed relief from one another. On their transatlantic crossing home, they had exchanged bitter words over Kenneth's love poems to Marthe. Marthe maintained that the lovers in those poems were not real, that their actual daily life with one another was far less idyllic, hardly imbued with the trust, consideration, and passion that Rexroth celebrates in the poems. Kenneth refused to acknowledge that his romanticized version of their life was illusory. At this juncture he would have been content if Marthe had retracted her statements about the poems and agreed instead to work toward living up to the image Rexroth had projected in them, even if he lacked that capacity. On his way to Texas, he wrote to Marthe about his distress over what he thought was her stubborn refusal to nurture and encourage him:

Surely you must know what I need so much. . . . Why do you scorn me for needing it? After all, everybody knows that this is what an artist needs. It does not answer to mock it by calling it "bolstering your ego." This is certainly not just a job, but the joy of an artist's wife. As far as that goes, it is what every husband expects—the little woman behind him urging him on.[30]

Rexroth did not stop to ponder what "every wife" expects. And he honestly believed that their years together should have made her feel "absolutely secure" in his abiding love.

Twenty-Four

FINAL THROES
1960–1961

B Y THE SPRING of 1960, Rexroth was back on the poetry and lecture circuit with a six-week tour that began on March 24 with a reading at Arizona State College.[1] He gave readings and lectures at Louisiana State University (Baton Rouge), the universities of North Carolina (Chapel Hill), Pittsburgh, Kansas City, and Pennsylvania (where, in addition to reading his poetry, he observed classes in ninteenth-century English poetry and twentieth-century European literature). He had gone to Washington, D.C., expecting to read at Howard, but the arrangements fell through. He was, however, able to spend three days until his next confirmed reading with Dick and Betty Eberhart, who were living in nearby Georgetown while Eberhart served as poetry consultant to the Library of Congress. It was a happy reunion.

After a reading in Pittsburgh, Rexroth lectured on the influence of the Far East on Western Tradition at New York University's Graduate Institute of Book Publishing, founded and directed by the noted writer and editor Stanley Burnshaw. Rexroth and Burnshaw had been corresponding since 1949, at which time Rexroth had asked Burnshaw to contribute some poems to a projected anthology of American poetry (it never materialized). They had last seen one another in December 1957 when Burnshaw, in San Francisco on business as president and editor-in-chief of Dryden Press, had taken Kenneth and Marthe out to dinner. Burnshaw also had met Marie: he dropped by the Eighth Avenue apartment one spring day of 1949 while Rexroth was in Europe; Marie was there and invited him in. Burnshaw was surprised to see Rexroth's pastels, which he thought had a very Eastern quality to them. He had not known that Kenneth was a painter as well as a poet.

Burnshaw's Institute modeled itself after the Pennsylvania School of Social Work. Students worked in publishing houses from nine to one, took technical courses from two to five, and attended some evening classes as well. Burnshaw had invited a number of prominent writers and scholars to participate in his course on the "Varieties of Literary Experience," including Lionel Trilling, Leon Edel, Cleanth Brooks, and Jacques Barzun. After the lecture, and over dinner at a nearby restaurant, Burnshaw was struck by Rexroth's eccentric behavior. During his lecture, Rexroth's voice had assumed an odd quality, sounding like a cross between a British accent and a Western drawl, almost as if he was poking fun at his audience or playing multiple roles as he read. Now, at dinner, his conversational voice returned to normal.[2] (Others would also comment on the strange variations in Rexroth's platform voice.) Rexroth and Burnshaw shared a similar political orientation, and talked freely about literature, Marxism, and the future of Western society. Burnshaw invited Rexroth to his Central Park West home for another evening of good food and conversation, after which he noted in his journal how impressed he was with Rexroth, that "his ideas are like mine, but he *knows* much more; he is still the little boy whose grandpa sat on the porch with Eugene Debs. I think his ideas are better grounded than mine."[3]

Rexroth went uptown to read at the Poetry Center at the 92nd Street Y on April 9. He was pleased with his audience, largely comprised of young academics who asked him sharp questions during the discussion period about the future direction of poetry. He singled out Denise Levertov as the best poet of her generation (which he would continue to do at lectures and in essays like "Bearded Barbarians or Real Bards," published in *The New York Times Book Review*, February 12, 1961, and in various collected essays). He also said that Robert Creeley was second best, a judgment "which seemed to please everybody."[4] Although he could not see her, Levertov was in the audience sitting next to Esther and Joseph Handler. Afterwards they all went out for beer along with Elizabeth Kray, the director of the Poetry Center—and a few Columbia students.

At the end of the evening he returned to his "lonely pillow and . . . folded quilt" at the Marlton Hotel on 8th Street in the Village. For him it was expensive, but he was able to save money by cooking his own meals. The food even in the best New York restaurants sickened him and he suspected that all the chefs used meat tenderizer. "Steak tastes like mush," he wrote Marthe.[5] He attended Palm Sunday Mass ("one of the greatest shows on earth") at the church of St. Mary the Virgin, and regretted that his family was not with him. He had sent Marthe extra money so that she could buy flowers for Easter. (He had been in the habit of ordering flowers to Scott Street, but did not do so this time because he was convinced that he was cheated every time he did it.) He insisted that Marthe take Mary to the major ceremonies of Holy Week.

These complaints notwithstanding, Rexroth had learned to adapt himself to the rigors of a poetry tour. He no longer needed to introduce himself to his audience, and he was never faced by a cool reception from his hosts. Students or faculty met him at the airport, his overnight accommodations were subsidized, and he was invited to dinners and parties. His readings were well attended. His press release, with fair accuracy, described him as "a leading figure in literary and intellectual circles on the West Coast," a pioneer in jazz poetry, and mentor to many key writers of the Beat Generation, although he now repudiated "some aspects" of the work typical of those writers. The essays he was publishing, especially those collected in *Bird in the Bush* (1959) demonstrated that he wanted to be valued as a scholarly (but not stuffy), sophisticated, hip critic.[6] He was one of the few critics to praise Donald Allen's *The New American Poetry* (1960), the first major anthology of open form poetry.

For KPFA, Rexroth taped some interviews with people for whom he had great respect, like Ornette Coleman and Charles Mingus. He saw "a great Monet show" at the Museum of Modern Art and a "very perverse play by Genet" Off-Broadway, probably *Death Watch*. But New York was a grind; everything, even pleasurable things like listening to music, felt like work. He showed no particular pleasure that the Great Jones Gallery would be exhibiting his pastels beginning April 12. He was not impressed with the political activity he observed, either. In sympathy with the freedom rides and sit-ins in the South, many New Yorkers were picketing the local branch chain stores. Rexroth thought they were wasting their time, that they were doing nothing more than inflating their own egos. Generally, New York remained a hateful place for Rexroth. Yet while he was there, he formed still another romantic attachment.

Gloria Oden, whose book of poems *Resurrections* (1978) was nominated for a Pulitzer Prize, had written to Rexroth in response to an advertisement he ran in *The Nation* for a place to stay while he was in the city. She was interested in hearing about Rexroth's views on the civil rights movement as she herself was black and she knew from his ad that he had been south, but she could offer him no accommodations.[7] Oden, the youngest of six children, came from a religious and politically active family. Her father, Reverend Redmon S. Oden, was pastor of A.M.E.Z. churches in Yonkers and New Rochelle. Oden had graduated from Howard University in 1948 and four years later earned a J.D. She was eager to break with the structure of her life, which had been fixed by her family. She lived not far from the Marlton Hotel, on East 4th Street, and was trying to write even though she held down a full-time job. When Rexroth called, she happily agreed to meet him.

Their first evening together made her feverish, literally. After dinner, Rexroth walked her home—she insisted on returning by nine o'clock so that she would get a full night's sleep—and at the door, she held out her hand. Instead, he kissed her on the forehead, and she became so flustered that she could not report for work the next morning.[8] Rexroth called that day, and not long afterward, they became lovers. More than once, Rexroth asked her to accompany him on social engagements because he enjoyed the "shock value" he thought their black / white relationship created. After Rexroth gave her the initial push, she began sending her work out to

journals and small magazines. Oden credited Rexroth for the break she
was able to make with a style overburdened by figurative language. One
evening, Rexroth introduced her to Ornette Coleman at the Five Spot,
and she transformed the occasion into a description of Rexroth's influence on her:

> His ferocious love,
> which burdened me to find
> my centre self and hold
> against sulfurous preachment,
> has fleshed me
> with curious armour;
> a bright-bonding girdle
> which, in my Father's stead,
> not only protects
> but also nullifies
> my power to betray
> sensibilities that
> continuously weigh and
> clarify existence.[9]

When Rexroth left New York, he and Gloria promised to correspond
regularly. But back in San Francisco, a fresh crisis awaited him. Marthe
had been reading Esther Handler's letters, and new fury was unleashed
in her. During a period when Kenneth had told her that their marriage
and family was more important to him than anything else—and that
without them he would no longer be able to write—he had not only
conducted an affair with Esther but established an intimate correspondence with her. Kenneth did not show much remorse during this confrontation, and surmised that it had a cathartic effect on Marthe: "having
got 2 years of surreptitiously read letters from Esther off her mind or
conscience, Marthe seems in better shape than she has been for years."[10]
Actually, the friendship between Rexroth and Esther had lost its intense
intimacy: "it was a true blow when it broke," he told Gloria Oden,[11] but he
was relieved to be free of Esther's "psychodramas." He was not bitter
about Esther: "she certainly gave me a great deal of quiet domestic happiness that Easter in St. Louis."[12] Rexroth instructed Gloria not to mail
letters that would arrive on the weekend or when he was away: "it is better
[Marthe] nevers know you exist."[13]

Another truce reached, Kenneth and Marthe worked out a program
for the summer when he would not be traveling much. (He participated
in the Chicago Poetry Seminar, June 3–5.) Marie had offered her house
in Lagunitas to Kenneth for early July when she would be visiting friends
in Denver, and Kenneth decided to bring Katharine there now that she
would be turning six. He had never spent time alone with her in the
country, as he had with Mary, and he thought this would be a perfect
opportunity to go walking and hiking with her and to teach her to read.

Mary was slated for two weeks at Camp Caniya near Sierra City in July, so no feelings would be bruised. Marthe stayed home, went to work, took Mary to her physical examination for camp, and typed one of Kenneth's articles. She hunted for a private school for Mary and Katharine, although Kenneth was not interested in spending money that way. If extra money was going to be spent on the children's education, he preferred to see it go for lessons in piano, dance, swimming, French, and organized nature hikes in the country.

Kenneth and Katharine enjoyed each other's company in Lagunitas. They took long walks and went on picnics in Devil's Gulch. Katharine progressed rapidly through the books that Kenneth taught her to read. Also, she was thrilled to discover that a deer and her faun had their covert behind Marie's house and she painted a picture of them for Marthe. For his part, Kenneth, having signed a contract with Doubleday, hoped to take full advantage of this quiet and harmonious time to complete a major section of his autobiography. That was not to happen. After Mary left for camp, coming home to an empty apartment every night made Marthe miserable. She had planned on spending part of the Fourth of July weekend in Lagunitas, but decided to come up for an overnight stay as well the week before. The preliminary visit turned into a domestic disaster: Kenneth and Marthe had a heated argument over the hopeless state of their marriage with Katharine as an audience. The next morning Marthe left, with Katharine in tow.

Their argument had touched on several familiar topics. Kenneth was especially angry because Marthe had balked at typing the manuscript of the autobiography once she realized he expected to complete it at a killing pace. Kenneth told Marthe that he had conceived the autobiography as a "testament" to her and the children, and now he regretted that, unlike other authors, he would not be able to write in the Preface: "This book is dedicated to my wife who typed the mss. and read the proofs and whose sometimes harsh but always enthusiastic criticism made this book possible."[14] Nor would Marthe yield to Kenneth's pressure to work on his translations of selected poems by Pierre Reverdy for New Directions while camping in the Sierras. She wanted to help him, but objected to unrealistic deadlines. If Kenneth had led Laughlin to believe the project was near completion, Marthe refused to be held accountable.

And then there was Kenneth's very real and lifelong yearning for a country place that he could call his own. Now that he was earning more money than he had ever had, the thought of buying land became feasible. Marthe agreed that this was a fine idea, but she was annoyed that Marie had offered to sell Kenneth some of her land in Lagunitas, and apparently hoped to oversee the construction of the cabin. Kenneth seemed to have some understanding of the dynamics of this arrangement, although he had to belittle Marthe to achieve it: "Marie and I—after all—we are both 55 years old and have know each other for 30 years. We are—for better or worse—the adults involved in this child's nightmare."[15] Nor did Marthe want to leave San Francisco permanently, or commit herself to spending every weekend out of town. Kenneth could have his cabin in Lagunitas, but she was not about to exile herself. These disagreements represented not only the couple's evolving resentment toward one another, but, more significantly, their ultimate incompatibility.

Kenneth became desperate after Marthe left with Katharine. He rushed down to San Francisco to make amends, but when he got to Scott Street, Marthe and Katharine were nowhere to be found. After two or three distraught phone calls to friends who might know where they were (in fact, Marthe had gone to visit the Tallmans, who were now living in Berkeley), he gave up the search and went back to Lagunitas. He had good reason to be frantic. He had struck Marthe several times during their argument, and Marthe responded furiously to this degrading treatment. She could no longer tolerate such behavior, especially when Kenneth told her that there was nothing extraordinary about husbands hitting their wives and that he did not feel disturbed by it. Marthe could not understand how he could rationalize such violence. "I am physically and morally incapable of such acceptance," she wrote him after she got back to Scott Street, and she referred him to his writings of pacifism. "I think," she added, "that much would be different between us if you started to believe what you do want to believe, what your write."[16]

Kenneth avoided the issue. Instead, he reiterated that frequently "young girls who marry older men become bitterly disillusioned."[17] He himself was incapable of living with a woman who felt trapped in his presence and who regarded his work with contempt. He had finally lost hope that their marriage would return to the "beautiful companionship" they had shared during their first four years together. But he was adamantly against a divorce. He wanted the children to grow up with both parents present, and he thought it best for him and Marthe to consult a marriage counselor. He believed, as in most American marriages he had observed, a way could be found for them to lead a decent and peaceful life together.

His domestic situation unresolved, Rexroth's work was suffering. He may have been writing a fair amount of journalism, but he was not producing many poems. He had written Laughlin from Provence that he was "quite sure" he would not be writing any more poetry. (The poems inspired by his European trip would not appear until 1964.) At fifty-five, he sensed that this was his last chance to be productive. He tried to impress this on Marthe. "I must get certain jobs done soon. This is a debt—not just to society—but to the society of generations to come. Of this failure to do my duty, I am always terrible aware."[18] As self-inflated as these words appear, they belong to a man who wanted to remain faithful to his vocation.

That August, in the aftermath of this turmoil, the Rexroths went camping together in the "cream" of the Sierras. By now, Kenneth was aware that Marthe did not want to spend her precious vacation time in an activity that exhausted rather than restored her before she returned to work, and he was careful to avoid steep climbing trails. He described this bittersweet family holiday to Gloria, who that summer was attending the Breadloaf Writers' Conference:

We had a fine pack trip. We shot the works and went deluxe. No donkeys, but all of us on horseback and with a packer to take to take care of the horses. Expensive but worth it. I'll probably never have the money to spend again and the girls will always remember it. They were in ecstasies especially Katharine—who had never really ridden before. She had a fine little sorrel mare and comported herself like a cavalry veteran.[19]

The trip had been a success, but the future still looked grim.

In September 1960, Marthe left the California Teachers Association to work on a project funded by the United States Office of Education. It was an inventory of the language and area centers in American colleges and universities that required an extended trip to Washington, D.C. Kenneth was left on his own to oversee life on Scott Street. He kept order with the help of a housecleaner, baby-sitters, and Marie, who wrote Marthe to reassure her that, in fact, the children were fine and "not living on hamburger."[20] Kenneth wanted Marthe to know that he was master of the situation—not to imply that her presence was superfluous, but that she was in reality free to carve out a meaningful career for herself. He urged her to make the most of the Washington experience, to visit the museums and test the French restaurants. "Maybe you can pick up a fascinating escort at the Iranian Embassy," he joked, "or at the Culture Office of the French."[21] He kept busy writing and going to the theater and opera. He took Mary to see *The Threepenny Opera,* which she thoroughly enjoyed. He was not sure how much of the satirical humor she actually understood, "but she laughed and scandalized all the squares."[22]

When Marthe returned from Washington, Kenneth proposed that they spend more time as a family with other families as a way of giving their lives stability. They had the Triests to visit in Sebastopol, and Kenneth resumed his friendship with Ephraim Doner, his painter friend in Big Sur who was now married and had a family. The Rexroths also befriended the family of Madefrey Odhner, who ran a chicken farm in Oakland. Rexroth had met Madefrey in the thirties. The son of a Swedenborgian clergyman, he was originally named "Made-Free-By-Truth." When Rexroth met him, he was writing poetry that made Rexroth think he wanted to be the successor to George Sterling. Rexroth was fond of him, even though he had been a captain in Army Intelligence during World War I.

Marthe enjoyed these outings, found them pleasant enough even if they did little to dispel her deep dissatisfaction with her marriage. She agreed to seek counseling, and upon the recommendation of Dr. Joseph

Henderson—the Jungian psychoanalyst who so many years ago had written up Kenneth's psychiatric examination for the draft board—she started to see Steven Schoen, a therapist who rented an office in the same building in which Henderson practiced. Schoen did not encourage Marthe to map out a strategy for living the rest of her life with Kenneth. Instead, he helped her understand that as long as she remained married to him, she might be miserable. In the process of therapy, Schoen, who himself was married with three children, and Marthe fell in love.

At the end of January 1961, Marthe finally left Kenneth, and on June 2 she sued him for divorce on the grounds of extreme cruelty. Although he did not contest the divorce, Kenneth had wanted to avoid this final break. If the battlefield aspect of their relationship had created new wounds and opened old ones, he still believed that their marriage should be preserved. Marthe should cope with his infidelities and his physical bullying; she should not mind his running her life. For his part, he remained willing to absorb the anger and hostility that Marthe directed against him, and to tolerate her rebuffs and sexual rejection—the legacy, Rexroth believed, of her aborted relationship with Creeley. "I do love Marthe," he wrote Gloria Oden. "I feel no real hostility towards her due to all this—only a terrible misery of sympathy."[23] In his weakest moments, however, Kenneth blamed his misery on Marthe's "violent, disorganized libido": he would distort their past and hold Marthe responsible for separating him from Marie.[24]

Rexroth had run out of techniques—which included loud cries of despair and threats of suicide—to persuade Marthe that she should remain married to him. Three years earlier, she had returned because she was afraid that he would kill himself. She no longer felt bound to respond to such threats. In part, Kenneth had lost his credibility; by all odds he should have done away with himself a while ago, if he had meant what he said. But Marthe also recognized that Kenneth, not she, bore the total responsibility for preserving his own life.

During their first year apart, Rexroth managed far better than he had predicted. Initially, Mary and Katharine lived with their mother. Kenneth was given liberal visiting rights, and he did not have to forego trips to the mountains with the children, or upcoming birthday celebrations—Mary would be turning eleven, Katharine seven. Three weeks after the divorce, he went camping with his daughters in Yosemite National Park. And at the end of the summer, they accompanied him to Aspen, Colorado, where he was a special guest from August 20 to September 2 at the Aspen Institute for Humanistic Studies.[25] He lectured mainly about anarchism and the lives of Emma Goldman and Alexander Berkman. Apparently, he presented a dapper image. He brought with him the suits he had designed himself and had made up by the London tailor, A. Lynes; according to Jonathan Williams, another Aspen fellow that summer, Rexroth looked like Robert Louis Stevenson at his best.[26] In addition to Rexroth

and Williams, Paul Goodman, John Hawkes, Jonas Salk, and W. W. Ros-
tow also visited the Institute.

Mary and Katharine went horseback riding and swimming, visited the
sled dogs up the mountains, and played tennis. Kenneth was very proud
of the way they behaved, "perfectly poised but still childlike." He told
Marthe how "everybody" loved their daughters and were sure they had
come from a happy home.[27] Unreconciled to their divorce, he wrote her
how he thought it was a "great tragedy" that she could not enjoy Aspen
with them. He missed her terribly. "I'm always seeing dresses I want to
buy you," he said after he sent her a dirndl skirt of beautifully patterned
material. He was very melancholy.

Dearest Marthe, surely you must know that I love you devotedly and want only to
see you happy and would do anything to help you. Never be afraid to let me know
if you need me. I will always respond. Certainly I need you always in every way. I
love you.[28]

Kenneth had repeatedly expressed such tender feelings before. As heartfelt and sincere as they were, Marthe could no longer respond to them
with the commitment to share her life with him.

Twenty-Five

A VICTORIAN MAN
ON THE TOWN
1961–1963

EXROTH CONTINUED to live on Scott Street after Marthe and the children moved to a five-room apartment with a big garden near Lincoln Park. The divorce agreement decreed that he would keep the ten thousand-volume library, "his security blanket." The $6,000 savings account went to Marthe, who in addition was awarded $275 monthy alimony and child support. Since he had his job on the *San Francisco Examiner* and his popularity at various art and poetry festivals carried healthy honoraria, the arrangement did not strap Rexroth. In March 1961, he was the featured speaker at the Idaho State College Festival of the Arts. That April he was dashing around New York City for two weeks, where he gave readings and lectures at New York University, Columbia, and City College, which patient Griselda Ohanessian at New Directions had arranged for him. At City College, he had lunch with Leo Hamalian, a professor of English in charge of readings, to whom he confided that the social revolution had degenerated into "pot and pussy." He also spoke before Harvard students and faculty. He participated in a television show called "The House We Live In" organized by Professor Ian McHarg at the University of Pennsylvania and broadcast on WCAU-CBS, Philadelphia. In 1961, his second volume of criticism, *Assays*, came out, and in 1962, his *Poems from the Greek Anthology* appeared.[1]

While Rexroth was in New York, he and Gloria Oden were together much of the time. They were now colleagues in writing: both had published in *The Urbanite: Images of the American Negro* (March 1961): Oden, "A Home, A Wilderness," the first chapter of a work in progress; Rexroth, "Who Am I? Where Am I Going???" a brief but hard-hitting attack on the notion that by 1961 the goals of the civil rights movement had been achieved. "If you are being raped in the kitchen or burned alive in the woods," Rexroth writes, "it is small consolation to know that all the world condemns your persecutors as evil men."[2] Further on, he adds:

The end of the road is total social indifference as to race, not in the Five Spot or the Blue Note; not in City College; not in a political rally. . . . It means that race won't make any difference if you're a plumber and go to the Plumber's Convention. It won't make a particle of difference with your neighbors in your apartment house or suburb. It won't make any difference to the kids your kids play with, or to the young men and women your sons and daughters choose to marry.[3]

The piece was written in part as a eulogy for Richard Wright, who had died on November 28, 1960.[4]

Rexroth and Oden developed a relationship that was warm, loving, and filled with a quiet and tender respect for one another's work. They seriously considered marriage, but Oden's strong sense of identity kept her in New York. She was fully aware that she would sacrifice her new-found independence if she moved to San Francisco, and there was no chance that Rexroth would move east. She had learned all about the chaos of Rexroth's life, and she also knew that she had not been his only "extra-marital" liaison. In spite of the love they shared, she felt that ultimately what Kenneth wanted from her, he could get from a paid housekeeper. Their relationship began to cool by the end of the summer of 1961, although it took nearly another year for their romantic involvement to dissolve.

Rexroth described the break-up to another friend and lover, Ruth Hartman, one of the more glamorous figures in San Francisco society, who lived in a lavender house in exclusive Seacliff (sometimes referred to as the "Golden Ghetto"). Rexroth had been introduced to Hartman by her daughter Margot Blum, whom he had recently met after praising in his *Examiner* column Blum's performance in the San Francisco Opera's Spring production of *Martha*. Rexroth pretended to be gallant and care-free about Oden's rejection—she had merely fallen in love with someone else. Rexroth surmised that she was on the brink of an important career (she eventually became professor of English at the University of Maryland), and that he "would have fouled up her life far more" than she would his if they had married.[5]

He pursued new romances and revived others, perhaps identifying with Paulos Silentiarios, whose poems he had translated so recently.

> Don't tell me I'm getting gray,
> That my eyes are red and bleared.
> It's just love having a romp.
> He kicks me where it hurts most,
> Sticks arrows in me for fun,
> Keeps me awake with lewd tales;
> My loins are prematurely
> Shriveled; my neck is scrawny;

I wane in a waxing fire.
If you would only relent—
I would grow plump at your touch,
And my hair turn black in a night.[6]

Rexroth's reputation as a man-on-the-prowl grew.[7] In his correspondence, he indulged in the kind of rhetoric more at home in men's locker
rooms. He continued to boast about sexual adventures during his at-
homes, and would recite off-color jokes and stories that offended as many
people as they amused. He still enjoyed ridiculing the sexual mores of the
middle class: "My god, they think if you do it on your side, you're a freak."
They were friends who thought Rexroth was intent on projecting a "bohemian mystique." Less philosophical observers called him an "old goat"
and left it at that. But however libertine Rexroth may have appeared, he
was not content to lead a life that went from one casual affair to the next.
He genuinely wanted another "Sacramental marriage." He saw no contradiction between his longing for a stable, profound relationship with one
woman and his predisposition to screw anyone within reach. When he
became determined to find a fourth wife, Rexroth ran into unexpected
obstacles, the kind he had encountered in his adolescence before he met
Andrée. The women to whom he proposed marriage wanted to be his
lover, his friend, but not the sympathetic self-sacrificing spouse he would
expect to take charge (as a secretary would) of the mundane aspects of a
writer's life.

During this period, 1961 to 1963, Rexroth became closer to Susan
Wiere, who was still living in Southern California. She would sometimes
fly up to San Francisco to spend the weekend with him, although after
her first visit she threatened never to return unless he devised a way to
heat the Scott Street apartment properly. The two space heaters that
Rexroth had set up were inadequate, and he thought he could solve the
problem by purchasing an electric blanket. He also cooked delicious meals
for her. They would stroll along the beach, and take romantic drives
through the mountains. Upon her return to Santa Monica, Rexroth would
dispatch a dozen yellow roses. Although the relationship was emotionally
intense, Susan refused to marry him. She had grown far too conscious of
his Victorian mentality and of the double standard that fixed his attitude
toward women. And she corroborated Rexroth's confession that he was
not marriageable. "I'm married to my work," he would say in moments of
melancholy candor. They did, however, remain friends. Phyllis Swig,
whose father owned the Fairmount Hotel in San Francisco, was another
woman whom Rexroth courted in his own fashion. She was living on Fifth
Avenue in New York at this time, and Rexroth called on her during his
trips east. In the fall of 1961, she came out to San Francisco for three
weeks. When she saw Rexroth in action, she put an end to their relationship. Rexroth dismissed her as a "frightfully unhappy woman . . . another

Marthe," even though she was "radiantly beautiful, wealthy with fine children."[8]

Another writer with whom Rexroth had been intimate during the early sixties was Ruth Stephan. Rexroth and Stephan were both in Chicago in the early twenties (Stephan was actually born there), but they were on opposite ends of the social ladder. Stephan was the only daughter of Charles R. Walgreen, who founded the successful drugstore chain and would have strongly disapproved of his daughter going to places like the Dill Pickle or listening to soapboxers in the Washington Square Bug Club condemn the capitalist system.[9] In 1939, she brought out a book of poetry, *Prelude to Poetry,* and with her second husband, the painter John Stephan, published *The Tiger's Eye,* a discriminating little magazine to which Rexroth contributed a review of Richard Blackmur's *The Good European* entitled "To Be or Not"[10] and an exquisite series of poems called "Hojoki."[11] Set in the lean-to hut in Devil's Gulch, these poems testify to Rexroth's great talent for expressing his moods and philosophical reverie in images of the natural world. Rexroth takes the title, which means "Monk's Record" or "Record of a Monk's Hut," from the collection of poetic essays written in A.D. 1212 by the Buddhist monk Kamond Chomei. In the closing poem, "Spring," he gently pokes fun at his serious, contemplative mood by remarking on how startled he is that the oak tree under which he is sitting seems to be purring, quivering, and breathing:

> I am startled until I
> Realize that the beehive
> In the hollow trunk will be
> Busy all night long tonight.[12]

These six tightly structured poems are particularly informative because they reveal so well an inner peace that contradicted the tenor of Rexroth's worldly, personal life.

> A thing unknown for years,
> Rain falls heavily in June,
> On the ripe cherries, and on
> The half cut hay.
> Above the glittering
> Grey water of the inlet,
> In the driving, light filled mist,
> A blue heron
> Catches mice in the green
> And copper and citron swathes.
> I walk on the rainy hills.
> It is enough.[13]

But clearly, Rexroth was not content with an exclusive diet of transcendental pleasure.

Although *The Tiger's Eye* was shortlived, Stephan and Rexroth had reason to remain in touch. Stephan wrote two novels, each presented as the memoirs of the seventeenth-century Queen Christina of Sweden who abdicated the throne to embrace Catholicism. At the same time she edited a collection of songs and tales of the Quechua people, the South American Indians who live in the Andean highlands. She was also becoming attracted to Asian culture. She increasingly felt the constraints of married life and from Reno, Nevada, she wrote Rexroth a rather amusing letter of complaint in which she declared she was a dinosaur. Unlike the people she observed around her, she had no aptitude for keeping up with the fast pace of life. Like Rexroth, she could not be both artist and spouse. She signed the letter "Stephanasaurus."[14]

Rexroth visited her at her Greenwich, Connecticut, home or Fifth Avenue apartment in New York City when he came east. In 1961 she divorced John Stephan and went to Kyoto, where she lived in a student house at Daitoku-ji, the compound of Zen Buddhist temples. She wrote to Rexroth from Japan and sent him some of the poems she had composed there. Over the next several years she traveled widely and saw Rexroth occasionally, sometimes when she passed through San Francisco on her way home from Japan. She met Mary, whom she liked and found very interesting. She proposed that Rexroth should join her on one of these jaunts as her guest, but his life in 1962 was too unstable for such a luxury.

He had, however, availed himself of Stephan's generosity in another way. In 1960 she founded the Ruth Stephan Poetry Center at the University of Arizona at Tuscon, and Rexroth was among a number of poets invited to the Center for readings, informal meetings with classes, and individual conferences with students writing poetry. (Other poets who came to the Center in the sixties were Robert Frost, Louise Bogan, Karl Shapiro, Robert Duncan, Allen Ginsberg, John Crowe Ransom, Cecil Day Lewis, Denise Levertov, Robert Creeley, and Owen Dodson.) She also became a civil rights activist, and helped organize Freedom Schools in the South. After an autobiographical novel of hers was rejected in 1969, she stayed home more in Greenwich with her third husband. By then, her friendship with Rexroth had faded, but he remained fond of her, and took numerous photographs of her when she visited him in San Francisco. (Stephan died in April 9, 1974, under circumstances which suggest suicide.)

Rexroth was still in demand for poetry readings and lectures. He spent the week of June 14, 1962, in Anchorage, Alaska, the first poet to be invited to the annual Alaska Festival of Music. He gave a reading, conducted workshops for Anchorage Community College students interested in writing poetry or journalism, and gave interviews to the local radio and television stations. He liked Alaska, partly because his reading was so enthusiastically received, but partly because there were many "widows"—as women whose husbands were working in the distant petroleum fields or posted at remote Army bases were known—who appreciated his presence. In July, Rexroth enjoyed the hospitality of another lover, Germaine Firth, who invited him to participate in "The Pursuit of Happiness," a conference she organized at the Old Strawberry Hotel, thirty-two miles east of Sonora. Rexroth oversaw two of the seminars: "Religious Restatement in an Age of Faithlessness," and "Beyond Institutions: The Family Redefined." He was adding to his repertory, expanding it beyond his two favorite subjects, poetry and anarchism.

Rexroth's lecture schedule was bursting with engagements—at the San Francisco Medical Center, the San Francisco Public Library, the Northern California Humanist Council, as well as the National Poetry Festival, held at the Library of Congress in October 1962. Not everyone appreciated his act. Louise Bogan, who attended the festival, retained a sharp recollection of Rexroth's reading, far more critical than her report of his Five Spot performance four years earlier: "Rexroth got up and roll[ed] his eyes around while telling stories about his exploits. Morton Dauwen Zabel [then editor of *Poetry*] witnessed the performance and was sickened by it."[15] Rexroth had also joined the faculty (teaching an art survey class) at the San Francisco Art Institute in September 1962, a position he held for the next six years.

Twelve-year-old Mary arrived on Scott Street that September, unannounced, suitcase in hand. Marthe and Steven Schoen were living together with his three children and Marthe's two, and Mary was miserable. Marthe had not wanted her to leave, but she felt enormous pressure—from Kenneth, from Mary, and from her new therapist—to honor Mary's preference for living with her father. But with Mary back home, Rexroth's responsibilities expanded, and he needed help. Moreover, he felt that there was something indecent about a father living alone with a daughter, especially one on the edge of puberty. He went so far as to register with the Scientific Marriage Center in search of a stepmother. Without success, the director, Rose Marie Marston, proposed three candidates—a thirty-two-year-old German physician, a fifty-five-year-old property owner, and a fifty-four-year-old church secretary. In total candor, Rexroth made his plight known during his broadcasts on KPFA, and one day early in 1963 Carol Tinker appeared at Scott Street ready to volunteer her secretarial services and anything else that was needed to keep the Rexroth domicile running smoothly.

Twenty-three years old, Carol was born in Pittsburgh, one of three children. She grew up in New York City, Japan, and Brandywine Hundred, Delaware. After attending Carnegie Mellon University, where she majored in the arts, she moved to San Francisco in 1962. She wanted to observe its cultural scene first hand, and specifically to meet Kenneth Rexroth. She liked saying that she "picked him out" from Delaware, and Kenneth used to tease her about her determination to meet him by calling her a "one-eyed Wabanaki," after the confederation of Algonquian-speaking Indian tribes who lived in Delaware.[16] A highly sensitive, intellectual woman, she painted and wrote poetry. With her pale skin, freckles, turned-up nose, and straight brown hair, she bore a striking resemblance to Rexroth's first wife, Andrée. Carol officially became Kenneth's housekeeper, secretary, and Girl Friday shortly before Marthe and Steven Schoen were married. She lived in her own apartment on Page Street for the first year and a half, but in 1965 moved into Scott Street, where she had her own room. From then on, Rexroth referred to her as his live-in secretary. As Rexroth wrote Laughlin, "it works out fine."[17]

At this juncture, Rexroth initiated a revisionist policy toward his work. New Directions was bringing out his next volume of poetry, *Natural Numbers: New and Selected Poems* (1964), which included five of the seven poems published in *In Defense of the Earth* under the general title "Seven Poems for Marthe, My Wife." Rexroth asked first that the general title be stricken, and then that Marthe's name be removed from individual titles of poems. So "Marthe Away" became "She Is Away." The dedication line beneath "The Old Song and Dance," which reads "On Marthe's Birthday," was removed.[18] Rexroth's bitterness at this juncture had surfaced and hardened, and he believed that eliminating Marthe from the record would magically be restorative. Seeking Laughlin's approval, he wrote that no matter how painful and distasteful it was, "everyone" had advised him to do it, including, he said, Mary. He added that his friends now regarded Marthe as "a totally malevolent woman" determined to hurt him and the children.[19]

Whether or not Rexroth thought that he was following sound advice by striking Marthe's name from his poetry, he was perhaps unconsciously conceding that Marthe spoke truly when she said that the poems provided a false, idealized version of their relationship. The poem "Marthe Growing," now entitled "Growing," illustrates Rexroth's doomed expectations: that Marthe would free him from "the past and the / Falling inertia of unreal, dead / Men and things"; and with his "warm heart's blood" he would nurture her spirit and creativity, which would bloom like an exotic plant, "one pale leaf / Unlike any other unfolding, / And then another, strange, new, / Utterly different."[20] Alluding to Martin Buber's philosophy of personal responsibility, the closing lines poignantly summarize the assumed responsibilities that Rexroth had hoped would be the basis of their marriage:

> I and thou, from the one to
> The dual, from the dual
> To the other, the wonderful,
> Unending, unfathomable
> Process of becoming each
> Our selves for each other.

Such editorial changes indicate that Rexroth felt humiliated and betrayed not only by Marthe, but also by his own dreams and self-delusions.

Another of the poems published in *Natural Numbers*, "Pacific Beach," had appeared nine months earlier in a booklet that accompanied an exhibition sponsored by Steuben Glass, entitled "Poetry in Crystal." It was dedicated to "Phyllis on her arrival in San Francisco," no doubt a reference to the trip Phyllis Swig made to San Francisco in 1961. It is a melancholy poem, set at night along the Pacific Coast highway, with a lonely Rexroth driving "eighty / Miles an hour through the still, / Moonfilled air."[21] The ocean tide, peaceful though it may be, reminds him of the vicissitudes of love and the easy shifting of love's loyalties. All that remains constant is the longing for true and lasting love. When this poem was printed in *The Collected Shorter Poems*, the dedication to Phyllis, like the ones to Marthe, was deleted. And ironically enough, this poem belongs to a sequence of eight love poems entitled "Air and Angels." No dedicatees are mentioned but Susan Wiere inspired the first poem, "This Night Only," and the fourth poem, "Coming," which describes Rexroth flying south to Los Angeles to his lover's "curving lips" and "ivory thighs," the presence of her last visit (presumably to Scott Street) fading like "the yellow rose buds that stood / On the commode."[22] The title of another poem, "Like Queen Christina," is an allusion to Ruth Stephan's persona in her two novels.

In "Maroon Bells," he describes a love that seems boundless:

> O my girl, mistress of all
> Illuminations and all
> Commonplaces, I love you
> Like the air and the water
> And the earth and the fire and
> The light love you and love you.[23]

All eight poems indicate that Rexroth was reaching a point where the women in his life had become a single Woman, grounded in the real world of ocean and sun, airports and mountains, highways and cities, subject to the weaknesses of human nature, but now anonymous, her passion and sensuality idealized along with her identity.

Twenty-Six

REWARDS
1963–1967

FOR THE TIME BEING, the domestic situation stabilized. During the next years, Rexroth plunged into a maze of activities. He spoke at the Esalen Institute, before the San Francisco Music Chamber Society, the University of Southern California, the University of California, Berkeley, Los Angeles, and Davis, the San Francisco Jewish Community Center, and Penn State. He continued to teach a poetry workshop at San Francisco State. He flew to Washington to attend the annual National Poetry Festivals, and in 1963 he was interviewed by D. G. Bridson for the Library of Congress. He was asked the questions he had been used to answering, questions about San Francisco, the Beats, poetry and jazz, the literary scene in England, poetry and the university. Bridson enjoyed the interview, which took place "over a couple of cigars and a bottle of whiskey" in the Washington Hotel, but he had a difficult time recording it. Rexroth sat in a chair tilted back so far that his position was nearly parallel to the ceiling. Bridson had to stretch out on the bed beside him in order to pick up Rexroth's voice with his microphone. Carol Tinker was the only upright person in the room.[1]

The next year, during February and March the Peacock Gallery on Union Street exhibited seventeen pastels by Rexroth. In the fall of 1965 he gave readings at Johns Hopkins, Temple University, the City College, and the 92nd Street Y, where he was introduced by Gilbert Sorrentino. His performances became more eccentric, marked by dialogue that he seemed to be conducting with himself sotto voce. Amazingly prolific, he still appeared in *The Nation* and *The New York Times Book Review*, and could now also be read in *Atlantic Monthly*, *New Leader*, *Contact*, *Chicago Review*, *Book Week*, and *Harper's* (despite the fact that Rexroth had nearly sued them for libel when they published "The New Cult of Sex and Anarchy" in 1947). New American Library commissioned him to write an Afterword for Frank Norris's *McTeague*. He produced a stunningly successful overview of this San Francisco novel, placing it firmly in American literary history without exaggerating its achievement. Although on more than

one occasion Rexroth stated that he did not care to read novels, this essay
reveals that he had thought carefully about prose fiction, its function and
its practitioners. He casually revealed his familiarity with the current
critical approaches to literature—making sure not only to talk about symbol and structure, tragedy, naturalism, Social Darwinism, and the interior
life, but also to keep such discussion accessible to the general reader. At
the risk of losing credibility as an objective critic, he injected into the essay
his own personal prejudices. Commenting on the clear craftsmanship of
Norris's prose, he denigrates the style of far greater writers. "It's been a
long time since I got worked up over the overeducated conversation of
the Karamazov brothers. I read Melville only when paid."[2] No doubt
Rexroth hoped to shock his readers with his irreverent pronouncements.
His popularity at KPFA did not suffer. Parties were sometimes scheduled
to coincide with his Sunday evening programs: guests would wait to hear
who would be insulted next.

Forced to use his time judiciously, Rexroth occasionally had to sacrifice a few moments in the spotlight. When the National Institute of Arts
and Letters awarded him $2,500 in May 1964, he did not fly to New York
to attend the ceremony. Malcolm Cowley made the presentation of the
award, and praised the absent Rexroth for "maintaining under difficult
circumstances, the integrity of the arts, and for communicating his understanding of experience with lucid candor, energy and compassion.
Memorably and movingly he presents both minute particulars and the
large vistas opened by his secular religiosity." For those people in the
audience who were familiar with the turmoil of Rexroth's private life,
Cowley's remarks regrettably underscored the split between the poet's
persona and the man himself. However, if in public he seemed to thrive
on being flamboyant and on the make, peppering his speech with provocative comments, at home he was establishing a new and proper routine.

Rexroth modulated the rhythms of his daily life so that he could work
efficiently, yet supervise Mary's education and free time. He lived according to a fixed weekday schedule.[3] Every morning, before Mary left for
school, he prepared her breakfast. Mary was not permitted to come to the
breakfast table in her bedclothes. After she left, around eight-thirty, he
worked with Carol Tinker on his correspondence until ten. From then
until mid-afternoon Rexroth would write or dictate the next essay for
publication or tape for KPFA. Between two and four in the afternoon, he
went marketing for the day, ran the laundry over, and tended to various
errands, including a trip to Raffetta's for dark roasted coffee beans and
the peculiar but friendly conversation with Mr. Raffetta, who spoke Italian only. There was now a refrigerator in the kitchen. Unless he had a
class to teach, or a segment to tape for the television station KQED (a
recent but shortlived association), by four Rexroth was back home and in
the bathtub, where he would stay for two hours reading and translating.
(Rexroth did his translating exclusively in the bathtub.) Mary's dance

classes at the San Francisco Ballet School often prevented her from getting home before eight, at which time she, her father, and Carol would
dine. Rexroth wore a jacket at the dinner table, set the table with cloth
napkins and candles, and served wine. (This was a far cry from the huge
spaghetti dinners he used to serve up in a dishpan, with cheap California
jug wine that he had decanted into empty bottles with fancy labels.) On
Friday nights, candles were lit in a menorah: since Rexroth's approach to
religion was home-grown ecumenical (at one time or another he was
drawn to Roman Catholicism, Anglicanism, the Greek Orthodox faith,
Buddhism, and Martin Buber's brand of Judaism), there was nothing
unusual in his eyes or Mary's about this ritual.[4]

On weekends, when Katharine came to stay, Rexroth did not observe
so rigid a routine. Nevertheless, to young Katharine, the atmosphere
around the house seemed tense and lifeless, and she felt timid and scared
around her father. He was quick to criticize her if she did something as
harmless as spilling honey on the table. She spent most of her time there
reading and playing with the cat.[5] Mary would often retreat to her room.
If Carol Tinker were free, she would make up stories with Katharine to
pass the time. Kenneth took the girls to the Kabuki theater and to just
about any production of Shakespeare. Sunday mornings they attended
mass at the Church of the Advent, after which Rexroth would usually
cook huge pancakes toughened by too many eggs. There was the Sunday
paper to read, but no Sunday comics. From the time Mary and Katharine
were little, Rexroth cut the comics out of the newspaper because he thought
they were too violent. For the same reason, television was forbidden. Yet
their father took them to see Samurai films in which Japanese heads and
hands were lopped off routinely.

Rexroth took advantage of San Francisco's booming cultural scene.
He frequently attended concerts, the ballet, or theater, although he rarely
had to pay his way since becoming a columnist on the *Examiner*. Rexroth
remained a popular figure and cultivated cordial relationships with directors and managers, including Leon Kalmios, managing director of the
San Francisco Ballet. (Rexroth wrote a libretto for *Original Sin*, a ballet
choreographed by Lew Christensen, with music by John Lewis and the
Modern Jazz Quartet.) Although Carol often was by his side, Mary was
usually his companion for special occasions, especially opening nights at
the opera. He told the San Francisco reading public via his column, with
perhaps some exaggeration, that by the time Mary had reached the age
of ten, she had "learned the techniques of the compleat opera goer. She
studies the people in the opposite boxes, compares their gowns to Renoir
and Clouet, compares the performance to a previous one in Europe, and,
I suppose, frightens the neighbors."[6] He took great pride in young Mary's
beauty, character, and precociousness. He had raised her to be brave and
independent, to fish and climb and shoot with a bow and arrow. He made
no concession to her gender except that he took great delight in dressing

her up. From the time she was a child, he had been in the habit of buying her a kimono or a mantilla for the new year to show her off, instead of a winter coat to keep her warm. Marie would usually come to the rescue at such times, taking Mary to lunch followed by a practical shopping excursion.

Rexroth had high expectations for both of his daughters, although Katharine was much more under the direction of Marthe. He wanted them to go to the best schools and colleges (as no doubt Marthe did), although he was disinclined to foot tuition bills. He also explained to Mary early on that he had settled on three criteria to determine whether or not her suitors were acceptable candidates for marriage.[7] First, the sleeve vent on the man's shirt had to button. This assured a reasonable level of cultivation and knowledge about English tailors. Second, the moons on all ten fingers had to show—a sure sign that the man knew how to take care of himself. (Rexroth was very particular about his own hands, which were delicate and small, and he had a great aversion to washing dishes as a result. His feet were so small that he could wear Marie's hiking boots.) And third, the man should know how to cook a light supper in formal evening dress. This would indicate that he owned evening dress, had the occasion to wear it, and knew his way around the kitchen. Rexroth had an original, creative system for judging a person's value as a possible son-in-law. No beatniks for his daughter. He wanted Mary to attend Radcliffe and marry a Harvard man.[8] His brand of egalitarianism did not extend to the future that he wanted for his daughters.

Rexroth had never lost his interest in a full-time teaching position, and nourished the hope that he would get one, preferably nearby. He was poet-in-residence from June 22 to July 17, 1964, at the University of Wisconsin, Milwaukee, where he taught a course on the metric principles of English poetry and befriended poet, critic, and teacher Morgan Gibson. His friend Joe Axelrod, who had been at San Francisco State, extended every effort to get him an appointment at California State College at Palos Verdes, which was slated for a new campus. Axelrod served on the planning staff for the new state college and had been appointed Dean of Humanities and Arts. Rexroth's appointment was tentatively approved by Leo Cain, president of the college, but the new campus never materialized. Axelrod returned to San Francisco State as Dean of Humanities, and Rexroth thought he had missed his last opportunity to achieve security in the academic world. He decided that it was finally time to do something commercial in the world of books. By this time, his Scott Street apartment could no longer accommodate his library. He had rented a small second apartment on the first floor of 250 Scott Street, but neither could that addition contain the overflow. When Horace Schwartz described his plans for opening a bookstore, Rexroth decided to cast his lot with him in hopes of supplementing his income through the sale of his superfluous books. Schwartz opened a small shop on the second floor of a Union Street building in a former antique store and called it "Kenneth Rexroth Books." It didn't last long.[9]

Rexroth and Schwartz had known one another since the early fifties, when Schwartz was running Goad Press. He had published a separate pamphlet of Rexroth's *Thou Shalt Not Kill: A Memorial for Dylan Thomas* in 1955. Schwartz, who made his living as an accountant, bought all the books Rexroth wanted to get rid of, and they shared the profit on the books sold.[10] Schwartz minded the store, which was quiet enough for him to work on the tax files of his clients. Rexroth rarely stopped in, but sometimes Mary would help out. Schwartz paid $75 a month to rent the space, and hardly made any money although every so often he would give Rexroth $20 or $30. Because the primary stock was Rexroth's cast-off review copies, there was no regular inventory to speak of. Schwartz liked to think of the place as a West Coast version of New York's Strand Bookstore, but that was a delusion of grandeur. And he enjoyed conversing with people who wandered into the bookstore under the impression they were going to meet the great Rexroth. One day Paul Bowles walked in, and after he learned that Rexroth was not around, asked Schwartz if he had one of his books and how much he was selling it for. When Schwartz told him it was two dollars, Bowles became furious and said he was being cheated. It dawned on Schwartz that Rexroth did in fact seem to know countless people—either through correspondence or actual meetings—in literature and the arts. On another occasion, Ira Gershwin came into the store asking for Rexroth. He told Schwartz he had known Rexroth in the thirties when they were both down in Santa Monica.

In the mid-sixties, Rexroth was so popular a San Francisco cultural figure that an official "Rexroth Birthday Committee" was created in honor of his sixtieth year and the forthcoming publication of his autobiography and collected shorter poems. Organized largely through the efforts of Carol Tinker, it was a gala black-tie event held at the Scottish Rite Building, during which a member of the Oakland Mayor's Office officially proclaimed Kenneth Rexroth an "honorary Negro." Rexroth's friend Dick Collins flew in from Long Beach to attend. Marie Rexroth, acting as one of the hosts, placed Collins at the head table, where the speeches and presentations were made, and from where he could easily hear the piano and flute softly playing the introductory music he had written for Rexroth's *Phaedra*, which had been performed at St. Louis University in the midfifties. Novelist Herbert Gold was also there as a member of the birthday committee. Gold had enjoyed more than a few of Rexroth's literary soirées and spaghetti dinners, and listened to Rexroth radio talks, which he said sounded as though Rexroth "was in bed with a bunch of books."[11] Gold, who had gone through marital crises himself, had helped nurse Rexroth through his divorce from Marthe by having lunch with him regularly.

Despite a killing schedule, Rexroth set aside time for younger writers.

An acquaintance on *The Wall Street Journal* showed him a sheaf of poems by Jessica Hagedorn, a fifteen-year-old girl who had recently immigrated from the Philippines with her mother to San Francisco, and who had never heard of Rexroth.[12] After Rexroth read the poems, he invited Jessica for dinner, a casual but elegant meal graciously served by Carol Tinker. Mary (a year younger than Hagedorn) was friendly but somewhat intimidating—she was a serious ballet student and very sophisticated. That evening marked the beginning of a friendship between Hagedorn and Rexroth, who reminded her of her Chicago grandfather—a lovable, sad, big, cranky man. Rexroth was "magical." He was very sympathetic to her artistic aspirations, her Filipino childhood, and her education. He set her on a course of reading—which included anthologies of black writers and French writers like Apollinaire, Artaud, and Clevel—and invited her to use his library whenever she liked. She lived nearby on Fell Street, and took advantage of Rexroth's offer.

Rexroth also encouraged her and Stephen Schwartz, the son of his "bookstore partner" Horace Schwartz, to attend his poetry workshop at San Francisco State after their classes over at Lowell High School next door. The size of the class varied, from twenty to thirty, but everyone in the room adored Rexroth. Rexroth decided that Jessica needed to develop her ear, and invited her to read with him at a small coffeehouse, the Blue Unicorn. Soon after her initiation into public performance, she appeared with Rexroth and the musical group Serpent Power at the Straight, a theater in the Haight. To give her fledgling career another boost, Rexroth cited, in his *Examiner* column, Hagedorn and Schwartz as the two best younger poets to appear recently in the Bay Area. Jessica was thrilled. He never tampered with her poetry, or condescended to her about it, but would suggest, for example, that she think more in terms of shape when she was writing. Jessica liked to hang out around Kenneth: he was an activist; he cared about people; he supported the underdog. He was also funny. She gleefully listened to the dirty stories he would tell over the dinner table, epecially the one about persimmons, which had several variations, all based on Rexroth's contention that the exotic fruit resembled a vagina.[13] Sometimes they would all eat out together—Rexroth, Mary, and Jessica—at Connie's, a West Indian restaurant where the specialty was coconut bread, and then go over to City Lights Bookstore where Mary and Jessica would eavesdrop on Kenneth's conversations with Shig, and with the poets who dropped by.

In the fall of 1965, Rexroth flew east for three days to read at the 92nd Street Y, and to discuss numerous writing assignments, including an article for *Holiday* on contemporary poetry. For *Saturday Review,* John Ciardi had invited him to write a series of pieces (he received $5,000 for the first twenty) on the classics, entitled "Classics Revisited." He had started off in March 1965 with "The Epic of Gilgamesh" and worked his way up, in two more series, to the modern period, with pieces on Homer and *The Kale-*

vala (where he emphasizes that the *Iliad* and *Odyssey* and *The Epic of Gil-gamesh* are works of literature, and "the notion that they were grunted out by Folk sitting about a fire and munching bones was a hallucination of a few nineteenth-century German scholars.").[14] He wrote about Sappho, Plato, Julius Caesar, and Plutarch; classic Japanese poetry, Lady Mura-saki, Marco Polo, and Malory; Casanova, Shakespeare, Stendhal, and Mark Twain. He demonstrated an overwhelming breadth of knowledge, but more importantly, his informal, conversational style made these works accessible to general readers who had learned to hate the classics in school.

As a member of the advisory board for the National Book Award, he attended its annual awards ceremony at New York's Lincoln Center. In the anteroom to Avery Fisher Hall, he nearly got into a brawl with James Dickey, whom he called a Fascist (Rexroth pronounced the word "Fasist"). During the ceremony, he sat on stage next to his friend Stanley Burnshaw, who had served on the committee for the translation award.[15] Over Rexroth's objections, Elizabeth Bishop had won the poetry award for *Questions of Travel*. When Robert Lowell (who according to Burnshaw practically blackmailed the committee into awarding Bishop the prize) accepted the award for her, he decided to read her poem about Ezra Pound, "Visits to St. Elizabeths." Written in nursery-rhyme style, it is an account of the various "mentally ill" people incarcerated in the Washington, D.C., hospital, "the house of Bedlam." The inmates include a crazy sailor, a boy who pats the floor "to see if the world is round or flat," Pound (who is never named but called the "cruel man," "tedious man," "wretched man"), and "Jew in a newspaper hat."[16] When Lowell was through, Rexroth stood up and announced that he wanted to go on record as protesting against "this anti-Semitic poem." The audience appeared divided on the issue on whether or not Rexroth's accusation was justified (it was not), and there was a brief flurry of discussion. The ceremony did not interfere with the pleasant dinner that Burnshaw and Rexroth shared afterwards with James Laughlin, in whose Bank Street apartment Rexroth was staying. Throughout his life, Rexroth would remain antipathetic to Bishop's poetry, but he regarded Robert Lowell as a "true Protestant, metaphysical, Baroque poet," whose dilemmas and spiritual conflicts gave his work "poignant immediacy."[17]

Rexroth's urge to travel outside the United States was stirring once again by 1966. He felt secure enough to consider leaving San Francisco for a while, especially since he could continue, as he had during his last European trip, to tape for KPFA. He thought he was ripe for a handsome grant, now that he had received the 1965 William Carlos Williams Award from *Contact*. Rexroth had been murmuring about going back to France and Italy, but he changed his plans when he was awarded a grant from the Rockefeller Foundation and another from the Akademische Aus-tauschdienst in West Germany, which essentially was an invitation to visit Berlin as a scholar/poet and live at the expense of the German government. He figured out that combined, these grants provided enough money to take Mary and Carol on a trip around the world. He was sure he could schedule lectures or readings along the way for supplemental income.

First, he had to sublet the Scott Street apartment. Luckily Paul Goodman, who at the request of the Associated Students Union had been running seminars at San Francisco State, told Rexroth that his old friend Edward Roditi wanted to teach for a year at the college. Rexroth asked Joe Axelrod if Roditi could be invited. As it happened, Axelrod had known Roditi in the late thirties when both were students at the University of Chicago. Axelrod arranged for Roditi to be named visiting professor for the 1966–67 academic year. This suited Rexroth perfectly, because Roditi could then live on Scott Street and watch over his valuable library. However, he feared that the apartment was too big for one person to manage. With Marie's help and Roditi's consent, he found a roommate for Roditi, Lois Borgman, a dietitian for the San Francisco Health Department. He knew the place would now be safe, and that his books and mail—he received on the average twenty pieces a day—would be taken care of. He also had to arrange for Mary's education. She was a student at the local high school, Polytechnic, which she had insisted on attending, over the protests of both her parents who thought the school (with a population of less than 10 percent white) was too dangerous. Rexroth arranged for her to continue her coursework and take her exams through correspondence. He also made sure that Mary would be able to attend ballet classes abroad.

After stopovers in London (where they visited Stuart Montgomery of Fulcrum Press), and Amsterdam, Kenneth, Mary, and Carol were in Berlin by October 1. They were not traveling light. Kenneth made Mary and Carol wear big skirts so that they could hide all the carry-on baggage he wanted to take, which came to be known as "the office." It consisted of two large cameras, two briefcases, and a portable metal file, none of which Kenneth carried. Much to Mary and Carol's horror, he insisted on wearing a plastic fold-up raincoat. All three got sick en route. In Berlin, "everything toxic, everything too expensive, everything square."[18] Nor was Rexroth impressed by the German people. "The *only* civilized Germans," he wrote Roditi (who had served as a translator during the Nuremberg Trials) "departed in smoke from the gas ovens."[19] Initially, there was not much hospitality.

Rexroth noticed a certain pattern developing. Readings, lectures, and parties in the process of being organized for him would "mysteriously stop."[20] He blamed some of the icy treatment on politics, suspecting in his own paranoid way that Lyndon Johnson ("Johnson the Second") had given orders to the people working at the U.S. Office of Information Services to avoid and isolate any U.S. citizen who was an outspoken dove, which Rexroth clearly was. On numerous occasions, he had made his anti-Vietnam position quite clear in the States. On January 7, 1961, he had given a paper on "The Intellectual and War: A Case History of Failure" at a conference sponsored by two pacifist organizations, the Committee of Correspondence and the American Friends Service Committee. He belonged to the National Advisory Council of the Student Peace Union, one of the organizations responsible for a peace demonstration in Washington, D.C., in February 1962, and had participated with I. F. Stone, Benjamin Spock, Mario Savio, Norman Thomas, Dick Gregory, Paul Krassner, Dave Dellinger, and Norman Mailer in the Vietnam Days Community Meeting, May 21 and 22, 1965, on the UC Berkeley campus.[21]

Still, by December, with the help of Walter Hasenkleber, who served as liaison between Rexroth and his host government, Rexroth was made to feel very welcome. Berlin had transformed itself into a wonderful city, and the sumptuous suite provided by the West German government in the old mansion by the Wannsee was peaceful and restful. Rexroth still suspected the government of "spy movie goings on,"[22] but he assumed that he was now considered a good guy. Unwilling to abandon his conspiracy theory altogether, he believed the authorities in Bonn and Washington had decided, for the sake of diplomacy, that it would be tactful to identify Rexroth as "a very important writer and public figure." So, after months of isolation, Rexroth was catapulted into the limelight, invited everywhere, and sought by the BBC. The only drawback was that Mary resented her afternoon classes at the Berlin Ballet School. She thought the students were unpleasant, out of shape, and poor dancers.[23]

In mid-December, the three left for a tour of Scandinavia, which Rexroth thoroughly enjoyed, especially their stay in Helsinki which, in his opinion, had the best people and the best theater. He wrote Roditi that he had bought a "very campy Aarhippa suit designed by a nymphomaniac,"[24] which made him look like "one of those naturally preserved fully dressed iron age gents." Back in Berlin in time for Christmas, Kenneth, Mary, Carol, and their cat "Herr Mule" celebrated in grand style. They decorated their tree with foil-wrapped chocolate, ate caviar and pheasant (Herr Mule got the bones), and drank fine champagne. Among all the presents Mary received, Kenneth liked the silver-fox hat and muff best because, he told Roditi jestingly, it made her look "very kinky." The generally festive atmosphere was enhanced by preparations for their trip around the world. He sent off their tentative itinerary to Marie, Roditi, and Lois Borgman. He wanted his mail forwarded, but he also asked them if they would notify the consulates, the cultural relations offices, the bureaus of tourism, and the airline public relations chiefs that a famous American poet and newspaper columnist was on his way.

The round-the-world trip began in February 1967. The first part included Brussels, Paris, and Barcelona, none of which lived up to Rexroth's expectations. Paris prices reminded him too much of New York, and he developed an aversion to Spanish culture.[25] He spoke no Spanish whatsoever, having worked from the French to produce the translations for

Thirty Spanish Poems of Love and Exile (City Lights) more than ten years ago. They proceeded to southern Italy, which Rexroth disliked almost as much as Spain, then on to Greece, Turkey, Iran, Afghanistan, and India. This was the first time Rexroth had been out of Western Europe. In New Delhi, he met the great Mexican poet Octavio Paz, who was at the time Ambassador to India. Over dinner, the two men discussed their common concern with the turbulent state of the world. Rexroth also communicated to Paz a growing enthusiasm for the culture of China and Japan, but not that of India.[26] In India, Kenneth, Mary, and Carol were not staying in the de luxe hotels most westerners patronized, but chose one where the restaurant menu consisted of "rice" days and "chapati" days,[27] and whose location did not shield them from India's great poverty. Every morning they would see death wagons picking up the most recent victims of the widespread famine that at this time plagued the country.

They avoided Vietnam where the war was raging, but visited Singapore, Thailand, and Australia, "a great place if you feel beachy."[28] In Sidney, he met the writer Frank Moorhouse, who would later write a fictionalized account of an excrutiatingly boring party he and his friends held for Rexroth and Carol Tinker. Entitled "The American Poet's Visit," the story paints an unflattering portrait of Rexroth (whom he calls Rextroth, Rexrotty, Rexrough, as well as Rexroth) as a pretentious, aging "all-American poet-revolutionary." Carol Tinker fares far worse as the "secretary"—she has no name—who wears "attacking spectacles" and speaks about political matters with the "enervating enthusiasm common to American business executives, folk singers and tourists."[29] On his part, Rexroth was not impressed with Australian diplomats. When the director of one of the Australians USIS offices revealed to Rexroth that he had never heard of him, Rexroth informed him that he was not qualified to hold his job.[30] Rexroth expected VIP treatment and was irritated when he did not get it.

From Australia, they flew to Hong Kong, Taipei, Tokyo, and Kyoto, where for a short while they stayed with Masa and Gary Snyder, who were living in Murasakino ("field of Murasaki flowers"), north of Daitoku-ji, the great Zen Buddhist complex. They slept in a tiny "3-mat" room. By Snyder's account,

Kenneth was too big for everything (as are any large foreigners). He was like Philip Whalen, when Phil first arrived, in that he had a literary knowledge of so much that anything he saw he had a story about it already. . . . His opinions, therefore, of restaurants, people, inns, objets d'art were wildly varied: sometimes right on, sometimes ludicrously bookish. Or Kennethish.[31]

With Snyder, Rexroth enjoyed excursions to the pre-Zen temples of the Nara area, but not to the Daitoku-ji monastery because, as Snyder has observed, Rexroth harbored a "relentless hostility" to the Zen branch of Buddhism, which he associated with reactionary Samurai politics.[32] (In

1958, Rexroth had told Jerome Rothenberg and David Antin that the Japanese thought that Zen was "Buddhism for white people.")[33] However, after the three had moved to a nearby *ryokan* (where they rented an apartment that included a small kitchen, a small study for Kenneth, and a living room furnished with futons on which Mary and Carol slept), they made several trips of their own to Daitoku-ji, ignoring Rexroth's reservations about Zen.[34]

With Professor Yuzuru Katagiri's assistance, a reading was arranged for Rexroth at Doshisha University in Kyoto, and two more were organized in Tokyo: one at a jazz place called the Pit-In, and another at a women's junior college. Katagiri served as translator at the Doshisha reading, which nearly ninety people attended (including Gary Snyder and Japan's mendicant poet-storyteller Nanao Sakaki, whom Rexroth had already met at a wild party at Snyder's house). No academics showed up. The audience was aware of Rexroth's connection to the Beats and was expecting a wild performance; instead, they heard a rather sedate man, dressed in a plaid shirt, bow tie, and German-styled green hunting jacket, read selections from his "Aix en Provence" series (from *Natural Numbers*); "Moonlight now on Malibu" (his poem to Susan Wiere), "Another Spring"; and "A Sword in a Cloud of Night," the poem where on Christmas Eve he walks hand-in-hand with Mary through the Fillmore District and urges her to believe in Orion, Christmas, and birthdays. At the end of this unexciting performance, Rexroth answered questions, mostly about the Beat writers. In Tokyo, the audience and the poet had a better time. Rexroth read the same poems but, with jazz accompaniment, "he really swinged," according to Professor Katagiri.[35] This was not to be his last tenure in Japan, the only country, he would say later on, that felt like home.

From Japan, they flew to Honolulu for a May 25 reading, entitled "An Evening with Kenneth Rexroth," and to visit the University of Hawaii campus. In December 1966, W. Todd Furniss, Dean of the College of Arts and Sciences, had invited Rexroth to be distinguished visiting writer, at his convenience, in one of the following years. Rexroth thought a stopover on the way home was in order because the position carried a salary of $25,000 (then the equivalent of about $75,000). But for the time being, he could not get a leave from the *Examiner* without jeopardizing his position. Moreover, Mary would not be able to get the dance training in Honolulu that she could in San Francisco.

Once back home on familiar turf, Rexroth was disinclined to leave the comfortable routines of Scott Street. But meeting the weekly deadline for the *Examiner* became a chore, if not a bore—the challenge of conducting a weekly forum on "the life of the community" had lost its glow. The job was using up "afflatus better channeled into more important work."[36] Furthermore, as lively as he kept his columns, management informed him that they were no longer boosting the sales of the *Examiner*. Rexroth might have sensed an ax falling somewhere down the road.

Twenty-Seven

ONE ERA ENDS,
A NEW ONE BEGINS
1967–1971

OR THE JULY 1967 ISSUE OF *Playboy* magazine, Rexroth had published an article which caused a local furor. Originally entitled "The Fuzz" (and later reprinted as "The Heat" in *The Alternative Society*, 1970, and *World Outside the Window* in 1987), it features a brief but incendiary interview Rexroth conducted with several members of the Berkeley police force, and an excerpt from a journal for police officers listing twenty different types who should be considered prime candidates for an interrogation (like those visibly "rattled" by the presence of a police officer). Rexroth wanted to validate his contention that the police were abusing their power, and imposing their system of ethics and morality on the city's population. Since returning from his round-the-world trip, he had observed that the police, with increased frequency, were stopping "suspicious looking" people (for example, interracial couples or adolescents wearing torn dungarees), asking for identification, and searching their cars for marijuana. Among his friends and associates, the general consensus was that the police were a corrupt lot, profiting off vice and poverty, wielding their power with unrestrained prejudice. Rexroth concurred: police were involved "in a symbiotic relationship within the illegal communities—narcotics peddlars, prostitutes, and gamblers—that function as subcultures in the society."[1] Rexroth suggested the situation might improve if policework became a profession requiring a "broadly humanistic" education, and offering a solid, middle-class salary.

In mid-October 1967, Rexroth went down to Santa Barbara to spend a long weekend with the Brothers of the Order of the Holy Cross at Mount Calvary, a monastery located in the mountains overlooking the Pacific Ocean. This Anglo-Catholic brotherhood also operated the Holy Cross Monastery in West Park, New York, where the youthful Rexroth had gone on retreat in 1925. He had recently completed his fourth long poem, *The Heart's Garden, The Garden's Heart,* and at Mount Calvary had written a poem dedicated to Gary Snyder entitled "A Song at the Wine-presses," in which he observes a water ouzel (a type of thrush) like one he had seen near Daitoku-ji, close to Gary and Masa's home, north of Kyoto. Both of the poems were published in *The Collected Longer Poems* in 1968.[2]

These works marked the dedicated shift toward Eastern philosophy and aesthetic form that characterized his later work—the original poems, not the translations. Rexroth had no need to reject Western religion, especially since the Western philosophy and theology to which he had always been attracted—Jakob Boehme's, for example, or Martin Buber's—was compatible with Eastern philosophy. In "A Song at the Wine-presses" he cites Richard Ste. Victoire, the medieval theologian chiefly remembered for his works on mysticism, whom Dante ranked with the greatest teachers of the Roman Catholic Church:

> "Contemplation is a power
> That coordinates the vast
> Variety of perception
> Into one all embracing
> Insight, fixed in wonder on
> Divine things—admiration,
> Awe, joy, gratitude—singular,
> Insuperable, but at rest."[3]

Although allusions to the landmarks and highlights of his life would continue to enliven his work, and his concern for social justice would remain steady, Rexroth was entering a new stage where he felt less inclined to mourn lost causes and was more interested in cultivating a vision that led to responsible results. Now Rexroth would rarely use European settings, as he had in *The Dragon and the Unicorn.* With the exception of a few very fine poems in the volume *New Poems* (1974), such as "The Family" and "Bei Wannsee," the East and its philosophy dominated his creative impulses.

Rexroth's long poems are a kind of cardiograph of his arduous journey from Christian conviction through agnostic doubt toward a highly individualistic interpretation of Buddhist equanimity. In *The Heart's Garden,* he says:

> What is the secret
> The reward of the right contemplation?
> The revelation that it is all
> Gravel and moss and rock and clipped
> Shrubbery. That it doesn't
> Symbolize anything at all.[4]

The search for enlightenment that informs *The Homestead Called Damascus, The Phoenix and the Tortoise,* and particularly *The Dragon and the Unicorn* seems wedded to the imperatives of Western metaphysics. In *The Heart's Garden,* the quest becomes vision that makes abstract discourse superfluous.

> The secret of the moss garden
> Is sprinkling it just enough
> Depending on the weather
> And sweeping it twice a day
> So lightly the leaves are removed
> And the moss is stimulated.[5]

If consciousness is centered on perfecting daily and mundane human experience (like sweeping the garden), the external world of nature and daily existence may be seen as reflection in inner experience or a human statement of that experience. Here is a landscape where life is acted out not as a mere worldly occurrence, divorced from the inner life, but as human experience in which the outward and the inward merge. It is more than a longing for order: in a sense, this is an ethical system, a Buddhist version of behaviorism, not far afield from an earlier statement Rexroth had made in one of his *San Francisco Examiner* columns about the nature of illumination:

The Catholic contemplative, the Sufi, the Buddhist monk follow counsels of perfection—illumination comes as the crown of a life of intense ethical activism, of honesty, loyalty, poverty, chastity, and above all charity, positive, outgoing love of all creatures. The good life creates the ambiance into which spiritual illumination flows like a sourceless, totally diffused light.[6]

On another level, however, these are the thoughts of a man who feels himself approaching the end of his years. Emotional and psychological crises are now muted. He has even resolved to tame his obsession with visionary experience: "the desire for vision is / The sin of gluttony," he writes.[7] His love of nature is as intense as ever, and he is "still wandering / Through the wooded hills . . . listening / Deep in his mind to music / Lost far off in space and time."[8] Rexroth's ability fully to articulate a Buddhist perspective coincided with his recognition that his physical powers were waning, that his social and political commentary had only a limited influence, and that in all likelihood, he was not going to achieve the kind of enduring ecstatic relationship with a woman that he had so long envisioned. In *The Heart's Garden,* he could still call up his first heartbreak: "She is inexhaustible / . . . It was a green jacket, a green / Jacket with a yellow lining."[9] And women in various forms—goddesses, prostitutes, dancing virgins—haunt the poem as though Rexroth could not forget his quest for romantic and erotic love. In these long poems, Rexroth was grappling with the question of how to apprehend reality, and had reached the point where he knew that it was vain either to grasp at any single aspect of it or to pursue it too aggressively.[10] While this is not an old man's poem, or a poem about an old man finding an old man's religion, it suggests that Rexroth at sixty-three knew that his psyche could no longer easily accommodate the struggles, challenges, and contradictions that had once fired him.

This new orientation brought him a fresh set of admirers, the young and creative college-age students of the sixties who opposed the Vietnam War. Alienated from the older generation, which they held responsible for the conflict, they sought a communal, often radical lifestyle that might nurture both body and spirit. For some of them, Rexroth already knew the secret. The young poet Antler met Rexroth at the Milwaukee home of Morgan Gibson, who had traveled with Rexroth on a reading tour of Wisconsin and Illinois in spring 1968. Alluding to Rexroth's meditative poem "Time Spirals," Antler describes him as a wise man, aging but "with the thought of salmon / shooting up the rapids of his brain."

> It was as if he were slowly falling asleep
> Sitting in that chair, while everyone at the party
>   asked him questions.
> Suddenly I wondered if someday I'd become a bard
> And if, as they asked me questions,
>   I'd tilt back my head and for a minute or so
>   pretend to doze, eyes peering under lids . . .[11]

Rexroth's sagelike appearance was enhanced now by gray-white hair that he had let grow long, "Halley's Comet hair," Antler called it, in honor of the poem Rexroth had written for Mary. First published in 1956 in *In Defense of the Earth*, "Halley's Comet" proudly but tenderly articulates his deepest hope that he has passed on to his daughter an understanding of the joy and sanctity inherent in the natural world.

> When in your middle years
> The great comet comes again
> Remember me, a child,
> Awake in the summer night,
> Standing in my crib and
> Watching that long-haired star
> So many years ago.
> Go out in the dark and see
> Its plume over water
> Dribbling on the liquid night,
> And think that life and glory
> Flickered on the rushing
> Bloodstream for me once, and for
> All who have gone before me,
> Vessels of the billion-year-long
> River that now flows in your veins.[12]

But as his observations in the *Playboy* article imply, the charm of San Francisco was beginning to pall for Rexroth. He was feeling rather cynical about the anti-war effort, and thought that the counterculture movement had collapsed, a pale shadow of the radical, Bohemian tradition that had once inspired people like himself. Violent crimes were on the rise, and racial tension was poisoning the atmosphere. A Black Panther storefront office had opened on Haight Street, a block away from Rexroth's apartment, an invitation to further violence from bigots. Moreover, he thought that the cultural life of San Francisco was deteriorating because City Hall was being run by the Italians, not the German Jews who had taken over the city more than fifty years earlier. These Italians "did not have the cultural values that would sustain art and music in the old way."[13] And while his "Classics Revisited" columns in *Harper's* remained popular, in the fall of 1968, he lost his job on the *Examiner,* and his courses were not renewed at either San Francisco State or the Art Institute. Rexroth claimed that after reading "The Heat," the chief of police wanted revenge: "The Boss Heat in San Francisco got me fired from three jobs at once, one of which I had held for almost ten years. Can I prove it? No. My informants refuse to testify."[14] On the other hand, his column had not significantly boosted the *Examiner's* circulation, and many younger poets in San Francisco were competing for teaching workshops.

Furthermore, many of his longtime colleagues—those who had been living in San Francisco for a while—were becoming gradually disenchanted with him. His Friday nights at home had lost much of their magic, in fact occasionally turned unpleasant or embarrassing when Rexroth's crude humor misfired. Others were no longer charmed by his stories and anecdotes, and wondered whether he did not take too much pleasure in the sound of his own voice. Even his friends were a little weary of his efforts to romanticize his life, what the sculptor Ronnie Bladen described as the "growing older" syndrome. Why couldn't he just accept the fact that with age he had developed a pot belly, people asked themselves, instead of blaming his infirmity on an encounter with a psychotic patient in San Francisco General so many years ago? Why did he lead people to believe that he—and not Ruth Witt-Diamant—had founded the San Francisco Poetry Center? Nor did his friends and associates appreciate the rumors and gossip that he liked to spread without regard to its often slanderous nature. For instance, Tom Parkinson had to live with Rexroth's story of how he had stolen Dylan Thomas's letters to Rexroth and how he had sold them to Serendipity Bookstore in order to finance a trip to England. Rexroth said that Serendipity had since sold the letters to the Bancroft Library. The letters never surfaced. Jack Shoemaker (who worked at Serendipity) finally confronted Rexroth about this incredible accusation, whereupon Rexroth apologized and withdrew it.[15] But the atmosphere had been sullied and the Rexroth mystique appeared to be very tired.

When Rexroth received an offer to teach at the University of California, Santa Barbara, for the 1968–69 academic year from Professor Edward Loomis, who had admired Rexroth's poetry from the days he himself lived in San Francisco during the late forties,[16] he accepted. For the first time Rexroth was going to have the kind of financial security that would make him independent of book royalties and freelance journalism. Uncertain of how long he would want to live in wealthy and conservative Santa Barbara, he sublet his Scott Street apartment.[17]

Katharine was still living in San Francisco, and Rexroth had come to terms with the likelihood that she would soon become an even smaller part of his life. This was complicated by a very delicate and serious matter: Katharine had come down with Hodgkin's disease in the fall of 1967 and was undergoing cobalt radiation treatment. Her condition had improved by March 1968, and that eased his guilt about leaving the city. He did not have to be concerned about missing Mary; she would be registering for classes as UCSB that fall.

Carol would be moving to Santa Barbara with Kenneth, although their relationship had developed kinks. Upon their return from Hawaii, there were signs that she was overwhelmed by her responsibilities as companion for Mary and secretary to Rexroth. For instance, she had failed to forward all of Edouard Roditi's mail to Brown University, where Roditi was teaching. She seemed unable to dissolve Mary's intermittent hostility toward her as an "intruder," which she had sensed from the outset of her life on Scott Street. To complicate an already trying situation, Carol's image of Rexroth as the independent spirit indifferent to money and materialism was beginning to change, especially when he complained that Katherine's illness was going to cost him a fortune (in actuality he did not have to spend a cent on it).[18] For Christmas 1967, Carol went back east to visit her ailing mother, and upon her return to San Francisco, moved out of Rexroth's apartment. Rexroth, who continued to support her, believed that she was on the verge of a nervous breakdown, and he was worried because she had spent all the money he had given her to live on. But somehow by summer 1968 she recovered enough so that she could be Rexroth's "live-in secretary" once again.

They arrived in Santa Barbara in time for the fall 1968 semester. Mary had made the trip separately with friends. By October, they had moved into a furnished house on Pimento Lane in Montecito, a posh suburb, and Kenneth went swimming in the ocean every day. Not long afterward they found the "Dower House" on East Pepper Lane, sitting on three acres of beautiful, heavily wooded property with a stream running through it and a small green cabin in front. Five rooms, nearly one hundred years old, the house had been the servants' quarters of a large estate; no one had lived there since 1925. Its closets were filled with beautiful linen and nineteenth-century watercolors. Surrounded by heavily scented geraniums, bougainvillea, flowering nasturtiums, oak, pine, walnut, eucalyptus and apricot trees, and a century-old pear tree, the house reminded Rexroth of an English cottage, especially the porch with its wrought-iron chairs.[19]

It was incredibly priced at $32,900, and Rexroth wisely bought it outright with cash. His financial situation had dramatically improved after he had negotiated a lucrative contract with Herder & Herder to publish five books, and, on Horace Schwartz's advice, had invested part of his advance in Pacific Gas and Electric stock.[20] He planted rose bushes wherever he could, and sycamore trees to hold the banks of the stream. He refused to cut down any trees, not even the eucalyptus that threatened to fall across the roof. He fixed the front patio so that on warm days he could take lunch outdoors. He covered the living-room floor, as he did all his others, with black and white linoleum, and shipped in his dark Victorian antique furniture, kitchen copper pots, water pipe, Edward Weston prints, and Juan Gris paintings from San Francisco. There he was, then, ensconced in one of the richest and most conservative communities in the United States. "Santa Barbara is Nixonville with a vengeance," he wrote Laughlin on January 31, 1969, "and the English Department [at the university] is completely dominated by avowed fascists." He was ready to conquer new vistas.

Rexroth's first impression of the Santa Barbara students was disappointing. "They're all stoned and they're all illiterate," he told Dick Collins.[21] But after an initial period of adjustment, his attitude mellowed and he became a great hit. He taught a three-hour class Monday night in a small auditorium. Formally listed in the catalogue as "Poetry and Song," it was also known as "Rexroth's NiteClub." He himself described it as "literary brainstorming." Students were required to make individual presentations of their "art"—recite their poems, play their flutes, perform skits or less structured kinds of "happenings"—and those presentations basically made up the content of the course. Rexroth would comment on each presentation and talk about some aspect of jazz, literature, or religion related to what the class had witnessed. Once, two women tried strapping miner's lights to their foreheads and circulating around the darkened auditorium as they poured a mild solution of hydrogen peroxide into everyone's left ear so they could learn, with the help of tape-recorded instructions, how to listen to ear wax dissolving.[22] During the class, Rexroth would sometimes repeat certain sayings that seemed to come from nowhere but had lodged themselves in his classroom repertoire. "It ain't no sin / To take off your skin / And jump around in your bones." "We made love on the American flag / and came all over the stars." Then there was the "haiku" by the wife of the Chinese ambassador: "Dinner at the American embassy / and all the plates were round."[23]

In the eyes of the students, Rexroth knew everything about everybody. He was a man of great erudition and sensitivity who could also tell a good joke. Whoever took this class received an A, although one semester he passed around his gradebook so that the students could enter their own grades (he may have been inspired by Michel Foucault, who once gave a horse registered in his philosophy class at the University of Paris the grade of A). Yet Rexroth was not being frivolous. He wanted the students to understand that, ultimately, they had to be their own judges. These grading practices did not endear him to the faculty, but Rexroth was indifferent to if not contemptuous of most of his colleagues, and often referred to them as "inmates of a fog factory." He remained polite to Edward Loomis, perhaps unaware that Loomis now regarded him as a self-inflated celebrity.[24] In the diary that he kept briefly during his first summer in Santa Barbara, Rexroth noted that the Santa Barbara professors thought that "Montessori is something with cheese and tomato sauce."[25]

Although "Poetry and Song" was all the university required of him, Rexroth also conducted a small seminar on Tuesday evenings, inviting selected participants to his home. The atmosphere was entirely different from the one on campus where, in a very real sense, anything went. Rexroth would sit in his favorite armchair silent until everyone had assembled. Early arrivals also remained silent, most of them awed by this famous poet whose walls were lined with books from floor to ceiling (although the major part of Rexroth's library was still in Scott Street) and whose living room seemed filled with artifacts. Once he got started, Rexroth talked non-stop on a variety of topics. Midway through the evening, Carol would serve tea from a cart ceremoniously rolled out of the kitchen. Rexroth was especially interested in preliterate poetry at this time, and had been in the process of putting together an anthology. He discussed African and American-Indian literature. He moved on to the literature of Japan and China and then changed gears entirely and discussed the international avant-garde, from Gunnar Eklund to Paul Celan to Lawrence Ferlinghetti. He also explored a growing interest in the Middle Eastern cultures (and wrote a piece for *Ararat* called "Who Are the Armenians?").[26] In many ways, these evenings were reminiscent of the literary soirées he once conducted at home in San Francisco, except that here he was surrounded by students who unequivocally found him inspiring. They gave him the kind of traditional respect and adulation that Rexroth had yearned for all his life. Another reward was also forthcoming. In May 1969, Rexroth was formally inducted into the National Institute of Arts and Letters, the congressionally chartered honor society for the arts. At sixty-four, he was the oldest inductee that year, among them Peter de Vries, Wallace Stegner, and painter John Heliker.

That spring the student community in nearby Isla Vista, protesting the Vietnam War, had burned down the Bank of America, but Rexroth's classes continued. During the riots he was able to conduct his class in "Poetry and Song" at St. Marks Church in Isla Vista, where many of the students lived. Often dressed like them, in denim overalls and leather sandals, a red bandana tied around his forehead to keep his long hair from falling into his eyes, he even managed to have the class performances broadcast over the local radio station. A few days after the bank was burned, Lawrence Ferlinghetti, Allen Ginsberg, and David Meltzer, in the role of lion-tamers, came down to Santa Barbara and with Rexroth read to an overflowing crowd at the Santa Barbara Unitarian Church. They were all in favor of anti-war demonstrations, but they feared that the chances for creating a new world order based on peace and love would be jeopardized by further acts of destruction and violence.

One year in Santa Barbara turned out to be enough for Mary, who had been as unimpressed by the UCSB faculty as Kenneth. She returned to San Francisco to study textiles at the California College of Arts and Crafts. Although they would never again live in the same city, Rexroth took her flight more or less in stride, later reporting the news to Laughlin in a letter written to thank him for two books of his poetry and to encourage him to write more.[27] He mentioned that Mary had gotten a job as a counselor at a place called the Modern Sex Institute, "a halfway house for people with mental illness," giving dance therapy and conducting a "sort of yogic dance class." She was studying printmaking and also writing poetry, which Rexroth urged Laughlin to publish in the next *New Directions Annual*. "She's lots better than Leonore Kandel," he wrote with fatherly pride. Rexroth thought Kandel's *They Are Killing* was a contemporary feminist classic.[28] Mary did not cut herself off from her father—there were visits and friendly correspondence, but she had declared her independence.

If the boundaries of Kenneth and Carol's relationship appeared murky, the arrangement itself was intact, even though Carol had lost her assignment as Mary's "companion." They both felt that Santa Barbara had become their home, and Rexroth shipped his library down from San Francisco. To house the massive collection, he had a barnlike building constructed, complete with a moon-viewing platform in back. Carol had arranged to have the books carefully packed according to categories, and when they arrived, in crates marked "Edible Beef Bones," Rexroth asked the members of the UCSB football team to unpack them. The players complied, disrupting any order in which they had been assembled. Carol was exasperated. The responsibilities of a live-in secretary—for which she received a salary—were many and diverse, but Kenneth did not always take care to provide amenable working conditions. For example, he had begun to tape the sequel to his autobiographical novel, and Carol was transcribing it. However, she had only a manual typewriter, and when she requested an electric machine, Rexroth accused her of being "just like Marthe."[29] (Eventually, he bought one.) Carol had less trouble when it came to a dishwasher. Rexroth had always taken good care of his hands, and regarded well-manicured nails as the sign of a gentleman, as he had told Mary when he lectured her about a prospective husband. He hated washing dishes. Whenever Carol was sick, Kenneth would demonstrate his domesticity by announcing that he had done the dishes.[30] As Carol began to share the cooking, she felt that a dishwasher was a necessity. Rexroth agreed.

In the fall of 1969, Barbara Szerlip, a student from the previous semester, had returned from a summer visit back east with her family to
Santa Barbara without a place to live. She was spending her nights in a
sleeping bag in a field on college property. When Rexroth discovered this,
he invited his former student to live at East Pepper Lane until she could
arrange something else. He informed Barbara that several people camping near the spot where she was sleeping had been molested—to frighten
her even more he added that fingers had been chopped off—and persuaded her to move into a tent behind the house. She ended up staying
for most of the academic year, and blended into the Dower House routine. Rexroth asked for neither rent, board, nor sex, although they enjoyed overt displays of affection. Her one major responsibility was to pick
up at the post office all the review copies sent to Rexroth.

On most evenings Rexroth, Carol Tinker, and Barbara Szerlip would
have dinner together. (Rexroth did the marketing, and the butcher at the
local Safeway market always called him when fresh buffalo steaks arrived.) The same elegant rules Rexroth observed at dinner on Scott Street
were enforced at East Pepper Lane. Always, there were candles, cloth
napkins, wine; everyone was expected to dress properly. Yet there was
room for mischief. One evening in the presence of a dinner guest, Rexroth
decided it was necessary to dispel any impression that the atmosphere was
ultra-refined.[31] He served one his favorite desserts that evening, persimmons kept in the freezer for an hour until they became slightly crispy.
The visitor, who was a nervous type, had never eaten a persimmon before
and did not know how to approach it. Rexroth, who had been waiting for
the right moment to make his play, picked up the persimmon, bit off the
pointed end, threw his head up, rolled back his eyes, and announced that
the persimmon tasted "just like Japanese pussy"—echoing a line (about
figs) of Rupert Birkin's in D. H. Lawrence's *Women in Love*. The dinner
guest excused himself from the table and retreated to the bathroom,
unable to enjoy the fruit as so many of Rexroth's guests had.[32]

Essentially, life was quiet on East Pepper Lane. Gary Snyder and his
family visited, and so did Diane and Jerome Rothenberg, whom Rexroth
regarded as a learned, highly skilled poet with a "profound understanding of the poetry of pre-literate people and of non-Western European life
attitudes."[33] David and Tina Meltzer also came, and in 1973 Rexroth
would choose the poems for *Tens*, David Meltzer's first collection of selected poetry. Jessica Hagedorn would show up, usually without warning.
Rexroth's hospitality was not diminished by accumulating health problems. His back was troubling him, a consequence of the injuries he sus-
tained many years before in San Francisco County when he was thrown
against the wall by a patient. During his round-the-world trip, he had
fallen down in Stockholm and hurt himself. And on a steep flight of stairs
in Japan, he had slipped and hit his heel, creating a bone chip that eventually calcified and became a chronic source of discomfort and pain.

Geared to his health, Rexroth's recreation was unstrenuous gardening and swimming, frequently at the end of the day when "the tide was full and there was a deep slow swell in the sea."[34] He had figured out that the best way to get through the dense kelp beds was to keep his body high and out of the tangle by swimming on his back, which gave him a vantage point from which to appreciate the scene around him: the schools of anchovies, the "paleontological looking pelicans," a three-masted vessel in the distance. He also indulged his preference for sleeping outdoors, even though he would often awake in the morning soaked with dew. For him, Santa Barbara's climate was ideal.

Over the next few years Rexroth enjoyed his leisurely life. He was an anti-establishment writer-in-residence living in a beautiful but unpretentious house, writing, painting, and extending hospitality to those whom he cared to see. He would often invite guests to stay in the little cabin that sat on the property right near the gate by East Pepper Lane. They were fortunate to have a nearby place to sleep: after he and Carol had served a magnificent Korean hotpot, Kenneth would talk, sometimes mumbling asides to himself, far into the night on all his favorite subjects, often outlasting the most durable guest. He was still in demand as a reader, largely at West Coast schools, including Fresno City State College and the newly established California Institute of the Arts in Valencia. At this time, he was especially interested in reciting his translations from the Chinese to music, and collaborated with composer and poet Lou Harrison to produce performances at the Twenty-Fifth Annual Ojai Festival (May 28–30, 1971) and at the Mark Taper Forum in Los Angeles (July 26, 1971).

With a group of young Los Angeles friends, Dana Gioia attended the performance at the Mark Taper Forum, entitled *The Jade Flower Palace*. The turnout was small, and Gioia had a front row seat.

The event . . . consisted mostly of traditional Chinese music performed by Harrison's ensemble, but between every piece Rexroth who had a magisterial stage presence would read one of his translations from the Chinese. It was a wonderful evening, and afterwards my friends and I went up to speak to him since he waited up front after the music finished. . . . We didn't talk all that long, but he was warm and encouraging. I realize now that he was also delighted to see that we had read at least some of his books.[35]

For five years Gioia had been a Rexroth fan, Rexroth's *One Hundred Poems from the Chinese* one of his favorite volumes of poetry. When Gioia discussed Tu Fu with other poets in LA or the Bay Area, "everyone based all of their opinions on Rexroth's translations and notes." Because he also admired Rexroth's "non-pedantic and engaging" criticism, every week he saved the "Classics Revisited" columns from *The Saturday Review*.

In fact, Rexroth's prose was being published at a fast clip. Herder & Herder had come out with a collection of Rexroth's essays, *With Eye and Ear* (1970), and his breezy, informal literary history of modern American poetry, *American Poetry in the Twentieth Century* (1971), which had originally been slated as an introduction for an anthology of modern American poetry. Noting that *With Eye and Ear* "reinstated book reviews as a serious form of criticism," Karl Shapiro qualified his praise of the book by portraying Rexroth's views as an "amazing mixture of judiciousness and cant."[36] Shapiro to the contrary, Rexroth's essay on Thomas Vaughan and "spiritual alchemy" is an ideal introduction to that seventeenth-century mystic's thought. However, Rexroth was still slinging insults. Leslie Fiedler, whom Rexroth once referred to as a "cow college professor," was now, by Rexroth's account, guilty of using the term "WASP" as his "favorite term of abuse." *American Poetry in the Twentieth Century* did not fare well. Robert Kirsch found the style too informal, and the writing bland.[37] But Rexroth's high praise for the work of Gary Snyder, Philip Whalen, and David Meltzer in that volume helped to compensate for the critical neglect these poets suffered at the time (Snyder did not receive the Pulitzer until 1975). Rexroth had not dropped out of the public eye, even though he had abandoned San Francisco.[38]

During these last few years, Rexroth had been seeing Mary and Katharine infrequently. Their relationship consisted largely of occasional newsy letters that sometimes contained requests for sums of money Rexroth had already agreed to give them, but had a difficult time parting with. (He did help pay for the two girls' trip to Europe in the late spring of 1972.) But Katharine went east for her college education—to Middlebury—and Mary was leading a busy life in San Francisco, establishing closer ties to her mother, who had a third daughter now and had recently married again for the third time. Beautiful, tall, and graceful, Mary had started to earn money belly-dancing in the Greek nightclubs on Columbus Avenue. She had also appeared in X-rated films, and had posed for a *Playboy* article entitled "The Porno Girls" (October 1971). The article discussed pornographic movie stars who frequently had conservative backgrounds. They were the "girl next door," or college student putting herself through school. In her letters, Mary spoke as freely about these activities as she did about the various art and music classes she was taking, or the newest apartment she had moved to. She made fun of the people who asked her if there was any correlation between these films and the rise in venereal disease.[39] The relationship between father and daughter was about as sophisticated as it could get. In his personal files, Rexroth kept a copy of "The Porno Girls."

Problems arose over Rexroth's tenure at UCSB in the spring of 1973. He was informed that the English Department would no longer allocate the $9,000 that his appointment carried because he was beyond the age of retirement. The university was also having trouble balancing its budget. Various people tried to reverse this decision. Rexroth did not need the money as much as he needed the love and respect of his students. As an Honorary Fellow of the University of California at Santa Cruz, Laughlin wrote to Frank Gardiner, Chair of the English Department, to vouch for Rexroth's stature and credentials. In May, a poetry reading was held in Campbell Hall in honor of Rexroth, and to protest the action taken by the university. Among the poets who participated were Allen Ginsberg, Lawrence Ferlinghetti, and Gary Snyder. Snyder talked about the first time he read Rexroth's poems, how impressed he was by Rexroth's ability to evoke life in the Sierras. He also spoke of how Rexroth's political awareness and understanding of Asian culture had influenced his own work. Ferlinghetti reminisced about the days when he first met Rexroth, before there was such a thing as the "San Francisco Literary Renaissance." Accompanied by flautists and a guitar player, Rexroth read some original poems and translations from the Chinese, for which he received a standing ovation. The three-hour reading, which drew a huge crowd—people had to sit on stage and in the aisles—was covered as an important event by the *San Francisco Examiner* (March 11, 1973).

Carol, with troubles of her own, could provide little comfort during this period. She was back east visiting her mother, who was on her deathbed. However, steady support came from Lagunitas, where Marie kept beaming optimistic reports that his battle with UCSB had been covered fully by the San Francisco papers. Rexroth's tenure was extended for one more year only.

Twenty-Eight

BORDER CROSSINGS
1972–1974

BUT REXROTH did not languish for long. He had not put his eggs into one basket. Seabury Press published two of his volumes. One was *The Elastic Retort: Essays in Literature and Ideas* (1973), which contained studies of Japanese poetry, fiction, drama, and Anglo-Catholicism and additional "Classics Revisited," including Aristotle's *Poetics, Uncle Tom's Cabin,* Ford Madox Ford's *Parade's End,* and Swift's *Gulliver's Travels,* where Rexroth observes iconoclastically that Swift's satire is a more innocent piece of writing than *Winnie the Pooh.*

The other book was *The Orchid Boat: Women Poets of China.*[1] Rexroth translated these poems with the help of Ling Chung, whom he had met in 1970 while she was a graduate student writing her doctoral dissertation on "Kenneth Rexroth and Chinese Poetry: Translation, Imitation and Adaptation" at the University of Wisconsin, Madison. She had flown out to Santa Barbara to interview him, and from the outset the two got along famously. By the third day of her visit they were in the barnlike library Rexroth had built behind the house, translating quatrains from the Sung Dynasty (which would be published in *New Poems* in 1974).[2] After Ling Chung returned to Madison, she and Rexroth corresponded for more than a year. She came back to Santa Barbara in 1972 to go over the final draft with him. Sometimes they disagreed about the way a certain poem had turned out. As a native speaker, Ling Chung had far more authority about exact meanings of words, but to her continuous amazement Rexroth was always ready "to grasp the pathos of the Chinese poet."[3] In his review, published in the November 1973 issue of the *Journal of Asian Studies,* Stephen Owen praised *The Orchid Boat* for the variety of poets represented. However, he noted that when the translating became difficult, their imaginations often supplied a solution "remarkable for its ingenuity and incorrectness."[4] Owen, like most reviewers, approved of the book, adding that "the liberties which the translators take with their texts are not in themselves objectionable: more often than not they create beautiful versions."

Why did Rexroth turn to translating women poets exclusively?[5] Only one poem by a woman appears in *Three Hundred Poems of the T'ang Dynasty*, edited by Witter Bynner, who in the twenties had introduced Rexroth to the poems of Tu Fu. It could be argued that Rexroth wanted to ride the wave of the new feminist consciousness which had surfaced in the sixties; but it is more likely that he was trying to understand why his three marriages had been such disasters, and why his relationship with his daughters was growing distant. Perhaps if he could enter the psyche of women poets, he would learn more about women than he had while living with them. Written by courtesans, Tao women priests, and contemporary Chinese women, the highly imagistic poems that appear in *The Orchid Boat* are about heartbreak and sexual longing, the excitement of a secret tryst, and by contrast, the contentment found in a lasting relationship. Occasionally they can be witty and sexually explicit, as in a poem by Huang O (1498–1519), who was happily married to the poet and dramatist Yang Shen.

> If you don't know how, why pretend?
> Maybe you can fool some girls,
> But you can't fool Heaven.
> I dreamed you'd play with the
> Locust blossom under my green jacket,
> Like a eunuch with a courtesan.
> But lo and behold
> All you can do is mumble.
> You've made me all wet and slippery,
> But no matter how hard you try
> Nothing happens. So stop.
> Go and make somebody else
> Unsatisfied.[6]

More often they express a yearning for the unity created by sexual passion—a recurrent theme in his own poetry—as in "Married Love" by the thirteenth-century poet, calligrapher, and painter Kuan Tao-sheng.

> You and I
> Have so much love,
> That it
> Burns like a fire,
> In which we bake a lump of clay
> Molded into a figure of you
> And a figure of me.
> Then we take both of them,
> And break them into pieces,
> And mix the pieces with water,
> And mold again a figure of you,

> And a figure of me.
> I am in your clay.
> You are in my clay.
> In life we share a single quilt,
> In death we will share one coffin.[7]

His interest in women poets of China and Japan would grow even stronger over the next few years.

Rexroth said his poems were about the ordinary things in his life—"the stuff I see, the girls I'm sleeping with, or something else like that."[8] He liked to sound casual: "The girl I fuck in this poem must now be about forty-five. I look her up sometimes."[9] However, it would be more accurate to say that the poems were a highly idealized and romanticized version of his daily life. All along, Rexroth's love poetry, which is infused with the enlightenment born out of sensuality and passion, had been inspired by Leslie Smith, Andrée Schafer, Marie Kass, Marthe Larsen, or a number of women with whom he had fallen in love or become infatuated. They do reflect the longing, disappointment, and conflict that tempered these relationships. But they do not reveal how responsible he was for their failure. That he chose during the last ten years of his life to devote the major part of his creative energy to translating the work of women poets from China and Japan reveals a transformation of both heart and mind. His sympathetic treatment of these works indicates that he had developed an exquisite sensibility about the struggles of individuals seeking love and fulfillment in an environment that essentially restricted them to passive roles. His identification with these poets suggests that, despite outward appearances, he too felt trapped.

However, unlike these women poets, Rexroth had the opportunity to break the bonds that oppressed him—a distinction that seems to have no function in his allegiance to these poets, unless that allegiance is another example of Rexroth romanticizing his life. Longing for her absent lover, the early-twelfth-century poet Chu Shu-chen recalls happier days spent with him "under the pear blossoms":

> Last night I was fulfilled in a dream.
> Speechless, we made love
> In mist and clouds.
> Alas, when I awoke
> The old agony returned.[10]

Helpless, Chu Shu-chen had no recourse but to reconcile herself to her fate. On the other hand, Rexroth could have changed the course of his life. But his obsession with the image he presented to the world—a wise libertine, a man of the world—doomed him to a life where he would feel betrayed by love, and disappointed by his family and friends. Unlike these women poets, Rexroth had built his own prison.

Rexroth continued to appear at various conferences—nasty and angry one moment, tenderly reading a poem the next. In 1972 he appeared in San Francisco to participate in a protest demonstration against U.S. intervention in Chile, sponsored by Glide Church. He returned to Japan for ten days in November 1972 to attend the PEN Japanologists Conference in Tokyo. He was amused to learn that he was considered a leading Japanologist even though he did not speak the language.[11] He delivered a rambling lecture entitled "The Influence of Classical Japanese Poetry on Modern American Poetry."[12] His main premise was that "classic Japanese culture provided those nutriments for which the West was starved." He cited contemporary American poets who were influenced by the classical forms of Japanese poetry: Robert Creeley, Gary Snyder, Philip Whalen, Cid Corman. And he praised Snyder and Whalen again for identifying with the spirit of Buddhism and for "talking about an ecological esthetic, a blending of American Indian and Far Eastern philosophies of cooperation with, rather than conquest of nature."[13] He came home from Japan determined to return for a longer time. He wanted to thrive again in that atmosphere himself. He thought first of applying for a teaching position at Doshisha's Women's College in Kyoto, but then decided to apply instead for a Fulbright fellowship.

Rexroth was invited by Robert Lewis to participate in the Fifth Annual Writer's Conference in Grand Forks, North Dakota, in March 1974. Some old friends were there, like Lawrence Ferlinghetti, Michael McClure, and Allen Ginsberg. On the evening of March 21, Rexroth read to a packed auditorium, but was disturbed initially by the antics of a manic Gregory Corso.[14] Every time Rexroth paused, Corso shouted out words of encouragement and praise, and kept calling Rexroth "Poppa." For more than fifteen years, Rexroth had labored to dissociate himself from his role as "father figure" to the Beats, and here was Corso demonstrating a disturbing and unexpected brand of filial respect. (Corso has made it a habit through the years to sing the praise of poets from his seat in the audience.) After Rexroth threatened to come down from the stage and silence him by force, Corso left. Rexroth and Corso would confront one another again at the conference, most notably on the last day, when they interrupted and yelled at each other during an "open mike" panel discussion, with each threatening to walk out. They resumed their seats only after Allen Ginsberg's diplomatic entreaties.[15]

The evening after his reading, Don Eades threw a party at his home. Students gathered around Rexroth, who had planted himself in a living-room chair and held forth as though he were conducting one of his seminars at East Pepper Lane, and listened open-mouthed. The next day during an extended interview with Lewis and his colleague James J. McKenzie, Rexroth spoke on a variety of topics with the understanding that he was saying "what comes into [his] head," which was not necessarily the truth.[16] But he spoke honestly enough on social issues, and turned the question about the relationship between African-American writers and the writers of the Beat Generation into a full-fledged discussion of how the media had only recently acknowledged the existence of talented African Americans. He remarked ironically that as bad a deal as Native Americans had gotten, at least their image had appeared on American currency.

Rexroth had established a good rapport with two of the finest African-American writers on the American literary scene—Amiri Baraka (Leroi Jones) and Ed Bullins—and during his reading at North Dakota, he had made specific reference to Baraka's transitory connection to the Beat and Black Mountain writers, while he was still Leroi Jones and was co-editor of *Yugen.* Rexroth and Baraka had maintained a distant but friendly respect for one another ever since Allen Ginsberg had introduced them in New York City in the early sixties. Soon after that, in August 1964, Baraka, whose *Dutchman* had won the Obie Award as Best American Play, went out to the West Coast to attend a Writer's Conference on "The Negro in American Literature" at Asilomar, a meeting site overlooking Monterey Bay. Sponsored by the Special Programs division of the University of California, and by Herbert Hill, Labor Secretary of the NAACP, the conference drew an audience of more than two hundred. Other speakers included the novelist Harvey Swados, the distinguished teacher and critic Saunders Redding, Gwendolyn Brooks, Arna Bontemps, journalist Nat Hentoff, Professor Robert Bone, author of the groundbreaking study *The Negro Novel in America,* and actor Ossie Davis. Attending as correspondent for *The Nation,* Rexroth reduced the conference's impact to a demonstration of a "characteristic social mechanism—the institutionalization of dissent and revolt. . . . Today, Malcolm X is invited to address executive seminars at Shangri-las nestled in the snow-clad Rockies."[17] But he loved the joint poetry reading by Brooks and Baraka.

After the conference, Baraka drove up to San Francisco and spent an evening at 250 Scott Street. Before meeting Rexroth, Baraka had read his translations from the Chinese and Japanese and had liked them enormously. After he learned where Rexroth stood politically, Baraka liked him even more for his "clarity about time and history."[18] Baraka remembered Rexroth as warm and irascible, and looked him up again in 1966 when he was back in San Francisco as a visiting professor at San Francisco State, working with playwright Ed Bullins, who had won an Obie for *The Fabulous Miss Marie,* and getting involved in various films and stage productions.[19]

Rexroth had also established a cordial relationship with Bullins in the mid-sixties. Bullins was working with San Francisco State College to get support and funding for his Black Arts / West Theater on Fillmore Street, and would keep Rexroth informed of all the activities he had planned, such as summer workshops in creative writing, black makeup, stage design, directing, and seminars on street plays, theater of cruelty, theater of reality, and so on. He kept in touch with Rexroth when he joined the New

Lafayette Theater in New York City. Rexroth wrote a letter of recommendation for Bullins when he applied for a $5,000 grant from the Rockefeller Foundation, and was delighted when he received the award in 1967, the same year that he won the Drama Desk-Vernon Rice Prize for "Outstanding Achievement of the Off Broadway Theater, 1967–1968 Season."

Three months after the North Dakota conference, Rexroth was conducting poetry workshops during the 1974 Santa Barbara Writer's Conference (June 21–28) at the Cate School, twelve miles south of Santa Barbara, in Carpinteria overlooking the Channel Islands. Among the well-known writers who participated were Joan Didion, John Gregory Dunne, Christopher Isherwood, Ray Bradbury, Alex Haley, Ross MacDonald, and Budd Schulberg. On the heels of the conference came word that Rexroth would be off the American lecture circuit for a while. He had been awarded a Senior Research Fulbright Fellowship to Japan for 1974–75, and would be leaving in September. Though expected to be available for lecture engagements and occasional classes in English and American literature, his chief responsibility was to write poetry. The timing was perfect since Rexroth's connection to UCSB was now formally at an end, and negotiations for a Distinguished Professorship at The City College in New York had fallen through, largely because Rexroth's name was barely known in New York academic circles.

However, one matter in particular had to be settled, and that was his ten-year-old relationship with Carol Tinker. To avoid passport and visa problems, Rexroth thought that they should be legally married. Unlike his first three marriages, his relationship with Carol did not appear to be passionate. Carol and Kenneth slept in separate bedrooms on Scott Street and East Pepper Lane, and from the start Kenneth had made no secret of his liaisons and encounters with other women. Thirty-five years his junior, Carol had sought him out as an admirer of his poetry, anxious to be of service. Clearly Rexroth depended on her for her intelligent companionship and secretarial skills. He solicited her linguistic acumen for his translations and her artistic talent for the brushwork that accompanied the poems in *The Silver Swan* which Rexroth would write in Kyoto during 1974–75. He also encouraged Carol to pursue her own poetry, and wrote the Introduction to *Four Young Women Poets* (1972), which included poetry by Carol Tinker, Jessica Hagedorn, Alice Karle, and Barbara Szerlip.[20] Eight years later Rexroth would write the Introduction to *The Pillow Book of Carol Tinker*.

Carol gave the impression of being cool and collected, but behind that composure was a fragile person vulnerable to emotional stress, and Kenneth worried about her. She was the first woman he had ever lived with who depended on him for financial support (she still received a salary from him as his secretary). He was aware that she had tried to establish a bona fide place in the Rexroth household, devoting herself with uneven success to winning over Mary and Katharine, who had from the outset resented her intimate presence. During their years together, he dedicated several of his books to her—not always exclusively. And the spare, resonant poems in the beautifully produced *Sky Sea Birds Trees Earth House Beasts Flowers* "are love poems for Carol."[21] Clearly, Carol and Kenneth loved one another, but it was not a conventional union. There were times when Carol wished Kenneth were an ordinary, and, perhaps, more urgent lover. In her poem "Gold Wires," she writes:

> What am I to tell you, alone in the dark
> I am quivering in empty space
> You are telling me that you are only sadly alone
> You who spin and wind and twist the wires
> Charged with message.[22]

Shortly before he and Carol were married, Marie came to Santa Barbara for a visit, and Kenneth proposed marriage to her in a last-ditch effort to secure for himself a strong female anchor. Although she had remained a devoted friend, Marie was leading a full life quite independent of Rexroth. She had retired in 1968 as a teacher and nursing supervisor at the San Francisco Department of Health, and worked on Marin County's commission on the aging (she served as chairperson). She played her viola and sang. She never gave up her active role as godmother to Mary and Katharine, nor had she lost interest in the twists and turns of Kenneth's professional career and personal life. But she had no desire to move down to Santa Barbara, accompany Kenneth to Japan, or resume conjugal life as Kenneth defined it.

With Rexroth's longtime friend Dick Collins serving as best man, Kenneth and Carol were married in Mount Calvary Church in August 1974. Carol's family attended, but neither Mary nor Katharine appeared. More than one observer noted that the ceremony and the reception at East Pepper Lane reflected a personal fulfillment for Carol, and a renewed sense of life for Kenneth. Kenneth actually carried Carol across the threshold when they got home. She was a proper bride in her Victorian lawn dress and hat.[23] For the reception, the garden was manicured, the house was decorated with festive Japanese kites, and good food and drink abounded. But the reception stretched far into the evening, and finally Carol decided to retire. Unable to find Kenneth among their wedding guests, she walked over to the library, thinking he might need some respite from the festivities. She found him at the library all right, but he was on the floor locked in the arms of a young woman. Far from naive about Kenneth's sexual activities, Carol has assumed that in honor of this rare occasion, he would behave himself. The sight of her husband *in flagrante delecto* made her hysterical, and she had to swallow a strong sedative prescribed by her doctor in order to sleep.[24]

As always, Carol forgave Kenneth, and two weeks later they were together in Japan. Just outside Tokyo, they stayed briefly at the home of John Solt, translator of Japanese poetry, editor, and former student of Kenneth's in Santa Barbara. Then moved on to Kyoto and their home base in Japan, a seven-hundred-year-old farmhouse in an embayment of Higashiyama, the Eastern Hills. The farmhouse was on a street that led up to the Yamashina Pass, near the forest of Sennuji, the complex of Shingon Temples where the ashes of the emperors of Japan are stored. Before long Carol and Kenneth were taking long walks through the forest and wildlife preserves that became the setting for the series of eight contemplative poems entitled *On Flower Wreathe Hill* (1976).[25] In these poems, Rexroth once again explores the meaning of his life. He is keenly aware, here, that he has lived far more many years than he has left, and yet he feels the enduring power of his meditation.

> There are more leaves on
> The ground than grew on the trees.
> I can no longer see the
> Path; I find my way without
> Stumbling; my heavy heart has
> Gone this way before. Until
> Life goes out memory will
> Not vanish, but grow stronger
> Night by night
> Aching nostalgia—
> In the darkness every moment
> Grows longer and longer, and
> I feel as timeless as the
> Two thousand year old cypress.[26]

The title is a Chinese and Japanese euphemism for cemetery, and it is also an allusion to one of the most profound and sacred sutras of Mahayana Buddhism. As Rexroth acknowledges in his notes to this slim volume, for these poems he borrowed freely from many Japanese poets, sometimes directly incorporating complete lines, which may appear to be plagiarism but is in fact an old Japanese device known as *honkadori*.[27] He truly wanted to embrace this culture.

Rexroth took it upon himself to appoint as his guardian, so to speak, Professor Sanehide Kodama, with whom he had been corresponding about living arrangements in Kyoto. Kodama soon became a good friend, visiting the Rexroths almost every week. He and his wife Kayoko were the first people to extend hospitality to the couple, and Kodama and Yasuyo Morita, who worked as secretary for Rexroth, helped him with the translations that appeared in *One Hundred More Poems from the Japanese* and *Women Poets of Japan* (1977). Rexroth dedicated the poems in *On Flower Wreathe Hill* to Morita, who did the calligraphies on the cover and title page and with whom he had become intimate. (Rexroth did the calligraphies in the text.) The Kodamas lent the Rexroths their extra television set, and to Kodama's amazement, Rexroth seemed to understand and enjoy the music and drama that were broadcast, and even the news programs.

In Kyoto, Kenneth and Carol were not without a circle of friends for long. Rexroth became friendly with Yuzuro Katagiri, who had been instrumental in arranging poetry readings on his last extended trip through Japan. Rexroth came to Katagiri's class at Kyoto Seika College to lecture about American poetry. And when Rexroth read at the Hon'yara-do Coffee Shop in Kyoto in January 1975, where nearly a hundred people packed into a space that normally accommodated half that number, Katagiri served as his translator. (Few academics showed up for this reading, just as they had not shown up for Rexroth's reading at Doshisha University in 1967.) Both professional and personal, these associations were important to Rexroth. When they returned to Santa Barbara, Kenneth and Carol would be visited by these dear friends. Yasuyo Morita stayed for two months in the fall of 1976, and was encouraged to feel that she could stay far longer if she chose. Professor Katagiri also visited Santa Barbara for a few days in September 1975, and Rexroth was able to return a small part of the hospitality Katagiri had shown him. Katagiri was invited to read some of his own poetry at one of the readings he attended in Santa Barbara.

In Kyoto, besides his former UCSB student John Solt, who was doing graduate work in Kyoto, Rexroth saw other westerners like Tim Reynolds, a promising young poet and translator of classics whom Rexroth had once rescued from a motorcyle accident on the Golden Gate Bridge; the poet Edith Shiffert (Rexroth would write the Introduction to her *New and Selected Poems*); and Monica Bethe, the daughter of nuclear physicist Hans Bethe and an expert on Noh. She was Rexroth's next-door neighbor, living in the house to which the farmhouse belonged.[28] Upon first arriving at the farmhouse, Rexroth had become distraught when he discovered that it had neither a desk nor a desk chair. Bethe was able to provide him with both, and from that time on, Rexroth introduced her as "the woman who made me a writer." Bethe enjoyed evenings with Carol and Kenneth, listening to him talk long into the night.

In 1974, Rexroth was a portly, grey haired man with a noble face and long delicate fingers. Living Japanese style did not quite suit his physique, but with great equanimity, he would sprawl out on the tatami, leaning back on one elbow which propped him up, and allowing his long, somewhat frail legs to extend out to the front. This left one hand free to gesture elegantly and punctuate his endless stories.[29]

This was also the year that Rexroth became closer to Morgan Gibson, whom he had met the summer of 1964 when he was poet-in-residence at the University of Wisconsin in Milwaukee. Two years earlier, Gibson had written *Kenneth Rexroth,* the first full-length study of Rexroth's work, and he had recently been appointed to teach at Osaka University.[30] As soon as he arrived in Kyoto, he visited Kenneth and Carol:

I found him sitting like a Buddha on *tatami* before an electric fan, framed by open sliding doors, eyes closed, naked but for shorts, sweating all over, perfectly still. I stood intoxicated by the heat of the overgrown garden, awed by his presence in the ancient house and the hypnotic music of cicadas, in a swarm of enormous dragonflies and mosquitos that I dared not swat for fear of disturbing him from sleep, a poem—or *satori?*[31]

When Rexroth finally opened his eyes, he showed Gibson around the house, simultaneously lecturing him on the various aspects of life in Japan, warning Gibson, for example, that he would "learn nothing from most Japanese monks about Buddhism, for monks were popularly regarded as funeral directors." Gibson believes that he learned more about Asian traditions and modern poetry from Rexroth than anyone else he had met in Japan. He was also able to read his own poetry with Rexroth at several scheduled readings.

Carol and Kenneth would also see the poet Kazuko Shiraishi, who was living in Tokyo. Shiraishi had been in the United States a year before and created quite a sensation when she read her highly charged and surreal poetry in English and Japanese to Rexroth's students in Santa Barbara. Rexroth helped her to publish a collection of her poems, *Seasons of Sacred Lust,* with New Directions in 1978. Her principal translator was her friend, the poet Ikuko Atsumi, who became Rexroth's co-translator for *Women Poets of Japan* (1977), a collection of seventy-seven poets from the Classic period to the contemporary. (She was assisted by John Solt; Rexroth, Yasuyo Morita, and Carol Tinker also helped during the stages of revision.)

The year in Japan was a fulfilling one. Once again, Rexroth had captured the imagination, love, and respect of a literary and artistic community. And Carol was able to assume a place where her own creative efforts took on power and significance. She was not burdened here with the history of Rexroth's life in San Francisco and Santa Barbara, and she was writing poetry and had begun a novel. In May, for example, both she and Rexroth participated in a bilingual Poetry Exchange with various Japanese and American poets. Rexroth gave lectures and readings on numerous occasions, in academic settings as well as in clubs and private residences, including one with Cid Corman at his place. Poet and editor of *Origin,* Corman had been living on and off in Europe and Japan since 1954, had written more than forty books, and had translated Basho, Kusano Shimpei, and Francis Ponge. Corman and Rexroth were in touch with one another, but they were not close. Corman had been back to San Francisco in the mid-fifties when Rexroth was desperate over Marthe's affair with Creeley, and he would not allow Rexroth to persuade him in a long conversation over the telephone that Creeley "had stolen" his wife. Nor, as Corman put it, had he ever been willing, as other younger writers had, to "play disciple to him."[32] Corman had returned to San Francisco in the early sixties, and from his apartment near Scott Street, he saw Rexroth frequently, largely because Corman's landlady and her friend were typing the manuscript for Rexroth's *Autobiographical Novel*. But whatever reservations Corman had about Rexroth's personality, he respected the man and his "small but genuine body of real work." There was no reason why they could not share a Kyoto literary evening together.

Although Rexroth had an aversion to Indian culture, that winter he traveled to India to attend a Writer's Conference in Bombay. He visited New Delhi as well, where he had the pleasure of meeting Darina Silone, widow of the novelist, short story writer, and anti-Fascist political leader Ignazio Silone. Air India had given her a complimentary first-class return ticket to Osaka, and although she had done nothing to prepare herself for such a trip, she decided to take advantage of this unexpected gift. When Rexroth heard that she would be visiting Kyoto, he gave her his address. In Kyoto, Rexroth gave her as much practical advice as she could use, and Darina Silone, at Kenneth and Carol's urging, spent nearly all of her evenings with them. "Kenneth explained Japan to me. I realized that he must be a wonderful translator of Chinese and Japanese poetry. . . . He literally devoted himself to explaining it to me.[33]

The year was sweetened further when Rexroth received the $10,000 Copernicus Award, which recognizes the lifetime achievement of a poet over forty-five years of age. (The award was given to three other poets between 1974 and 1977: Robert Lowell, Robert Penn Warren, and Muriel Rukeyser.) Rexroth decided to share some of the reward. To help young women poets in Japan, he established the Kenneth Rexroth Award, to which he contributed $100 annually.

In a very real sense, this year was more than a watershed for Rexroth. It was the culmination of his career, a new peak of achievement. His powers as a poet were restored in Japan, his skills as a "sympathetic translator" sharpened and further refined. The landscape of the Higashiyama touched him so significantly that it became an enduring poetic landscape, as poem "XVII" of *The Morning Star* so clearly and beautifully suggests. His own garden in East Pepper Lane, created in the spirit of a Buddhist setting, has become Higashiyama. He leaves his desk after a night of reading:

> I go out
> Into the wooded garden
> And walk, nude, except for my
> Sandals, through light and dark banded
> Like a field of sleeping tigers.
> Our racoons watch me from the
> Walnut tree, the opossums
> Glide out of sight under the
> Woodpile. My dog Ch'ing is asleep.[34]

The quiet peace of his surroundings, and the philosophical resolution that permeates a poem like *The Heart's Garden, the Garden's Heart,* infiltrates this poem also. The long-dead princess whose tumulus (burial mound) was close to Kenneth and Carol's farmhouse in Kyoto and which inspired Rexroth's *On Flower Wreath Hill,* appears in this poem as "the naked girl." She is the agent, both erotic and spiritual, who helps the poet transcend the limitations of mundane life without losing the joy the natural world assuredly provides. Her body enters his, his "self vanishes," and he achieves "another kind of knowing / Of an all encompassing / Love" where time, space, "grasping and consequence" do not exist. And yet immediately after his revelation, Rexroth becomes gloriously conscious of the brilliance of the morning sun just risen. His erotic pleasures had become etherealized, but he expresses his spiritual ecstasy with sense-ridden images of nature.

Twenty-Nine

OLD BONES, FRESH CONTRADICTIONS
1974–1980

WHILE LIVING IN JAPAN, Rexroth's disillusionment with American life had hardened into disgust. He described his native land to James Laughlin as "a long dead corpse full of fighting maggots cannibalizing each other."[1] No doubt such harsh words grew from his reaction to the many Americans who had prospered from the Vietnam War, and the erosion of the idealism and political commitment that less than a decade earlier had fostered the anti-war movement and civil rights activism. In his opinion, the consciousness-raising of the sixties had been undermined by a bourgeois mentality. As he wrote in his fast-paced survey of communal societies, *Communalism* (1974), people were sadly mistaken if they thought a commune was "a twelve-room Riverside Drive apartment occupied by lawyers, professors, psychiatrists, and social workers who share expenses, [and] play musical beds"; or a farm where some effort was made at self-sufficiency but with an open-gate policy that attracted "loafers and sociopaths" who abandoned children and dogs.[2] Moreover, Rexroth thought it supremely ironic that the few communes like the Hutterite colonies in North Dakota, or Sunburst Farms near Santa Barbara, which were in fact successful, were located near silos for intercontinental ballistic missiles and military air bases.[3]

In contrast, Japan and much of Asian culture represented an alternative perspective. In the paper he had delivered to the Tokyo PEN Conference in November 1972, he had asserted, some fifteen years before such a view became accepted, that in spite of its aggressive capitalist economy, modern-day Japan was a country that did not thrive on defense spending. "Japanese businessmen are only too well aware that they owe their ever expanding economy to the fact that seventy percent of their taxes do not go for wars, past, present and future," Rexroth wrote in his essay "Japan and the Second Greater East Asia Co-Prosperity Sphere."[4]

But, as he told his audience in Tokyo, it was the distant, classic culture of Japan that provided him with a metaphor for a dream world:

a world of exquisite sensibility, elaborate courtesy, self-sacrificing love, and utterly anti-materialistic religion, but a dream in the literal sense, too, a nightside where the inadequacies and frustrations of the American life were overcome, the repressions were liberated and the distortions were healed.[5]

The Buddhist perspective (in combination with another philosophy alien to the thought of most American citizens—that of the Native Americans) created what Rexroth called an "ecological aesthetic" that was in counterpoint with the dominant American outlook because it worked in "cooperation with rather than the conquest of nature." Not that modern Japan had remained immune to side effects of high technology. It had its share of urban sprawl, jerry-built housing, smog. "Take a walk through the mountains, past waterfalls and through forests," Rexroth advises. "Everywhere's there's garbage."[6] However, he added, once environmental pollution became a problem, the ecological movement became popular with the Japanese establishment—the government, the "giant trusts"—not just "the freaks, hippies and New Left intellectuals."

In the last decade of his life, Rexroth did a very curious thing: he published a book of his own poems but identified them as translations from the work of Marichiko, "the pen name of a contemporary young woman who lives near the temple of Marishi-ben in Kyoto."[7] Marishi-ben is the patron goddess of geisha, prostitutes, women in childbirth, and lovers. At first, he tried to fool his readers, his publishers, and his friends into believing this writer actually existed. In the Marichiko poems, he explored every aspect of what he imagined to be one woman's psyche in order to come to terms with how he as a man who had professed great love for women, could at last acquire a rudimentary understanding of woman's nature. If his ruse succeeded, then, perhaps, he could be sure that he had achieved a deeper empathy with women.

While he was still in Japan, Rexroth had asked his dear friend Yasuyo Morita to help him translate the poems into Japanese, and she brought a young woman tanka poet with her one day to Morgan Gibson's home in Osaka to see if she could do so. However, Rexroth was not satisfied with her work, largely because he felt that she was not putting the erotic passion of the originals into the translations.[8] Morgan Gibson has shown that Marichiko is modeled after Yosano Akiko (1878–1942), whose poems Rexroth had translated, and whom he regarded as "the greatest woman poet and love poet of modern Japan," an inspiration to feminists and antiwar activists.[9] Although Rexroth's readers eventually caught on to his trick, some perceived that the Marichiko poems were extraordinary acts of the imagination. Professor Katagiri, who knew the poems were Rexroth's own creations, liked them so much that he translated them into Japanese, calling his work "An Attempt at Reconstructing Love Songs of Marichiko."[10]

Eliot Weinberger, for one, regarded these poems, as well as Rexroth's translations (with Ling Chung) of the Sung dynasty poet Li Ch'ing-chao,[11] as "master works of remembered passion."[12] The poems focus on the yearnings of a young woman for her absent lover:

> As the wheel follows the hoof
> Of the ox that pulls the cart,
> My sorrow follows your footsteps,
> As you leave me in the dawn.[13]

Throughout the entire sequence of sixty poems, Rexroth consistently conveys in the simplest language, and with the finest sensitivity, the pathos of this young woman's desire for a lover's devotion. However, this is hardly an original theme. Had the Japanese experience transformed his woman-as-object perpective, or was he merely fantasizing about the "perfect" woman of his dreams, the one who had always eluded him in life? Was he cultivating the "feminine" side of his own nature, or was he promoting the stereotype of "woman-as-victim"?

At the Third Annual Santa Cruz Poetry Festival in November 1975, Rexroth offended many women among the three-thousand people who filled the civic auditorium by identifying Marichiko as his Japanese paramour (a variation on his standard "this is about a girl I used to screw" introduction). Although he gave a memorable reading to music composed by Lou Harrison, some people in the audience began to hiss. He did not seem distressed, but tried to defend himself. "I may not look that way," he said, "but I was a feminist before most of your mothers were born." Such remarks did not mollify his detractors, and they continued to harass him. On numerous other occasions, Rexroth declared that he came from generations of liberated women, and in a news story that covered his attendance at the Second Annual San Francisco Poetry Festival in the fall of 1977, he is quoted as saying that he wrote poetry to "please women—not to bitch about them."[14] Such patronizing commentary turned off many feminist readers who might otherwise have appreciated Rexroth's recent work.[15]

Back in Santa Barbara, Kenneth and Carol had resumed a peaceful rhythm of life. By and large they were isolated from mainstream Santa Barbara, although they cultivated relationships with such people as the art historian Beatrice Farwell and Ed Loomis (who liked Rexroth better now that he was retired), the painter Irma Cavat, the television journalist Christine Craft, Capra publisher Noel Young and the novelist Thomas Sanchez, who had known Marie Rexroth before he met Kenneth. They gave small parties, usually an eclectic mix of literary and artistic people, young and old. Irma Cavat's teen-aged daughter Nika was sometimes a guest. On one occasion, Kenneth put his tongue in her mouth, but she did not tell anyone.[16] If she had, she would have discovered that Kenneth enjoyed greeting other female guests in the same manner. Kenneth and Carol also asked her to clean their house for them, but that was really an invitation to spend the afternoon with Carol, sipping green tea and eating dainty cakes beneath the eucalyptus trees in front of the house.

Rexroth established an especially close friendship with a young man very new to the Santa Barbara, the novelist Bradford Morrow, a former Danforth Fellow at Yale who was working at Maurice F. Neville Rare Books while he completed a study of Wyndham Lewis. At a party held at Neville's bookstore, he and Rexroth were introduced by Melissa Mytinger, who had published *The Love Poems of Marichiko* for Christopher's Books in 1978. Morrow and Rexroth discovered a mutual interest in Lewis—Rexroth liked his paintings and satiric novels *Tarr, The Apes of God,* and the trilogy *The Human Age.* A bond of trust quickly grew between the two men. Morrow appreciated Rexroth's perspective on Santa Barbara's social elite ("Never trust a bourgeois millionaire," Rexroth was fond of repeating), but their long talks in the privacy of Rexroth's library were what Morrow enjoyed most. Rexroth used Morrow as a sounding board for his ideas, and Morrow would bring to his attention new trends in contemporary fiction and jazz, and talk about the progress he was making on the Wyndham Lewis book. They liked to call one another "Doc" in honor of their lack of Ph.D's—and, in fact, Morrow continued to live in Santa Barbara only because Rexroth was there.

He took me on as an unenrolled student and amanuensis of sorts, directing me less to texts than giving me on at least a weekly basis an impromptu lecture back in the library. He lightheartedly propounded theories about matters as diverse as the purported homosexual affair that Richard Nixon carried on with Bebe Rebozo in the back seat of New York cabs and that male members of the human species were genetically inferior to females and that this may have had something to do with the depletion of ozone layer. Serious subjects were centered on the history of politics and economics, and literature—here primarily modern and contemporary literature.[17]

Rexroth soon asked Morrow if he would agree to act as literary executor upon his death, and Morrow accepted the responsibility.

These two friends did their fair share of clowning around. Once Rexroth showed Morrow a color Polaroid of a beautiful Japanese woman and told him that she was the real Marichiko, but he never revealed her identity. On that same day, he composed two rather lewd poems and wrote them out for Morrow in Japanese on fine handmade paper:

Two Irregular Senuryu

I

Love Poem

All over the world
At this moment, beautiful
Women are wiping
Their assholes.

II

Prostatic Hypertrophy

They also piss
Who merely stand & wait.

Both poems were signed. At the bottom of the second, Rexroth wrote (in English): "Uttered 16 Oct 78 for Brad Morrow."[18]

Morrow encouraged Rexroth to "write" (that is, tape) a sequel to *An Autobiographical Novel*. He was especially interested in hearing Rexroth's account of the San Francisco scene in the fifties and sixties, and sometimes Rexroth would rehearse recollections and opinions that showed up later in the transcribed manuscript. To make a living, Morrow had started his own small rare manuscripts and bookshop (he had quit Neville's), and his experience in this area helped Rexroth.[19] He offered to publish a selection of chapters from the book-in-progress. Quick on the uptake, Rexroth thought it should be a de luxe autographed edition, and Morrow eventually brought out *Excerpts from a Life;* the cover, which was printed by Patrick Reagh of Los Angeles, reproduced one of Rexroth's early paintings, which he referred to as "Sailor with a Hornpipe." Furthermore, when Rexroth told Morrow that UCLA had stopped picking up his papers and manuscripts (an arrangement Lawrence Clark Powell had worked out in the early sixties that provided Rexroth with a neat $1,000 every year), Morrow took it upon himself to sell the abandoned material to USC. Rexroth, who had given up wine because alcohol made him ill, celebrated by bringing a vintage bottle of champagne up from the wine cellar, ceremoniously popping the cork.

Rexroth cultivated friendships with other young people as well. Jeffrey Miller, who had also worked at Maurice Neville Rare Books and later went on to become publisher of Cadmus Books, came by, and so did former students at UCSB like flautist David Tolegian, poet Bill O'Daley, and Melissa Mytinger. On the average of twice a week, Rexroth would telephone Missy Mytinger, keeping her on the line for two hours at a time, turning over ideas and gossip, a monologue to which Mytinger could only listen attentively. Mytinger helped Rexroth to catalogue his enormous library with the possibility of starting a bookstore, a plan Morrow and Rexroth had spun one afternoon back in the library but which never materialized. She also got saddled with the responsibility for running a sort of renegade poetry series in Santa Barbara.[20] Rexroth would call her up, announce, "Denise [Levertov] is coming to town," and expect Mytinger immediately to organize and announce a poetry reading, at which Rexroth would make the introductory remarks.

Mytinger often invited Rexroth to dinner parties at her home, although he liked to create havoc. One evening he got into a terrible row with a dinner guest over the *Kenyon Review* and John Crowe Ranson (whom Rexroth called "a bag of shit"), with the two men on the verge of throwing chairs at one another before Rexroth walked out. The next day Rexroth had totally put the argument out of his mind.

Missy attended one of Rexroth's formal birthday parties during which guests would pay their respects and enjoy the good food. He would appear after everyone had arrived and sit in a large chair slightly removed from the crowd, from where he could French-kiss his women guests. Carol Tinker regarded these celebrations with some trepidation and amusement. In her poem "Thank You for Your Birthday," she writes:

> Memories
> as expensive as
> Ambiguous friends
> have come
> To tell stories
> to go away
> And surely these
> People
> never forget
> what bites.[21]

With a great sense of ceremony, Carol served coffee and birthday cake from the trolley she brought from the kitchen. (Rexroth had always been very particular about his birthday cake. In 1942, Robert Duncan recalled that Rexroth stormed out of the Potrero Hill house in "an infantile rage" because Marie had ordered the wrong kind of cake.) Guests did not linger long after.

Sam Hamill, who along with Tree Swenson had founded Copper Canyon Press in 1972, became a most loyal friend. Actually, Rexroth and Hamill had met in front of City Lights Bookstore in 1958, one of the first places Hamill visited after he fled the orphanages of Utah at the age of sixteen. Hamill was leaving the bookstore with a copy of *Thirty Spanish Poems of Love and Exile,* and there was Rexroth himself strolling down Columbus Avenue. After he asked Rexroth to sign the book, the two began talking and before long Hamill, who had been sacking out in the back of his 1941 Ford, found himself elevated to Scott Street.[22] Hamill stayed with the Rexroths the next four weeks or so, and got a big dose of literary night life. He saw close up people like Michael McClure, Philip Whalen, Diane Di Prima, and Gary Snyder. And he watched Jack Kerouac, "drunk and full of himself," seek Rexroth's approval time after time despite Rexroth's rebuffs. More important, however, was the example Rexroth set for Hamill at this time in terms of what it meant to lead a writer's life. He saw that Rexroth isolated himself for a good part of the day. He heard Rexroth tell him to quit smoking dope and shooting pool for a dollar a game. Rexroth advised him to read more Pablo Neruda, and he did. He directed him to the French poets, but Hamill never liked them. Rexroth gave him an entry into the classics, taught him how to listen to Thelonious Monk, and how to escape the tyranny of iambic pentameter.

When the two men ended up in Santa Barbara ten years later, they resumed their relationship, although by now Hamill was no longer a young acolyte and "did not want to sit on Kenneth's doorstep." He had spent several years in Asia, first in the Marine Corps, then as a conscientious objector, and had studied Zen Buddhism, Taoism, and Confucianism in a monastery. Hamill and Rexroth were often at odds with one another because Rexroth felt betrayed by Hamill's decision to do graduate work with Hugh Kenner on Ezra Pound, and because Hamill liked Confucius, whose philosophy Rexroth regarded as reactionary. And Hamill, who was going through his own serious consciousness-raising after reading Audre Lorde, Adrienne Rich, and Denise Levertov, would not hesitate to chastise Rexroth for ordering Carol Tinker about, or speaking to her in a tone that clearly lacked respect. Rexroth was more amused than annoyed by Hamill's criticism since he had once given him similar advice. Long ago, after reading a few sonnets Hamill had written, Rexroth had told Hamill that he did not like women and should make friends with a few.

Rexroth extended the same kind of warmth and hospitality to Hamill in Santa Barbara as he had in San Francisco. Hamill appreciated Rexroth's encouragement and constructive criticism. Sometimes he felt that Rexroth made no distinction between encouraging him and any other young poet down the road, but Rexroth never failed to let Hamill know in some quiet way that he thought his work was special. And although they never discussed it directly, Rexroth understood Hamill's isolation—he barely had enough money to feed himself in those days and was going through personal crises that drained his emotions and creativity. Rexroth may have seen some of his younger self in Hamill, while Hamill took pleasure in seeing Rexroth as an old man loved by his hand-selected community.[23]

Rexroth continued to attend conferences, including the Portland Poetry Festival (August 11–15, 1976), which was dedicated to his work. In conjunction with the festival, the Wentz Gallery ran an exhibition of sixteen of Rexroth's pastels. The festival theme grew out of a perspective on American poetry which Rexroth had articulated in his *American Poetry in the Twentieth Century,* that is, that American poetry had become a public, performance art, and since 1955, a "tribal, pre-literate relationship between the poet and the audience" once again existed. Indeed, Rexroth's readings to jazz violin, piano, saxophone, bass, and drums, and to Asian music played on the flute, koto, and shakuhachi, were as popular as ever.[24]

The man on whom he relied most for his poetry and jazz performances at this point was still Dick Collins, whom he would call to gather up a band for him three weeks to a month before he was scheduled to appear. Collins always played the trumpet, but the other performers varied, whether they played the sax, bass, drums, clarinet, violin, or the koto or shakuhachi. Rexroth was not the easiest person to work with, and no two performances were ever alike.[25] Collins truly enjoyed accompanying him, and made sure the music was there to enhance rather than overpower the poetry. He preferred not to contradict Rexroth when he insisted that terms like "topsy" and "zonky" were identical and that a tune like "La Vie en Rose" had the same resonance for his audience as it did for him. Rexroth decided which music was to be played, sometimes writing it himself, other times transposing a piece for a soprano saxophone.

When the band played, Collins would keep the poetry on the floor beside him so that the performance would not become a concert. Rexroth never seemed to mind if the poetry ended before the music, and would stand aside and calmly wait until the performers finished. There would usually be a small rehearsal before the show but the musicians for the most part did not understand the connection between what they were playing and what Rexroth was reading. They did know that when Rexroth started rocking back and forth, they were free to go with it. The last time Collins appeared with Rexroth was on November 29, 1977, at the University of California, Santa Barbara.[26] One hour before they were due on stage, Rexroth asked Collins to write a dirge to accompany "For Eli Jacobson." He obliged, and the music slipped neatly into the random pattern of vaudeville, French café, pop, be-bop, and classical numbers of the band's repertory. As Collins described it, this was "poetry and music dada."

When Rexroth performed, he was very well received but he was not the same person who read at the Cellar or the Black Hawk twenty years earlier. His health had declined, and anyone who remembered the Rexroth of the late forties through the early sixties could see that his appearance had radically changed. With age, Rexroth had become overweight and his pace had slowed as walking on a calcified heel became painful. Far more serious was the discomfort he had to endure while his physicians tried to find a suitable medication to control his high blood pressure. Before the Portland Festival, in March 1976, he went into severe shock from a new medication he had been taking. The effects of an alternative prescribed drug were in evidence later that summer when he was teaching at a conference in poetry and fiction in Port Townsend, Washington. The drugs had made him drowsy, and students in his workshop reported that he had once dozed off in class. Some of them transferred to a section taught by Philip Levine.[27]

Levine had long been an admirer of Rexroth's poetry and translations from the Japanese and Chinese, and through the mid-sixties a regular listener to his KPFA Radio programs. He remembered Rexroth boasting about how in 1928 he knew "everyone who mattered" on the avant-garde literary scene because in those days "there were fewer people who mattered than the number of people smoking dope on the corner of Haight and Ashbury." He had not spoken to Rexroth since 1968 when the two participated in a panel discussion on academic freedom after poet Robert Mezey had lost his job at Fresno State. (The panel discussion came to an abrupt halt with the announcement that Martin Luther King, Jr., had been assassinated.) Now seventy-one, Rexroth was not the overpowering poet that Levine remembered. The blood pressure medication interfered with his memory, and he wanted Levine, the "next oldest, next best-read" person around to stick by him for when he forgot "the name of the poet who wrote the essay about rhyme." Carol Tinker, who ordinarily helped Rexroth with such details, had not accompanied him this time. Rexroth also wanted Levine to help him shake loose a young woman at the conference who thought she could seduce Rexroth, but whom he did not want to oblige.

At the Port Townsend Conference, Rexroth's behavior was far from exemplary. He goaded Madeline Defrees by insisting that she discuss the evils of the Catholic Church. In 1973, Defrees had received dispensation from her religious vows, and she was extremely uncomfortable with Rexroth's acid observations. After Robin Skelton finished reading a poem about his ordeal in a Japanese camp for prisoners of war, Rexroth accused him of lying, and insisted that during the war the Japanese had treated their prisoners kindly. Rexroth added the rather peculiar assertion that anti-Semitism did not exist in Mussolini's Italy. At a book-signing party— one of the scheduled conference events—Rexroth got hold a large book of prints by Gustav Klimt, turned the pages until he came upon a portrait of a red-headed woman wearing a large hat, and told Levine that it was a portrait of his mother. "Klimt caught her looking like the Austrian whore she wanted to look like rather than the bourgeios matron she was." (Actually there is a strong resemblance between photographs of Delia Rexroth and the woman Klimt painted.) Levine was also surprised that after twenty years Rexroth still seemed to harbor enormous hostility toward Robert Creeley. Once, when he heard someone at the conference refer to Creeley, Rexroth became furious. "Don't mention that name in my presence," he said. "I'll beat the shit out of him if I ever see him again."

Nearly a year later, another of Rexroth's bursts of temper caused a serious falling out with Gary Snyder. Awarded the Pulitzer Prize in 1975 for *Turtle Island,* Snyder was working without salary on the California Arts Council for Governor Jerry Brown. In the winter of 1977, Snyder proposed that Rexroth be officially honored as California Artist of the Year. When he told him of his intention over the telephone, Rexroth became furious, called Brown a Fascist, and declared emphatically that he wanted no part of this honor.[28] Rexroth believed that Brown had "discovered the use of the rhetoric of radical politics for reactionary purposes."[29] For example, he wanted to know why Brown supported an annual award for a distinguished poet and then cut funds for the poet-in-the-schools program. Snyder, though annoyed that Rexroth had become so angry, was willing to explain his alliance with Brown. But Rexroth was not interested. His calculations permitted him to accept funds from the U.S. State Department for travel to Asia without feeling that he was compromising his principles, but accepting an award from his home state he regarded as a betrayal of those feelings. He and Snyder never managed to straighten out this misunderstanding. However, "the best" of Rexroth's poetry continued to radiate for Snyder "a notable serenity and wisdom," which initially gave him "the nerve to draw on Far Eastern material" for his own purposes. At the core of Rexroth's poetry, Snyder perceived "Buddha's sense of compassion . . . the sense of mutuality and good manners inherent in many preliterate cultural world views, grandmotherly wisdom."[30]

Rexroth's health improved enough for him to fly to New York City, where he talked about his background and the influences on his life at the annual "Education of the Poet" talk sponsored by the Academy of American Poets in April 1977. The following year he and Carol returned to Japan in April, and with Rexroth giving lectures under the State Department's sponsorship, they were able to tour South Korea, the Philippines, Hong Kong, Singapore, and Thailand. In Japan they saw many friends again, including Professor Kodama at Doshisha Women's College, Professor Yuzuru Katagiri at Kyoto Seika College, and Professor Morgan Gibson at Osaka University. The Kenneth Rexroth Award winners gave him a welcome reading (1984 was the last year the award was made). John Solt saw Rexroth at Meiji Gakuin University, where he read his poetry and answered questions from the audience. When one student asked where American poetry was going, Rexroth said with a faint smile, "It's gone."[31] Actually, Rexroth did not believe the contemporary poetry scene in the States was dead; he thought that the pulse of American literature now belonged to women.

Indeed, one of the topics on which Rexroth lectured was contemporary American women poets. Through the years Rexroth had been supportive of many women writers, praising the talent of Mina Loy, Muriel Rukeyser, Lenore Kandel, Denise Levertov, Ann Stanford, Gloria Oden, Babette Deutsch, and Louise Bogan while they were still relatively unknown, and more recently in his Introduction to *Four Young Women Poets*, Carol Tinker, Jessica Hagedorn, Barbara Szerlip, and Alice Karle.[32] He grew certain during the following years that women writers were the stars of contemporary literature. His interest in Chinese and Japanese women poets was a logical extension of that belief.

Yet there was an unsettling aspect to Rexroth's interest when, on a personal level, he treated the women whom he lived with as though their chief function was to create a domestic environment conducive to his own writing. If he had exploited some women on the personal level, he had, on the other hand, helped many others professionally. To more than one friend he confided that the presence of young women, especially poets, aroused his erotic impulses and charged his own wellsprings of creative energy.

Perhaps Rexroth's remarks about poet Carolyn Forché illustrate best his perspective. Rexroth met her at a private poetry reading in Santa Barbara in 1976, the year she won the Yale Series of Younger Poets' award. A warm correspondence soon sprang up between the two poets— who had a mutual friend in Irma Cavat—while Forché was traveling from her San Diego home base around the country and to Europe. They were separated in age by nearly five decades, yet Forché's letters indicate that an intense, heady attachment existed between them, innocent as it may have been. Forché was his "gypsy, with her passion and caring."[33] She wrote: "I miss you. You have an inward steadiness, a radiance, a calm. I sometimes wish to be near it when I am not, and then somehow I sense you with me."[34] In the *American Poetry Review* (November–December 1976) Rexroth lauded her first book, *Gathering the Tribes,* praising her as the "best woman poet" selected as a Yale Younger Poet since Muriel Rukeyser. Six years later Forché would receive numerous awards for *The Country Between Us,* but Rexroth had already singled out her talent (as he had Denise Levertov's more than twenty-five years before). Tongue-in-cheek Rexroth welcomed her to the "bearshit-on-the-trail" school of poetry, and was especially pleased with her poem "Kalaloch" because its setting was the trails along the Pacific Coast where he and Andrée had once camped. He liked her proletarian background, her strong sense of place, and the controlled but fluent cadence of her verse, all of which contributed to what he perceived to be "pure feminist poetry . . . of a human being in her late 20's moving in perfect freedom and independence (not the same thing) through life experiences that are reserved for young males."[35]

Yet by the late seventies, many Bay Area people had wearied of Rexroth's version of himself as an aging but active satyr. Some critical readers continued to believe that Rexroth's limited knowledge of Chinese and Japanese did not qualify him to translate from those languages. Others remembered Rexroth's outbursts of temper, and as James Broughton has pointed out, when Robert Duncan dubbed Rexroth "The Terrible Tempered Mr. Bangs," it was a sign that he was being taken less seriously. A few of his friends, now less amused by his self-inflating stories and gossip, relished the fact that his autobiography had to be called a "novel."[36] When, at the invitation of Jack Shoemaker, Rexroth read at the San

Francisco Museum of Art in 1979, he apparently stirred a general disaffection. San Francisco's poetry-reading audience packed the auditorium, but some of Rexroth's erstwhile colleagues decided not to attend. Duncan, asked to introduce Rexroth, begged off on the grounds that the night of the reading, a Thursday, was his time for watching television. Gary Snyder also declined the honor. Lawrence Ferlinghetti and Shig Murao came to the reading twenty minutes late and stayed for only half an hour.[37] Ferlinghetti may have still been reacting to Rexroth's angry disapproval of his decision not to publish Kazuko Shiraishi.[38] What was perceived as his chronic petulance led many of his readers to feel regretfully that the great Rexroth had outlived his time.

Rexroth outwardly gave no indication that any of this disturbed him. Capacity audiences attended his readings; he had the support of a loyal community in Santa Barbara, and poets of the next generation were sending him manuscripts to read, seeking his advice and approval. Geoffrey Gardner was gathering material for *The Ark*, a festschrift for Rexroth, and though he had originally set out to produce a manuscript of 150 pages, he ended up with a book of more than 400 pages that included such notables as Octavio Paz, Josephine Miles (Rexroth would sometimes refer to her as "Miss Josephine"), Jonathan Williams, Denise Levertov, James Wright, Robert Kelly, Kathleen Raine, Philip Whalen, Ted Weiss, Marge Piercy, Jerome Rothenberg, Muriel Rukeyser, Nathaniel Tarn, and Ann Stanford. Even Rexroth's publishers joined the celebration. Justus George Lawler, of Herder & Herder, who had accompanied Rexroth— once with his three young sons—long ago on reading tours in Michigan and Indiana, contributed a memoir, and James Laughlin a poem.

In addition, he was formally connected to the International College, a non-accredited institution based in Westwood that arranged apprentice-ships between students and tutors. Also on the staff were Ravi Shankar, Lawrence Durrell, Marshall McLuhan, and Anaïs Nin. Many people applied for instruction from Rexroth, but he was highly selective and chose only a few aspiring writers. Invitations to read from respectable places like the University of Michigan and the 92nd Street Y continued to roll in (he decided that a trip to New York would be too rigorous for a seventy-four-year old).

Rexroth's health was deteriorating alarmingly. He refused, however, to stay home. He flew up to Seattle in early spring 1980, and after being warmly introduced to his audience by Sam Hamill, gave a wonderful performance. Hamill later registered his reaction to Rexroth's reading:

He sat at a table, and placed his wallet directly in front of him. To his left, a Japanese woman sat at a koto. A Japanese gentleman who must have been nearly Rexroth's age stood to her left rear, shakuhachi in hand. And Rexroth *sang* in Japanese, then in English, his translations as they were meant to be heard. With his wallet he BANGED the table for punctuation. Throughout his reading, I wept,—not because I knew he was dying which seemed clear despite his boundless good humor or because I feared I would never seem him again which also proved to be true, but because the poems were magnificent; because his delivery was perfect.[39]

The next day he went on an hour's drive north to visit the Skagit Valley and gave a reading in La Conner.[40] He had last seen that landscape some fifty years ago when he had come west with Andrée.

That same spring, at the invitation of the poet and anthologist Al Poulin, Rexroth flew to Rochester, New York, to attend a literary festival sponsored by the New York State Literary Center, which Poulin co-directed with Dale Davis. The highlight of the three-day conference on April 24–26 was a ceremony honoring James Laughlin for his lifelong support and encouragement of contemporary writers. Rexroth was suffering from a hernia, constantly medicated to control his high blood pressure, and subject to daily enemas. Although largely confined to a wheelchair, he was in good spirits. When Dale Davis and Eliot Weinberger met him at the airport, the flight attendants were fawning all over him. He had requested that a "pretty woman" act as a guide for the duration of the conference, but was glad to see Weinberger—"the one person who understands me"—waiting for him. Davis arranged a special dinner for Rexroth at the old local fire hall, attended by a coterie that included Weinberger, and Ann and James Laughlin (who paid for the dinner). For Rexroth the twelve-course meal, prepared by the Zen Center, resembled "Temple food," but he enjoyed the royal treatment.[41] As they left the table, Rexroth's gait was slow and deliberate, and he reminded poet Joe Bruchac of a turtle, "one who stays within his shell, not sticking his neck out until he has checked things out, but also holding on fiercely when he decides to bite." Clayton Eshleman, with whom Rexroth had quarreled, kept his diplomatic distance.[42]

Toward the end of the festival, at a nearby church, Rexroth read, in honor of Laughlin, selections from the Marichiko poems to the accompaniment of a woman koto player from the Rochester School of Music. With wide sweeping gestures of his hands, he gave the koto player her cues. His audience was mesmerized by the performance. Joe Bruchac observed that "the difficult old man had been replaced by the bright-eyed strength of a poet in full voice, his body old, but his spirit still as young as the lovers in those poems."

Feisty and energetic despite his ills, he went up to San Francisco in June 1980 to read at the International Poetry Festival. Joyce Jenkins, the organizer of the conference, thought of scheduling Rexroth and Kazuko Shiraishi to appear on stage together, he reading a poem in English, she in Japanese. When he heard of the plan, Rexroth called up Jenkins at 7:00 a.m. and roared: "I am San Francisco," convincing Jenkins that Rexroth should have his own undivided time on stage. Until Rexroth appeared at the reading, Jenkins had no idea that he had been so seriously ill. His body was bloated (his belly protuding like a balloon), his step slow, and his eyes constantly downcast. She had a vision of "tubes being ripped away" once she learned that he had "escaped from some medical situation." And yet when he reached the podium, he gave a performance that was "magnificent, so full of knowledge and life." Indeed, if any one person can represent a place, Rexroth was San Francisco.[43]

A new relationship had been established around this time between Rexroth and Fr. Albert Huerta, who in December 1979 was a part-time teacher at the University of San Francisco (where they had a mutual friend, Fr. William Monihan). Huerta was completing his doctoral dissertation in Hispanic languages and literatures at UCSB and requested an interview with Rexroth in order to talk about the work of Arturo Serrano-Plaja and Jorge de Sena, both of whom had been professors at UCSB. Huerta approached Rexroth for his insights into Spanish and Portuguese poets because he knew that upon his recommendation, a poetry reading had been arranged for Jorge de Sena at the Unitarian church; and he had also read Rexroth's *Thirty Spanish Poems of Love and Exile*. Huerta had called upon the Rexroths when he was staying at the Jesuit Novitiate in Santa Barbara, and the two men quickly discovered that they shared ideas about literature and theology.

Concurrently, Rexroth remained in touch with a number of women writers, among them Carolyn Forché and Kathy Acker, whose punk novels *Great Expectations* and *Blood and Guts in High School* had created a sensation. He was still giving advice to unestablished writers like Kerry Tomlinson and Elizabeth Sutherland.[44] Nor was Rexroth shy about entering the controversy swirling around Chögyam Trungpa, the high Tibetan lama who had fled Tibet in 1959, graduated from Oxford University, and founded the first Tibetan Buddhist meditation center in Scotland where he met Robert Bly. After Trungpa married, he left for Vermont and established the Vajradhatu Seminary, a three-month Buddhist retreat that took place in various resorts around the country and attracted several American writers and artists, including Allen Ginsberg. In 1974 he founded the Naropa Institute in Boulder, Colorado. It housed the Jack Kerouac School of Disembodied Poetics, directed by Allen Ginsberg and Anne Waldman.[45] Among those who became associated with it were Robert Creeley, William Burroughs, John Cage, Gary Snyder (who in 1972 had participated with Robert Bly in a benefit reading for Trungpa but soon disassociated himself from the Buddhist leader when he got drunk during the fund-raiser), Joni Mitchell, Amiri Baraka, John Ashbery, Robert Duncan, Jerome Rothenberg, and W. S. Merwin. During a fall 1975 retreat—an advanced seminar in Tantric buddhism—and under the orders of Chögyam Trungpa, Merwin and his companion the poet Dana Naone were dragged from their room and forced to attend a drunken Halloween party where they were stripped of their clothes. Trungpa's confederates had broken through plate glass to get their hands on them, and Merwin himself began swinging a broken beer bottle. The next day, after a conference between Trungpa, Merwin, and Naone, the two poets stayed for another month, until the next gala party was announced.

Several versions of this spectacle began to spread, and two small books were written about it: *The Party*, a straightforward account by Ed Sanders and his class at the School of Disembodied Poetics; and *The Great Naropa Poetry Wars*, by Tom Clark, a book that views the incident as clear-cut evidence that Trungpa's church was inherently Fascist. Some observers put the fracas in the category of a drunken fraternity party; others commended it as a form of Buddhist pedagogy which "shocked" the Western mind. There was no confusion about Rexroth's attitude toward Trungpa. On the back cover of Tom Clark's book, he called Trungpa a "counter Buddha, sometimes considered his brother, who always goes about seeking whom he may devour with ignorance and trying to destroy the Buddha word."[46] In more down-to-earth terms, Rexroth compared Trungpa to the Satanist Aleister Crowley, and suggested that he be deported to a farming commune in Northwest Tibet.

Jeffrey Miller, Clark's publisher, thought Rexroth was courageous to embroil himself in yet another ferocious controversy. Allen Ginsberg had asked Miller to take *The Great Naropa Poetry Wars* out of print,[47] but Rexroth told Miller to tell Ginsberg to see him if any trouble arose. It was not the first time Rexroth and Ginsberg had disagreed over the worthiness and integrity of another man. Jack Kerouac had been the source of an earlier rift. Rexroth was very unhappy about Ginsberg's defense of Trungpa, and felt Ginsberg's actions detracted from the positive influence that Buddhism could exert in the United States. He asked Geoffrey Gardner, who was still working on his Rexroth festschrift (*The Ark* was published in 1980), to exclude the poem that Ginsberg had written in response to Gardiner's request for material, even though he considered Ginsberg to be one of the most important poets in the United States, his influence enormous, "as great in India or Sweden or underground behind the Iron Curtain as it is in America."[48]

Thirty

AN UNEASY DEATH
1981–1982

REXROTH SUFFERED a severe heart attack in late December 1980, and was forced to spend the next several months bedridden at home. There was a nurse to help, but Rexroth was slow in mending, and measured his progress in the number of level city blocks he could walk. The scope of his reading began to narrow, focusing on the neoplatonist Plotinus and the Modernist Father George Tyrrell, about whom Rexroth used to have long talks with his friend Justus George Lawler, who shared with him "regrets at the destruction of the old liturgy in both churches and the accompanying linguistic and ceremonial debasement."[1] His friendship with Bradford Morrow flourished, and the two men, nearly fifty years apart, spoke to one another on the telephone every day. For Rexroth's seventy-fifth birthday, "with a full measure of rascality," Morrow had printed *Saucy Limericks and Christmas Cheer,* seventeen limericks by a Rexroth who still enjoyed risqué humor. Here is a fair example:

> Hannibal whispered in Punic
> In the ear of his favorite eunuch
> "I love the sweet ass
> Of this Roman lass,
> Would you kindly hold up her tunic?"[2]

In return, Rexroth gave Morrow a birthday present of the only short story he ever wrote, entitled "Vivienne Renaud," an erotic tale of an afternoon's love in the forest near Versailles.[3]

They also worked out the details for a new journal of contemporary writing that Morrow would edit, to be called *Conjunctions.* Among the initial group of contributing editors were Rexroth's friends, poet and translator Nathaniel Tarn and Edouard Roditi. Morrow and Rexroth decided to make the first issue a festschrift for Laughlin. Rexroth telephoned for his approval. He gave it, Rexroth told Morrow, with the fervor of "a blushing bride being carried upstairs to the nuptial bed-room." Early in 1981, having gone over the list with Rexroth, Morrow sent out over seventy-five invitations to prospective contributors. As a special feature, Morrow interviewed Rexroth in February of 1981 about Laughlin and the various writers that New Directions had published. Rexroth was still razzing Laughlin about the way he ran his book com-pany: "I just write him abusive letters about literature, saying why does he publish such shit in New Directions." But on a serious note, Rexroth declared that he "wouldn't have had a career without Laughlin, and I look on Laughlin as, I suppose, my best friend, and always a good com-rade."[4]

Two months later, Rexroth suffered his first stroke. After Carol Tinker brought him to Cottage Hospital, she called Morrow, who came immedi-ately to see if he could be useful. The admitting nurse, Angela Jaffrey, observed that Rexroth was very angry and looked like "a lion in pain." He could not talk, but his eyes were glaring and his body restless.[5] He was still in the emergency room when Morrow arrived, but was permitted to see only next of kin. Morrow announced he was Rexroth's grandson, and a nurse led him to Rexroth's blindingly bright and noisy room. As soon as she left, Rexroth said in a fake-thug accent, "Come on, man, we're getting out of here." Morrow stayed for about twenty minutes, refolded his blue jeans for him, and brushed his hair back. When Rexroth was released from the hospital, his right side was still paralyzed and he required the attention of a nurse and physical therapist at home. Although he had been a practicing Anglican, on Easter on 1981 he was received into the Roman Catholic Church by Father Huerta. Both his mother and father had been on their deathbeds when they converted.

But Rexroth scorned his illness. From July 3 to August 9, 1981, the Santa Barbara Museum of Art held an exhibit of his paintings, and Rexroth attended the opening and the celebration supper that followed in his favorite sushi restaurant, the Suisshin ("Tipsy Heart"). He refused to use the special contraption that would enable him to get from his wheelchair into the car, and insisted that Bradford Morrow lift him. At the end of the summer, he suffered a second stroke. When Morrow visited him this time, Rexroth was as rebellious as ever, and gestured to Morrow (his speech was too slurred to be easily understood) that he wanted his cathe-ter removed. "His hands and eyes were very full of life and even mis-chief," Morrow remembered. Morrow urged him to keep working with his speech therapist so that he could continue to tape his autobiography, but the distractions were frequent. There was a steady stream of visitors that included a core of UCSB faculty, among them Beatrice Farwell, who had written the brochure for the exhibition at the Santa Barbara Museum of Art, and Ed Loomis, who came almost daily, feeling ambivalent about Rexroth's inability now to dominate the conversation. Rexroth never recovered enough to work again. One afternoon while Carol Tinker, Ku-zuko Shiraishi, and John Solt (who was back from Japan) were visiting him, he announced to them that he was dying.

Rexroth desperately wanted to leave the hospital; however, his con-dition required round-the-clock nursing which Medicare and Blue Cross would not cover. James Laughlin stepped in. By the end of September, Laughlin had sent more than $15,000 to cover the cost of home care. Laughlin visited Rexroth in December 1981, but was not able to stay for Rexroth's seventy-sixth birthday, which was celebrated, in a manner of speaking, with Marie, Katharine, and Mariana (in order to get rid of "excess baggage," Mary had changed her name from Mary Delia Andrée Rexroth to Mariana Rexroth in May 1975). But by New Year's Eve he was back in the hospital, in the intensive-care unit. The series of afflictions from which Rexroth suffered during the last six months of his life is staggering: congestive heart failure, another minor stroke, kidney fail-ure, severe muscle spasms, an inoperable hernia, and paralysis. There were long periods when he could not talk at all. His memory would fade in and out, yet true to form he remembered the long, polysyllabic words more easily than simple ones like "duck" or "football." James Laughlin said the only person he ever knew to call him during a superbowl game was Rexroth, which helps to explain why "football" so easily slipped out of his vocabulary.

How did Rexroth get through these months? He spent most of the nights awake, cared for by Angela Jaffrey, the attractive young nurse who had admitted him to Cottage Hospital the night of his first stroke and who had now become his private nurse. She got to know him very well. She would arrive around 11:00 p.m., and often find him groaning in pain in his small, ascetic-looking bedroom just off the living room. After a while she discovered the kinds of activities that would distract him, if not give him real pleasure. She would put him in his wheelchair, take him into the living room, and put on a piece of classical music. He would sit there, tears running down his face, yearning to talk about the music he loved but unable to speak a coherent sentence. Sometimes he would stare for hours at the shadows that moved along the walls and windows, imag-ining what private ghosts of the past only he could know. He liked Angela to talk about herself, but he was also extremely considerate of her and would motion for her to lie down on the sofa and sleep when she became tired. He had a small blackboard to communicate his needs. He would point to "Call Carol" or "I want to get up" or "I'm hungry." When Angela asked if she could listen to a recording of one of his readings, he refused to give her permission (she never heard him read until she listened to a tape after his death). But Angela found his facial expressions eloquent, and without speaking he managed to communicate well. Sometimes he liked to go to the kitchen and supervise his meals, which most usually consisted of eggs scrambled with large quantities of butter; frozen yogurt;

and rice cooked to the consistency of mush. Food preparation remained a major concern for Rexroth even though he could not consume anything very palatable. Also, he insisted on appearing well groomed. Angela regularly manicured his fingernails, and he was always cleanly shaved. He wore beautiful kimonos and Angela would often catch him staring at the full-length mirror in his small room.

He was not always the most accommodating of patients. He had a wide if faulty knowledge of medicine and pharmaceuticals (thanks to reading Merck's *Manual of Medicine* at bedtime for forty years), and believed that he knew more about the medication he should take than his doctor did. He became adamant about the fallibility of prescriptions, especially those for pain. He had actually become addicted to paregoric (for its opium), and once summoned the strength to grab a bottle of it out of Angela's hand. For a while he was taking nuvane, a synthetic form of morphine, until near the end he was given straight morphine. He would become incredibly angry when he was denied relief from his suffering, especially from mysterious muscular spasms that defied diagnosis. He did have a steady stream of visitors who lifted his spirits, but Angela believed that he was giving up the will to live.[6] As his mother Delia had done fifty-six years ago, Rexroth picked out the clothes he wanted to be buried in.

When his physicians gradually reduced his medications, his health rallied. He actually regained his ability to speak and began eating solid food again. On June 3, Carol Tinker called Brad Morrow, who had moved to New York City, and said very cheerfully, "There's someone here who wants to talk with you." Partially recovered, Rexroth conversed with Morrow for several minutes and was pleased to learn that *Conjunctions* was making its mark. Morrow promised to fly out and visit him within the next couple of weeks. But in the late afternoon of June 6, Rexroth's heart began fluttering, and he experienced a massive and fatal heart attack early that evening. An electrocardiogram machine registered his death by blowing a fuse.

Rexroth was buried the following Friday, June 11, 1982. His funeral demonstrated that he died a Catholic, and a Buddhist. (Carol Tinker remained certain that Kenneth was essentially a Buddhist, but she also knew that he believed he should observe the rituals of the culture to which he was closest by birth.)[7] An ecumenical funeral was conducted by four Jesuit priests. Alberto Huerta delivered the eulogy at the mid-morning mass of Christian burial at Mount Carmel Catholic Church; however, the sisters from the Santa Barbara Vedanta Temple were also present, chanting in Sanskrit. David Tolegian, his Santa Barbara student, played music composed by Rexroth's dear longtime friend Dick Collins, and Esther Handler read from "On Flower Wreath Hill." Michael McClure, who could not catch a plane in time to attend the funeral, telephoned Morrow and asked him to read a poem he had written in Rexroth's memory. In one verse, he sought to describe the relationship of the younger San

Francisco poets to the departed Rexroth: "We are the sculptures on the urn. / We are the flames of the candles / that do not burn.[8] The pallbearers were Bradford Morrow, John Tinker (Carol Tinker's brother), Ed Loomis, Tom Adler, Jeffrey Miller, and John McBride, Mariana's husband at the time and editor of *Invisible City*[9]

Rexroth was buried with a Tibetan statue by his side in the Santa Barbara cemetery, his gravestone facing the ocean. On the stone appears one of the poems from *The Silver Swan:*

> As the full moon rises
> The swan sings
> In sleep
> On the lake of the mind.[10]

The nearby Pacific Ocean would have to absorb the contradictions that marked Kenneth Rexroth's life and followed him through death. Present at the luncheon that followed were his three wives, two daughters, John McBride, Bradford Morrow, Father Huerta, Father Monahan, Jeffrey Miller, Dick Collins, and his oldest friend Frank Triest, who had taken the bus down from San Francisco.

KPFA broadcast a Rexroth memorial on the day he died. Lawrence Ferlinghetti reported that he had the sensation Rexroth was "hovering over us at that moment, in the form of a giant Monarch butterfly dreaming it's a Chinese philosopher." Although Rexroth had not been a part of the San Francisco Bay literary scene for the last fourteen years, his friends and acquaintances—despite whatever offenses they may have suffered—wanted to acknowledge his passing respectfully. Mariana was quite aware of this, especially after the Santa Barbara funeral where she and Katharine, and Marthe and Marie, felt as though they had attended the funeral of a stranger. The day after Rexroth's funeral Mariana arranged a memorial service, a *panakeda,* to be held at the Greek Orthodox Holy Trinity Cathedral on June 12, 1982. It provided a dignified ritual for Rexroth's friends to observe his passing and to express their sadness. City Lights announced the service, as did the daily newspapers, and there was a huge turnout of poets, musicians, and painters. People from long ago also came, including Masha Zakheim Jewett, whose father Bernard Zakheim had painted Rexroth into his Coit tower murals (she brought the portrait of Rexroth her father had painted in the thirties). Hazel Takeshita, one of the women Rexroth and Marie Rexroth had helped avoid the internment camps during World War II, attended. Later that month, Gary Snyder, who had heard of Rexroth's death over a friend's CB radio, organized with his friends Will Staple, Dale Pendell, and Steve Sanfield an outdoor memorial under the stars around a bonfire. They read their favorite poems by Rexroth and among other things discovered again "the depth of his anarchistic critique of government and civilization."[12] The following year memorial services were held at the Marishiten Temple in

Tokyo, and a memorial program was organized by Professor Katagiri at the Kyoto American Center, during which both he and Morgan Gibson read from *The Heart's Garden* to the piano accompaniment of Ron Hadley.

Rexroth would have approved of these rituals, but he would have been unhappy to read the various obituaries which persisted, with a few exceptions, in identifying him as the father of the Beat poets. Nor would he have been pleased with the chaos that followed his last will and testament, through which he intended to create a memorial to himself by turning the Dower House into a small research center for writers and scholars. It would be sponsored by the Jesuits (to whom Rexroth bequeathed the house, his library, and paintings), and was to provide both a safe haven for Carol Tinker—who was left only with her mother's small inheritance)—and a sure method for avoiding taxation. He had not bothered to inform his lawyer friend Ruth Pokrass, whom he had met while househunting with Carol in 1968, that he had appointed her executor of his estate, nor had he ever discussed with her the terms of his will.[13]

After he died, the Jesuits decided that the responsibility of running a Kenneth Rexroth research center was more than they could handle, but they did not relinquish the financial control that Rexroth had bequeathed to them. For a while Carol Tinker was in an extremely precarious situation. Her physical and mental health suffered, and Pokrass worked hard to prevent a disaster. After gaining approval from the Attorney General, Pokrass enacted a reformation of trusts which enabled her to liquidate the estate's assets. She found a buyer for the East Pepper Lane house, and Carol Tinker moved to a house on Calle Rosales in Santa Barbara. Mariana and Katharine received the residual of stocks, cash, and royalties. In 1987, Rexroth's massive library was sold by California bookseller Soren Edgren to a new Japanese university. The Jesuits received the remainder of the proceeds of the sale of the East Pepper Lane house, Rexroth's library, and furniture. If the healthy response to Rexroth's posthumous publications is any indication, the man who was buried in that pleasant pasture overlooking the Pacific remains tangibly alive in the minds of his friends and readers.

EPILOGUE

K ENNETH REXROTH'S LIFE was surely a tissue of contradictions. In his personal relationships he professed great love for women in general, and for his mother, wives, and daughters in particular. And yet the women married to him were forced to accept his premise that it was proper for him to dedicate himself first and finally to his art, everything else being secondary. He refused to be controlled or confined by the constraints of a regular job, nor did he adhere to the conventions of a middle-class marriage. A wife of his had to endure sexual infidelity, verbal and intermittent physical abuse, and the jealous rage of a man who could not take what he dished out. But he immortalized them in some of the most exquisite love poems in the English language, and became frantic when threatened by their departure. He insisted that his daughters be photographed for the cover of his *Collected Shorter Poems,* which contains many examples of his pride and delight in fatherhood. He passed on to them a lasting love for art, culture, and nature, and endowed them with a profound worldliness. But too frequently his behavior—in both small and large ways—reflected a paradoxical detachment, especially in the case of Katharine, about whose paternity at one time he expressed doubts. He gave neither Mariana nor Katharine the handsome Bern Porter edition of *A Bestiary for My Daughters,* a small example perhaps of his neglect; nor did he provide much financial support for their education. Both girls suffered periods of alienation that went beyond the ordinary rite of passage children experience while they are asserting their independence, whether or not their parents are divorced. Even his love for his mother created conflict. He was Delia Rexroth's only child and because her marriage had periods of turmoil, he became the great object of her attention and affection without competition. She died when he was eleven, which encouraged an idealized memory of her—that no other woman seemed capable of replacing. Moreover, he felt betrayed and abandoned by her early death, and similar feelings surfaced when his marriages began to deteriorate.

Rexroth's public behavior was also puzzling. He extended warmth and hospitality to countless younger poets, encouraging them to pursue their art and to resist a lifestyle that left them little freedom. He put the weight of his influence behind many of these writers, whose reputations in several instances would later outshine his. Others can recall the sound advice he would give them about establishing their status as conscientious objectors during the Korean and Vietnam wars. His friends and acquaintances were truly impressed with the breadth and range of his knowledge, and were shocked when they learned that Rexroth had never been graduated from high school. Harder still was it for them to accept the various confabulations Rexroth would relate about his encounters with the famous and the infamous. On one hand, he was a highly cultivated individual capable of discussing the Kronstadt rebellion, Baron von Hugel, the poetry of preliterate societies, and Lady Murasaki all in the same book review program. On the other hand, there was within the same body the semblance of a bourgeois cad with a sense of humor straight out of the gutter, and a temperament so vindictive that some of his dearest friends turned their backs on him. If he was a pacifist-anarchist, how was he able to write a column for a Hearst newspaper? If he could not tolerate pretentious people—he liked to quote his mother as saying, "A snob is a person who imitates the manners of the class above him"—why did he pour cheap wine into empty bottles with expensive labels at his dinner parties?

Rexroth tended to take sides with unpopular figures, or make statements that indicated he was speaking against the grain of established thought and perspective. And while there is nothing contradictory about taking such a position, he often carelessly alienated many people who would have been glad to agree with him. His personal radar system for detecting anti-democratic behavior in political organizations made it tenuous if not impossible for him to affiliate himself with any particular action group. Long before many people became disillusioned with the Communist Party, Rexroth labeled it a fascistic organization. Unlike most Americans, he felt World War II was a war fought between two capitalist systems, but he never made clear what he thought should be done about the millions of Europeans perishing on the battlefields and in concentration camps. Yet his sensitivity to the plight of Japanese Americans in the United States was ennobling. Later, after the war, by accusing them of unfairly dominating the agenda of meetings, he angered his anarchist-pacifist allies, people whose political orientation was most similar to his. Although he had many acquaintances in nearly every corner of the country, and was a familiar figure in the Bay Area, during one of his lower moments when he was keeping his early Santa Barbara diary, he wondered if he had made a single friend other than Marie in the forty years he had lived in San Francisco.

Nor did he tolerate academics and literary critics who thought art and politics could be separated. He despised the New Criticism, and as a result, his work was put into a kind of literary coventry. He could stomach neither the Fugitive poets nor Ezra Pound, although his admiration for D. H. Lawrence, the writer, rarely waivered. He devised a system of critical standards which could be seen as a precursor for late-twentieth-century Deconstruction. He relegated Henry James to the status of an "Ouida in a frock coat" because he based his characters on types—the Boston Brahmin, the American millionaire, and the British aristocrat—who had become icons for him. Rexroth wrote in 1960 that the paintings of James McNeill Whistler (who believed that art must be divorced from social significance) are like "highbrow movies . . . this is our kind of corn, designed specifically to take in our caste," and that once observers realize this, they are left "with little more than an entertaining afternoon of sophisticated nostalgia, like three hours spent with *La Traviata* or *The Merry Widow*."

Rexroth knew he risked displeasing his readers when he criticized their taste, and upset the standards their teachers had passed down to them. But this was all part of the public persona he had carved out for himself, the renegade blessed with culture and an encyclopedic memory. His orientation endeared him to many people, but rarely those who passed out teaching positions and poet-in-residencies. And though he wrote a stack's worth of job inquiries to various institutions of higher learning, he was contemptuous of American universities and colleges. When Black Mountain, the one college that seemed to suit his political orientation, offered him a position, his financial conditions undermined the offer. The man who had expressed so much contempt for the marketplace used it as a measuring stick for making one of the most important decisions in his life.

Kenneth Rexroth was a man of talent and imagination whose life reflected the more passionate and dedicated aspects of modern literary life in the United States. He yearned in the twenties for fresh idioms and the breakdown of artificial boundaries between art forms. He confronted the dilemmas created by the social and political crises of the thirties and beyond. He helped pave the way for the fusion of Eastern perspective and Western pragmatism that can be found in the poetry of the generation that followed him. In his poetry, he balanced aesthetics and politics, love and nature. Rexroth was also the first to speak with authority about the literary energy that seemed to burst forth in San Francisco during the mid-fifties. Although he might have loathed to hear it, he started out as any typical young American hero might, ready for adventure, anxious to prove that he was a man who could think for himself, indeed educate himself, and be fooled by absolutely no one. He developed the intellectual toughness to perceive the worst in American politics, but had the energy needed to endure it. He knew how to survive in the wilderness.

Rexroth assumed he had the right to try his hand at anything he chose, and produced as a result a collection of oils and watercolors that show talent, though a derivative one. If he wanted to translate from the Chinese, he did so, with the aid of self-designed flash cards to help him learn the characters, and some direct consultation with French translators and Chinese-speaking colleagues. Here is old-fashioned American ingenuity. He went from being a public ward of Chicago and a high school dropout to being a published poet, a recipient of prestigious literary awards, a newspaper columnist, and a widely read book reviewer. A street in San Francisco, formerly "Tracy Place," is now "Kenneth Rexroth Place." While in the eyes of the Federal Bureau of Investigation he was subversive and unpatriotic, he felt, for the majority of his life, most at home in the United States, as a good American in the tradition of Midwestern radicalism. Unfortunately, Rexroth built into this image a nasty level of sexism that went beyond the norm for the all-American hero.

Every so often, Rexroth would declare that the life he truly desired was the monastic one. His period of residence with the Brothers of the Holy Cross Monastery in West Park, New York, and Santa Barbara provided important although relatively brief respites from his often turbulent life, as did his extended visits to Japan, where the rituals of the meditative life were more significant for him. But the great delight he took in the beauty and harmony of the natural world, his love for his wives and daughters, his intense enjoyment of art, music, dance, and social discourse, and his interest in creating an international pacifist consciousness were bound to keep him in the throes of everyday life. He was a deeply contemplative man who immersed himself in both Western and Eastern philosophy and theology in his search—and a very intense search it was—for spiritual fulfillment. But he was too much in the world.

He resolved this conflict, as he did most nearly all the conflicts of his life, by writing verse. The style that emerged in his most successful volumes—*The Phoenix and the Tortoise, The Signature of All Things, In Defense of the Earth, Natural Numbers*—was one of direct statement and clear images, a poetry that with uncanny, breathtaking precision reproduces his observations of the physical world. Or to quote Jonathan Williams, "It's what really rings in your ear and stays in your head." Within the context of his art, Rexroth's perceptions exude accuracy—about love, loneliness, political commitment and disillusionment, hope, courage, despair, and transitory moments of revelation. However, the events of his life reveal that like many of us, he could not always get his head and his heart to work together. His poems as well as his translations, especially from the Chinese and Japanese, reveal a marvelous sensitivity about the struggle to do precisely that. If one consistent pattern ran through Kenneth Rexroth's life, it was that he was genuine in his poems the way he could not always be in his life. His vocation became his salvation.

ABBREVIATIONS

AAN	*An Autobiographical Novel*
AAN-II	Unpublished sequel to *An Autobiographical Novel*
APTC	*American Poetry in the Twentieth Century*
AS	*The Alternative Society*
AWW	*The Art of Worldly Wisdom*
BIB	*Bird in the Bush: Obvious Essays*
BM	*Beyond the Mountains*
CLP	*The Collected Longer Poems*
CR	*Classics Revisited*
CSP	*The Collected Shorter Poems*
D&U	*The Dragon and the Unicorn* (long poem and volume)
ER	*The Elastic Retort*
HCD	*The Homestead Called Damascus*
IDE	*In Defense of the Earth*
IWH	*In What Hour*
KR	Kenneth Rexroth
LH	Linda Hamalian
NN	*Natural Numbers*
P&T	*The Phoenix and the Tortoise* (long poem and volume)
SAT	*The Signature of All Things* (long poem and volume)
SP	*Selected Poems*
WEE	*With Eye and Ear*
WOW	*World Outside the Window: The Selected Essays of Kenneth Rexroth*

NOTES

One
THE EARLY YEARS 1905–1918

1. The 1906 South Bend City Directory spells the name "Rextroth."
2. Rexroth confirmed the facts of this special friendship in his March–April 1969 correspondence with Olive Carpenter, of the Northern Indiana Historical Society, UCLA.
3. In AAN, Rexroth says that the family moved to Franklin Street, but I found no listing in the Elkhart City Directory for this address. I suspect Rexroth means the house on Marion Street when he refers to the house on Franklin Street. Rexroth's editors at Doubleday insisted that in order to avoid lawsuits, he call his autobiography, which covers the years 1905–27, a "novel."
4. So he described her to poet Weldon Kees, August 20, 1940, UCLA.
5. AAN, p. 50.
6. Although Helen was to stay behind and marry a urologist named Milo Lundt, with whom she raised a son, and Kenneth was to spend the major part of his life in California, the two remained in touch for sixty-five years. "She is the lady," Rexroth wrote in that same letter to Weldon Kees, "of the long number on Sacco and Vanzetti—and the kitchen sink—August 22, 1939" and the Helen to whom "The New Year" is dedicated. Both poems appear in IWH. While on his poetry circuits

through the Midwest, Rexroth would visit the Lundts. When he was given the Indiana Authors Day Award at the Indiana University Writers Conference on April 20, 1969, the Lundts picked up the prize and brought it to him after he and Carol Tinker had moved to Santa Barbara.

7. See ANN, p. 51.
8. P&T, CSP, p. 158.
9. Founder of the Postum Cereal Company, Post had been a patient at the Battle Creek Sanatorium, founded by Seventh-Day Adventists who believed that the consumption of meat was the source of many illnesses. He recognized the sales potential of the cereal he had eaten, by J. H. Kellogg. When Post started a breakfast food company, W. H. Kellogg, Kellogg's brother, did the same, and so began the cornflakes business in the United States, with many small-time investors hoping for a share of the profits.
10. Rexroth's memory of his home as palatial is born out by a letter from a latter-day occupant, Marion McIntyre, dated July 7, 1971. After reading an excerpt from AAN in the local Battle Creek newspaper, Mrs. McIntyre wrote to Rexroth to say that although the house had been

painted white and converted into apartments, she knew the tall purple-brown Victorian mansion "could be none other than the house in which I now live. Each succeeding description, right down to the 'four-horse barn' and your mother's 'boudoir that seemed as big as a bowling alley,' confirmed this. You have been so true and accurate in your description as [sic] only someone actually living in this house could ever be"—UCLA

11. Kenneth nearly duplicated the event some sixty years later when he overturned his 1968 Dodge Dart in a Santa Barbara ditch (photographed on the front page of the *Santa Barbara News Press*).

12. Interview of KR by Lester Ferris, December 1, 1978 *Between Two Wars* (Athens, OH: Richard Bigus *Labyrinth Editions*, 1982). IN AAN, p. 6, Rexroth writes that his grandfather and Debs ate roast chicken and sipped straight whiskey from a quart bottle that each had beside him.

13. The Rexroths lived next door to the Posts and heard the shot from the hunting rifle that Post used to kill himself.

14. Susan Edmiston and Linda D. Cirino, *Literary New York: A History and*

Guide (Boston: Houghton Mifflin, 1976), pp. 60–61.

15. Ibid., pp. 55–57.

16. The book was not published until 1970, by Frontier Press. Rexroth believed that Berkman was "a typical political assassin, naive, isolated, and fanatical," and that his prison years "turned him into a man of exceptional maturity and wisdom," his memoirs "the record of a personal reformation quite the opposite of that expected by the prison system." Bradford Morrow made available a copy of Rexroth's essay on Berkman in manuscript.

17. From "Delia Rexroth," *Pacific*, II (April 1947); SAT, NN, CSP, p. 186.

18. New Directions Press published the *Selected Poems* by D. H. Lawrence with an introduction by Rexroth in 1947.

19. AAN, p. 89.

20. From "Gic to Har," *New Republic*, August 9, 1939; IWH, CLP, p. 108.

21. AAN, p. 95.

22. See "Portrait of the Author as a Young Anarchist," IDE, CSP, p. 298.

23. NN, *Norfolk Virginia Pilot* (January 5, 1964), *CSP*, p. 320.

24. AAN, p. 99.

25. AAN, p. 87.

Two

A PRECOCIOUS ADOLESCENCE 1919–1924

1. AAN, p. 102.

2. IDE, *Europe* (French translation, February–March, 1959), NN, CSP, p. 258.

3. IDE, CSP, p. 252.

4. Because draftees were needed by the U.S. Army in World War I, high school students were being required to undergo rudimentary military training as part of their physical education course.

5. *The WPA Guide to Illinois* (New York: Pantheon Books, 1984), p. 112.

6. Emmet Dedmon, *Fabulous Chicago* (New York: Random House, 1953), p. 206.

7. In an April 6, 1966, letter to Rexroth, Floyd Dell writes that in his memory Chicago remains a romantic place, UCLA.

8. AAN, p. 129.

9. When I was checking the Chicago City Directory for 1923, I found the following entry: "Loeb, Jacob M. Pres Eliel & Loeb Co., 1737 West Jackson Boulevard." Is "Eliel" here related to the same man who helped Charles Rexroth get started in the wholesale pharmaceuticals business?

10. AAN, p. 129.

11. In a letter to Rexroth on February

3, 1960, David Galler mentions a friend "who says that she knew you, and Larry Lipton to a lesser extent, many years ago in Chicago. I don't know Esther's maiden name; but she tells us that her father used to throw parties to which you would go on occasion. Without distorting it, I can say that she remembers you very warmly." UCLA.

12. See Lawrence's letter to Mrs. Bessie Freeman, August ?28, 1923, *The Collected Letters of D. H. Lawrence,* Vol. 2 (London: William Heinemann, 1962), p. 751.

13. It is on Walton Street, between Dearborn and Clark.

14. *The WPA Guide to Illinois,* p. 247.

15. AAN, p. 105.

16. At least two other people remember Rexroth being there. On January 10, 1949, a man named Edwin Upson from Ellis Avenue in Chicago wrote to Rexroth: "I am curious to know if you are the Mr. Rexroth who lived in Chicago during the 1920's and attended the Washington Park open forum, better known as the 'Bug Club.' " And one Arthur Kramer from Evansville, Wisconsin, asks on August 5, 1956, if Rexroth remembered him from the Dill Pickle days. Correspondence File, UCLA.

17. AAN, pp. 105–106.

18. Harvey Warren Zorbaugh, *The Gold Coast and the Slum* (Chicago: University of Chicago Press, 1929), p. 115.

19. Dale Kramer, *Chicago Renaissance* (New York: Appleton-Century, 1966), p. 334.

20. See AAN, pp. 135–136, for a colorful and vivid description of this man.

21. Kramer, p. 334.

22. Edmmet Dedman, *Fabulous Chicago* (New York: Random House, 1953), p. 282.

23. For a lively biography of Reitman, see Roger A. Bruns, *The Damndest Radical* (Champaign, IL: University of Illinois Press, 1987).

24. AAN, pp. 138–139.

25. January 20, 1953, letter to Lawrence Lipton. For further discussion of Lipton, see Chapter 4, note 6.

26. January 20, 1953, letter to Lawrence Lipton.

27. Kramer, p. 286.

28. Kenneth's enthusiasm for these poets, however, did not mean, as some critics might assume, that he was rejecting his father, who preferred the pastoral elegies of Francis Jammes. Both father and son gravitated toward Rainer Maria Rilke, a poet who celebrated the utter transience of the world, accepting life and death as a single holiness.

29. AAN, p. 146.

30. Kramer, p. 287.

31. AAN, p. 146.

32. The original Little Theater functioned in a fourth-floor room in the Fine Arts Building between 1912 and 1915, run by Ellen Van Volkenberg and Maurice Browne.

33. Another letter from Arthur Kramer dated August 5, 1967, from Evansville, Wisconsin, confirms Rexroth's presence in these spots: "It's many a year since the early 1920's, the Radical Bookshop, the Dill Pickle, etc. etc., and maybe you don't even remember me. However, I have seen your name cropping up here and there of late years—I've lately read some of your poetry (good stuff) and a couple of late reviews," UCLA.

34. Verifying Rexroth's IWW membership is tricky business. In a June 27, 1984, telephone conversation with me in Chicago, Fred Thompson, sawmill and construction worker who joined the IWW in 1922 and who co-authored *The I.W.W.: Its First Seventy Years,* said he did not know Kenneth Rexroth. He explained that the appearance of Rexroth's name on a membership list does not necessarily mean that name identified only one person. "There could be two Kenneth Rexroths," he observed. In 1917 the

Chicago offices of the IWW were raided and all records seized; the offices were raided and records seized again in 1925. The only way, said Mr. Thompson, to ascertain whether or not a person was a member of the IWW is if somebody knew that person's identity and revealed it.

35. Rexroth calls him Jimmy Feely and Willy McCauley in AAN, but in a January 20, 1953, letter to Lawrence Lipton, he refers to him as McKenzie. He tells Lipton in another letter he wrote five days earlier that McKenzie was still alive, living in Staten Island.

36. AAN, p. 169.

37. Rose (Kalish) Hecht wrote to Rexroth in 1966 to tell him how much she enjoyed An Autobiographical Novel, and how angry she was at the reviewer who referred to her husband as a forgotten writer.

38. "One night a skinny little boy came in with a whole mess of drums. For once we realized we had a great artist. It was Dick Rough [sic] the first and greatest of the hipsters and one of the few really great musicians in the history of jazz," AAN p. 163.

39. Putnam was also associate editor of Edward Titus's This Quarter Magazine, co-editor of European Caravan (New York: Brewer, Warren & Putnam, 1931), author of Paris Was Our Mistress (New York: Viking Press, 1947), and translator of Don Quixote.

40. AAN, p. 162.

41. See Rexroth's January 15, 1953, letter to Lawrence Lipton in which he reminisces about the Green Mask crowd. "It will never be again," he writes Lipton, "but it sure was good while it lasted."

42. Rexroth and Farrell did not meet until they were middle-aged. They began corresponding in the winter of 1948—initially over a political

action group called the "Writers Mobilization for Peace."

43. James Farrell, Young Lonigan (New York: Vanguard Press, 1932), p. 140.

44. Ibid., p. 142.

45. Ibid., p. 144.

46. Ibid., p. 146.

47. Ibid., p. 39.

48. In AAN, p. 155, Rexroth places this apartment on Calumet Avenue near 54th Street, which is very close to the Prairie Avenue apartment, listed as Rexroth's residence in Polk's 1923 City Directory.

49. Harvey Warren Zorbaugh, The Gold Coast and the Slum (Chicago: University of Chicago Press, 1929), p. 70.

50. AAN, p. 176.

51. AAN, p. 185.

52. AAN, p. 180.

53. Rexroth refers to this restaurant as "Schlogel's" in AAN, p. 181.

54. AAN, p. 185.

55. AAN, p. 180.

56. Thomas B. Littlewood, Horner of Illinois (Evanston, IL: Northwestern University Press, 1969), p. 37.

57. The last official document, an accounting of cash withdrawn from the estate, mostly to Minnie Monahan between 1921 and 1923, is dated January 4, 1927. This document is on file with the Chief Deputy Clerk, Probate Division, Cook County, Chicago.

58. I tried to confirm the dates of Rexroth's incarceration, but in a September 19, 1985, letter to me, Officer D. L. Earnest, Supervisor of the Old Records Department of the Cook County Department of Corrections, indicated that no records could be located for this time period. One explanation could be that Rexroth gave the authorities a pseudonym, J. Rand Talbot, the name Rexroth would use for literary purposes several years later.

Three
First Loves 1922–1924

1. AAN, p. 158.
2. AAN, p. 158.
3. AAN, p. 191.
4. AAN, p. 156. Rexroth claims that he developed a brief but passionate friendship with this teacher after she caught him reading Remy de Gourmont instead of conjugating irregular verbs.
5. It is possible that some of these poems are part of a mysterious, unpublished manuscript entitled "A Lantern and a Shadow," a collection of twenty-five poems that made a reappearance, so to speak, in 1967. The poems had been found by a woman named Marion Kravetz in Chicago among the papers of Max Kahn. Rexroth had known a man named Max Kahn in San Francisco, not Chicago, and had never met Marion Kravetz. In a brief flurry of correspondence, Rexroth on his way home from his trip around the world with his daughter Mary and Carol Tinker, expressed surprise that these poems, which Kravetz believed to date from the twenties, still existed. Bradford Morrow points out in "An Outline of Unpublished Manuscripts" (*Sagetrieb*, II, 3 [Winter 1983] that there is no way to confirm whether these poems—obviously juvenilia with themes that Rexroth would later take up—were written during the twenties or forty years afterward, since there are no known holographs to work against. The single handwritten correction, while clearly Rexroth's, could have been made at any time because his calligraphy did not vary with time.
6. Early versions of parts of this poem can be found in the file marked "Earliest Poems" in the Rexroth Archives at UCLA.
7. AAN, p. 199.
8. The entire poem first published in *The Phoenix and the Tortoise* under the title ". . . about the cool water"

also appeared in a volume called *Erotic Poetry*, edited by William Cole for Random House in 1963, the same year it was reprinted in *Natural Numbers*. See CSP, pp. 139–142.
9. AAN, p. 203.
10. Leslie Smith to KR, October 7, 1923, UCLA.
11. Leslie Smith to KR, October 12, 1923, UCLA.
12. CLP, p. 9.
13. Katherine Anne Porter also liked Romany Marie's, whose owner she described as a "swarthy, weathered, beautiful woman in early middle life," who wore four or five long and gaily colored ruffled skirts at a time and who was known to use her bare feet to extinguish cigarettes. See "Romany Marie, Joe Gould—Two Legends Come to Life," *Collected Essays* (New York: Delacorte, 1976).
14. Rexroth says it was located on the corner of Michigan and Ontario, but the letter he received from Leslie is addressed to Wrightwood Avenue.
15. Rexroth said that marijuana merely made him feel "sexier" than usual. He thought its reputed effects were "largely group induced hysteria." See AAN, p. 217. Of course, Rexroth may have been using stronger substances. Or he may have known just what stories would upset Leslie.
16. AAN, p. 214.
17. Nancy Banks, "The World's Most Beautiful Ballrooms," *Chicago History*, II, 4 (Fall–Winter 1973), p. 206.
18. In 1967, an earlier version of this poem surfaced in the already mentioned typescript of twenty-five poems entitled "A Lantern and a Shadow." This poem reveals Kenneth's precocity as a writer, even if the latter version, less sentimental and more concise, is clearly better. The development of his genius may be traced by comparing the untitled and very likely first complete ver-

sion of the poem as it appears in typescript, with its errors and typos, to the final version above:

I pass your home in a slow vermilion dawn,
the blinds are drawn and a window is open.
the subtle breeze from the lake is as your breath upon my cheek

All day long I walk in an intermittent rainfall,
I pluck a vermilion tulip in the city gardens
tasting the delicate raindrops that cling to its petals—
four o'clock and it is a lone clour in the city.   '

I pass your home in a rainy evening your figure is a fiant gesture amongst lighted walls.
Late into the night I sit before a hwite shee of paper—
till a wet vermilion quivers in my hand.

19. KR to Lawrence Lipton, January 1, 1953. Lipton Archives, UCLA.

20. In *AAN*, Rexroth gives Milly two persona: Milly Tokarsky, "an Armenoid Jew, a raving beauty ... [with a] personality which went with her appearance: a solemn, brooding sensitivity of a kind I had never seen before"; and Ruth, "a mathematics graduate student [who] knew a great deal more than most girls I had met up to that time."

21. Milly Tokarsky lived with her husband, the Sumerologist Samuel Kramer (d. 1990), in Philadelphia. Much of the discussion of Milly's friendship with Kenneth comes from an interview at her home, February 7, 1987.

22. AAN, p. 257.

23. CSP, p. 195. The poem could also be dedicated to Mildred Brock, a young woman Rexroth knew in the mid–forties.

24. A glance through his correspondence with Lawrence Lipton confirms this.

25. AWW, CSP, p. 36.

26. AAN, p. 136.

Four
THE RADICAL BOHEMIAN / THE TENTATIVE POSTULANT 1924–1926

1. Gary Snyder would occupy that same position some forty years afterward.

2. AAN, p. 282.

3. AAN, p. 291.

4. Rexroth refers to her as Doris in AAN. In an undated letter to Lawrence Lipton, he boasts that he "got her in a sort of package, along with two friends—Josephine Bennett who was the prima assaoluta and another girl—Marian Schillo who was plainer but brawnier and hotter." In his correspondence with Marion Kravetz, Rexroth refers to Marian Schillo as a high school friend. See Bradford Morrow, "An Outline of Unpublished Manuscripts," *Sagetrieb*, II, 3 (Winter 1983), p. 143.

5. In notes that Rexroth gave to Lawrence Lipton as Lipton was preparing his Introduction to *The Homestead* for its first version in Theodore and Renée Weiss's *Quarterly Review of Literature*, he says that Dorothy "figures in no way in the narrative of the poem." Lawrence Lipton Archives, UCLA.

6. Lawrence (née Isadore) Lipton is best remembered for his pioneer study of the Beat movement, *The Holy Barbarians* (New York: Julian Messner, 1959). He often refers to Rexroth to explain the philosophy behind the Beats, regarding him as a kind of absentee guru of the movement.

7. From "I Was a Poet for the F.B.I." in *Bruno in Venice West & Other Poems* (Van Nuys, CA: 1976), p. 54.

8. Carol Tinker revealed this in a

postcard she wrote to me, August 28, 1985.

9. CLP, p. 13, II, 7. In a March 8, 1957, letter to Lawrence Lipton, Rexroth writes: "That girl actually existed, still exists, but not a dancer, a musician." Lawrence Lipton Archives, UCLA

10. KR to Lipton, July 7, 1957.

11. Later in the forties, Angulo recorded a series of programs on folktales of the American Indians for KPFA in Berkeley, and in 1953 Hill & Wang published his *Indian Tales*.

12. Evidence suggests that their discussion about Chinese poetry did occur at this time. In a review of Elsa Gidlow's *Sapphic Songs* for the January–February 1978 issue of the *American Poetry Review*, Rexroth mentions that he met Bynner the same time that he met Gidlow, shortly before she left *Pearson's* magazine in New York City. In an interview with me at her home in Muir Woods, Marin County, California, August 13, 1984, Gidlow says that she left *Pearson's* in 1925, so that in the fall of 1924, Rexroth would have had the opportunity to meet both Gidlow in New York City (when he was living in the Dominic Street commune) and Bynner in Santa Fe. However, Gidlow could not remember meeting Rexroth in New York.

13. George N. Caylor to KR, July 7, 1967, UCLA.

14. Rexroth has an amusing account of this ruse in AAN, pp. 324–325.

15. In her interview with me, Milly Tokarsky remembered that Rexroth had lived in a similarly decorated room when she knew him.

16. Sherry (McKenzie) Abel related this to me in a telephone conversation, June 6, 1987.

17. This man turned out to be Arnold Gingrich, who later founded *Esquire*. Rexroth would see Gingrich again in his New York City office many years later.

18. Edmiston and Cirino, *Literary New York*, pp. 108–109, and 73.

19. AAN, p. 332.

20. "Protoplasm of Light," *The Lights in the Sky Are Stars*, IDE, CSP, p. 241. The Bronx is also the setting for "3 Local Men Vanquish Monster in Fight," a section of "Phronesis," Rexroth's spoof on *The Waste Land*, particularly on Eliot's use of myth and his willingness to follow Pound's advice that he burn his transitional bridges: "Draw up a chair / boys it's warmer over here. The neoplatonists / like servants of the Fisher King bear past a flame enveloped object. Does anybody know what it is?" See p. 42, CSP. The title of this poem, which swings from journalistic prose to surrealistic imagery, seems to be derived from *phronimos*, meaning "sane" or "sensible" in Greek. Rexroth continues to express his antipathy to Eliot in "Easy Lessons in Geography," which he dedicates to his onetime neighbor Hart Crane, and the publisher of Black Sun Press, Harry Crosby, whose wife, Caresse, Rexroth would get to know rather well in Europe in 1948–49.

21. Florence Becker Lerner, who was to become a Lewis Carroll scholar, and who would run a weekly poetry program over WEVD in New York during the fifties, remembered that party well: it coincided with the night she married Sam Becker, who got very sick afterwards from drinking too much cheap wine. See Florence Becker Lerner to KR, October 23, 1957, UCLA.

22. Rexroth recalled this meeting in an undated letter to Laughlin. He was under the impression that Midner had been in and out of psychiatric hospitals, but wanted Laughlin to tell Djuna Barnes (with whom Rexroth claims to have spent an uproarious two nights in bed) that Midner had resurfaced and was cured.

23. AAN, p. 334.

24. These include the evening party that

the two chief characters, Sebastian and Thomas, attend with their friend Leslie; and Sebastian's trip to New York City, across the bridge (no longer functioning) about a mile south of the Vanderbilt mansion. The tower that Thomas climbs could be the one recently completed at the monastery in 1922. And the panthers in the crocus, the Doric columns, and privet gardens that appear in the poem could have sprung from a mansion upstream which is now the property of the Marist Brothers.

25. The cabin is still there and can be visited by first writing to the John Burroughs Nature Sanctuary Memorial Association.

26. AAN, p. 337.

27. AAN, p. 339.

28. AAN, p. 342.

29. AAN, p. 343.

30. Rexroth made a gift of this poem to Bradford Morrow in the mid-seventies. In AAN, p. 149, Rexroth said his first poem was published in Steen Heindriksen's small magazine *The Wave*, but he did not remember the title, nor whether he gave his real name as author.

31. Kep Thorpe sent a copy of the St. John the Beloved poem which he "found in an old envelope of odds and ends" in 1979. He also sent Rexroth a poem, "Greyhound Chicago South," which he hoped Rexroth would help him publish. Thorpe to KR, June 25, 1979, UCLA.

32. The Thorpes eventually returned to Nashville.

33. Andrée actually had more than one name, probably because she was a member of the Communist Party. In more than one place, she is referred to as Andrée Dutcher and Myrtle Schafer.

34. AAN, p. 347.

35. Most of this information was gleaned from a biographical account that Andrée herself gave to the writers for the Federal Art Project, San Francisco. It is at the Ryerson and Burnham Libraries of the Art Institute of Chicago, under the call number "California Art Research, Series 1."

36. "Andrée Rexroth," P&T, CSP, p. 154.

37. AAN, p. 351.

Five

A Promising Future 1927–1929

1. However, Monroe asked Rexroth if she could publish excerpts of the 1931 letter that Rexroth had sent along with the poem, UCLA.

2. In a January 1, 1953, to Lawrence Lipton, Rexroth reminisces about his Chicago friends and talks about plans of compiling a kind of Spoon River anthology of Chicago 1920–27, with a few additional characters from the Far West of those days: "In a sense it will be my autobiography. What a cast!" Apparently those plans never came to fruition. Lipton Collection, UCLA.

3. AAN, p. 362.

4. Rexroth thought as recently as 1975 that "strangers"—blacks and Asians—were still unwelcome in Del Norte, Siskiyou, and Modoc counties.

5. AAN, p. 364.

6. Her work also appeared in such magazines as *Pearson's*, *Emerson Quarterly*, *New Masses*, *The Liberator*. Her *Sapphic Songs, Seventeen to Seventy* appeared in 1978 and was very favorably reviewed by Rexroth in *The American Poetry Review*.

7. AAN-II.

8. She estimates the year as 1932, but in her interview with me (Muir Wood, CA., Aug. 13, 1984) she marks the meeting as 1927, which sounds far more likely. See "Random Memories of a Many-Faceted

Friend," *Ark*, Geoffrey Gardner, ed. (1980), p. 38.

9. Gidlow interview.

10. "Random Memories of a Many-Faceted Friend," p. 38.

11. Ibid.

12. Charles Erskine Scott Wood had undergone his conversion by this time. A graduate of West Point who had participated in several campaigns to exterminate Native Americans, he changed his perspective when he married the feminist poet Sara Bard Field. During World War I he wrote for *The Masses*. See *Literary San Francisco*, edited by Lawrence Ferlinghetti and Nancy J. Peters (New York: Harper & Row, 1980), p. 139.

13. *Elsa: I Come with My Songs* (San Francisco: Bootlegger Press & Druid Heights Books, 1986), p. 203.

14. Ibid.

15. In an undated, antagonistic letter to writer / critic Rolfe Humphries, who served as poetry editor for *New Masses* and who had once called him "a provincial," Rexroth asserts that he always got along fine with Sara Field. So Gidlow apparently did take the Rexroths along to Field's "Los Gatos and other places." Humphries would later in *The New Republic* attack Rexroth's *In What Hour* as excessively abstract. In *Excerpts from a Life* (Santa Barbara, CA: A Conjunctions Book, 1981), p. 25, Rexroth obliquely refers to Humphries as a "Stalinist hatchet man," a term Rexroth would apply to other people he did not like.

16. Built in 1852, this building is reputed to have been home for more than two thousand writers and artists. Originally, the marble-floored chandeliered saloons and restaurants on the ground floor made it popular with reporters and mining investors. By the end of the nineteenth century, the neighborhood had changed and smaller businesses, banks, tailors, Chinese herb dealers, and attorneys had taken over. The avant-garde of the Bay Area patronized the Monkey Block restaurant known as Coppa's, where local artists and writers had covered the walls with grafitti and murals. It was one of the few buildings to survive the San Francisco earthquake of 1906. For a fuller history, see *Literary San Francisco*, p. 96.

17. See Hayden Herrera, *Frida* (New York: Harper & Row, 1983), pp. 116–120, for an interesting discussion of Rivera and Kahlo's stay in San Francisco.

18. Rexroth scribbled this observation in a rough draft of a letter to Louis Zukofsky, UCLA.

19. Porter Chaffee letter to LH, July 17, 1986. Both Chaffee and Rexroth later became editors on the Federal Writers' Project.

20. In an August 7, 1984, interview with me, Frank Triest, Rexroth's long-time friend, confirmed that the two did work on the same canvas.

21. This statement is excerpted from a three-page letter written in pencil, addressee unknown, n.d., box 14, UCLA.

22. AAN-II.

23. Rexroth played an active role in preventing United States Route 101 from going through the city.

24. "Andrée Rexroth," P&T, CSP, pp. 191–192.

25. Rexroth, after describing him as perhaps the most remarkable man in California, referred to him (in his November 24, 1967, broadcast on KPFA) as "Little Leo Eleosser who lived into his nineties, the last years in a remote area of Mexico." He was one of the few doctors Frida Kahlo trusted and she painted a portrait of him that captures the intensity of his personality. See pp. 120–122 of Herrera's *Frida* for a full description of Eleosser and his relationship with Kahlo and Rivera. The Rexroths counted Eleosser and their Montgomery Block neighbor Ralph Stackpole among the few people of the older generation who connected them to a cosmopolitan world.

26. KPFA broadcast, November 24, 1967.
27. AAN-II.
28. AAN-II.
29. Rexroth held a significant place beside other poets who appeared in *Blues*—including H.D., William Carlos Williams, Horace Gregory, and Parker Tyler. Eugene Jolas, editor of *transition*, contributed to these issues of *Blues*, as did James Farrell, Gertrude Stein, and Harry Crosby. Like Ford, William Carlos Williams valued Rexroth's contributions, and was not offended by Rexroth's view that he should have given a better explanation of what was wrong with conservative, academic verse. See Paul Mariani's *William Carlos Williams* (New York: McGraw-Hill, 1981), pp. 289–292, for a detailed discussion.
30. Ford to Rexroth, April 25, 1929, UCLA.
31. See his June 15, 1929, letter to Rexroth, UCLA.
32. Ford to Rexroth, April 25, 1929, UCLA.
33. Ford to Rexroth, June 15, 1929, UCLA.
34. So reports Ford in a December 10, 1929, letter to Rexroth, UCLA.
35. Undated fragment to Ford, UCLA.
36. Rexroth to Ford, May 20, 1929. *Action Française* was initially a republican anti-Dreyfusard group that launched a newspaper (1908–44) to promote the restoration of a strong, hereditary French monarchy, to save France from a century of decay caused by the bureaucratic centralization of the Republic and "immigrant" infiltrations. Winters did not identify with this group.
37. Later on, Rexroth declared that Stein had a commonplace mind and that "a great deal of her writing was covert lesbian humor," AAN-II.
38. He reported this to Malcolm Cowley in an undated letter (see Cowley Papers, Newberry Library). He had also apprised Ford of this proposed perspective.
39. During World War II, Ford and Tyler devoted themselves to Surrealist theory and discovered many American Surrealist painters and poets. With Philip Lamantia as their associate editor (his first volume of verse, *Erotic Poems*, published by Bern Porter in 1946, contains an introduction by Kenneth Rexroth), they ran the magazine *View*. Ten years later, when Rexroth was living in Vicenza, he resumed a brief correspondence with Ford.
40. Rexroth to Ford, n.d., UCLA.
41. Janet Lewis described this visit to me in a July 6, 1985, letter. I also interviewed her at her home in Los Altos on August 15, 1984.
42. Lewis interview.
43. Winters expressed this opinion in a postcard (n.d., early forties likely) to KR. Lewis learned of Rexroth's collection in 1984 when Stanford University held a commemorative exhibition of her work and her husband's entitled "Poets and Poetry in Lives of Yvor Winters and Janet Lewis." Winters himself had banished the poems into obscurity until 1968, when he published *The Early Poems of Yvor Winters*. In the brochure that describes the exhibit, Rexroth is quoted as terming Lewis a poet who "uses reason to veil and adorn the flesh of feeling and intuition," a method he ascribes to "the great poets."
44. Jackson did publish a poem of Rexroth's, "Education," in *Continent's End: A Collection of California Writing* (New York: Whittlesey House, 1944), p. 73.
45. Delarney and Brown are pseudonyms.
46. The exact circumstances of his first meeting with Rexroth are unclear. In a May 20, 1929, letter to Charles Henri Ford, Rexroth writes that he was recently in Seattle "for about three weeks visiting Kliorin (whom I had never met)." He reports Kliorin has been expelled from the university because "one of Marx's wiskers [sic] was found on his lapel." However, in another version

of their first meeting (AAN-II), San Francisco poet Ben Hamilton, then a student at the University of Washington, sent Kliorin to the Rexroths after they agreed to put him up for a short time in their studio while he looked for his own place.

Six
SANTA MONICA RESPITE, New York Journey 1929–1931

1. CLP, p. 261.
2. In AAN-II, Rexroth says that he thinks they have all disappeared except one or two owned by Joseph Rabinowitch. See Rabinowitch to Rexroth, November 7, 1931. According to the brief biography of Andrée published in the California Art Research Series under the Federal Writers' Project, Rabinowitch owned three of her oil paintings. There is no indication in this pamphlet, on file at the Ryerson and Burnham Libraries of the Chicago Art Institute, that Kenneth helped her with these particular paintings.
3. AAN-II.
4. In a January 29, 1932, entry in his diary, Weston mentions that Rexroth is writing about him. See Nancy Newhall, ed., *The Daybooks of Edward Weston*, Vol. II (New York: Aperture, 1973), p. 240. Rexroth owned several Weston photographs.
5. AAN-II.
6. AAN-II.
7. AAN-II. Rexroth mistakenly reports that he and Andrée saw Yvor Winters and Janet Lewis in Pasadena during this time. According to Rexroth, he told Winters that Crane was homosexual and a violently abusive drunk. Winters, anticipating his first meeting with the poet whose work he admired greatly, became so outraged by Kenneth's remarks that he asked Kenneth and Andrée to leave even though they had been invited to dinner. Two weeks later, Janet Lewis called to apologize and reinvite them. When Rexroth asked how their meeting went with Crane, Winters replied that Crane was a vagrant. Lewis says this episode is entirely invented, and

that they only saw Rexroth in the Bay Area. "My husband did not need any advice from Rexroth on Crane and he did not order R. off the premises. I did not ever phone to apologize for any action of my husband" (July 6, 1985, letter to LH). Rexroth also liked to tell a story about how a young lamb that Winters was raising made a scene at dinner by jumping from the table where Winters was showing him off to the bookcase to a chair to the floor, "whereupon it squatted to piss. Winters, his face frozen with embarrassment, tackled it around the shoulders and rushed out with it still spouting piss" (*Excerpts from a Life*, p. 19).
8. CSP, p. 120.
9. He wrote these remarks to Louis Zukofsky on March 10, 1931.
10. AAN, p. 105.
11. AAN-II.
12. CLP, p. 3.
13. CLP, p. 17.
14. Triest interview, August 11, 1984, Woodacre, California.
15. AAN-II.
16. Daniel Aaron, *Writers on the Left* (New York: Harcourt, Brace & World, 1961), p. 214. Aaron also spells out Gold's objectives for *New Masses* on pp. 208–209.
17. Rexroth says that as a boy he met Reed but did not like him, although he had "certain breezy characteristics that I did enjoy because it always shocked Eastern Left intellectuals. They say that at the First World Congress of the Comintern, he kept hitching up his pants and just absolutely horrified Lenin." See *Excerpts from a Life*, p. 29.
18. AAN-II.
19. Nancy Lynn Schwartz, *The Holly-*

wood Writers' Wars (New York: Knopf, 1982), p. 40.
20. *Compass,* II (February 1940); IWH, CSP, p. 89.
21. AAN-II.

22. AAN-II.
23. AAN-II. A Dymaxion house is factory-assembled, air-deliverable, and contains its own utilities.

Seven
EARLY DEPRESSION DAYS 1931–1933

1. For more information about Zeitlin, see Lawrence Clark Powell's *California Classics.* Zeitlin, who resembles a graying Picasso, was running a bookstore on North Cienega Boulevard in Los Angeles as recently as 1983.
2. Andrée Rexroth to Jake Zeitlin, UCLA.
3. KR to Jake Zeitlin, UCLA, May 21, 1948.
4. Joe Rabinowitch to KR, UCLA, n.d.
5. Joe Rabinowitch to KR, November 22, 1931, UCLA.
6. Rexroth thought it was Andrée's canvas that he saw in Stockholm in 1966. See AAN-II.
7. AAN-II.
8. As further evidence of Andrée's extraordinary intelligence, Rexroth said the Andrée also beat Marcel Duchamp at chess in the home of Walter H. Annenberg, the philanthropist and art collector who served as Ambassador to Great Britain and Ireland. In a conversation we had in my home in the spring of 1986, Mariana Rexroth said that she had seen photographs of Andrée sitting on Duchamp's lap.
9. AAN-II.
10. See "A Public Letter for William Carlos Williams' Seventy-fifth Birthday," *Assays,* pp. 202–205.
11. Paul Mariani, *William Carlos Williams: A New World Naked* (New York: McGraw-Hill, 1981), p. 314.
12. Ferren to KR, UCLA.
13. AAN-II.
14. AAN-II.
15. AAN-II.
16. AAN-II.
17. AAN-II.
18. Freeman became increasingly conflicted over these often bitter struggles to control the Reed movement, which he described in his autobiography *An American Testament: A Narrative of Rebels and Romantics* (New York: Farrar & Rinehart, 1936).
19. KR to Malcolm Cowley, n.d., Newberry Library.
20. Aaron, *Writers on the Left,* p. 227.
21. Interview with Frank Triest, August 7, 1984, San Francisco.
22. His unsuccessful attempt to secure a steady assignment from editors of *The Fortnightly,* a little magazine that operated out of a North Beach cottage, was fairly typical. Willis Foster, one of the editors, told him that their orientation was not avant-garde, was "mostly concerned with the established symphonies, opera, art, and books," and that they did not pay for contributions. Willis Foster letter to LH, June 4, 1989.
23. KR to Louis Zukofsky, November 20, 1930, UCLA.
24. KR to Zukofsky, n.d., UCLA.
25. KR to Zukofsky, December 25, 1930, UCLA.
26. Harriet Monroe to KR, UCLA. Twenty-four years later, *Poetry's* editor Henry Rago asked Rexroth (April 8, 1955) if he would do a 1,200-to 1,500-word article on West Coast writing and publishing. Rexroth replied with a nasty attack on Rago and his colleagues as "squares [who] just don't want to know what the younger generation is doing or won't face the evidence" (April 13). And yet he was willing to do the article, provided there would be no editorial cuts, and in spite of his opinion that no one did less for the Chicago Renaissance than Harriet Monroe—"in fact I think USA let-

ters would be much better off had she and her magazine never existed." Conceding that he had not been attacked personally, Rago wrote (April 25) that he was still eager to read Rexroth's article, but could not promise to accept it without editing. At that point, Rexroth precipitously cut off communication.

27. See Rexroth's Introduction to *The New British Poets*, (New York: New Directions, 1949), p. viii.

28. See Zukofsky's Preface to *An "Objectivists" Anthology* (Le Beusset, Var, France: TO, 1932). Michael Heller's *Conviction's Net of Branches: Essays on the Objectivist Poets and Poetry* (Carbondale: Southern Illinois University Press, 1985) is essential for understanding Objectivist poetry.

29. See Zukofsky, *Prepositions: The Collected Critical Essays of Louis Zukofsky, Expanded Edition* (Berkeley and Los Angeles: University of California Press, 1981). Also see Zukofsky's"—'Her Soil's Birth'" in *An "Objectivists" Anthology*, p. 182, for a clear and accessible example.

30. *American Poetry in the Twentieth Century* (New York: Herder & Herder, 1971), p. 111. See also KR to Babette Deutsch, January 26, 1949, Special Collections, Washington University Libraries.

31. Interview, August 8, 1984, in Rakosi's Irving Street apartment in San Francisco. Rakosi called his brief encounters with Rexroth "nonmeetings." Rexroth had told several people that Rakosi was a Hungarian Stalinist agent, his way of explaining the twenty-year hiatus in Rakosi's writing career. In 1973, they both participated in a National Poetry Conference in Ann Arbor, Michigan, honoring Zukofsky. Suffering from a bad back and in a vile mood, Rexroth had shown up a day late. He stormed into the conference dining room and cried, "They can't do this to me." Without saying hello, he walked by the table where Mary and George Oppen, Robert Duncan, Leah and Carl Rakosi were sitting. He was irritated that he had been given a bunk in student quarters, like everyone else. During the conference he kept to himself and the students.

32. Rexroth also claims that the publisher, George Decker, was murdered. Decker outlived Rexroth.

33. CSP, p. 45.

34. CLP, p. 54.

35. KR to Babette Deutsch, January 26, 1949. In *Poetry in Our Time* (New York: Henry Holt, 1952), Deutsch briefly discusses Rexroth's early Objectivist poetry—see pp. 91–92. She prefers Rexroth's mature work, which adopts a style "that answers the imagists' call for palpable definiteness of statement and deep truth of feeling. . . . His slowly moving, considered, heavily weighted verse is more disciplined than that of Lawrence, more nostalgic than that of Williams, and has a larger literary allusiveness than either found acceptable."

36. AAN-II.

37. KR to Babette Deutsch, January 26, 1949.

38. Pound to KR, August 20, 1931, UCLA.

39. Robert McAlmon to KR, October 5, 1931, UCLA.

40. Brita Lindberg-Seyersted, ed., *Pound / Ford: The Story of a Literary Friendship* (New York: New Directions), p. 93.

41. Williams to KR, ?August, 1931.

42. KR to Zukofsky, March 10, 1931, UCLA.

43. KR to Zukofsky, March 10, 1931, UCLA.

Eight
CRUMBLING INSTITUTIONS, 1933–1936

1. This information is contained in the FBI file on Rexroth's application to become a CO.
2. See Masha Zakheim Jewett, *Coit Tower San Francisco* (San Francisco: Volcano Press, 1983), for the history and background of the Public Works Art Project.
3. Shirley Staschen Triest to LH, interview, August 11, 1984, Woodacre, California.
4. Interview of KR by Les Ferris, Santa Barbara, December 1, 1978, in *Between Two Wars*, n.p.
5. Rexroth identified many of the figures for Masha Zakheim Jewett while she was writing *Coit Tower*. See p. 82 there.
6. *San Francisco: The Bay and Its Cities* (New York: Hastings House, 1940).
7. See Houston Peterson, *The Melody of Chaos* (New York: Longman, Green & Co., 1931).
8. She is best known for her study *The English Novel: Form and Function* (New York: Rinehart & Company, 1953). She also taught at SUNY, Buffalo.
9. AAN-II. Rexroth claimed that Roger Van Ghent was actually a dockworker from Antwerp. The birth certificate of his son indicates that, in San Francisco, Van Ghent was a book salesman.
10. She also wrote about Gertrude Stein and Laura Riding.
11. Interview with Frank and Shirley Triest, August 11, 1984, Woodacre, California.
12. Rexroth regarded Hagedorn as one of the finest draftsmen he had ever known, producing work that was "completely original, representational Surrealism" (AAN-II). Hagedorn stopped speaking to Rexroth after Rexroth sent photographs of his paintings to Eugene Jolas to be reproduced in *transition*, the monthly literary magazine for experimental writing that Jolas and Elliot Paul ran for ten years in Paris. Works by Gertrude Stein, e.e. cummings, Ernest Hemingway, Hart Crane, and James Joyce appeared on its pages. Rexroth and Hagedorn were reconciled in 1952 after Peregrine Press published *Fourteen Poems,* Rexroth's translations of O. V. de L. Milosz, with illustrations by Edward Hagedorn. In *Common Soldiers* (San Francisco: Archer, 19779), p. 312, Janet Richards reports that Hagedorn had rejected Rexroth for many years and that when *An Autobiographical Novel* appeared, he "declared it to be a fabrication from start to finish—without having read it."
13. Correspondence of May 15, 1944 (?), and January 29, 1950, from her indicates that she provided helpful criticism for Rexroth's collection of plays, *Beyond the Mountains* (1951). She is a main character in Susan Sherman's *Give Me Myself* and in John Aldridge's *Party at Cranford.* Van Ghent died in Rome on January 18, 1967.
14. This magazine, entitled *Material Gathered on Federal Writers Project,* is on file at UCLA.
15. Through its ominous ambiance and heavily stressed syllables, the poem entitled "The Crisis" reflects Rexroth's despair over the current political scene. It appears in AWW, p. 94, dedicated to Dorothy Van Ghent. In CSP, p. 62, it is Part I of a five-part poem.
16. Rexroth also claims in his contributor's note that at the age of fifteen he was writing for *Industrial Society.*
17. September 30, 1940, statement to the Fellowship of Reconciliation. Frank Triest said Rexroth played an active role in organizing this union, but he never liked to attend the meetings. Interview, January 18, 1987, Hayes Street, San Francisco.
18. Ferris / Rexroth interview, *Between Two Wars.*
19. IWH, CSP, p. 84. It also appeared

in *New Masses* on August 3, 1937.

20. *Material Gathered on Federal Writers Project*, p. 56, UCLA.
21. *Material Gathered on Federal Writers Project*, p. 57, UCLA.
22. *WPA Guide to California* (New York: Pantheon, 1984), p. xxii.
23. KR: Kees, n.d., UCLA.
24. These manuscripts are on file at UCLA.
25. This information is contained in a personnel security investigation on Harry S. Westfall. I received this document under my Freedom of Information Act request #255,870.
26. Ferris / Rexroth interview, *Between Two Wars*.
27. *Camping in the Western Mountains*, p. 74, UCLA.
28. Aaron, *Writers on the Left*, p. 307.
29. On file at UCLA. First published in 1986 in *World Outside the Window*.
30. See Rahv's October 6, 1936, letter to KR. In June 1936, Rahv had published Rexroth's "Remember now there were others before this," a strident poem prompted by the dangers of institutionalized governmental repression. Initially a response to Stalin's purges, it would be entitled "from the Paris Commune to the Kronstadt Rebellion" when it appeared later in IWH.
31. Yvor Winters: KR, September 12, 1936, UCLA.
32. KR: Winters, UCLA, n.d.
33. Nancy Lynn Schwartz, *The Hollywood Writers' War*, p. 117.
34. AAN-II.
35. AAN-II.
36. AAN-II.
37. Gidlow interview, August 13, 1984.

Nine
POTRERO HILL 1936–1939

1. AAN-II.
2. AAN-II.
3. AAN-II.
4. Rexroth was not the only person filled with memorable stories about Marie. Nearly everyone who knew her liked to reminisce about her warm, off-beat personality. Her serious, wide-eyed curiosity sometimes made her the butt of jokes. Her friends liked to talk about the time Kenneth sent her out to get a nail set. After three hours she came back and said, "I've been to every hardware store in San Francisco, but not one has a full set of nails."
5. Some of the children who attended this camp became part of San Francisco's social and cultural elite, among them former San Francisco mayor Diane Feinstein, and Sanford Burstein, the noted psychiatrist and Lewis Carroll bibliophile who is married to Elizabeth Burstein, once an intimate of Rexroth's.
6. AAN-II.
7. AAN-II.
8. "Love Sacred and Profane: The Erotic Lyrics of Kenneth Rexroth," *Sagetrieb* (Winter 1983), pp. 108–109.
9. P&T, CSP, p. 149.
10. P&T, CSP, p. 144.
11. AAN-II.
12. Interview with Michael Baranchek, aired on KPFA, Berkeley, and KCRW, August 12, 1983. Marie credited her Socialist father and her European background for her liberated attitude.
13. Like Rexroth, Saroyan respected Winters greatly and had sent him a poem about a Brancusi sculpture for *The Hound and Horn*, on whose editorial staff he served. Although Winters did not accept the poem, he encouraged Saroyan to keep writing and suggested that he get in touch with Rexroth. Long after Rexroth left, Potrero Hill continued to attract writers and artists. Lawrence Ferlinghetti moved to Wisconsin Street in 1958, and until 1972 writers like Jack Kerouac, Neal

Cassady, Allen Ginsberg, Peter Orlovsky, Gary Snyder, and Michael
McClure used to stop by.

14. IWH, CSP p. 106.
15. This information comes from
E. Graydon Carter, "James Laughlin of New Directions," *Avenue* (December–January 1985), pp. 134–
147.
16. "An Interview with Kenneth
Rexroth," conducted by Bradford
Morrow, *Conjunctions, 1* (1981), p.
49.
17. "Inhale and Exhale: A Letter from
Bill," *William Saroyan: The Man and
the Writer Remembered*, edited by Leo
Hamaliam (Cranbury, N.J.: Associated Universities Press, 1987), p.
220.
18. Letter from Aram Saroyan to LH,
n.d.
19. Saroyan sent Rexroth a copy of his
July 11, 1958, letter to Freed, UCLA.
20. Laura Riding to KR, May 24, 1936,
UCLA.
21. In Paris with his wife Caresse Crosby,
Harry Crosby ran the Black Sun
Press, which published D. H. Lawrence, James Joyce, Kay Boyle, and
Hart Crane.
22. James Laughlin to LH, interview,
January 19, 1986, Norfolk.
23. KR to James Laughlin, n.d.
24. James Laughlin to Richard Zieg-
field, July 19–20, 1982, interview,
*Writers at Work: The Paris Review In-
terviews* (New York: The Viking
Press, 1988), p. 172.
25. The remains of the hut, located in
what is now officially called Samuel
P. Taylor State Park, are the focus
of the *Samuel P. Taylor State Park
Cultural Resource Inventory* written by
Frances Miller, archeological specialist, in June 1987. It is on file with
the California Department of Parks
and Recreation in Santa Rosa, CA.
    Elsa Gidlow and her friend Vee
borrowed this same car to look for
land in Marin County. Gidlow had
inherited $800 worth of stock from
her former lover Tommy. She felt
uncomfortable about owning stocks,
and thought investment in land

would suit her better. Although she
didn't find anything with Vee, in
1940 she bought her own place in
Fairfax, Marin County, "a huddle
of wood that no one else would consider house," on a steep and beautiful hillside, the site of several
abandoned summer cabins. See *Elsa:
I Come with My Songs*, p. 289. In 1956
she found another home, two miles
from the Pacific Ocean, which she
named "Druid Heights." She transformed the site into a lush, green
dwelling place, and "unintentional
community" that became home to
many artists, including Alan Watts
and Jano Watts. See Abigail Hem-
street's Foreword to Gidlow's *Sapphic
Songs* (Mill Valley, CA.: Druid
Heights Books, 1982).
26. James Laughlin to LH, interview,
January 19, 1986.
27. Books that discuss Malraux's tour
are Pierre Galante, *Malraux*, trans.
Haakon Chevalier (New York:
Cowles Book Co., 1971), pp. 115–
117; and Jean Lecouture, *André
Malraux*, trans. Alan Sheridan (New
York: Pantheon, 1975), pp. 267–
270.
28. Frank Triest confirmed this in an
August 20, 1986, letter to me: "most
of Kenneth's 'so-called' stories were
factual. (Believe it or not)."
    In "Why Is American Poetry
Culturally Deprived?" Rexroth reports that shortly after the war, in a
conversation about the role of the
intellectual in contemporary literature, Malraux told him that "Orass
Mikwa" was the most significant
writer in the United States. After
some thought, Rexroth figured out
that Malraux was referring to "the
semi-literate pulp magazine writer
of the blood-on-the-bikini school,
Horace McCoy." See AS, p. 50. This
essay was reprinted in WOW, pp.
209–217.
29. Baranchek interview.
30. Marie Rexroth: KR, n.d., UCLA
31. Gidlow interview.
32. A final decree was entered on April
29, 1938.

33. See his "Literary Argument," *New Republic*, November 11, 1940, for a more detailed discussion.
34. Robert McAlmon to KR, n.d., pp. 663–664, UCLA.
35. Secker & Warburg first published McAlmon's autobiography in 1938. The University of Nebraska reprinted it in 1962. Kay Boyle extended it by adding interchapters based on her own memoirs. Doubleday published the revised version in 1968.
36. See Rexroth's review of Robert Knoll's *McAlmon and the Lost Generation*, reprinted in WEE, pp. 180–184, for more of Rexroth's often blunt impressions of McAlmon.
37. Marie Rexroth to KR, n.d., UCLA.
38. See Zukofsky's January 4, 1936, letter to Rexroth, UCLA.
39. Rexroth had no remarks or grades for another story entitled "Lee Wah," about a lonely, stoical forty-year-old man who has been hospitalized for arthritis. Rexroth's one short story, "Vivienne Renaud," was published posthumously in *Conjunctions*, (Spring–Summer 1982).
40. There is a discrepancy with dates here. In the unpublished second part of his autobiography, Rexroth states that "at the time of Munich" he quit his WPA job to work as a psychiatric orderly. However, in a letter to the San Francisco draft board, Rexroth states that as of December 11, 1942, he would be employed as a psychiatric orderly.
41. "Memorandum submitted to Local Board 77 at hearing December 18, 1942," FBI file.
42. AAN-II.
43. AAN-II.
44. AAN-II.
45. This poem was translated into German and published in *Das Lot* (March 1948), p. 74. In a July 7, 1986, letter to me, John Montgomery wrote that the woman in the poem was an eighteen-year-old blond student at Berkeley named Louise Lude. She and Kenneth remained strangers to one another.

Ten
SUBVERTING THE WAR EFFORT 1939–1942

1. *The New Republic*, October 4, 1939, pp. 245–246.
2. *The New Republic*, October 11, 1939, p. 73.
3. In February 1988, Soviet officialdom rehabilitated his reputation.
4. Broun had also been very active organizing the New York Newspaper Guild, and had been among the early protesters against German fascism.
5. By 1943 he had won critical praise for his poems and short stories appearing in *The New Yorker, Partisan Review*, and *Harper's*. During World War II, encouraged by this success, Kees moved to New York, where he worked as a critic for *Time* magazine, a writer for Paramount newsreels, and art critic for *The Nation*. He wrote several novels that were never published. In addition to four one-man shows of paintings at the Peridot Gallery, he exhibited with rising abstract expressionists such as Hans Hoffman and William de Kooning. After moving in 1947 to San Francisco, he became involved in composing and playing jazz, and with Michael Grieg organized *Poets' Follies*, a literary burlesque. On July 18, 1955, his car was found abandoned at the Golden Gate Bridge and he was never seen again.
6. The review appeared in *Prairie Schooner*, 12 (Spring 1938). Kees was alluding to two of Rexroth's difficult Cubist poems, "Easy Lessons in Geophagy" and "Organon."
7. *Weldon Kees and the Mid-Century Generation. Letters 1935–1955*, edited by Robert E. Knoll (Lincoln and London: University of Nebraska Press, 1986), p. 46.

8. KR: Kees, c. October 1939, UCLA.

9. Although Marie had joined the FOR in 1939, Rexroth had not bothered to apply formally for membership until June 1941, even though he had been corresponding with the organization in order to air his views. On May 29, 1941, A. J. Muste invited Rexroth to write an article about his social-pacifist philosophy for the organization's magazine *Fellowship*.

10. Paul Mariani, *William Carlos Williams*, p. 430.

11. KR: Kees, November 10, 1939.

12. *New Masses*, May 10, 1938; IWH, CSP, p. 95.

13. Eleanor Slater to KR, July 15, 1940, UCLA.

14. "Falling Leaves and Early Snow," IWH, CSP, p. 109.

15. Rolphe Humphries, "Too Much Abstraction," *The New Republic*, August 12, 1940, p. 221.

16. "Gic to Har," IWH, CSP, p. 108. Part of this poem appears in Chapter One, p. 8.

17. Nearly twenty years later in *The Nation*, Rexroth would get his revenge. Humphries as a translator of Latin poets was "dogged":

> He's kep' at it. And once in a while he achieves a certain felicity, but it is so brief that you wonder if it hasn't been an accident. As the Fuller Brush men say, "Just keep at it and the Law of Averages will take care of you."

See "On Translating Roman Verse," *With Eye and Ear* (New York: Herder & Herder, p. 146.

18. See William Fitzgerald, "Twenty Years of Hard Labor," *Poetry* (November 1940), p. 158.

19. Richard Foster, "The Voice of the Poet: Kenneth Rexroth," *Minnesota Review*, II, 3 (Spring 1962), pp. 377–384.

20. "Requiem for the Spanish Dead," IWH, CSP, p. 86.

21. Horace Gregory and Marya Zatu-
renska, *A History of American Poetry 1940–46* (New York: Harcourt, Brace, 1946), p. 494.

22. Robert Hass, "Some Notes on the San Francisco Bay Area As a Culture Region: A Memoir," *Twentieth Century Pleasures* (New York: Ecco Press, 1984), pp. 223–224.

23. Gidlow related the circumstances surrounding Andrée's death in the interview already cited.

24. "Andrée Rexroth," P&T, CSP, p. 154.

25. "Andrée Rexroth," P&T, CSP, p. 166.

26. "Andrée Rexroth," SAT, CSP, pp. 190–191.

27. KR: Weldon Kees, c. October 10, 1940.

28. However, Rexroth's reasons are rather incredible. One, he said, believed that homosexuals fantasized when they talked about the anus as "an organ of accommodation." The other believed, according to Rexroth, that "a diagnostic sign of schizophrenia was red hair."

29. ANN-II.

30. AAN-II.

31. AAN-II.

32. AAN-II.

33. In retrospect, Rexroth said that the only people he thought should ever receive capital punishment were the doctors who ordered shock therapy and lobotomies for their patients. See AAN-II.

34. See Rexroth's Foreword to his *Poems from the Greek Anthology* (Ann Arbor: University of Michigan Press), 1962. The poem, on p. 99, is also an epigraph to "When We with Sappho." At sixteen with Clay Mac Cauley's *Hyakunin-Isshu* and Arthur Waley's *Japanese Poetry* (1919) beside him, he had tried translating Japanese.

35. *The Latin Portrait: An Anthology of English Verse Translations from the Greek Poets*, edited by George Ross Trevor-Hamilton (London: Nonesuch Press, 1934).

Eleven

PACIFIST BARRICADES 1942–1943

1. "Strength through Joy," P&T, CSP, p. 156.
2. Quoted in Ailene S. Kraditor, *The Radical Persuasion, 1890–1917* (Baton Rouge and London: Louisiana State University Press, 1981), pp. 178–179.
3. KR to James Laughlin, December 28, 1941, Norfolk.
4. Interview with Michael Grieg, August 11, 1984, San Francisco. During the mid-fifties, Grieg would participate (with Weldon Kees among others) in the *Poets' Follies* (theatrical events that were precursors for the "happenings" of the sixties) before he became an editor of the *San Francisco Chronicle*.
5. FN: AAN-II.
6. AAN-II.
7. Mariana Rexroth said that at the memorial service (known as a *panakeda*) she held for her father at Holy Trinity Cathedral in San Francisco on June 12, 1982, a Japanese woman whom nobody seemed to know came with $20 to pay her respects. She said Rexroth had sponsored her during the Japanese-American evacuation (August 9, 1984, interview).
8. AAN-II.
9. AAN-II.
10. *P&T*, CLP, p. 64
11. KR to Franklin Folsom, May 12, 1941, UCLA.
12. KR to Malcolm Cowley, 1940?, Newberry Library.
13. KR to Malcolm Cowley, October 3, 1941.
14. KR to Weldon Kees, August 8, 1940, UCLA.
15. AAN-II.
16. AAN, p. 152.
17. AAN, p. 77.
18. This brief summary comes from my reading of Nicolas Berdyaev, "Unground and Freedom," introductory essay to *Jacob Boehme, Six Theosophic Points and Other Writings* (Ann Arbor: University of Michigan Press, 1958), and Franz Hartman, Introduction, *Personal Christianity: The Doctrines of Jacob Boehme* (New York: Frederick Ungar, 1958).
19. AAN-II. It is obvious that he had also discovered D. H. Lawrence at this time.
20. AAN-II.
21. At the end of his life, when a stroke left him paralyzed, the stomach disorder intensified, causing excruciating pain that could not be relieved by medication.
22. AAN-II.
23. Rexroth used the cabin well into the fifties, but it collapsed with time, the steep gulley washing out the trail during rainstorms.
24. October 21, 1942, letter to Local Board 77, Selective Service, 832 Pacific Building, San Francisco, UCLA.
25. Under the Freedom of Information Act, I was able to obtain a partial record of the FBI's investigation. The U.S. Department of Justice reviewed ten pages of his file and released ten pages with the names of informants blacked out. Rexroth's name appears in other files where he is not the primary subject, so-called "see" references, which continue until 1971. All my requests to see uncensored copies of these documents were denied.
26. In Rexroth's FBI file, the name of the examining physician is blacked out. However, in a telephone interview in San Francisco on August 15, 1984, Henderson identified himself as the doctor who was examining inductees for psychiatric disorders.
27. Joseph Henderson: LH, August 15, 1984.
28. AAN-II. Many of the instances Rexroth cites do not appear in the FBI file I received. However, as the record of my correspondence with the Department of Justice indicates, I was sent a censored and incomplete file.

29. AAN-II. FBI reports do cite the remarks of a woman who worked with
Rexroth on the Federal Writers'

Project from November 1934 to July
1936.

Twelve

PRIVATE BATTLES 1943–1944

1. Marie Rexroth to KR, n.d., UCLA.
2. Marie Rexroth to KR, n.d., UCLA.
3. CSP, p. 142.
4. There it is listed in the table of contents as ". . . about the cool water."
In 1963, the poem appeared in *Erotic
Poetry*, edited by William Cole (New
York: Random House). It is also included in NN and SP.
5. Marie Rexroth to KR, n.d., UCLA.
6. P&T, CSP, 161. The poem closes
with people sitting around a radio
listening to voices three thousand
miles away. In unpublished notes to
this poem, Rexroth identifies the
voices as issuing from a radio program out of the Trappist monastery in Kentucky, probably the
Cisterian monastery in Gethsemani
where Thomas Merton had been
living since 1938. UCLA.
7. Marie Rexroth to KR, n.d., UCLA.
8. Marie Rexroth to KR, n.d., UCLA.
9. KR to James Laughlin, n.d., Norfolk.
10. No matter how his paintings are
judged, they were vital to Rexroth's
entire sense of himself as an artist.
11. KR to James Laughlin, n.d., Norfolk.
12. CSP, p. 142.
13. Robert Duncan: LH interview, May
18, 1982. An abbreviated version of
this interview appears in *Conjunctions*, 4 (1983), pp. 85–95. The following comments by Duncan are
from this interview.
14. KR to James Laughlin, n.d., Norfolk.
15. AAN-II.
16. Henry Miller to KR, March 18, 1945,
UCLA.
17. *The Diary of Anaïs Nin*, Vol. 6, 1955–
66 (New York & London: Harcourt
Brace Jovanovich, 1976), p. 375.
18. She is now living in Paris, known as
"Julie Man Ray."
19. *Big Sur and the Oranges of Hierony-
mous Bosch* (New York: New Directions. 1957), p. 197.
20. AAN-II.
21. AAN-II.
22. Confirmation of Kenneth's 4-E status can be found in a summary of
his application for CO status on file
with the FBI. This summary was
made in 1962 after the Attorney
General had requested information about participants in the National Poetry Festival held that year.
23. William Carlos Williams to KR, July
31, 1942, UCLA.
24. Marie Rexroth to KR, n.d., UCLA.
25. Marie Rexroth to KR, n.d., UCLA.
26. Shirley Triest to LH, letter, September 20, 1986.
27. Writer and Sierra Club mountain
climber John Montgomery wrote
this to me in a July 7, 1986, postcard.
28. KR to James Laughlin, n.d., Norfolk.
29. P&T, CSP, p. 146.
30. KR to James Laughlin, n.d., Norfolk.
31. Marie Rexroth to KR, n.d., UCLA.
32. "Martial—XII, LII," P&T, CSP, p.
164.
33. CSP, p. 171.
34. Miller's exact words are: "The proletariat are the zombies of the earth."
See *Sunday After the War*, (New York:
New Directions, 1944), p. 47.
35. Marie to KR, n.d., UCLA.
36. KR to James Laughlin, n.d., Norfolk.
37. Marie Rexroth to KR, n.d., UCLA.
38. James Laughlin to Marie, n.d.
Laughlin is referring to the community of affluent Jewish people
who lived in Pacific Heights.
39. Marie Rexroth to KR, n.d., UCLA.

Thirteen

HAPPY DAYS 1945–1947

1. The title poem first appeared in *New Directions 1944,* which is dedicated to Rexroth.
2. *Quarterly Review of Literature,* 2 (1945), pp. 145–149.
3. William Carlos Williams to KR, September 21, 1945, UCLA.
4. William Carlos Williams to James Laughlin, November 1, 1944. *William Carlos Williams and James Laughlin: Selected Letters,* edited by Hugh Witemeyer (New York: Norton, 1989), p. 104.

   The following year, Williams published his own "The Phoenix and the Tortoise," in which he refers to Rexroth as "Barnum / Barnum our Aeschylus." See *Pacific* (Oakland, CA, November 1945), pp. 47–48; or *The Collected Earlier Poems of William Carlos Williams,* (New York: New Directions, 1951) where the poem appears on p. 465 even though it is not listed in the Contents.
5. In 1949, Lenoir established the Vesuvio Bar, a popular Bohemian hangout in North Beach.
6. In subsequent editions of this volume, in CSP and CLP, KR changed the table of contents.
7. Yvor Winter, to KR, January 6, 1944. UCLA.
8. "Floating," P&T, CSP, p. 144.
9. Yvor Winters to KR, August 27, 1940.
10. Janet Lewis to LH, interview, August 15, 1984.
11. AAN-II.
12. KR to Theodore Weiss, n.d. Private collection of Theodore and Renée Weiss, Princeton. The Weisses shared their impressions of Rexroth with me on January 16, 1990. For a different perspective on Winters, see Thomas Parkinson's remarks in John Tritica's "Regarding Rexroth: Interviews with Thomas Parkinson and William Everson," *American Poetry* (Fall 1989), pp. 71–87. Parkinson regards Winters as a "pretty good scholar and a first rate critic" (p. 72) whose strong family ties and whose affiliation with Stanford University gave him a healthy sense of community that Parkinson thought was lacking in Rexroth.
13. "The Giant Weapon," SAT, CSP, p. 198.
14. See the *Quarterly Review of Literature,* II, 2 (1945), pp. 107–109.
15. *American Poetry in the Twentieth Century* (New York: Herder & Herder, 1971), p. 93. When Winters died in 1968, Rexroth asked radio station KPFA, television station KQED, and the Poetry Center at San Francisco State College to broadcast a memorial program on Winters, but he was refused.
16. Janet Lewis's personal collection. Rexroth claimed to have met Janet Lewis when she was a graduate student with a page-boy haircut at the University of Chicago. Lewis, who had long hair in 1922, did not recall the meeting. In the brochure for an exhibition in honor of Winters and Lewis at Stanford University Library, March 11 to April 9, 1984 (nearly two years after Rexroth died), "Poets and Poetry in the Lives of Yvor Winters and Janet Lewis," Rexroth is quoted as having praised Lewis for using reason "to veil and adorn the flesh of feeling and intuition."
17. After fighting in the Spanish Civil War on the republican side, Hamilton Tyler came to Berkeley, audited classes at the university, worked as a welder in the shipyards, and married Mary. See Lee Bartlett, *William Everson: The Life of Brother Antoninus* (New York: New Directions, 1988), p. 82, for a fuller description of the evening Rexroth read "Phaedra." See also Ekbert Fass, *Young Robert Duncan* (Santa Barbara: Black Sparrow, 1983), pp. 185–187, for more details about life at Pond Farm.

18. James Laughlin to LH, interview, January 19, 1986.

19. Information about Waldport comes from David Meltzer's interview with William Everson in *Golden Gate: Interviews with 5 San Francisco Poets* (Berkeley: Wingbow Press, 1976), pp. 67–115; and from Lee Bartlett, "From Waldport to San Francisco: Art & Politics Make Peace," a paper delivered in San Francisco, December 1987, at the Modern Language Convention. The paper was published in *The Literary Review* (Fall 1988). Further information comes from a telephone conversation with actor Joyce Lancaster Wilson, January 19, 1987. She is writing a book about Waldport, and collaborated on many projects with her husband Adrian.

20. Introduction to William Everson's "The Poem as Icon—Reflections on Printing as a Fine Art," an "informal discourse" Rexroth gave April 16, 1976, for National Book Week at UC, Santa Barbara. Reprinted in *Earth Poetry: Selected Essays & Interviews of William Everson 1950–1977*, edited by Lee Bartlett (Berkeley: Oyez, 1980), p. 143.

21. William Everson to LH, interview, April 9, 1982, Davenport, California.

22. Published in 1946 by the former nuclear physicist Bern Porter, the first person to publish a volume of poetry by Robert Duncan, entitled *Heavenly City, Earthly City.* He co-edited the little magazine *Circle* with George Leite and *Berkeley* with James Schevill, a brilliant young Californian who would become director of the Poetry Center and a professor at Brown University. In addition to Lamantia and Duncan, Porter published between the mid-forties to the mid-fifties such other writers as Henry Miller, Parker Tyler, Kenneth Patchen, Leonard Woolf, Kenneth Rexroth, and James D. Harmon. Porter had quit his position in the Physics Department at the University of California in Berkeley after Hiroshima was bombed. Schevill has written a biography of Porter, *Roaring Market, Silent Tomb,* for Dog Ear Press.

23. KR to James Laughlin, n.d., Norfolk. Graves was known for his mystical art in which spiritual states are expressed by Buddhist motifs and elemental symbols like birds and flowers. Having grown up in the Pacific Northwest, Graves had dropped out of high school and headed for Japan. He became closely linked with the visionary, Asian-influenced group of Northwest artists led by Mark Tobey, and virtually achieved overnight success in 1942 when his work appeared in a famous series of shows devoted to new American art organized by Dorothy C. Miller at the Museum of Modern Art. Graves spent a few weeks as Visiting Artist at the CO camp in Waldport. Rexroth's essay. "The Visionary Painting of Morris Graves," first published in *Perspectives USA* (Winter 1955) and collected in *Bird in the Bush* (New York: New Directions, 1959) is a fine introduction to the man and his work.

24. The Eberharts talked at length with me about their friendship with the Rexroths in their home near the Dartmouth campus in Hanover, November 30, 1985.

25. *The Long Reach: New and Uncollected Poems 1948–1984* (New York: New Directions, 1984), p. 163.

26. Thomas Parkinson, "The Poets Take Over: New Forums for Literature in the San Francisco Bay Area," *The Literary Review* (Fall 1988), p. 19.

27. This information comes from "A Guide to the New American Poetry: San Francisco Bay Scene 1918–1960" by Eloyde Tovey, who worked at the Bancroft Library until she retired in 1983.

28. "Gas or Novacain," P&T, CSP, p. 151.

29. It also served as headquarters for the Arbeiter's Ring, also known as the Workman's Circle, a working-class community organization that

provided social and practical services (like medical insurance) for its members.

30. AAN-II.

31. A copy of this reading list was given to me by Richard Moore. In a January 20, 1987, letter to me, he writes that the "original is a very worn and frayed sheet with Kenneth's typescript on both sides." I also consulted William Everson's copy of a 1947 "Rexroth Discussion Group" in *American Poetry* (Winter 1984), pp. 65–66.

32. "Robert Duncan on Kenneth Rexroth," interview conducted by LH, *Conjunctions* 4 (1983), p. 89.

33. Bladen's austere and assertive sculptures in steel, wood, and aluminum can be seen at the Museum of Modern Art, the Federal Reserve Bank in Boston, and the Albany State Office Building. Accompanied by his wife Connie, he recalled his days with Rexroth for me during an interview on December 13, 1987, at the Old Town Bar, a favorite haunt in New York. The following February, he died.

34. William Everson, *Archetype West: The Pacific Coast as a Literary Region* (Berkeley: Oyez, 1976), p. 107.

35. AAN, p. 152.

36. Rexroth reluctantly gave Pound credit for his translations from the Chinese. In the annotated bibliography of *One Hundred Poems from the Chinese* (New York: New Directions, 1956), Rexroth's comment on Pound's *The Classic Anthology* reads: "The less said the better" (p. 47).

37. *Classics Revisited*, pp. 127–128.

38. *One Hundred Poems from the Chinese*, p. 10.

39. IWH, CSP, p. 102.

40. "Andrée Rexroth: Mt. Tamalpais," SAT, CSP, p. 190.

41. SAT, CSP, p. 204.

42. Thomas Parkinson talked at length about the history of *Circle* in "The Poets Take Over: New Forums for Literature in the Bay Area," *Literary Review*, (Fall 1985), pp. 16–20.

43. These are Eloyde Tovey's words in her "Guide to the New American Poetry: San Francisco Bay Scene, 1918–1960," unpublished.

44. Copies of *The Ark* are scarce. See Lawrence Ferlinghetti and Nancy Peters, *Literary San Francisco* (New York: Harper & Row, 1980), pp. 155–158, and Eloyde Tovey for a fuller description.

45. KR later dedicated this poem to William Everson.

46. William Everson to LH, April 9, 1982, Davenport, California.

47. Duncan made this remark to Dale Davis, director of the New York State Literary Center, at the "A Matter of Occasion" conference she organized at Nazareth College in 1981.

48. See Parkinson's "Phenomenon of Generation," *A Casebook on the Beat*, edited by Thomas Parkinson (New York: Crowell, 1961), p. 282.

49. "The Poets Take Over," p. 20.

50. KR to James Laughlin, n.d., Norfolk.

51. KR to Charles Wrey Gardiner, January 25, 1947, Harry Ransom Research Center, University of Texas at Austin.

52. William Everson to LH, April 9, 1982.

53. See Introduction, *The New British Poets* (New York: New Directions, 1949), p. VI. In his Introduction, Rexroth expressed antipathy toward Auden and his circle, making an exception only of Stephen Spender, whose verse contained "no cheap-jack solutions, no political or religious confidence games, no smart aleck stylistic trickery."

54. He had mocked the war or ignored it and cared only about publishing work of the highest quality. See Noel Annan, "Oh What A Lovely War!" *The New York Review of Books*, September 28, 1989, p. 3.

55. Rexroth related this incident in a January 25, 1947, letter to Charles Wrey Gardiner.

56. William Everson to LH, April 9, 1982.

57. AAN-II.

58. In the September 1968 issue of *Art News,* Rexroth reviewed two of Crehan's one-man shows held in San Francisco that summer. Crehan painted "an extremely quick, unrealistically colored" portrait of Rexroth, which Rexroth praised for its accuracy of tone.

Fourteen

OLD PROBLEMS, NEW SOLUTIONS 1947–1948

1. Mildred Edy Brady, "The New Cult of Sex and Anarchy," *Harper's* (April 1947), p. 319.
2. See David Meltzer's interview with Everson in *Golden Gate: Interviews with 5 San Francisco Poets,* p. 91.
3. James Laughlin to KR: April 20, 194?, Lausanne, UCLA.
4. In one respect, Mildred Brady was right about this new generation of anarchists: women were looked upon as second-class citizens, she said, who should learn "to keep their mouths shut, to play the role of the quiet and yielding vessel through which man finds the cosmos." Moreover, "the accepted view of both the women and the men seems to be that woman steps out of her cosmic destiny when the goal of her endeavor shifts beyond bed and board. ... Most of the girls hold down jobs. But the job is significant only in that it contributes to a more satisfactory board" (p. 320). A glance at the contributors' page of the little magazines appearing on the West Coast reveals a paucity of female names.
5. See Everson's May 11, 1948, letter to KR.
6. James Laughlin to KR: February 18, 194?, UCLA.
7. See Everson file, UCLA.
8. KR to James Laughlin, May 5, 1948, Norfolk.
9. William Everson to KR: November 31, 1948, UCLA.
10. George Woodcock, "Elegy for an Anarchist," *London Review of Books,* 19 January–1 February 1984, p. 20. Woodcock met Rexroth in 1951 when he came to the United States and lived for a while near Sebastopol, an area that remained popular with California anarchists.
11. "Lyell's Hypothesis Again," SAT, CSP, p. 181.
12. "Yugao," SAT, NN, CSP, p. 184.
13. KR to James Laughlin, n.d., Norfolk.
14. On one of her jobs, during Christmas 1946 at the White House bookstore, Marthe worked beside Pru and Robert Stock, who later invited Pru and Marthe to his parties.
15. In 1979, Janet Richards published her memoirs, *Common Soldiers* (Archer Press). It contains several allusions to Rexroth.
16. AAN-II.
17. William Carlos Williams to KR, April 19, 1948, UCLA.
18. William Carlos Williams to KR, September 21, 1945, UCLA.
19. "A Letter to William Carlos Williams," *Briarcliff Quarterly* (October 1946), SAT, CSP, p. 193.
20. As Williams recalled on April 19, 1948, Rexroth had stood in his front parlor and in "an accusing voice rumbling from the upper edge of [Rexroth's] asshole" asked Williams if he was a Jew. In the left-hand margin of this letter, Rexroth scribbled: "This is an hallucination." In his May 1, 1948, letter, Williams could not identify the culprit. There had been two men who "walked across the continent" from Los Angeles, and one was a disciple of Yvor Winters who made sure that he attended early Sunday mass. Rexroth had traveled east in 1931 with John Ferren, but it seems unlikely that he would behave in such an obnoxious manner since he visited Rutherford to articulate his enormous respect for Williams.
21. Day first met Gordon when Gordon

was working for the League for Spanish Democracy.

22. KR to Marthe Larsen, May 19, 1948. Private collection of Marthe Whitcomb.

23. KR to Eduoard Roditi, March 3, 1948. Roditi Collection, UCLA.

24. Edouard Roditi told me this story April 1, 1982.

25. James Laughlin to KR: March 8, 194?, UCLA.

26. Edouard Roditi would say that when Laughlin initially rejected Rexroth's translations, Rexroth became envious of Ezra Pound with whom he thought Laughlin was obsessed.

27. KR: Marthe Larsen, June 24, 1948. Private collection of Marthe Whitcomb.

28. James Farrell to KR, March 6, 1948, UCLA.

29. KR to Marie Rexroth, "Monday," UCLA.

30. Marie to KR, September 4, 1948, UCLA.

31. KR to Marie, "Monday," UCLA.

32. KR to James Laughlin, n.d., UCLA.

33. Marie Rexroth to KR, September 4, 1948, UCLA.

34. KR to James Laughlin, n.d., UCLA.

35. Creekmore included thirty-five of Rexroth's translations from the Japanese in *A Little Treasury of World Poetry* (New York: Scribner's, 1952), along with his version of Abelard's "Rumor Laetalis."

36. KR to Marie Rexroth, "Monday," UCLA.

Fifteen

ON THE ROAD 1948–1949

1. KR to Marthe Larsen, October 9, 1948. Private collection of Marthe Whitcomb. Rexroth's relationship to the gay community is puzzling. The homophobia he harbored seems to have been limited to bad jokes and sophomoric remarks, but they had no impact on his political activities and commitment to civil rights.

2. Parts I and II were published in *New Directions in Prose and Poetry*, XII and XIII, in 1950 and 1951, and together in 1952.

3. D&U, CLP, p. 97.

4. KR to Marthe Larsen, October 9, 1948.

5. "Delia Rexroth," SAT, CSP, p. 186.

6. October 6, 1948.

7. The epigram appeared in Rexroth's *Poems from the Greek Anthology*, p. 2.

8. *Cronos* also carried "A Note for Geraldine Udell."

9. KR to Marthe Larsen, October 8, 1948.

10. In his correspondence he never refers to Mrs. Abbott except to mention casually that the house in which the Abbotts lived, really a big old farm, had belonged to her family

for generations and had once been the showplace of the community.

11. KR to Marthe Larsen, October 9, 1948.

12. KR to Marthe Larsen, October 11, 1948.

13. KR to Marthe Larsen, October 9, 1948.

14. KR to Marthe Larsen, October 14, 1948.

15. See Section II, "The Autumn of Many Years," *The Homestead Called Damascus*, CLP, pp. 10–17.

16. KR to Marthe Larsen, October 19, 1948.

17. See September 5, 1948, handwritten version of this letter, UCLA; and the typed version, n.d., UCLA, and in Selden Rodman's private collection.

18. Foreword, Louise Kertesz, *The Poetic Vision of Muriel Rukeyser* (Baton Rouge: Louisiana State University Press, 1980), pp. xi–xii.

19. See Lawrence Lipton, in "Notes Towards an Understanding of Kenneth Rexroth with Special Attention to 'The Homestead Called Damascus.' " *Quarterly Review of Literature*, 9 (1957), p. 42.

20. John Gould Fletcher to KR, April 12, 1946, UCLA.
21. Philip Whalen to LH, interview, March 19, 1987, New York City.
22. This is from a typed letter, n.d., to Rodman, UCLA, and Selden Rodman's private collection. The September 5, 1948, handwritten version begins: "Your poetry seems much the best to me when it drops the aesthetic object impersonality of highbrow verse and gets into your own bowels—or your wife's or girl's or your friends or whoever."
23. Rodman would reprint two of Rexroth's poems, "A Letter to William Carlos Williams" and "Lyell's Hypothesis Again," in his *100 Modern Poems* (New York: Pellegrini & Cudahy) in 1949. Rodman liked "A Letter to William Carlos Williams" so well that he read it several years later when he appeared at the San Francisco Poetry Center in 1956, described in Chapter Nineteen. James Laughlin read it at the Centenary Celebration of William Carlos Williams's birthday at the 1983 annual convention of the Modern Language Association in New York City.
24. Selden Rodman to LH, interview, January 28, 1988, Oakland, New Jersey.
25. See statement attached to Rodman's December 29, 1951, letter.
26. KR to Marthe Larsen, November 5, 1948.
27. Cid Corman to LH, letter, February 27, 1988.
28. KR to Marthe Larsen, November 9, 1948.
29. See *Groves of Academe* (New York: Harcourt, Brace 1951) pp. 234–294, passim. Mary McCarthy vaguely remembers that Rexroth attended a poetry conference at Bard, which was something like the one she describes in another setting in her 1951 novel *Groves of Academe* (first published in 1951). That was the only time she met him, and she is not sure if they ever talked, even on that occasion (April 1, 1987, letter to LH).

Ten years later Rexroth wrote to James H. Case, Jr., President of Bard College, and asked to be considered for a faculty position there. He listed all his qualifications—books, fellowships, awards, teaching experience. He also noted that he had read and lectured at campuses across the country. He knew better than to mention specifically that he had read at Bard. Nothing came of his inquiry.
30. *William Carlos Williams and James Laughlin: Selected Letters,* edited by Witemeyer, p. 168.
31. KR to Marthe Larsen, November 10, 1948.
32. KR to Marthe Larsen, November 10, 1948.
33. So Rexroth wrote to Marthe on November 16, 1948.
34. Robert Duncan to LH, interview, May 18, 1982, New York City.
35. KR to Marthe Larsen, November 16, 1948.
36. Rexroth related this information to Professor Sanehide Kodama at Rakucho Bekkan, Kyoto, June 13, 1978. Professor of English at Doshisha Women's College in Kyoto, Kodama met Rexroth in 1973 when Rexroth came to Japan on a Fulbright. The two men saw one another regularly during that year. Kodama devotes a chapter of his *American Poetry and Japanese Culture* (Hamden, CN: Archon Books, 1984) to Rexroth's poetry.
37. P&T, CLP, p. 85.
38. See pp. 126–127 in Kodama's *American Poetry and Japanese Culture* for a full discussion of how Rexroth incorporated the work of these poets into his own.
39. KR to Marthe Larsen, November 20, 1948.
40. Marie Rexroth to KR, October 12, 1948, UCLA.
41. Michael Greig to LH, letter, February 6, 1987.
42. David Koven made a similar observation in a February 21, 1987, letter to me.
43. According to David Koven, Jim

Harmon described Rexroth's sexual behavior in these words. February 21, 1987, letter to LH.

44. This is from a fragment of a letter KR wrote to Marie from Eighth Avenue shortly before he left for Europe.

45. Ivan Raner to LH, interview, January 17, 1987, Berkeley.

46. KR to Marthe Larsen, March 26, 1949.

47. Rexroth erroneously blamed the book's delayed publication on the publisher's death. In his Author's Note to the 1953 edition of *The Art of Worldly Wisdom,* he wrote that Decker had been murdered.

48. KR to Marthe Larsen, April 5, 1948.

49. Michael Grieg to LH, letter, February 6, 1987.

50. Weldon Kees to Norris Getty, April 11, 1949. *Weldon Kees and the Midcentury Generation: Letters 1935–1955,* edited by Robert E. Knoll (Lincoln: University of Nebraska, 1986), p. 119.

51. Levertov recalled this in the *American Poetry Review* (January–February 1983), p. 19. Mitchell Goodman also recounted Rexroth's faulty predictions in a taped interview he gave me in December 1985.

52. KR to Marthe Larsen, March 26, 1949.

53. Marthe Larsen to KR, n.d.

Sixteen
An American in Europe 1949

1. Rexroth is referring to *The Signature of All Things.* This letter to Marthe is dated "First day out at sea."

2. KR to Marthe Larsen, April 7, 1949.

3. D&U, CLP, p. 100. On April 23, 1978 Rexroth told Sanehide Kodama that he had devised flexible masks for the play and arranged for flute, recorder, drum, and zittern to serve as both orchestra and chorus. See *American Poetry and Japanese Culture* (Hamden, CT: Archon, 1984), p. 229, note 17.

4. KR to Marthe Larsen, May 8, 1949.

5. D&U, CLP, p. 101.

6. D&U, CLP, p. 101.

7. KR to Marthe Larsen, April 21, 1949.

8. D&U, CLP, p. 107.

9. D&U, CLP, p. 107.

10. Derek Savage's letters to KR are on file at UCLA.

11. P&T, CSP, p. 146.

12. Derek Savage to LH, February 6, 1986, UCLA.

13. Derek Savage to LH, February 6, 1986, UCLA.

14. Marie Rexroth to KR, May 29, 1949, UCLA.

15. D&U, CLP, p. 116. KR used nearly identical phrasing in his May 5, 1949, letter to Marthe Larsen.

16. KR to Marthe Larsen, May 8, 1949.

17. Kathleen Raine talked to me about her meetings with Rexroth on June 1, 1985, at her home, 47 Paultons Square, across the park from the flat where she had met Rexroth.

18. "Stone and Flower," SAT, CSP, p. 206.

19. KR to Marthe Larsen, May 8, 1949. Yet Rexroth gave Comfort his due. After Herbert Read, Rexroth regarded Comfort as "the nearest thing to a systematic Romantic" in postwar England. Editor of *Poetry Folios,* a little magazine that appeared irregularly, Comfort had published four of Rexroth's poems in 1946: "Climbing Milestone Mountain, August 22nd, 1937," "Un Bel Di Vedremo," "Harmodius and Aristogeiton," and "Requiem for the Spanish Dead," as well as an excerpt from *The Phoenix and the Tortoise,* and the dance play *Iphigenia at Aulis.*

20. This poem has the title "Monads" in CSP.

21. This poem has the title "No!" in SAT, CSP, p. 203.

22. SAT, CSP, 183.

23. Introduction, NBP, p. xxxv.

24. KR to C. W. Gardiner, September 10, 1946. Harry Ransom Humanities Research Center, University of Texas at Austin.

25. KR to Gardiner, February 28, 1947.

26. KR to Gardiner, February 28, 1947.

27. KR to Marthe Larsen, May 17, 1949.

28. None of the food he had eaten in England had satisfied him. He wrote Marthe on May 17, 1949, "that everytime they set a plate in front of you in a restaurant, you feel like suing the management.... They can spoil anything. All they have to do is take food out of a package or tin and put in on a plate and it becomes inedible."

29. KR to Marthe Larsen, May 19, 1949.

30. KR to Marthe Larsen, May 23, 1949.

31. KR to Marthe Larsen, May 23, 1949. In *The Dragon and the Unicorn*, Rexroth cited Emma Goldman as inspiration for this commentary, with a slight variation in wording: "You're not British anarchists,/ You're just British," CSP, p. 118.

32. George Woodcock to KR, June 28, 1949, UCLA.

33. KR to Marthe Larsen, May 10, 1949.

34. See KR's August ?, 194?, letter to Tambimutto on file at Harry Ransom Research Center, University of Texas at Austin.

35. KR to Marthe Larsen, May 22, 1949.

36. Robin Blaser to LH, letter, August 5, 1984.

37. D&U, CLP, pp. 165–166. See pp. 162–168 for other examples.

38. Actually there were two rounds of these letters between Kenneth and Marie, in May–June 1949 and October 1949. They essentially repeated each other.

39. KR to Marthe Larsen, May 21, 1949.

40. KR to Marthe Larsen, May 30?, 1949.

41. The following summary of Marie's response comes from her June 5, 1949, letter.

42. Some of her friends, like Frank and Shirley Triest, suspected that she might be jealous of Kenneth's talent, and that this feeling led to bursts of resentment. "She wanted to be a writer," said Frank Triest. "She was very intelligent, coherent, articulate, but she couldn't become a writer" (August 11, 1984, interview, Woodacre). Other friends, however, like social worker Belle Rainer, a Berkeley undergraduate, and a regular participant in the Libertarian meetings and the Rexroth literary soirées, thought Marie was comfortable with her role as a poet's wife and amanuensis— interview with Belle Raner, January 17, 1987.

43. KR to James Laughlin, July 8, 1949.

44. Selden Rodman Collection in Oakland, New Jersey, and the University of Wyoming.

45. KR to Marthe Larsen, June 8?, 1949.

46. KR to Selden Rodman, May 22, 1946.

47. KR to Selden Rodman May ?, 1946.

48. "On a Flyleaf of Rime—Gaspara Stampa," IDE, CSP, p. 246.

49. KR to Marthe Larsen, n.d.

50. KR to Marthe Larsen, June 22?, 1949.

51. The Cincinnati foundation had previously awarded her a special scholarship after graduating from high school. She had used that money to help pay living expenses during her freshman year at Ohio Wesleyan. She had transferred to Mills College in her sophomore year.

Seventeen

TRUTH AND CONSEQUENCES 1949

1. Marthe Whitcomb to LH, interview, January 19, 1987, Palo Alto.

2. Mariana Rexroth to LH, interview, September 16, 1986, New York City.

3. It is likely that "Vivienne Renaud," his short story about a torrid sexual

encounter in a small forest near Versailles, is based on one such encounter. See *Conjunctions*, 2 (Spring–Summer 1982).

4. D&U, CLP, p. 124.
5. Marthe Whitcomb to LH, interview, January 19, 1987, Palo Alto.
6. KR to James Laughlin, n.d.
7. Marthe Whitcomb made available to me a log she recorded of the major events of her life with KR.
8. D&U, CLP, p. 154.

9. KR: JL, n.d.
10. Marie Rexroth to KR, n.d., UCLA.
11. D&U, CLP, pp. 222–223.
12. D&U, CLP, p. 226.
13. D&U, CLP, p. 230.
14. KR to Marthe Larsen, n.d.
15. D&U, CLP, pp. 262–263.
16. KR to Marthe Larsen, December 27, 1949.
17. D&U, CLP, p. 268.
18. KR to Marthe Larsen, December 27, 1949.

Eighteen
NEW LIVES 1950–1952

1. KR to Marthe Larsen, January 4, 1950.
2. Marie Rexroth to KR, "Tuesday."
3. Marie Rexroth to KR, "Tuesday."
4. Shirley Triest to LH, interview, August 11, 1984.
5. KR to James Laughlin, n.d.
6. D&U, CLP, p. 123.
7. *Quarterly Review of Literature*, IV, 3 (1948), pp. 255–292.
8. See James Schevill, "Mirrors for a 'Renaissance,' " *Literary Review* (Fall 1988), p. 29–35 for a fuller description of this episode.
9. KR to Marthe Larsen, n.d.
10. KR to Charles Wrey Gardiner, January 2, 1951, Harry Ransom Humanities Research Center, The University of Texas at Austin
11. KR to Marthe Larsen, February 27, 1950.
12. *Fourteen Poems by O. V. de L. Milosz* (San Francisco: Peregrine Press, 1952; reprinted in 1983 by Copper Canyon Press).
13. "Thirteen" (Copper Canyon, n.p.).
14. Marie Rexroth to James Laughlin, April 4, 1951.
15. Marthe Larsen to KR, n.d., UCLA.
16. KR to James Laughlin, n.d.
17. D&U, CLP, p. 136.
18. D&U, CLP, p. 145.
19. D&U, CLP, p. 150.
20. D&U, CLP, p. 128.
21. D&U, CLP, p. 131–132.
22. D&U, CLP, p. 126.

23. This comes from a form letter KR sent out to solicit review copies. UCLA.
24. KR to Babette Deutsch, October 28, 1952, Washington University. His review appeared October 26, 1952.
25. Weldon Kees to Tony Myrer and Judith Rothschild, February 24, 1951. *Weldon Kees and the Midcentury Generation*, edited by Robert E. Knoll (Lincoln: University of Nebraska Press, 1986), p. 150.
26. Afterword to *McTeague* by Frank Norris (New York: NAL, 1964), p. 347.
27. D&U, CLP, p. 118.
28. KR to Marthe Larsen, June 23, 1952.
29. D&U, CLP, p. 246.
30. D&U, CLP, p. 249.
31. William Everson, *Archetype West* (Berkeley: Oyez, 1976), p. 104. For example, Everson believed *The Phoenix and the Tortoise*, whose setting is a deserted California beach, is Rexroth's great masterpiece. Another poet, Peter Viereck, placed *The Dragon and the Unicorn* in the tradition of "global travelogues of broken-up prose . . . interspersed with Yeatsian refrains of Earthly Ecstasy," a style Viereck defined as "mating Crazy Jane with Rand McNally." See Peter Viereck, "The Last Decade in Poetry: New Dilemmas and New Solutions," *Literature in the Modern World* (Nashville: Bu-

reau of Publications, George Pea-
body College for Teachers, 1954),
p. 51. He preferred a poem like *The
Signature of all Things*, because it was
full of "refreshing spontaneity," and
grounded in the California landscape that inspired Rexroth's talent. If Viereck shortchanged *The
Dragon and the Unicorn*, he nonetheless accurately singles out a major—
and nature-bound—strength of
Rexroth's poetry.

32. James Harmon to KR, May 23, 1952,
UCLA.
33. Laughlin said he could not recall
the specific details that would explain why, but he suspected the
magazine was too conservative to
accommodate Rexroth's taste.
Laughlin to LH, June 17, 1988.
34. "The Great Nebula of Andromeda," CSP, p. 238.
35. KR to Babette Deutsch, September
17, 1952, Washington University.

Nineteen
ALIVE IN THE SILENT DECADE 1953–1955

1. Ferlinghetti and Peters, *Literary San
Francisco*, p. 191.
2. Both Thomas Parkinson and James
Schevill discuss this era of the Bay
Area's literary and political scene in
the Fall 1988 *Literary Review*.
3. Mariani, *William Carlos Williams: A
New World Naked*, p. 625.
4. Rexroth used to say that he and
Ferlinghetti met in Paris during
Rexroth's Guggenheim year, and
that Rexroth had persuaded Ferlinghetti to come to San Francisco.
Ferlinghetti, who was living with a
French family at the time and
studying for his doctorate, avoided
contact with English-speaking people and could not recall meeting
Rexroth in Paris. Lawrence Ferlinghetti to LH, interview, August
13, 1984, San Francisco.
5. Lawrence Ferlinghetti to LH, interview, August 13, 1984, San Francisco.
6. Martin sold his interest in the store
when he moved back to New York
in 1955. Martin was the son of the
famous anarchist Carlo Tresca.
7. Ferlinghetti's father had shortened
the family name to Ferling, but in
1954 Ferlinghetti decided he preferred the original. Rexroth liked
to claim that he encouraged Ferlinghetti to do this.

8. *San Francisco Chronicle*, February 7,
1954.
9. The long poem was published separately by New Directions in 1952.
10. This quotation appears in Allen
Ginsberg and Ted Berrigan's "Kenneth Rexroth: 1905–1982," *Third
Rail*, Issue 8 (1987), p. 10.
11. *San Francisco Chronicle*, October 16,
1955.
12. Ferlinghetti thanks KR for this in a
January 11, 1952, postcard, UCLA.
13. Jonathan Williams to KR, November 14, 1950, UCLA.
14. KR to Jonathan Williams, May 1,
1951. The Jonathan Williams Papers are housed in the Poetry / Rare
Books Collection, University Libraries, the University of Buffalo
(SUNYAB).
15. KR to Jonathan Williams, November 21, 1950, SUNYAB.
16. KR to Jonathan Williams, November 21, 1950, SUNYAB.
17. KR to Jonathan Williams, November 25, 1951, SUNYAB.
18. Jonathan Williams to KR: April 17,
1951, UCLA.
19. KR to Judith Malina and Julian
Beck, October 8, 1951, Harry Ransom Humanities Research Center,
University of Texas at Austin.
20. Beck and Malina talked about the
production with me on June 29,

1983, in their quarters at 10 rue Oberkampf, Paris.

21. William Carlos Williams, *The New York Times Book Review*, January 28, 1951, p. 5.

22. In *Revolutionary Rexroth: Poet of East-West Wisdom* (Hamden, CT: Archon, 1986), Morgan Gibson discusses the plays in detail, with useful insights about the influence of Euripides, Sophocles, Yeats, and Noh drama. See Chapter 4, pp. 88–95.

23. Julian Beck to KR, May 5, 1952, UCLA.

24. Jonathan Williams to LH, interview, January 4, 1986.

25. Jonathan Williams, *Portrait Photographs* (Frankfort, KY: Gnomon Press, 1979), p. 8.

26. Rexroth's records were stolen when he moved to Santa Barbara in 1968.

27. Professor Ralph A. Raimi, Professor of Mathematics at the University of Rochester, and a friend of Herbert Gold, sublet Rexroth's Scott Street apartment from September 5, 1968, until January 5, 1969. He was kind enough to provide me with a list of recordings he had taped from Rexroth's collection.

28. "Disengagement: The Art of the Beat Generation," *The Alternative Society* (New York: Herder & Herder, 1972), p. 2. All quotations will be from this text. The essay originally appeared in *New World Writing* in 1957 and was reprinted in *World Outside the Window.*

29. Ross Russell, *Bird Lives!* (New York: Charterhouse Press, 1973), pp. 309, 323, 327.

30. William Carlos Williams, "Two New Books by Kenneth Rexroth," *Poetry*, XC (June 1957), p. 83.

31. Gibson, *Revolutionary Rexroth*, p. 61.

32. Gibson, *Kenneth Rexroth* (New York: Twayne, 1972), p. 96. Robert Penn Warren also uses this refrain in his poem "Variation: Ode to Fear."

33. "Thou Shalt Not Kill," CSP, p. 273.

34. "Thou Shalt Not Kill," CSP, p. 272.

35. "Thou Shalt Not Kill," CSP, p. 274.

36. "Thou Shalt Not Kill," CSP, p. 273.

37. "Disengagement: The Art of the Beat Generation," p. 3.

38. Introduction, *The New British Poets*, p. xx.

39. See Rexroth's lengthy discussion of "The New Apocalypse" poets in his Introduction, *The New British Poets*, pp. xxi–xxiii.

40. Ibid., p. xx.

41. Ibid., pp. xviii–xix.

42. A news story in the *Daily Californian* (April 20, 1955) covered Shapiro's lecture. The quotations are from the newspaper article.

43. "Disengagement: The Art of the Beat Generation," p. 14.

44. Ferlinghetti said that KR picked him out to read at the Cellar. August 13, 1984, interview. An amused Robert Duncan was in the audience one night, wearing a Brooks Brothers suit.

45. "From Red Hill to the Renaissance: Rehearsing the Resistance," *The Literary Review* (Fall 1988), p 22. Rexroth did not perform "Thou Shalt Kill" that particular evening but as an epigraph for "The Iron Curtain" chapter of *The Impossible Theater*. Blau took two lines from "Thou Shalt Not Kill" ("Who killed the bright-headed bird? / You did, you son of a bitch").

46. These comments and many of those that follow in the discussion of Snyder's early acquaintance with Rexroth are from a series of questions Snyder was kind enough to answer by cassette recorder, July 25, 1982. Details about Snyder's biography are also taken from the interview Snyder gave to David Kherdian, which appears in *Six San Francisco Poets*. (Fresno: The Giligia Press, 1965), pp. 21–26.

47. Gary Snyder to LH, interview, July 25, 1982.

48. Bob Steuding, *Gary Snyder* (Boston: G. K. Hall, 1976), p. 112. Steuding does not suggest that Snyder's early work merely imitates Rexroth, and he illustrates some real differences. For example, he points out how their

tones can be dramatically different—Rexroth is often elegaic while
Snyder is buoyant, optimistic.
49. Gary Snyder to KR, "Wednesday,"
UCLA.
50. "A Berry Feast," *The Back Country*
(New York: New Directions, 1968),
p. 13.
51. Gary Snyder to KR, "Wednesday,"
UCLA.
52. *American Poetry in the Twentieth Century*, p. 177.
53. Professor Donald Gutierrez told me
about this one. He himself had called
Rexroth during the early fifties for
advice about the draft and made the
mistake of repeating the rumor to
Rexroth. Gutierrez has published
several important articles on
Rexroth's poetry, including "Going
Upstream: Kenneth Rexroth's Lyric
'Time Spirals,' " in *Notes on Modern
American Literature* in (Autumn
1982); "Natural Supernaturalism:
The Nature Poetry of KR," in *The
Literary Review* (Spring 1983); "Love
Sacred and Profane: The Erotic
Lyrics of KR," in *Sagetrieb* (Winter
1983), pp. 101–112; "Musing with
Sappho: KR's Love Poem 'When We
with Sappho' as Reverie," in *Ameri-
can Poetry* (Fall 1986); and "KR: "*The
Signature of All Things*," in *American
Poetry* (Fall 1989).
54. Norman Rush to LH, interview,
January 23, 1986, New York City.
Rexroth died before Rush received
widespread acclaim for his collec-
tion of short stories, *Whites.*
55. Although in a January 7, 1953, let-

ter to Laughlin, Rexroth mentioned that "Eli Jacobson dropped
dead recently," to others Rexroth
would relate a grisly and totally unfounded story about Jacobson's
death. He said that in December
1952, Jacobson's body was found
floating in San Francisco Bay. His
fingers had been severely beaten, as
though he had been struggling to
hold on to a ledge of a building, or
in this case perhaps a bridge. A few
days before his death, Jacobson had
called Rexroth up to tell that he was
cutting his last remaining connections to the Communist Party because he had discovered at this late
date that Stalin was an anti-Semite.
Rexroth begged him not to break
so abruptly with his comrades, and
arranged to meet him in Sausalito
before he took any action. Jacobson
never appeared. Rexroth had told
June Oppen of his proposed ren-
dezvous, and he suspected she
"warned" her brother, poet George
Oppen, about Jacobson's change of
heart. Rexroth absurdly speculated
that Oppen was working as a "hit
man" for the Party, and then he had
murdered Jacobson. In an interview nearly thirty years later,
Rexroth would describe Oppen as
a "remarkable poet." See "An Interview with Kenneth Rexroth,"
conducted by Bradford Morrow,
Conjunctions, 1 (1981), p. 60.
56. "For Eli Jacobson," CSP, p. 244.
57. "Fish Peddler and Cobbler," CSP,
p. 319.

Twenty
THE BEATS ARRIVE 1955–1956

1. Robert Creeley to KR, December 12,
1953, UCLA.
2. KR to Creeley, July 1, 1951, Washington University Libraries, St.
Louis.
3. Pym-Randall Press reprinted these
translations in 1972.
4. KR to Robert Creeley, n.d., Washington University Libraries.

5. See Laughlin's Introduction to the
"World Poets Series" edition of *The
Homestead Called Damascus* (New
York: New Directions, 1963).
6. In 1944, two sections of the poem—
"Adonis in Summer" and "Adonis
in Winter"—were published in *The
Phoenix and the Tortoise.* "Adonis in
Summer" first appeared in *Modern*

Verse, 1 (July 1941), pp. 16–17, under the title of "The Lotophagi with their silly hands."

7. Lawrence Lipton to KR, July 27, 1955, UCLA.

8. Lawrence Lipton to KR, August 20, 1955, UCLA.

9. The last work that Divers Press printed was Robert Duncan's *Caesar's Gate*, with financial backing from Duncan himself. Creeley was willing to consider publishing *The Homestead* in *Black Mountain Review*. See KR to Creeley, n.d., Washington University Libraries.

10. "Hermaios," the third of the four-play series *Beyond the Mountains*, also appeared in the *Quarterly Review of Literature*, IV, 3 (1948).

11. New American Library published this edition in 1955.

12. This description appears in Janet Richards's *Common Soldiers* (San Francisco: Archer Press, 1979). She reports that Rexroth and Kees disliked one another intensely for reasons unknown to her.

13. Reviewing *The Collected Poems of Weldon Kees*, edited by Donald Justice (Iowa City: Stone Wall Press, 1960), Rexroth reiterated his conviction that Kees was among the most significant poets of his generation, that he was a genuine, alienated poetic hero. See *Assays*, p. 236.

14. The manuscript eventually turned into *Empty Mirror: Early Poems*. Williams's Introduction first appeared in *Black Mountain Review* in Fall 1957, six years after he wrote it.

15. See Barry Miles, *Ginsberg: A Biography* (New York: Simon & Schuster, 1989), for a detailed account of Ginsberg's activities in the Bay Area during this period.

16. Allen Ginsberg to LH, interview, July 9, 1985, New York City.

17. Allen Ginsberg to KR, June 15, 1955, UCLA. Donald Davie thinks *Howl* had its roots in Rexroth. He writes in *The Poet in the Imaginary Museum* (New York: Persea Press, 1977) "From under the shadow of Rexroth himself, came Allen Ginsberg's prophetic-confessional poem *Howl!* And ever since, confessional poems have been the order of the day" (p. 142).

18. These comments, and those that follow, are from my interview with Michael McClure on August 12, 1984, in his San Francisco home on Downey Street. He has since moved to Oakland.

19. While living in Paris, Lowenfels had contributed regularly to *transition*, and in the late twenties and thirties began a series of elegies to writers whom he admired, including Apollinaire, Rimbaud, Hart Crane, and D. H. Lawrence, which would be called "Some Deaths." He left Europe to become the editor of the Philadelphia edition of *The Daily Worker* and stopped writing verse for twenty years. After he was convicted in 1954 under the Smith Act, which outlawed the Communist Party (the first poet to earn this distinction), he returned to writing poetry. Earlier, on July 16, 1937, from New York City, Lowenfels had written Rexroth a letter praising "the authentic ring" of his poem "Requiem for the Spanish Dead," UCLA.

20. Allen Ginsberg to LH, interview, July 9, 1985, New York City. For a somewhat different account of the genesis of the reading, see Barry Miles, *Ginsberg: A Biography*, pp. 193–195. Several other versions exist, but all indicate that Ginsberg was the major organizer of the event.

21. Cassady is the model for Dean Moriarty in Kerouac's *On the Road* and for Cody Pomeray in *Dharma Bums*, *Desolation Angels*, and *Book of Dreams*.

22. Gerald Nicosia, *Memory Babe* (New York: Grove Press, 1983), p. 492.

23. Gregory Corso, *The Vestal Lady on Brattle and Other Poems* (Cambridge, MA: Richard Bruckenfeld, 1955; reprinted San Francisco: City Lights, 1967).

24. Philip Whalen to LH, interview, March 19, 1987, New York City.

25. From *The Literary Revolution in*

America, by Allen Ginsberg and Gregory Corso. Appendix II, *Howl*, edited by Barry Miles (New York: Harper & Row, 1986), p. 165.

26. Nicosia, *Memory Babe*, p. 492.

27. Bruce Cook, *The Beat Generation* (New York: Scribner's, 1971), p. 65.

28. From *The Literary Revolution in America*, Appendix II, *Howl*, p. 165.

29. He reviewed Leonie Adams, Louise Bogan, and Babette Deutsch for the *New York Herald Tribune Book Review* in the summer of 1954, had spoken highly of Muriel Rukeyser's poetry, and more than any critic of his time was responsible for directing younger poets to the work of Mina Loy. See Roger Conover's Introduction to Mina Loy's *The Last Lunar Baedeker*, edited by Roger Conover, with a note by Jonathan Williams (Highlands, NC: The Jargon Society, 1982). The book is dedicated to Rexroth.

30. Allen Ginsberg to LH, interview, July 9, 1985, New York City.

31. *One Hundred Poems from the Chinese*, p. 111.

32. Philip Whalen to LH, interview, March 19, 1987, New York City.

33. Allen Ginsberg to LH, interview, July 9, 1985, New York City. Ginsberg's behavior may in part have provoked Rexroth, more than fifteen years later, to give a rather sneering history of Ginsberg's activities in *American Poetry in the Twentieth Century:*

> Ginsberg had been a rather conventional, witty poet influenced by his New Jersey *Landsman* William Carlos Williams, and taught his letters at Columbia by Mark Van Doren, Lionel Trilling, and Jacques Barzun. He was very much a catecumen of the highly select Trotskyite-Southern Agrarian Establishment, and destined by his elders to step into the thinning ranks of their youth brigade alongside Norman Podhoretz and Susan Sontag and others of that ilk and kidney. He inhaled the libertarian atmosphere of San Francisco and exploded. (p. 41)

Oddly enough, in the very same book, Rexroth relays the same information in a far more positive tone thirty pages later—perhaps the consequence of collecting scattered essays into a book.

34. Selden Rodman, February 11, 1956, journal entry, Rodman's private collection, Oakland, New Jersey, and Yale University Library.

35. Selden Rodman, February 13, 1956, journal entry.

36. IDE, CSP, p. 281.

37. IDE, CSP, p. 282.

Twenty-One

REXROTH IN MISERY 1956–1957

1. Robert Creeley, "On Black Mountain Review,' *The Little Magazine in America* (Yonkers, NY: Pushcart, 1978), p. 260.

2. In a January 23, 1988, letter, Janelle-Therese Viglini told me that during this period Rexroth provided her shelter while she hunted for a new home for herself and her six-month-old baby—she had recently fled from Langley-Porter, the neuro-psychiatric institute at the University of California. While Marthe was at work, she and Rexroth enjoyed "*grossière intervention corporelle*" (her expression) for two weeks.

3. Allen Ginsberg to LH, July 9, 1985.

4. KR wrote this to Laughlin and urged him to write to Marthe reassuring her that she possessed all these attributes.

5. He could not remember if it was "Sunflower Sutra" or "America."

6. KR to Laughlin, n.d.
7. KR to Marthe, n.d., Private collection of Marthe Whitcomb.
8. KR to Marthe, "Sunday night," Private collection of Marthe Whitcomb.
9. KR to Marthe, "Sunday night," Private collection of Marthe Whitcomb.
10. "Marthe Away," IDE, CSP ("She Is Away"), pp. 228–229.
11. Frank Triest to LH, interview, January 18, 1987, San Francisco.
12. Marie Rexroth to Laughlin, letter, June 12, 1956.
13. Marthe to KR, "Tuesday a.m."
14. James Laughlin to LH, interview, January 19, 1986, Norfolk.
15. KR to Laughlin, June 28, 1956, Norfolk.
16. "The Great Nebula of Andromeda," IDE, CSP, p. 238
17. "A Sword in a Cloud of Light," IDE, CSP, pp. 240–241.
18. "Quietly," IDE, CSP, p. 243.
19. "Marthe Lonely," IDE, CSP ("Loneliness"), p. 230.
20. KR to Henry Miller, January 13, 1957, Henry Miller Collection, UCLA.
21. Robert Duncan to Robert Creeley, May 22, 1965. Robert Creeley Papers, Special Collections, Washington University Libraries, St. Louis.
22. Robert Duncan to KR, May 14, 1956, UCLA.
23. Robert Duncan to Marthe, n.d., Robert Creeley Papers.
24. Duncan to Creeley, May 18, 1956, Robert Creeley Papers.
25. Gary Snyder to KR, August 10, 1956.
26. Kerouac to KR, December 13, 1956.
27. For a full history of the *Howl* trial, see Lawrence Ferlinghetti, "Horn on *Howl*," *Evergreen Review*, I, 4 (1957), pp. 145–158. Also see "Appendix III: Legal History of "Howl," pp. 169–174, *Howl* annotated by

Allen Ginsberg, edited by Barry Miles.
28. Ferlinghetti, "Horn on *Howl*," *A Casebook on the Beat*, edited by Thomas Parkinson (New York: Crowell, 1961), p. 132.
29. AS, p. 11.
30. AS, p. 12.
31. AS, p. 12.
32. AS, p. 13.
33. *The Nation*, February 23, 1957, p. 161.
34. *Evergreen Review*, I, 2(1957); WOW, p. 59.
35. Barry Gifford to LH, interview, August 18, 1984, Berkeley.
36. Allen Ginsberg to LH, interview, July 9, 1985.
37. See *The Village Voice Reader* (Garden City, NY: Doubleday, 1962), p. 339; *San Francisco Chronicle*, "This World," February 16, 1958, p. 23; and *The New Yorker*, May 3, 1958, p. 29. For a more detailed summary of Rexroth's reviews of Kerouac, see Tom Clark's *Jack Kerouac* (New York: Harcourt Brace Jovanovich, 1984).
38. *The New York Times Book Review*, November 29, 1959, p. 14.
39. Allen Ginsberg to LH, interview, July 9, 1985.
40. Eugene Burdick, *The Reporter*, April 3, 1958, p. 31.
41. Norman Podhoretz, "A Howl of Protest in San Francisco," *The New Republic*, September 16, 1957, p. 20.
42. Dan Jacobson, "America's 'Angry Young Men: How Rebellious are the San Francisco Rebels?" *Commentary* (December 1957), p. 477.
43. "Mark Tobey: Painter of the Humane Abstract," *Art News* (May 1951), BIB, p. 176.
44. *Time*, December 2, 1957, p. 71.
45. KR to Marthe, Venice, California (late fall 1957).

Twenty-Two
ON THE EDGE 1957–1958

1. Robert Duncan to Robert Creeley, Creeley Papers, Special Collections, Washington University, St. Louis, November 26, 1957.

2. Duncan to Creeley, November 26, 1957.

3. Duncan to KR, January 11, 1958.

4. KR to Marthe, June 14, 1957.

5. "Homer in Basic," NN, CSP, p. 317.

6. "Fish Peddler and Cobbler," NN, CSP, p. 320.

7. KR to Lipton, October 17, 1957.

8. KR to Marthe, December 1, 1957.

9. Richard Collins to LH, interview, July 25, 1984, Los Angeles.

10. KR to Marthe, n.d.

11. KR to Marthe, "Tuesday."

12. D&U, CLP, p. 202.

13. Richard Collins to LH, letter, September 3, 1987.

14. Susan Wiere to LH, interview, January 24, 1987, Los Angeles.

15. Twenty years alter Rexroth would tell Dick Collins that life deteriorated among the flower children of Haight-Ashbury because "nobody did the dishes: they were screwing one another and everybody got diseases. it was love time. No one cleaned the bathrooms, the kitchen, the urinals." July 25, 1984, interview with Collins.

16. KR to Lipton, December 26, 1957.

17. KR to Lipton, December 26, 1957.

18. "This Night Only," NN, CSP, p. 338.

19. So reports Rexroth in "Kenneth Rexroth Live from Santa Barbara," on tape, Audio-Forum, Guilford, CT, 06473.

20. KR to Marthe, January 19, 1958.

21. See "Jazz Poetry," WOW, pp. 68–72.

22. KR to Marthe, January 25, 1958.

23. KR to Marthe, March 21?, 1958.

24. Esther Handler to LH, interview, August 20, 1985, Chevy Chase, Maryland.

25. KR to Marthe, March, 29, 1958.

26. KR to Marthe, n.d., St. Louis.

27. Marthe to KR, March 20, 1958.

28. KR to Marthe, April 22, 1958. By this time, Rush had served nine months in a federal prison, been graduated from Swarthmore, and had settled in New York City where he worked as an antiquarian book dealer and wrote fiction.

29. KR to Marthe, Mary, and Katharine, April 14, 1958.

30. The New Yorker, May 3, 1958, p. 30.

31. Alice Denham, AMO (New York: Coward, McCann, Geoghegan, 1975), pp. 54–55.

32. See Literary San Francisco, p. 186. Rexroth ranked Kaufman's poetry in Solitudes Crowded with Loneliness (New Directions, 1965) and in Golden Sardine (City Lights, 1967) with the best produced by the Beat writers. See American Poetry in the Twentieth Century, pp. 156–157.

33. Jerome Rothenberg made this interview available to me. It is also on file at Special Collections, University of California, San Diego Library.

34. Marthe to KR, April 21, 1958.

35. See American Poetry Review (January–February 1983), p. 19. Mitchell Goodman was also impressed with the "good and interesting things" Rexroth said about Creeley's poetry—Goodman to LH, interview, December 1985. In 1967, Denise Levertov, Kenneth Rexroth, William Carlos Williams was published by Penguin Books (Harmondsworth, Middlesex). Five years later, Levertov dedicated "3 a.m., September 1, 1969" to Rexroth. The poem, which appears in Footprints (New York: New Directions, 1972), p. 72, indicates that Levertov associates Rexroth with the spirituality she found in nature.

36. KR to Marthe, April 20, 1958.

37. KR to Marthe, April 23, 1958.

38. KR to Marthe, April 22.

39. KR to Ciardi, October 29, 1955, USC.

40. KR to Ciardi, October 10, 1955.

41. The New York Times Book Review, August 3, 1958, p. 6.

42. KR to Ciardi, October 10, 1955. How Does a Poem Mean? was published in 1959 by Houghton Mifflin.

43. One Hundred Poems from the Chinese, p. 48, 1971. This translation suggests that Rexroth, like the speaker in the poem, may have gone through

a period of heavy drinking. Although he was known to get drunk on occasion, as Lew Welch reported in a December 6, 1957, letter to Gary Snyder in *I Remain: The Letters of Lew Welch & the Correspondence of His Friends,* Vol. I, *1949–1960* (Bolinas, CA: Grey Fox, 1980), p. 121, Rexroth regarded himself as a moderate drinker.

44. KR to Marthe, July 1?, 1958.
45. BIB, p. 126.
46. KR to Marthe, July 18, 1958.
47. KR to Marthe, July ?, 1958.

Twenty-Three
A CHANGE OF SCENE IS NOT ENOUGH 1958–1960

1. KR: Jonathan Williams, October 7, 1958.
2. KR: G. d'Andelot Belin, Jr., March 8, 1959, UCLA.
3. See Janet Richards, *Common Soldiers,* pp. 265–287, for her reminiscences of Rexroth.
4. Marie Rexroth to KR, November 16, 1958, UCLA.
5. Marie Rexroth to KR, November 16, 1958, UCLA.
6. Rexroth's detailed account of French inhospitality appeared in an undated letter he wrote from Aix to writer Renaud de Jouvenel, UCLA.
7. In the February–March 1959 issue of *Europe,* Renaud de Jouvenel translated four of Rexroth's poems: "Pour Eli Jacobson," "Marthe au Loin," "Les Mauvais Jours Ancien," and "L'été de 1918." Rexroth's essay, "L'influence de la poésie Française sur la poésie Américaine," appeared in the same issue.
8. A. Alvarez to LH, letter, November 13, 1989.
9. KR to Renaud de Jouvenel, n.d.
10. "Christmas," NN, CSP, p. 323.
11. "On the Eve of the Plebiscite," NN, CSP, p. 326.
12. These poems can be found in *Gödel's Proof,* CSP, pp. 9, 10, 11.
13. "Camargue," CSP, p. 10. See also "High Provence" and "Leaving L'Atelier Aix-en-Provence,' p. 11.
14. KR to Laughlin, May 17, 1959.
15. See p. 329, "Ascension Night," NN, CSP, p. 329.
16. Mariana Rexroth to LH, September 26, 1986, New York City.
17. Robert Hatch to KR, March 19, 1959, UCLA.
18. KR to James Laughlin, January 25, 1959.
19. "Rotation Days," NN, CSP, p. 329.
20. "Ascension Night," NN, CSP, p. 329.
21. "Observations in a Cornish Teashop," NN, CSP, p. 331.
22. This information, and the description of Rexroth's summer in England, comes from the Derek Savage correspondence file, UCLA, and from a February 6, 1986, letter Mr. Savage wrote to me in which he very generously answered a series of questions.
23. According to Janet Richards, Rexroth could be generous about giving books away—he received so many free copies for reviews. But he refused to loan anyone books from his private collection. A small sign that announced "No books loaned" was displayed on his bookshelves. The first time Allen Ginsberg visited Rexroth, Rexroth pointed to this sign after Ginsberg asked if he could borrow a few out-of-print volumes (see *Common Soldiers,* p. 286). Richard Kostelanetz encountered the same response when in Santa Barbara he asked Rexroth for one of two review copies of his own book on Moholy-Nagy so that he could give it to poet Harry Reese, who had driven Kostelanetz to Rexroth's house. Richard Kostelanetz to LH, post card, June 20, 1989.
24. Allen Tate and David Cecil, *Modern Verse in English* (New York: Macmillan, 1958).
25. CSP, p. 282.
26. *The Fireside Book of Humorous Poetry*

(New York: Simon & Schuster, 1959), p. 448.

27. *Poetry for Pleasure* (Garden City, NY: Doubleday, 1960), pp. 308, 89–90.

28. William Arrowsmith and Roger Shattuck, *The Craft and Context of*

Translation, (Austin: University of Texas Press, 1961), pp. 22–37.

29. William Arrowsmith to LH, letter, July 26, 1984.

30. KR to Marthe, November 16, 1959.

Twenty-Four
FINAL THROES 1960–1961

1. The academic community had awakened to his presence without fully accepting him. The distinguished literary critic and historian Frederick J. Hoffman had written to Rexroth earlier that winter to tell him how much he enjoyed *Bird in the Bush,* that he appreciated Rexroth's range of knowledge and depth of insight. He especially valued the clear and sharp style of "Some Thoughts on Jazz," "The Hasidim of Martin Buber," and "Poetry, Regeneration and D. H. Lawrence"—January 8, 1960, UCLA. Rexroth assumed Hoffman would be glad to invite him to read at the University of of Wisconsin, and mailed the letter straight off to Elizabeth Kray, who had helped Rexroth arrange this tour. She promptly wrote to Hoffman, but he was disinclined to pay a $350 fee and was affronted by what he considered to be Rexroth's "making a career of commercializing talent." Frederick Hoffman to Elizabeth Kray, February 8, 1960, UCLA.

2. Stanley Burnshaw to LH, interview, December 11, 1987, New York City.

3. Mr. Burnshaw graciously typed out this journal entry for me, December 12, 1987.

4. KR to Marthe, April 10, 1960.

5. KR to Marthe, "Holy Saturday," April 1960.

6. Thomas Parkinson wrote a highly favorable review of *Bird in the Bush* for the *San Francisco Sunday Chronicle* (Jan. 31, 1960) and, as Frederick Hoffman had in his letter to Rexroth, singled out the Lawrence

and Buber essays for being profound.

7. Over the summer Rexroth would publish several essays about the civil rights movement, such as "The Students Take Over" in *The Nation,* July 2, 1960, and "A Hopeful Journey Through the South" in *The Carolina Quarterly* (Summer 1960).

8. Gloria Oden to LH, interview, August 20, 1985, New York City.

9. Gloria Oden, "Ornette to Rexroth." Dr. Oden kindly gave me a copy of this poem, and permission to reprint it here.

10. KR to Gloria Oden, May 6, 1960. Gloria C. Oden's private collection.

11. KR to Gloria Oden, June 10, 1960.

12. KR to Gloria Oden, May 6, 1960.

13. KR to Gloria Oden, June 1, 1960.

14. KR to Marthe, July 5, 1960.

15. KR made this observation to Gloria Oden in a February 17, 1961, letter in which he analyzes Marthe's behavior during the final weeks she lived with him.

16. Marthe to KR, July 7, 1960.

17. KR to Marthe, July 5, 1960.

18. KR to Marthe, July 5, 1960.

19. KR to Gloria Oden, August 9, 1960.

20. Marie to Marthe, "Tuesday noon."

21. KR to Marthe, September 13, 1960.

22. KR to Marthe, September 13, 1960.

23. KR to Gloria Oden, February 14, 1961.

24. KR to Gloria Oden, February 17, 1961.

25. Laughlin was a trustee of the Institute.

26. Williams liked Rexroth's suits so much that he had his own Rexroth design made up by Lynes. Jonathan Williams to LH, interview, January

4, 1986, Highlands, North Carolina.

27. KR to Marthe, August 29, 1961.
28. KR to Marthe, August 24, 1961.

Twenty-Five
A VICTORIAN MAN ON THE TOWN 1961–1963

1. A University of Michigan Press book, this volume was originally going to be published by Jargon Press and illustrated with line drawings by Shirley Triest.
2. "Who Am I? Where Am I Going???" *Assays,* p. 16.
3. "Who Am I? Where Am I going???" *Assays,* p. 17.
4. In this essay, Rexroth says that he met Wright in Chicago at a John Reed "Left Ball" and that he met him subsequently although he does not say where. Neither Michel Fabre in *The Unfinished Quest of Richard Wright* (New York: William Morrow, 1973) nor Constance Webb, in *Richard Wright* (New York: Putnam, 1968) mentions these subsequent meetings. Both Wright and Rexroth were at the First National Conference of the John Reed Club held in May 1932.
5. KR to Ruth Hartman, August 27, 1961. From the private papers of Margot Blum, who is also the wife of poet James Schevill.
6. Untitled, *Poems from the Greek Anthology* (Ann Arbor: University of Michigan Press, 1962), p. 79.
7. Some people said that "he'd screw anything that moved—male or female, two-legged or four."
8. KR to Gloria Oden, November 9, 1961.
9. Carol Tinker told me August 7, 1985, that Rexroth met Stephan "at the Walgreen residence in Chicago or Michigan." Rexroth did work as a drug-store clerk, but not for Walgreen. A summary of Ruth Stephan's life, by her son John J. Stephan, appeared in the *Yale University Library Gazette* (April 1976).
10. *The Tiger's Eye* (March 1948), pp. 69–70.
11. *The Tiger's Eye* (October 1949), pp. 98–100.
12. "Spring," SAT, CSP, p. 189. Rexroth may have also learned to listen to trees from D. H. Lawrence.
13. "Summer," SAT, CSP, p. 188.
14. Ruth Stephan to KR, September 28, 1959, UCLA.
15. *What the Woman Lived: Selected Letters of Louise Bogan 1920–1970,* edited by Ruth Limmer (New York: Harcourt, Brace, 1973), p. 348.
16. Carol Tinker to LH, interview, December 22, 1982, New York City.
17. KR to James Laughlin, March 28, 1963.
18. When *The Collected Shorter Poems* was published in 1966, the order of the Marthe poems was rearranged and her name excised from all poems, including "The Great Canzon for Marthe."
19. KR to James Laughlin, n.d., probably soon after May 15, 1963.
20. "Growing," CSP, p. 233.
21. "Pacific Beach," CSP, pp. 340–341.
22. "Coming," CSP, p. 340.
23. "Maroon Bells," CSP, p. 341.

Twenty-Six
REWARDS 1963–1967

1. D. G. Bridson's interview with Rexroth was pre-recorded on June 10, 1963, and transmitted on June 16, 1963.
2. See p. 347 of KR's Afterword to *McTeague*
3. Mariana Rexroth to LH, interviews, September 18, March 23, and

December 19, 1986, New York City.

4. Gloria Oden believed that Rexroth wanted "some kind of Jewish ancestry." Gloria Oden to LH, August 20, 1985.

5. Katharine Rexroth shared some of these observations with me during an interview in Ann Arbor, October 31, 1985.

6. *San Francisco Examiner,* October 9, 1960. Ken Knabb brought this column to my attention.

7. Mariana Rexroth to LH, September 18, 1986.

8. Mariana Rexroth to LH, March 23, 1987.

9. Although the store bore Rexroth's name, he owned no part of it. Carol Tinker to LH, telephone conversation, March 29, 1990.

10. Horace Schwartz to LH, August 11, 1984, San Francisco.

11. Herbert Gold to LH, December 10, 1982, New York.

12. Jessica Hagedorn to LH, June 29, 1989, New York.

13. Hagedorn loosely drew on her impressions of Kenneth, Mary, and Carol for her book *Pet Food & Tropical Apparitions* (San Francisco: Momo's Press, 1981). They appear as Silver Daddy, Porno, and Tinkerbell. Hagedorn's most recent work is *Dogeaters* (New York: Pantheon, 1990), a novel about life in Manila during the Marcos years.

14. *"The Kalevala,"* CR (New Directions, 1986), p. 25.

15. Burnshaw related this episode to me on December 11, 1987, New York City.

16. Elizabeth Bishop, "Visits to St. Elizabeths," *The Complete Poems 1927–1979* (New York: Farrar, Straus, 1983), pp. 133–135.

17. APTC, p. 175.

18. KR to Edouard Roditi, n.d., Roditi Collection, UCLA.

19. KR to Roditi, October 1, 1966.

20. KR to Roditi, November 1, 1966.

21. The Federal Bureau of Investigation had a record of these activities, as they did of his 1939 membership in the Writers Division of the Committee for the Arts Project (along with people like Clifford Odets, Alfred Kreymborg, Muriel Rukeyser, Malcolm Cowley, and Granville Hicks), and that his poem "Gentlemen, I Address You Publicly" was included for publication in *New Masses* (June 29, 1937). The Committee on Un-American Activities had made note of Rexroth's membership of the League of American Writers. His application for CO status in 1943 had been preserved. A "name check request" by the FBI of the thirty-five individuals who participated in the National Poetry Festival in October 1962 at the Institute of Contemporary Arts in Washington, D.C., produced a two-page summary of Rexroth's personal history.

22. KR to Roditi, December 4, 1966.

23. Carol Tinker to LH, telephone conversation, March 28, 1990.

24. KR to Roditi, December 25, 1966.

25. Mariana Rexroth told me that he absolutely hated Spanish culture—September 20, 1986.

26. Octavio Paz to LH, telephone conversation, October 14, 1987, New York City. Paz told me that he thought Rexroth wrote "exquisite love poems," and that his translations of Pierre Reverdy were very good. Paz believed that if Rexroth was not in the main current, he was in a more powerful one: "making the connection between life, society and poetry. See his recent *Sombres des ombres* for a poignant eulogy to Rexroth.

27. Carol Tinker to LH, July 5, 1988.

28. KR to Roditi, April 16, 1967.

29. "The American Poet's Visit," *The Americans, Baby* (New York: Harcourt, Brace, 1972), p. 155.

30. Gary Snyder related this story to me in an August 27, 1987, letter.

31. Gary Snyder to LH, letter, August 27, 1987.

32. Gary Snyder to LH, letter, August 27, 1987.

33. KR to Jerome Rothenberg and David Antin, unpublished inter-

view, University of California San Diego Libraries.

34. Carol Tinker to LH, telephone conversation, July 5, 1988.

35. Professor Yuzuro Katagiri de-scribed Rexroth's first readings in Japan in a February 24, 1988, letter to me.

36. KR to W. Todd Furniss, June 26, 1967.

Twenty-Seven
ONE ERA ENDS, A NEW ONE BEGINS 1967–1971

1. AS, p. 81.
2. Pym-Randall Press published *The Heart's Garden* separately in 1967.
3. "A Song at the Winepresses," CLP, p. 305.
4. *The Heart's Garden*, CLP, p. 297.
5. *The Heart's Garden*, CLP, p. 297.
6. *San Francisco Examiner* column, Box 7, UCLA.
7. *The Heart's Garden*, CLP, p. 295.
8. *The Heart's Garden*, CLP, p. 283.
9. *The Heart's Garden*, CLP, p. 283.
10. See Cyrena Pondrum's interview of Rexroth in *Contemporary Literature* (Summer 1969), pp. 313–331, for a fuller discussion of Rexroth's attitudes toward the mystical and Buddhist elements in his poetry.
11. "Rexroth As He Appeared to Exist, March 24, 1968, 9:00 P.M." *Poetry Flash* (August 1982), p. 10. The poem also appears in Antler's *Last Words* (New York: Ballantine Books' Available Press, 1986).
12. "Halley's Comet," IDE, CSP, p. 237.
13. Rexroth made this observation to Dr. Ralph A. Raimie, Professor of Mathematics at the University of Rochester, who with his wife and daughter sublet the Scott Street apartment from September 1968 to January 1969. He reported these remarks in a December 13, 1987, letter to me.
14. "The Heat," AS, p. 96.
15. Jack Shoemaker to LH, telephone conversation, August 15, 1984.
16. Edward Loomis to LH, interview, July 29, 1984, Santa Barbara.
17. Herbert Gold had introduced Rexroth to his tenant, Professor Ralph Raimi. Raimi was spending a leave of absence at the University of California at Berkeley, and the Scott Street apartment with its 30,000 books appealed to this cultured professor of mathematics, who was especially impressed by an entire wall of books devoted to cooking, one six-foot shelf for wine alone. In order to make Raimi and his family feel more secure in this volatile neighborhood, Rexroth had built before their arrival a locked iron gate for the entrance to his apartment building. Rexroth dined with the Raimis a few times when he came up to San Francisco during the next six months. On those occasions, he slept on the floor in a sleeping bag in the downstairs flat which he leased for book storage— November 20, 1987, letter from Raimi to LH. When the Raimis vacated the apartment in early January, Marie rented it to two young men from the Public Health Department.

18. Carol Tinker to LH, telephone conversation, June 30, 1987.
19. Carol Tinker to LH, interview, January 23, 1987, Santa Barbara.
20. The five-book contract was worth $50,000—interview with Horace Schwartz, August 11, 1984. Rexroth produced three of the books: a collection of essays entitled *With Ear and Eye* (1970); *American Poetry in the Twentieth Century* (1971), an informal history of modern American poetry that originally was to serve as an introduction to an anthology of modern American poetry; and anther collection of essays, *The Alternative Society* (New York: Herder & Herder, 1972).
21. Dick Collins to LH, interview, July 25, 1984.

22. See Barbara Szerlip, "Kenneth Rexroth: Experience as Consequential," *Alcatraz,* 2 (Santa Cruz, 1982), pp. 215–219. Comments also come from an interview Barbara Szerlip gave me on August 7, 1982, San Francisco.

23. Karen Feinberg, another student and later a performance artist, jotted down some of these expressions in her journal. Karen Feinberg to LH, August 20, 1985, New York City.

24. Edward Loomis to LH, September 29, 1988.

25. "A Crystal Out of Time and Space: The Only Diary," *Conjunctions,* 8 (1985), p. 79. See also David Meltzer's interview with Rexroth in *Golden Gate: Interviews with 5 San Francisco Poets* for more Rexroth observations on his colleagues at UCSB.

26. Rexroth described this evening seminar in an interview he gave to James J. McKenzie and Robert W. Lewis, March 22, 1974, at the University of North Dakota, Grand Forks, where with Gregory Corso, Michael McClure, Gary Snyder, Lawrence Ferlinghetti, and Allen Ginsberg he attended the English Department's Fifth Annual Writer's Conference. See *North Dakota Quarterly* (Summer 1976), pp. 7–33, for the interview. He also discussed it in a January 10, 1972, letter to Leo Hamalian.

27. KR to James Laughlin, July 31, 1970.

28. In 1970, Two Windows Press published a twelve-page chapbook entitled *The Coffee Should Be Warm Now,* by Mary Rexroth.

29. Carol Tinker to LH, January 23, 1987.

30. Carol Tinker to LH, January 23, 1987.

31. Barbara Szerlip told me this story in the August 7, 1984, interview, San Francisco.

32. Rexroth once told a friend that he was afraid he had damaged his mouth and throat from too much oral sex.

33. APTC, p. 177.

34. "A Crystal Out of Time and Space: The Only Diary," *Conjunctions,* 8 (1985), p. 64.

35. Dana Gioia to LH, letter, November 17, 1988.

36. *Los Angeles Times Book Review,* January 24, 1971, pp. 10–12.

37. *Los Angeles Times,* July 9, 1971, Section IV, p. 3.

38. There is an amusing story about Rexroth, Robert Kirsch, and Susan Wiere. Rexroth was convinced that Wiere and Kirsch had had an affair, though in fact they hadn't. Rexroth would badger Wiere with accusations which she refused to take seriously. However, Rexroth told Wiere that shortly before Kirsch died, he had "confessed" to him that they had been lovers. He had devised his own evidence to support his unshakable belief.

39. Mary Rexroth to KR, May 1, 1971.

Twenty-Eight

BORDER CROSSINGS 1972–1974

1. New Directions had published *One Hundred More Poems from the Chinese* in 1970.

2. For a detailed discussion of the Ling Chung's meetings with Rexroth, see "Forty Years in Between": *For Rexroth,* edited by Geoffrey Gardiner (New York: The Ark, 1980), pp. 11–13. I also interviewed Ling Chung, July 31, 1984, in Pasadena.

3. Ling Chung, "Forty Years in Between," p. 12.

4. Stephen Owen, *Journal of Asian Studies* (November 1973), p. 105.

5. Rexroth had included a number of women poets in both the very popular *One Hundred Poems from the Chinese* and *One Hundred Poems from the Japanese.*

6. Huang O, "To the Tune 'Red Em-

broidered Shoes,' " *The Orchid Boat* (New York: Seabury Press, 1972), p. 61.

7. Kuan Tao-sheng, "Married Love," *The Orchid Boat*, p. 53.

8. James J. McKenzie and Robert W. Lewis, "That Rexroth—He'll Argue You Into Anything," (an interview), *North Dakota Quarterly* (Summer 1976), p. 26.

9. See Stephen Spender, *The Thirties and After: Poetry, Politics, People, 1930's–1970's* (New York: Random House, 1978), p. 187. He attributes this remark to a poet named "Waxwrath."

10. Chu Shu-chen, "Spring Joy," *The Orchid Boat*, p. 45.

11. He made this observation in an October 17, 1972, letter to Leo Hamalian.

12. This essay was collected in *The Elastic Retort* (New York: Seabury Press, 1973) and reprinted in *World Outside the Window* (New York: New Directions, 1987).

13. *WOW*, p. 273.

14. Robert W. Lewis, Chair of the English Department, described the reading to me in an April 3, 1987, letter. Lewis introduced Rexroth that evening.

15. For more details about this incident, see James McKenzie, "Interview with Allen Ginsberg," *Kerouac and the Beats*, edited by Arthur and Kit Knight (New York: Paragon House, 1988), p. 229.

16. "That Rexroth," p. 7.

17. "Black Writers—Black or White Readers," *The Alternative Society* (New York: Herder & Herder, 1972), p. 22. A version of this essay appeared in *The Nation*, September 7, 1964, under the title "Panelizing Dissent."

18. Amiri Baraka to LH, May 6, 1984. Hamilton Hall, Columbia University.

19. Baraka reminisces about Rexroth in his poem "Was He Some Ken to You?" in *Third Rail*, Issue 8 (1987), p. 15.

20. *Four Young Women Poets* was published by McGraw-Hill in 1972.

21. Rexroth dedicated *Sky Sea Birds Trees Earth House Beasts Flowers* (Santa Barbara: Unicorn Press, 1973) to Gary Snyder, hoping that Snyder might use them as love poems for his wife Masa.

22. "Gold Wires," *The Pillow Book of Carol Tinker* (Santa Barbara: Cadmus, 1980), p. 25.

23. James Laughlin had sent Carol $100 with which he hoped she would buy a wedding dress. Instead, Carol gave Karen Feinberg, one of Kenneth's favorite students, $90 for a piece of sculpture (whose figures resembled Harpo Marx) which she placed in their garden, and spent the remaining $10 on a tea set. Carol Tinker to LH, telephone conversation, September 6, 1986.

24. Carol Tinker told me about her wedding night on two occasions: once at her Calle Rosales home in Santa Barbara, January 23, 1987; and again during a telephone conversation, June 22, 1987. A wedding guest also recounted this episode to me.

25. It is also the setting for several other poems, including those found in *The Silver Swan*.

26. II, *On Flower Wreath Hill* (n.p. Blackfish Press) reprinted in *The Morning Star* (New York: New Directions, 1979), p. 36.

27. For a full discussion of this technique, see Sanehide Kodama, *American Poetry and the Japanese Culture*, pp. 150–152.

28. Both the farmhouse and the house were owned by a former professor at Kyoto University whose wife and son were still living there. Shortly after Rexroth left, the house was torn down and the farmhouse was moved to the campus of Doshisha University.

29. Monica Bethe to LH, letter, June 1, 1988.

30. *Kenneth Rexroth* was published by Twayne in 1972. In 1986, Gibson published his newly interpreted vision of Rexroth in *Revolutionary*

Rexroth, Poet of East-West Wisdom.
31. *Poetry Flash* (August 1982), p. 2.
32. Cid Corman to LH, letter, February 27, 1988.
33. Darina Silone to LH, letter, December 1, 1987.
34. XVII, *The Morning Star,* p. 19.

Twenty-Nine
OLD BONES, FRESH CONTRADICTIONS 1974–1980

1. KR to James Laughlin, August 27, 1975.
2. *Communalism* (New York: Seabury Press, 1974), p. 303.
3. *Communalism,* p. 304.
4. "Japan and the Second Greater East Asia Co-Prosperity Sphere" was originally published in *San Francisco Magazine* and collected in *The Elastic Retort* in 1973.
5. "The Influence of Classical Japanese Poetry on Modern American Poetry," WOW, p. 268. This essay is based on the paper Rexroth delivered at the Tokyo PEN Conference. It also appeared in *The Elastic Retort.*
6. "Japan and the Second Greater East Asia Co-Prosperity Sphere," *The Elastic Retort,* p. 139.
7. "Notes," *The Love Poems of Marichiko, The Morning Star* (New York: New Directions, 1979), p. 85. Poems by "Marichiko" had appeared earlier in *One Hundred More Poems from the Japanese, New Poems, New Directions in Prose and Poetry 29, The Silver Swan,* and *Flower Wreathe Hill.* There is also a Christopher's Books edition.
8. Morgan Gibson to LH, letter, January 30, 1988.
9. See Gibson, *Revolutionary Rexroth,* p. 83. In a January 30, 1988, letter to me, Gibson speculates that Kimiko Nakazawa, a Japanese woman who was an intimate friend of Rexroth's during this period, might be the real-life prototype for Marichiko.
10. Yuzuru Katagiri to LH, letter, February 24, 1988.
11. See *Li Ch' ing-chao: Complete Poems* (New York: New Directions, 1979).
12. Eliot Weinberger, "At the Death of Kenneth Rexroth," *Sagetrieb* (Winter 1983), p. 51.
13. "XL," *The Morning Star,* p. 72.
14. *San Francisco Chronicle,* November 18, 1977.
15. Other writers who participated in the conference included Philip Levine, Kay Boyle, Bob Kaufman, George Hitchcock, Lawrence Ferlinghetti, Carol Lee Sanchez, Jessica Hagedorn, and Ken Kesey.
16. Nika Cavat to Leo Hamalian, letter, September 12, 1988.
17. Bradford Morrow, notes written to LH, November 30, 1987.
18. Bradford Morrow, November 30, 1987.
19. Bradford Morrow to LH, interview, July 1, 1985, New York City.
20. Melissa Mytinger to LH, interview, August 19, 1984, Oakland, California.
21. *The Pillow Book of Carol Tinker,* p. 42.
22. Sam Hamill to LH, interview, May 7, 1985, New York City.
23. Several years later, Hamill published under the guise of a review of Rexroth's *Selected Poems* a first-rate evaluation of Rexroth in *American Poetry Review.* (May–June 1986) where he evokes an essence of Rexroth's work that he himself worked so hard to create in his own poems: "the articulation of human experience as close to perfection as human articulation can be."
24. Rexroth performed in such places as California State College, Stanislaus, Fresno, and Los Angeles, University of California, San Diego, The San Francisco Art Institute, and Laguna Mouton Playhouse.
25. Dick Collins to LH, interview, July 25, 1984.

26. This performance was recorded and is available on the Watershed tape, "A Sword in a Cloud of Light."

27. Levine told me about the conference in a January 22, 1987, interview at his home in Fresno. I also talked to Sam Hamill about Rexroth's participation at this conference.

28. Gary Snyder told me about this during a telephone conversation on May 6, 1986, several hours before he gave the yearly "Education of a Poet" lecture sponsored by the Academy of American Poets at the Guggenheim Museum, New York City.

29. See Ruth Steine's article / interview with Rexroth in the *San Francisco Chronicle*, November 18, 1977.

30. Gary Snyder to LH, interview, July 25, 1982.

31. See John Solt, "Remembering Kenneth Rexroth," *Third Rail*, Issue 8 (1987), p. 21.

32. The volume was in production so long that the poets feared they would have to change the title to "Four Old Lady Poets."

33. Carolyn Forché to KR, June 30, USC.

34. Carolyn Forché to KR, December 2, USC.

35. "Kenneth Rexroth on Carolyn Forché," *American Poetry Review* (November–December 1976), p. 44.

36. See James Broughton, "A Big Bang for Mr. Bangs," *Sagetrieb* (Winter 1983), pp. 33–35.

37. Jack Shoemaker to LH, telephone interview, August 16, 1984, San Francisco.

38. New Directions published Shiraishi's *Seasons of Sacred Lust* in 1978.

39. Sam Hamill, "Poetry & Jazz: A Memoir," *Sagetrieb* (Winter 1983), p. 54.

40. See Robert Sund's *This Flower* (La Conner, WA: The Great Blue Heron Society, 1982) for another poet's impressions of Rexroth's reading there.

41. Dale Davis to LH, telephone interview, September 15, 1989.

42. Joe Bruchac attended this festival, which he described to me in a March 2, 1988, letter. I am relying here on his impressions of Rexroth.

43. Joyce Jenkins, "Rexroth at the San Francisco International Poetry Festival," *Poetry Flash*, p. 9. Scheduled to appear on the same evening was Maya Angelou, Jayne Cortez, Philip Lamantia, and Ted Joans.

44. See KR's Introductions to Tomlinson's *Time Payments* (1978) and Sutherland's *Mouth of the Whale* (1978), both published in Santa Barbara by Mudborn Press.

45. Eliot Weinberger's "Dharma Demagogy"—a review of two books, *The Party* edited by Ed Sanders, and *The Great Naropa Poetry Wars* by Tom Clark, and which appears in *The Nation*, April 19, 1980—provides one summary of the events surrounding the controversy, as does Paul L. Berman's review, "Buddahgate: The Trashing of Allen Ginsberg," *The Village Voice*, July 23–29, 1980. The synopsis of this controversy comes from these two sources.

46. See Tom Clark, *The Great Naropa Poetry Wars* (Santa Barbara: Cadmus, 1980), back cover.

47. Jeffrey Miller to LH, telephone interview, January 19, 1987.

48. APTC, p. 171.

Thirty
An Uneasy Death 1981–1982

1. Justus George Lawler, "Rexroth: A Personal Memoir," *For Rexroth* (New York: The Ark, 1980), p. 55.

2. #16, *Saucy Limericks & Christmas Cheer* (Santa Barbara: Bradford Morrow, 1980).

3. "Vivienne Renaud," *Conjunctions*, 2 (Spring–Summer 1982), pp. 54–59.

4. Bradford Morrow, "An Interview with Kenneth Rexroth," *Conjunctions,* (Winter 1981–82), p. 67.

5. Angela Jaffrey to LH, interview, January 21, 1987, Berkeley.

6. I visited Rexroth with my husband in April 1982. His steely brilliant blue eyes lit up in recognition, but only a series of grunts issued from his mouth.

7. Carol Tinker to LH, interview, December 22, 1982.

8. Michael McClure, PLANH, *Poetry Flash* (August 1982), p. 3; *Sagetrieb* (Winter 1983), p. 26; *Third Rail,* Issue 8 (1987), p. 13.

9. In November 1977, McBride published an interview of Rexroth by Paul Portuges and Paul Vangelisti. He also ran Red Hill Press.

10. The lettering was designed by Richard Bigus, who printed Rexroth's *Between Two Wars,* a collection of Rexroth's thirties poems, with an interview with Rexroth by Lester Ferris and an introduction by Bradford Morrow. The poem first appeared in *The Silver Swan* (Port Townsend, WA: Copper Canyon, 1976). It was reprinted in *The Morning Star* (New York: New Directions, 1979), p. 4.

11. Lawrence Ferlinghetti, *Poetry Flash* (August 1982), p. 8.

12. Gary Snyder to LH, taped interview, July 25, 1982.

13. Ruth Pokrass to LH, interview, April 8, 1988, New York City.

SELECTED WORKS BY KENNETH REXROTH

Poetry

In What Hour. New York: Macmillan, 1940.

The Phoenix and the Tortoise. New York: New Directions, 1944.

The Art of Worldly Wisdom. Prairie City, IL: Decker Press, 1949. Sausalito, CA.: Golden Goose Press, 1953, 1973. Santa Barbara, CA.: Morrow and Covici, 1980.

The Signature of All Things. New York: New Directions, 1950.

The Dragon and the Unicorn. Norfolk, Conn.: New Directions, 1952.

A Bestiary for My Daughters Mary and Katharine. San Francisco: Bern Porter, 1955.

Thou Shalt Not Kill: A Memorial for Dylan Thomas. Sunnyvale, CA.: Goad, 1955.

In Defense of the Earth. New York: New Directions, 1956; London: Hutchinson, 1959.

The Homestead Called Damascus. New York: New Directions, 1963.

Natural Numbers: New and Selected Poems. New York: New Directions, 1963.

The Collected Shorter Poems. New York: New Directions, 1966. 1967. 1976.

The Heart's Garden, The Garden's Heart. Cambridge, MA: Pym-Randall Press, 1967.

The Spark in the Tinder of Knowing. Cambridge, MA: Pym-Randall Press, 1968.

The Collected Longer Poems. New York: New Directions, 1968. 1970.

Sky Sea Birds Trees Earth House Beasts Flowers. Santa Barbara, CA: Unicorn Press, 1971, 1973.

The Kenneth Rexroth Reader, Eric Mottram, ed. London: Cape, 1972.

New Poems. New York: New Directions, 1974.

The Silver Swan. Port Townsend, WA: Copper Canyon Press, 1976.

On Flower Wreath Hill. Burnaby, British Columbia: Blackfish Press, 1976.

The Love Poems of Marichiko, Santa Barbara, CA: Christopher's Books, 1978.

The Morning Star—includes *The Silver Swan, On Flower Wreath Hill, The Loves Poems of Marichiko.* New York: New Directions, 1979.

Saucy Limericks and Christmas Cheer. Santa Barbara, CA: Bradford Morrow, 1980.

Between Two Wars. Richard Bigus, ed. Fourteen poems from *In What Hour.* Introduction by Bradford Morrow. Interview with Rexroth by Lester Ferris. Athens, OH: Labyrinth Editions, and San Francisco: Iris Press, 1982.

Selected Poems. Edited with an introduction by Bradford Morrow. New York: New Directions, 1984.

Verse Plays

Beyond the Mountains. New York: New Directions, 1951; San Francisco: City Lights, n.d.; London: Routledge, 1951.

Translations

Fourteen Poems by O. V. de L. Milosz. San Francisco: Peregrine Press, 1952; Seattle: Copper Canyon Press, 1982.
One Hundred Poems from the French. Highlands, N.C.: Jargon Society, 1955; Cambridge, MA: Pym-Randall, 1972.
One Hundred Poems from the Japanese. New York: New Directions, 1955. 1957. 1964.
One Hundred Poems from the Chinese. New York: New Directions, 1956, 1965, 1970.
Thirty Spanish Poems of Love and Exile. San Francisco: City Lights, 1956.
Poems from the Greek Anthology. Ann Arbor: University of Michigan Press, 1962.
Pierre Reverdy: Selected Poems. New York: New Directions, 1969. London: Cape, 1973.
Love in the Turning Year: One Hundred More Poems from the Chinese. New York: New Directions, 1970.
The Orchid Boat: Women Poets of China. With Ling Chung. New York: Herder & Herder, McGraw-Hill, 1972.
One Hundred More Poems from the Japanese. New York: New Directions, 1974, 1976.
The Burning Heart: Women Poets of Japan. With Ikuko Atsumi. New York: Seabury Press, 1977.
Seasons of Sacred Lust: Selected Poems of Kazuko Shiraishi. With Carol Tinker, Ikuko Atsumi, John Solt, and Yasuyo Morita. New York: New Directions, 1978.
Li Ch'ing Chao: Complete Poems. With Ling Chung. New York: New Directions, 1979.

Essays and Criticism

Bird in the Bush: Obvious Essays. New York: New Directions, 1959. 1979.
Assays. New York: New Directions, 1961.
Classics Revisited. Chicago: Quadrangle Books, 1968.
The Alternative Society. New York: Herder & Herder, 1970, 1974.
With Eye and Ear. New York: Herder & Herder, 1970, 1974.
American Poetry in the Twentieth Century, New York: Herder & Herder, 1971, Seabury Press, 1973.
The Elastic Retort: Essays in Literature and Ideas. New York: Seabury Press, 1973.
Communalism: Its Origins to the Twentieth Century. New York: Seabury Press, 1974.
Classics Revisited, Bradford Morrow, ed. New York: New Directions, 1986.
World Outside the Window: The Selected Essays of Kenneth Rexroth. Bradford Morrow, ed. New York: New Directions, 1987.
More Classics Revisited, Bradford Morrow, ed. New York: New Directions, 1989.

Autobiography

An Autobiographical Novel. Garden City, NY: Doubleday, 1966. Weybridge, England: Whittet, 1977; Santa Barbara, CA: Ross-Erikson, 1978.

Excerpts from a Life. Foreword by Ekbert Faas. Santa Barbara, CA: Conjunctions,
1981. Sections reprinted in *Conjunctions* 4 (1983): 96–114, and in *Sagetrieb* 2 (Winter 1983): 9–17.
"A Crystal Out of Time and Space: The Poet's Diary." *Conjunctions,* 8 (1985): 62–
85.

Fiction

"Vivienne Renaud." *Conjunctions,* 2 (Summer 1982): 54–59.

Recordings

San Francisco Poets. New York: Evergreen Records 1, n.d.
Poetry Readings in "The Cellar." San Francisco: Fantasy Records 7002, 1957.
Kenneth Rexroth at the Black Hawk. San Francisco: Fantasy Records 7008, 1960.
A Sword in a Cloud of Light. Washington, D.C.: The Watershed Foundation, 1977
(tape).

Bibliography

James Hartzell and Richard Zumwinkle, *Kenneth Rexroth: A Checklist of His Published Writings,* with a foreword by Lawrence Clark Powell (Los Angeles: Friends of the University of California at Los Angeles Library,
1967).
Bradford Morrow, "An Outline of Unpublished Rexroth Manuscripts, with an
Introductory Note to Three Chapters from the Sequel to *An Autobiographical Novel," Sagetrieb* (Winter 1983): 135–144.
Morgan Gibson, "Bibliography," *Revolutionary Rexroth: Poet of East-West Wisdom*
(Hamden, CT: Archon Books, 1986): 125–148.

INDEX

Mardersteig, Giovanni, 208
Mariani, Paul, 388
Marichiko, 352–54, 420
"Marine Cemetery, The" (Valèry), 54
Marius the Epicurean (Pater), 23
"Maroon Bells", 314
Marshall, John, 156
Marston, Rose Marie, 312
"Marthe Away", 260, 313
"Marthe Growing", 313
"Marthe Lonely", 264–65
"Martial—XII, LII", 139
Martin, Peter, 225, 227, 406
Marx, Karl, 60, 72
"Mary and the Seasons", 263
Masses, The, 13
Masson, Andrè, 66, 153
Masters, Edgar Lee, 13, 18, 44
Material Gathered on Federal Writers Project,
    390–91
Matthiesson, F. O., 184
Mattick, Ilse, 184, 209
Mattick, Paul, 174, 184, 204, 309
Maurice Neville Rare Books, 354, 355
"Maximian, Elgy V", 29
Maximianus, 29
Mayakovski, Vladimir, 17
Medieval Mind, The (Taylor), 59
Meltzer, David, 269, 333, 335, 337, 398,
    418
Meltzer, Tina, 335
Menninger, Karl, 130
Merlin, Milton, 52, 53, 55, 56, 58, 60, 65, 75,
    81
Merriam, Eve, 175
Merwin, W. S., 364–65
"Metaphysics" (Ginsberg), 241
Mexico City Blues (Kerouac), 270
Mezey, Robert, 359
Midner, Frances, 30, 36–37, 383
Midwest, 58
Miles, Josephine, 148, 153, 225, 362, 562
Milhaud, Darius, 223
Miller, Henry, 134–35, 140, 147, 152, 153,
    157, 215, 220, 223, 226, 228, 240, 265,
    398
Miller, Jeffrey, 355, 365, 370
Mills, Dickie, 234
Milosz, O. V. de L., 217
Mingus, Charles, 283, 300
Mitchell, Joni, 364
Mitchell, Tennessee, 44
Modern Scottish Poetry (Lindsay), 155
Modern Verse in English (Cecil & Tate), 296
Modotti, Tina, 40
Moholy-Nagy, Laszlo, 65
"Monads", 403
Monahan, Minnie, 5, 7, 11, 18, 19, 21, 125,
    178, 183, 380
    photograph of, 121

Monahan, Paul, 18, 19, 21
Monk, Thelonious, 357
Monkey Block, 48
Monroe, Harriet, 13, 44, 70–71, 384, 388–89
Montgomery, John, 393
Montgomery, Stuart, 322
Montgomery Block, 48
Moody, William Vaughan, 177
Mooney, Tom, 10
"Moonlight now on Malibu", 325
"Moon Shines on the Moonshine, The", 36
Moore, Marianne, 256, 274
Moore, Richard, 133, 153, 156
Moore, Ward, 164
Moorhouse, Frank, 324
Morada, 51–52
Moran, Bugsy, 28
Morita, Yasuyo, 346, 347, 348, 352
Morning Star, The, 349, 353, 422
Morrow, Bradford, 354–55, 366–67, 369, 370,
    381, 382, 384, 422
Moses Coulee Apple Growers Cooperative, 33
Mother Earth, 25
"Motto on the Sundial, The", 58, 106
Munson, Gorham, 92, 103
Murao, Shigeyoshhi, 267, 362
Murder the Murderers (Miller), 157
Museum Without Walls (Malraux), 95
Muste, A. J., 394
Myrer, Tony, 405
"myriad deaths were yours to die alone, A", 40
Mytinger, Melissa, 354, 355–56

NAACP, 68
Nakazawa, Kimiko, 420
Naone, Dana, 364–65
Naropa Institute, 364
Nation, The, 95, 221, 240, 267, 269, 278–79,
    292–93, 295, 300, 315
National Book Award, 321
National Committee for Conscientious Objec-
    tors, 116
National Council for the Prevention of War,
    103
National Institute of Arts and Letters, 266, 316,
    333
National Maritime Union, 82
Natural Numbers: New and Selected Poems,
    313, 314, 325, 375, 381
Negro Novel in America, The (Bone), 343
Neruda, Pablo, 282, 357
Neurotica, 279
New American Library, 315, 409
New American Poetry, The (Allen), 300
New and Selected Poems (Shiffert), 347
New Anthology of Modern Poetry, 174
New British Poets, The, 165, 184, 188, 190–
    91, 194, 214, 217, 233, 236, 286
New Criticism, 150, 156, 226, 238, 293